"*Life is a dream for the wise, a game for the fool, a comedy for the rich, a tragedy for the poor.*"

SHOLEM ALEICHEM

"*The pursuit of knowledge for its own sake, an almost fanatical love of justice, and the desire for personal independence—these are the features of Jewish tradition which make me thank my stars that I belong to it.*"

ALBERT EINSTEIN,
The World as I See It

Other Books by Leo Rosten

ROME WASN'T BURNED IN A DAY: THE MISCHIEF OF LANGUAGE

PEOPLE I HAVE LOVED, KNOWN OR ADMIRED

A TRUMPET FOR REASON

THE JOYS OF YIDDISH

A MOST PRIVATE INTRIGUE

THE MANY WORLDS OF LEO ROSTEN

CAPTAIN NEWMAN, M.D.

RELIGIONS IN AMERICA (ed.)

THE STORY BEHIND THE PAINTING

THE RETURN OF H*Y*M*A*N K*A*P*L*A*N

A GUIDE TO THE RELIGIONS OF AMERICA (ed.)

THE DARK CORNER

112 GRIPES ABOUT THE FRENCH (WAR DEPARTMENT)

HOLLYWOOD: THE MOVIE COLONY, THE MOVIE MAKERS

DATELINE: EUROPE

THE STRANGEST PLACES

THE WASHINGTON CORRESPONDENTS

THE EDUCATION OF H*Y*M*A*N K*A*P*L*A*N

LEO ROSTEN'S
TREASURY OF JEWISH
QUOTATIONS

A DAZZLEMENT
OF 4,500 PROVERBS,
FOLK SAYINGS, WITTICISMS,
INSIGHTS, MAXIMS AND
MORALISMS—
COLLECTED OVER 58 YEARS,
FRESHLY TRANSLATED OR
REWRITTEN, AND
GARNISHED WITH IRONY,
PARADOX AND
TRUTH

LEO ROSTEN'S TREASURY

of

JEWISH QUOTATIONS

McGRAW-HILL BOOK COMPANY

NEW YORK   ST. LOUIS   SAN FRANCISCO

SYDNEY   DÜSSELDORF   MEXICO   PANAMA

LONDON   TORONTO

23456789BPBP798765432

Library of Congress Cataloging in Publication Data

Rosten, Leo Calvin, date
    Leo Rosten's treasury of Jewish quotations.
    Includes bibliographical references.
    1. Quotations, Jewish. I. Title. II. Title:
Treasury of Jewish quotations.
PN6095.J4R6   808.88'2   72-298
ISBN 0-07-053978-2

BOOK DESIGN: HERB JOHNSON
ART DIRECTION: HARRIS LEWINE

All translations from the Hebrew/Aramaic texts used for this anthology—whether the Torah, the Talmud, collections of *midrashim,* memoirs, essays, letters, poems, autobiographies—were made by Rabbis Solomon D. Goldfarb, Aaron Kriegel and Jay Rovner; and all translations were freely rephrased in English by Leo Rosten. Translations for Yiddish sources were made by Mr. Rosten, Rabbi Goldfarb and various consultants.

TO

the scholars, rabbis, poets, philosophers

and plain men of good sense

from whose words, quoted in these pages,

I have learned so much.

CONTENTS

AUTHOR'S PREFACE: THE STORY
OF THIS BOOK   1

*How the Obsession Began / The Bonus of Bernstein
/ The Power of Proverbs / Proverbs and the Jews /
The Pedigree of Proverbs / Proverbs and Jewish Women /
Detour: Yiddish / The Torments of Translation / The
Importance (and Misdemeanors) of Translation / On
Translating Yiddish / On Translating Proverbs / How
My Translations Were Made / A Word to Non-Jews /
Cosmetic Devices That May Interest Linguists and
Grammarians / Who Is Left Out? / Acknowledgments*

HELPFUL HINTS TO THE READER   59

*WHAT PROVERBS/FOLK SAYINGS ARE
     INCLUDED?*   61

ON ARRANGEMENT   61

ON REPETITIONS   62

*SOURCES AND ATTRIBUTIONS OF THE
     AUTHORS QUOTED*   63

GUIDE NOTES ON TORAH AND TALMUD   65

  A. *THE TORAH*   67
    (1) ENGLISH AND HEBREW NOMENCLATURE   67
    (2) TORAH: LARGER MEANING   68

  B. *THE TALMUD*   68
    (1) WHICH TALMUD?   68
    (2) WHAT IS THE TALMUD?   69
    (3) WHAT THE TALMUD IS NOT   70
    (4) THE NAMES OF THE TALMUD'S SIX ORDERS (BOOKS)   71
    (5) THE NAMES OF THE 63 TRACTATES   71
    (6) "THE MINOR TRACTATES OF THE TALMUD"   71

  C. *THE MISHNAH*   72

  D. *THE MIDRASH AND HAGGADA*   74

  E. *THE GEMARA*   76

  F. *THE RESPONSA*   76

REFERENCE NOTES   79

A NOTE ON THE NAMES OF AUTHORS CITED   85

ANTHOLOGY OF JEWISH QUOTATIONS   87

APPENDICES

  I. *ON THE ENGLISH SPELLING OF HEBREW AND YIDDISH WORDS*   571

  II. *ON TRANSLATING HEBREW*   573

  III. *BIOGRAPHICAL VIGNETTES of the AUTHORS QUOTED*   577

  IV. *GLOSSARY: Some Hebrew, Aramaic and Yiddish words; words and names used in and for the Torah;*

the tractates of the Talmud; the Mishnah, Apocry-
pha, etc., including the more important foreign
names of books, essays or poems cited in the
anthology.   641

V.   SELECTED BIBLIOGRAPHY   699

   1.   BOOKS AND ARTICLES PUBLISHED IN ENGLISH   699

   2.   BOOKS PUBLISHED IN YIDDISH ONLY   707

   3.   BOOKS PUBLISHED IN HEBREW ONLY   707

   4.   BOOKS PUBLISHED IN GERMAN ONLY   710

INDEX   711

THE STORY
of
THIS BOOK

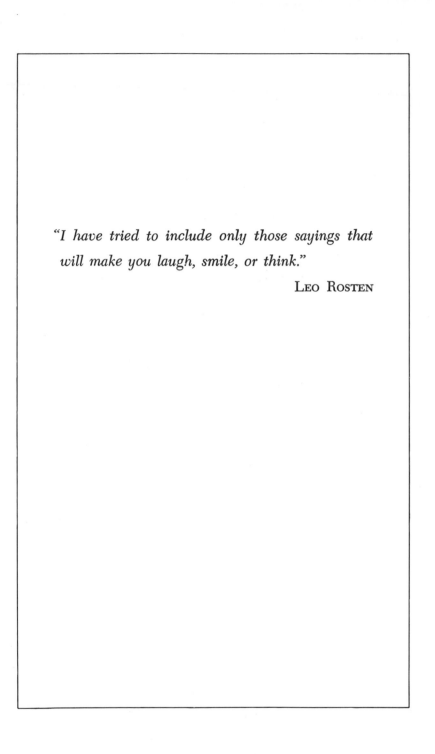

"*I have tried to include only those sayings that will make you laugh, smile, or think.*"

LEO ROSTEN

"I never met a man in whom I failed to recognize some quality superior to myself; if he was older, I said he has done more good than I; if he was younger, I said he has sinned less; if richer, I said he has given more to charity; if poorer, I said he has suffered more; if wiser, I paid honor to his wisdom; if not wiser, I judged his faults less severely. Take this to heart, my son."

The Testament of
Judah ben
Jehiel Asher (1250–1327)

How the Obsession Began

I STARTED this book when I was six years old. I did not, of
course, know that I was becoming an anthologist, nor that I
would spend fifty-eight years collecting gems—verbal gems of
wit, insight and wisdom, particularly those used and loved by
Jews.

I was raised by a mother and father who simply leaped at
the chance to utter a folk saying, in Yiddish, in the day-by-day
rearing of their children. And so proverbs, epigrams, maxims,
vitsen of every conceivable sort were woven into the fabric of my
daily life. No aspect of my conduct escaped comment or instruction, chastisement or praise—through an adage. Had I forgotten
a chore? Torn my shirt? Not finished my milk? ... Was I protest-
ing too much? Excusing too long? Explaining too little? ... Had
I arrived too late? Left too early? Neglected my homework? ...
Was I guilty of insufficient consideration to a widow, an old man,
a beggar, a clerk? Not helped a neighbor, hurried the grocer, ignored a greeting, fudged on a promise? ... Was I being stubborn,
jealous, willful, vain? Would Mr. Becker think me unfriendly or
Mrs. Feibush unkind, Joey Tiven insensitive or Molly Shulman
unjust?

For even the possibility of having committed some breach of
decorum, I heard a mighty precept that might teach me—heir of
all the ages—how better to conquer my thoughtlessness, guard
my tongue, refine my conduct, so that I might one day be worthy
to be called a *mentsh*. My tender age, the normal distractions of
youth, innocent impulsiveness—all received short shrift from my

[5]

mother, a lady of indomitable will, who sought perfection and discounted my explanations (God forbid they should be *excuses*) for the errors of my boyish ways.

So it was through the proverbs and parables of the Jews that I was introduced to the kingdoms of ethics, reason, psychology, philosophy. The words of ancient sages and scholars poured into my ears—to teach me the imperatives of honor, the ingredients of manners, the dimensions of duty, guilt, shame, self-respect... I tell you, as I look back on it now, the building of the Pyramids involved no greater complexities of analysis and choice than accompanied the simple business of living out one day in what I can only call the ethical furnace of my home.

Now, the maxims I heard from my mother and father were, of course, not original with them: they were folk sayings—heard from his or her father, who had heard it from his or her mother, who had heard it from his or her uncle, who was quoting a friend who was only repeating what some rabbi had told him a sage, quoted in the Talmud as "speaking for" another seer, had once said.*[1] And *that* patriarch, had my parents known it, was interpreting Hillel or Rabban Gamaliel, who was repeating an adage first heard in Judea or Babylon or Alexandria—and *that* aphorism, for all anyone knows, had been refurbished by some twelfth-century scholar in Cordova or some sixteenth-century mystic in Safed, some eighteenth-century rabbi in Vilna or some twentieth-century *hasid* in Dubno or Berdichev or Brooklyn.

And there was another bottomless well of folk wisdom that gushed sweet waters into our Chicago home. Each night, as soon as we finished dinner (we called it "supper"), my father would open the *Daily Forward* ("Forvits" is how it is rendered in Yiddish). How he loved that journal! It served as chronicle, town crier, telephone, movies, radio, television, almanac, encyclopedia —all in one. The news was a daily bazaar of human deeds and follies; a circus of the singular, the fanciful, the brutal, the grotesque; a recessional of the wonders and crimes, the glories and horrors the race of man each day created.

My father would spread the *Forvits* across the table under the gas lamps, and would proceed to read; and as he read he would mumble and cluck and sigh, muttering astonishment or approval,

---

* Numbered references are identified or expanded at the end of this Preface, pp. 79–84.

marveling over this miracle or deploring that disaster. The most noteworthy items he read aloud to my mother and me; and so, even as a boy, I apprehended snatches of meaning from the reports about the movers and shakers of the world: breadlines in Warsaw, maneuvers off Jutland, a *brouhaha* in Washington, a small pogrom in Rumania, a large one in the Ukraine ... To all these reverberations of the great world in our warm little kitchen my father counterpointed his own commentary—admiration or dismay or disgust, eloquent grunts or scoffing snorts, an epiphany of "Mnh!" and "Mnyeh!"s, shocked "Oy!"s, affirmative "Ai-ai-ai!"s, cynical 'Hoo-hah!"s—all replaced, as his Americanization proceeded, with ungreenhornish "My!"s and "Imagine!"s, "Fakers!" or (in outraged regression) *"Paskudnyaks!"*

When the reading of the news was completed, my father turned to the *"Bintl Brief"* ("Bundle of Letters"), the "agony column" of Letters to the Editor that was a veritable Vanity Fair: and now I heard about raffish boarders making advances to respectable young landladies; consumptive men forced to live on the pittances of in-laws; Socialist seamstresses who lamented their swains' indifference to the Class Struggle; sad tales of lost children, abandoned sweethearts, greedy relatives, heartless sons, unforeseen pregnancies—every conceivable experience that cast fate's harsh shadow across unprepared lives. The *Bintl Brief* threw onto the public stage of print the high hopes and brave dreams, the aching disillusionments and small miseries of life in this shimmering New World to which the immigrant hordes had come.

The letters to the *Forward* often asked for advice: "Should I marry him?" "Is such a woman to be trusted?" "Will capitalism change only through revolution?" "How can a mother's heart bear such shame?" "Does a business partner need a *written* promise?" And the editor, famed Abe Cahan, often answered the questions himself, in consoling, indignant, or magisterial words. Many of the letters, and more of the answers, contained Jewish folk sayings, which my father read or improved ("Sleep faster: we need the pillows"), and the adages sank roots in my mind:

"When you're hungry, sing; when you're hurt, laugh."

"When a father helps a son, both laugh; when a son helps his father, both cry."

" 'For instance' is not proof."

"It's better to be embarrassed than ashamed."

"Safeguarding a girl in love is harder than guarding a sackful of fleas."

"A man is not honest just because he had no chance to steal."

"Dear God: let us not suffer all that we may be able to endure."

"A fool measures water with a sieve."

"A saloon can't corrupt a good man, and a synagogue can't reform a bad one."

"Little children don't let you sleep; big children won't let you live."

"He only lies twice a year—in summer and in winter."

After the daily, delicious heartthrobs of the *Bintl Brief* came the climax to each night's vicarious dramas: the reading of a short story—a tale by Cahan himself, or by I. J. Singer, the great Sholem Asch, or the incomparable Sholem Aleichem. My father read very well; he had a faultless sense of comic timing and significant pauses; he was a marvelous mimic. And those stories held me in thrall.

To this day, I remember the textures, if not the plots, of the tales these as-yet-unheralded writers spun out: about an impending *shidakh* or a calamitous purchase, an encounter with an anti-Semite or an uneasy deposit in that novel institution (likely to swindle its depositors at any moment) known as a Bank (the deposit was promptly withdrawn). Sages and salesmen, yearning widows and shameless philanderers; overworked men, undernourished wives; the dreamy, the lazy, the successful, the *shlemiels;* men burning with idealism, men soured by life; the favors and fevers of love sought, love lost, love gained, love not requited; *shtetl* customs and American foibles; *brises,* betrothals, betrayals, Bar Mitzvahs; the pleasure of wine in a *gleyzele,* the danger of *schnapps* in a glass; children who flourished, children who perished; the laugh in the doorway, the cry in the night—I can hear them all again, faint old music as from a calliope, playing its accompaniment to the kaleidoscope of characters that turns in my memory.

And here, too, in the tales told by fine writers, lay a cornucopia of folk sayings they knew or witticisms they coined. It was from Sholem Aleichem, if I am right, that I first learned:

"To a marriage, walk; to a divorce, run."

"Gossip is nature's telephone."

"April Fool: a joke repeated 365 times a year."

"A bachelor is a man who comes to work each morning from a different direction."

"The girl who can't dance says the band can't keep time."

"When a poor Jew eats a chicken, one of them is sick."

I do not think we can ever recover the freshness of childhood; yet our minds are populated by people from the past. In my memory, none move more merrily, more vividly, in more magical measure, than the characters in those stories my father read to me when both I and he—*olevasholem*—were so very young.

*　　*　　*

I was lucky to be an immigrant child, and to grow up in a bilingual world; nothing so sharpens the ear to the subtleties that differentiate words as constantly shuttling between two vocabularies. A language, in Walter Nash's phrase, is "a palisade of verbal custom."

> In language I make . . . effigies and create ikons. In words, whispering, stumbling words, in the litter and ceaseless drift of words, is my searching for my own identity . . . and the articulation that will go on, at the heart of all experience, till at last all burdens are laid down and I need no more words, not even amen and good night.[2]

And as I grew older, it was from storekeepers or soapbox orators, at meetings of the Workmen's Circle or on picnics of Chicago's Lodzer colony, that I heard more and still more scintillating sayings:

"When a young man marries, he divorces his mother."

"Out of snow, you can't make cheesecake."

"The man who marries for money will earn it."

"A rabbi whose congregation doesn't want to run him out of town isn't a rabbi; and a rabbi whose congregation does run him out of town isn't a man."

"When you go to a restaurant, choose a table near a waiter."

The folk sayings were not only sardonic or scathing: some stopped my heart:

"I felt sorry for myself because I had no shoes—until I met a man who had no feet."

"The rich have heirs, not children."
"Pity was invented by the weak."
"When you add to the truth, you subtract from it."
"No one is as deaf as the man who will not listen."

      ❁ ❁ ❁

The adages I heard struck me, even in my puberty, as much more than little homilies. They were illuminations, electrifying flashes of perception and perspicuity. And, perhaps because I dimly dreamed of someday being a writer, they struck me as masterpieces of precision: the use of small words to teach huge truths. Even the homeliest folk saying impressed me as having a certain beauty; for there *is* beauty—or, at least, elegance—in the economy and pungency with which a simple saying can convey a profound verity.

Words must surely be counted among the most powerful drugs man ever invented. In my adolescence, I became an absolute nut about aphorisms. I collected epigrams the way some boys collect stamps. For years, obsessed with a fear of forgetting anything, I wrote down every *bon mot* I read or heard. My pockets became filing cases for tersities of wisdom (scribbled on scraps of paper, backs of envelopes, margins torn from newspapers), a hodgepodge of verbal wonders—from O. O. McIntyre or Will Rogers to "Kin" Hubbard and the true masters: Mark Twain, G. K. Chesterton, Oscar Wilde, Bernard Shaw, H. L. Mencken (the most neglected humorist in American letters). In a spree of affluence, I bought a 4-by-6-inch card catalogue, and packets of lined cards, and blank index guides on which to write my categories: "Fate . . . Lust . . . Honor . . . Folly . . ."—and so began to systematize my own precious Bartlett.

I devoured any anthology that offered the cream of the jests of Bacon, Montaigne, Sydney Smith, La Rochefoucauld. I still remember my rapture on discovering Ambrose Bierce's *Devil's Dictionary,* or my jubilation in collected quotations of Epictetus, Marcus Aurelius, Balthasar Gracian, Heinrich Heine. I reveled in admiration over the genius that could marshal words, metaphors, irony, paradox with so much originality, to achieve such deft insight. In a way, I honed my mind on the whetstones of epigrams. I came to suspect, long before I encountered Sigmund Freud, that witticisms are "strategems to evade the censors of the self," that "comedy is a complex masquerade [and] murder oft peeps through the masks of our wit," that "humor is the messenger of truths that churn behind the camouflage of levity."[3]

And then, with the audacity of the young, I turned aphorist myself, selling an article to the *New Republic*, entitled: "Political Lexicon"; it was a twenty-four-year-old's broadside, dripping cynicism, against the stupid, heartless, hypocritical System. One line will give you the flavor:

> *Rules of War:* The rules, solemnly observed by sovereign nations, which make it illegal to hit below the toes.

I was, of course, too young to *know* very much: to distinguish grievances from truth; to suspect the sardonic, which is so attractive to youth, and respect the expedient, which enrages the impatient.

I now tried to distinguish adages from apothegms from aphorisms. What makes an epigram different from a precept or proverb, a folk saying from a maxim? I cannot say that I did much more than tone up my semantic muscles in this foredoomed exercise; but I did begin to think of folk sayings as proverbs' homely brothers—and of both as packaged common sense. An adage, I decided, is sober, an aphorism arresting, but an epigram must tickle the ribs. Proverbs deal with universals; epigrams deal with anything. An adage may be trite; an aphorism is no aphorism if it is. Proverbs are encapsulated experience; epigrams are flashes of fun. Proverbs are the primers we inherit from the past; epigrams are often new, young, in vogue—and may pass out of use. Epigrams, I concluded, are displays of wit traceable to a known man, often more clever than true, prized more by intellectuals than by the masses.

It may amuse you to know that I was so lost in my obsession that I visualized aphorisms as dressed in silk, epigrams as bedecked with sequins, proverbs as wrapped in fur. Folk sayings, obviously, ran around in honest homespun.

❖   ❖   ❖

It occurred to me that witticisms achieve the greatest longevity of a writer's output. How few of us have read a page by the

authors of lines we remember with that special gratitude we accord the wickedly apposite.

"If triangles had a God, He would have three sides."

"The doctor who treats himself has a fool for a doctor—and
a fool for a patient."

"No one forgets where he buried the hatchet."

"Conscience is the inner voice that tells us that someone is
watching."

"An idealist is one who, upon observing that a rose smells
better than a cabbage, concludes that it will also make better
soup."[4]

❋   ❋   ❋

The more I read, down the years, the more I found myself
plumbing beneath and beyond the surfaces of wit. I came to see
that the sayings of a people reflect its particular history, values,
and sensibilities; that any people, whether nation, tribe, or sect,
possesses a distinctive style of thought, special patterns of esteem
or scorn, characteristic reflexes of affection and contempt and
moral outrage—and all these are mirrored in the adages men
prize.

Yet the more I studied proverbs, the more I found certain
common themes running through all of them: whatever a people's
experience or ethos or faith, men ultimately voice the bitter conclusion that life is unjust, fate blind, fortune heartless. And I began to understand that all men, whether Zulu or Christian or Jew,
desperately try, through the reiterated sorcery of words, to fortify
their faith in a passionate necessity to believe that virtue *will* be
rewarded, that evil will be punished, that truth will somehow triumph in the end.

The Bonus of Bernstein

I WENT to study in London in 1934, and in that glorious hodge-podge of villages nestling around the Thames I discovered secondhand-book stores such as I had never dreamed of before. There were thousands of them, crammed from floor to ceiling, spilling their frayed bodies across sagging shelves, indoor counters and outdoor bins. The shops stood like noble beggars—near the British Museum, off Russell Square, in alien Soho; but most of them were crowded along Charing Cross Road, unshaved cheek by untidy jowl, and overflowed into the lanes and alleyways that web off that paradise for bibliophiles. Foyles, bulging out the seams of four high buildings, was but the largest athenaeum: St. Martin's Lane, which is not a lane but a traffic jam, shimmered with frumpy shops for antiquarians, faddists, collectors of anything ever written on Aztec gold or Battersea boxes; the empires of Assyria, China, Islam; the art of Mogul miniatures or Mithraic amulets; the politics of Sparta, Solon, Suleiman, Samarkand.

How many hypnotized hours I spent in those dusty dungeons, reading as much as browsing, and browsing much more than buying (I was living on $1.50 a day), I cannot remember. One day, my eye, traveling along a decrepit shelf, fell upon a thick, greenish volume whose title, in shining gilt, was *Jüdische Sprichwörter und Redensarten.* I took the book down. The text was Yiddish, on the right-hand pages, with Roman-letter phonetic renditions on the left; and the pages were numbered "backwards," as Hebrew books are, starting from what would be the end of an English volume.

The volume was a collection of folk sayings compiled by one Ignaz Bernstein. I glanced through the pages idly, then with excitement—for not only did I recognize a great many old friends from home: I read quiddities I had never heard before. (Many were totally incomprehensible, for they contained Russian, Polish,

Lithuanian words, or "inside" phrases of Galitizianer Jews.)

Once or twice a week, after that, I went back to the shelf in that stall in that shop (could it have been in Cecil Court?) where Ignaz Bernstein's work mutely rested. I would plunge into its pages, scribbling notes; and when I returned to the Commons Room of the London School of Economics, I would with assumed aplomb toss off verbal firecrackers—to friends, an opponent at the chess table, the usual covey of kibitzers: "There's a Yiddish folk saying that goes..."

How I longed to buy Bernstein! But how could I? The volume was selling for 15 shillings, I think—a fearful sum for my budget. But my yearnings grew, my continued pirating made me feel guilty, and the desiccated Scrooge who owned the book store was giving me glances that increased in nastiness with each visit. It all made me covet Ignaz Bernstein as I coveted few books before or since.

One day I noticed something on the title page: my heart leaped. Bernstein's work had been published the very year of my birth—and in Warsaw, which is but seventy miles from Lodz, where I was born. I felt like Saul on his way to Damascus. Had destiny drawn me to this seedy shop in a sunless lane in a far-off land? The subject, the place of publication, the date, even the author's initials, "I.B." (which the madness of desire made me moan *"Ich bin"*: "I am")—were these not magical omens? I swiftly figured that if I cut down on three breakfasts, skipped four lunches, say, and trimmed the costs of three dinners ... I handed fifteen precious shillings to the startled owner and hurried back to my digs in Brunswick Square.

Every night thereafter, when the long days' studies were completed, I rewarded myself with a dip into Bernstein, reading the Yiddish, slogging through the phonetic explications of idioms I could not fathom, lost in a remote yet vaguely familiar world of *shtetl* sayings and rustic adages ...

Then tragedy struck. Bernstein disappeared. I searched through my skimble-skamble of notes, papers, journals, textbooks, books borrowed from the library or the student on the floor above. But I could not find Bernstein. I searched again, quickly, with no success, then reassured myself by thinking he would turn up tomorrow —perhaps under my bed, in the closet, fallen behind the bookcase. But I was wrong. He did not. Bernstein had really disappeared!

Where, when, by whose hand? Lost? Stolen? Thrown out by the harpy widow (of a *pukka sahib* slain in "Indja") to whom I paid rent? Committed to the "dust bin" by my slovenly char? To be sold to some bookseller in Bloomsbury or on voracious Charing Cross Road? To end in a dump in Bethnal Green or as kindling for some fireplace in Chelsea? Oh, God! (Nay, *Gotenyu!*)

On and off, during the years that followed, I would think of *Jüdische Sprichwörter und Redensarten:* but I never ran across another copy—not in London or New York or Hollywood. I wrote to several book dealers on Fourth Avenue, and to bookfinding services; but the months passed, year in, year out, and the pain wore off and in time I became too deeply involved in work and Washington to take up the chase again.

It is a strange thing, wholly mystifying to (and inexplicable by) me that it was not until thirty years later, as I was finishing the present anthology, that I suddenly remembered Ignaz Bernstein again. I phoned a librarian friend and asked if he knew of Bernstein's compendium. He told me the book had just been reprinted —in Oldsheim, Germany—and suggested I try certain booksellers on the Lower East Side. Need I say how swiftly I phoned them? The first had never heard of Bernstein; the second offered to order the book ("You should have it in eight weeks"); but the third dealer whispered, "I have a copy . . . quite expensive, I'm afraid . . . oh, not the new edition; the old 1908 . . ." I did not let him finish. "Are you sure? Will you check? Please." In a moment I heard the miraculous truth, and within an hour, dear Ignaz Bernstein, published in 1908, was in my hands once more.

The first thing I did, naturally, was turn to the flyleaf. Could fortune be so kind as to have resurrected the very volume I had owned in Brunswick Square over three decades ago? Alas: no signature, in my handwriting or any one else's, was inscribed on the olive-green paper.

Whose copy of Bernstein I now own I shall never know. But how grateful I am to whoever it was who bought it, received it, stole it, lost it, or sold it so that it could once more become mine! I still find many of its local locutions odd, many of its nouns and names furiously incomprehensible, many of its provincial idioms impenetrable; yet I treasure the more durable of those old, all-but-forgotten pearls, some of which I added to my final draft of the volume you hold in your hands.

The Power of Proverbs

BUT let us return to the theme of this preface. My love of proverbs was in no way unusual. The truth is this: Men quote proverbs "the better to express *themselves*." Adages are the wit of the inarticulate. Proverbs are the gospel of the poor. Folk sayings are the college of the masses.

More important: Proverbs are what a people—any people— believe, cherish, and teach their young. They are those gleanings of knowledge and experience with which the dead dower each generation of the living. Shakespeare has a phrasing that runs: "We patch grief with proverbs." I think we do more than that. We patch our ignorance and our impotence with them, too.

Proverbs clarify our thinking, crystallize our hopes, assuage our immense anxiety about the immensities of what we do not, unaided, understand. They flash light into places where reason falters for lack of it. Indeed, the proverb is often reason laid bare, argument stripped of fat, complexity clarified beyond misinterpretation.

You may retort that proverbs often contradict one another (as any reader of anthologies, including this one, soon discovers). The sagacity that advises us to look before we leap promptly warns us that if we hesitate we are lost; that absence makes the heart grow fonder, but out of sight, out of mind. What can one believe? Simply that life is full of contradictions, that proverbs reflect and express them, and that many apothegms are more witty than true. Examples:

"Honest men marry soon, wise men not at all." Well, now, was Solomon not wise? Are wise men never honest? Are no bachelors fools? Do no thieves marry young?

"He who does not rise early never does a day's work." This is an agrarian cliché: Do watchmen perform no service? Do no scholars or poets or composers work far into the night?

"Not to advance is to retreat." Really? Not to advance may be to escape disaster. Advance—or retreat—when and *why?* The Charge of the Light Brigade was insanity, pure and simpleminded, as Cecil Woodham-Smith's superb retelling shows us.[5]

"There is no wisdom like silence." How can you judge what is not said? Are mutes then paragons of wisdom?

But I should not press the case: a foolish consistency, "the hobgoblin of little minds," is secondary. Folk sayings are born singly; they are not *designed* for consistency: they are not, indeed, designed at all: they occur. So I have tried to make this compendium not an assemblage of the consistent or the undebatable, but a collection of insights that are often not on speaking terms with one another. What they add up to, because of their very flouting of consistency, is a treasury of precepts which can extricate a man from any predicament. (That is a Hindu saying.)

Proverbs, said Emerson, are "the sanctuary of our intuitions." But they are more: they are the precious distillation of what man has *learned* from centuries of experience. Aristotle considered apothegms the product of intellectual maturity and, recognizing their enormous power, declared it "unbecoming" for the young to utter maxims![6]

"Respect [these] discoveries of the wise," the author of *Ecclesiasticus* tells us, "for of them shalt thou learn instruction." Yet it is much more than instruction that we receive from "the discoveries of the wise": it is insight—and delight, pleasure in the precision of phrasing, the music of alliteration, the felicity of verbal counterpoint and balanced construction, all orchestrated by that special genius that can popularize the profound.

Proverbs and the Jews

THAT the ancient Hebrews set great store by proverbs scarcely needs to be said: consider how lavishly they are strewn through the Old Testament, or were presented separately—in the Book of Proverbs, the books of the prophets, "wisdom literature"*—the Apocrypha.[7]

The Talmud, that monumental compendium of 1200 years of dialectics (from the 5th century before, to the 8th century of, the Christian Era) and commentaries, discussion and debate on the Torah (the first five books of the Old Testament) and the post-Biblical sages, is an inexhaustible treasure trove of pithy sagacities (in Aramaic) on every conceivable aspect of faith, life, law, man, virtue, evil, customs, morals and mores.[8] The names of over 2,000 rabbi-teachers appear in the Talmud; so far as I know, no one has counted the apothegms.[9]

It is wise to remember that proverbs preceded printing by thousands and thousands of years: it was by oral transmission that the meat and marrow of wisdom circulated among the tribes of man. Collections of sayings (first handwritten, which few men could afford, and later printed) were very popular with the Jewish masses.

The so-called "wisdom literature" was rooted in and flowered from popular wisdom; the scholars and poets who collected folk sayings often improved upon them—but their origins remain the masses. Proverbs are an "international genre"—with separate classes for verbal instruction and moral exhortation. ("Happy is the man who . . ." straddles both.) Sayings are still used as pedagogy by primitive (preliterate) groups, and were more formally employed by the ancient Chinese, Hindus, Persians, Egyptians to train civil

---

* "Wisdom literature" is the overall term used to designate the Book of Proverbs, Ecclesiastes, certain Psalms, and the Apocrypha: Ecclesiasticus, the Wisdom of Solomon, IV Maccabees.

servants. As early as King Solomon, the Hebrews used oral precepts for vocational training—and to educate an elite, a new class, the officials of the ancient state of Israel. Religious/moralistic sayings spread among the Israelites to transmit the essence of monotheism, of "Yahwistic piety," and as exhortations to obey the Law. Proverbs disseminated not only elementary knowledge and skills, but a whole code of morals, a system of ethics, a set of sanctions for a new way of life.[10]

The lucidity and vitality of proverbs made them priceless for instruction; and the rabbis preferred to teach orally rather than from written texts. They feared that if repeated disputations about the meaning of Holy Scripture were written, they would attain undesirable authority. Worse, once a judicial interpretation is written down (the scholars of Judaism reasoned) men tend to feel that what is written is superior to what is told. Above all, the rabbis wanted to preserve a direct, lively, intimate rapport with their students. The Talmud told them: "Prayer should not be recited as if a man is reading from a document."

The rabbis, seeking to keep their audiences alert (during a discussion, no less than a sermon), would often toss Greek, Latin, Arabic, Persian words into their exposition: this was sure to excite interest and provoke questioning.[11] The Haggadah (see Guide Note D, below), an enormous repository of folklore, fables, parables, allegories, witticisms, is studded with foreign words and phrases —which are then explained. The preachers of Judaism found a folk saying more effective than a sermon, in the same way that a scalpel is more precise than a club. "Epigrams stab to the heart."[12]

The marvelous sayings of Jesus ben Sirach (*Ecclesiasticus*) and the matchless *Pirke Abot* ("Saying of the Fathers"), which embraced six centuries of Jewish wisdom and wit (from the third century before, to the third century after, the Christian Era), were and are among the most beloved of Jewish books. In the Middle Ages, Jewish thinkers and psalmists published literally thousands of different collections of Talmudic and folk wisdom.[13] And in each new generation, new teachers, prophets, poets, philosophers, legalists and local wits, some famous, some obscure, kept adding (or embellishing) sayings and profundities to the unclosed treasury of Jewish thought: Rashi's classic commentaries, Bahya ibn Paquda's *Duties of the Heart*, Maimonides' majestic code, Judah Ha-Levi's noble *Kuzari*, the mystical revelations of the *Zohar*.

In the eighteenth and nineteenth centuries, an immense treasure of aphorisms poured into Jewish thought from the hasidim of Eastern Europe, who preached religious ecstasy and glorified saintly souls. The hasidim were rabbis (often not formally ordained), mystics, holy men, whose every rumination was seized upon by disciples: "Our hasid is wiser than your hasid" was a refrain that encouraged the competitive production of aphorisms.[14]

In the nineteenth and twentieth centuries, new men of letters invigorated the old tradition: Chaim Bialik, the leading poet in the renaissance of Hebrew, published a huge *Sefer Ha-Agadah* (in collaboration with Ravnitzki) and a smaller "assemblage" of apothegms. Nathan Stutchkoff's *Der Oytser fun der Yidisher Sprakh* ("Thesaurus—or Treasure—of the Yiddish Language") is a cornucopia of folklore and folk sayings. My hero Ignaz Bernstein has preserved for history almost four thousand *vitsn.* A short, excellent culling of proverbs from the Talmud was published in 1900 by one Madison C. Peters, who seems to have drawn heavily on preceding anthologies and translations.[15]

In recent years, American publishers have given us English translations of Mendele Mocher Seforim, Sholem Aleichem, the remarkable aphorist "The Chofetz Chaim" (Rabbi Israel Meir Kahan), Hebrew poets from Spain, post-Biblical writers and philosophers—to say nothing of miscellaneous collections, in English, of Jewish proverbs compiled by Lewis Browne, Joseph L. Baron, Hanan Ayalti, Fred Kogos, et alia.

*   *   *

A lovely passage in Midrash* (*Canticles,* 1b) runs:

Scorn not the *mashal* [proverb], for through it thou mayest gain a firm hold upon the Law, like a king who lost a piece of gold [and] by means of a wick, which is worth but a trifle, was able to find it again.

"A firm hold upon the Law ..." History inflicted such a succession of catastrophes on the Jews, from Babylon to Buchenwald, that special utility became attached to what was not destructible. Proverbs are portable. Wisdom takes up no room. Adages were the one Jewish treasure no Pilate could plunder, no inquisitor burn, no

* For descriptions of Midrash, Mishnah, Talmud, see the Guide Notes, pp. 68–76.

Cossack loot, no Nazi defile or destroy. Proverbs were the jewels concealed in Jewish minds.

The voluminous output of sayings, ironies, insights and paradoxes flowed from the Jews' untiring exercise of analytic intelligence, their training in introspection, their need to be astute observers (i.e., to anticipate the acts of tyrants or bullies or brigands)—and their literacy.

> When the overwhelming majority of mankind was illiterate, it was hard to find a Jewish lad over six who could not read and write. Most adult male Jews handled at least *three* languages: Hebrew in synagogues and "houses of study," Yiddish at home, and—to Gentiles—the language of the land in which they lived. My father, a workingman denied the equivalent of a high-school education, handled Yiddish, Hebrew, Polish and English.... Jews were linguists of necessity.[16]

A dominant proportion of the sayings in this volume deal with man's behavior, and cast a dazzling light on man's inner drives and moral dilemmas. Many Jewish folk sayings—about sex, dreams, pride, lust—seem fresher than Freud, though they may be older than King David. Yet this should not surprise us; for if a people hold themselves responsible to God for their every thought, if their teachers persuade them that their fate for all eternity depends on how they live, you may expect them to become intensely self-aware, self-examining, and self-critical. Psychology begins in introspection; philosophy begins in asking "Why?," "How?," "To what end?"

The Pedigree of Proverbs

I MUST add that the sayings loved and repeated by the Jews were not limited to what only their ancestors had created. Historians, archaeologists, philologists and ethnologists have so expanded and enriched our knowledge of the past that we now know how polyphonic was the life and growth of cultures, and how remarkable are the similarities of legend and myth in widely separated portions of our globe. (This is no new idea: Josephus, after recounting the story of Moses and the Red Sea, reminds us that Alexander the Great was also said to have marched his forces through a parting, by God's will, of the Pamphylian Sea.)

Since the Israelites lived within the teeming interplay of cultures that made up the civilization of the Middle East, they were long exposed to Hittite, Phoenician, Chaldean, and Arabic wisdom; then to Greek philosophy, the lore of Persia and the fables of Hindus; then to the writings of the Romans and the thought of Muslims and Moors.[17] And after the Jews were expelled from Spain, they came into close contact with French, Dutch, Italian, German, English, Rumanian, Polish, Russian (indeed all Slavonic) culture, as we shall see.

The enrichment which migrations and persecutions (as a by-product) conferred on Judaic thought and cosmopolitanism is impossible to appraise. What is clear (and rarely remarked upon) is that the children of Israel *had* to become anthropologists. It should not surprise us that Hebrew proverbs incorporated the wisdom of many other peoples: the *degree* to which such sayings and folklore filtered into the consciousness of the Jews is beyond measure. "A drowning man does not care about getting wet" is an Arabic saying —but the same idea is echoed in various forms in various tongues. The same is certainly true of "Penny wise, pound foolish," or "If you seek honey, expect bee stings"—which was cited long ago by al-Mutanabbi, an Arab who must have been quoting the greatest of proverbists: Anonymous.

What all this adds up to is this: the parentage of a folk saying is often as difficult to determine as the posthumous location of "Abraham's bosom." Of the eighty-two fables we attribute to Aesop, for instance, only one, according to Aristotle (*Rhetoric*, II), can safely be called original. Aesop, a slave in Samos, collected and transcribed the animalized lore of countless centuries—and a hodgepodge of peoples. How memorable is Thackeray's summation:

> The tales were told ages before Aesop; and asses under lions' manes roared in Hebrew; and sly foxes flattered in Etruscan; and wolves in sheep's clothing gnashed their teeth in Sanskrit, no doubt.[18]

I think you will be surprised by the number of aphorisms attributed to other sources or persons that are to be found in the

Talmud, which often alludes to popular sayings and often clinches an argument, for one or another technical point of law, by citing a piece of folk wisdom.[19]

> "Give every man the benefit of the doubt."
> "Look at the contents, not at the bottle."
> "Don't threaten a child: either punish or forgive him."
> "A dream uninterpreted is like a letter unopened."
> "It is better to die on your feet than live on your knees."
> "Experience is the name we give our mistakes."
> "In our dreams, it is not we who sin—but the dream."
> "All is well that ends well."

I hope all this will impress you as much as I was impressed when, in my salad days, reading John Wycliffe's preface to his translation of the Bible, I learned that he had undertaken the awesome labor because he felt the Bible is meant "for the government of the people, by the people, and for the people."

      ✿   ✿   ✿

Last year in London I purchased a dish towel on which I found block-printed:

> "Little dogs make the most noise."
> "No one needs help to get into trouble."
> "An obedient wife commands her man."
> "Idle young men become unhappy old men."

Are not these lovely sayings characteristically "Jewish"? They certainly are; but they happen to come from the storehouse of horse sense of the Maoris of New Zealand.

But the following, surely, are Jewish in style, mood, and substance:

> "A nation's treasure is its scholars."
> "Don't open a shop unless you like to smile."
> "With virtue, you can't be entirely poor;
> without virtue, you can't really be rich."
> "Deep doubts, deep wisdom; small doubts,
> little wisdom."

But they are old Chinese proverbs.

Are there, then, any special qualities, any singular psychology or philosophical stance, which distinguish the proverbs of Jews from those of other people? I think so; and I think you will think so, too, if you scan the pages of the anthology that follows.

At this point, however, let me explore one important aspect of the role which proverbs have played in Jewish life—a role which has not, in my judgment, been sufficiently emphasized.

Proverbs and Jewish Women

J EWISH boys would begin to study Hebrew as early as the age of three, and very rarely (unless mentally deficient) remained illiterate past the age of six. On his first day in the *cheder*, the elementary Hebrew school, the little boy's parents would take him to the *melamed* (teacher) and would stand over the child as the letters of the Hebrew alphabet were pointed to and pronounced: "*Aleph ... beyz ... gimel ...*" Sometimes the letters would be printed on a slate and coated with honey, for the young scholar to lick off as he repeated the sounds; sometimes the mother would have popped cookies, shaped in the form of Hebrew letters, into the little scholar's mouth before he was taken to the *cheder;* sometimes the mother would reward the boy with a honey-cookie, shaped in the form of the letter the lad pronounced, as soon as he uttered the name; sometimes the mother or *melamed* would place a drop of honey on the child's tongue, asking, "How does that taste?" "Sweet," the boy would of course reply. "The study of Torah," the *melamed* or mother would reply, "is sweeter." And at the end of the child's first lesson, his mother would enfold him, with a shawl or veil, and utter a prayer that her son "fulfill his life with years of study [Torah], marriage and good deeds."[20]

Every Jewish male over thirteen hurried to the synagogue to pray at least three times a day: in the morning (*shahrith*), in the afternoon (*minhah*), after sundown (*maarib*).

> The synagogue, from its inception, was a place for both prayer and study, and the distinction between the two is exceedingly difficult to draw. . . . Study and prayer, or (better)

study-prayer, was the most potent mortar in Jewish life. It was the linchpin in a Jew's self-esteem. It lent meaning and purpose to the most difficult and desperate of existences. It illuminated life. It ennobled, inspired, redeemed. It admitted even the humblest Jew to the company of sages, prophets, scholars, saints.[21]

Now, learning in *groups* and discussion in groups were especially favored; the Talmud (*Berakoth*, 63) says: "Learning is achieved only in company." So:

> Virtually all of male Jewry participated in a perpetual seminar. Even the cobblers. Even the tailors. The drivers and diggers, farmhands and carpenters. The peddlers and beggars and shopkeepers. . . . They were all arguers, dialecticians, amateur theologians.[22]

And in the *Beth Midrash* ("house of study") every Jew sat "like [an] intellectual magnate. . . . When a problem came up, there was immediately a host of people pouring out opinions, arguments, quotations. . . . The stomachs were empty, the homes barren, but the minds were crammed with the riches of the Torah."[23] One may learn a good deal about Jewish life by remembering that it was customary for Jews, when they met or whiled away an hour, to ask one another: *"Zug mir a shtikl Torah"* ("Tell me a piece of Torah"). Then discussion—fervent, contentious, casuistic, all-absorbing—was launched.

The point I now want to stress is this: when a Jew came home, he would tell his wife what "portion" of Torah he had read or discussed or heard discussed; what maxim from Akiba or the Saadia Gaon, what fresh explications of a man's duty to his parents, children, brothers, sisters, the old, the sick, the poor; what revelations of the Messiah's coming, or the nature of immortality, or the rewards in the "world-to-come" for the bitter travails of this life on earth.

Such majestic mysteries, conveyed to a mother or wife or child, required prodigious simplification—not only because they are themselves saturated in complexity, but because even the discussions of Jewish laymen were extremely technical, cloaked in theological conundrums, flecked with such a profusion of split hairs that they torment ordinary reason. (Anyone who has plowed through a page of Talmud will know what I mean.)

And no device proved more useful to the Jewish husband, in imparting quick summaries, than—proverbs, parables, folk sayings. The meaning of a metaphor in Genesis or a parable in the Haggadah; the reduction of a logical dilemma to a nutshell; the rendition of Rabbi Meir's paradox or Yitskhok the Tailor's question—all were borne down that verbal stream in which the core of the sacred teachings, and their embroidering by prophets and scholars, moved from the temple of God through the houses of study into the streets and home to the kitchens.

In this endless process, it was folk sayings that made the hallowed homely, the sacred secular, the lofty cozy. And since Yiddish was the language through which Eastern European Jewish mothers could participate in the savoring of Talmudic law and lore, Yiddish was the language they used to transmit the great tradition to their children.

So it was that I, like any other Jewish boy, heard—from my mother or father or uncle—some bit of wit or wisdom or wonder, coined twenty centuries ago, which lay within the forbidding forests of the Talmud, or which (I would discover forty years later) was a saying of Rab Ashi or some disciple of some illustrious sage who had adorned one or another school of thought in some academy in Jerusalem or Babylon.

A word about Yiddish is in order.

Detour: Yiddish

T HE journeyings of the Jews presented them with the necessity of learning the languages of the territories through which they wandered, or the provinces in which—for a week or a decade or a century—they were permitted to settle. In order to live, to work or trade or raise their sustenance, Jews had to become at least bilingual (they carried Hebrew with them, of course).

The ancient rabbis and scholars knew Greek and Latin. As

groups of Jews moved eastward into the Middle and Far East, they picked up new languages—in what is now Turkey, Persia, India, even China.

During the first century before the Christian era, Jewish settlements were established in Greece and along the entire Eastern Mediterranean from Asia Minor to Alexandria. In succeeding migrations, Jews moved into the Crimea and the Balkans. When the Eastern Catholic successors to Constantine launched their savage persecutions, Jews were driven farther up into the Ukraine, up the Volga, into Kiev and places under the hegemony of barbaric Slavs. (Rabbinical letters allude to Jews whose native tongue had become Russian, and who read the Torah in Russian.) When the Tartar hordes overran the Russian steppes and decimated the Ukraine, Jewish (and Slavic) survivors fled into the Carpathians, up into Poland and Lithuania and provinces of Muscovite Russia. (Early Polish coins contain Hebrew lettering, and suggest that Polish rulers authorized Jews to mint their money.) A Jewish community settled in Vienna in the eighth or ninth century.

In migrations *westward* from Palestine and Egypt, Jews settled in Rome, along the Mediterranean, in Germany (Jewish groups accompanied the Romans into Teutonic regions as early as the fourth century), in Spain and France. In the Middle Ages, merchant Jews criss-crossed Europe, some settling in various localities.

The Crusades inflicted hideous catastrophes on Jews all along the Crusaders' routes, driving them from the Rhineland and the Danube deeper into Central Europe, Bohemia, the Balkans and the territories from which, in time, a Polish suzerainty was formed. In the thirteenth century, when the Jews were brutally expelled from France and England (as, in the fifteenth, they were hounded out of Spain and Portugal), masses of Jews wandered back into North Africa, Egypt, Palestine; or into the Netherlands, Germany, Italy, *mittel-Europa.*

Now, in each of these historic convulsions, the Jews learned new parlances. Jews learned Arabic, Dutch, several Slavic tongues, and languages born of Latin: Italian, Spanish, Portuguese, French.

The odd story of a new tongue, Yiddish, begins (so far as recent scholarship has reconstructed it) in the tenth and eleventh centuries, when Jews from Northern France came down the Rhineland, where they picked up the Germanic dialects of places in which they sank roots: Cologne, Trier, Coblenz, Mainz. Jews who

filtered farther eastward learned the regional parlance of Frankfurt, Wurzburg, Stuttgart. So grew up a vernacular, Judaeo-German, that was to become the foundation of Yiddish (the name
comes from the German *Jüdisch*). And when Jews were invited
(!) to come to reside in Poland, to form an economic class between ignorant peasants and indolent noblemen, they brought Hebrew and German with them. It was in the settlements of Middle
and Eastern Europe—in Galicia, Hungary, Rumania, the Ukraine,
Poland, Russia, Lithuania—that, after the seventeenth century, an
unique Jewish language flowered and a novel literature grew up.

Yiddish, let me emphasize, was scorned by the rabbis and
detested by the intellectuals of Judaism—especially by German
Jews, to whom Yiddish was "a loathsome jargon," "vulgar," "pig-
gish." Jewish intellectuals preferred the established languages of
Europe, languages with a "proper" vocabulary, an accepted grammar, a dignified history and literature. But the Jewish masses
clung to their beloved vernacular, and embroidered and enriched
it *ad libitum.* . . . Hebrew, after all, was "God's tongue," far too
sacred to be demeaned by earthly, earthy uses. More and more,
Yiddish became the workaday tongue for everyday life, for sharing the vicissitudes of daily and domestic affairs. Eastern European Jews were often trilingual; and Yiddish became the vehicle
for irreverent folk sayings which Hebrew could not countenance,
and homely anecdotes Hebrew would not trifle with.

There is no slang, for instance, in Hebrew; in Yiddish, slang
was invented, embraced, relished and embellished with gusto.
Hebrew possessed no colloquial words for genital organs; Yiddish
showed no hesitation in coining explicit words, vulgar or euphe-
mistic, for the instruments of sex and the rondos of copulation.

And so Yiddish, "the Robin Hood of languages," has practiced
the most buoyant banditry among the words of every land in
which its practitioners wandered. In the course of twenty-four
hours, a son of Judah, speaking Yiddish today, may, without being
aware of it, raid over two dozen other languages.*

I always marvel over how ingenious Yiddish became in de-
veloping a vocabulary of psychological insight; how fertile in dis-

---

* For example: Hebrew (*mezuza*), English (*donton* = "downtown"), Aramaic
(*alevay*), Russian (*kishke*), Polish (*pisk*), Ukrainian (*paskudnyak*), Rumanian (*grid-
zhe*), Czech (*nebish*), Ukrainian (*blints*), Italian (*yente*), French (*davn*), Spanish
(*Schnaiur*, a name derived from *señor*), Turkish (*kave*).

covering nuances for the observation of man and society; how resourceful in perfecting words to describe the marvelous gallery of human character types;* above all, how perceptive in understanding that baffling interplay of comedy, tragedy, fantasy, and farce that is human life. I am not unaware of the risks one runs in generalizing, but surely there is good reason to call German ponderous, French lean and logical, Italian lyrical, Russian melancholy, Arabic flowery, English powerful. And Yiddish?

> Steeped in sentiment, it is sluiced with sarcasm. It loves the ruminative, because it rests on a rueful past; it favors paradox, because it knows that only paradox can do justice to the injustices of life; it adores irony, because the only way the Jews could retain their sanity was to view a dreadful world with sardonic eyes.[24]

What does all this have to do with proverbs and folk sayings? A very great deal. Maurice Samuel tells us:

> The Yiddish masses were strangers to earthy joys that lightened the lives of their . . . neighbors. Their consolations were to a large extent [those] of the imagination, and therefore their language, besides serving a normal need, had an esoteric function unimaginable to their neighbors. All languages have their peculiarities and impenetrable privacies. . . . The spirit of Yiddish sets it apart from contiguous languages. The difficulty of translating Yiddish . . . lies less in the absence of corresponding vocabularies than in the Jewish-Yiddish conception of the meaning of life and the destiny of the people.[25]

All this is by way of prelude to saying that Jewish proverbs, like Jewish life, are freighted with emotion, laden with ornate metaphors and purple exaggerations, glutinous benedictions and fearsome maledictions:

> "May the cholera seize him!"
> "May his insides sound like a music box!"
> "May all his teeth fall out, save one" (so that he may
>   have a permanent toothache).

---

* Examples: *nudnik, nebbech, shlepper, shlump, shmendrick, shlemiel, Kuni Lemmel, tummler, kibitz, gonif, shnuk, Moyshe Kapoyr, kochleffel, platkemacher, shtunk, yachneh, Khaim* (or *Chaim*) *Yonkel, bulbenik, plosher, etcetera* (which is not Yiddish).

"I would like to treat him like a treasure—bury him in the ground with loving care."

The folk sayings in this volume are drawn from Yiddish and Hebrew (the former often translated from Hebrew), and Yiddish is a "a tongue that never takes its tongue out of its cheek. . . . In its innermost heart, Yiddish swings from shmaltz to derision."[26]

It is the proverbs and folk sayings which enrich that language, and which do indeed have a unique flavor, that I collected for over fifty years. Then arose a perplexing question: how best translate them?

The Torments of Translation

EVERY language spoken by man (there are over 2,800) is combed with uniqueness. Human languages are as different as peas in a pod (if you examine them under a microscope). What human tongues have in common is only purpose: the use of words to try to describe, understand and communicate the measureless sensations of existence, the swarm of impressions on the self, the marvelous symbolic productions of the human mind, the infinite fantasies of the imagination, the divine and the wretched parameters of the human condition:

Of all man's marvelous inventions, language is surely the most amazing. It is the *sine qua non* of man's estate; it distinguishes him from his animal cousins; it permits experience to be accumulated and transmitted; it makes abstract thought —generalization, discrimination, analysis, hypothesis—possible. Without language, there could be nothing remotely like science or technology: no poetry or physics; no transistor or computer; no laser, maser, zipper or Hollandaise sauce. . . .

The Bible says, "In the beginning was the word." If that means anything, it means that language existed *before* man. . . . The great Rabbi Akiba's disciples took it for granted

that an alphabet existed before God created the world. I
have no way of proving this, but there is no way of dis-
proving it either."[27]

A language is a *Weltanschauung*. Even languages very close
in origin, history and structure develop surprising differences. The
English "conscience" is not the same as the French *conscience*
(which means "consciousness" or "conscientiousness"). German
had no word for "bully" until the twentieth century (a mordant
comment on Teutonic values) and can only render the Englishman's idea of "fair play" as "*'fair' Spielen*." If this be true of
tongues so close to each other in birth, so laden with cognates,
so cross-fertilized by usage and literature, how much more does
it intrude when one tries to translate Yiddish or Hebrew into
English?

Translation is not simply a matter of dexterity in transferring
synonyms. Translation does not contend with words, but with
meanings. To translate is to decode: to transpose one mode of
thinking, feeling, fearing, appraising, into the word patterns of
another. No language can be separated from its historical skeleton,
its psychological skin, or its sociological garments. Languages are
acculturated verbalizations of experience and thought.

Christian missionaries in the Orient, for instance, were sorely
perplexed because Chinese had neither a word for "word" nor a
word for, or an idea of, "sin." (The closest was *tsui*, which meant
"crime"). And in Africa or Polynesia, the Christian messengers of
the Lord found bewildering difficulty in trying to communicate
the idea of God—i.e., one supreme deity—to people mystified by
such an impoverished theology. In language, which is a system
of "culturally ordained categories," each of us "builds the house
of his consciousness."[28]

One of the translators at the United Nations tells us that
when an English or American speaker says, "I assume," interpreters render that in French as "I deduce" and in Russian as "I consider."[29]

It is hard for us truly to believe that each culture teaches
its people what to say about what that culture has taught them
to think, feel, see, or even hear. The pioneering studies of Edward
Sapir (whom I was fortunate to know) and Benjamin Lee Whorf
have forced us to consider the surprising degree to which our

sensations, our thoughts, even our actions, are influenced by the particular system of sounds and symbols we inherit. We all tend to assume that we are experiencing the real world, "but in many cases we are free only to experience the possibilities and limitations of grammar."[30]

For instance: Do you think dogs go *"woof-woof," "bow-wow"* or *"arf-arf"*? In English prose, they bark that way. But in German, dogs go *"wau-wau,"* in Chinese *"wang-wang,"* in Vietnamese *"gau-gau,"* and in Japanese *"wan-wan."* In Yiddish, dogs go *"how-how,"* and there is a saying: "The dog who barks *'ho-ho'* is not dangerous, but the one who growls *'how-how'* is." (I cannot help wondering how a Laplander or Litvak would translate "going to the dogs.")

In German, frogs are said to croak *"quak-quak,"* which would confuse an American duck. Scottish roosters would surely be flabbergasted to learn that French roosters go *"cocorico"* (at least in French novels). As for Arabian donkeys, which Arabian writers tell us go *"ham-ham,"* I quail to think of what they would think if they learned that in Rumanian it is dogs that go *"ham-ham."* I leave it to zoologists to decide whether, perhaps, different breeds make different sounds.

Any sensible American will tell you that scissors go *"snip-snip," "snip-snap,"* or *"snap-snap."* But to a Greek, believe it or not, scissors go *"kritz-kritz."* And to a Chinese, scissors hiss *"su-su."* As for Spaniards, Italians, and Portuguese, their scissors retain as marked a national identity as any other, being written respectively as *"ri-ri," "kri-kri,"* and *"terre-terre."*[31]

All this may disturb your comforting assumption that in onomatopoeia, at least, there is universal agreement; that everyone, whether Choctaw or Irish or Cypriot, produces the same oral renditions of and for the same heard sounds; that different languages must employ the same vocalizations for objectively uniform acoustics.

But the notion that onomatopoeia crosses the frontiers of language rests on the misconception that verbal allusions accurately mirror "real" sounds: they do not; they record and reflect those sounds our culture has instructed us to hear, or predisposed us *not* to hear. A German child is taught to hear the buzzing of a bee not as *"bzz-bzz"* (which English bees do, apparently in order to validate our word "buzzing") but as *"sum-sum."* If you will repeat *"sum-sum"* for a while, you may come to prefer it to "*bzz-bzz*"—or you may, in the interest of world peace, henceforth describe all bees as going "*bzz-bzz sum-sum.*"

Do you think that in every society men grow so angry they "see red"? Well, "our classification of the spectrum into . . . red, orange, yellow, green, blue and violet is culturally arbitrary, and persons in other cultures divide the spectrum quite differently. Perception itself is an aspect of human *behavior.*"[32]

Optical recordings often express learned ways of seeing and inferring. I once wrote: "We see things as *we* are, not as they are." Professor E. H. Gombrich tells us that ancient artists drew eyelashes on the lower lids of horses' eyes (the drawings *they* had seen and studied showed eyelashes on horses' lower lids); but lower eyelashes do not happen to exist on real, undrawn horses . . . . As Degas once blurted: "Drawing is not what one sees, but what others must be made to see."

Have I wandered from proverbs and translation? Only to illustrate, I hope, how complicated simple things become if we examine them with care. The mere change of sound, in translating, can alter the sensual glow and hum of the original. I commend to you Bernard Berenson's appraisal of critics: They break a watch into its parts, to hear how it ticks. Changing one word's *position* can alter meaning dramatically: "What is harder than getting a pregnant elephant in a Volkswagen? Getting an elephant pregnant in a Volkswagen."

The most tormenting aspect of translation is this: What is idiomatic in one tongue is idiotic in another. Think for a moment of what happens if a translator of English does not realize that "Tell it to Sweeney" is a rebuff, not a request; that "a Northern Spy" may have been an undercover agent for Ulysses S. Grant— or only a variety of apple; that Occam never used his razor for shaving, any more than Cleopatra used her needle for sewing; that "Jack-in-the-pulpit" does not mean the preacher's name is Jack; that "behind the 8-ball" is gibberish in nine tenths of the world; and that when athletes engage in a "rhubarb" they do not sit down to eat the stuff.

It gives me the greatest pleasure to inform you that Russian physicists believe that the first nuclear atomic pile in history was constructed in a pumpkin field—that being their natural translation of "squash court," the site in the concrete bowels of the stadium ("Stagg Field") of the University of Chicago.

As for poetry, I can do no better than give you Chaim Bialik's despairing dictum: "Reading poetry in translation is like kissing a woman through a veil."

* * *

I cannot help feeling that where a translator, however fine a scholar, is not a writer, translation starts under a deadly handicap. For if a writer is anything he is one who is sensitive to words, who loves their texture, their nuances, their conceptual echoes and overtones. An empathy for language—which is to say, a refined and heightened awareness of words—is simply a *sine qua non* (how do you say that in English?) for translators. The man who hears not the beat of a word, much less a sentence, or who is indifferent to simile and metaphor, or who does not savor parallel construction, or who is word-blind and cadence-deaf, is bound to butcher his task. A seventeenth-century man of letters, John Denham, bristled:

> Such is our pride, our folly and our fate
> That only those who cannot write, translate.

The Bill of Rights composed by the 1971 International Conference on Literary Translation reads:

> The translator's chief obligation is to create the work in a new language with the appropriate music and the utmost response to the silences of the original.[33]

As an admirer of the manifesto, I wish that its writers had said "another," not "a new," language: translators are surely not obliged to invent a tongue from scratch.

"A good translation," said Benedetto Croce, "is a work of art."

The Importance (and Misdemeanors) of Translation

Not until I was immersed in this work did a perfectly obvious thought occur to me: how monumental a role translators have played in human history. Indeed, what we know of history, or of the lore, legends and literature of other peoples, is almost entirely a product of translators. Except for scholars who are multilingual, education itself, for most of us, is rooted in translated works. How many of us have read Thucydides in Greek? Or tackled Livy in Latin? Or, for that matter, savored Dante, Cervantes, Goethe, Tolstoy, in the original? As Miles Smith of Oxford wrote in 1611, in a preface to the King James Version of the Bible:

> Translation it is that openeth the window, to let in the light; that breaketh the shell, that we may eat the kernel; that putteth aside the curtaine, that we may looke into the most Holy place. . . .

The entire web of our culture is interlaced with translations; interpreters may properly be called the carriers of civilization, and its true cross-fertilizers. Take the great books of Greek philosophy, science, geography, astronomy, medicine. The words of Euclid, Aristotle, Aristarchus of Samos (who held that the earth revolves on its own axis, and moves around the sun), Plato, Galen, and later Ptolemy, were (except for a small band of scholars) unknown to the Europeans of the twelfth and thirteenth centuries, until those words were translated into Latin—from Arabic, into which tongue they had been rendered from Syriac, into which language they had been translated from the Greek. These Latin texts, thrice removed from the original, flowed into Europe's monasteries and universities to transform the late medieval world. The first complete translation of Plato into Latin was not made until 1482.[34]

Plutarch and Suetonius provided kings and princes with political lessons from their predecessors. It was from translations of Machiavelli that one or another Anglo-Saxon, Nordic or Slavic ruler learned stratagems of statecraft, power politics, diplomacy. It was from translations of Castiglione that Europe's royal courts learned the rudiments of manners. And the poets of the Renaissance, like the playwrights of Elizabethan England, were profoundly influenced by their reading of translated classics; Ben Jonson tells us that Shakespeare "had small Latin and less Greek," yet Shakespeare based six plays on Greek history, and six of his greatest on Roman.[35]

Suppose I make the point another way: Had translations *not* been made, would Homer, Vergil, Erasmus, Montaigne, be recognized outside of our universities? Were translations forbidden what would you or I know of Sumeria or Confucius, Carthage or Copernicus or Montezuma? Of the Mongol hordes or the Moghul dynasts? Of life in medieval Kyoto? Of the Crusades—or Dostoevski? Of what happened this morning in Peking, Moscow, Tokyo, Berlin?

✿   ✿   ✿

But what we do know about history, through translations, is pitted with astonishing errors because of translation. (The Italians say, *"Traduttore traditori"*: translators are traitors.) Take a simple example: Do our history books tell us that Greek tyrants were not tyrannical? They should: for among the ancient Greeks a tyrant (*tyrannos*) was simply one who had seized power; many Greek "tyrants" were liberal, popular and far from tyrannical.

Now take a more important body of errors in translation, if one contemplates the consequences: the Bible. I first became aware of the farrago of boners in English translations of Holy Scripture when I spent a year studying comparative religion in the Divinity School of the University of Chicago. (Mind you, I had not the slightest intention of becoming a divine, divine though the idea may sound; I was simply fascinated by the varieties of men's faith, the psychology of belief, the anatomy of man's accumulated knowledge about gods and God.) It was no small revelation, to me, to learn such simple but startling facts as these: That the Bible (from the Greek *biblia*) is a collection of "little books"; that these books were not written at one time, and not by one man, but by a good many men across a stretch of at least 1,300 years (if you date the earliest parts of the Old Testament prior to 1,200 before the Christian Era, and the last of the New Testament post-100); that the holy books were gathered together, in far from systematic fashion, down the centuries—according to the haphazard judgment of religious leaders, rabbis, kings, preachers, priests; that the Bible was not even called "Bible" until the fourteenth century—and not "Holy" until 1568; that the immortal King James Version (1611) was the *third* English translation authorized; that the Wycliffe Bible (c. 1388) was branded heresy; that Tyndale's great translation of 1525* so fixed the English style and mood that all later versions "must be looked upon as revisions . . . not independent translations";[36] that from 1611 to 1697 the New Testament was revised seven different times; that a revised Revised Version appeared in 1885, and at least twenty variant translations have appeared since then.[37]

At the University, I met Professor Edgar J. Goodspeed, who had completed his "American" (that is what he named it) translation of the New Testament. I was simply astounded to learn how many solemnly printed passages in the Old and New Testaments were questionable, misleading, or downright *wrong*, when compared with the earliest Hebrew/Aramaic/Greek manuscripts. "Candles" and "candlesticks," for instance, are historical impossibilities (torches or oil lamps were what the Hebrews used); "the Three Wise Men" were not wise men at all: they were astrologers or soothsayers (the rendering of the Greek *magoi* or the Latin *magi* as "wise men" is just false). "Servant" in the Bible often means "slave" (slavery was rife in the ancient world); and to "add one cubit unto his stature" (Matthew 6 : 27) is a bit ludicrous, since a cubit is about 18 inches.

The King James version uses a late sixteenth century idiom

---

* Tyndale's story is as fascinating as it was tragic. He started to translate the New Testament, but found such hostility to this in England that he went to Germany. A Church injunction stopped him in Cologne; he fled to Worms. Copies of his translation reached England in 1526, and were denounced and suppressed by the bishops. Cardinal Wolsey sent an order to have Tyndale arrested in Worms. Tyndale worked in a hideaway and published his translation of the Pentateuch in 1520. His defenses of the Reformation were denounced by Thomas More; his criticism of Henry VIII's divorce incurred the monarch's wrath. Wolsey's agents captured Tyndale in Antwerp, where he was correcting some translations; he was tried for heresy, condemned, and strangled at the stake. Then, on orders of Emperor Charles V, his body was burned. . . .

I tell this story at length to suggest the perils which translators sometimes confronted.

(already somewhat archaic by the time that great Bible was printed[38]) that lends glory to the text—and discombobulating ambiguity: What on earth is meant by "Ye are not straitened in us"? Or "We do you to wit of the grace of God"? Or take the misleading references to money: a "penny" was not a trifle to the Hebrews; it was the going rate for twelve hard hours of work. Or take the fallacious impressions of time: "the third hour" leads a modern reader to think that what is meant is 3 A.M. or 3 P.M.; but what "the third hour" meant was the third hour after dawn: i.e., 8 or 9 in the morning.

In many unhappy cases, the original meaning of a word is precisely *opposite* the meaning we derive from it in the translation by King James's reverent scholars. The phrase "by and by" meant, to the Hebrews, not "in a little while," but "immediately." And to the King Jamesians, so apparently simple a word as "comprehend" signified not "comprehension," as we today assume, but "overcoming an obstacle."[39]

Of greater consequence are the startling changes in the translations of gospel recently made, and jointly agreed upon, by committees of scholars themselves Protestant, Catholic, Jewish. Let me mention a few:

(1) "In the beginning God created the heaven and the earth" is now rendered, in several modern translations, as: "When God began to create the heaven and the earth." (Obviously, God existed before He created anything.)

(2) The Third Commandment now reads: "Thou shalt not swear falsely by the name of the Lord your God; for the Lord will not clear one *who swears falsely* by His name" (my italics). The change is of cardinal importance; for in the new translations man is commanded to avoid *perjury,* not profanity (as the King James "take the name of the Lord in vain" seemed to signify).

(3) The Israelites, fleeing from their pursuers, did not cross the Red Sea. They were nowhere near the Red Sea at the time. What the Israelites cross, in modern translations, is the "Sea of Reeds" or "The Sea of Bulrushes," either of which is accurate English for the Hebrew *Yam Suf* of the ancient texts.[40] (I wish I could say the error made was tantamount to mistaking "Reed Sea" for "Red Sea"—an instantly plausible and visual mistake.) The change to "Sea of Reeds" offers us a crutch for credibility; after all, the rushes in a marsh part more readily, without divine

intervention, than the waters of a sea. (But how were the pursuing Egyptians drowned?)

(4) The most historic change, surely, has been made in Isaiah 7 : 14 (and therefore in Matthew 1:22–21, which quotes Isaiah 7 : 14). The King James Bible, as do portions of the bibles in over 1,431 different translations, recounts how Isaiah promised Hezekiah (a king of the Jews who was defending himself against two enemy armies) that his aggressors will be destroyed:

> Therefore the Lord himself shall give you a sign; Behold, a virgin shall conceive, and bear a son . . .

But new translations render this passage as:

> Therefore the Lord himself shall give you a sign: A young woman is with child, and she will bear a son . . .

The word Isaiah used was *almah,* which in Hebrew does not mean "virgin," but "young woman." (The Hebrew word for "virgin" is *betulah.*) Isaiah used the word he meant, which Greek and Latin translators later misinterpreted. (I hasten to add that faith in the Virgin Birth does not depend simply on how one translates this passage.)

Since my student days, over a dozen excellent new translations of the Bible have appeared, many of them inspired by the dramatic discovery of ancient documents that predate all earlier manuscripts (the most famous and significant, of course, are the Dead Sea Scrolls). And the new translations agree on the corrections I have sketched above.[41]

Before you vent too much wrath on errant scribes and scholars, or their modern correctors, let us consider with charity the pitfalls and phantoms that make any translator's life a misery: Let us return to some special problems Yiddish presents to the translator.

On Translating Yiddish

To translate, we have seen, is to recreate portions of a culture in words which are comprehensible to someone to whom that culture is unknown or but thinly comprehended. To translate Yiddish is to translate a certain style of life, a construct of apperceptions, a system of values, intricate subtleties of thinking and feeling which are imbedded in the language of Eastern European Jews and their descendants.

To translate Yiddish into English is quite different from translating, say, French into Italian: for a common religion (Christianity), equalities of statehood, shared political ideas and whilom sovereigns—all these endow English, French, Italian, German, Spanish, with a common (or close) inventory of experience, common codes of etiquette, common models of masculinity or ideals of femininity, assumptions about salvation, hunting, drinking, passions—all of which are worlds removed from Jewish experience and ideology. The translator of Yiddish is therefore compelled to build cultural-psychological bridges across chasms that do not separate other peoples from one another—or do not separate them so widely.

Many Yiddish words and phrases are exasperatingly difficult to translate—at least, to my finicky satisfaction. To render Yiddish (or German or French) word-by-word would be to produce such barbarisms as "It grows a pain," or "It comes a child." And I'm afraid there are only pallid equivalents in English for a whole symphony of vivid and delectable Yiddish words. Consider these hallowed few:

> *chutspa:* monumental gall, colossal effrontery;
> *mishpokhe:* a family unit that embraces relatives far, near,
>   remote, and numerous;
> *kvel:* a beaming pride in a child's achievements, or an un-

worthy (but ever-so-pleasurable) gloating over an enemy's humiliation;

kvetsh: a chronic griper-complainer-drip-sourpuss;

tchotchke or *tsatske:* a toy, a trinket; but also a mistress, a playgirl, a pretty, brainless young thing—whether wife or girlfriend;

paskudnyak: a gross, greedy, contemptible man or woman;

shlemiel: a simpleton in spades, a maladroit pipsqueak; a butter-fingered bumpkin: "A *shlemiel* falls on his back and breaks his nose";

shlimazl: a born loser, a football to fate, a man who buys a suit with two pairs of pants and promptly burns a hole in the jacket;

zaftik: juicy; but a *zaftik* woman is inviting to the touch and seductive to the glands.[42]

Or take the Slavic particle *zhe,* which is used in Yiddish to add a note of needling, in impatience or accusation, to the commonplace. If you want to say, "For heaven's sake, when will you be ready?" you say *"Venzhe vest di zayn greyt?"* ("When already will you be ready?") If you want to end a conversation with a courteous but unmistakable hint, you say *"Zayt zhe mir gezunt,"* which Englishes abominably as "Be already to me well..." but means: "go already—in good health."

And if Yiddish words can perplex a translator, consider how their arrangement can derange their substance:

"He should live so long" is not an amiable hope but a creamy curse.

"From this he makes a *living?*" is not a question; it is a put-down.

"*This* I need?" is a contemptuous rejection of what it appears to be asking, for it means, "Of all the things in the world I do *not* need, this leads the list."

"Do you want it to sing, too?" when asked of a customer who returns a canary merely because it is mute, turns a reasonable expectation upside down, and thus means: "How carping of you to expect this beautiful bird, which has so splendid an array of nonvocal attributes, to sing, *too.*"

When Yiddish phrases or idioms are to be translated, the difficulties become magnified yet further. A translator who renders *"Vus makhst du?"* as "What are you making?" is absolutely right

—*if* the question is being asked of a relative or friend (*du*) who is standing over an anvil; but the translation is cockamamy nonsense if the speaker is greeting someone—for "*Vus makhst du?*" only means "How are you?"

The unwary reader of the Yiddish phrase "*Hak nisht* (or *nit*) *kayn tschainik*," translating the words literally as "Don't knock a teapot" (it *means* "Don't yak, yak, *yak* so much"), will be as deluded as the inexpert translator of the Polish phrase "He is underpinned with a child" who does not know it means "In every man, a child is hidden."

To render the Yiddish *broyges* as "angry" is to destroy the distinctions between *broyges, beyz* and *onkast*: To be *broyges* is to be "on the outs with"; a man who is "*broyges*" is not on speaking terms with you. In the bygone Bronx, "*broyges*" was cleverly, if inelegantly, translated "mad on," as in this indignant declaration, heard on Tremont Avenue: "Invite her to my party? Never! I'm mad on her."

* * *

The most crushing ripostes, the most taunting acerbities, bloom and thrive in Yiddish, which seems limitless in devices that sow seeds of sarcasm in the soil of ordinary discourse: Let me expand on this point, which I sketched out, in briefer form, in the *Joys of Yiddish:*

(1) *Emphasis by transplanting a predicate adjective:*
"Funny, he isn't."
("He isn't funny" is not funny; but "Funny, he isn't," is—for it means "There are many things you can say about him, even fine, flattering things, but the one thing you can *not* say is that he is funny.")

(2) *Demolition of a virtue through repetition with a prefatory "shm-":*
"Good-shmood, he eats like a horse."

(3) *Emphasizing a defect by repeating a word with the "shm"-gambit:*
"Fat-shmat, she has to dance the Watusi."

(4) *Stressing an asset through "shm"-prefaced reiteration.*
"Poor-shmoor, he'd give his shirt to a beggar."

(5) *Dismissing an idea out-of-hand by framing it as a question:*

"I should invite him to my son's *Bar Mitzvah?*"

(When a question is framed "I should . . . ?" instead of "Should I . . . ?" you may be pretty sure you are being told, not asked.)

(6) *Sarcasm via the addition to a straightforward sentence of* "only," "just" *or* "merely": this transforms the forthright into the murderous:

"Why did he leave her? She only tried to poison him —once a week."

"She was an angel about the divorce; she just wanted his seven gold teeth."

"We were merely three hours late—on a two-hour flight."

(7) *Inferential aspersion through innocent interrogation:*

"Already he's not satisfied?"

"For *that* you blame me?"

"For that you *blame* me?"

(8) *Scathing disdain by placing the object before the subject:*

"*Thanks* she expected for arriving so late?"

(9) *Maximizing indignation by repeating a question in the exact form in which it was asked.* In this ploy, my using Question B as a reply to your Question A (B being identical to A) indicates that the answer to your question is so obvious that its use by you constituted an affront to me that is best erased by umbrage via echo. Note three exquisite variations:

I

Q. "Did you send flowers to the hospital?"

A. "Did I send flowers to the hospital?"

(Meaning: "How can you insult me by doubting it?")

II

Q. "Did you send flowers to the hospital?"

A. "Did I send flowers to the hospital!"

(This converts a boorish question into an aggrieved affirmation, meaning, "I practically bought out the florist's shop.")

III

Q. "Did you send flowers to the hospital?"

A. "Did I send flowers to the hospital?!"
   (Meaning: "How could any decent human being *not* send flowers to the hospital?")

(10) *Imputing stupidity through sardonic reprise:*
   Q. "Would you like some cheesecake?"
   A. "Would I like some cheesecake?"
      (Shorthand for, "Who in his right mind would not jump at the chance to eat some cheesecake?")

(11) *Rejection by repetition in which ridicule is implied:*
   Q. "Will you take twenty dollars for it?"
   A. "Will *I* take twenty dollars for it?"
      (This expresses incredulity at so ridiculous an offer.)

(12) *Noble forbearance by repeating a question without comment on it:*
   Q. "Will you take twenty dollars for it?"
   A. (*sighing*) "Will I take twenty dollars for it?"
      (This calls attention to my reasonable character—despite your cheap offer.)

(13) *Tactical acquiescence without binding acceptance:*
   Q. "Will you take fifty dollars for it?"
   A. "Will I take fifty dollars for it?"
      (This hedges too-prompt acceptance, which might lead you to wonder whether you had been too generous.)

(14) *Underlining asininity by holding up a mirror to it:*
   Q. "Don't you want to get well and spend the winter in Palm Beach?"
   A. "No, I don't want to get well and spend the winter in Palm Beach."

(15) *Underlining asininity by holding a contrary mirror before it:*
   Q. "How would you like a free week in the Virgin Islands?"
   A. "I'd rather rent a basement in a home for the aged."

(16) *Contempt by concurrence:*
      Q. "But won't you die if they don't operate?"
      A. "Yes, I'll die if they don't operate."
         (Meaning, "Only an idiot asks such a question.")

(17) *Deflation by magnified concurrence:*
      Q. "A bird in the hand is worth two in the bush, so accept the offer."
      A. "Any bird in the hand is worth two in the bush!"
         (Meaning: "In that case I should accept any offer.")

(18) *Scorn through stressing one word:*
    "Her he *loves?*"
    (This casts doubt on the sanity of the lover.)

(19) *Criticism by stressing another word in the same sentence.*
    "*Her* he loves?"
    (This suggests that the loved one lacks any semblance of those qualities that might make a sane man love her.)

(20) *Relieving guilt by linking a curse to instant but only nominal cancellation:*
    "May darkness invade his eyes, God forbid!"
    "May a fire rage in his bowels, let God prevent that!"
    "May God avoid driving her crazy with shingles!"

But I must not strain your patience by extending mine. (For the difficulties of translating Hebrew, see Appendix II.

On Translating Proverbs

I N translating proverbs and folk sayings, insensitivity to the cadences of a culture, no less than the overtones and resonances of its language, can prove fatal. If euphony is expelled from an epigram, its very heart is stilled; if alliteration is abolished, the playfulness of a saying may be destroyed; if mushiness replaces succinctness, an aphorism becomes a banality. Earnest but inept translators can turn a bit of wisdom into a pile of nonsense.

Take this line, exactly as I found it, attributed to "the Talmud":

> Bad matches beget good children.

On the face of it, the sentence struck me as absurd. Why? (1) If bad marriages produce good children, then what kind of offspring do good marriages produce? (2) Do *both* bad and good marriages beget good children? (3) Is the happiness or integrity of a marriage irrelevant to the character of the offspring? (4) How could one of the Talmudic sages, who were exceptionally rigorous in reasoning, let pass so many-forked a proposition?

I brought my problem to one of my experts, who traced the sentence to its source and translated the passage in which it appeared. Then I reduced the passage, which contained involutions which need not detain us, to:

> *Even* a bad marriage can beget good children.

I have the greatest sympathy for immigrants who had to learn English, a most difficult and perverse tongue, in their adulthood; but just as my sympathy turns sour when a tone-deaf fiddler plays Mozart, my patience runs out when an inveterate bungler commits a translation.*

Many English translations of Yiddish folk sayings simply boggle the mind; others offend the ear; and some are so insipid that they turn wit into waffles. Do you think my judgment harsh? Then come with me through a rogue's gallery of semantic misdemeanors I found in one or another place:

(1) "Worms eat you when dead..." I regret to tell you I never knew a dead worm who could eat.

(2) "Regard the speech, not the speaker." Does "regard" mean look at, respect, appraise, think about, be fond of? The irritating confusion is easily removed:

> "Judge the speech, not the speaker."

(3) Even immortal Hillel cries to be rescued from translators, one of whom quotes him:

---

* One translator of Yiddish regularly renders *fraylikh* as "laugh" (it means "cheerful"), *beyz* as "wicked" (in contexts which dictate "angry"), "too much" as the English for *a sakh* (which means "much" or "a lot," but *not* "too much"), and *vill redn* into "has a lot to say" (it can only mean "wants to talk").

"Who does not increase, decreases." What Hillel *meant,* I submit, was: "The man who does not grow [in knowledge], grows smaller."

(4) "What the eyes don't see the heart will not hurt." This abortion confuses the coronary with the myopic. Should it not read: "What the eyes don't see, the heart won't feel"?

(5) One earnest Yiddishist translated a saying into: "What's straight talk to your face is falsehood when spoken behind your back." "Straight talk" is ungainly, and its antonym is not "falsehood" (straight talk can be erroneous, and truth can be oblique); and is falsehood false only when "spoken"? The triple excrescense is readily remedied:

"What is candor to your face is slander behind your back." (My rhyming of "candor" and "slander" is an unexpected bonus.)

(6) A scholar I need not name quotes a *midrash:* "Is then evil good? Yes; for . . ." I could not believe this translation to be accurate. How could the rabbis, so ferocious in their indictment of "the Evil Impulse," possibly call Evil "good"? I guessed that the original passage might mean that the Evil Impulse may sometimes *serve* the good—which is as far a cry from being good as being sick is from being sickening. I discussed this (evil, not sickness) with my experts on Talmud and my guess turned out to be correct.

(7) Is not English massacred in "You must not take an offense on anything a fool does"? The sentence has a dislocated spine. The adage can be phrased briskly: "Never be offended by a fool."

(8) Or take this well-known folk-saying: "On their gravestones, all Jews are good men." What the saying *means* is ironic: "In their epitaphs, all men are good." You may decide for yourself whether "epitaph" is more exact than "gravestones."

(9) "Those who want people to think they are wise, agree with them." Here is a stew of pronouns gone misreferent: who are "they"? I prefer to rephrase the thought this way:

"If you want people to think you wise, agree with everyone."

(10) I cannot believe that anyone with a sense of style will prefer: "What a deaf man does not hear, he figures out for himself," to "The deaf imagine what they cannot hear." Thank you.

(11) "Who is a hero? He who keeps down a retort." Well,

"keeps down" is un-English; and a *vits* is not a retort. Another translator (Keeps Down's brother) cripples the same saying as: "Who is a hero? He who does not make a witticism." Well, ordinarily, "witticism" is *vits* in English; but *vitsn* come in various flavors, some pleasant, some sour, some joyous, some bitter. The saying is most effective, I think, in these words:

"Who is a hero? He who represses a wisecrack."

(12) "A lock is good only for an honest man." But what in the world did the translator mean by "good"? Did he think a lock works well only on the door of an honest man? Did he believe locks are prejudiced against crooks? The original lends itself to transplanting that will preserve a shrewd observation:

"Locks keep out only the honest."

(13) "*Az men maynt, genart men zikh*" has been translated as: "To assume is to be deceived." This is grossly inaccurate; the epigram should read:

"To assume is to deceive one's self."

Deception is as different from self-deception as trust is from delusion.

(14) "There is no barber that cuts his hair." Once I stopped shuddering over that "that," I had no qualms about changing the saying to:

"No barber cuts his own hair."

(15) "He is a giant who has many dwarfs about him." Not bad, I suppose; but my discontent is eased by rewriting:

"That man is a giant who is surrounded by dwarfs."

After all, you can have a good many dwarfs "about" and yet be leagues (as dwarfs go) away from being surrounded by them.

By now you no doubt suspect how therapeutic I found it to rewrite those translators who bury bright sayings in the mausoleums of their prose.

The last word is Proust's: "When I read another writer, I set my inner metronome to his rhythm."

How My Translations Were Made

L EST you credit me with linguistic powers I do not pretend to command, I hasten to tell you that my only reading of Aramaic, Hebrew, or Arabic sources has been in translations, a great number of which have, happily, been showered upon us within the past fifty years.[43]

Most of the sayings in this book *have been freshly translated from either Yiddish, Hebrew, or English* (which peculiarity I explain below). I checked my own translations of Yiddish folk sayings with Rabbi Solomon D. Goldfarb, who worked with me for many months, producing translations of Hebrew works (from the Talmud, post-Biblical philosophers, ancient theologians, medieval poets) which I then rephrased—condensed or expanded, decorated or denuded—into that English formulation I considered most accurate, which means most harmonious or pointed, lofty or impish, noble or sardonic or paradoxical. Where amiable differences arose, I took advantage of the independent judgment of scholars at the Jewish Theological Seminary. On technical problems in linguistics and philology, I tapped the multilingual abilities of Dr. Felix Kaufmann.

I alone must take responsibility for each sentence, and therefore each interpretation, in the pages that follow. If, on one or another point, you take exception to my rendition, I can only say that I have tried to be faithful to the meaning, not just the wording, of each proverb; and I sought to strengthen, sharpen, or enliven that meaning by the English into which I reworded it. What I have tried to do is recreate aspects of the life and life-style of the Jewish people, through their sayings. This means that I have tried to retrieve the substance and flavor of ideas which are often phrased in such archaic language, or concealed within such esoteric contexts, that their meaning is incomprehensible to modern readers (except those who have been immersed in the Talmud, Jewish customs, lore and law).

Above, I used the odd phrase "translated from English." What I mean by this is that in a lifetime of reading and socializing, I collected thousands of Yiddish and Hebrew apothegms—in English. When I assembled all my notes to compile this anthology, I read my hoard with a fresh eye—and a sinking heart. I realized that I simply had to rephrase or jettison and replace much of the English. The labor this involved is too painful to describe. Suffice it to say that I was often driven to translate the English of an epigram back into Yiddish—and the Yiddish back into clearer, deeper, or (I trust) wittier English.

Speaking of English suggests that a short side-excursion may help non-Jews understand what often makes them wince: the emotional flamboyance of some of their best friends.

A Word to Non-Jews

S INCE a language is a vehicle for a culture, it contains within itself that invisible scale of proportions which (along with a thousand other subtleties) the culture assigns to the expression of emotions. Compare the ethos of the Jews in this respect with, say, that of the English.

Englishmen prize privacy; Jews prize intimacy. The English dislike displaying their feelings; Jews think feelings are meant to be verbalized.

Englishmen understate the serious ("The riot was a bit of a mess") and overstate the trivial ("What a *frightfully* amusing hat!"); Jews tend to inflate what is important ("That will blacken his name for all time!") and pooh-pooh what is not cataclysmic ("Stroke-shmoke, he can still wink with one eye!").

The English repress uneasiness; Jews feed it banquets of nourishment. An Englishman treats a disaster as unfortunate; a Jew thinks a hangnail an injustice.

The English are embarrassed by confidences; Jews are let down by "coldness."

The English place a premium on the concealment of emotion (in a crisis, John Bull does "fly into a calm"); they voice a deep conviction as if it were a tentative opinion; they are made uncomfortable by a raised voice or a trickled tear; they disapprove of the dogmatic—and all of this puzzles people (besides Jews) who were steeped in other modalities of affect.

Where Egypt wails, England blinks. Where Hindu women tear their hair, English women study their nails. An Italian explodes invective; an Englishman sniffs "Really?" When the Russians thunder "*Averyone* knows . . ." the English demur "But I should think that . . ." Where Americans cry, "It's terrific!" Englishmen concede, "Rather impressive." And where Englishmen murmur "What a pity," Jews cry "What a disaster!"

These differences in what anthropologists call "character structure" are crucial to anyone who tries to understand values which are foreign to his own, or comprehend conduct which departs from his ingrained expectations. Jews may strike Anglo-Saxons as verbose and melodramatic because Jews are early taught (as I was) to feel an *obligation* to respond to the misfortunes of others with visible, audible sympathy—so that no one can possibly fail to recognize the depth and sensitivity of one's compassion. To Jews, emotions are not meant to be nursed in private: they are meant to be dramatized and displayed—so that they can be *shared*. What is sweeter than a tearful or gleeful *shmus:* a juicy exchange of feelings or frustrations, dreams and experience? Not to do this, O Albion, is to lack "true feeling," to be blinded by selfish preoccupations, to fail in one's duty as a man.

I suppose that whereas a psychiatrist regards "empathy" as feeling for others, a Jew considers empathy heartless if it does not give equal time to himself. It is not that Jews (or Greeks or Arabs) are genetically maudlin, and wallow in wailing and hyperbole; they have just been taught that it is healthier to express than repress; that one must help those in stress by echoing their lamentations (which reduces their burden); that to embroider your own emotions is an obligation to your fellow men—who are entitled to participate in your miseries, no less than your triumphs, as you are in theirs.

The English think "a stiff upper lip" is a sign of courage;

(12) I sometimes change intransitive verbs to transitive: "One who is envious of . . ." is inferior, to my mind, to "The man who envies . . ."

(13) I sharpen or simplify wherever meaning can be strengthened: Maimonides' *Guide to the Perplexed,* I, 31 is often given in English as: "We naturally like whatever is familiar, and dislike whatever is strange." I prefer to make this: "By nature we like the familiar and dislike the strange."

(14) I try to refurbish such diction as: "What's easy to utter may be hard to carry." I felt no guilt in making this: "What's easy to say may be hard to bear."

(15) Wherever possible, I try to heighten accuracy: "Who does not please his parents will have sons who don't obey," I change to: "The man who disobeys his father will have disobedient sons." The congruence of "man . . . father . . . sons" (instead of "who . . . parents . . . sons"), and the counterpointing of "disobeys" and "disobedient," tighten the muscle to the thought.

(16) I sometimes *join* sentences whose ideas gain in power from union: "He gives little who gives with a frown. He gives much who gives little with a smile" is enriched by combination and, therefore, immediate contrast: "The man who gives little with a smile gives more than the man who gives much with a frown."

(17) I see no excuse for perpetuating abominable diction: "Better experience an injustice than do one." "Experience" makes the reader hesitate (is it a noun or a verb?); the lazy "do" should not march by the side of the mighty "injustice"; injustices sound more unjust when "committed" than when "done"; and surely "experience" is less eloquent than "suffer." So I frame this memorable injunction: "It is better to suffer an injustice than to commit one."

(18) Wherever possible, I seek to abolish ambiguity: "As you put a fence around your vineyard, so . . ." There is no way of knowing what that "as" means until the reader reaches the "so." Is the following not clearer: "Just as you build a fence around your vineyard, so . . ."?

(19) In a few cases, I combine two folk sayings to emphasize the ironic intention of each: "All brides are beautiful" and "All dead men are pious." I placed each of these, as a separate saying,

in its appropriate category in the anthology, but added a new, combined aphorism: "All brides are beautiful, and all dead men look pious."

Few men reject a free bonus.

Who Is Left Out?

THERE is a gallimaufry of witticisms by Jews from Heinrich Heine to Groucho Marx that I have not included,* because their quips, however funny or memorable, are not folk sayings or proverbs or maxims. Where I *have* included the words of a modern writer (Sholem Aleichem, or Rabbi Israel Meir Kahan, "The Chofetz Chaim") it is because they are clearly in the tradition of Jewish thought.

I have included some sayings of recent paternity because any jury would agree that they are "Jewish" in content and ambience: "When you go to a restaurant, take a seat near a waiter."

That tidbit might well have been uttered in Beersheba, Barcelona, or Bialystok.

❊   ❊   ❊

Thus endeth my Preface to the Reader, may you live in good health unto 120! The reason "120" is used by Jews in exchanging felicities, is that that is the age at which Moses died. One exuberant gentleman I knew used to say, "May you live until 121!"—and when asked why, replied, "Because I wouldn't want you to die suddenly."

LEO ROSTEN

May 20, 1972
New York, New York

---

* With two exceptions, for Heine, too haunting to be excluded; see GOD and OLD AGE in the collection.

✿ ✿ ✿

Acknowledgments

I EXTEND deep thanks to Rabbi Solomon D. Goldfarb; his vast knowledge of the Talmud and the sprawling *corpus* of rabbinical literature, his capacity for identifying obscure quotations or tracing them to their source, and his friendly encouragement during many difficult stretches of my labors were true *mitzvahs*.

For help on countless technical problems, I owe thanks to my patient friend Professor Seymour Siegel of the Jewish Theological Seminary. For valuable comments on anthropological aspects of the Preface, I am grateful to Dr. Margaret Mead. For a battery of invaluable editorial/historical/philological suggestions, I thank my multilingual colleague, the memory expert of the Chaos Cub, Dr. Felix Kaufmann. The staff of the New York Public Library were unfailingly helpful; their expertise merits the gratitude of any author.

In the final stage of preparing the manuscript, I was helped with Talmudic and rabbinical verifications by Rabbis Aaron Kriegel, Jay Rovner, and Leslie Friedman, all of whom are a credit to their Seminary, whose librarian, Dr. Menahem Schmelzer, enriched my source materials with many recommendations. Other research aid was conscientiously executed by Angelika Wolff. Gale Picard provided tireless assistance in organizing the collocation. Froso Calise's equanimity and efficiency were a boon. Rita Callahan supplied secretarial first-aid on many crucial occasions.

Many friends answered my many inquiries, to give me nuggets of Jewish wit I had not heard or read before. My mother and Mr. and Mrs. George Echt followed the finest principles of *mishpokhe* by surveying their memories and circle of acquaintances to give me dozens of delightful folk sayings, plus a hundred more from their acquaintances in the rabbinate. Abe Altrovitz of the Minneapolis *Star* sent me columns in which he had published adages submitted by his readers. At least 250 owners of *The Joys of Yiddish* wrote me sayings they had heard from their parents—who came from Bucharest, Johannesburg, Frankfurt, Budapest, Rio de Janeiro, Lisbon, Tokyo.

My wife, as always, deserves a bouquet for allowing our house to be transformed into a research factory, and for amiably suffering, for so long, a husband possessed and obsessed by an enterprise that often seemed to have no end. Many good friends gave me asylum when I feared I was ready for one.

LEO ROSTEN

HELPFUL HINTS
to the
READER

What Proverbs/Folk Sayings Are Included?

I HAVE not included many proverbs (from the Old Testament or the Apocrypha) because they are so familiar that they have come to be hackneyed through over-usage. What I *have* tried to include in this anthology are only those Jewish sayings that will make you laugh or smile or think. Since this is an emphatically personal compendium, I have excluded any saying that did not make *me* smile or laugh or think.

On Arrangement

I FIRST intended to arrange the quotations, within a category, according to their pungency, risibility, or surprise—placing the funniest or most striking sayings at the beginning, and the longer, legalistic sayings at the end. In this, I followed the advice in the Talmud which tells us that a teacher should begin a lesson with something amusing. It is lamentable that so few teachers know this, and that those who do are often elephantine in their levity.

In the end, however, the material seemed to fall best into the following order: folk sayings; quotations from the Torah, the

Talmud and rabbinical literature; selections from individual aphorists.

I salvaged my original intention by calling the reader's attention to my favorites—I just could not restrain myself—by using a special symbol (❧, which printers charmingly call a "fleuron").

On Repetitions

(1) You will find some sayings repeated—that is, appearing in different wordings in different places, under different topic categories. This is intentional, not accidental. I repeat entries in different sections because:

   (a) content sometimes embraces more than one category: e.g.,
   "To a drunkard, no liquor is bad; to a merchant, no money is tainted; to a lecher, no woman is ugly."
   This saying clamors for inclusion under DRUNKARDS, BUSINESS, MONEY, LUST.

   (b) it seemed advisable to give those readers who will use this anthology as a reference work a maximum number of places in which to find an adage;

   (c) some adages are so good that they deserve to be repeated;

   (d) who is hurt?

(2) You will sometimes find different versions of the same saying. This is also intentional. Example:
   "Small children disturb your sleep;
       big children disturb your life."
   "Little children won't let you sleep;
       big children won't let you rest."
   "Little children don't let you sleep,
       and big children won't let you live."

Each has its own distinctive thrust. To choose one and omit two others would be to exclude varying insights on the same theme.

Sources and Attributions of the Authors Quoted

(1) THE largest number of adages in this collection are not credited to a given book or person because they are folk sayings.

(2) Wherever possible, I cite the name of the scholar, rabbi, philosopher or poet whom I quote; but please remember that in the Talmud a sage often uses a popular saying to buttress his point; he did not necessarily coin the proverb—though it is sometimes attributed to him.

(3) Exact attribution becomes particularly difficult because the names of 2,000 scholars appear in the Talmud, and many are quoting other rabbis or sources, and many names are identical: for instance, I have noted some 25 Simeons, 20 Joses, 14 Eleazar/ Eliezers. To be sure, many names are further identified (e.g., Simeon the Just, Simeon ben Lakish, Simeon of Teman; or Eleazar of Modi'im, Eliezer ben Eliezer bar Kappara); but hasty quoters often drop a place-name or patronym which tells us which Simeon or Eleazar is being quoted. By my count, in the index to the Talmud, "Rab," for instance, appears 1,330 times; "Abaya" 1,225 . . . but who can be certain when either was quoting? And how many times does one or another great teacher say, "As our people know . . ." Therefore:

(4) It is sometimes impossible to guarantee the originality of a line: to be sure that an apothegm in the *Pirke Abot* ("Sayings of the Fathers"), say, or in an eleventh-century poem by Ibn Gabirol was invented there, fresh and new; for the scholar may have been echoing a folk saying, the poet quoting or paraphrasing. And a humorist like "Mendele" (Mocher Seforim) or Sholem Aleichem loved to repeat (or deliberately butcher) a saying well-known to his readers. Where an aphorism *is* credited to an individual, in this anthology, it is because the weight of evidence or expert opinion strongly confirms his paternity.

(5) A large number of quotations come or are adapted from the Talmud; these are more specifically identified (contrary to much contrary and irritating practice) by book, tractate and page number.

(6) All editions and translations of the Talmud preserve the same pagination, which was established by its first printer, Daniel Bomberg (who was not a Jew), in Venice, early in the sixteenth century. My references can be verified in the English translation published by the Soncino Press (London, 1935–1952). But I should caution the reader that my quotations often do not coincide *verbatim* with the Soncino text—for I found many of my quotations, during decades of readings, in one or another of Heaven-knows-how-many essays and books; or the particular passage may have been translated for me from the Hebrew Talmud by Dr. S. D. Goldfarb—and was then sharpened, shortened, polished or reworded by me, according to my own judgment about style, pungence or context. I defend the license of translators as strongly as that of poets.

(7) In the BIBLIOGRAPHY, I have listed the more important printed sources read or consulted. I hope I need not again stress that a very great number of the sayings in these pages I *heard* (see ACKNOWLEDGMENTS) from my parents, relatives, friends, rabbis, colleagues in seminars I was privileged to attend for six years at the Jewish Theological Seminary, or received from readers of *The Joys of Yiddish*.

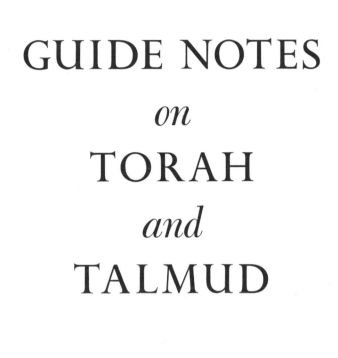

GUIDE NOTES

on

TORAH

and

TALMUD

A · *The Torah:*

1. ENGLISH AND HEBREW NOMENCLATURE

THE Torah (from Hebrew, "doctrine" or "teachings") refers to the first five books of the Old Testament, called "the books of Moses" by Jews[44] and the Pentateuch in Greek and English:

Genesis: Greek for "origin" or "creation"; in Hebrew, this book is called *Bereshith,* from *Be-Reshith:* "In the beginning" (originally, the name was *Sefer Maaseh Bereshith:* "Book of Creation").

Exodus: Greek for "road out"; in Hebrew, the book is named after its opening word, *Shemot:* "Names."

Leviticus: Late Latin for the Greek *Leutikos;* in Hebrew, this book is known as *Vayyikra* or *Va-Yikra,* the opening word: "And He called." (This book was once called *Torat Kohanim,* "the priestly code.")

Numbers: Known in Hebrew as *Bemidbar,* from *Be-Midbar:* "In the wilderness."

Deuteronomy: Known in Hebrew as *Dvarim* ("Words"), after the second word of the text (the first word means "These are the . . ."); this book was also called *Mishneh Torah,* "Repetition of the Law," from which came the Greek *Deuteronomion.*

2. TORAH: LARGER MEANING

In general discourse, "Torah" can mean not only the first five books of the Old Testament, but also:

(1) The actual Scroll, containing the five books of Moses, hand-written on parchment (kept in the "ark," in a synagogue or temple, behind the high altar), from which specified readings are publicly given on the Sabbath, on Mondays and Thursdays, and during festivals.

(2) The divine teachings of the Lord.

(3) The Old Testament as a whole.

(4) All Jewish Law, including the oral tradition of Judaic religion and moral precepts.

(5) Living in accordance with the teachings of Judaism; "to live Torah," "to live by Torah," "to practice Torah," mean to practice Judaism's prescriptions about faith, compassion, study, and duty to one's fellow man.

B · *The Talmud*

1) WHICH TALMUD?

W HEREVER "Talmud" is cited in the anthology of quotations, the standard Talmud (Babylonian) is meant; when the less-frequently used Jerusalem Talmud is cited, the attribution is worded "Talmud J."

The great Palestinian and the Babylonian academies produced separate Talmuds: the *Talmud Yerushalmi* (of Jerusalem), which was compiled and collated around the fifth century; and the *Talmud Babli* (Babylonian), written in Aramaic and Hebrew, about a century later. When we speak of the Talmud today, *we generally refer to the Babylonian Talmud:* it had a much greater influence on Jewish law and life; the Jerusalem text, which is shorter and incomplete, was not preserved *in toto;* the Babylonian Talmud contains about 2,500,000 words, more than three times the number in the Jerusalem Talmud.

The English translation of the Babylonian Talmud was published in 35 volumes and in 12 volumes (which do not include all the voluminous commentaries) by Soncino Press, London, from 1935 to 1952.

Page numbering is identical in all editions and translations of the Talmud; "62b," for instance, was the reverse side of the original sheet, "62a"; this form has been preserved down the centuries.

2) What Is the Talmud?

The Talmud is not the Bible. It is not the Old Testament. It is not "a" book.

The best way to think of the Talmud is as the minutes of a symposium on religion, law, philosophy, ethics, that lasted without interruption (but with contantly changing scholars and authorities) for 1,200 years, from the fifth century before, to the eighth century after, the Christian Era, "when [the Babylonian Talmud] was substantially in its present state."[45] (The name "Talmud" was first used in the middle of the eighth century; it comes from Hebrew *lamad,* "study," or *limed,* "teach.")

The Talmud is a monumental compendium of 63 *massekhet* (books) that record this 1,200 year-long seminar of oral analysis, debates, commentaries, commentaries *upon* commentaries of the Torah (the first five books of the Old Testament) by over 2,000 scholar-rabbis who devoted their lives to interpreting "the Law" so that its majestic teaching could be applied to religious rites and obligations in countless new, everyday problems.

The Talmud is a work of immense size, intricate structure, multifarious topics, enmazed subtleties, archaic dilemmas, mind-boggling feats of intellectual skill—and casuistries that exasperate the modern mentality. (One is tempted to scorn the dialectical acrobatics, the sophistry and hair-splittings; but in all fairness one should remember that the rabbis were steeped in an intellectual tradition not unique to them, but shared by apostles of scholasticism in other fields and faiths; for all were imprisoned within ironbound suppositions and "sacred" rules of explication; rare was the mind blessed, in those distant days, with the kind of critical/historical capacity that would liberate intellectual operations.)

I know of no work remotely the Talmud's equivalent: so universal in scope; so profound in its explorations of the nature of wisdom, virtue, truth, morals, ethics, laws; and often so quaint, parochial, and superstitious.

The discussions in the Talmud range from astronomy to urination, from the structure of the cosmos to the planting of Egyptian beans, from God's purposes to man's tragedies ("A man who crosses a river behind a woman will be excluded from the world-to-come" —because she will have to lift her skirts and he will be struck by unchaste thoughts).

The Talmud encompasses everything from religion to metaphysics, history, medicine, epistemology, pedagogy, hygiene, etc. It revolves around the enduring central questions that characterize the human condition: the nature of God, the purpose of life, the meaning of truth, the mystery of death, the duties of man, the hopes of a hereafter, the forms of punishment for evil and rewards for virtue.

The Talmud is, in one sense, the university in which every Jew for centuries studied and in which he was trained.

3) What the Talmud Is Not

The Talmud does not offer Jews a codified or consistent system of belief (though the scholars weave threads of unity within its complex whole).

The Talmud is not a legal code, though it bursts with cases, arguments, ecclesiastical decisions. (For "the code," see *Shulhan Aruk* in the GLOSSARY.)

The Talmud is not a history, though it is crammed with invaluable information about the ancients.

It is not a treatise on philosophy, though it is a philosopher's treasure—and nightmare.

> The Talmud ... was not only a book of philosophy or devotion, it was a reservoir of national life; it was the faithful mirror of the civilization of Babylon and Judea; at the same time it was a magical phantasmagoria of all the wild dreams, the fables, the legends, the scraps of science ... the reveries,

the audacious theories discovered by the Wandering Jew in his endless travels. Every generation of Judaism had accumulated its facts and fancies there.[46]

The Talmud is not a book of ethics, though it is unique in the richness and range of its discourses on moral problems.

It is not a text in anthropology, though it contains invaluable data on folklore, customs, mores, superstitions, early cosmologies. The Talmud is—the Talmud.

> Say what you will of the Judaism of the Middle Ages; call it narrow; deride it as superstitious ... [but] for sweetness and spirituality of life, the Jew of the Ghetto, the Jew of the Middle Ages, the Jew under the yoke of the Talmud, challenges the world.[47]

4) THE NAMES OF THE TALMUD'S SIX ORDERS (BOOKS)*

1. ZERAIM ("Seeds," or the laws of agriculture)
2. MO'ED ("Festivals, set feasts")
3. NASHIM ("Women")
4. NEZIKIN ("Damages": civil and criminal law)
5. KIDDUSHIN ("Sacred or Hallowed Things")
6. TOHOROTH ("Cleannesses" or "ritual purity")

5) THE NAMES OF THE 63 TRACTATES

Relevant ones are identified by name in the GLOSSARY.

6) "THE MINOR TRACTATES OF THE TALMUD"

(more properly "The Minor Tractates added to the Talmud"):

ABOTH D' RABBI NATHAN; SOFERIM; SEMAHOTH; KALLAH; KALLAH RABBATI; DEREKH ERETZ RABBAH; DEREKH ERETS ZUTA; PEREK HASHALOM; GERIM; KUTHIM; ABADIM; SEFER TORAH; TEPHILLIN; ZIZITH; MEZUZAH.
These have been translated into English.[48]

---

* Soncino Press, London, (12 vols.) 1936 to 1952.

C · *The Mishnah*

THE original six "orders" of legal material, arranged by topics, which are the base of the Talmud, are called the Mishnah (from a Hebrew root meaning "to review" or "to repeat" [learning], a collection of interpretations of Biblical passages and laws as they were applied to social conditions in Palestine between the fifth century before, and the second century of, the Christian Era.

These laws included ecclesiastical court decisions, regulations on ritual, ethical teachings, etc. They were originally transmitted by rabbis orally, so as not to impair the sanctity of the written Law: i.e., the Torah. The Mishnah is the collocated "Oral Law." What often confuses laymen (like me) is that "Mishnah" is used to mean either the six fundamental orders of the Talmud, or a particular paragraph or interpretation of the text, or for a collection of earlier teachings: "The Mishnah of Rabbi Meir," "The Mishnah of Rabbi Akiba," etc.

The Mishnah was written in simple Hebrew (with some loan-words from Aramaic, Greek, and Latin), and was authoritatively redacted or edited by Judah ha-Nasi ("the Prince"), around the year 200. The first printed edition appeared in 1492, in Naples, published by Soncino.

A Mishnah opens the six "orders" (*Sedarim*) and sixty-three tractates (*Massekhot*) of the Talmud (see above). Each of the Mishnah's sixty-three tractates is divided into chapters (*Perakim*), of which there are 523; each chapter is set forth in paragraphs.

The Mishnah is not the work of any one man, school, or time; nor were its contents new. The Mishnah was the end result of four to six centuries of analysis and teaching in Palestine.

The work had its origins after the return of the Hebrews to Judea from their Babylonian exile (537 B.C.E.), when the scholars of the Great Assembly, the Jews' religious and legislative body, established basic rules for the interpretation of Jewish law. The scribes (*Sopherim*) were official copyist/teachers; later sages (*Tannaim*) continued to interpret Biblical laws, in the context of changing historical, political, social conditions.

Hillel made one of the earliest attempts to codify the vast and entangled body of oral teachings, but no one knows what became of that enterprise. Akiba performed the pioneer work of collecting and classifying oral decisions and precedents into a *Mishnah* or "review" and Akiba's work was continued and completed by Judah ha-Nasi, also known simply as "Rabbi," who declared the canon closed around the year 200.*

The Mishnah thus serves as the central commentary used in both the Babylonian and Jerusalem Talmuds.

The Mishnah was such a formidable achievement that it was accepted by the rabbis as *the* authority in interpreting the Old Testament, and was elevated to a station which only the Torah could supersede.

The Mishnah has been translated into English, with prodigious scholarship and footnotes, by Dr. Herbert Danby (Canon of St. George's Cathedral, Jerusalem), Oxford University Press, London, 1933.

I am fond of an old rumination:

> The Mishnah begins with an open *mem* and ends with a closed *mem*—to teach us that when a man begins to study, he believes all the mansions of knowledge are open to him; but when he finishes, he discovers how much knowledge is still behind doors closed to him.[49]

---

* For biographical vignettes of these and other scholars, see BIOGRAPHIES, Appendix III.

D · *The Midrash and Haggada*

ROM the time of Ezra (the fifth century before the Christian
Era), a group of scholars known as *Sopherim* (scribes) were
"skilled in the laws of Moses." These men were teachers of
"the Oral Law," as derived from the Torah.

The effort to "investigate" Scripture, in order to find its true
meaning and implications, was known as *Midrash* (from *darash,* the
Hebrew for "investigate"). The *midrashim* are efforts to "penetrate"
a text and illuminate its inner spirit.*

The first *midrashim* were strictly legal in nature, and are
known as *halaka.* At the same time, a different kind of Midrash
was growing: colloquial and moralistic, not juridical: this was the
Midrash *Haggadah* (from the Hebrew: "to tell").

The Haggada presents its lessons in informal, sometimes
homely, often imaginative, amusing and poetic ways—as a roving
commentary on and about those portions of Scripture which are
not the Law, but which are anecdotal, legendary, or folklore. From
the Midrash Haggada come many of the moral lessons the rabbis
used to inspire Jews to greater piety and virtue. From haggadic
parts of the Talmud (about a third of its contents) one can glean a
marvelous harvest of historical and medical data, wonderful legends
and unforgettable anecdotes.

The Haggada is often a collection of sermons, delivered on the
afternoons of the Sabbath, when Jews gathered to hear Scripture
taught, explained and discussed.

The earliest haggadic *midrashim* were collections of sayings,
lyrical verses, moralisms, by the most revered rabbis. Called the

---

* Four types of interpretation of the holy Torah were devised: *pshat,* the simple, literal meaning; *remez,* hints of meaning, or clues to content; *drush,* homily
exposition of a text; and *sod,* the secret, mystical, esoteric meaning contained beneath the surface of a word or passage. But the sacred texts remain indisputable;
in the Talmud, *Shabbat* (63a), the rabbis ruled: "Nothing can supersede the *plain*
meaning of the text" [my italics].

Pirke Abot, or "Sayings of the Fathers," this is the most popular, most beloved and most quoted work in rabbinical literature. (You will find more than a hundred passages from *Pirke Abot* in the present collection.)

The Midrash was written in Hebrew, with occasional passages in Aramaic. A volume of the Midrash often bears the name of the book of the Bible under discussion.

Midrash Rabbah ("Great Midrash") is a misnomer; it consists of ten books: one for each volume of the Pentateuch (Torah) and one for each of the five "scrolls" (Song of Songs, Ruth, Lamentations, Ecclesiastes, Esther). The names of some other volumes of Midrash are: *Mekilta, Sifre, Sifra, Pesikta de Rab Kahana, Tanhuma.* (For each, see the GLOSSARY.)

A set of strict rules (hermeneutics) was agreed upon by the rabbis—regulations which defined and delimited the ways in which Scripture could be interpreted in order to provide new rulings or to justify new teachings. The seven rules established by the great Hillel, plus forty-five by two later scholars, remain the authoritative guidelines of Biblical exegesis in Judaism. (Incidentally, one of the things that upset the rabbinical authorities about Jesus of Nazareth was the fact that he expounded the Law without attention to these principles, offering teachings on his own authority; the Jews could not concede that Jesus was the Messiah,[50] even though many of them respected and supported Jesus' noble teachings.)

Until the seventh century, scholars continued to make additions, albeit minor, to the Talmud. These men were called *Seboraim* ("reasoners"). Until the twelfth century, rabbis continued to write their commentaries—as works of Midrash.

The whole process of interpreting Holy Scripture, to make it relevant to changing life, to keep it fresh as a source of inspiration, authority and faith, continued in the period known as the Talmudic or Rabbinic era.

The total body of teachings contained in the Talmud, Midrash and Responsa (see F, below) is known as Rabbinical Judaism.

E · *The Gemara*

The second division of the Talmud is the *Gemara* (from the Aramaic "completion"), or commentaries upon the Mishnah. (The language of the Gemara is Aramaic, but contains a great deal of Hebrew.)

There are two Gemaras: one is the work of the Palestinian schools, and was edited around the year 380 in Tiberias. The other Gemara, the work of the Babylonian School, is much larger and more widely known, and is included when the word "Talmud" is used. This Gemara was edited around the year 500 by Rabbi Ashi and his disciple Rabbi José, and is usually published with the commentary of the celebrated sage Rashi.* It contains further comments which are called *Tosephoth,* the work of French and German scholars in the twelfth to the fourteenth centuries.

Note: The Gemaras of both the Palestinian and the Babylonian Talmuds do not represent a complete commentary on the complete Mishnah. Large sections are missing from both Gemaras.

F · *The Responsa*

The widely dispersed communities of Jews often needed authoritative rulings on a thousand and one aspects of life not explicitly covered in the Torah. During the Babylonian exile, letters were sent to great scholars asking for their interpretations of, and rulings on, the Law to be followed. The scholars'

---

* For more information on these and other scholars, see BIOGRAPHIES in Appendix III.

replies, known as *responsa*, were of critical importance in preserving and adapting Judaism to new political and social pressures.

Over 500,000 *responsa*, published in over 1,000 compilations, have been found, from such illustrious scholars as Alfasi, Rashi, Maimonides, the *tosephists* of France and Germany in the twelfth to the fourteenth centuries, Joseph Caro, who assembled the great *Shulhan Aruk* (Set Table) of regulatory laws, and others.

Another aspect of the importance of *responsa* correspondence is worth mentioning. During many periods, the reading or study of the Talmud was forbidden to Jews by hostile sovereignties. (In 1242, the Church, in Paris, ordered all Talmudic literature to be burned: twenty-four cartloads vanished in the flames; in 1553, a huge number of volumes were destroyed in Rome; in 1757, thousands of Talmud volumes were burned in Poland, by order of a bishop; and the depredations of the Nazis in Germany, Austria, and conquered parts of Poland and Russia need not be detailed.) In these tragic and critical times, the *responsa* were a means of circumventing the prohibitions.

The *responsa* remain priceless repositories of contemporary data on the intellectual life, historical events, social conditions, philosophical disputations, etc., of all the places in which Jews lived, or to which they traveled. *Responsa* are still being written —e.g., to answer questions concerning, say, the times of prayer, which will surely need reinterpretation in the age of space travel.

Here are some striking examples:

> May *challa* [braided bread, for the Sabbath] be sliced by the bakery's machine?
>
> May a rabbi officiate at a wedding where the groom is under a psychiatrist's care, trying to be cured of impotence?
>
> May a physician hasten the end of the sufferings of a patient with terminal cancer—where the family agrees, and one of the doctors, the patient's own son, concurs with the others, who recommend the withdrawal of intravenous fluids?
>
> May a man wear a toupee during a religious service?
>
> What can be decided, by Jewish Law, about operations to change a male to a female, or vice versa? (The surgery sterilizes the person.)
>
> What are the religious implications in a case where a Jew's heart stops beating, but is restarted in open-heart surgery?

May a Jewish officer wear his sword, as part of his full-dress uniform, during a wedding ceremony?

Our hospital has one mechanical-kidney machine. How should a Jewish doctor decide which patient to save, among all who need it?

Can Jewish Law protect the operator of a television station who has done a worthy public-service job from another Jewish operator who has applied for an F.C.C. license—to replace the first operator? Is this unfair competition?[51]

Reference Notes

1. Example: "Rabbi Bizna ben Zabda said in the name of Rabbi Akiba who had heard it from Rabbi Panda who had it from Rabbi Nahum who had had it from Rabbi Biryam who was reporting the words of a certain elder—and who was that? Rabbi Bana'ah . . ." Talmud, *Berakoth,* 55b, Soncino, London and New York, 1948.

2. Walter Nash, *Our Experience of Language,* Batsford, London, 1971, p. 192.

3. Leo Rosten, *Rome Wasn't Burned in a Day: The Mischief of Language,* Introduction, Doubleday, New York, 1972.

4. These epigrams were coined by, respectively, Voltaire, William Osler, "Kin" Hubbard, H. L. Mencken, and Mencken again.

5. Cecil Woodham-Smith, *The Reason Why,* Constable, London, 1953.

6. Aristotle, *Rhetoric,* II, any edition.

7. The Apocrypha and Pseudepigrapha are not in the formal, closed canon, produced from the time of the Second Temple (about 538 B.C.E.) to the defeat of Bar Kochba's rebellion against the Romans (135 C.E.). See *Apocrypha* in the GLOSSARY. An excellent work is R. Travers Herford, *Talmud and Apocrypha,* KTAV, New York, 1970.

8. The span of time covered by the Talmud is the subject of considerable difference of opinion among experts (I am certainly not one). The "orthodox," often dogmatic figure for the number of years encompassed by the Talmud is 600. But if one remembers that the Old Testament is the "source" for,

and subject matter of, the Talmud, this would extend the time period to "about ten centuries." (See the Introduction to *The New English Bible,* Oxford University Press and Cambridge University Press, London and New York, 1961, 1970.) The most recent researches of Rabbi Louis Finkelstein, Chancellor emeritus of the Jewish Theological Seminary, supports the startling judgment that many passages in the *Mishnah* (see Guide Note C, pp. 72–73) and other rabbinical works were written *before* or during the Babylonian exile—that is to say, six or more centuries prior to what has, until recently, been the consensus of the experts. This justifies my "1200 years" figure. (See Louis Finkelstein, *New Light from the Prophets,* Basic Books, New York, 1969, pp. 1–13).

9. Aramaic was the Semitic language spoken, millennia ago, around the Tigris and Euphrates rivers. During their exile in Babylonia, the Hebrews adopted Aramaic as their language. For a scholarly survey of proverbs in the Bible, Apocrypha, and Talmud, see *The Jewish Encyclopedia,* Vol. X, KTAV Publishing House, New York (no date cited), pp. 226–231, where several hundred Aramaic sayings and "Judaeo-German" (i.e., Yiddish) proverbs are included.

10. William McKane, *Proverbs: A New Approach,* SCM Press, London, 1970, pp. 6–17.

11. See Samuel Rapaport, *A Treasury of the Midrash,* KTAV, New York, 1968, p. 5.

12. Alexander Smith, in *Dreamthorp: A Book of Essays Written in the Country,* J. E. Tilton Co., Boston, 1864; reprinted, Peter Pauper Press, Mount Vernon, New York, 1947.

13. Collections of proverbs were numerous and popular among Jews for many centuries: Rabbi Hai Gaon's *Musar ha-Sekhel* ("The Ethics of Wisdom"), Samuel ha-Nagid's *Ben Mishle,* Moses ibn Ezra's *Tarshish,* and a good many works translated from Arabic (in which many Hebrew poets and scholars framed their words): Ibn Gabirol's great *Mibhar ha-Peninim* ("Choice of Pearls") and *Tikun Midot ha-Nefesh* ("The Improvement of the Qualities of the Soul"), Abraham ben Hasdai's *Ben ha-Melekh ve-ha-Nazir* (a story of the Buddha), *Mahberot Immanuel* ("The Compositions of Immanuel of Rome") etc. Many of the originals, especially those in Arabic, were

lost for centuries; many have been found and reprinted within the last hundred years.

14. The hasidim produced many remarkable folk-sages, most notably Nachman of Bratslav ("The Bratslaver") whose brilliant sayings were published as *Sefer ha-Midot*. Leaders of the *Haskalah* ("Enlightenment") movement which waged ideological warfare against the "medievalist" hasidim, collected the apothegms of *their* brightest minds (e.g., the *Sefer ha-Midot* of Solomon Rubin).

15. Ludwig Seligman (*Parabeln, Legenden und Gedanken aus dem Talmud*), Emanuel Deutsch (*The Talmud*), Rabbi Henry Cohen (*Talmudic Sayings*), Leopold Dukes (*Rabbinische Blumenlese*), and others.

16. Leo Rosten, *Joys of Yiddish*, McGraw-Hill, New York, 1968, p. xx.

17. The amount of legend, custom, and demonology that is common to the people of the Old Testament and other peoples (whether Masai tribes or Polynesian clans) has been thoroughly documented by James Frazer (*Folklore in the Old Testament*) and greatly expanded by Theodor H. Gaster (*Myth, Legend and Custom in the Old Testament*). And as I write these words, a book just published in England lies before me: Professor William McKane's *Proverbs: A New Approach* (S.C.M. Press, London, 1970), a *tour de force* of cross-analysis of the old sayings of Assyria, Babylon, and Egypt.

18. William Thackeray, *The Newcomes* (any edition).

19. Evidence for prior collections of folk sayings is found in the Talmud: *Baba Kamma* (92b, 93a) and *Yebamoth* (118b): see the *Babylonian Talmud* (12 vols.), translated into English by various authors, edited by I. Epstein, Soncino Press, London, 1935–1952.

20. For a survey of educational practices among Jews, see Simon Greenberg, "Jewish Educational Institutions," in *The Jews: Their History, Culture and Religion*, edited by Louis Finkelstein, Vol. II, third edition, Harper, 1960.

21. *Joys of Yiddish*, *op. cit.*, p. 39.

22. *Ibid.*, pp. 41–42.

23. A. J. Heschel, *The Earth Is the Lord's*, Abelard-Schuman, New York, 1964, p. 46.

24. *Joys of Yiddish, op. cit.*, p. viii.
25. Maurice Samuel, *In Praise of Yiddish,* Cowles, New York, 1971, pp. 14–15.
26. *Joys of Yiddish, op. cit.*, p. xviii.
27. This quotation combines a passage from *Joys of Yiddish* with my article, "Is It Greek to You, Too?" *Look,* February 7, 1967, p. 8.
28. See John L. Mish, in *The World of Translation*, P.E.N. Conference, New York, 1970, pp. 241–47. The definition of language is from Walter Nash, *op. cit.,* p. 252.
29. Peter T. White, "The Interpreter: Linguist Plus Diplomat," *The New York Times Magazine,* November 6, 1955.
30. Walter Nash, *op. cit.,* p. 18. I have been greatly influenced by Edward Sapir's ideas and by his classic *Language,* Harcourt Brace, New York, 1921; by Richard Lee Whorf, *Language, Thought, and Reality,* ed. John B. Carroll, M.I.T. Press, Cambridge, Mass. 1956; by H. N. Shenton, E. Sapir, and O. Jesperson, *International Communication,* London, 1931. Readers interested in variant positions may peruse the work in linguistics of Roman Jakobson, C. K. Ogden and I. A. Richards, Leonard Bloomfield, Harry Hoijer, and Noam Chomsky. For a Roman Catholic exposition, see David Crystal, *Linguistics, Language and Religion,* Burns and Oates, London, 1965.
31. For all of these animal sounds, see Helmut Braem's delightful and illuminating chapter, "Languages Are Common Yet Unique," in *The World of Translation, op. cit.,* pp. 121–134.
32. M. H. Segall, D. Campbell and M. J. Herskovits, in *The Influence of Culture on Visual Perception,* Bobbs-Merrill, 1966, pp. 37, 213.
33. Quoted in *The World of Translation, op. cit.,* p. 8.,
34. See Lewis Galantière, "An Ancient Art," in *Translator: An Occasional Publication,* P.E.N., New York, Vol. 1, No. 1, May 1963, pp. 5–6.
35. See Gilbert Highet, *The Classical Tradition,* Oxford University Press, 1949, pp. 196, 217.
36. See A. F. Polland, *Records of the English Bible,* Oxford University Press, 1911.
37. For data to support the various items, see the relevant entries in *Dictionary of the Bible,* edited by James Hastings, revised edition edited by Frederick C. Grant and H. H. Rowley,

Scribner's, New York, 1963; *Peake's Commentary on the Bible,* edited by Matthew Block and H. H. Rowley, Nelson, London, 1967; the *New Standard Jewish Encyclopedia,* edited by Cecil Roth and Geoffrey Wigoder, Doubleday, New York, 1966; Frederick C. Grant, *The Gospels: Their Origin and Their Growth,* Faber and Faber, London, 1957: and other standard sources on the Bible, its history, recent discoveries, and alterations.

38. Donald Ebor, Chairman of the Joint Committee for *The New English Bible,* Oxford & Cambridge University Presses, London, 1970, p. v.

39. See various footnotes in *The Goodspeed Parallel New Testament: The American Translation and the King James Version,* University of Chicago Press, 1943; for Old Testament data see *The Cambridge History of the Bible,* Vol. I: *From the Beginnings to Jerome,* edited by P. R. Ackroyd and C. F. Evans, Cambridge University Press, London, 1970, and the introductions to *The New English Bible, with the Apocrypha,* Oxford and Cambridge University Presses, 1970.

40. *Ibid.* Also see *The Torah: A new translation of the Holy Scriptures according to the Masoretic text,* Jewish Publication Society of America, Philadelphia, 1967. A summary of the changes made will be found in New York *Times,* October 12, 1962, p. 1 ff.

41. See the Bibles cited above, plus *The Anchor Bible,* edited by William F. Albright, Doubleday, 1958; *The New American Bible,* translated by Members of the Catholic Biblical Association of America (carrying the imprimatur of Patrick Cardinal O'Boyle, Archbishop of Washington), P. J. Kennedy & Sons, New York and Collier-Macmillan, London, 1970; *The Jerusalem Bible* (based on *La Bible de Jérusalem, Paris*), Darton, Longman & Todd, London, 1966, 1968.

42. The insatiable reader can find these and 400 other words explained and illustrated, in depth, in *The Joys of Yiddish, op. cit.*

43. I cite particularly the Soncino Press (London), whose English translation of the entire Talmud is an historic achievement (one can only regret that the English prose of the scholars is so often turgid); the Jewish Publication Society of Philadelphia, which has translated the Torah and many invaluable

I rashly decided to write a biographical vignette for each of the men to whom more than one quotation in my dictionary is attributed (see BIOGRAPHIES, Appendix III). I did that because it exasperates me to run across the name of an author, in an anthology, about whom I can learn more only by consulting a dozen reference works—often without success: for some names are variously spelled; pseudonyms are often not identified; some names do not appear in standard sources; and, alas, so on. The obstacles encountered, the time consumed, the pitfalls dug by earlier investigators, sometimes appear to be the work of demonic forces. Let me illustrate:

(1) The story of Rabbi Meir, the second-century collator of Mishnah, must be sifted out from twenty-four other "Meirs" listed in the admirably thorough *Jewish Encyclopedia* of 1904.

(2) The often-quoted "Ibn Ezra" may be Moses or Abraham (ben Meir)—both eleventh-twelfth century Spanish-Jewish scholars; and Moses is Moses ben Jacob Ka-Sallah, or, as he is known in Arabic literature, Abu Harun Musa.

(3) "Ha-Nakdan" *may* be traced back to Berechiah ben Natronai, or Berechya ben Berechiah ben Natronai, or Berechya ben Natronai, or Benedict le Pointeur ("the punctuator").

(4) "Falaquera," a distinguished Spanish-Jewish philosopher-translator of the thirteenth century, sometimes appears as Palquera, or Shem Tob Palquera, or Ibn Falaquera.

(5) The immortal Ibn Paquda, eleventh-twelfth century philosopher and *dayan* (ecclesiastical judge), author of the classic *Duties of the Heart,* may first be met under Bahya ibn Pakuda, or "Bachya the Saint," or Bachya ben Joseph ibn Pakuda.

It both relieved and amused me to discover that such vexations do not die with time. Try, for instance, to find out who Malcolm de Chazal is (or was): he coined some of the wittiest epigrams in the *Viking Book of Aphorisms,* edited by W. H. Auden and Louis Kronenberger, who cannily offer no dates or biographical data. (Chazal, so far as I can discover, is a hermitlike postmaster in a small town in a southern province of France.)

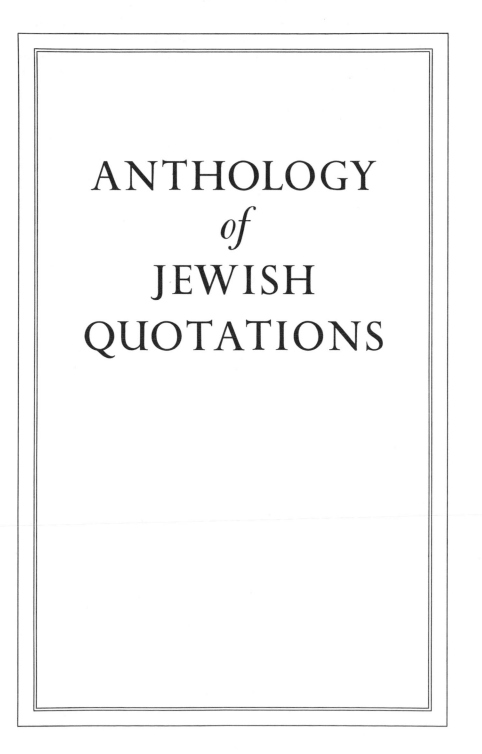

ANTHOLOGY
of
JEWISH
QUOTATIONS

"Certainly the heroism of the defenders of every other creed fades into insignificance before this martyr people, who for thirteen centuries confronted all the evils that the fiercest fanaticism could devise, enduring obloquy and spoliation, the violation of the dearest ties and the infliction of the most hideous sufferings, rather than abandon their faith."

W. E. H. Lecky, Spirit of Rationalism, *vol. II,* p. 270.

(Use of the fleuron [⋅୫] denotes that a quotation is a favorite of the author's.)

ABILITY

See: CAPABILITY

ABSOLUTISM

⋅୫ If you insist too long that you're right, you're wrong.

See also: GOVERNMENT, LAW, POLITICS

ABSTINENCE

He who denies himself (a little) wine is a sinner; how much more so, then, is the man who denies himself too many things.
TALMUD: Nedarim, 10a

Are not enough things prohibited you in the Law? Must you prohibit yourself still others?   TALMUD J.: *Nedarim,* 41

The man who causes himself pain by not enjoying what is not sinful may be called a sinner.   TALMUD: *Nazir,* 19a

Those who abstain are physicians of faith and healers of souls.
                    BAHYA IBN PAQUDA, *Duties of the Heart*

See also: ASCETICS/ASCETICISM, EXCESS, FASTING, GLUTTONY, TEMPFR-
ANCE

ABUSE

The man who hears himself abused and remains silent will be
    spared many other abuses.   TALMUD: *Sanhedrin,* 7a

See also: GOSSIP, LIARS/LIES

ADAM

Note. Genesis tells us that God created man from *adamah* ("dust
    of the ground"). In the Talmud (*Sanhedrin,* 38a, b), the rev-
    ered Rab says that Adam's head was made of earth from the
    Holy Land, his body from the soil of Babylonia, his limbs from
    the earth of other lands.
        The curious *Sybilline Oracles** (3 : 24–26), written by
    unknown Greek, Jewish, and Christian hands, incorporating
    six centuries of polyglot legends, offers us the charming theory
    that Adam's name consists of the first letters of four Hellen-
    istic words which encompass the world: "A" for *anatole*
    (east), "D" for *dysis* (west), "A" for *arktos* (north), "M" for
    mesembria (south).
        The rabbis thought Adam "of an extreme beauty and
    brightness, like the sun" (Talmud: *Baba Bathra,* 58a), soon
    clothed in garments made of light, not animal skins (*Genesis
    Rabbah,* 20). As we all know, Adam grievously sinned and so
    was deprived of all glory, and "the light of the world was
    robbed of its brightness, which will not return until the Mes-
    siah comes." (*Zohar*)

                                                            —L.R.
God saw that heaven and earth were jealous of each other, so
    He created man out of earth—and his soul out of heaven.

_____
* Translated from the Greek by H. N. Bate, Society for the Promotion of Christian Knowledge, London, 1937.

Adam would never have taken a wife if he hadn't been put to sleep first.

Adam invented writing.   —A legend

◄§ Why did God create only one man? So that no one could say virtue and vice are hereditary.   TALMUD: *Sanhedrin,* 4a

When a man uses a die to stamp out coins, they all come out alike; but God stamped all men with the die of Adam, yet each is different: So everyone has a right to say, "For my sake was the world created."   TALMUD: *Sanhedrin,* 4 : 5

Why did God create Adam alone? In order to teach us that whoever destroys a single life is as guilty as though he had destroyed the entire world; and that whoever saves one life, earns as much merit as though he had saved the entire world.
TALMUD, J.: *Sanhedrin,* 4 : 5

◄§ Why did God create but one man? So that no one of his descendants should be able to say, "My father is better than your father."   TALMUD: *Sanhedrin,* 37a

Why was man created a solitary human being, without a companion? So that it could never be said that some races are better than others.   TALMUD: *Sanhedrin,* 37a

God acted as Adam's best man.   TALMUD: *Berakoth,* 61a

When Adam first saw the sun go down, and beheld an ever-deepening gloom enfold the world, he was possessed by terror. And God took pity and endowed Adam with divine intuition: to take two stones—one named Darkness, the other The Shadow of Death—and rub them hard against each other, and in that way discover fire. And when Adam did this, he exclaimed, "Blessed be the Creator of Light!"   TALMUD

When the pious reproach Adam, who is seated at the gates, for having sinned and brought death to them, Adam answers: "I died with only one sin, but you committed many; because of them, not me, have you died."   *Tanhuma Hukkat,* 16

Adam was the first to enter Hades.   *Sibylline Oracles,* 1 : 81

Adam sits at the gates, weeping for the multitude of souls who
pass through the wide gate to receive their punishment, and
filled with joy for the virtuous few who enter the narrow
gate to receive their reward. *The Testament of Abraham*

Adam's dust was collected from all parts of the world.
RABBI MEIR in TALMUD: *Sanhedrin,* 38a

If God really loved Man, would He have created Adam?

See also: ADAM'S RIB, ANCESTORS, EVE, GOD AND MAN, MAN

ADAM'S RIB

Note. The Old Testament's story of the creation of the first woman
from the first man's rib is far from being unique. Similar tales
are found among Polynesians, Burmese, Siberian Tatars, the
Yuki and Salinan Indians of California, etc. . . . Such fables will
enchant anyone who reads Frazer's *Golden Bough,* but elementary courses in anthropology suggest that these myths may simply be echoes of Biblical accounts told to the natives' grandfathers by Christian missionaries.* (See CONVERTS.)

—L.R.

ADULTERY

There is no worse adultery than that of the woman who, while
making love with her husband, thinks of another man.
MIDRASH: *Tanhuma*

See also: DIVORCE, MARRIAGE, MEN AND WOMEN

ADVERSITY

Adversity is the best college.

* For a dizzying succession of data, see Theodor H. Gaster, *Myth, Legend and
Custom in the Old Testament,* Harper & Row, New York, 1969, pp. 21, 330–31;
and in V. Lauternari's intriguing *The Religions of the Oppressed,* Macgibbon & Kee,
London, 1963, and Knopf, New York, 1963, *passim.*

Uphill, we always climb with caution; downhill, we dash carefree.

Even life's smoothest path is studded with stones.

See also: CONFLICT, HAPPINESS, LIFE: ITS ADVERSITY, MISFORTUNE, QUARRELS

ADVICE

◄§ Love can't take advice, and lovers won't.

A good saying at the right moment is like a piece of bread during a famine.

Sweet words won't warm you, but sweet thoughts will.

◄§ Teach your tongue to say "I do not know," lest you invent something.   TALMUD: *Berakoth*, 4a

Set a fence around your words.
                          HILLEL in TALMUD: *Niddah*, 3b

Who is this that darkeneth counsel by words without knowledge?
                          Book of Job, 38 : 2

ADVICE: EXAMPLES OF

◄§ When you're hungry, sing; when you're hurt, laugh.

◄§ If you're going to do something wrong, at least enjoy it.

◄§ Never consult a woman about her rival, a coward about a war, or a merchant about a bargain.

Words should be weighed, not counted.

If you can't bite, don't show your teeth.

◄§ In a restaurant, choose a table near a waiter.

If you want to be a barber, practice on someone else's beard.

If you eat your bagel, you'll have nothing left but the hole.

◦§ If things aren't the way you like, like them the way they are.

You can't fill a sack that's full of holes.

◦§ It is better to be embarrassed than ashamed.

Don't pat your stomach while the fish is still in the pond.

◦§ What you can do, do; what you have, hold; what you know, keep to yourself.

If you know, tell; if you can, do; if you have, hold on to it.

◦§ For a long, happy life, breathe through your nose and keep your mouth shut.

◦§ He who has butter on his head should not walk in the sun.

If you sit home, you won't wear out your shoes.

◦§ When you flee from fire, you may run into water.

If a dog barks, go in; if a bitch barks, stay out.

◦§ Don't offer pearls to men who deal in onions.

Don't ask questions about fairy tales.

◦§ The man who bends his back shouldn't complain if it's beaten.

Don't hitch a horse and an ox to the same wagon.

◦§ Only a genius or a fool rushes into print.

Better ask ten times than get lost once.

Don't feed your horse too much too often: he'll become rebellious.

◦§ Better be ridiculed than shamed.

Treat him like a rabbi and watch him like a thief.

Because of the thorns, don't uproot the garden.

◄§ Don't worry about what may happen tomorrow; just correct what you spoiled yesterday.

Hire a helper and do it yourself.

If you don't run so far, the way back will be shorter.
MIDRASH: Ecclesiastes Rabbah, 11 : 9

Give every man the benefit of the doubt.
Sayings of the Fathers, 1 : 7

Be pliable—like a reed, not rigid—like a cedar.
TALMUD: Ta'anith, 20b

Be obscure, that you may endure.
TALMUD: Sanhedrin, 14a

See also: GOSSIP, KNOWLEDGE, SILENCE, TALK, WISDOM, WORDS

AGE

◄§ Two things grow weaker with the years: teeth and memory.

The man who wants to know everything gets old fast.

◄§ If you don't want to get old, hang yourself while young.

A man can be gray at the sideburns and silly in the head.

◄§ Gray hair is a sign of age, not wisdom.

To lose years is far worse than to lose dollars.

At seventy, a man is as he was at seven.

Fortunate are those who actually enjoy old age.

Three kinds of people grow old before their time: those who raise chickens for a living; those who give orders but are not obeyed; and those who live on an upper floor.

The old who are not wise should not be called venerable.
TALMUD: Yebamoth, 80b

Four things make a man age prematurely: fear, anger, children, and a bad-tempered wife.   MIDRASH: *Tanhuma*

AGNOSTICS

See: FAITH, GOD: COMPLAINTS ABOUT, HEREAFTER, PRAYER: IRONIC COMMENTS ON, RELIGION, SKEPTICISM, VIRTUE

ALIMONY

Note. In the first century before the Christian Era, Jewish wives began to receive a specified and secure sum, in case of a husband's death or a divorce, from the husband's estate. The *ketubah* ("marriage settlement contract") granted a wife a legal lien on her husband's estate; and by rabbinical laws, a wife was not permitted to release her husband from this obligation. (This protected women from the amorous chicanery of men who might seek financial concessions before committing themselves to matrimony.)

Orthodox Jews still maintain the form and guarantees of the *ketubah*.

—L.R.

See: FAMILY, MARRIAGE, MEN and WOMEN, WIVES

ALTRUISM

The world goes on only because of those who disregard their own existence.   TALMUD: *Hullin,* 89a

See also: COMPASSION, GOOD DEEDS, HELP, PITY, SELFISHNESS

AMBITION

ᴥ§ The Jew who can't be a cobbler dreams of being a professor.

If you don't climb too high, you won't have far to fall.

If you look up to the heights, hold your hat.

◆§ Eggs want to be smarter than hens.

Man strives and God laughs.

A human being must either climb up or climb down.
TALMUD: Erubin, 21a

Fire rises—and goes out; water descends—and is not lost.
Berechiah ben Natronai, ha-Nakdan, Fox Fables

Man's obsession to add to his wealth and honor is the chief source
of his misery.
MAIMONIDES: Guide to the Perplexed, 3 : 39

Ambition is bondage.
IBN GABIROL, Choice of Pearls

See also: CONTENTMENT, HAPPINESS

ANCESTORS

Note. Jews accord special honor (*koved*) to a man or woman
because of the notable merits, virtue, good deeds, or learning
of his or her ancestors. The commandment to "honor thy
father and mother" carries power in Jewish thought second
only to that accorded the Almighty.

Affluent Jews would try to marry their daughters to young
men of illustrious intellectual background, however poor; and
for their sons they sought scholars' daughters as brides. (See
headnotes for FAMILY and SCHOLARS.)
—L.R.

God prefers your deeds to your ancestors' virtues.
MIDRASH: Genesis Rabbah, 74

See also: ADAM, CHILDREN, FAMILY, FATHERS, HONOR, MOTHERS

ANGELS

&s The virtue of angels is that they cannot deteriorate; their flaw is that they cannot improve. Man's flaw is that he can deteriorate; and his virtue is that he can improve.

—Hasidic saying

&s There was a time when angels walked the earth; today, they are not found even in heaven.

Two angels always accompany everyone—and they testify for or against him.   TALMUD: *Ta'anith,* 11a

True dreams come from angels; false dreams come from demons.

adapted from TALMUD: *Berakoth,* 55b

Those who pray in Aramaic will get no aid from the angels: angels do not understand Aramaic.   TALMUD: *Shabbath,* 12b

Man was made a little lower than the angels.

adapted from *Book of Psalms,* 8 : 5

Through intelligence and knowledge man comes to resemble the character of the angels.   adapted from IBN GABIROL

Man is not an angel, whose reasoning works perfectly.

JOSEPH CASPI, *Yore Deah*

Angels do not eat; they merely appear to be eating; hence we learn a man should not turn aside from local custom.

Rashi, *Commentaries on the Pentateuch, Genesis*

See also: GOD, HEAVEN, HELL, HEREAFTER, SAGES, SATAN

ANGER

Because you're angry at the rabbi, why refuse to say *"Amen!"* to the prayer?

Anger is a fool.

A boiling kettle overflows.

Whoever is consumed by rage hears no thunder and sees no lightning.

⌐§ Never try to pacify someone at the height of his rage.

An angry man is unfit to pray.   NACHMAN OF BRATSLAV

He who curbs his wrath merits forgiveness for his sins.

When you give vent to your feelings, anger leaves you.

Anger and temper shorten our years.

Anger in a house is like a worm in a plant.

All Hell rules over the man who is angry.
                              TALMUD: *Nedarim,* 22a

When a sage is angry, he is no longer a sage.
                              TALMUD: *Pesahim,* 66a

⌐§ Never anger a heathen, a snake, or a pupil.
                              TALMUD: *Pesahim,* 113a

Observe people when they are angry, for it is then that their true
    nature is revealed.   *Zohar*

A gentle answer turns away wrath; but harsh words stir up anger.
                              Book of Proverbs

⌐§ Anger begins with madness and ends in regret.
                    HASDAI, *Ben ha-Melekh ve-ha-Nazir*
                    (The King's son and the Nazirite)

Smoking a pipe helps mellow our anger.   THE LUBLINER RABBI

See also: CONTENTMENT, HATE, HEALTH, PASSION, PEACE, TEMPER

ANIMALS

Note. The wry, dry, percipient adages that follow deal, nominally,
    with the animal kingdom; but each cocks a sidelong glance at

Man: his nature, his dilemmas, his propensities for obtuseness, folly, and paralogic. Jews are not unique in this, of course: fairy tales and folk epics and nursery rhymes have always employed the majesty of the lion or the cunning of the fox, the gluttony of the pig or the helplessness of the lamb, as devices for communicating comments about the lords of creation.

Aesop's *Fables* are, of course, the most famous of parables. And a long line of continuity can be traced from Aesop to Rudyard Kipling's *Jungle Books* to the altogether unique genius of Walt Disney. Such a line would run through the folk tales of India or Araby, the matchless anecdotes of the Chinese, the rich Brahman bestiary of the *Panchatantra* (written in Sanskrit). You will find fables in Herodotus, and in Horace's *Satires.* Perhaps the shrewdest fabulist since Aesop was Jean de La Fontaine. And Gotthold Lessing, who disliked the cynical French tales, created new ones in German.

All these mythical stories about animals are designed to teach, to moralize, to make sharp and sometimes sardonic observations on the conduct and character of Man. So are the Jewish witticisms I cite below.

—L.R.

◄§ If a horse had anything to say, he would speak up.

Animals have long tongues, but they can't say a blessing.

Even a flea can bite.

The goat is God's creature, too—but why must he stink?

If you set geese among oats, they'll starve to death.

The dog who follows you is devoted—to the crumbs he expects.

◄§ The camel wanted horns—so they took away his ears.

No one is as poor as a dog, or as rich as a pig.

An ox doesn't know his own strength.

You can't get fur from the hide of a dog.

If a horse realized how small a man is, it would trample him at once.

Birds only come down where there are seeds to pick.

Gazelles are the animals most loved by God ... because a gazelle harms no one, and never disturbs the peace.

MIDRASH: *Midrash Samuel,* 9

If you throw a bone to a dog, he will lick even the dust on your feet.   *Zohar*

Don't show a beaten dog a cane.

See also: CHARACTER, CLEANLINESS, GREED, SAFETY, SURVIVAL

ANTI-SEMITISM

Note. The Jews are not hated because they have evil qualities; evil qualities are sought for in them, because they are hated.

MAX NORDAU

What was their crime? Only that they were born .... That is why the Portuguese burnt them.

VOLTAIRE, *Sermon du Rabi Akib'*

The study of the history of Europe teaches [this] lesson: the nations which dealt fairly with the Jew have prospered; the nations that tortured and oppressed him wrote out their own curse.

OLIVE SCHREINER

The literature on anti-Semitism is immense, fascinating, partisan, vicious, horrifying, and as complex as any subject so steeped in demagoguery, psychopathology, xenophobia, superstition, paranoia, and poisonous prejudice must be. For two recent interesting excursions into this realm, see Arland Ussher's *The Magic People: An Irishman Appraises the Jews* (Devin-Adair, New York, 1951) and Jean-Paul Sartre, *Anti-Semite and Jew* (Schocken, New York, 1965).

—L.R.

God told Moses to accept His holy mission—but be prepared for beatings and curse.

The happiness of Jews is never entirely free from fear.

◆§ Dear God, if you really loved the Jews why did you make them "the chosen people"?

When a Jew is right, he is beaten twice as hard.

◆§ Calamity may be blind, but it has a remarkable talent for locating Jews.

Why are there so many Hamans, but only one Purim? [Haman tried to exterminate all the Jews in Persia; Purim is the festival that commemorates Esther's success in foiling Haman.]

Whatever can happen to all Jews will happen to one Jew.

Misfortune favors Jews; fortune greets them last.

One day, a Jew passed the imperial train and saluted the Emperor Hadrian, who waxed furious: "You, a Jew, dare to greet the Emperor! You shall pay for this with your life!" Later that day, another Jew passed the Emperor and did not greet him. "A Jew dares pass a Roman Emperor without saluting?" Hadrian exclaimed. "You shall be killed!" To his puzzled courtiers, Hadrian explained, "I hate Jews, so I use any excuse to destroy them."   —adapted from TALMUD

To be a Jew means to be ready to be a martyr.
                              MIDRASH: *Exodus Rabbah*, 42 : 9

The sufferings of the Jews in one year could not be recorded even if all the seas were full of ink, and all the reeds were pens, and all men were set to work writing the story.
              —adapted from MIDRASH: *Megillath Ta'anith*

See also: **HATE, HOSTILITY, INQUISITION, INTOLERANCE, JEWS, PERSECUTION, POGROMS, PREJUDICE**

ANXIETY

꙳ Only one type of worry is correct: to worry because you worry too much.

Riches bring anxiety: wisdom gives peace of mind.

IBN GABIROL

See also: CONSCIENCE, LIFE, SUFFERING, TROUBLE, WORRY

APOSTATES

See: PROSELYTES

APPEARANCE

If velvet and silk hang in your closet, you can step out in rags.

At night, all cows look black.

꙳ A homely patch is prettier than a beautiful hole.

It is the worm that lures the fish, not the fisherman and not the rod.

Not everyone at whom dogs bark is a thief.

A man looks to you the way you look at him.

When you have a new coat hanging on the wall, your old one doesn't feel ashamed.

Men see what we wear, not what we eat.

The man who lives in a house did not necessarily build it.

꙳ A goat has a beard—but that doesn't make him a rabbi.

Don't look at the pitcher, but at its contents: for a new pitcher may be full of old wine, and an old pitcher may be empty.

Sayings of the Fathers, 4 : 20

◦§ If you judge by beards and girth, goats are the wisest creatures on earth.   JOSEPH SOLOMON DELMEDIGO

See also: CONDUCT, DECEIT, DECORUM, DRESS, FACE, ILLUSION

ARBITRATION

Arbitration is justice blended with charity.
                                        NACHMAN OF BRATSLAV

See also: COMPROMISE, LAW

ARGUMENT

◦§ The man with an unimpressive argument rattles off many of them.

One strong point is worth ten weak ones.

◦§ If you protest long enough that you're right, you're wrong.

A woman will argue even with the Angel of Death.

He who seeks the truth must listen to his opponent.
                        ISAAC SAMUEL REGGIO, *Torah and Philosophy*

See also: CAUSE AND EFFECT, LAW, PROOF, QUARRELS, TALK

ARROGANCE

◦§ The man who praises himself will shame himself.

The man who despises little things will gradually fail.

Arrogance is a kingdom—without a crown.
                                        TALMUD: *Sanhedrin*, 105a

◦§ When you turn proud, remember that a flea preceded you in the order of divine creation.   TOSEPHTA: *Sanhedrin*

How great some men would be, were they not arrogant.
                                                TALMUD: *Kallah Rabbathi,* 3

The unrepentant go to Hell, the shamefaced to Eden.
                                                Sayings of the Fathers, 5 : 20

Chutzpa [arrogance, gall] prevails even in heaven.
                                                TALMUD: *Sanhedrin,* 205a

See also: CONCEIT, HUMILITY, PRIDE

ASCETICS/ASCETICISM

Those who are spiritually healthy, yet become ascetics, will become
    morally ill.   MAIMONIDES, *Mishneh Torah*

The Torah tells us to follow the path of moderation ... not to dwell
    in the wilderness, nor in the mountains, nor to don hair gar-
    ments, nor to afflict the body.
                                    MAIMONIDES, *Mishneh Torah,* Deut 3 : 1

See also: ABSTINENCE, FASTING, GLUTTONY

ASHKENAZIM

See: GLOSSARY

ASTROLOGY

Note. The ancient Hebrews, like the Babylonians, Egyptians, and
    Greeks, were impressed by astrology. In the Bible, the Hebrew
    word *mazel* referred to a planet or a constellation of the zodiac,
    and the word was invoked when "fate" was involved. Later,
    Talmudic sages sternly warned the Jews to eschew soothsaying
    and diviners. Perplexed believing Jews had a hard time know-
    ing what to think: The Bible, after all, talks of the "signs of
    heaven"—Jeremiah, for instance, and Isaiah. But the Midrash

teaches: "The Holy One forbade astrology in Israel"; and it is said that God made Abraham "a prophet, not an astrologer." The great Maimonides called astrology "a disease, not a science."

Nonetheless, Jews continue to utter "*Mazl tov!*" The supernatural or divinational aspects are forgotten (just as "God be with you" became "good-bye"), and *mazel* has become simply "luck," "*Mazl tov!*", "Congratulations."

—L.R.

Do not believe the astrologers ... our Torah [holds] that a man's conduct is in his own hands, that no external compulsion prevents a man from being virtuous or vicious—except as he may be so constituted, by nature, and finds it easy or hard to do a certain thing. But that a man must do, or refrain from doing, something [because of the stars] is entirely untrue. . . . Astrology is a disease, not a science.

MAIMONIDES, *Hilhoth Tshuvah* (Laws of Repentance)

So it is with all astrologers (says the Talmud): they see something but do not understand what they see.

RASHI, *Commentaries on the Pentateuch, Numbers*

See also: DESTINY, FATE

ATHEISTS

True faith needs no evidence.

❧ Don't ask questions of God: He may say, "If you're so anxious for answers, come up here."

Many who say they don't believe in God, ask His mercy.

❧ Few sailors are atheists, for they are in daily peril.

The fool has said in his heart, "There is no God."

Book of Psalms, 14 : 1

See also: FAITH, GOD, SKEPTICISM

AUTHORITY

Note. Political scientists have always seemed to me to underesti-
mate the enormous impact on secular authority of the Hebrew
concept of monotheism—and the historic line which monotheism drew to limit the legitimacy and power of the temporal.
Ancient monarchs—in Assyria, China, Egypt, Central America,
the Hellenic world—were omnipotent; their authority was un-
challengeable. The law was the King's Law, and his subjects
had no separate, higher, moral or philosophical authority
through which to question or resist royal power. The monarch
was beholden to no one, "owed" nothing to the people, and
could change or ignore laws to suit the royal whim.

But among the Hebrews, the king became subordinate to,
and an agent of, God—who alone deserved unquestioning
obedience. No king of Israel could dream of "divine rights,"
or sacrifices to *him* (as Persian, Babylonian, Sumerian, Roman,
Incan kings did). One historic consequence of monotheism lay
in the fact that any monarch was held responsible to God (who,
presumably, had chosen him). A king or queen was commis-
sioned, as it were, to protect the people's *rights*, the property
and integrity of those over whom he reigned. The Jews clung to
the idea of "limited monarchy"—a concept that was inconceiva-
ble to many of the emperors and conquerors under whose hegemony they fell.

—L.R.

No office can dignify a man, but many a man dignifies his office.

When people who have led hard lives are given authority, they are
harsher than tyrants.

Alas for the possession of that authority that buries its possessor!
SAADIA GAON

The man who cannot control himself becomes absurd when he
wants to rule over others.
ISAAC ARAMA

See also: DEMOCRACY, GOVERNMENT, INFLUENCE, LAW, POLITICS,
POWER

B

BACHELORS

Note. Great social pressure was exerted, in a Jewish community, for every young man to get married—and while young. An unmarried male was looked upon as insensitive to his duty, even something of a sinner. He was evading the responsibility to "multiply," as God commanded; to perpetuate life itself; to honor the solemn debt that attends the gift of having been born; to provide himself with a *Kaddish* to mourn his death and honor his name.

A man who remained unmarried after the age of twenty was considered unblessed, living without joy, derelict in his duty to Jewry—for who knew what learned sons, what marvelous *talmide khakhomin* ("disciples of the wise"), he might have sired?

Yet paradoxically, as in so many other matters, Jews remarked on the sagacity of bachelors by poking fun at those deluded by the illusion of marital bliss.

See headnote: MARRIAGE.

—L.R.

Bachelor: A man who comes to work each morning from a different direction.

A cow can't be a butcher, nor can a bachelor be a matchmaker.

When a bachelor dies, girls are avenged.

Man is not even called man until he is united with woman.
Zohar

When a bachelor reaches twenty and is still unmarried, the Holy One says, "Let him rot!" TALMUD: *Kiddushin,* 29b

Unmarried teachers are as arrogant as kings, but their minds are like those of children.   —adapted from MIDRASH

See also: MARRIAGE

BAD

See: EVIL, VIRTUE, WICKED/WICKEDNESS

BAPTISM

Note. "This was the time of Nicholas I. Some of these 'soldiers of Nicholas,' as they were called, were taken as [Jewish] boys of seven or eight—snatched from their mothers' laps. They were carried to distant villages . . . and turned over to some peasant, who used them like slaves. . . . No two were ever left together, and they were given false names . . . entirely cut off from their own world. And then the lonely child was turned over to the priests, and he was flogged and starved and terrified . . . but still refused to be baptized. . . . After he entered the army, he was bribed with promises of promotions and honors . . . and endured the cruellest discipline [but would not agree to be baptized].

"When he was discharged, at the age of forty, he was a broken man, without a home, without a clue to his origin, and he spent the rest of his life wandering among Jewish settlements, searching for his family, hiding the scars of torture under his rags, begging his way from door to door.

"There were men in our town whose faces made you old in a minute. They had served Nicholas I, and come back, unbaptized." Mary Antin, *The Promised Land*, Heinemann, London, 1911.*

---

* For an historical account of child martyrdoms, see Simon Dubnow, *History of the Jews in Russia and Poland*, J. P. S. A., 1918, Vol. II, pp. 18–29.

BARBARIANS

Whoever helps or caters to a barbarian causes the exile of his children.

See also: GOVERNMENT

BASTARDS

Note. You must bear with some careful distinctions here. What we call "illegitimate" is not quite bastardy, in Jewish law and tradition. A *mamzer* (bastard), in rabbinical law, is a child born of an adulterous or incestuous union. But if the father of the child can be identified, the child is not, technically, a *mamzer*. He is, alas, a *mamzer* if his paternity is uncertain or unprovable.

But note this: Under Talmudic law, the Jewish community is solemnly obligated to pay for the feeding, clothing, and education of such children. Apart from the compassion for the mother and the innocent child, the social value of this custom should be noted: many a bastard turned out to be a scholar, or a success through whom Judaism benefited. Indeed, there is a well-known saying that a *mamzer* who is a *talmid khokhem* ("disciple of the wise"), one of the wisest of the wise, is preferable to a high priest who is ignorant. And one of the affectionate terms Jews use about an especially bright, articulate, or ingenious person is, "Oh, what a *mamzer!*"

Mamzeyrim (plural) were not allowed to marry non-*mamzeyrim;* they were expected and encouraged to marry other *mamzeyrim*—otherwise their offspring were classified as not legitimate. This Orthodox religious dictum is being strongly protested in Israel today. On November 9, 1971, a National Bastard Day dramatized the wide opposition to the rabbinate's "monopoly" of rituals and rights in marriage. A bill has been introduced into the Israeli parliament (Knesset) to institute civil marriages—which would ignore the "legitimacy" of those seeking to wed.

Conservative and Reform rabbis strongly support this. After all, the Talmud tells us that in the world to come all the *mamzeyrim* will appear and the blessed Messiah will himself take up their cause. I trust they will receive restitution for the stigma, sufferings, or injustices that befell them, innocent souls, in this world below. (I also think that the way things are going these days among the rebellious, "emancipated" young, this issue may become as academic as their conduct, on or off campuses, is unacademic.)

—L.R.

Blood never turns into water.

A learned bastard stands higher than an ignorant high priest.
                              MIDRASH: *Numbers Rabbah* 6 : 1

No one has the gall of a bastard.
                              MIDRASH: *Haneelam,* Genesis, 118

Most bastards have a just complaint.
                              TALMUD J.: *Kiddushin,* 4 : 11

A fool is worse than a bastard—if the bastard is wise.
                              TALMUD J.: *Kiddushin,* 4 : 11

❧ If there were fewer swine, there would be fewer bastards.

See also: FAMILY, SONS

BEAUTY

❧ It is good to look at the fair—and live with the wise.

What good is beauty without luck?

Too beautiful is sometimes a fault.

A pretty face costs money.

How many lament their looks, and how few lament their brains!

Better a little with beauty than much without it.

꙰ It is not that that which is beautiful pleases us, but that that which pleases us is called beautiful.

The beautiful is not dear; but the dear is beautiful.

Beauty fades, but a good name endures.
                                        APOCRYPHA, *Ahikar*, 2 : 49

A beautiful ornament looks best on a beautiful woman.
                                        TALMUD J.: *Nedarim*

Charms are deceptive, and beauty is a breath; but a woman who reveres the Lord will be praised.   *Book of Proverbs*

Do not look too long on the beauty that belongs to someone else.
                                        BEN SIRACH, *Ecclesiasticus*

See also: CHARACTER, NATURE, VIRTUE

BEGGARS/BEGGING

It is better to strip a carcass of its hide than to beg.

A beggar does more for an alms-giver than the alms-giver does for the beggar.

Better be a servant in a temple for heathens than accept alms.
                                        TALMUD J.: *Berakoth*, 9

꙰ I have tasted everything, and found nothing as bitter as begging.   IBN GABIROL, *Choice of Pearls*

See also: BORROWERS/BORROWING, CHARITY, GOOD DEEDS, THE POOR/ POOR MEN

BENEVOLENCE

See CHARITY, GOOD DEEDS, KINDNESS

BETRAYAL

If you betray your cause, you support the other's.

See also: TREACHERY

BIBLE

Note. "The whole drama of mankind is contained in this, the
Book of Books... Mahomet, I think, called the Jews the
'People of the Book.' That Book is their country. Within its
boundaries they live and enjoy inalienable citizenship and
cannot be dislodged. . . . Around them, nations rose and disappeared; states flourished, decayed, vanished; revolutions
raged across the world. But the Jews sat poring over this
Book, oblivious to the wild chase of time that rushed over
their heads."   HEINRICH HEINE

"There is not a verse [of the Bible], not a word, but is thick-
studded with human emotion."   WALT WHITMAN

See: GOD, ISRAEL, JEWS, TORAH; also see Preface; and GUIDE NOTE A,
p. 67.

BIRTH

The world is new to us every morning—this is God's gift; and
every man should believe he is reborn each day.
                                               BAAL SHEM TOV

BITTERNESS

᷾ All sentences that start with "God forbid" describe what is
possible.

Every man knows his own bitterness,
And in his joy no stranger can share.
                              Book of Proverbs 14 : 10

See also: ENVY, JEALOUSY

BLAME

Better pray for yourself than blame someone else.

When a fool does something wrong, he blames others; the seeker
of wisdom who does wrong blames himself; but the wise man
blames neither himself nor others, for he is pious.

IBN GABIROL, *Choice of Pearls*

See also: CONSCIENCE, GUILT, WISDOM

BLIND

The blind like to hear tales of wonder.

BOASTERS

Note. Our ancestors, Jew and non-Jew alike, were fearful that
man's boastings, his very successes might offend some god—
and boomerang into disaster. An envious or jealous mortal
could cast an evil spell on another's luck or health.

Among Jews, *keyn eyn-oreh* ("no evil eye") is a magical
phrase uttered to: (a) ward off the evil eye; (b) protect a
child or loved one; (c) show that one's praises are not contaminated by envy. Jews have a long tradition of scorn for
the vainglorious.

—L.R.

He who has a wide mouth has a narrow heart.

One coin in a bottle rattles; the bottle filled with coins makes
no sound.   TALMUD: *Baba Mezi'a,* 85b

Barren trees make more noise than fruit-bearing trees.... They
ask fruit-bearing trees: "Why don't you make any noise?"—
to which the trees reply, "Our fruits are sufficient advertisement."   MIDRASH: *Genesis Rabbah,* 16 : 3

Burning thorns crackle, as if to say, "We too are wood!"
                              MIDRASH: *Ecclesiastes Rabbah*, 7 : 6

More smoke than roast.   —Rabbinic saying

Like wind-blown clouds that bring no rain is he who boasts of
    gifts he does not give.   *Book of Proverbs*

Don't boast about tomorrow; you don't know what one day can
    bring.   adapted from *Book of Proverbs*, 27 : 1

⤜§ Both the boaster and the fool don't know the proper time
    for silence.   BEN SIRACH, *Ecclesiasticus* 20 : 6

He who advertises his name, loses it.
                    HILLEL in *Sayings of the Fathers*, 1 : 14

See also: **ARROGANCE, CONCEIT, FOOLS, PRIDE, VANITY.**

BOOKS

Note. I have always loved the idea of those pious Jews who en-
    visaged "the world to come" as an immense library, where
    all the truly good books written by man would be available
    to the righteous dead. In the *Sefer Hasidim* ("Book of the
    Pious"), there is an enchanting folk tale about books being
    placed on tables in cemeteries, so that the souls of the dead
    would be able to read and study, should they want to, as they
    did in life. One Sabbath eve a group of gentiles passed a
    Jewish cemetery, and to their astonishment beheld an old
    Jew seated at a table near his grave, lost in thought, his head
    propped on one hand as the other turned the pages of a
    book. . . .

To an extent unequalled among other sections of humanity, Jews
    have been interested in books. . . . (The Jew) copied books. He
    owned books. He patronized literature. He was interested in in-
    tellectual life and . . . movements. Even in the most soul-de-
    stroying period of oppression, it might be assumed that almost

every ghetto Jew, however humble his circumstances and however lowly his calling, was likely to have his modest library. A
book was not to him, as to his neighbor, an object of veneration,
of mystery, of distrust. It was a sheer necessity of everyday
life.*

CECIL ROTH

Jewish literature is crammed with references to the nobility
of books. In the fifth century before the Christian Era, Nehemiah,
Governor of Judah for the Persian King Artaxerxes I, "founding a
library, gathered the acts of the kings, and of the prophets, and
of David, and the epistles of the kings concerning holy gifts." (II
Maccabees, 2 : 13)

By tradition, books were treated by Jews as special, treasured
objects: when they grew old or frayed, it was thought sacrilegious
to throw them out; old books were placed in a synagogue's attic;
when space ran out, books were solemnly buried, in a ceremony
fit for the burial of a saint. Even books the Jews hated were
never burned, but were called "apocryphal" or "outside," and were
locked away or hidden.

Rabbinical literature is full of admonitions about the solemn
duty of a Jew to lend books to others, even enemies (so that
learning will be increased); of the obligation of every community
of Jews to build a library; of meticulous advice about the binding,
airing, care, and preservation of books and manuscripts. Along
with the *mitzvah* attached to the ransom of enslaved Jews, was
one for Jews who bought back books which had been captured
by brigands, pirates, or the robbers of synagogues. Thousands of
prized Talmuds and rabbinical writings, stolen from Jews, were
bought back—by them, or other Jews.

But not all: we must remember the vast number of books
that were destroyed forever. After the expulsion from Spain, thousands of Jews fled to Lisbon; the authorities there soon issued a
decree that anyone owning a Hebrew book would be put to
death. In Venice, in 1553, in "the Bitter Month," officials burned
Talmuds and thousands of other volumes. So did the Romans, who
ransacked all Jewish homes and burned their books in the Campo
dei Fiori. . . . Countless precious Hebrew manuscripts and incu-
nabula before the year 1500 no longer exist. Indeed, the complete

---

* In *Essays on Jewish Booklore*, KTAV, New York, 1971, p. 179.

text of the Babylonian Talmud has survived in only one ancient manuscript! (See headnote: VANDALISM).

My own boyhood was gloriously enriched by an eccentric classmate, "Potch," who stored 300 beautiful volumes in my bedroom closet. He claimed that the books—all new, in fresh cartons —were presents, but I soon learned they had been stolen. . . . What delicious hours, for all the moral qualms I suffered, were mine! (If you care to explore this conflict between conscience and bibliomania, consult *People I Have Loved, Known, or Admired*, McGraw-Hill, New York, 1970, pp. 121–30.)

—L.R.

~§ If you drop gold and books, pick up the books first, then the gold.

~§ The Archangel Metatron, the librarian of heaven, brings new books to the Holy One, who then presents them to the Academy on High, for careful study.   —A legend

~§ Whenever the shelves in the Library of Heaven were entirely full, and a new, worthy book appeared, all the books in the celestial collection pressed themselves closer together, and made room.   —A legend

Of the making of books, there is no end.   *Ecclesiastes*, 12

~§ Those who consider a thing proved simply because it is in print are fools.   MAIMONIDES, *Letter to Yemenite Jews*

Every author should weigh his work and ask, "Will humanity gain any benefit from it?"   NACHMAN OF BRATSLAV

Whoever is able to write a book and does not, is as if he has lost a child.   NACHMAN OF BRATSLAV

Not by chance are son and book named in Latin by the same word: *liber*.
JOSEPH SOLOMON DELMEDIGO, *Noblot Hokhmah* ("Notes of Wisdom")

My pen is my harp and my lyre; my library is my garden and my orchard.   JUDAH HA-LEVI

◅§ A man's wisdom extends only as far as his books, and a man should sell all he may possess to buy books. For as our sages said: "He who increases books, increases wisdom."

JUDAH CAMPANTON

◅§ Books should be placed in stately array near the dead, so that the souls of the righteous may in death study as they did on earth.

—Judah of Regensburg, *Sefer Hasidim* ("Book of Saints")

◅§ Should a man face straitened circumstances, he should first sell his gold and jewels, then his house and estate, but not—until the very end, when he has nothing left—his library.

—Judah of Regensburg, *Sefer Hasidim* ("Book of Saints")

A book should not be used as a missile, a shield, or an object for punishment.

JUDAH OF REGENSBURG

◅§ If you have one son who does not like to lend his books, and another son who does, leave your library to the second, even if he is the younger.

JUDAH OF REGENSBURG

◅§ You must not refuse to lend a book even to an enemy, for the cause of learning will suffer.

—a pious Jew, quoted by JUDAH OF REGENSBURG

Never use a pen or a tablet as a bookmark [for you may injure the book].

JUDAH OF REGENSBURG

Never refuse to lend books to anyone who cannot afford to purchase them, but lend books only to those who can be trusted to return them.

IBN TIBBON

Cover your bookcases with rugs or linens of fine quality; preserve them from dampness and mice and injury; for it is your books that are your true treasure.

IBN TIBBON

Handle books with respect: never put a book underneath paper when you line the paper for writing.

IBN TIBBON

Make books your companions; let your bookshelves be your gardens: bask in their beauty, gather their fruit, pluck their roses, take their spices and myrrh. And when your soul be weary, change from garden to garden, and from prospect to prospect.   IBN TIBBON

ᗞᔦ My book is like my beloved; does a man lend his beloved to others?   MOSES BEN ABRAHAM DARI

ᗞᔦ Those who refuse to lend their books . . . shall be fined.
—minutes of the Latvian Jewish Community Council, 1736

When a man travels and finds books which are not known in his hometown, it is his duty to buy them, rather than anything else, and bring the books back home with him.
—Judah of Regensburg, *Sefer Hasidim* ("Book of Saints")

ᗞᔦ Three possessions should you prize: a field, a friend, and a book.   HAI GAON

ᗞᔦ Lend books to the poor before you lend them to the rich.
                                    JUDAH THE PIOUS

Read only brief or systematic books, one at a time, and books beautifully written, on fine paper and attractively bound. Read in an attractive room, and from time to time let your eyes gaze upon beautiful objects so that you will come to love what you read.
    PROFIAT DURAN, *"Maaseh Ephod"* (a Hebrew grammar)

ᗞᔦ It is a man's duty to keep an eye on the honor of his books. . . . If you keep a box of books in your bedroom, place it at the head, not at the foot, of your bed . . .
                                    JUDAH THE PIOUS

See also: KNOWLEDGE, LEARNING, SCHOLARSHIP, STUDY, TRUTH, WISDOM

BOORS

A boor does not fear sin, and a vulgar man cannot be a saint.
                    HILLEL in *Sayings of the Fathers,* 2 : 5

See also: CONDUCT, DECORUM, SENSITIVITY

BORE

ᶜᵍ When a bore leaves the room, you feel as if someone came in.

See also: FOOL, NEBECH, SHLEMIEL.

BOREDOM

We get tired even of *kneydlekh* [dumplings].

Let things get worse—just so they're different!

See also: EXCESS, IDLENESS, MODERATION

BORROWERS/BORROWING

Note. The use of borrowed money is a *sine qua non* of economic growth; yet lending for interest was long hobbled (see Deuteronomy 23 : 20) by simplistic laws, theological taboos, and moral opprobrium—which is often sanctimonious self-indulgence, and seems endemic to man.

Roman law held that a debt is personal, so promissory notes could not be transferred and could not become claims against an estate. In Germany, a debt died when a creditor died. Even in England, up to the middle of the nineteenth century, some debts were not transferrable. But the Talmud ruled that for Jews all debts must be honored—even after a debtor or creditor dies; the Talmudists understood the importance of the negotiable—yet they, too, wrestled with what economists now consider unproductive misconceptions about "usury." The Talmud developed remarkably modern rules governing property, trade, contracts, insurance—but forbade any Jew to accept "excessive" interest in loans; it was left to the rabbis to determine "equitable" rates.

In the year 1200, Maimonides saw that economic growth required that money be used, by being lent, and said that charging interest was neither usurious nor wicked, but served a salutary economic function.

Popes and kings, noblemen and entrepreneurs, long enlisted or preempted the aid of Jews to finance the building of cathedrals, palaces, estates—in this way transferring the medieval sin of "usury" to those outside the Christian fold, souls so doomed to perdition that added transgressions did not matter. Thus the Jews were forced to become moneylenders, and often royal treasurers; and then—but for the rest, see the headnotes for LENDING, MONEY, and USURY.

—L.R.

◄§ If you laugh when you borrow, you'll cry when you pay.

The biggest worriers can't pay the smallest debts.

Borrow, and you'll sorrow.

◄§ Borrowing, like scratching, is only good for a while.

He who need not borrow lives without worry,

You can't borrow money on the basis of "I would" or "I should."

The man who habitually borrows is not fit to be a judge.
                                    TALMUD: *Kethuboth,* 105b

◄§ The man who greets his creditors too warmly is guilty of usury in words.
                          —adapted from Talmud: *Baba Mezi'a,* 75b

◄§ The borrower is the servant of the lender.
                                    Book of Proverbs, 28 : 1

The borrower is liable for any accident [to the thing he borrows].
           RASHI, *Commentaries on the Pentateuch, Exodus*

See also: BEGGARS/BEGGING, BUSINESS, CREDITORS, LENDING

BRAINS

◄§ Prejudice is a blindness in the brain.

◄§ If you harden your heart with pride, you soften your brain with it, too.

&ampsmall God looks first into our hearts, then at our brains.

The tongue is the messenger of the brain.

&ampsmall Many complain of their looks, but who complains about his brains?

See also: INTELLECT, INTELLIGENCE, REASON, WISDOM

BRIBERY

If you don't bribe, you won't ride.

&ampsmall It is surprising how many spots on the character are removed by a solution of gold.

When bribery increased, the span of life decreased,

TALMUD: *Sotah,* 47b

If a man, even one wise in Torah, takes a bribe, his mind will ultimately become confused; what he has learned will be forgotten.

RASHI, *Commentaries on the Pentateuch, Exodus*

If you grease the wheels, you can ride. SHOLEM ALEICHEM

See also: CONSCIENCE, HONOR

BRIDES

Note. Every Jewish bride, however poor, wore a wedding gown and had a trousseau: a collection in even the poorest Jewish community insured that. Wedding guests were obligated to praise the bride and extol her beauties. It was traditional for the groom to give the bride a simple ring (the rabbis wanted to minimize differences between the wealthy and the poor), and for the bride to give the groom a new *talis* (prayer shawl).

—L.R.

◈§ All brides are beautiful—and all corpses look pious.

The bride with beautiful eyes need not worry about her figure.

A groom and a bride have glass eyes. [They see no faults in each other.]

When the groom is desired, the bride needs no words.

Three kinds of mortals need to be protected from others: a patient, a groom, and a bride.   TALMUD: *Berakoth,* 54b

Every bride is beautiful.
          BET (school of) HILLEL in TALMUD: *Kethuboth,* 17a

See also: GIRLS, IRONY: EXAMPLES, MARRIAGE, WEDDINGS

BROTHERS

Whoever seeks a faultless brother will have to remain brotherless.

◈§ If my brother steals, it is the thief who is hanged—not my brother.

A brother turned enemy is an enemy for life.

A brother helped by a brother is like a fortified city.
                                             Book of Proverbs

A friend is friendly at all times.
But a brother is born for adversity.   *Book of Proverbs*

Honor your father and mother, and include your oldest brother.
                                     TALMUD: *Kethuboth,* 103a

If you do not give to your poor brother, in the end you will have to receive from him.   *Sifre—Deuteronomy,* 116

See also: DUTY, FAMILY

BURIAL

The deceased rich once were buried in ornate caskets, and the poor in cheap coffins; so the rabbis have decreed that all who die, however rich or poor, be buried in plain caskets.

TALMUD: *Mo'ed Katan*, 27a

Walk reverently in a cemetery, lest the dead say: Tomorrow they will join us, yet today they mock us!

TALMUD: *Berakoth*, 18a

See also: DEATH, THE HEREAFTER

BUSINESS

Note. Anyone tempted to jump to uncomplimentary conclusions (after reading the number of sayings Jews bandy about concerning trade, business, commerce) might remember that for centuries Jews were forbidden to own land, or farm it, or enter a profession, or enroll in a college.

The supposed "natural shrewdness" of Jews as businessmen has never impressed me; my early years in Chicago were spent among Jews who were conspicuously unaffluent. I thought of Jews as laborers, artisans, craftsmen: our streets were lined with little shops—grocers, tailors, barbers, bakers, butchers, shoemakers—and but one small bank in ten large blocks.

When I lived in England, I was surprised by the dry acerbic comments of the English anent the "native cunning" of the Welsh, the "hunger-for-money" of the Scots, the "instinctive cleverness" of the Irish. And when I traveled through Vermont and New Hampshire I came to know what "shrewd Yankee" really means: parsimony, thrift, and a shrewdness for which Jews are customarily belabored.

As a peripheral comment, it is Italy that gave English most of its business vocabulary: "bank . . . credit . . . net . . . account . . . debit . . ." et cetera.

—L.R.

If you invest in a fever, your profit is a disease.

&§ When you send a fool to market, the merchants rejoice.

Trade may make you a king but it robs you of leisure.

The dough must be bad, indeed, if the baker admits it.

&§ The saloonkeeper may love the drunkard, but will he let him marry his daughter?

Make one sale, and already some call you a merchant.

&§ I trust you completely, but please send cash.

It's easier to get into something [business] than to get out of it.

When you are the only buyer, buy; when other buyers are present, act uninterested.

Don't open a shop unless you know how to smile.

The best broker is cash.

&§ If you invest a needle, you won't win more than a needle.

A nearby penny is worth a distant dollar.

&§ Entrances are wide; exits are narrow.

Business is not brotherhood.

Better a steady dime than a rare dollar.

You don't make big fortunes by peddling little things in the street.

The man who studies can't conduct a business; and a businessman can't devote enough time to study.

Hasty purchases are not good.

False scales are an abomination to the Lord;
But a just weight is his delight.   *Book of Proverbs* 11 : 1

"It is nothing, it is nothing," says the buyer; but when he leaves,
he boasts.   —adapted from *Book of Proverbs,* 14

While the sand is yet on your feet, sell.
Talmud: Pesahim, 113a

Better a small profit at home than a large one from abroad.
Talmud: Pesahim, 113a

◆§ The pot that belongs to partners is neither hot nor cold.
Talmud: Erubin, 3a

Three possess a certain charm: a place to its occupants, a woman
to her husband, and a bargain to the customer.
Talmud: Sotah, 47a

In business, everything depends on aid from heaven.
Talmud: Megillah, 6b

Fifty productive men are better than two hundred who are not.
Talmud J.: Pe'ah, 8 : 8

This is the manner of merchants: first they show the poor stuff
and then they show the best.
Rashi, Commentaries on the Pentateuch, Numbers

As a peg stays between the joinings of stones, so sin [greed] in-
trudes between buyer and seller.
Ben Sirach, Ecclesiasticus, 27 : 2

A man's drive for profit should be prompted by the desire to give
charity.   Nachman of Bratslav

See also: GAMBLING, GOLD, LENDING, MONEY, THRIFT, USURY

CABALA

Note. "The pupils of the Ari ["the holy lion"],* of blessed memory, once asked him why he had never written a book on the
Kabbalah. He replied that it was impossible, because the moment he plunged into a subject a veritable torrent of thoughts
overwhelmed him, one subject leading him irresistibly to another and another and another. Even when he speaks to his
disciples, said the Ari, he must exert strenuous effort to keep
his thoughts to one subject."**
                    —adapted from a collection by S. Y. AGNON

See GLOSSARY: CABALA, ZOHAR

CANTORS

Note. The cantor (*khazn*) is the professional singer who sings
long passages of the liturgy—not as a chant or in a singsong
(as the laity do) but with truly virtuoso singing, especially in
the sweet falsettoes. Emotion is expressed with intensity; the
cantor speaks for the worshippers (he is known as *shaleah
tsibur,* or "emissary of the congregation") in expressing the
emotions embedded in the sacred texts.
     The cantor has come to be regarded as a simple man—
even a simpleton: hence the many jokes and gibes at his ex-
pense. It is even libeled that *khazn* is an acronym formed
from the first letters of "*Khazonim zaynen naronim*": "Cantors
are fools."
     For more than ten centuries, no music was heard in a

---

* Rabbi Isaac ben Solomon Luria (*q.v.*), BIOGRAPHIES, p. 614.
** *Essays on Jewish Booklore,* KTAV, New York, 1942–1971.

synagogue; but as Catholic and Protestant religious services grew more and more opulent, Jewish worshippers, too, sought musical enrichment. Toward the end of the Renaissance, in a radical departure from tradition, congregations began to employ professional cantors; in Eastern Europe, the idea was anathema. In time, the special bravura style of rendering prayer won over even the fundamentalists.

—L.R.

All cantors are fools, but not all fools are cantors.

ﻬ Any Jew can be a cantor, except that at this moment he happens to be hoarse.

One man is an expert on folklore, another on brushes, but everyone is an expert on cantors.

A *khazn* without a voice is like a sheep without wool.

When a *khazn* knows no Hebrew, he is called a cantor.

ﻬ A cantor is a fool: he stands on a platform but thinks he's on a pedestal.   IBN ZABARA, *Book of Delight*, ch. 5

See also: PRAYER, RABBIS, WORSHIP

CAPABILITY

ﻬ Corn can't grow on the ceiling.

If you can't do what you want, do what you can.

You can't make a beaver hat out of a pig's tail.

You can't make ten when even one doesn't exist.

A nut tree will not grow apples.

No cloth is so fine that moths are unable to eat it.

Though his tongue be long, an ox can't blow the shophar [the ram's horn blown in the synagogue during the High Holy

Days; it symbolizes how God reprieved Abraham by allowing him to sacrifice a ram instead of Isaac, his son].

The flute which makes sweet music for princes is not appreciated
   by weavers.   TALMUD: *Yoma*, 20 : 2

Even an angel can't do two things at the same time.
                          MIDRASH: *Genesis Rabbah*, 50 : 2

See also: INTELLIGENCE, REASON

CAPITAL PUNISHMENT

"In those old, wild, barbarous days, when neither life nor the death
   of anyone counted for anything, Rabbi Akiba openly condemned capital punishment, a practice today recognized as
   highly uncivilized."   LEO TOLSTOY

See COURTS, JUDGES, LAW

CAUSE AND EFFECT

If you don't eat garlic, you won't smell.

 &s; If cats wore gloves, they would catch no mice.

 &s; If you eat your bagel, you'll have nothing left but the hole.

If you're busy with tar, your hands will get dirty.

When one link snaps. the whole chain collapses.

 &s; If everyone sweeps in front of his door, the whole city will
   be clean.

Ropes drawn too taut break.

Storms pass, but their driftwood remains.

 &s; When one blind man leads another, both fall into the pit.

If the shepherd is lame and the goats are swift, there will be an accounting at the gate.

Can fire be near tow and not singe it?

TALMUD: *Sanhedrin*, 37a

The pace of the ass depends on the amount of feed he gets.

TALMUD: *Shabbath*, 51b

⋙ The hole, not the mouse, is the thief.

TALMUD: *Gittin*, 45a

They have sown the wind, and they shall reap the whirlwind.

Book of Hosea, 8 : 7

From a tiny spark comes a great conflagration.

BEN SIRACH, *Ecclesiasticus*, 11 : 32

See also: ARGUMENT, CIRCUMSTANCES, ENDS AND MEANS, FORGETTING

CAUTION

⋙ Caution at first is better than tears at last.

Don't let go of a lion in your grip; he will devour you.

⋙ Better measure ten times and cut once, instead of measuring once and cutting ten times.

Never expose yourself unnecessarily to danger: A miracle may not save you . . . and if it does, it will be deducted from your store of luck—or merit.   TALMUD: *Shabbath*, 32a

Caution should not be overcautious.

BAHYA IBN PAQUDA, *Duties of the Heart*

Don't be like the bird that sees the grain but not the trap.

JUDAH IBN TIBBON, *A Father's Admonition*

See also: FORESIGHT, HASTE, JUDGMENT, PRUDENCE

CENSORSHIP

Note. The Talmud (*Sanhedrin* 100b) lists the immortal sayings of Ecclesiasticus (Jesus ben Sirach) as one of the "forbidden" books—that is, a work "outside" the canon. But Ecclesiasticus was greatly loved by Jews, widely quoted by rabbis, and swiftly translated from Hebrew into Aramaic (the language of the Israelites in Babylon, and in Palestine in 180 when Ben Sirach wrote his masterpiece).

According to each one's bent, the rabbis periodically responded to "secular" books with alarm, anger, or warnings to the laity. Their motives were pure enough (what censor's are not?): They were determined to keep the religious and intellectual life of their Jewish communities pure, unpolluted by reading that might disturb faith with agnostic, heretical, Greek or Christian thought—or by secular science. By "secular" the rabbis meant books about philosophy, poetic celebrations of paganism or pantheism, the classics of Greece and Rome, works in sciences that appeared to threaten the Talmud's cosmology.

Maimonides' *Guide for the Perplexed* (1190), which asserted that Judaism rested on reason and could be comprehended best on Aristotelian principles, created a furor in the learned circles of Europe. The book was much admired by Muslim and Christian thinkers (Aquinas, Leibniz), but fervently opposed by rabbis, who, in 1305, forbade Jews to read philosophical works of this kind until they were twenty-five. Those under twenty-five who disregarded the ban, designed to last fifty years, were threatened with anathematization. (In the eighteenth and nineteenth centuries, Maimonides' work became "the Bible of the enlightened.")

Other important Jewish writers who were taboo, at one time or another, include Levi ben Gershon, Isaac ben Moses Arama, the cabalists, hasidim, Reformists, the Baal Shem. See BIOGRAPHIES in the present volume.

—L.R.

See BOOKS, EROTICA, READING, STUDY

CERTAINTY

If there is room for question, something is wrong.

Better a small certainty than a large doubt.

If you insist you're right long enough, you'll be wrong.

Between "sure" and "perhaps," "sure" prevails.
TALMUD: *Kethuboth*, 12b

◆§ Don't rely on If and Perhaps.
BACHYA IBN PAQUDA, *Duties of the Heart*

There is no certainty without some doubt.
ELIAS LEVITA, *Tishbi*

Those who grieve over the doubtful will rejoice over the sure.
MOSES IBN EZRA, *Shirat Yisrael*

See also: CONTEXT, JUDGMENT, LAW, PRUDENCE

CHARACTER

◆§ Salaoons can't corrupt good men, and synagogues can't reform bad ones.

Spots on the character can be removed—with a little gold.

◆§ It is better to have nobility of character than nobility of birth.

A giant is very tall even though he stands in a well.

Better a crooked foot than a crooked mind.

Every innkeeper praises his beer.

It *may* be that you will find an honest saloonkeeper, or a shepherd who is a thief.

What's in a man is sure to come out, one way or another.

Spit in a whore's face and she'll say, "It's raining."

❧ If the light is crooked, the shadow is crooked.

The cloak of a saint may cover the character of a scoundrel.

The man who is not good for himself is not good for others.

Should a peasant become a king, he still would not take the basket off his head.

Rub him with honey and he'll still smell of tar.

To accept an excuse shows a good character.

He enjoys giving so much that he hopes others will be in need, so that he may help them.

❧ To drunkards, no liquor is bad; to merchants, no money is tainted; to lechers, no woman is ugly.

❧ He is the kind of man who first prepares the bandage, then inflicts the wound.   TALMUD: *Megillah,* 13a

❧ What a man wants, he does not have; what he has, he does not prize.

There are three types of "doers": If a man says, "I shall do it soon," his character is poor; if he says, "I am ready to do it," his character is average; if he says, "I am doing it," his character is praiseworthy.   —Hasidic saying

God decides what shall befall a man, but not whether he shall be righteous or wicked.   TALMUD: *Niddah,* 16b

❧ You can know a man by three signs: his tips, his tippling, and his temper.   —adapted from the TALMUD

There are four types among men:
The ordinary one says: "What is mine is mine, and what is yours is yours."
The queer one says: "What is mine is yours, and what is yours is mine."

The saintly one says: "What is mine is yours, and what is yours
is yours."
The wicked one says: "What is mine is mine, and what is yours
is mine."
Sayings of the Fathers, 5 : 16

Like garden, like gardener.   TALMUD J.: *Sanhedrin*, 2 : 6

As the breath of the potter, so the shape of the vessel.
Zohar

Remember the virtues you lack and the faults you have; forget
the good you did and the wrong you received.
Orhot Tsadikim ("Ways of the Saints")

In this world, one who is a dog can become a lion, and one who
is a lion can become a dog.
MIDRASH: *Ruth Rabbah*, 3 : 2

◄§ Character is tested through three things: business, wine, and
conversation.   *Abot de Rabbi Nathan*, ch. 31

As is its fuel, so will be the fire.
BEN SIRACH, *Ecclesiasticus*, 28 : 10

Watching for other people's blemishes prevents me from investi-
gating my own—which task is more urgent.
BAHYA IBN PAQUDA, *Duties of the Heart*

Moral conduct is a preparation for intellectual progress: only that
man whose character is pure, calm and steadfast can reach
correct conceptions.
MAIMONIDES, *Guide to the Perplexed*, 1 : 34

The man who keeps silent in the face of abuse is a true Hasid.
NACHMAN OF BRATSLAV

See also: ANIMALS, DISCIPLINE, HONESTY, MAN

CHARACTER ILLUSTRATED VIA ANIMALS

A dog without teeth is no longer a dog.

One recognizes the chick by its pecking.

The dog who barks "ho-ho" is not dangerous; the one who growls "how-how" is.

You can deck a pig in palms, but he will still act like a pig.

You can't make an arrow out of a pig's tail.

What, besides beef, can you expect from an ox?

⮸ An eagle doesn't catch flies.

Let a dog on your bench and he'll jump to your table.

A lion should not weep in the presence of a fox.

⮸ The goat has a beard, but still is no rabbi.

CHARACTER OF THINGS

Three things grow overnight: profit, rent, and daughters.

Though a castle totter, it is still called a castle; should a dunghill be built to the sky, it is still a dunghill.

⮸ Said the cat: "If I had eyes of silver and ears of gold, I still would not stop stealing."   APOCRYPHA: *Ahikar*

See also: EVIL, HONESTY, HONOR, MAN, VIRTUE

CHARITY

Note. The Judaic admonition to be righteous, compassionate and, above all, help one's fellow man is called *tsedakah—* *"righteousness." This is the closest word for "charity" in He-* *brew or Yiddish;* for Jews never separated charity from duty —that is, from moral and religious obligation. Deuteronomy (15:11) says, "For the poor shall never cease out of the land; therefore I command thee, saying, thou shalt open thine hand wide unto thy brother ..."

Jews are forbidden to turn away anyone who asks for help. The poor and needy must, moreover, be spared embarrassment. Every Jewish community contained a hostel attached to the synagogue, for travelers or itinerants. Jews place great stress on helping the poor, the sick, the handicapped—and refugees, who have always been a part of the history of Jews

Every community had a special fund for the needy; every holiday includes philanthropic activities; every home once contained little boxes into which coins for various charities were dropped. Every Jewish child was taught early in life to feel a duty to help those who needed help. Orphans were supported by communal funds. Fatherless or poor girls received a wedding gown, trousseau, and dowry from the community. The penniless received free burial. And even paupers were obligated to contribute nominal sums to the community fund.

All these obligations, incidentally, were superseded by the duty to ransom Jewish captives or slaves. A moving account of this side of the Jewish experience was written by Cecil Roth in the chapter, "A Community of Slaves," in *Personalities and Events in Jewish History*.

Maimonides analyzed and rated the different forms of *tsedakah*. The highest form, he said, is to help someone to help himself; after that, to help a man anonymously and secretly—so that the benefactor does not know whom he helps, and the benefactee does not know (so cannot feel obligated to) the one who helped him. I have never heard an improvement upon this.

—L.R.

ᴇᴚ The longest road in the world is the one that leads from your pocket.

ᴇᴚ If charity cost nothing, the world would be full of philanthropists.

To steal for charity is still stealing.

Charity is also a habit.

A sick person should be asked; a healthy one—given.

He is a philanthropist—with other people's money.

His charity stops at his pocketbook.

He who gives, lives; he who does not give, does not.

 ঙ§ Lend before witnesses, but give without them.

Rather give charity to a cripple than to a needy scholar.

The best charity is good will.

A man gives little if he gives much with a frown; he gives much if
 he gives little with a smile.

If you won't give to Jacob you will have to give to Esau.

Charity is the very salt of riches.   Talmud: *Kethuboth,* 66b

The man who refuses to live within his means, but seeks to be
 supported by charity, must not be helped.
        Talmud: *Kethuboth,* 67b

We should be grateful for the presence of rogues among the poor;
 for if not for them, we would sin each time we ignored an
 appeal for alms.
        Talmud: *Kethuboth,* 68a

To shut one's eye to charity is like worshipping idols.
        Talmud: *Kethuboth,* 68b

 ঙ§ The greatest charity is to enable the poor to earn a living.
        Talmud: *Shabbath,* 63a

Charity knows neither race nor creed. Talmud: *Gittin,* 61a

[When a rabbi saw a man give a penny to a beggar in public:]
 "Better had you given him nothing than put him to shame."
        Talmud: *Hagigah,* 5a

He who gives alms in secret is greater than Moses.
        Talmud: *Baba Bathra,* 9b

Whoever gives the poor money is blessed sixfold; whoever does it
with a kind word is blessed sevenfold.

Talmud: *Baba Bathra*, 9b

Better be a servant in a heathen temple than take alms.

Talmud J.: *Berakoth*, 9

When the year has been prosperous, people become more brotherly.

Midrash: *Genesis Rabbah*, 89 : 4

As a torch is not diminished though it kindles a million candles, so
will he not lose who gives to a good cause.

Midrash: *Exodus Rabbah*, 30 : 3

Better is he who gives little to charity—from money honestly
earned, than he who gives much—from money acquired by
fraud.   Midrash: *Ecclesiastes Rabbah*, 4

He who closes his ear against the cry of the poor will himself one
day call and not be heard.

—adapted from *Book of Proverbs*

He who lengthens the life of a poor man [through charity] will
have his own life lengthened when his time to die comes.

Zohar

There are four kinds of almsgivers: the one who gives, but does not
want others to give; the one who gives and wants others to
give; the one who neither gives nor wants others to give.

Sayings of the Fathers, 5 : 19

Do not harden your heart against your poor brother; if you do not
give to him, you will, in the end, have to receive from him.

Sifre—Deuteronomy, 116

The door which is not opened for a beggar will open for a
doctor.   *Pesikta Rabati*, 42b

Man is worthy of being called Man only if he is charitable.

Yalkut Ruveni

There is a kind of charity which is pernicious: that of the man who
gives alms to an adulterer, or to a glutton, or to a drunkard...

or who supplies weapons to murderers . . . or who gives food to
robbers.

Sefer Hasidim

To give everything to religion is not piety but folly: it impoverishes
a man so that he must come to depend on charity. We need
show no compassion for such a man, for he belongs to those
described by the sages as "pious fools who destroy the world."
MAIMONIDES, *Mishneh Torah:* 8 : 13

The sages would sometimes tie money in a cloth bag and throw
it behind their backs for poor men to pick up, so that the poor
should not feel shame.
MAIMONIDES, *Mishneh Torah*, 10 : 1–14

The great sages used to go about throwing money through the doors
of the poor [and hurrying away, not to be seen]: this is
virtuous.
MAIMONIDES, *Mishneh Torah*, 10 : 1–14

If a poor man asks for alms, and you have nothing to give,
console him with words; for it is forbidden to chastise a poor
man or raise your voice against him, since his heart is broken.
MAIMONIDES, *Mishneh Torah*, 10 : 1–14

Poor men, required to give to charity, may fulfill their obligations
by exchanging alms.   JOSEPH CARO, *Shulhan Aruk*

No man is ever impoverished by giving alms, nor is harm ever
caused by it.   JOSEPH CARO, *Shulhan Aruk*

He who refuses aid which he has the power to give is accountable
to justice.   JOSEPHUS, *Against Apion*, II, 27

A poor but humble man who gives nothing to charity is preferable
to a rich but haughty man who does.
NACHMAN OF BRATSLAV

Charity cures heartaches.   NACHMAN OF BRATSLAV

A *mitzvah* [good deed] that costs money is worth more than one
that costs nothing.   NACHMAN OF BRATSLAV

Always help the persecuted. NACHMAN OF BRATSLAV

Before reciting his prayers, a man should give to charity.
NACHMAN OF BRATSLAV

Charity with a smile shows the donor's character.
NACHMAN OF BRATSLAV

Even the poor should give some token of charity.
NACHMAN OF BRATSLAV

He gives twice who gives quickly.
LEONE DA MODENA, *Tsemah Tsadik*

Don't use the chutzpa of a beggar as an excuse for not helping
him. RABBI SHMELKE OF NICKELSBURG

◄§ Men are always close—to their pockets.
SHOLEM ALEICHEM

See also: COMPASSION, DUTY, GENEROSITY, GOOD DEEDS, GIVING & TAK-
ING, KINDNESS, MERCY, OBLIGATION, PITY, RESPONSIBILITY

CHARM

Two things can't be bought: charm and luck.

◄§ The charming don't have to be beautiful.

Charm surpasses beauty.

A little charm does no harm.

Charm can't be bought at the grocer's.

If you open a shop, stock up on charm.

See also: BEAUTY, DECORUM

CHASTITY

◄§ Jews have no nunneries.

CHEAP

 What's cheap is expensive.

Cheap *borsht* (beet soup) is a blessing to the toothless.

To the poor, *borsht* (beet soup) tastes as good as caviar to the rich.

If you can't afford the expensive, be grateful for the cheap.

The cheapest man can be very generous—with the money of others.

See also: BUSINESS, JUDGMENT, VALUE

CHILDREN

Little children, little troubles; big children, big troubles.

 Little children won't let you sleep; big children won't let you live.

The *nakhes* [pleasures] we get from children are far more precious than gold.

Children bring joy, children bring sorrows.

Little children don't let you chew, and with big ones you can't afford the new.

Each child brings his own blessing into the world.

You can tell a Jew by how he treats his children.

Whom God would punish, he sends bad children.

Children—and money—form a happy world.

 One father can support ten children, but ten children seem unable to support one father.

Children are like grass: some blossom and some fade.

A boy, a blessing; a girl, a worry.

A child's tears move the heavens themselves.

◆§ If you're a child at twenty, you're a jackass at twenty-one.

If the world will ever be redeemed, it will be through the virtues of children.

Even a child is known by his deeds.

A mother's blow never disables a child.

◆§ A child's simple sense is a kind of wisdom.

For children, we tear the world apart.

The apple doesn't fall far from the tree.

Sometimes a dog is more loyal than a child.

◆§ A little child is a pig; a big child is a wolf.

Don't gossip about the children of others while yours are still growing up.

Your child may be a robber, yet you dance at his wedding.

◆§ Five fingers on one hand—yet no two are alike.

One [child] is not enough.

It is better not to have had children than to bury them.

Those who marry for money will have unworthy children.

◆§ Take care of the children of the poor, for they will be the ones who advance knowledge.   TALMUD: *Nedarim,* 81a

A child is a staff for the hand—and a hoe for the grave.
                                        TALMUD: *Yebamoth,* 65b

◆§ Every child tends to exaggerate its own importance.
                                        TALMUD: *Sukkah,* 21a

No kids, no wethers; no wethers, no sheep . . . No children, no adults; no adults, no sages.
                                MIDRASH: *Genesis Rabbah,* 42 : 3

Don't fret over married children; they will take care of themselves.
NACHMAN OF BRATSLAV

We each have the kind of children we deserve.
NACHMAN OF BRATSLAV

◄§ Children without a childhood are tragic.
MENDELE MOCHER SEFARIM

◄§ It is better that children cry than that their fathers cry.

See also: ANCESTORS, DAUGHTERS, FAMILY, FATHERS, MOTHERS, SONS

CHILDREN: ON BEGETTING THEM

Of children and glasses, one never has too many. [Both are fragile.]

A man without children is like a piece of wood which, though kindled, does not light—or give off light.

He who begets a fool does it to his sorrow;
And the father of a dolt will have no joy of him.
Book of Proverbs

Let not the fear of bad offspring deter you from having children; you must do your duty and God will do what pleases Him.
TALMUD: *Berakoth,* 10a

Not to beget children is to impair the divine image.
MIDRASH: *Genesis Rabbah,* 34 : 14

CHILDREN: ON TEACHING THEM

He who does not bring up his son to some honest calling brings him up to be a thief.

Don't limit a child to your own learning, for he was born in another time.   —Rabbinic saying

◄§ If you teach your children in their youth, they won't have to teach you in your old age.   —Hasidic saying

We learn best what our heart prepares us to learn.

TALMUD: *'Abodah Zarah,* 19a

If you don't teach the ox to plow when he is young, it will be
    difficult to teach him when he is grown.

MIDRASH: *Midrash Proverbs,* 22

Teach a child good manners during babyhood.

NACHMAN OF BRATSLAV

CHILDREN: ON RAISING THEM

It is easier to have children than raise them.

Train a child in the way he should take,
And when he is old, he will not depart from it.

Book of Proverbs 22 : 6

It is important for a growing child to be given things he can break:
    Rabbah often bought imperfect earthenware for his little ones
    to smash, should they want to.   TALMUD: *Yomah,* 78b

Never promise something to a child and not give it to him, because
    in that way he learns to lie.   TALMUD: *Sukkah,* 46b

When the chicks of a hen are young, she gathers them to her; when
    they are grown, she drives them away.

MIDRASH: *Leviticus Rabbah,* 25 : 5

Love your children equally, even though the favored disappoint
    you and the neglected make you happy.

BERECHIAH BEN NATRONAI HA-NAKDAN, *Fox Fables*

৶৽ The man who disobeys his father will have disobedient sons.

Wherever children are learning, there dwells the Divine Presence.

At five, your son is your master; at ten, your slave; at fifteen, your
    double; and after that, he is your friend or foe—depending on
    how you raised him.

The man who spares the rod hates his son.

—adapted from *Book of Proverbs,* 13 : 24

Play no favorites: when Joseph got a many-colored coat, his
brothers came to hate him.
                          MIDRASH: *Genesis Rabbah*, 84 : 8

◄§ If you don't respect your parents, your child will not respect
you.   MAIMONIDES, *Guide to the Perplexed*, 3 : 9

See also: DISCIPLINE, KNOWLEDGE, LEARNING, PIETY

CHILDREN: ON PUNISHING THEM

◄§ If you must beat a child, use a string.
                              TALMUD: *Baba Bathra*, 21a

Don't threaten a child: Either punish him or forgive him.
                                                    TALMUD

The rod of correction creates wisdom; but a child left to himself
brings disgrace to his mother.   *Book of Proverbs*

The branch sprung from violence has no tender twig.
                              BEN SIRACH, *Ecclesiasticus*, 40 : 15

A mother's curse roots up the young plant.
                              BEN SIRACH, *Ecclesiasticus*, 3 : 9

Gold must be hammered, and sometimes a child must be beaten.
                              Alphabet of Ben Sirach, 4

◄§ When a father is quick-tempered, his children are confused.
                                    NACHMAN OF BRATSLAV

A strict master will not have understanding sons.
                                    NACHMAN OF BRATSLAV

CHILDREN: AND PARENTS

◄§ It is better that a child should cry than its parents.

◄§ About his children, every parent is blind.

◆§ The rich don't have children: they have heirs.

◆§ One father can support ten children; but ten children don't seem to be able to support one father.

◆§ Parents once taught their children to talk; today children teach their parents to be quiet.

Pity the child who has been banished from his father's table.

It is better not to live than to be dependent on your children.

◆§ The talk of the child in the street is that of his father or mother at home.

Though parents have a dozen children, each is the only one.

Crooked parents can produce straight children.

Any finger hurts as much as any other. [All children are equally loved.]

To its parents, no child is superfluous.

The follies of children are termites to their fathers' possessions.

A father loves his children; but they love their children.
                              TALMUD: *Sotah,* 49a

As my fathers planted for me, so do I plant for my children.
                              TALMUD: *Ta'anith,* 23a

It is normal for a child to fear his father more than his mother; it is normal for a child to love his mother more than his father.
                  RASHI, *Commentaries on the Pentateuch, Exodus*

See also: FAMILY, FATHERS, MOTHERS

CHILDREN: GRANDCHILDREN

◆§ When you have a grandchild, you have two children.

Grandchildren are like children.   TALMUD: *Yebamoth,* 62b

A man appreciates the love of his grandchildren more than the love
of his children.   *Zohar*

See also: **FAMILY, FATHERS, MOTHERS**

CHUTZPA

◦§ After murdering his father and mother, he asked the court to
be merciful because he was an orphan.

While beating you up, he cries, "Help! Help!"

See: **ARROGANCE**

CIRCUMSTANCES

There's no need to light a lamp at noon.

◦§ The same sun bleaches linen and blackens gypsies.

A little coin in a large jar makes a great noise.

◦§ If things are not as you like, like them as they are.

◦§ Entrances are wide, but exits are narrow.

When an old man takes a young wife, he gets young and she gets
old.

A cat and a rat will make peace over a carcass.

◦§ A thief takes one path; his pursuers confront ten.

◦§ What is bread for one is death for another.

A heavy load [of bread] is no burden.

When the wet leaves [on a tree] burn, what can the dry ones say?

When the light goes out, the mice dance.

◦§ When a teacher fights with his wife, it's tough on his students.

At the seashore, thornbushes are veritable fir trees.

> Talmud: *Pesahim,* 4a

◦§ The man who makes arrows is often slain by one of them.

> Talmud: *Pesahim,* 28a

If the victim is fat enough, a cat and a weasel feast together.

> Talmud: *Sanhedrin,* 105a

If a man goes into a tannery, the smell does not leave him all day, even though he bought nothing.

> *Abot de Rabbi Nathan,* 11 : 14b

Silence is not commendable in the presence of absurdities; wrath is, when voiced over sin.   Ibn Gabirol

See also: ADVICE, ANIMALS, CAUSE AND EFFECT, COMPROMISE, CONTENTMENT, CONTEXT, COOPERATION, DEPENDENCY, ENDS AND MEANS, INFLUENCE, WISDOM

CIVILIZATION

Note. "In the infancy of civilization, when our island was as savage as New Guinea, when letters and arts were still unknown to Athens, when scarcely a thatched hut stood on what was afterwards the site of Rome, this condemned people (Jews) had fenced cities and cedar palaces, their splendid Temple, their fleets of merchant ships, their schools of sacred learning, their great statesmen and soldiers, their natural philosophers, their historians, and their poets. What nation ever contended more manfully against overwhelming odds for its independence and religion? What nation ever, in its last agonies, gave such signal proofs of what may be accomplished by a brave despair?"*

> Thomas Babington Macaulay

"The Roman *patria* applied only to the city of Rome. . . . The ancient Greeks concentrated their colonization on localities abutting great bodies of water. The ancient Hebrews followed the changing centers of civilization. Ensconced at first around the shores of the Euphrates and the Tigris, they pulled up

---

* *Essay and Speech on Jewish Disabilities,* Jewish Historical Society of England, London, 1910.

stakes and journeyed to the Nile when it became the hub of
civilization. For a long period they settled in Egypt, but the
magnetic, gravitational 'pull' of onmarching civilization . . .
again attracted them into its orbit, propelling them into centers
that had been established along the eastern shores of the
Mediterranean."*

ALAN STEINBACH

See BOOKS, COMMUNITY, GOVERNMENT, HISTORY, ISRAEL, LAW, POLITICS

CLEANLINESS

Note. Talmudic deliberations contain the most extraordinary, detailed, "modern" prescriptions about personal cleanliness, which
is considered an obligation to the body God gave man. Christians often remarked on the unusual emphasis Jews placed
upon cleanliness and hygiene; some medieval commentators
said this amounted to a "cult of purity." Such a "cult" was of
immense value in keeping Jewish families healthier than they
might otherwise have been. Every Jewish community was
required by Talmudic law to maintain a public bathhouse.
Bathing could only have helped fortify a sense of self-respect.
This seems all the more significant, I think, if one considers the
differences in hygiene and sanitation that existed between
Jewish and other communities in the Middle East.

—L.R.

ᴈ Poverty comes from God, but dirt does not.

A scholar with one spot on his garments deserves the worst.

TALMUD: *Shabbath,* 114a

"Cleanliness is next to godliness," it is said. Carefulness leads to
cleanliness, cleanliness to purity, purity to humility, humility to
saintliness, saintliness to fear of sin, fear of sin to holiness, and
holiness to immortality.   TALMUD

See also: ANIMALS, CLOTHING, CONDUCT, DECORUM, POVERTY, SCHOLARS

---

* *Essays on Jewish Booklore,* KTAV, New York, 1971, p. xviii. For interesting
essays on this and related themes, see Cecil Roth, *The Jewish Contribution to Civilization,* Macmillan, London, 1938.

CLOTHES/CLOTHING

Fools see men's clothes; wise men see men's spirits.

Our clothes conceal our blemishes.

A homely patch is more beautiful than a beautiful hole.

◄§ The clothes of other people do not warm us.

In your town, your reputation counts; in another, your clothes do.
TALMUD: *Shabboth,* 14b

The man who does not respect clothes will not benefit from them.
TALMUD: *Berakoth,* 62a

Man's honor [dignity] accompanies his dress.
MIDRASH: *Exodus Rabbah*

The dress of a wise man must be free of stains; he should not wear the apparel of princes, to attract attention, nor the raiment of paupers, which incurs disrespect.
MAIMONIDES, *Mishneh Torah,* 5 : 7–13

Eat less and dress better.   —adapted from IBN TIBBON

See also: CONDUCT, DECORUM, STATUS

CLUMSY MEN

He can't even tie the tail of a cat.

If he were to fall on his back he would break his jaw.

See also: SHLEMIELS, SHLIMAZLS

COMFORT

It breaks no law to be comfortable.

The change from trouble to comfort gives us more pleasure than
uninterrupted comfort does.
> MAIMONIDES, *Guide to the Perplexed,* 3 : 24

See also: COMPASSION

COMMANDMENT

Live by the commandments; do not die by them.
> TALMUD: *Sanhedrin,* 74a

Six hundred and thirteen commandments were given to Moses:
365 negative, corresponding to the days of the year, and 248
positive, corresponding to the number of joints in the human
body.
> TALMUD: *Makkoth,* 23b

A commandment is to the Torah what a lamp is to the sun.
> MIDRASH: *Psalms,* 17 : 7

See also: LAW

COMMON SENSE

⋟ No barber cuts his own hair.

A thread is always found on a tailor.

⋟ A meowing cat won't catch a mouse.

Just to look costs nothing.

You can catch flies better with honey than with vinegar.

The scholar who sets forth to look for a bride would be well advised to take an ignorant but sensible man along.

⋟ Some scholars have the sense of donkeys: they only carry a lot
of books.
> —adapted from BAHYA IBN PAQUDA, *Duties of the Heart*

See also: CIRCUMSTANCE, JUDGMENT, REASON, WISDOM

COMMUNITY

The man who avoids society is inclined to wickedness.

If fire strikes the wet, what chance have the dry?

Nine rabbis cannot make a *minyan,* but ten shoemakers can. [To "make a minyan" means to constitute a quorum of ten for prayers or other religious services.]

❧ When the sheep are sheared, the lambs tremble.

Let us be like the lines that lead to the center of a circle—uniting there, and not like parallel lines, which never join.
                                                        —Hasidic saying

A community is too heavy for any man to carry alone.

The wolf will grab the sheep that strays from the flock.
                                        Moses Ibn Ezra, *Shirat Yisrael*

See also: GOVERNMENT, LAW, POLITICS, PUBLIC, PUBLIC WELFARE

COMPANIONS

❧ If you lie with dogs, you rise with fleas.

With men, as with apples, one rotten spoils the others.

We need comrades—both for joy and for sorrow.

Give me comradeship, or give me death.
                                        Talmud: *Ta'anith,* 23a

❧ How can a jar and a kettle associate happily when, whichever is struck, the same one is always smashed?
                                        Ben Sirach, *Ecclesiasticus,* 13 : 2

When one of my friends died, one of my limbs perished.
                                        Ibn Gabirol

A companion who tells you your faults is better than a companion
who hands you a gold coin.

IBN GABIROL

See also: DEVIL, FRIENDS/FRIENDSHIP

COMPASSION

Note. Rakhmones, which in Yiddish usage means "pity" or "compassion," is a quintessential word that lies at the heart of
Jewish thought. All of Judaism's philosophy, ethics, ethos,
learning, education, are saturated with a sense of, and a
heightened sensitivity to, the primacy and nobility of *rakhmones.*

God is often called the God of Mercy and Compassion
(*Adonai El Rahum ve-Hanun*). The writings of the ancient
prophets are permeated with appeals for *rachamim,* which is
considered a divine attribute.

Rakhmones is not found in the Bible; *rahamim* is—in an
unforgettable way: The Lord decided that a world governed
by justice alone would be impossible; for human beings to
endure requires that compassion (*rahamim*) be added.

Women's Liberation Movementeers may be interested to
know that the Hebrew root *rehem* means "a mother's womb,"
and that the rabbis said that men and women should give
others the same love that a mother feels for the issue of her
womb.

—L.R.

One heart is mirror to another.

◦§ Some men can't even spare a sigh.

When a man has compassion for others, God has compassion for
him.   TALMUD: *Bezah,* 32a

The man who begs aid for his comrade, while himself in need,
is answered first.   TALMUD: *Baba Kamma,* 92a

◦§ When the Egyptians were drowning in the Red Sea, the angels in heaven began to break forth in songs of jubilation,

but the Holy One, blessed be He, silenced them: "My creatures are perishing—and ye are ready to sing!"
—adapted from TALMUD

Never beat or inflict pain on any animal, beast, bird, or insect.
Sefer Hasidim

✑ Can you ask a cruel man's advice about compassion?
BEN SIRACH, *Ecclesiasticus*, 37

If one is cruel to himself, how can we expect him to be compassionate with others?
HASDAI, *Ben ha-Melekh, ve-Ha-Nazir*

Whoever fails to visit a sick, friendless person is as if he shed his
blood. AKIBA in TALMUD: *Nedarim,* 40a

Where there is no compassion, crime increases.
NACHMAN OF BRATSLAV

✑ If we do not help a man in trouble, it is as if we caused the
trouble. NACHMAN OF BRATSLAV

Toothaches afflict those who have no compassion for animals.
NACHMAN OF BRATSLAV

See also: ALTRUISM, FORGIVENESS, GENTILES, GOD, GRATITUDE, GRIEF,
HEART, HEAVEN, HELP, KINDNESS, MERCY, PITY, SENSITIVITY

COMPLAINT

✑ Dear God: I know you will provide, but why don't you provide *until* you provide?

If you're not in pain, why are you moaning?

The bad wheel usually creaks the most. (The least deserving make
the most noise.)

Don't grumble; it may lead to other sins. *Derekh Erets Zuta*

See also: CONTENTMENT, ENVY, GREED, HAPPINESS, JEALOUSY

COMPROMISE

A mountain cannot meet with a mountain, but one man can meet
with another.

The profits of compromise are nothing compared to its losses.
"The Chofetz Chaim"

See also: ARBITRATION, CIRCUMSTANCES, COOPERATION, DEMOCRACY,
GOVERNMENT, LAW, TALK.

CONCEIT

Money leads to conceit, and conceit to sin.

The *khokhem* [wise man] who parades his knowledge is worth
less than the stupid man who, ashamed, hides his ignorance.

No one is as ugly as the man who is conceited.

If you harden your heart with pride, you soften your brain
with it, too.

Conceit and poverty make a wretched combination.

If a man always praises himself, it tells us that he knows nothing.
Zohar

The conceited man is not a sinner but a fool.
"The Chofetz Chaim"

See also: ARROGANCE, MONEY, PRIDE, VANITY

CONDUCT

Don't be too sweet, lest you be eaten up; don't be too bitter, lest
you be spewed out.

The spittle a man throws upward falls back on his own face.
Midrash: *Ecclesiastes Rabbah,* 7 : 9

If you have paid a fine in court, sing and walk away.
TALMUD: *Baba Kamma,* 7

When you see a man stronger than you, rise.
APOCRYPHA: *Ahikar,* 2 : 61

The way a man walks tells us whether he is wise or foolish, learned or ignorant.
MAIMONIDES: *Mishneh Torah,* 5 : 7–13

See also: APPEARANCES, BOORS, CHARM, CLEANLINESS, CLOTHING, COURTESY, DECORUM, MANNERS, STATUS

CONFESSION

If we were to recount all our sins, we would never complete the list. Therefore, we use the alphabetical form: The alphabet has a beginning and an end. The [Yom Kippur] confessional is in the plural because every Jew is responsible for all other Jews.
SEYMOUR SIEGEL

See also: GOD *and* MAN, REPENTANCE, SALVATION, SIN

CONFIDENCE

The man who has confidence in himself gains the confidence of others.
—Hasidic saying

Don't be too sure of yourself till the day you die.
HILLEL in *Sayings of the Fathers,* 2 : 5

See also: JUDGMENT, SELF-ESTEEM

CONFLICT

◈ The cat loves fish—but doesn't want to wet her paws.

See also: COMPROMISE, FORESIGHT, PRUDENCE

CONFORMITY

The man who follows the gait of others will sway from side to side.

⋙ If you want people to think you wise, just agree with them.

Where many go, no grass will grow.

Had not a great man praised you, I might have objected to what you say.

When one dog barks, he easily finds others to bark with him.
                              MIDRASH: *Exodus Rabbah,* 31 : 9

If you meet a lion, roar; if you meet a donkey, bray.
                                                    FALAQUERA

To accept tradition without examining it, with intelligence and judgment, is like the blind blindly following others.
                              Bahya ibn Paquda, *Duties of the Heart*

See also: INDIVIDUALITY, MASSES, POPULARITY

CONSCIENCE

⋙ You can wash your hands, but not your conscience.

A guilty conscience is a snake in the heart.

Only the things you do can leave a clear conscience.

⋙ Be the master of your will, and the slave of your conscience.
                                                    —Hasidic saying

The pangs of conscience are better than floggings.
                                        TALMUD: *Berakoth,* 7a

What restrains beasts from doing harm is something external—a bridle or a bit; but man's restraints lie within himself.
                              MAIMONIDES *Commentary on the Mishnah*

See also: DECEIT, DISCIPLE, DUTY, FALSEHOOD, FRAUD, GUILT, LIES, SIN

CONSIDERATION (FOR OTHERS)

⇜ Don't drain your well as long as others may need water.

Too courteous is discourteous.

Never address a slave as "slave," for the very name is contemptible.

When you come to a new city, follow its customs.

Don't taunt your neighbor for your own blemishes.
TALMUD: Baba Mezi'a, 59b

The family servant should eat after the meal is over; but if especially good meat or old wine is served, he should receive his portion immediately, so that he be spared the pain of waiting.   TALMUD: *Kethuboth,* 61a

Never wait until a shy employee asks for his wages; pay him before he asks.   GERSONIDES

⇜ Among those who stand, do not sit; among those who sit, do not stand. Among those who laugh, do not weep; among those who weep, do not laugh.   Hillel in *Tosefta Berakoth,* 2

Never rebuke a man in such a way as to shame him in public.
RASHI, Commentaries on the Pentateuch, Leviticus

See also: DECORUM, DISCRETION, GRIEF, HEART, HELP, MANNERS, SENSITIVITY, TACT, THOUGHTFULNESS

CONSOLATION

An apt utterance is a joy to a man, and a word in season—how good is it!   *Book of Proverbs,* 15 : 23

CONTENTMENT

Why seek honey when sugar is so sweet?

⇜ To pursue happiness is to flee from contentment.

Three things soften a man's heart: a pleasant melody, a pleasant
scene, and a fragrant odor. TALMUD: *Berakoth,* 57b

Two things never come together—contentment and envy.
IBN GABIROL

The worst bondage is exile from peace of mind.
THE BELZER RABBI

See also: AMBITION, ANGER, CIRCUMSTANCES, COMPLAINT, ENVY,
GREED, HABIT, HAPPINESS, JEALOUSY

CONTEXT

All colors look alike in the dark.

◦§ A heavy rain may be good for the fields but is bad for the
roads.

Near golden wagons you will find golden nails.

The man who has not tasted the bitter does not know what the
sweet is.

There is no quality so deplorable but that it sometimes serves
a use, and no quality so praiseworthy but that it sometimes is
lamentable: Silence is a commendable trait, but it is detestable
when preserved while listening to absurdities; wrath is reprehensible, but if expressed over transgressions, it is praiseworthy. IBN GABIROL

See also: CAUSE and EFFECT, CERTAINTY, CIRCUMSTANCES, ENDS and
MEANS, PARADOXES, RELATIVITY

CONVERTS

Note. By tradition, rabbis are obliged to try to dissuade non-Jews
from formal conversion. (This may have originated as an effort to test the intensity of the desire to be converted.) A

long period of study and training in Judaism's practices and principles of faith is mandatory, and discourages those swayed by transient impulse. Converts are accorded complete equality of status under Jewish law: The one legal (halakic) taboo is against a rabbi's marrying a woman proselyte.

The history of conversion to Judaism is worth sketching. Converts to Judaism have been known since the days recorded in the Bible (e.g., Ruth) and there were a considerable number of proselytes to Judaism during the aggressive Hasmonean (or Hashmonai) dynasty in Judea, in the second century. Some very great rabbis were thought to be descended from proselytes (e.g., Akiba).

Some Talmudists held that one reason God dispersed the Jews was to spread the True Faith and make converts everywhere.

Converts continued to adopt Judaism in modest numbers during the Middle Ages, despite the fact that it was a capital offense carrying gruesome, fatal penalties. In the eighth century, the Khazar tribes of southern Russia turned Jewish. (See Judah ha-Levi, in BIOGRAPHIES.) Some converts came to Judaism from the ranks of the Catholic clergy: French, English, German, Dutch. Proselytes from Islam were not uncommon, nor later from the Protestant ranks. Russian peasants in the nineteenth century were caught up in the "Sabbotnik" (a Judaistic) movement. Balkan and Italian converts emigrated to the state of Israel after 1948.

My favorite story in the proselytic zone involves one Te-Ua, a Maori, converted to the Anglican faith, early in the nineteenth century, who then started a local Israelite cult that sang hymns in a blissful mélange of Hebrew, Greek, English, and German. He became known as "Tiu" ("Jew"), and his faith was so potent that he declared himself the Moses of his people and proclaimed New Zealand the new Canaan.*

In the United States, there has been a noticeable increase in the number of proselytes to Judaism, because of the grow-

---

* See Theodor H. Gaster, *op. cit.*, pp. 330–31. Also see Vittorio Lauternari's fascinating *Religions of the Oppressed* (tr. Lisa Sergio), Macgibbon and Kee, London, 1963; Knopf, New York, 1963.

ing number of mixed marriages, in which the majority of the grooms are Jewish and the brides gentile.*

—L.R.

The true convert is dearer to God than the Israelites, for had not the Israelites seen the thunder and lightning on Mount Sinai, the shaking mountain and blaring trumpets, they might not have accepted holy Torah. But the proselyte who saw none of these has opened his heart to the Holy One. Who can be dearer to God?   MIDRASH: *Tanhuma*

When anyone says he wants to become a convert, the rabbis (should) ask: "Why? Do you not know the Israelites are hounded and persecuted?" If the answer is, "Yes, I know, and want only to be worthy," the rabbis should accept him.

TALMUD: *Yebamoth,* 47a

See also: FAITH, ISRAEL, PROSELYTES, RELIGION

COOPERATION

We fall down by ourselves, but it takes a friendly hand to lift us up.

If a moron holds a cow by the ears, a clever man can milk her.

See also: CAUSE and EFFECT, CIRCUMSTANCES, COMPROMISE, HELPING

COUNSEL

It is better to ask the way ten times than take the wrong road once.

If you ask, you won't err.

Many come for counsel, but not all are helped by it.

For want of counsel, a people will fall;
But safety lies in a wealth of counselors.

Book of Proverbs, 11 : 14

---

* *New Standard Jewish Encyclopedia, op. cit.,* p. 1570.

Before trouble comes, obtain advice; after it comes, advice is useless.　　　　　　　　　　IBN ZABARA, *Book of Delight*, ch. 2

ৎঌ The best of animals needs a whip, the purest of women a husband, the cleverest of men advice.　　　　IBN GABIROL

See also: ADVICE, FORESIGHT, JUDGMENT

COURAGE

ৎঌ When there is no money, half is gone; when there is no courage, all is gone.

He who has nothing to lose can try anything.

Nerve succeeds.

He who does not dare, will not get his share.

ৎঌ Don't consult a coward about war.

To lose courage is worse than to lose an army.

See also: COWARDICE, ENDURANCE, FORTITUDE, HONOR, OPTIMISM,
VALOR

COURTESY

Too much courtesy is a discourtesy.

The most courteous man is one who bears with the discourteous.

See also: CONDUCT, CONSIDERATION, DECORUM, MANNERS

COURTS

ৎঌ Where there is room for question, something is wrong.

Justice delayed is worse than injustice.

From litigation you can never recover your losses.

&§ An oath [in court] is worthless if it affirms the impossible: for instance, that you saw a camel fly.
                              TALMUD: *Shebuoth,* 29a

Silence [in a court] may be equivalent to confession.
                              TALMUD: *Yebamoth,* 87b

A man may not accuse himself of a crime.
                              TALMUD: *Yebamoth,* 25b

No man can be declared guilty in his absence [from the court-room].   TALMUD: *Kethuboth,* 11a

A benefit may be conferred, but not a disability imposed, on a man in his absence.   TALMUD: *Erubin,* 7 : 11

&§ When a court has pronounced a sentence of death, its members [judges] should taste nothing for the rest of that day.
                              TALMUD: *Sanhedrin,* 63a

If your cloak is taken from you by a court of law, sing a song and go your way. [You are saved from theft.]
                              —adapted from TALMUD: *Sanhedrin,* 7a

See also: EVIDENCE, JUDGES, JUSTICE, LAW

COURTSHIP

&§ One man gets caressed for a pinch, another gets slapped.

It costs nothing to make sweet promises.

Love makes us blind, deaf, and dumb.

The right mate comes with the first date.

Those who can't love, flatter.

Flattery is a device for theft.

If you want the daughter, flatter the mother.

Before a rooster approaches a hen, he promises her: "Come to me and I shall give you a gown of many colors." But afterwards he says, "May I lose the comb on my head if I have the means to buy such a thing."   TALMUD: *Erubin,* 100b

It is natural for a man to woo a woman, not for a woman to woo a man, for it is the loser who seeks what he lost [the rib].
                          TALMUD: *Niddah,* 31b

See also: DECEIT, DECORUM, FLATTERY, LOVE, MARRIAGE

COWARDS, COWARDICE

◁§ There is no cure for cowardice.

If you have nothing to lose, at least be brave.

◁§ Never consult a woman about her rival, nor a coward about war.

When you lose all your money, you have lost half, but when you lose courage you have lost all.

You'd be surprised by how often nerve succeeds.

If you have no choice, you lose nothing by being brave.

Soldiers grow brave after eating.

Don't enter the forest if you fear leaves.

If you carry a lantern, you will not fear the darkness.

See also: COURAGE, FEAR, HONOR, VALOR

CREDITORS

◁§ No man shows impatience with his creditors.

Fear pays no debts.

Lending makes enemies.

If you are owed money by a man who is unable to repay it, do
not keep crossing his path.   TALMUD: *Baba Mezi'a,* 75b

Better eat vegetables and fear no creditors, than eat duck and
hide from them.   TALMUD: *Pesahim,* 114a

See also: BORROWERS, DEBT, LENDING, MONEY

CRITICISM

The man who can't bear to hear a word of criticism will have to
hear many.

It is easier to negate than to affirm.

⋅§ It's easier to find faults in others than virtues in oneself.

Reprove not a scorner, lest he hate you; reprove a wise man, and
he will love you.   *Book of Proverbs,* 9 : 8

A rebuke sinks deeper into a man of intelligence than a hundred
lashes into a fool.   *Book of Proverbs,* 17 : 10

⋅§ He who winks makes trouble; he who openly reproves makes
peace.   *Book of Proverbs,* 16 : 7

Wheat needs grinding, and men need correction.
TALMUD: *Abodah Zarah,* 44a

In honoring, we begin with the most prominent; in censuring, we
begin with the least important.   TALMUD: *Berakoth,* 61a

A man's mind is hidden in his writings; criticism brings it to light.
IBN GABIROL, *Choice of Pearls*

Include yourself in any reproof.   NACHMAN OF BRATSLAV

He who cannot accept reproof cannot become great.
NACHMAN OF BRATSLAV

A man can detect a speck in another's hair, but can't see the flies
on his own nose.   MENDELE MOCHER SEFORIM

See also: EGOTISM, FLATTERY, GREAT MEN, INTELLIGENCE, WISE
MEN, WRITING

CRUCIFIXION

Note. "Your madness goes so far as to say that we [Jews] are
scattered because our fathers condemned to death Him whom
you worship. O ye pious tigers, ye fanatical panthers, who ...
have no better way of supporting your sect than by executioners, can you not see that it was only the Romans who
condemned Him? We [Jews] had not at that time the right
to inflict death; we were governed by Quirinus, Varus, Pilate.
No crucifixion was ever practised among us. Not a single trace
of that form of punishment is to be found. Stop punishing a
whole nation for an event for which it cannot be responsible.
Would it be just to burn the Pope and all the Monsignori in
Rome because the first Romans ravished the Sabines and pillaged the Samnites? Amen."
     VOLTAIRE, *Sermon du Rabin Akib.*

See: ANTI-SEMITISM, INTOLERANCE, JEWS, PERSECUTION, POGROMS,
PREJUDICE

CRUELTY

Even the mercy of the wicked is cruel.

❧ He is the kind of man who first prepares the bandage, then
inflicts the wound.   TALMUD: *Megillah,* 13a

It is cruel not to forgive one who begs for forgiveness.
     RASHI, *Commentaries on the Pentateuch, Numbers*

See also: CONSCIENCE, COMPASSION, GOOD DEEDS, KINDNESS, SIN, VIR-
TUE

CURSES

Note. Anglo-Saxons may well marvel over the opulent repertoire of curses available to the peoples in Mideastern cultures, where oral maledictions are a sort of popular art form.

Among Jews, swearing is rare but cursing is common; let me explain. By "swearing" I mean the venting of frustration or anger in obscene phrases directed at no one in particular; by "cursing" I mean the invocation of calamity (pain, injury, death) upon someone—hoping that God, though not directly asked to do so (indeed, usually asked *not* to), will direct his wrath upon the one cursed and in the form requested. For example: "*Damn* this hammer!" is swearing; "May he be buried in the ground and bake bagels, God forbid" is cursing.

One reason why ornamental cursing gives pleasure to Jews is that since fighting was so despised, *verbalized* hostility came to be correspondingly prized. Consider: If you break my jaw, you have merely demonstrated the power of your muscle—which an animal, ignoramus or barbarian can do. If, instead, you hurl a juicy execration at me, you act like a man, not a beast; you use the wits God gave you—instead of fists, feet, teeth, claws or fangs.

How much sweeter than a blow is the malediction: "May all your teeth fall out—except one!" (Why "except one?" So that you will retain the capacity to be afflicted by toothaches.)

Robert Graves, I think, observed that the more lurid a curse, the less poison it carries; and Maurice Samuel, in his charming *In Praise of Yiddish*, characterizes the flamboyance of Oriental curses as "arabesques of affliction and gratification [that] dizzy the mind."

The elaboration of Jewish curses reaches staggering heights of picturesqueness: "May his intestines sound like a music box"; "May he own a hundred houses, and in each a hundred rooms, and in each room a hundred beds; and may he go from bed to bed in search of one moment's sleep!"

I, for one, am awed by such ingenuity in the catharsis of disaffection.

—L.R.

◆§ I would like to treat him like a treasure: bury him with care and affection.

◆§ God grant him so much breath that he should always be able to ask what the weather is like—outside.

May God send a fool to help him.

◆§ May his stomach churn like a music box.

May his navel turn dizzy.

May a *kazarnya* [armory] fall on his head!

May he grow sick from his satisfactions.

◆§ May his buttocks drop off!

Let bunions grow on his bunions, and on his carbuncles—boils.

May he get sick—and remember it.

May I dance over his corpse and spit prune pits into his eyes.

◆§ May he own five ships of gold—all wrecked.

May a child be named after him soon. [Ashkenazic Jews were forbidden to name a child after a living person.]

If he had twice as much sense he would be an idiot.

Don't wish him even on his enemies.

May all his teeth fall out—except one [so he can have a toothache].

May a flood pour over him.

May a thunderbolt find his head.

Like a beet should he grow—with his head in the earth.

A *shvarts* [dark] year upon him!

◆§ Let onions grow in his navel.

May he have to crawl on all fours.

He should swell up like ten mountains.

May his name return without his body.

May cramps parade through his bowels.

May delirium guide even his words.

May he need a prescription.

Let him lie in the earth and bake bagels.

May he spend all he has on physicians.

May he beat his head against the wall.

May he be seized by the cholera.

May he be seized by a nine-year convulsion.

May prolonged nausea overcome him.

BUT REMEMBER, PLEASE:

A curse does not arrive as fast as a telegram. [Don't take curses too
  seriously.]

Like a sparrow flitting, a swallow fluttering,
The curse that is groundless will not reach home.
Book of Proverbs, 26 : 2

A curse uttered by a sage will be fulfilled, even if it was undeserved.
TALMUD: *Berakoth,* 56a

CUSTOMS

Old tunes can be found for many a new song.

◖§ Customs are more powerful than laws.
TALMUD: *Yebamoth,* 61a

See how the people act, and that is the law.

TALMUD: *Berakoth,* 45a

When you come to a city, follow its customs.

MIDRASH: *Exodus Rabbah,* 47

Some of the roads most used lead nowhere.

See also: COMMUNITY, HABIT, LAW, TRADITION

CYNICISM

If you want men to like you, agree with them.

—Hasidic saying

🙠 The Torah spread light, but it is money that gives warmth.

DANGER

I have escaped with the skin of my teeth.   *Book of Job,* 19 : 20

See also: ADVERSITY, SUFFERING, TROUBLE

DAUGHTERS

🙠 What the daughter does, the mother did.

The man who marries off a daughter doesn't regret the dowry.

He who seeks the daughter flatters the mother.

ঙ্গ A good daughter makes a good daughter-in-law.

Fill your house with guests and you'll marry off your daughter.

A married daughter is like a piece of bread—cut off.

To marry off a daughter is like removing a hump from your back.

A daughter is a treasure—and a cause of sleeplessness.
                    BEN SIRACH, *Ecclesiasticus*, 42 : 9

Some daughters are more precious than sons.
                                        RABBI HAI GAON

A beautiful daughter is worth—half her dowry.
                                        SHOLEM ALEICHEM

It is hard to raise sons; and much harder to raise daughters.
                                        SHOLEM ALEICHEM

See also: FAMILY, FATHERS, GIRLS, MOTHERS, WOMEN

DAUGHTERS-IN-LAW

ঙ্গ A daughter-in-law is always a bit of a mother-in-law.

One can talk to a daughter, yet mean the daughter-in-law.

The daughter is scolded, but the daughter-in-law is meant.

A daughter-in-law can no more live under the same roof with her
    mother-in-law than a goat can live in the same barn with a
    tiger.

See also: FAMILY, MOTHERS-IN-LAW, SONS-IN-LAW, WOMEN

DEATH

Note. Judaic law forbids display or ostentation at a funeral. The
    rabbis instituted simple burial rites to enforce the idea of
    "democracy in death," so that no family, however poor, would
    be shamed by the simplicity of coffin or shroud.

The prayer for the dead is called the *Kaddish,* which extols God, but contains not a single reference to death or mourning. Sholem Aleichem has left us this delightful memory of the *Kaddish* he and his five brothers recited in mourning for their mother:

You should have heard us deliver that *Kaddish!* A pleasure! All our relatives beamed with pride, and strangers envied us. One of our relatives . . . exclaimed, 'When a woman has six sons like that to say *Kaddish* after her, she will surely go straight to paradise. Either that or the world is coming to an end!'*

On the anniversary of a death, a memorial candle or lamp is lighted in the home, and another in the synagogue, to burn from sunset to sunset. A burning light is connected with the idea of immortality—perhaps as suggested in Proverbs (20 : 27): "The spirit of man is the candle of the Lord . . ."

It is considered both a *mitzvah* and a duty to attend a funeral. In a small community, everyone was expected to attend—except the teacher (*melamed*), who was enjoined not to interrupt instructing the children, unless a saintly sage or relative had died. At Orthodox funerals, collectors for charity pass among the mourners.

Note to attorneys: Jewish law does not contain the idea of a "legal death"—i.e., a period of time, say seven years, after which a court can declare someone "officially" dead for legal purposes. Changes are being made in Israel and America to allow for missing-in-action cases.

—L.R.

When you start thinking of death, you are no longer certain of life.

◄§ Dying while you are young is a great boon in your old age.

◄§ It's astonishing how important a man becomes when he dies.

How odd is death: the old often survive the young.

Every man knows he will die, but no man wants to believe it.

◄§ All corpses look pious.

As long as one limb moves, men reject the grave.

---

* Quoted in Maurice Samuel, *The World of Sholom Aleichem,* p. 37.

Death may be free—but it costs a life.

⋞§ For dying, you always have plenty of time.

Bread and death: everything revolves around them.

We are never late for two occasions: marrying and dying.

It is better not to have had children than to bury them.

Better a noble death than a wretched life.

Death does not knock on the door.

Is there a bad mother, or a good death?

From a cemetery, you cannot "take back."

Better ten times sick than once dead.

⋞§ The death of the rich is smelled far away.

Better ten times ruined than dead once.

Life is only loaned to man; death is the creditor—who one day will
claim it.

All corpses' faces look alike.

⋞§ To die, you don't need a calendar.

While men live, the whole world is too small—once dead, the grave
is large enough.

⋞§ The road to a cemetery is paved with suffering.

The homeliest life is better than the prettiest death.

When Elijah is the coachman, you travel fast.

No one knows who will see tomorrow.

No man dies before his time.

⋞§ An old woman, visiting a cemetery, addressed the graves:

"How peacefully you sleep, good souls! Still, if you don't mind, I would rather not join you."

Even the best horse, when dead, is only a carcass.

Up to seventy, we learn wisdom—then we die fools.

Death is merely moving from one home to another.
THE KOTZKER RABBI

It is better to go to a house of mourning than to a house of feasting.
Ecclesiastes, 2

[When dust returns to dust] the spirit shall return to God, who gave it.   *Ecclesiastes, 7*

The world, which was made for us, abides; but we, for whom it was made, depart.   APOCRYPHA: *II Baruch, 14 : 5*

Love is as strong as death.   *Song of Solomon, 8 : 6*

◄§ In death, two worlds meet with a kiss: the world going out and the future coming in.   TALMUD J.: *Yebamoth, 57a*

The dead don't feel the scalpel.   TALMUD: *Shabbath, 13b*

When a sage dies, all men should mourn.
TALMUD: *Shabbath, 105b*

No man dies with even half his desires fulfilled.

Don't question God: He may say, "If you're so anxious for answers, come up here."

The death of a woman is felt by no one so keenly as by her husband.   TALMUD: *Sanhedrin, 22*

Sleep is a sixtieth of death.   TALMUD, *Berakoth, 57b*

When you take leave of the dead, say not "Go to peace," but "Go in peace."   TALMUD, *Berakoth, 64a*

◄§ In a harbor, two ships sailed: one setting forth on a voyage, the other coming home to port. Everyone cheered the ship going out, but the ship sailing in was scarcely noticed. And a wise man said: "Do not rejoice over a ship that is setting out to sea, for you cannot know what storms it may encounter, what fearful dangers it may have to endure. But rejoice rather over a ship that has safely reached port, and brings home all its passengers in peace."

And this is the way of the world: when a child is born, all rejoice; when a man or woman dies, all weep. We should do the opposite. No one can tell what trials and travails await a child; but when a mortal dies in peace, we should rejoice, for he has completed his long journey, and is leaving this world with the imperishable crown of a good name.

—adapted from the TALMUD

When Death summons a man to appear before his Creator, three friends are his: The first, whom he loves most, is money, but money cannot accompany him one step; his second friend is relatives, but they can only accompany him to the grave, and cannot defend him before the Judge. It is his third friend, whom he does not highly esteem, his good deeds, who can go with him, and can appear before the King, and can obtain his acquittal.   TALMUD

It is nobler to visit a house of mourning than a house of feasting.
Ecclesiastes, 2

When the time comes for an accounting of man's deeds, it is too late to do anything about them.
MIDRASH: *Genesis Rabbah,* 84 : 12

◄§ Man enters the world with closed hands, as if to say, "The world is mine"; he leaves with open hands, as if to say, "I take nothing with me."   MIDRASH: *Ecclesiastes Rabbah,* 5 : 14

The world weeps when a fruit tree is cut down.
Yalkut Ruveni

On the day of his death, a man feels he has lived but a single day.
Zohar

"When my time comes to die," said the frog, "I go down to the sea, there to be swallowed by one of its creatures; thus even my death is a deed of kindness."   *Yalkut Shimoni*

Fear not death, for it is your destiny.

> BEN SIRACH, *Ecclesiasticus*, 41 : 3

What is it that troubles you? Death? Who lives forever?

> SAMUEL HA-NAGID

ᦤ Death, the terror of the rich, is the desire of the poor.

> IBN ZABARA, *Book of Delight*, 7 : 25

What is the cause of death? Life.

> —adapted from IBN ZABARA, *Book of Delight*, 7 : 27

A short life with wisdom is better than a long life without it.

> MOSES IBN EZRA, *Shirat Yisrael*, 119

God gave us the blessed hope of immortality, through which we may console ourselves for the vanity of life, and overcome the fear of death.   JEDAIA BEN BEDERSI

See also: ANGELS, BREAD, BURIAL, DESTINY, FAILURE, FUTURE, GOD, THE HEREAFTER, LAZY, LIFE, LIFE and DEATH, MAN, RESURRECTION, SUICIDE, WEALTH, WIDOW

DEATH: ANGEL OF DEATH

To summon Death's Angel, send a lazy messenger.

ᦤ Don't try to swap jokes with the Angel of Death.

The Angel of Death doesn't look at calendars.

The Angel of Death always manages to find an excuse.

ᦤ It is the Angel of Death who nourishes our synagogues, for if not for the *Kaddish* [prayer for the dead] how many men would attend them?

The Angel of Death may slaughter—but he is always right.

Death's Angel won't let you take money along.

The Angel of Death does not care whether a dead man has a shroud.

ها§ If the rich could hire the poor to die for them, the poor would make a very good living.

The Angel of Death has many eyes.

Both the doctor and the Angel of Death kill—but the doctor charges a fee for it.   IBN ZABARA, *Book of Delight*

DEBT

ها§ Tears pay no debts.

You can't pay a debt with your pedigree.

You can't pay debts without regrets.

The greatest of worries won't pay the smallest of debts.

Never take the clothes of a woman or a child in repayment of a debt.   —adapted from *Exodus,* 22 : 25–6

It is better to eat herbs and fear no creditors, than eat meat and have to hide from them.   TALMUD: *Pesahim,* 114a

The man who does not pay his debts but gives alms commits robbery.   *Sefer Hasidim*

Better go to sleep without supper than get up in debt.
                    JUDAH IBN TIBBON, *A Father's Admonition*

See also: BORROWING, CREDITORS, LENDING, TEARS

DECEIT

If his word was a bridge, men would be afraid to cross it.

It's not hard to deceive people—once.

He who deceives me lets shame fall upon him; if he deceives me twice, let shame fall on me.

ها§ From afar you fool people; nearby, you fool only yourself.

Like a madman who hurls deadly firebrands is the man who deceives his neighbors and says, "Was I not joking?"
Book of Proverbs, 26 : 19

The kiss of an enemy is full of deceit.
adapted from *Book of Proverbs*, 27 : 6

Deception in words is worse than deception in money.
Talmud: *Baba Mezi'a*, 58

See also: APPEARANCES, CONSCIENCE, COURTSHIP, FALSEHOOD, FLAT-
TERY, FRAUD, FRIENDS/FRIENDSHIP, FRIENDS: FALSE FRIENDS,
IDEAS, LIARS/LIES, SELF-DECEPTION

DECORUM

When the guest coughs, he needs a spoon.

ເຈ Better be embarrassed than ashamed.

Never address a slave as "slave" for to do so is to humiliate him.

A rabbi's daughter is not allowed to do what a bath-keeper's
daughter is.

Don't humiliate a beggar by giving him alms in a way that attracts
attention.

Before taking leave, one should not finish an ordinary conversation
with idle talk, but with some comment on halaka [law].
—adapted from Talmud, *Berakoth*, 31a

For a well-bred man, a little is adequate.
Ben Sirach: *Ecclesiasticus*, 31 : 19

When your neighbor is in trouble, abstain from visible pleasures.
Gersonides

Among those who stand, do not sit; among those who sit, do not
stand; among those who laugh, do not weep; among those who
weep, do not laugh.   Hillel in *Tosefta Berakoth*, 2

The wise man should not walk with a haughty expression; nor
   should he walk with a slow gait, like a woman; or run about
   like a madman; or stoop like a hunchback; he should gaze
   downward, as though in prayer, and walk like a man pre-
   occupied.   MAIMONIDES, *Mishneh Torah*, 5 : 7–13

See also: APPEARANCES, BOORS, CHARM, CLEANLINESS, CLOTHING, CON-
   DUCT, CONSIDERATION, COURTESY, HONOR/HONORS, MANNERS

DEEDS

If a man does despicable deeds, let him not depend upon the merits
   of his parents.

Deeds are male, words female.

They say to fruit-bearing trees, "Why do you not make any noise?"
   and the trees reply, "Our fruits are sufficient advertisement."
                              MIDRASH: *Genesis Rabbah*, 16 : 3

Whether Jew or Gentile, man or woman, rich or poor—it is according to deeds that God's Presence descends.
                              MIDRASH: *Eliahu Rabbah*, 8

෴ What is hateful to you, do not to your fellow man: that is the
   whole Law; all the rest is interpretation.
                         HILLEL in TALMUD: *Shabbath*, 31b

Nothing accomplishes nothing.   BAHYA IBN PAQUDA

The intention is the foundation of the deed.
                    MOSES IBN EZRA, *Shirat Yisrael*, p. 141

See also: BOASTING, CONDUCT, GOOD DEEDS, TALK, VIRTUE

DEMOCRACY

The many (people) have more wisdom than the few.

In the multitude of counsellors there is safety.
                              Book of Proverbs, 11 : 14

We must not appoint a leader over the community without first
consulting the people.   TALMUD: *Berakoth,* 55a

ｇ Happy is the time where the great listen to the small, for in
such a generation the small will listen to the great.
                              TALMUD: *Rosh Hashanah,* 25b

ｇ The Torah can be interpreted in forty-nine different ways; and
God instructed Moses, "Decide according to the majority."
                              TALMUD J.: *Sanhedrin,* 4 : 2

See also: EQUALITY, GOVERNMENT, LAW, MASSES, POLITICS

DEMONS

A demon is at home with demons.

The world is full of demons; at least drive them out of yourself.

Obsessions are worse than diseases.

False dreams are the works of demons.

See also: DEVIL, DISEASE, EVIL, HELL, SATAN, SIN, VIRTUE

DEPENDENCY

The fruit should pray for the welfare of the leaves.

ｇ If the hunter can't shoot, his hound goes hungry, too.

See also: CAUSE AND EFFECT, CIRCUMSTANCES, INDEPENDENCE

DESIRE

No man leaves this world with even half of his desires satisfied.

Desire confuses the senses.

Desire can blind the wise.

Desires are the net of folly.   MOSES IBN EZRA, *Shirat Yisrael*

The greatest misers with money are the biggest spendthrifts with
desires.   MOSES IBN EZRA, *Shirat Yisrael*

The man who is not careful about obeying the law against stealing
will be less careful about the law against coveting; whatever
his eyes see, his heart will desire—and with a longing that can
never be satisfied.   LEONE DA MODENA

See also: ENVY, GREED, JEALOUSY, LUST, SIN

DESPAIR

⋑ A drowning man will grab even the point of a sword.

You can't drive away the darkness with sticks or weapons. The only
way is to light a candle and the darkness will disappear by
itself. Our candle is the Torah.
                    "THE CHOFETZ CHAIM"

See also: HOPE, PESSIMISM, RESIGNATION, SUFFERING, TORAH

DESTINY

⋑ The man who is destined to drown will drown in a glass of
water.

God is our father, destiny our step-father.

What can't be avoided can be welcomed.

Weep for the man who knows not his good fortune, and laugh for
him who knows not his destiny.
                    TALMUD: *Sanhedrin*, 103a

See also: ASTROLOGY, DEATH, FATE, FORTUNE, HEREAFTER, LUCK

DETERMINATION

The hardest rock will yield to those who drill with determination.

Where men truly wish to go, there their feet will manage to take
them.   TALMUD: *Sukkah,* 53a

See also: PERSEVERANCE, WILL

DEVIL

Note. Though Jewish theology and literature are rife with references to the Evil One, Jews seem to have no concept quite as
anthropomorphic as the Devil. The idea of Satan (in Job) is
the closest Jews came to a physical image of the incarnation of
evil, a cunning and maleficent tempter; the rabbis, instead,
preferred to refer to "the Evil Impulse." (See headnote for
EVIL).   —L.R.

If you live with a devil, you become a devil.

A man who looks better than the Devil is promptly called handsome.

▷ The moment you sit down to a really big meal, the Devil sends
you a guest.

Should the Devil [Evil Impulse] say: "Sin—God will forgive you,"
don't believe him.   TALMUD: *Hagigah,* 16a

Satan is especially active at the time of danger.
                    RASHI, *Commentaries on the Pentateuch, Genesis*

See also: COMPANIONS, DEMONS, EVIL, HELL, IMPULSE, SATAN, SIN,
VIRTUE

DIASPORA

Note. "History relates very few measures that produced so vast an
amount of calamity. In three short months, all unconverted

Jews were obliged, under pain of death, to abandon the Spanish soil. Multitudes, falling into the hands of the pirates who swarmed around the coast, were plundered of all they possessed and reduced to slavery; multitudes died of famine or of plague, or were murdered or tortured with horrible cruelty by the African savages. About 80,000 (Jews) took refuge in Portugal, relying on the promise of the king. Spanish priests lashed the Portuguese into fury, and the king was persuaded to issue an edict which threw even that of Isabella into the shade. All the adult Jews were banished from Portugal; but first all their children below the age of fourteen were taken from them to be educated as Christians. Then, indeed, the cup of bitterness was filled to the brim. The serene fortitude with which the exiled people had borne so many and such grievous calamities gave way, and was replaced by the wildest paroxysms of despair. When at last, childless and broken-hearted, they sought to leave the land, they found that the ships had been purposely detained, and the allotted time having expired, they were reduced to slavery and baptized by force. A great peal of rejoicing filled the Peninsula, and proclaimed that the triumph of the Spanish priests was complete."
—W. E. H. LECKY, *History of Rationalism in Europe,* vol. II

"The Greeks, I hear, would weep when a babe was born, and rejoice when an old man died; it seemed fitting to cry for the newborn, since he is entering the valley of weeping; and it is fitting to rejoice for the dead, since they have gone to the final place of rest. But Jews ought to weep when they are born and when they die and in the days between. They suffer the sorrows and evils of exile; their enemies seek every occasion to harm or humiliate them. . . . I grieve for them not because they are Jews, but because they are poor, powerless and lowly. We Jews have no other kingdom except that which the Lord of all the Universe gave us. He said to Isaiah: " 'I will look on him who is poor and contrite in spirit.' "
—adapted from SOLOMON IBN VERGA, *Shebet Yehuda,* 29

See: HEREAFTER, ISRAEL, JEWS, PERSECUTION, SABBATH; and GLOSSARY: DIASPORA

DISCIPLES

There are four kinds of disciples: Quick to learn, but quick to
forget: in him the gift is canceled by the failing; slow to learn,
but slow to forget: in him the failing is canceled by the gift;
quick to learn and slow to forget: his is a fortunate lot; slow to
learn and quick to forget: his is an evil plight.

Sayings of the Fathers, 5 : 18

See also: **PROSELYTES, SCHOLARS, STUDY**

DISCIPLINE

Good men need no discipline, and bad men are beyond its help.

The man who spares the rod hates his son.

Book of Proverbs, 13 : 24

Don't make a fence that is more important [expensive] than what
is fenced in.　　　　MIDRASH: *Genesis Rabbah*, 19 : 3

See also: **CHARACTER, CHILDREN, CONSCIENCE, TEMPER**

DISCRETION

As a jewel of gold in a swine's snout, so is a pretty woman who is
without discretion.　　　　*Book of Proverbs*, 11 : 22

◄§ Your friend has a friend, and your friend's friend has a friend
[so be discreet].　　　　TALMUD: *Kethuboth*, 109b

Don't say "Hang this up for me" to one from a family where there
was a hanging.　　　　TALMUD: *Baba Mezi'a*, 59b

Never shame a man by rebuking him in public.

Rashi, *Commentaries on the Pentateuch, Leviticus*

When you speak at night lower your voice; when you speak by day,
look around first.　　　　IBN GABIROL, *Choice of Pearls*

The fewer a man's words, the fewer his mistakes.
>> IBN GABIROL, *Choice of Pearls*

See also: CONSIDERATION, JUDGMENT, MANNERS, PRUDENCE, TACT

DISEASE

∾ An *aynredenish* [obsession] is worse than a disease.

Don't tell a sick man to get up, or a healthy one to lie down.

If you're not in pain, don't cry "Oy!"

∾ No matter where you place a sick man, he's still in pain.

Sometimes the remedy is worse than the ailment.

∾ When there's a cure, it was only half a disease.

Melancholy creates diseases—which happiness cures.

Envy is a disease that gnaws at the soul.

The door closed to good deeds opens to disease.

God sends cures for diseases.

Poverty in a home is worse than fifty plagues.
>> TALMUD: *Baba Bathra,* 116a

For one sick, six things are good: to sneeze, to perspire, to open the
bowels, to emit semen, to sleep, and to dream.
>> —adapted from TALMUD, *Berakoth,* 57b

The fox does not get sick from breathing the dust of his own den.
>> —adapted from TALMUD: *Kethuboth,* 71b

∾ The words of Torah heal the soul, not the body.
>> MAIMONIDES, *Mishneh Torah*

The idle man, even if he has all he needs, will end in weakness,
insanity and disease.   SAADIA GAON

It is a serious disease to worry over what has not occurred.

IBN GABIROL

See also: DOCTORS, HEALTH, MEDICINE, PAIN, SICKNESS, SUFFERING.

DISHONESTY

◄§ When a crook kisses you, count your teeth.

What he says he doesn't mean, and what he means he doesn't say.

One crook can't fool another.

He who does not take care of the property of another is dishonest.

TALMUD: *Baba Mezi'a,* 24a

See also: DECEIT, HONESTY, LIARS/LIES, THIEVES

DIVORCE

Note. As with the status of women in Jewish life, so the conditions of divorce are often misinterpreted by those who read and run. Ancient texts are quoted by those ignorant of the subsequent profound changes in rabbinical decisions, and in actual practice among Jews.

The Torah gives a husband the right to divorce his wife —but *not,* as is sometimes assumed, easily or arbitrarily. Divorce was regarded as a calamity, a blow to the integrity of the home, a defeat for the perpetuation of the community. The Talmudic rabbis, following the prophet Malachi, who condemned divorce, said that "the very altar sheds tears" for the man who divorces his wife (Sanhedrin, 22).

The marriage contract (*ketubah*), from very early times, protected a Jewish wife from her husband's hasty, selfish, or capricious desire for an abrogation of the marriage. Alimony, totally unknown in the Biblical era, was begun to help Jewish women in the first century before the Christian Era. Since the year 1000, a religious (as distinguished from a civil) divorce terminates a marriage among Orthodox Jews *only if both hus-band and wife agree to it*—and if the civil courts grant a civil divorce. (Reform rabbis do not ask for a religious divorce, in addition to a civil divorce, before a husband or wife may remarry.)

Down the ages, Jewish laws on divorce have been modified in favor of the wife. The denigration of European women in the Middle Ages found no counterpart in Jewish mores—where, indeed, the status of women was heightened. Maimonides declared that if a husband was not satisfying his wife's conjugal rights, or was repulsive to her, she could win a divorce. "A woman," said Maimonides, "is not like a captive, compelled to consort with a man against her will."

In general, divorce is discouraged—in whatever branch of Judaism; rabbis are bound by their office to try to exhaust every possibility for reconciliation. Where it is unmistakable that domestic discords cannot be healed, that marital harmony and love have died, divorce is permitted.

A useful summary of Jewish attitudes to, and laws about, divorce will be found in *Jews and Divorce* (edited by Jacob Fried, KTAV Publishing House, New York, 1968).   —L.R.

Each day they decide to divorce, but each night they head for bed.

If a woman can't make a *kugl* [noodle or potato pudding], divorce her.

◆§ When a divorced man marries a divorced woman, four go to bed.   TALMUD: *Pesahim*, 112a

◆§ A man should not marry a woman with the mental reservation that, after all, he can divorce her.
                                     TALMUD: *Yebamoth* 37b

◆§ Tears fall on God's altar for whoever divorces his first wife.
                                     TALMUD: *Gittin*, 90a

See also: ADULTERY, MARRIAGE, MEN AND WOMEN, WIVES

DOCTORS

⇜ Don't ask the doctor; ask the patient.

A new doctor has one blind eye. [The family doctor knows you better.]

Don't live in a town where there are no doctors.

The greatest doctor is time.

Doctors and gravediggers are partners.

The door that is closed to good deeds opens up for doctors.

A great doctor works with an angel at his side.

All physicians, even good ones, will end in Hell. *

Doctors can cure anything except poverty.

⇜ No physician can cure a prejudice, which is a blindness in the mind.

⇜ Where there is no wine, drugs are useful.
> TALMUD: *Baba Bathra,* 58b

A physician who takes no fee is worth no fee.
> TALMUD: *Baba Kamma,* 85a

Pay homage to the physician before you need him.
> MIDRASH: *Exodus Rabbah,* 21 : 7

See also: DISEASE, HEALTH, MEDICINE

DOWRY

Sell even the Holy Scrolls to make sure that a poor girl has a dowry.

Beauty is half the dowry.

---

* I do not understand why.—L.R.

You can't get a scholar without a dowry.

The more defects a girl has, the larger the dowry she needs.

See also: DAUGHTERS, MARRIAGE, OBLIGATION

DREAMS

Note. Man sleeps. Man dreams. No matter what his creed or race, culture or time. In ancient Gaza or medieval Japan, modern Iceland or (certainly) Beverly Hills. Whether cave man, Confucian, Inca—or space man heading for the moon.

Men dream in joy or terror, or in phantasmagoria of wonders not seen on land or sea. No people has ever been indifferent to the mystery and magic of dreams. No people has failed to convert them into omens, prophecies, divinations.

The Old Testament assigned great importance to dreams, which were thought to be one way in which the Almighty (blessed be He) makes known His wishes—especially to the prophets: thus, the revelations to Joseph and Daniel, and the dreams Yahweh sent non-Jews: Pharaoh, in the Book of Genesis, and Balaam, in the Book of Numbers.

Jews, traditionally, believe that the soul returns to God each night and is returned, by God's blessing, upon awakening; the lovely prayer said upon awakening thanks the Lord "for returning my soul unto me." The ancient Egyptians thought that dreams foretell the future. The Greeks held that dreams cure sickness. The Romans prayed to Mercury before retiring, asking the god to send them good visions. Natives of the Fiji Islands, like a thousand other groupings of mankind, believe that their souls leave their bodies in a dream. The Iroquois regarded dreams as supernatural commands, which had to be executed.

Calpurnia's dream might have saved Caesar and changed the world. Constantine's apparition of a luminous cross, inscribed *In hoc signo vinces,* drove him to march against Maxentius at Saxa Rubra, and the dreamer entered Rome in triumph, behind a purple banner on which was emblazoned what he said he had beheld: a Greek *Chi* and *Rho,* the first two letters of "Christos." Many a historian has speculated on what turns our history would have made had not Constantine lifted a small, harassed faith onto the very throne of imperial power, made Christianity the state religion, and sent Roman legions to the Bosphorus, to build a new Jerusalem there ... all because of a dream.

Long before Sigmund Freud, this immortal passage was written:

> Every man appears to have certain instincts, but in some men these passions are controlled by reason and, the nobler desires prevailing over them, the instincts are either wholly suppressed or reduced in strength. I mean particularly those desires which are awake when the taming power of the personality is asleep. For it is in sleep that the wild beast in our nature rears up and walks about naked. And there is no conceivable folly or shame or crime, however unnatural, not excepting incest or parricide, of which such a nature may not be guilty. In all of us, even in good men, there is a latent wild beast, who peers out in sleep.

The author was Plato.

I find it surprising that except for Joseph and Daniel, no one in the Old Testament *interpreted* a dream. This singular gap was remedied in the Talmud, where one of the longest haggadic sequences, with no digressions, sought to analyze dreams (*Berakoth:* 55b–57a). The interpretations are often quaint, often cryptic, often saturated in superstition. One smiles over the fanciful meanings read into dreamed elephants, asses, horses, snakes; or the solemn adjudication that if in Palestine you dream you are naked that is a sign of virtue, but if in Babylon, it reveals a failure to perform enough good deeds.

Yet, some rabbinical insights about the kingdom of sleep are astonishing. It is these, and the charming folk sayings Jews made up about the phantoms of the night, I now give you.

—L.R.

◦§ In sleep, it is not we who sin—but our dreams.

Only in dreams are carrots as big as bears.

◦§ The dumplings in a dream are not dumplings, but dreams.

A dream is a fool—for it is sleep that is the master.

Ask for three things: a good wife, a good year, a good dream.

ஃ Thieves have easy jobs, but bad dreams.

We can make the dream more important than the night.

In dreams, fools get rich easily.

What good is a sweet dream if the dawn is cold?

A fool dreams foolish dreams.

In bed, thoughts come into your mind so that you may know the
thoughts of your heart.
                    —adapted from the *Book of Daniel*, 2 : 20–30

I [God] do speak . . . in a dream.   *Book of Numbers*, 12 : 6

ஃ During the night [dream], a man's soul testifies as to what he
did during the day.   *Zohar*

ஃ A dream not interpreted is like a letter not read—so what
harm can it do?   —adapted from TALMUD: *Berakoth*, 55b

Just as wheat cannot be without some straw, so no dream is without
some nonsense.   TALMUD: *Berakoth*, 55a

ஃ Men see in their dreams only that which is suggested by their
own thoughts.   TALMUD: *Berakoth*, 55a

Any dream is better than that of being hungry.
                        —adapted from TALMUD: *Berakoth*, 55a

Neither a happy dream nor a bad one is ever entirely fulfilled.
                        —adapted from TALMUD: *Berakoth*, 55a

All dreams "follow the mouth"—i.e., the interpretation; hence, are
fulfilled.   —adapted from TALMUD: *Berakoth*, 55b

The sadness of a bad dream, like the pleasures of a good one, are
sufficient [they need not be fulfilled].
                        —adapted from TALMUD: *Berakoth*, 55b

If you have a dream which makes you sad, have it interpreted—in
  the presence of three others.
                              —adapted from TALMUD, *Berakoth,* 55b

When a dream speaks truth, it is through an angel; when a dream
  speaks falsely, it is through a demon.
                              RABA, in TALMUD: *Berakoth,* 55b

There are twenty-four dream interpreters in Jerusalem—and each
  gives a different interpretation.
                              —adapted from TALMUD, *Berakoth,* 55b

To those who paid him, Bar Hedya interpreted a dream favorably;
  to those who did not, he interpreted a dream unfavorably.
                              —adapted from TALMUD: *Berakoth,* 56a

If one dreams of intercourse with one's mother, it means he can
  expect to get understanding—for it is written, "Yea, thou wilt
  call understanding 'mother.'"
    TALMUD: *Berakoth,* 57a (the quotation is adapted from the
                              Book of Proverbs, 2 : 3)

If one dreams of intercourse with his sister, he can expect to gain
  wisdom, for it has been written: "Say to wisdom, thou art my
  sister."
              TALMUD, *Berakoth,* 57a (the quotation is from
                              Book of Proverbs, 7 : 4)

If you see King David in a dream, you may hope for piety; if you
  see King Solomon, you may hope for wisdom; if you see King
  Ahab, fear for punishment.   TALMUD: *Berakoth,* 57b

If, in a dream, you see the Book of Psalms, you may hope to gain
  piety; if you see the Book of Proverbs, you may hope to gain
  wisdom; if you see the Book of Job, fear punishment.
                              TALMUD: *Berakoth,* 57b

O Lord: as Thou turned the curse of Balaam into a blessing, so
  turn all my dreams into something good.
                  in the Siddur (prayer book) recited between
                  benedictions in some congregations

There is reality in any dream—except a dream during a fast.
                                —adapted from *Shulhan Aruk*

Dreams lift up fools.   Ben Sirach, *Ecclesiasticus*, 34 : 1

A good man has a bad dream to urge him to repentance; a bad
   man has a good dream to give him some reward in this world.
                —adapted from Rashi, Commentary on *Berakoth*

Three kinds of dreams are fulfilled: the dream of early morning, a
   friend's dream about you, and the dream that is interpreted
   within the dream. To which some add: the dream which is
   repeated.   Rabbi Johanan, in Talmud: *Berakoth*, 55a

The joy a blind man gets from a dream nullifies itself.
            —adapted from Rabbi Joseph in Talmud: *Berakoth*, 55a

A bad dream can be worse than a flogging.
                adapted from Rabbi Hisda in Talmud: *Berakoth*, 55a

A part of a dream may be fulfilled, but never the whole.
            —adapted from Rabbi Hisda in Talmud: *Berakoth*, 55a

See also: FOOLS, ILLUSION, SLEEP

DRESS

Eat according to your means, but dress above them.

◦§ Men greet you according to your dress; they say good-bye
   according to your sense [wisdom].

See also: APPEARANCE, CONDUCT, DECORUM, ILLUSION, VANITY

DRUNKARDS

Note. Jewish drunkards are exceedingly rare (even proportionately,
   in these bibulous times), and the souse is almost unknown in
   Jewish literature. Yet drinking is not foreign to Jewish culture.
   A Jewish child may be introduced to a sip of wine at an early

age, and the blessing over wine sanctifies each Sabbath. The goodness of wine is often mentioned in the Bible; and many Biblical metaphors use wine as an allusion to prosperity and good times. The Talmud holds that drinking wine in moderation "unfolds a man's brain," and some *hasidim* said a teetotaler cannot possess great wisdom.

The rabbis believed that wine possessed curative properties: "Wine is the greatest of all medicines." "Where wine is lacking, drugs are necessary," Rabbi Huna said. "Wine helps to open the heart to reasoning." But the sages always stressed moderation in drinking, as in everything else—except study.

Jews have a certain contempt for anyone who loses control of his faculties, or acts in an uncouth, "bestial" manner.

> ... drunkards were rarely seen among Jews. When night came and a man wanted to pass away time, he did not hasten to a tavern to take a drink, but went to pore over a book or joined a group which—either with or without a teacher—revered books.... Physically worn out by their day's toil, they sat over open volumes, playing the austere music of the Talmud ... or the sweet melodies of ... piety of the ancient sages.*

Drinking, if not drunkenness, has clearly increased among American Jews; I do *not* attribute this to the delightful injunction in the Talmud: "When a man faces his Maker, he will also have to account for those pleasures of life he failed to enjoy."

Traditional Jewish pride in sobriety is eloquently expressed by Israel Zangwill, in his classic *Children of the Ghetto***:

> On thousands of squalid homes the light of Sinai shone. . . . The Ghetto welcomed the Sabbath Bride with proud sound and humble feast.... All around, their neighbors sought distraction in the public-houses, and their tipsy bellowings resounded through the streets.... Here and there the voice of a beaten woman rose on the air. But no Son of the Convenant was among the [drunken] revellers or the wife-beaters. The Jews remained a chosen race, a peculiar people, faulty enough, but redeemed at least from the grosser vices—a little human islet won from the waters of animalism by the genius of ancient engineers.   —L.R.

---

* A. J. Heschel, *The Earth Is the Lord's,* Abelard-Schuman, New York, 1964, p. 45.
    ** Jewish Publication Society, 1892.

◄§ When one man tells you you're drunk, hesitate; when two tell you, think it over; when three tell you—lie down.

The tongue of the drunk reveals what is on the minds of the sober.

◄§ It's better to be dead drunk than dead hungry.

When drink enters, judgment leaves.

◄§ When a drunkard has no whiskey, he talks of whiskey.

◄§ A saloonkeeper may love a drunkard—but won't let him marry his daughter.

◄§ A drunkard can't help harming someone.

◄§ Drunkenness exiles a man from his family.

The workman who is a drunkard will never get rich.

They reel to and fro, and stagger like drunken men, and are at their wit's end.   *Book of Psalms*, 107 : 27

Wine is a mocker, strong drink a brawler; none who reels under them is wise.   *The Book of Proverbs*, 20 : 1

A drunkard cannot plead his case.   NACHMAN OF BRATSLAV

A teetotaler is rarely wise.   THE KORETSER RABBI

See also: FOOD AND DRINK, LIQUOR, TEMPERANCE, WINE

DUTY

A scholar profanes the Name of God if he does not pay the butcher at once.   —adapted from TALMUD: *Yomah*, 86a

When Rabbi Ammi's hour to die came, he wept bitterly; and his nephew asked, "But why do you weep? Is there any Torah you have not learned and taught? Is there any kindness you have not practiced? And you never accepted public office, or sat in judgment on others." The Rabbi replied: "That is why I weep:

I was given the ability to establish justice, but never carried it out." MIDRASH: *Tanhuma on Mishpatim*

When a man knows any evidence in favor of a defendant, he is not free to keep silent, for in doing so he may become responsible for the defendant's death.

MIDRASH: *Sifre Kedoshim,* 19

Man should perform his duties to his fellow men even as to God. MISHNAH: *Shekalim*

Those who warn the wicked are saved from blame, even if the warning goes unheeded. *Zohar*

A man should remember three things: that he has only one day to live; that he has only the page before him to study; and that he is the only Jew on whom the survival of Torah depends.

"THE CHOFETZ CHAIM"

See also: CHARITY, EVIDENCE, GOOD DEEDS, LAW, OBLIGATION, RESPONSIBILITY, STUDY

E

EARS

Ears have flaps, to cover them when slander is uttered.

◦§ Ears are the doors to the heart.

◦§ Your ears belong to yourself, but your tongue is heard by others.

Even a road has ears. MIDRASH: *Leviticus Rabbah,* 32

If the ear is stuffed, what use is the [warning] bell?

IBN GABIROL, *Choice of Pearls*

Ears are the gates to the mind.

MOSES IBN EZRA, *Shirat Yisrael*

The ear is more useful than the eye for knowledge.   GERONDI

See also: FACE, LEARNING, SLANDER

EATING AND DRINKING
(*See:* FOOD)

EDEN

See HEAVENS, PARADISE

EDUCATION

"In an unlettered world, when even kings could not sign their names, they had already developed a system of universal education, so that an illiterate Jew was, even in the Dark Ages, a contradiction in terms."*

CECIL ROTH

Note. It is remarkable how powerful and pervasive the role of education became among Jews, wherever they lived. Jews felt that knowledge about God's Torah must be perpetuated—and depended on the amount of learning transmitted to the young; hence every Jewish community provided an education—no matter how poor the community or how lowly the young scholar. Rabbinical authority even forbade a Jew to reside in any village that had no teacher of Hebrew for the young.

Jewish boys began studying as early as the age of three. They would study six to ten hours a day, six days a week. Many received their Hebrew education in a room (*cheder*) in the home of a *melamed* (teacher); in the larger (*Talmud*

---

* In *Essays in Jewish Booklore*, KTAV, New York, 1971, p. 179.

Torah) schools, there were several rooms and more than one teacher. These schools customarily were supported by the community and charged no tuition. A student of Abelard wrote:

> Christians educate their sons . . . for gain. . . . A Jew, however poor, had he ten sons would put them all to letters, not for gain . . . but to the understanding of God's laws; and not only his sons, but his daughters.*

Centuries before "adult education" courses were instituted, such education was common in Jewish communities as an obligation of religion. Each morning before going to work, and each evening after work, Jews gathered—in the synagogue, or outside its entrance, or in the House of Study attached—for communal study and colloquia on the Torah, Talmud, the work of great sages and scholars, the on-going, never-interrupted interpretations of the Law.

The Jews' extreme emphasis on education was expressed not only in the most intense effort to educate one's sons, but in the longing for a son-in-law who would be a scholar. This was considered a great honor. It was quite common for a family, as part of a girl's dowry, to pledge the support of the young couple for a number of years. The son-in-law often would move into his in-laws' home, there to receive free room and board, and devote himself solely to Talmudic studies.

In Eastern Europe, many women supported their husbands for a lifetime so that the men need never do anything but study Talmud, frequent the Bet Midrash ("house of study") and the synagogue, and thus add to Israel's glory and the Jews' hopes of salvation from the miseries of life on earth.   —L.R.

~§ In time, even a bear can be taught to dance.

If the student is good, so is the teacher.

~§ To educate fools is folly.
>   —adapted from *Book of Proverbs*, 16 : 11

A village without a school should be abolished.
>   TALMUD: *Shabbath*, 119a

---

* *Great Jewish Personalities in Ancient and Medieval Times*, edited by Simon Novick, B'nai Brith Publishers, New York, p. 240.

The very world rests on the breath of children in the schoolhouse.
TALMUD: *Shabbath,* 119b

Educating a fool is putting him in chains.
—adapted from BEN SIRACH, *Ecclesiasticus,* 21 : 19

The education of children must never be interrupted, even to rebuild the Temple.   TALMUD: *Shabbath,* 119b

Six things are not fit for an educated man: to walk in the street perfumed, to walk alone at night, to wear worn shoes, to dally with a woman too long in the street, to sit at table with illiterate men, to arrive late at the synagogue.
TALMUD: *Berakoth,* 43b

If you don't teach the ox to plow when he's young, it will be difficult to teach him when he is grown.
MIDRASH: *Midrash Mishle,* 22

Don't poke fun at an uneducated man: you may mock your own ancestors.   BEN SIRACH, *Ecclesiasticus,* 8 : 4

See also: LEARNING, SCHOLARS, SCHOLARSHIP, STUDY, TEACHERS

EFFORT

When you must, you can.

⇜ Peeling an egg does not put it into your mouth.

Roasted doves don't fly into your mouth unaided.

If you sweep the whole house, you will find everything.

See also: DETERMINATION, LAZINESS

EGOTISM

⇜ He thinks he can hear a flea cough and a roach sneeze.

⇜ There is no one more lonely than those who love only themselves.

They are madly in love, he with himself, she with herself.

Egotists always grumble, for egotism can never be satisfied.

I cannot be the judge in the case of a student of the Law, because
    I love him as myself—and no one can see a fault in himself.
               RAB ASHI in TALMUD: *Shabbath,* 119a

There is more hope for a fool than for a man wise in his own
    eyes.   *Book of Proverbs,* 29 : 20

Man cannot see anything to his own disadvantage.
                     TALMUD: *Shabbath* 119a

See also: CONCEIT, PRIDE, SELF-CENTEREDNESS, SELF-ESTEEM, SELFISH-
NESS, VANITY

EMOTIONS

Every heart has its own secrets.

Secrets are betrayed by the face.

An orphan eats much, an unhappy heart talks much.

◆§ Sugar in the mouth won't help bitterness in the heart.

When the eyes don't see, the heart won't feel.

Feelings that don't show on the face lie on the heart.

One heart sympathizes with another.

◆§ When the heart is full, the eyes overflow.
                     SHOLEM ALEICHEM

See also: GRIEF, HEART, PASSION, SORROW, SUFFERING

ENDS AND MEANS

◆§ You can't chew with someone else's teeth.

Without a hand, you can't make a fist.

He who has bread will find a knife.

⋙ Those who want to beat a dog always find a stick.

Every pot finds its cover.

To cite the end is no justification of the means.
                                    —adapted from TALMUD

The man who needs the fire must fan it.
                                    MIDRASH: *Samuel Rabbah,* 9

See also: CAUSE AND EFFECT, CIRCUMSTANCES, CONTEXT

ENDURANCE

(*See:* FORTITUDE)

ENEMY

Only one God—but so many enemies.

No enemy can do a man as much harm as he does himself.

A tongue is a dangerous enemy.

Enemies don't come free, you must pay for them.

⋙ "Rejoice not at thine enemy's fall"—but don't rush to pick him up either.

When you get a slap, you get an enemy, too.

⋙ A friend you have to buy; enemies you get for nothing.

⋙ Whether rabbi or street cleaner, everyone has enemies.

Better a good enemy than a bad friend.

Be careful when your enemy speaks honey.

It's easy to get an enemy, but hard to find a friend.

ᴥᵹ It is better that my enemy see good in me than that I see bad in him.

Who is a hero? He who turns an enemy into a friend.
Abot de Rabbi Nathan, ch. 23

Peace after enmity is sweeter than sweetness.

If your enemy is hungry, give him bread; if he is thirsty, give him water. *Book of Proverbs,* 25 : 21

Sincere are the words of a friend;
But deceitful are the kisses of an enemy.
Book of Proverbs, 27 : 6

The kisses of an enemy are deceitful.
Book of Proverbs, 27 : 6

Oh, that mine adversary had written a book!
Book of Job, 31 : 35

If two men claim your help and one is your enemy, help him first.
Talmud: *Baba Mezi'a,* 32b

Dogs in a kennel snarl at each other; but when a wolf comes along, they become allies. Talmud: *Sanhedrin,* 105a

An enemy is not hidden in adversity.
Ben Sirach, *Ecclesiasticus:* 12.8

ᴥᵹ Every type of enmity contains the possibility of being cured, except that of the man who hates you out of envy.
Ibn Gabirol, *Choice of Pearls*

A needle's eye is not too narrow for two lovers, but the whole world is not wide enough for two enemies.
Ibn Gabirol, *Choice of Pearls*

Every man's enemy is under his own ribs . . .
Bahya ibn Paquda, *Duties of the Heart*

One enemy is one too many. Asher ben Jehiel

See also: ENVY, FRIENDS/FRIENDSHIP; FRIENDSHIP: FALSE FRIENDS, HATE, JEALOUSY, LONELINESS, QUARRELS, WAR

ENVY

◦§ Don't count the teeth in someone else's mouth.

◦§ He is less upset by his poverty than by your wealth.

◦§ Envy turns into hate.

An envious man grows lean over the fatness of his neighbor.

That place seems good where we are not.

Envy destroys contentment.

Another man's tidbit always smells sweet.

Envy is like a disease—it consumes the soul.

A man envies everyone, except the accomplishments of his son
  or his pupil.

How appetizing is the fish on the other man's table.

Envy, cupidity and ambition drive a man from the world.
                              Sayings of the Fathers, 4 : 30

Without envy, the world could not abide, for then no one would
  marry or build a house.   MIDRASH: *Genesis Rabbah,* 9 : 9

Your revenge over the man who envies you is how he responds to
  your good fortune. . . . No one hurts himself more: his mourning is ceaseless, his soul grieves, his intellect deteriorates, his
  heart is in turmoil. Such a man is only cheered up by the misfortune of others.
          IBN GABIROL, *Choice of Pearls* (my paraphrase—L.R.)

All types of hatred are curable except that which flows from envy.
                              IBN GABIROL, *Choice of Pearls*

No man can be called wise unless he possesses three qualities:
  never to scorn one, less learned, who seeks knowledge; never
  to envy someone richer; and never to accept a fee for his
  learning.   IBN GABIROL

◦§ Envy is hatred without a cure.
>BAHYA BEN ASHER, *Kad ha-Kemah*

◦§ Don't envy a sinner: you don't know what awaits him.
>—adapted from BEN SIRACH, *Ecclesiasticus,* 9 : 11

The man who covets is guilty of robbery in thought.
>NACHMAN OF BRATSLAV

See also: BITTERNESS, CIRCUMSTANCES, COMPLAINT, DESIRE, ENEMY, GRATITUDE, GREED, HATE, HEALTH, JEALOUSY, UTILITY

EQUALITY

Nine rabbis can't make a minyan [quorum for prayers] but ten cobblers can.

In the public baths, all men are equal.

◦§ The masses aren't asses.

Be sure you have the support of your equals before you challenge your superiors.

The rich and the poor meet face to face, for the Lord is the creator of them both.   *Book of Proverbs,* 22 : 2

Before the Eternal One, the highest of men and the lowliest of men are equal.   MENDEL OF VITEBSK

See also: DEMOCRACY, GOVERNMENT, LAW, MASSES, POLITICS, POWER, STATUS

EROTICA

Note. In the literature of the Jews, erotic material rarely appeared —and where it did, the books were swiftly locked away and their reading banned. The *Shulhan Aruk* of Joseph Caro chastises Immanuel of Rome (*q.v.*) for his lusty verses in his *Mahbarot* ("Compositions"); other rabbis, fearing its "immoral" potentialities, urged publishers and copyists not to disseminate such morally offensive works.

More important than the occasional condemnation of erotica (most of which reads like *Rebecca of Sunnybrook Farm,* compared to our contemporary writings) was the rabbis' fear of, and hostility to, "secular" writings: *i.e.,* books on philosophy, logic, science, the Greeks, the Romans. See headnote: CENSORSHIP

—L.R.

See LUST, PASSION, SEX

ERROR

⋙ The man who answers speedily errs speedily.

⋙ Experience is our name for accumulated errors.

Error that comes from lack of study is a sin.

Rabbinical maxim

Once error creeps in, it stays.   TALMUD: *Baba Bathra,* 21a

God forgets those who reject proof that they are wrong.

NACHMAN OF BRATSLAV

⋙ Men make mistakes not because they think they know when they do not know, but because they think others do not know.

SHOLEM ALEICHEM

See also: KNOWLEDGE, LEARNING, REASON, SIN, TRUTH

EVE

Note. Considering the unprecedented brouhaha Eve let loose in the world, it is surprising how small a role she is actually allotted in Genesis: "little more than a personification of human life, which is perpetuated by woman."*

---

* *Dictionary of the Bible,* ed. J. Hastings, F. C. Grant and H. H. Rowley, Scribners, New York, 1963, p. 277.

The first reference to Adam's mate, in the Masoretic text (Genesis, 2 : 23), calls her *ishah* (translated as "woman") because she was taken from *ish* ("man"). Not until Genesis, 3 : 20, does Adam break free from the generic "woman" or "wife" to coin a name for his mate: *havah,* "because she was the mother of all the living [*hai*]."*

Now, eyewitness (or earwitness) testimony about the naming of Eve is, alas, lacking. And lest you think I flirt with blasphemy, let me enlist the authority of the *Encyclopedia of the Jewish Religion,* which disposes of Eve in nine crisp lines, informing us that modern Bible scholars treat the story of Eve as a traditional fable conceived by primitive peoples to explain the origin of mankind, the reason for menstruation and labor pains, and the subordinate position of women in the world: "The rabbis did not propound a doctrine of original sin, and the taint of Eve's sin was in any case removed by the Israelites' acceptance of the Law."**

I, for one, have always wanted to know more about Eve's legendary predecessor, Lilith (*q.v.*). However you feel about either, it is hard not to admire the astute answer Gamaliel's daughter gave to a sacrilegious king, in the last entry below.

—L.R.

◆§ Adam would never have had Eve had God not put him to sleep first.

"If you know everything," said the cynic to the sage, "tell me what Eve did whenever Adam came home?"
"She counted his ribs," said the sage.

Adam's last will and testament read: "Don't believe Eve's version."

The King said to Rabbi Gamaliel: "Your God is a thief, for He put Adam to sleep, then stole one of his ribs!"

---

* *The Torah: The Five Books of Moses, a new translation according to the Masoretic text,* J.P.S.A., Philadelphia, 1962. But *havah* is a nettlesome word to philologists, who say it was not strictly Hebrew in origin; and its alleged sonic resemblance to *ha-ra* ("evil") offers other scholars a portentous, if fragile, linkage between the name of woman and the conception of sin. Further titillation lies in the observation that it bears a resemblance to an Arabic word for serpent. (See *Dictionary of the Bible, op. cit.,* pp. 266–67, and *Encyclopedia of the Jewish Religion,* ed. Werblowsky and Wigoder, Holt, Rinehart, Winston, Israel, 1965, p. 136).
** *Encyclopedia of the Jewish Religion, op. cit.,* p. 136.

At this, the Rabbi's daughter cried out, "Police! Police!"

"What happened?" asked the King.

"A thief stole into my house," she replied, "and took my silver pitcher—and left a gold one in its place."

The King said: "If only such a thief would come to me!"

To which Gamaliel's daughter replied, "Then why do you mock our God? He took one rib from Adam only to enrich him with Eve."

—adapted from Talmud: Sanhedrin, 39a

See also: ADAM, ADAM'S RIB, ANCESTORS, GOD, LILITH, MEN and WOMEN, MARRIAGE, SERPENT, SIN, WIVES

EVIDENCE

No answer is a type of answer.

To assume is to fool one's self.

The drunkard smells of whiskey—but so does the bartender.

Where there's a flame there must be a fire; and there is no smoke except from fire.

Half an answer also tells you something.

You don't have to see the lion if you see his lair.

A man's death-trap may be between his cheeks [his words or testimony].

When all people cry "Crazy!" believe them.

If one man says, "You're a donkey," don't mind; if two say so, be worried; if three say so, get a saddle.

—adapted from Midrash: Genesis Rabbah, 45 : 10

A man should be able to classify everything he believes, so that he can say: "This I believe because it is handed down from the Prophets; this I believe from the evidence of my senses; and this I believe from reason." Whoever believes anything

that does not fall within these three categories, to him apply
the saying: "The thoughtless believeth every word." (Proverbs
14 : 15)   MAIMONIDES, *Responsa II*, 25a

See also: ERROR, JUDGES, LAW, LOGIC, REASON, TRUTH

EVIL

Note. Since God is just, observing Jews hold, He will not treat
the wicked and the virtuous in the same way: the former will
be punished, the latter rewarded. But the rabbis sought to
avoid a morality based on expedience. They stressed that personal reward is not a proper reason for either faith, virtue, or
righteousness. It is the love of God, fidelity to His commandments, the endless performance of good deeds, that must govern men's lives. (Moses said this in Deuteronomy, and the
prophets, elders and rabbis echoed it down the centuries.)
   Now, this attitude presented many difficulties in a world
where the evil often do flourish, and where the good and innocent do suffer and perish—as Job's three friends and
Jeremiah complained, asking for God's explanation. There was
none. "It is not in our power," said Rabbi Jannai and a hundred seers since him, "to explain the prosperity of the wicked
—or the sufferings of the righteous." But Jews continued
to try to explain, and to complain, and clung to faith in ultimate justice—in heaven, if not on earth.

                                                    —L.R.

God is everywhere, even in evil thoughts.

◄§ Evil is a two-edged sword.

◄§ If there were fewer swine, there would be fewer bastards.

The good is remembered; the bad is felt.

It is easier to abandon evil traits today than tomorrow.
                                        Hasidic saying

The Evil Impulse springs up in children not at five or six—but at
   ten, and from there on.   Rabbinical saying

The righteous man studies what he should answer,
But the mouth of the wicked pours out evil.
Book of Proverbs, 15 : 28

He who returns evil for good—evil will never depart from his
house.   *Book of Proverbs*, 17 : 13

Say not, "I will repay evil." Wait for the Lord to help you.
Book of Proverbs, 20 : 22

Both right and wrong are the work of our hands.
Apocrypha: *Psalms of Solomon*, 9 : 4

The greater the man the greater his potential for evil, too.
Talmud: *Sukkah*, 52a

The Evil Will lures man in this world, then testifies against him
in the world to come.   Talmud: *Sukkah*, 52a

God created the Evil Impulse, but He also created its antidote,
the Torah.   Talmud: *Kiddushin*, 30b

When the righteous man departs, evil enters.
Talmud: *Sanhedrin*, 113b

~§ Evil is sweet in the beginning but bitter in the end.
Talmud J.: *Shabbath*, 14 : 3

Israel argues, "Even though we sin, and Thou art angry, Thou
shouldst not forsake us: for if the potter makes a jug and
leaves a pebble in the clay, is it not inevitable that the jug
should leak? Thou didst create in us from our childhood the
Evil Inclination, therefore we beseech thee, cause the inclination to pass away so that we may do Thy will." And God
replies, "I shall do so—in the world to come."
Midrash: *Exodus Rabbah*, 46 : 4

Does the Evil Impulse ever serve good? Yes, for if not for the
Evil Impulse, no man would build a house, nor marry a wife,
nor beget children, nor engage in trade.
Midrash: *Ecclesiastes Rabbah*, 3 : 11

✑ The Evil Urge begins as a guest and proceeds like the host.
MIDRASH: *Genesis Rabbah,* 22 : 6

Don't court evil, and evil won't come to you.
MIDRASH: *Genesis Rabbah,* 22 : 8

We must expect that even in the millennium, evil will be weakened, but not totally extinguished. *Zohar*

He is called a man who masters his evil desires. *Zohar*

He who returns evil for evil acts wrongly; he should be patient,
and let God help him. *Zohar*

When the Evil Impulse comes to you, it is like iron still cold: If
you do not drive it out, it becomes molten—as if transformed
by fire. *Zohar*

The Evil Impulse is like a cake of yeast: placed in one spot, it
ferments throughout. *Zohar*

✑ The world was created for the sake of those who are ashamed
to do evil. Introduction to *Tikune Zohar*

Keep three things in mind and you will escape the toils of wickedness: Know whence you came, whither you are going, and
before Whom you will have to give a strict account.
Sayings of the Fathers, 3 : 1

Feel no sadness because of evil thoughts: it only strengthens them.
NACHMAN OF BRATSLAV

See also: GOD, GOOD AND EVIL, GOOD MEN, HABIT, HEREAFTER, SATAN,
SIN, WICKEDNESS

EXCELLENCE

Excellence comes from men's rivalry with each other.
—adapted from *Ecclesiastes,* 4 : 40

See also: CHARACTER, SCHOLARS, WISE MEN

EXCESS

ᴥᶘ Where there is too much, something is missing.

He who is everywhere is nowhere.

Too much means left over.

Three things are good in a little measure, and bad in large: yeast, salt, and hesitation.   TALMUD: *Berakoth,* 34a

Food prepared by two cooks is neither hot nor cold.
                                                        TALMUD: *Erubin,* 3a

Too much oil will quench the wick.   *Psalms*

Lamps are more often extinguished by too much oil than by too little.   TESTAMENT OF JUDAH ASHERI

Fast so that you may condemn excess. Do not believe that much eating and drinking make the body grow, or enlarge the understanding; the reverse is true.
                                              MAIMONIDES, *Responsa II,* 39a

Too much good food is worse than too little bad food.
                                              FALAQUERA, *Sefer ha-Mevakesh*

Nothing is more precious than light, yet too much of it is blinding.
                                                        JOSEPH DELMEDIGO

See also: ABSTINENCE, BOREDOM, FASTING, FOOD, GLUTTONY, HEALTH, JUDGMENT, MODERATION

EXCUSES

Oh Lord, give me an excuse!

Gluttons find ample excuses for gorging.

ᴥᶘ Girls who can't dance say the musicians can't keep time.

◦§ Ten excuses are less persuasive than one.

Not to answer is one kind of answer.

Don't do what you'll have to find an excuse for.

◦§ To be cheated once is understandable; to be cheated thrice is inexcusable.

◦§ Fools always find an excuse for their folly.

◦§ If you measure before you cut, you'll avoid the need for excuses.

Don't repent so much—just don't sin so often.

◦§ The guilty make excuses before they are accused.

◦§ There is no excuse for not helping someone when you can.

EXPERIENCE

◦§ Experience is the name people give their mistakes.

◦§ Some of the most well-trodden roads lead nowhere.

◦§ The man who has been bitten by a snake is afraid of a piece of rope.

◦§ You can't run past the moon.

If you lie on the ground, you can't fall.

◦§ Once a man has been burned by the hot, he blows on the cool.

◦§ A thread is always found on a tailor.

The sun shines brighter after it rains.

No one can know where the shoe pinches except the one who walks in it.

Where there is honey, there are flies.

◄§ The best preacher is the human heart; the best teacher is time; the best book is the world; the best friend is God.

On black earth, the best corn grows. [Simple folk often have the best hearts.]

Only the one who eats the dish knows how it tastes.
MIDRASH: *Deuteronomy Rabbah*

Without experience there can be little wisdom.
BEN SIRACH, *Ecclesiasticus*

Only those accustomed to the sun can endure its glare.
JUDAH ARYEH MOSCATO

No dog is smarter than one who has been beaten.
SHOLEM ALEICHEM

See also: FEAR, HABIT, LEARNING

EXPERTS

◄§ Those who can't sing can still be experts on singing.

See also: EXPERIENCE, JUDGMENT

EYES

One eye has more faith than two.

Truth is in the eyes; lies stay behind them.

The eye is small, yet it sees the whole world.

◄§ The eye does not see as well as the heart.

◄§ Even those with big eyes do not see their own faults.

The eye and heart are spies for the body: the eyes see, the heart covets—and the body commits the sin.
RASHI, *Commentaries on the Pentateuch, Numbers*

What has been created that is worse than the eye? It sheds tears
    on every face.
        —adapted from BEN SIRACH, *Ecclesiasticus*, 31 : 13

For learning, the eyes is less useful than the ear.
        —adapted from GERONDI

See also: FACE, TRUTH, VANITY

FACE

◆§ The worst informer is the face.

The face will betray a secret.

Troubles that don't show on your face lie on your heart.

He who shuts his eyes is hatching some scheme;
He who tightens his lips is planning some mischief.
        Book of Proverbs, 17 : 20

The face of one man is as different from the face of another as
    the thought of one from another.
        TALMUD: *Berakoth*, 58a

Looks explain words.
        —adapted from MOSES IBN EZRA, *Shirat Yisrael*

◆§ An ugly face is the best guardian of a woman's virtue.
        IMMANUEL OF ROME, *Mahberot*

See also: APPEARANCE, EARS, EYES

FAITH

⊷ I know the Lord will help—but help me, Lord, *until* you help.

Most sailors are religious: daily peril makes them so.

Truth is in your prayerbook.

⊷ What God does is best—probably.

Faith is shown in charity.

True faith needs neither evidence nor research.

If a thousand hasidim [pious men] gathered around a block of
wood, it, too, could work miracles.

⊷ God requires no synagogue—except in the heart.

Hasidic saying

The true proselyte is dearer to God than the Israelites were at
Mount Sinai: for had not the Israelites seen the thunder and
lightning, the quaking mountain and the sounding trumpets,
they would not have accepted the Torah; but the true proselyte, who saw none of these things, has surrendered to the
Holy One. Can anyone be dearer to God?

MIDRASH: Tanhuma

⊷ If the Greek gods steal, by whom shall their faithful swear?
APOCRYPHA: Ahikar, 8 : 22

Rivers full of water don't freeze as quickly as rivers with little
water. [The deeply learned will not "grow cold" to faith, as
the superficially learned may.] Zohar

God conceals Himself from our minds, but reveals Himself to our
hearts. —adapted from Zohar

⊷ With faith, there are no questions; without faith, there are
no answers. "THE CHOFETZ CHAIM"

A man should believe in God through faith, not because of miracles. NACHMAN OF BRATSLAV

Man must not rely on pure reason; he must mix faith with it.
                                        NACHMAN OF BRATSLAV

Better a superstitious believer than a rational unbeliever.
                                        NACHMAN OF BRATSLAV

Faith·is not only in the heart; it should be put into words.
                                        NACHMAN OF BRATSLAV

See also: FASTING, GOD, HERETICS, HOLINESS, MIRACLES, PRAYER, REA-
    SON, RELIGION, TRUTH

FALSEHOOD

God created everything except falsehood.

Half-truths are falsehoods.

Young liars turn into old thieves.

If you deal in falsehoods, perfect your memory.

᪥ Flattery grows into falsehood.

See also: DECEIT, FRAUD, HONESTY, LIARS/LIES, TRUTH

FAME

See: GLORY, GREAT MEN, HONOR, REPUTATION

FAMILY

Note. Pride of lineage is strong among Jews, but *yikhes* refers to
    more than pedigree, for *yikhes* must be earned as well as
    inherited. The crucial ingredients of *yikhes* are: learning, vir-
    tue, philanthropy, service to the community. One who does
    not live up to his family's past record swiftly "loses" his
    yikhes. The highest *yikhes* attaches to the man of learning.

Wealth or success never confer such *yikhes* on a family or its descendants as comes from the respect accorded knowledge. "All Jews are *mishpokhe*" means that Jews are one family: a common heritage, common obligations, common values. The state of Israel accepts, without exception, Jewish immigrants of the widest, sharpest cultural difference.

—L.R.

Blood never turns into water.

ఆ§ There are no praises and no blessings for those who are ashamed of their families.

ఆ§ A successful man's family always provides him with at least one *nukhshleper* [sycophant].

Measure your *mishpokhe* [relatives] not in length but in width.

A little hurt from one of your kin is worse than a big hurt from a stranger.

ఆ§ Before you marry a girl, study her brothers.

A nobleman worries about his horses and dogs, a Jew worries about his wife and children.

There are three partners in any man: God, his father, and his mother.

Look for the good, not the evil, in the conduct of members of the family.

Better a morsel of dry bread, with peace, than a house full of feasting, with strife.   *Book of Proverbs,* 17 : 1

An advantage over a kinsman is the worst kind of disadvantage.
                              APOCRYPHA II, *Maccabees,* 5 : 6

See also: ANCESTORS, BASTARDS, BROTHERS, CHILDREN, DAUGHTERS, DAUGHTERS-IN-LAW, FATHERS, MOTHERS, MOTHERS-IN-LAW, PARENTS, SONS, WIVES

FASTING

It's good to fast—with a chicken leg and a bottle of wine.

◦§ Our rabbi is so poor that if he didn't fast every Monday and Thursday, he'd starve to death.

It is good to fast—when the table is covered with fish.

Fasting is more effective than charity, for the latter is done with money, but the former can be done only by one's own person.
TALMUD: *Berakoth*, 32b

Do not fast in excess. [It weakens the capacity to perform good deeds.]   TALMUD: *Ta'anith*, 11a

See also: ABSTINENCE, ASCETICS/ASCETICISM, EXCESS, FAITH, FOOD and DRINK, WINE

FATE

◦§ When things don't get better, don't worry—they may get worse.

◦§ The man fated to drown will drown in a glass of water.

God is a father, fate is a stepfather.

What you can't avoid—welcome.

Even the biggest ball of twine unwinds.

There are two types of men: One who is first-rate, and fate made him last; the other who should be last, and fate put him first.
MOSES IBN EZRA, *Shirat Yisrael*

The man who ascribes things to accident sees a bird's nest and thinks it has no special purpose.
BAHYA BEN ASHER, *Kad ha-Kemah*

See also: ASTROLOGY, DEATH, DESTINY, FORTUNE, FUTURE, LUCK

FATHERS

❧ When a father helps a son, both smile; when a son must help
his father, both cry.

One may tell the truth—even to one's father.

It is better that the child cry than the father.

Fathers are always trying to make their sons good Jews; when will
they try to be good Jews instead of leaving the task to their
sons?

A father should be treated like a king.

A child should not sit in the place his father habitually uses.

❧ If in anger you push your wife or child away with one hand,
let the other bring them back to your heart.

No man in the world loves one more than one's father.

It is better to beg for bread than be dependent on your son.

Children's children are the crown of old men;
And fathers are the pride of their children.
                                                    Book of Proverbs, 17 : 6

The only time a son should disobey his father is if the father orders
him to commit a sin.   TALMUD, *Yebamoth*, 5b

Whoever teaches his son teaches not only his son but also his son's
son—and so on to the end of generations.
                                        TALMUD: *Kiddushin*, 30a

Should a father tell his son to throw gold into the sea, the son
should obey.   TALMUD: *Kiddushin*, 32a

❧ Even a rabbi should rise [in the presence of his pupils] when
his father enters.
                            —adapted from TALMUD: *Horayat*, 13b

He who raises a child is to be called its father, not the man who
   only gave it birth.   MIDRASH: *Exodus Rabbah,* 46 : 5

A father suffers for the troubles of his son.
                                        Midrash Sekhel Tov

It is because Esau respected his father that his descendants rule the
   world.   *Zohar*

Our sages recommended that a father should spend less than his
   means on food, up to his means on dress, and beyond his means
   for his wife and children.
                         MAIMONIDES: *Mishneh Torah,* Deot V

A man's father is his king.   *Pirke de Rabbi Eliezer,* 39

When a father is quick to lose his temper, his sons are fools.
                                        NACHMAN OF BRATSLAV

When a father complains that his son has taken to evil ways, what
   should he do? Love him more than ever.
                                             BAAL SHEM TOV

See also: ANCESTORS, CHILDREN, DAUGHTERS, FAMILY, MOTHERS,
PARENTS, SONS, WIVES

FEAR

⋙ When you have no choice, don't be afraid.

⋙ The man afraid of leaves should not enter a forest.

⋙ When the sheep are shorn, the lambs tremble.

⋙ Fear is the father of hate.

If a man carries his own lantern, he need not fear darkness.
                                             Hasidic saying

⋙ Fear only two: God, and the man who has no fear of God.
                                             Hasidic saying

◦§ Fear the man who fears you.   Hasidic saying

Obeying out of love is better than obeying out of fear.
RASHI, *Commentaries in the Pentateuch, Deuteronomy*

Whoever fears the Lord is afraid of nothing.
BEN SIRACH, *Ecclesiasticus*, 34 : 14

If you come near a king, you come near a lion:
Others will fear you, but your fear will be great, too.
HAI GAON, *Musar Haskel*

See also: **COURAGE, COWARDS, EXPERIENCE, GOD, RESIGNATION**

FEELINGS

See: **EMOTIONS**

FIGHTING

◦§ When a miller fights a chimneysweep, the miller gets black and
the chimneysweep gets white.

See also: **HATE, QUARRELS, VIOLENCE, WAR**

FLATTERY

◦§ If you can't love, learn how to flatter.

To flatter is to steal.

Flattery must lead to falsehoods.

A lying tongue brings destruction to itself; and a flattering mouth
works its own ruin.   *Book of Proverbs*, 26 : 28

He who reproves men will get more thanks in the end than he who
flatters them.   *Book of Proverbs*, 28 : 23

A man may flatter his wife for the sake of peace; his creditor, to get an extension; and his teacher, to get special attention.

Otsar Midrashim

Flattery leads to vulgarity; the flatterer is despised.

NACHMAN OF BRATSLAV

◦§ Flattery is unavoidable, needed by all men, so I may as well become a rabbi.   THE RUPSHITZER RABBI

Flattery is permissible only to promote peace.

THE KORETSER RABBI

See also: CRITICISM, DECEIT, LIARS/LIES, PRAISE

FOLKLORE

See: ADVICE, CIRCUMSTANCES, CUSTOMS, LAW, WISDOM

FOLLY

◦§ Of what use is wisdom, when folly reigns?

◦§ What's left over from the thief is spent on the fortune teller.

A stranger's folly produces laughter; your own creates shame.

◦§ It's folly to try to run past the moon.

Any man who understands his own foolishnesses is already a little wise.

◦§ A fool who wants to hang himself grabs a knife.

Wisdom may increase with the years, but so does folly.

Man does not commit a sin unless he is possessed by folly.

TALMUD: *Sotah,* 3a

See also: EGOTISM, FOOLS, IGNORANCE, ILLOGIC, INTELLIGENCE, MAN, NONSENSE, WISDOM/WISE MEN

FOOD AND DRINK

Note. Eating and drinking, to the ancient Hebrews, involved grave religious obligations and reinforced the idea of the Jews as a people "set apart," chosen by the Lord as "Mine . . ." (Leviticus). Strict dietary laws were believed to strengthen the dedication of a Jew to his role as one of God's instruments for the redemption of mankind.

Genesis 9 : 4 forbade the consuming of animal blood to all the seed of Noah. Moses, in Leviticus and Deuteronomy, forbade Jews to eat internal fat or suet, carrion, or the carcass of any animal that has died instead of having been slain in the ritual manner. The Talmud says forbidden foods "pollute the body and the soul." (Paul, in Acts 21 : 25, asked Christians to shun the blood of meat and the meat of strangled animals.)

For over 2000 years rabbis developed and refined an elaborate code of regulations concerning food. The ritualistic details became so minute that a major part of the rabbis' expertise lay in their mastery of the rules: what is proscribed and what permitted; when one food or another is allowed; how food must be prepared, how cooked, etc. An authorized slaughterer of animals, the *shokhet,* was and is still supervised by rabbis.

Whatever it was that originally prompted the taboo on pork was fortunate, for pork is the carrier of the parasites of trichinosis. Similarly, hepatitis has been traced to contaminated clams, which (even uncontaminated) are taboo to observing Jews.

Food taboos are quite common, of course, among the races of man: Egyptians ate no cow, bull, or cat (which were deities); Babylonians ate no birds of prey; Muslims are forbidden to eat pig—as are Borneans, Laplanders, Navajos or the Yakuts of Turkey. In many parts of Polynesia, the eel is taboo. Iranians will eat no scaleless or finless *pisces.* I could exhaust you with a more exhaustive catalogue of culinary taboos.

For a clear, simple explanation of the *kosher* laws, see Samuel H. Dresner, *The Jewish Dietary Laws: Their Meaning for Our Time*, including Seymour Siegel, *A Guide to Observance*, Burning Bush Press, New York, 1959.

—L.R.

FOOD .

ఆకి How just is our Lord: The rich He gives food—and the poor He gives appetite.

A man can forget absolutely everything—except to eat.

What is the proper time to eat? If rich, when you will; if poor, when you can.

Borsht and bread make your cheeks red.

ఆకి One man has no appetite for his food, while another has no food for his appetite.

Meat, not hay, makes the lion roar.

Only from your own table can you go away full.

Meat without salt is fit only for dogs.

At other people's parties, one eats heartily.

Anyone who eats in the street is like a dog.

If you eat pudding on the Sabbath, you'll be full all week.

ఆకి Soldiers become much smarter after eating.

More people die from overeating than from undernourishment.
TALMUD: *Shabbath*, 33a

ఆకి Miracles do occur, but they rarely provide food.
TALMUD: *Shabbath*, 53b

Food is better than drink up to the age of forty; after forty, drink is better. TALMUD: *Shabbath*, 152a

If you have a fine meal, enjoy it in a good light.
TALMUD: *Yomah*, 74b

❧ Feed your animals before you sit down to eat.

TALMUD: *Berakoth*, 40a

Man can live without spices, but not without wheat.

MIDRASH: *Psalms*, 2 : 16

Consider your table as a table before the Lord: Chew well and
hurry not.　　　　　　　　　　　　　　　　　　　　*Zohar*

Too much good food does more harm than too little bad food.

FALAQUERA, *Sefer ha-Mevakesh*

❧ Man eats to live; he does not live to eat.

ABRAHAM IBN EZRA, *Yesod Mora*

Food to a man is like oil to a lamp: If it has much, it shines, if too
little, it is quenched; yet a lamp is sooner extinguished by too
much oil than by too little.

The Testament of Judah Asheri

Eat sparingly and lengthen your life.

THE KORETSER RABBI

A man should eat slowly, properly, even if he eats alone.

NACHMAN OF BRATSLAV

Don't dance before you eat.　　　　　SHOLEM ALEICHEM

See also: EXCESS, GLUTTONY, MODERATION

FOOD: EATING AND DRINKING

❧ "For dust thou art, and unto dust shalt thou return"—in between, can a little drink hurt?

The rich eat when they want, the poor when they can.

Snatch and eat, snatch and drink, for this world is like a wedding.

TALMUD: *Erubin*, 54a

❧ Eat a third, drink a third, and leave a third of your stomach
empty; then, should anger seize you, there will be room for its
rage.　　　　　　　—adapted from TALMUD: *Gittin*, 70a

If a man eats and drinks only to satisfy himself, that is not praiseworthy: He should eat and drink to preserve life, in order to
serve his Creator.

JOSEPH CARO, *Shulhan Aruk*

You cannot pursue knowledge without eating and drinking; if men
engaged only in the pursuit of knowledge, the human species
would die out.   SAADIA GAON

To eat and drink much does not enlarge the understanding; the
opposite is achieved.

—adapted from MAIMONIDES, *Responsa* II : 39a

See also: DRUNKARDS, EXCESS, GLUTTONY, TEMPERANCE, WINE

FOOLS

◄§ A fool can ask more questions in an hour than ten wise men
can answer in a year.

◄§ That fools are fond of sweets is a discovery of the wise.

◄§ A fool who wants to hang himself grabs a knife.

When a fool goes to market, the merchants rejoice.

◄§ A fool has to figure out how to find a notch in a saw.

One fool can buy more than ten wise men can sell.

Never show a fool half-completed work.

Don't ask a fool a question—or give him an explanation.

A fool needs many shoes.

◄§ Drunkards sober up, but fools remain fools.

God protects fools—who else?

If he were not my fool, I'd be laughing, too.

A fool forgets the first blow by the time you raise the stick for the
second.

∾ A fool measures water with a sieve.

∾ If you send a fool to close the shutters, he'll close them all over town.

When a fool laughs, he raises his voice.

Were you to grind him up in a mortar, he'd say you were after the pepper.

∾ If a fool says nothing, you can't tell whether he's a fool or a sage.

∾ Whatever is on a fool's mind is on his tongue.

∾ Don't approach a goat from the front, a horse from the back, or a fool from any side.

When the Messiah comes, all the sick will be healed—but fools will stay fools.

The biggest cripple of all is the fool.

Fools need not be sown; they sprout by themselves.

Fools don't get gray.

Fools search always for yesterday.

There is no remedy for a fool.

∾ Why is it that fools generally have pretty wives?

Fools don't seem to age.

∾ You can educate a fool but you can't make him think.

A dead man is mourned for seven days, a fool is mourned for a lifetime.

God gave fools hands and feet—and let them run.

∾ Foolishness sometimes succeeds, but it is still foolishness.

Every village has its idiot.

◆§ A fool if rich is treated like a lord.

A fool is a fool forever.

We laugh at strange fools, but are ashamed of our own.

◆§ In a fool, the tongue is superfluous.

The worst fool is clever for himself.

From a fool, what do you get? Trouble.

You can tell an ass by his long ears, a fool by his long tongue.

◆§ A fool can be an expert—on other fools.

◆§ When you praise a fool, you water his folly.

Even a fool sometimes says something clever.

One fool makes many fools.

If all men were fools, they wouldn't be known as fools.

You'll find sense in a fool when you see an ass mount a ladder.

A half-fool may be a real sage.

A fool can't be questioned—or explained.

Fools, like weeds, flourish without rain.

If you keep quiet, you're half a fool; if you talk, you're a whole fool.

Dare not do business with fools.

◆§ Only a fool or a genius rushes into print.

◆§ The biggest foolishness of the fool is this: he thinks he's smart.

To try to be smarter than everybody is the greatest foolishness.

A fool is his own informer.

The world is a pleasant place—for fools.

He who has little in his head, must have plenty in his feet. [Fools
    run fast.]

❧ A fool complains of the cold in July.

Never be offended by a fool.

The only thing you can do with idiots and thorns is get rid of them.

❧ The fools who sing all summer weep all winter.

The wicked can't conceal his wickedness, nor the fool his folly.

Who is a fool? He who sleeps in a cemetery.
TALMUD: Hagigah, 3b

The world is in the hands of fools.   TALMUD: Sanhedrin, 46b

A fool is worse than a bastard—if the bastard is wise.
TALMUD J.: Kiddushin, 4 : 11

The pious fool sees a child drowning and says, "As soon as I take
    off my phylacteries, I'll save him"; while he does so, the child
    drowns.   TALMUD J.: Sotah, 3 : 4

A fool considers his ways right.   Book of Proverbs, 12 : 15

Understanding is a wellspring of life unto him that hath it: but the
    instruction of fools is folly.   Book of Proverbs, 16 : 11

Of what use is money in the hand of a fool:
To buy wisdom, when he has no sense?
Book of Proverbs, 17 : 16

When a fool holds his tongue, he too is thought clever.
Book of Proverbs, 17 : 28

A whip for the horse, a bridle for the ass, and a rod for the back of
    fools.   Book of Proverbs, 26 : 3

Answer not a fool according to his folly, lest you become like him.
Book of Proverbs, 26 : 4

Like a stick brandished by a drunkard is a parable in the mouth of
   fools.   *Book of Proverbs*, 26 : 9

As a dog returns to his vomit, a fool repeats his folly.
                                           Book of Proverbs, 26 : 11

A stone is heavy, and sand is weighty; but a fool's vexation is
   heavier than both.   *Book of Proverbs*, 27 : 3

He cuts off his feet who sends a message by a fool.
                                           Book of Proverbs, 26 : 6

Better be met by a bear robbed of her cubs than by a fool in his
   folly.   *Book of Proverbs*, 17 : 12

A fool thinks everyone else is a fool.
                               MIDRASH: *Ecclesiastes Rabbah*, 10

A parable from a fool is worthless, because he tells it at the wrong
   time.   BEN SIRACH, *Ecclesiasticus*, 20 : 20

The head of a fool is like a broken dish; it will not hold knowledge.
                             BEN SIRACH, *Ecclesiasticus*, 21 : 14

❧ The talk of a fool is like a heavy pack on a journey.
                             BEN SIRACH, *Ecclesiasticus*, 21 : 16

To a fool, wisdom is like a ruined house.
                             BEN SIRACH, *Ecclesiasticus*, 21 : 18

To the fool, instruction is chains on his feet.
                             BEN SIRACH, *Ecclesiasticus*, 21 : 19

❧ Teaching a fool is like gluing a broken pot.
                             BEN SIRACH, *Ecclesiasticus*, 22 : 7

The love of a fool is only a transient whim.
                                                    RABBENU TAM

It is easier to tolerate a whole fool than a half-fool—that is, a fool
   who tries to act clever.   IBN GABIROL, *Choice of Pearls*

Beware of the fool who is pious.
                                   IBN GABIROL, *Choice of Pearls*

Man does not live in peace, except for fools: they love tranquillity.
MOSES CHEFETZ, *Mlehet Mahshevet*

When a fool talks, he grinds much and produces little.
SHOLEM ALEICHEM

FOOLS AND WISE MEN

A fool says what he knows, a sage knows what he says.

⋑ Two kinds of men are always embarrassed: a fool among wise men, and a wise man among fools.

⋑ When a wise man talks to a fool, two fools are conversing.

What embitters the wise cheers up the foolish.

With the wise, the older the wiser; with the ignorant, the older the more foolish.

⋑ A blow from a sage is better than a kiss from a fool.

What one fool can spoil, ten sages can't fix.

⋑ If a fool keeps his mouth shut, he sounds like a sage.

A fool can throw a stone into a well—and a hundred wise men can't recover it.

One fool can ask more questions than ten wise men can answer.

When a fool holds a cow by the horns, a wise man can milk her.

The fool who, ashamed, hides his ignorance is better than the *khokhem* [wise man] who parades his wisdom.

Better to be in Gehenna [Hell] with a wise man than in *Gan Eden* [Paradise] with a fool.

A fool takes two steps where a wise man takes none.

The wise man eats to live; the fool lives to eat.

It is better to lose to a wise man than win from a fool.

Better a fool who has traveled than a wise man who remained home.

A fool loses, a smart man finds.

The wise man conceals his intelligence; the fool reveals his foolishness.

Of what use is wisdom when folly reigns?

He who walks with wise men will become smart; but the companion of fools will smart for it.
> —adapted from *Book of Proverbs*, 13 : 20

A fool's ways are right in his own eyes, but a wise man listens to advice.   —adapted from *Book of Proverbs*, 12 : 15

◆§ Give the wise a wink, the fool a fist.
> MIDRASH: *Midrash Proverbs*

A fool laughs, but a wise man smiles.
> BEN SIRACH, *Ecclesiasticus*, 21 : 20

◆§ The wise reports what he saw, the fool what he heard.
> HASDAI, *Ben ha-Melekh ve-ha-Nazir*

Wise men are pleased when they discover truth, fools when they discover falsehood.   IBN GABIROL, *Choice of Pearls*

Man is wise only while he searches for wisdom; if he thinks he has found it, he is a fool.
> IBN GABIROL, *Choice of Pearls*

See also: **FOLLY, ILLOGIC, ILLUSION, MAN: HUMAN TYPES, NEBEKH, SHLEMIELS, WISDOM, WISE MEN**

FORESIGHT

Better ask the way ten times than get lost once.

◆§ The man who lives without a plan will die without a shroud.

Fortune is more powerful than foresight.

◈ If you sing all summer, you'll weep in winter.

◈ When you go to a restaurant, choose a table near a waiter.

Better an egg today than a chicken tomorrow.

Don't throw away the dirty before you have the clean.

◈ Better measure ten times before you cut, or you may have to cut ten times before you measure.

Don't throw stones into the well from which you drink.

Woe to him who makes a door before he has a house, or builds a gate and has no yard.   TALMUD: *Shabbath*, 31b

If you don't plow in summer, what will you eat in winter?
                              MIDRASH: *Midrash Proverbs*

◈ A wealthy Jew fell sick; and when near death he asked a scribe to write his last will and testament, dictating these clauses: "To the faithful slave who brings this document and all my wealth, I leave all my property. To my only son, in Judea, I leave any one thing he may choose out of all my possessions." The slave returned with all the wealth of his dead master and showed the will to a rabbi, who said to the Jew's son: "If your father had left everything to you, the slave would have fled with the wealth; now he has brought everything safely to you, and you may choose *him,* according to the will: for all the property of a slave belongs to his master."
                —adapted from MIDRASH: *Tanhuma Bereshit*

Before a wise man ventures into a pit, he lowers a ladder—so that he can climb out.   SAMUEL HA-NAGID, *Ben Mishle*

◈ Plan for this world as if you expect to live forever; but plan for the hereafter as if you expect to die tomorrow.
                              IBN GABIROL, *Choice of Pearls*

See also: CAUSE AND EFFECT, CAUTION, CONFLICT, FORTUNE, JUDG-MENT, LUCK, MISFORTUNE, PRUDENCE

FORGETTING

٤ Men can forget anything—except when to eat.

What is learned in one's youth is not easily forgotten.

٤ Memory and teeth grow weaker with time.

If not for our ability to forget, we would never be free from grief.
—adapted from BAHYA IBN PAQUDA, *Duties of the Heart*, 2 : 5

In two years, a man can forget what it took him twenty to learn.
Abot de Rabbi Nathan, 24 : 6

See also: CAUSE AND EFFECT, LEARNING, MEMORY

FORGIVENESS

Those who want to be forgiven must learn to forgive.

٤ If you take revenge, you will regret it; if you forgive, you will rejoice.

Regard as enormous the little wrong you did to others, and as trifling the great wrong done to you.
TALMUD: *Derekh Erets Zuta* 1 : 29

One who is begged for forgiveness should not be so cruel as not to forgive.
RASHI, *Commentaries on the Pentateuch, Numbers*

Forgive the man who has done you ill, and give to the man who has refused you.
SAADIA GAON

Learn to receive blows, and to forgive those who insult you.
Abot de Rabbi Nathan, 41

See also: COMPASSION, GOD, GOOD DEEDS, JUDGMENT, JUSTICE

FORTITUDE

◦§ When you have no choice, at least be brave.

◦§ Pray that you will never have to suffer all that you are able to endure.

Fortitude is enlarged by food.

The man who cannot survive bad times will not see good times.
                                        Hasidic saying

If you carry your own lantern, you will endure the dark.
                                        Hasidic saying

See also: COURAGE, ENDURANCE, FREEDOM, STRENGTH, VALOR

FORTUNE

When fortune calls, quick!—offer her a chair.

One ounce of fortune is worth a pound of forecast.

◦§ From fortune to misfortune is but the span of a hand; but from misfortune to fortune is an immensity.

When thieves fall out, the peasant keeps his cow.

Fortune is a wheel that turns with great speed.

◦§ The fortune of this world is like a wheel with two buckets: the full becomes empty and the empty becomes full.

◦§ The man who does not rely on fortune postpones misfortune.
                              TALMUD: *Berakoth,* 64a

Show not your power in a time of might, for fortune is given to flight.   IBN GABIROL, *Choice of Pearls*

See also: FATE, FUTURE, GAMBLING, GOLD, HAPPINESS, LUCK, MISFORTUNE, POWER

FRAUD

Fraud with words is worse than with money.

You may defraud others, from a distance; but close up, you defraud
yourself.

It's not hard to cheat successfully—once.

Bread won by fraud tastes sweet to a man;
But afterwards his mouth will be filled with gravel.
                                             Book of Proverbs, 20 : 17

See also: CONSCIENCE, DECEIT, FALSEHOOD, LAW, LIARS/LIES, SIN

FREEDOM

❧ Thought is a universe of freedom.

❧ A slave is a free man if he is content with his lot; a free man is
a slave if he seeks more than that.

To be too proud is to be in a prison.

❧ The only free man is the one who studies Torah.
                                             Sayings of the Fathers, 6 : 2

Freedom is the world of joy.   NACHMAN OF BRATSLAV

To be immobile is to be in chains.
                                             MOSES IBN EZRA, *Shirat Yisrael*

See also: DEMOCRACY, EQUALITY, GOVERNMENT, LAW, MASSES, PRISON,
POLITICS, POWER

FRIENDS/FRIENDSHIP

❧ If you can't help a friend with money, at least give a *krekhts*
[sigh].

⋙ The man who seeks a faultless friend will remain friendless.

One enemy is too many; and a hundred friends are not enough.

⋙ It's not good to be alone—even in Paradise.

⋙ One's best friend is in the mirror.

Descend a step in taking a wife; ascend a step in choosing a friend.

A big blow from a stranger hurts less than a small blow from a friend.

⋙ The man who has no money to lend friends makes no enemies.

Better one old friend than two new ones.

A friend you get for nothing, an enemy you have to pay for.

Men become like those they associate with.

Old friends, like old wine, don't lose their flavor.

Better one friend with a dish of food than a hundred with a gripe.

⋙ We all remain better friends—at a slight distance.

With a glass of wine, you can find many friends.

It's good to eat with a friend, but not from one plate.

⋙ Your friend has a friend—so tell him no secrets.

Friendship is stronger than kinship.

⋙ If your friend is honey, don't lick him up altogether.

Many crowd the gate of abundance but even friends pass the door of misery.

One is none. [It is better to have others than be alone.]

⋙ Man can eat alone, but not work alone.

You can't patch up a torn friendship.

Sometimes a good friend is better than a brother.

◦§ The man who thinks he can live without others is mistaken; the one who thinks others can't live without him is even more deluded. Hasidic saying

If two logs are dry and one is wet, the kindling of the two will kindle the wet one, too.
TALMUD: *Sanhedrin,* 93b

◦§ My friend is he who will tell me my faults, in private.
IBN GABIROL, *Choice of Pearls*

A man without friends is like a left hand without a right.
IBN GABIROL, *Choice of Pearls*

Do not give your love to a friend all at once.
IBN GABIROL, *Choice of Pearls*

The meek becomes known in anger, the hero in war, and a friend in time of need. IBN GABIROL, *Choice of Pearls*

There are three types of friends: those like food, without which you can't live; those like medicine, which you need occasionally; and those like an illness, which you never want.
IBN GABIROL

Were I to break off with friends who sin, I would be friendless.
—adapted from IBN GABIROL

A good friend is a tower of strength; to find one is to find a treasure.
BEN SIRACH: *Ecclesiasticus,* 6 : 14

◦§ Question a friend: perhaps he did not say what you think, or if he did, so that he will not say it again.
BEN SIRACH: *Ecclesiasticus,* 19 : 14

Do not condemn your friend: you do not know what you would have done in his place.
HILLEL, in *Sayings of the Fathers,* 2 : 5

It is better to have a friend in the market place than gold in the coffer. LEONE DA MODENA

◦§ Your best friend is the one who is a friend without expecting anything.   LEONE DA MODENA

A man has three friends: his sons, his wealth, and his good deeds.
                                    Pirke de Rabbi Eliezer, 34

Friendship: one heart in two bodies.
                    IBN ZABARA, *Book of Delight*, ch. 7

A real friend feels no need to excuse himself for some failing.
                                    THE LUBLINER RABBI

To pull a friend out of the mire, don't hesitate to get dirty.
                                    BAAL SHEM TOV

See also: DECEIT, ENEMY, FALSE FRIENDS, FAMILY, HATE, NEIGHBORS, WEALTH

FRIENDS: FALSE FRIENDS

◦§ The good fellow to everyone is a good friend to no one.

Some friends remain friends only up to the pocket.

◦§ The man who takes offense for no reason gets friendly for no reason.

When you have a pretty wife, you are a bad friend.

A false friend is worse than a dog.

The man who puts a friend to public shame is as guilty as a murderer.

◦§ False friends are like migratory birds; they fly away in cold weather.   Hasidic saying

People treat each other in a friendly fashion—when times are good.
                    MIDRASH: *Genesis Rabbah*, 9 : 5

Stay away from your enemies, but guard yourself against friends.
                    BEN SIRACH: *Ecclesiasticus*, 6 : 13

See also: DECEIT, ENEMY, FAMILY

FUNCTION

See: CAUSE AND EFFECT, UTILITY

FUTURE

 Yesterday is your past; today is your future—because your tomorrow is unknown.

See also: DEATH, FATE, FORTUNE, HEREAFTER, LIFE

G

GAMBLING

Sick men need not be gamblers, but congenital gamblers are sick.

Gamblers show no mercy when gambling.

Gambling is an obsession.

Those who don't rely on luck lessen their bad luck.

See also: BUSINESS, FORTUNE, LUCK, MONEY, SIN

GEHENNA

See: HELL

GENEROSITY

◦§ The man who gives little with a smile gives more than the man who gives much with a frown.

◦§ Give with a warm hand, not a cold one [i.e., in your will].

The generous man will be enriched;
And he who waters will himself be watered.
                                    Book of Proverbs, 11 : 25

Be grateful to your benefactors, even though their generosity is not without self-interest: to gain status, or a place in the world to come.   —adapted from BAHYA IBN PAQUDA

The truly wise are as liberal with their wisdom as clouds are with their rain.   MOSES IBN EZRA, *Shirat Israel*

See also: CHARITY, GOOD DEEDS, GRATITUDE, PHILANTHROPY

GENTILES

Note. We must be careful not to confuse the Jews' use of the word "goy" ("gentile") with the word "Christian." Very often, a Jewish proverb meant to criticize *heathens* has been translated as if it is anti-Christian. The barbs of the Jews about *goyim* were often directed against pagans, not Christians; against barbarians, not Greeks; against those who practiced savagery, idolatry, licentious rites. Many folk-sayings about *goyim* preceded Christianity.

An old rabbinical saying goes: "The righteous of all nations will share in the world to come." The great Rashi reminded Jews that "Gentiles of the present age are not heathens." The *Sefer Hasidim* ("Book of the Pious") says: "If a Jew attempts to kill a non-Jew, help the non-Jew."

Respect for others, woven into the values of pluralism, forms an old and integral part of Jewish tradition. The rabbis taught: "Whether Jew or gentile, man or woman, rich or poor —according to a man's deeds does God's Presence rest on him."

The highest traditional contempt of Jews is reserved for those who are cruel, uncivilized, or unlearned; those who hurt, torment, exploit, or kill others.

Yet it would be dishonest to deny that relentless persecution, century after century, in nation after nation, has left Jews a legacy of bitter sayings: "*Dos ken nor a goy*" ("That only a *goy* is capable of doing"); "*A goy blaybt a goy*" ("A gentile remains a gentile," or, less literally, "What did you expect: once an anti-Semite, always an anti-Semite").

Experience is a bitter teacher, and it made many Jews feel that gentiles are not always gentle.

—L.R.

Gentiles aren't used to Jewish troubles.

God says: "Both the gentiles and the Israelites are My handiwork: Can I let the former perish on account of the latter?"
TALMUD: *Sanhedrin,* 98b

The Jew is urged to aid gentiles in administering the affairs of his community.　　　　TALMUD J.: *Gittin,* 5 : 9

If a non-Jew blesses you, respond "Amen," for it is written: "Thou shalt be blessed by all peoples."
TALMUD J.: *Berakoth,* 8b

For a Jew to cheat a gentile is worse than to cheat a Jew, for in addition to breaking the moral law, it brings Jews into contempt.　　　　TALMUD, *Baba Kama,* 113b

◆§ If you permit your tongue to speak evil of gentiles, it will end by speaking evil of Israelites.
MIDRASH: *Deuteronomy Rabbah,* 6 : 3

See also: COMPASSION, DUTY, JEWS

GIRLS

Note. The position of the girl in the family, the assumptions of what her duties and future duties as a wife would be, the physiological determinants and limits of female work, menstruation, pregnancy, breast feeding, the care of babies, the subordinate social status of girls—all these show great similarity in most of the cultures and tribes of antiquity. Farming, stock tending, nomadic life, the division of labor that automatically assigned cooking, feeding, the care of the young to the female (and hunting, heavy labor, war, defense, etc., to the male)—all these, despite some conspicuous exceptions, explain a good deal about the status of women in religious hierarchies, in pre-industrial society, in medieval court circles, in the working and middle classes produced in post-agrarian societies.

But the particular rights and protections given Jewish girls (female orphans, e.g., were required by law to be helped before males—so that girls would never be forced to beg) are too often misconstrued by historians, and can only be understood in the context of those facts and laws of Jewish life that governed family relations. For a brief description of this background, see the headnote for WOMEN.

—L.R.

A baby girl is a good omen.

❦ The girl who can't dance says the band can't keep time.

❦ An ugly girl hates the mirror.

If everybody looks for a pretty bride, what happens to the ugly girls?

❦ It is easier to guard a sack of fleas than a girl in love.

❦ Homely girls are easily seduced.

Jews have no nunneries.

With nets you catch birds, with presents—girls.

❦ When a girl has no other virtues, a freckle can be considered one.

A maiden is like velvet—fondle her.

It is not wise to borrow from a poor man—or kiss an ugly girl.

All girls lap up sweet words.

Girls should marry before boys do, for the shame of a woman is greater than the shame of a man.

Talmud: *Kethuboth*, 67b

Help the girl orphan before the boy orphan; the boy may beg, but not the girl.   —adapted from Talmud: *Kethuboth*, 67b

Little girl, don't be so sweet—lest you be consumed.

Yemenite proverb

Go understand a girl: she can't wait for the wedding, yet weeps on the way to the canopy.   Sholem Aleichem

See also: DAUGHTERS, MEN AND WOMEN

GIVING AND TAKING

The man who likes to take does not like to give.

⋗ Lend before witnesses, but give without them.

If you put something in, there is something to take out.

If you are given, take; if someone else takes, cry "Help!"

Let not your hand be stretched out to take, and withdrawn at the time of giving back.   Ben Sirach: *Ecclesiasticus*, 4 : 31

See also: CHARITY, GENEROSITY, GREED, JEALOUSY, PHILANTHROPY

GLORY

Too much glory can be half disgrace.

Honor is more precious than glory.

⋗ Any man surrounded by dwarfs looks like a giant.

Glory avoids those who chase after it, and is endowed on many who did not try to pursue it.

❧ Good men need no monuments: their acts remain their shrines.
—adapted from *Mishneh Shekalim,* 5 : 2

See also: HONOR AND HONORS

GLUTTONY

The eye is small, but can devour all.

❧ Those who have wide mouths have narrow hearts.

One beggar can't be at two fairs.

One man can't eat with two mouths.

The glutton for cake often loses the bread.

What a fat belly cost, I wish I had; what a fat belly does, I wish on my enemies.

Gluttons dig their graves with their teeth.

The man who increases his flesh increases food for the worms.
Sayings of the Fathers, 2 : 8

If you feel driven to eat, get up in the middle of a meal—and stop.   BEN SIRACH: *Ecclesiasticus,* 31 : 21

The glutton is like a dog who is never satiated; he becomes disgusting to everyone and, being subject to diarrhea, his body becomes like a sieve . . .   SAADIA GAON

Heavy eating is worse than daggers.   JUDAH BEN ASHER

More men die from overeating than undernourishment.
NACHMAN OF BRATSLAV

See also: EXCESS, FOOD, GREED, WINE

GOD

Note. The following tale is to be found in the *Baba Mezi'a* tractate of the Jerusalem Talmud:

> When a certain rabbi went to Rome, he chanced to find a jeweled bracelet that belonged to the Empress. An official crier went about proclaiming: "Whoever returns the Empress's bracelet within thirty days shall receive a reward; but if it be found upon him after thirty days—his head will be cut off."
>
> The rabbi returned the bracelet on the thirty-first day. The Empress asked him: "Did you not hear my proclamation?"
>
> "Yes," answered the rabbi.
>
> "Then why did you not return the jewel within the thirty days?"
>
> "In order," said the rabbi, "that you should not say that I feared you; I returned it because I fear God."
>
> Whereupon the Empress said, "Blessed be the God of the Jews."
>
> —L.R.

See GOD and MAN, GOD: WHERE DOTH HE RESIDE?, GOD: HIS POWER, GOD: COMPLAINTS ABOUT, GOD: IN HIS BEHALF

GOD'S NAME

Note. Four Hebrew letters, YHVH (which appear 6,823 times in the Old Testament), form the Hebrew name for God: *Adonai* is a substitute for these sacred letters. *Adonai* is never pronounced by pious Jews except during solemn prayer, and with head covered. When God is mentioned in ordinary discourse, a devout Jew changes even the substitute names: instead of *"Adonai"* he says *"Adoshem";* when saying *"Elohim"* he makes it *"Elokhim."* Orthodox Jews, writing or printing the name of the Lord, omit the vowel, to make G-d.

We do not know how YHVH was pronounced by the ancients: There are no vowel letters in Hebrew; vowel *sounds* are indicated by diacritical marks (dots, dashes). Today, YHVH is rendered vocally as "Yahveh." ("Jehovah," which first appeared in Christian texts in 1516, is simply incorrect—

based on a German papal scribe's reading of YHVH with the diacritical marks meant for *Adonai,* which had been added in the margins of a scroll, as aids to pronunciation; so YHVH became, in transliterated Latin, YeHoVaH.) The King James version of the Bible usually translates YHVH as "Lord."

—L.R.

GOD AND MAN

⋙ Truth rests with God alone—and a little with me.

When God does a favor, He doesn't boast about it.

Before God, weep; before people, laugh.

The rainbow is a sign that God has forgiven us.

⋙ God is closest to those whose hearts are broken.

Man reaches God through truth.

No one ever lost anything to God.

When God gives bread, men provide butter.

⋙ God waits long, but He pays with interest.

We get life from God, but make a living from men.

Dear God: Save me from having but one shirt, one eye, or one child.

Of God's purpose, one should not ask questions.

⋙ God punishes; it is man who takes revenge.

About tomorrow, let God worry.

Man needs woman, woman needs man, and both need God.

⋙ Some don't believe in God, yet ask His mercy.

God sends the remedy before the disease.

God punishes with one hand—but blesses with the other.

❧ Don't try to bargain with the Lord.

We don't know what to thank God for.

He who gave us teeth will give us bread.

It is better to receive from God by the spoonful than from man by the bushel.

What God does not choose to give, you cannot take.

God has no riches of his own; it's what he takes from one that he gives to another.

The spirit of God is pleased with one whom the spirit of man finds pleasing.

When we are young, God forgives our stumblings; when we mature, God weighs our works; when we grow old, God waits— for our repentance.

❧ Oh God: Spare us what we can learn to endure.

❧ Oh Lord, give me a good excuse.

There is no mediator between God's children and God.
                                    TALMUD J.: *Berakoth*, 9 : 1

Keep me as the apple of Thine eye, and hide me under the shadow of Thy wings.   *Book of Psalms*, 17 : 8

God loves these three: the one who does not get angry; the one who does not get drunk; and the one who does not insist upon his privileges.   TALMUD: *Pesahim*, 113a

Lord of the world, rather a bitter olive given by Thee than sweets provided by man.   TALMUD: *Sanhedrin*, 108b

❧ To love God truly, you must first love man. And if anyone tells you that he loves God but does not love his fellow man, he is lying.   Hasidic saying

His glory is on me—and mine on Him. *Hymn of Glory*

A broken and contrite heart, Oh God, [do] not despise.
Book of Psalms, 51 : 17

He who hears himself cursed and remains silent becomes a partner of God—for does not the Lord hear nations blame Him, yet remain silent. MIDRASH: *Psalms*, 86 : 1

☙ If God really loved man, would He have created him?

Who displeases man displeases God.
Sayings of the Fathers, 3 : 10

☙ If the [Greek] gods steal, by whom shall their believers swear?
APOCRYPHA: *Ahikar*, 8 : 22

Lord, be Thou neither against us nor for us!
BAR KOCHBA, before going into battle;
in TALMUD J.: *Ta'anith*, 4 : 6

He who flees from God flees into himself. PHILO

☙ God: Make an opening for me no wider than a needle's eye, and I will open for you a gate through which armies can pass.
Pesikta de Rabbi Kahana

God gave man the power to reason, which makes man capable of perfection. MAIMONIDES, *Guide to the Perplexed*, 1 : 2

Reason is the mediator between God and man.
ABRAHAM IBN EZRA, *Comentary to Pentateuch*

Man was created to serve God and to cleave to Him, not to accumulate wealth and erect buildings which he must leave behind. IBN EZRA, *Yesod Mora*

As man acts, God reacts. BAAL SHEM TOV

I don't want to know why I suffer, but whether it is for Thy sake.
THE BERDICHEVER RABBI

It is my desire to do God's will, not that God do my will.
THE GERER RABBI

When young, remember that service to the Lord is like food—
best when fresh; and when old, remember that service to God
is like wine—best when old.   THE KOBRINER RABBI

Don't ask God for what you think is good; ask Him for what he
thinks is good for you.   "THE CHOFETZ CHAIM"

⁓§ God will forgive me: *c'est son métier* ["it's his business"].
                                              HEINRICH HEINE

See also: HELL, HEREAFTER, HEREDITY, HERETICS, HOLINESS, MAR-
RIAGE, WOMEN

GOD:—WHERE DOTH HE RESIDE?

God said: Wherever you find the mark of a man's foot, there I
am revealed to you.

⁓§ The favorite place of God is in the heart of man.

Have not I commanded thee: Be strong and of good courage; be
not affrighted, neither be thou dismayed: for the Lord thy
God is with thee whithersoever thou goest.
                                    Book of Joshua, 1 : 9

Oh burning bush: Not because you are tall, but because you are
lowly, did God reveal Himself in you.
                                    TALMUD: *Shabbath*, 67a

⁓§ God conceals himself from man's mind, but reveals himself to
his heart.   *Zohar*

Thou art far, farther than the heaven of heavens, and near, nearer
than my body is to me. BAHYA BEN ASHER, *Kad ha-Kemah*

⁓§ A house testifies that there was a builder, a dress that there
was a weaver, a door that there was a carpenter; so our World
by its existence proclaims its Creator, God.
     —adapted from RABBI AKIBA, *Midrash Temura*, ch. 3

GOD: HIS POWER

He who took care of the parents will also provide for the children.

◆§ God is not kind to those who are not kind to others.

◆§ Were God to will it, a broom would shoot.

Only God can judge.

Man drives, but it is God who holds the reins.

If God doesn't approve, a fly doesn't move.

God gives nothing for nothing.

◆§ Man makes plans; God changes them.

God does not bargain, nor does He change.

Whom God would punish, he sends bad children.

God sends the frost according to the clothes.

◆§ Rome's Hebrew elders were asked, "If your God takes no pleasure in the worship of idols, why does He not destroy them?" The Hebrews replied, "If men worshipped what the world does not need, God would have destroyed them; but men worship the sun, the moon, the stars, the planets; is God then to destroy His world because of the fools?"

The Roman replied, "Then He ought to destroy the things the world does not need, and leave the others." To which the Hebrew elders said, "Then the worshippers of the stars, sun, and moon would be strengthened in their idolatry, for they would say, 'Behold, these verily are true gods, for they have not been destroyed.'"

—adapted from TALMUD: *'Abodah Zarah*, 54b

Everything is in God's hands, except the fear of God.

TALMUD: *Berakoth*, 32b

◦§ When we appear before His Throne, God will not ask, "Have you believed in God?" but "Have you dealt honorably with your fellow men?"

—adapted from TALMUD: *Shabbath*, 3a

God is long-suffering, but He collects His due.

TALMUD J.: *Ta'anith*, 2 : 1

◦§ Wherever you find man's footprints, there God was before you.

Mekilta to Exodus, 17 : 6

A day in the mind of God is like a millennium in the reckoning of man.   *Book of Psalms*, 90 : 4

The ways of man are pure in his own eyes; but the Lord weighs the motives.   *Book of Proverbs*, 16 : 2

◦§ God left unfinished the north corner of the world, saying: "Whoever claims to be a god, let him complete that."

Pirke de Rabbi Eliezer, ch. 3

God is everywhere, even in evil thoughts.

THE KORETSER RABBI

GOD: COMPLAINTS ABOUT

Note. One of the most interesting, surprising, and (to me) endearing aspects of the attitude of Jews to the Lord is the candor of their complaints about Him: grievances phrased with such tact, felicity, irony or wit that they manage to stop just this side of the sacrilegious.

To be both pious and critical, loving and sardonic, fearful and unafraid, respectful and indignant, represents a most delicate and sophisticated feat.

I think that the complaints against the Lord are managed without guilt, which is the most remarkable aspect of all, because believing Jews hold that:

(a) God made a covenant with the Hebrews, according to the Holy Torah;

(b) a contract requires responsible performance from both

sides, however vast the disparity in the status, virtue or power of the contracting parties;

(c) reciprocal responsibility justifies a complaint by either party about the imperfect conduct or nonperformance of the other;

(d) the relation between a Jew and the Lord is one-to-one, since the entire structure of the Jewish faith rests on the assertion, in the Talmud, that there are no mediators, no intermediaries, between God and man (rabbis are not agents of the Lord);

(e) since Jews hold that God gave each man a Conscience, by which to decide for himself whether to observe His commandments or not; and Reason, through which to analyze everything under the sun; and Free Will, which contains the capacity to err, sin or blaspheme (and take the consequences), Jews simply exercise these God-given gifts to the full;

(f) the Lord of the Universe is surely far too great, kind, just and all-knowing to mind little man's efforts to lighten life's burdens by the play and pleasure of levity, for—

(g) it would be a humorless, therefore imperfect, God who did not understand the preciousness of laughter in a world so laden with suffering and tragedy.

What I am trying to explain may come down to the simple fact that a robust people, if not their solemn pedants, simply take it for granted that God has a sense of humor, too. How else could He put up with *His* problems?

—L.R.

❧ Dear God, You help strangers, so why not me?

❧ "Thou hast chosen us from among all the nations"—but why did you have to pick on the Jews?

God will provide—but if only He would provide *until* He provides.

❧ If God lived on earth, people would knock out all His windows.

❧ Don't question God, for He may reply: "If you're so anxious for answers, come up here."

O, Lord: glance down from heaven and take a good look at Your world.

Don't play games with God—first, because you shouldn't; second, because He won't let you.

ఇ§ Dear God, help me get up: I can fall down by myself.

God loves the poor, but He helps the rich.

ఇ§ What God does is best—probably.

Whom God loves, He punishes.

Man thinks, and God laughs.

Father in heaven, You don't have to raise me up, but don't throw me down.

God pays well, but He is often in arrears.

ఇ§ God, if you don't help me, I'll ask my uncle in America.

GOD: COMPLAINTS IN HIS BEHALF

ఇ§ Men fear the gallows more than God.

If only Man were worth as much as God can give.

There is only one God—and so many enemies.

God made Man in three stages: when he is young, God forgives his stumblings; when he is man, God weighs his purpose; when he grows old, God waits until he repents.

If men thanked God for good things, they wouldn't have time to complain about the bad.

There is no room for God in the man who is full of himself.
Hasidic saying

God decides what a man shall be, and what shall befall him, but not whether he shall be righteous or wicked.
TALMUD: Niddah 16b

⋑ An old man was invited into Abraham's tent, but Abraham learned that the man was a fire worshipper and turned him out. That night, God appeared to Abraham, and said, "I have borne with that fool for seventy years; could you not have endured him for one brief night?"

> —Old story, attributed to *Poor Richard's Almanack,* which credits no earlier source

Because the prophets had to speak in a language understood by the masses, they said He is a jealous and avenging God.

> JOSEPH ALBO, *Sefer Ikarim,* 2 : 4

Men are wrong to think that outside of the Bible nothing persuades belief in the Eternal; many other proofs of God exist . . .

> SAADIA GAON

Don't ask God to change the laws of nature for you.

> NACHMAN OF BRATSLAV

See also: ADAM, FAITH, GOOD DEEDS, HEREAFTER, PIETY, PRAYER, SABBATH, SATAN, VIRTUE, WORSHIP

GOLD

⋑ The age of gold was the age when gold did not rule.

Gold has a dirty father (the earth) but is honored everywhere.

Gold shines—even in mud.

⋑ The key of gold opens all doors.

A little gold can lighten up your world.

Gold is attracted to gold.

Gossip is silenced with gold.

Gold confers authority.

Gold can't accompany a man to heaven.

The love of gold leads to madness.

See also: BUSINESS, FORTUNE, GREED, MONEY, RICHES, WEALTH

GOOD

Note. "Love thy neighbor as thyself" comes from Leviticus
(19 : 18). This so-called Golden Rule is basic to Judaism; it is
extensively cited in Rabbinical literature; it is found in the
sayings of Ben Sirach (*Ecclesiasticus*), in the Testament of
the Twelve Patriots, in Tobit; it is in Philo, in Josephus, and,
of course, is told of Hillel, who said: "What is hateful to thee,
do not unto others: that is the whole Law—all the rest is
commentary." (See headnotes for GOOD DEEDS, VIRTUE.)

—L.R.

⋐§ Too good is bad for you.

The man who is far from his good is near his harm.

Whether you do little or much, let it be out of good intentions.
TALMUD: *Shebu'oth,* 15b

The Evil Impulse serves goodness, for if not for the Evil Impulse
no man would marry or beget children, or engage in trade.
—adapted from MIDRASH: *Ecclesiastes Rabbah,* 3 : 11

See also: EVIL, GOOD DEEDS, GOOD AND EVIL, GOOD MEN, SELFISHNESS,
SIN, VIRTUE

GOOD DEEDS

Note. Kiddush ha-Shem is the cardinal conception that men become sanctified by following God's commandments and in so
doing "sanctify His name." In Leviticus (22 : 32), the Lord
says: "I will be hallowed among the children of Israel; I am
the Lord which hallows you." (The opposite of *Kiddush ha-
Shem* is *Hillul ha-Shem,* "the profaning of God's name.")
Kiddush ha-Shem involves the idea that any generous,
altruistic deed honors all Jews, for the Jews are "a kingdom

of priests," and each Jew must bear a responsibility to act in such a way as to honor all Jewry.

As a case of true *Kiddush ha-Shem,* the Talmud cites the case of a Jew's returning to an Arab, from whom he had purchased a camel, a jewel he had found around the camel's neck, saying: "I bought a camel, not a gem." And the Arab cried, "Blessed be the God of Israel."

—L.R.

A good deed has many claimants.

ᐱᔥ Troubles no one wants to steal from you; good deeds no one can.

ᐱᔥ The man who comforts a pretty young widow does not only mean to perform a good deed.

The beggar does more good for the giver than the giver does for the beggar.

ᐱᔥ He who has fed strangers may have fed angels.

That man deserves the highest honors who does not ask for them, but performs worthy deeds.

If a man intends to perform a good deed but is prevented from doing so, he is to be treated as though he has done it.
TALMUD: *Kiddushin,* 40a

Happy he who performs a good deed: for he may tip the scales for himself and the world.   TALMUD: *Kiddushin,* 40 : 2

The one who causes a good deed to be performed is as meritorious as the one who performs it.   TALMUD: *Sanhedrin,* 99b

ᐱᔥ The beginning and the end (of Torah) is the performance of lovingkindness.   TALMUD: *Sotah,* 14a

ᐱᔥ The whole value of a benevolent deed lies in the love that inspires it.   TALMUD: *Sukkah,* 49b

Good deeds are better than creeds.
—adapted from *Sayings of the Fathers*

Deeds of kindness weigh as much as all the commandments.

TALMUD J.: *Pe'ah,* 1 : 1

He who does not himself do good cannot depend on his father's
works and merits.　　MIDRASH: *Midrash Psalms,* 1 : 64

The door that is closed to a good deed will open to a doctor.

MIDRASH: *Song of Songs Rabbah,* 6 : 1

ᴥᎪ Happy is the man whose deeds are greater than his learning.

MIDRASH: *Eliyahu Rabbah,* 17

Be like a helmsman—on the lookout for good deeds.

MIDRASH: *Leviticus Rabbah,* 21 : 4

ᴥᎪ It is better to visit a house of mourning than a house of
feasting.　　*Ecclesiastes,* 2

The man whose good deeds exceed his wisdom is like a tree with
few branches and many roots: all the raging winds will not
move him.　　*Sayings of the Fathers,* 3 : 17

The reward of a *mitzvah?* Another *mitzvah.*

—adapted from *Sayings of the Fathers*

One *mitzvah* [good deed] leads to another, just as one *averah*
[sin] leads to another.　　*Sayings of the Fathers,* 4 : 5

Whoever performs one good action gains an advocate; whoever
commits a sin procures an accuser.

Sayings of the Fathers, 4 : 15

ᴥᎪ That good deed is most meritorious of which no one knows.

—adapted from MAIMONIDES

ᴥᎪ Naked a man comes into the world, and naked he leaves it;
after all his toil, he carries away nothing—except the deeds
he leaves behind.　　—adapted from RASHI

To revive a man is no slight thing.

NACHMAN OF BRATSLAV

A man's good deeds are used by the Lord as seeds for planting
   trees in the Garden of Eden: thus, each man creates his own
   Paradise.   THE MEZERITZER RABBI

Let a good man do good deeds with the same zeal that the evil
   man does bad ones.   THE BELZER RABBI

⋙ Good deeds bring a man immortality.
                                              THE SASSOVOR RABBI

When Akaybya was on his death-bed, his son asked, "Father, com-
   mend me to your friends."
"No, my son," said Akaybya, "I shall not."
"Have you found anything unworthy in me?" asked the son.
"No, my son. But it is your deeds that can bring you close to men,
   and your deeds can drive you from them."
                              —adapted from ELEAZAR ROKEACH

See also: ALTRUISM, CHARITY, DUTY, EVIL, FORGIVENESS, GENEROSITY,
   GOD, GOOD, GOOD AND EVIL, GOOD MEN, GRATITUDE, GRIEF, GUILT,
   HEART, HEAVEN, HELP, HEREAFTER, HEREDITY, HOLINESS, JEAL-
   OUSY, SELFISHNESS, SIN

GOOD AND EVIL

Good and a little is better than bad and a lot.

⋙ Better the bad of the good [men] than the good of the bad
   [ones].

It is better to see good than to hear bad.

Both good and evil are the work of our own hands.
                              APOCRYPHA: *Psalms of Solomon,* 9 : 4

The potter does not test cracked vessels, because to tap them
   even once is to break them; but he does test good vessels, because no matter how many times he taps them they do not
   break; so God tests not the wicked but the righteous.
                              MIDRASH: *Genesis Rabbah,* 32 : 3

There is no good without some evil in its midst.

MIDRASH: *Genesis Rabbah*, 68 : 10

The path of goodness begins in a thicket of thorns, but soon emerges into an open plain; the way of evil begins as a plain, but soon runs into thorns.   *Sifre Deuteronomy*, 11 : 6

◈§ Man is lucky that during childhood he cannot tell good from evil, for if he had mature powers of perception he would die of grief.   BAHYA IBN PAQUDA, *Duties of the Heart*

See not evil in others and good in yourself, but the good in the other and the failings in yourself. THE BERDICHEVER RABBI

See also: EVIL, GOD, GOOD, GOOD MEN, JEALOUSY, SELFISHNESS, SIN, VIRTUE

GOOD MEN

He is a good man, but his dog won't let you near him.

Good men need no recommendation, and bad men it won't help.

◈§ Where the good pay, the bad demand.

Be on the best of terms with all men, including the heathen: you may be beloved above and well liked below.

TALMUD: *Berakoth*, 17a

When the good die, they live (in the example they provide).

TALMUD: *Berakoth*, 18b

Good men promise little and perform much; wicked men promise much and perform nothing.   TALMUD: *Nedarim*, 21b

The man who asks mercy for another while both are in peril will be answered first.   TALMUD: *Baba Kamma*, 92a

To a fool it is like sport to do wrong; but is it hateful to a man of sense.   *Book of Proverbs*, 10 : 23

We cannot understand either the prosperity of the evil or the sufferings of the virtuous. *Sayings of the Father*, 4 : 21

Good men are hard to provoke and easy to calm.
                    —adapted from *Sayings of the Fathers*, 5 : 17

Good men need no monuments: their deeds are their shrines.
                                        Mishne Shekalim, 5 : 2

I dislike the man who is like snow: at first white and pure; later
    muddy and soiled.   THE RIZINER RABBI

&⸱ As between a pious man and a clever man, the pious one
    is superior; as between a pious man and a kind man, the
    kind man is superior.   THE KORETSER RABBI

In freezing weather, one man keeps warm by donning a coat, the
    other by heating his house; the first is selfish, the second is
    humane.   THE KOTZKER RABBI

&⸱ I don't like the good man who preens himself on his good-
    ness.   THE LUBLINER RABBI

The man who has led a good life will find many allies.
                                    NACHMAN OF BRATSLAV

See also: EVIL, GOOD, GOOD DEEDS, GOOD AND EVIL, HEATHEN, HERE-
AFTER, PIETY, SIN, VIRTUE

GOSSIP

&⸱ What's easy to say may be hard to bear.

What you don't see with your eyes, don't invent with your mouth.

&⸱ The tongue has no bones—so it's loose.

&⸱ If you want to find out what's happening in your house, talk
    to your neighbors.

It's easier to hear a secret than to keep it.

&⸱ A tongue can be a dangerous weapon.

You can't close *all* the mouths on earth.

◄§ Loose tongues are worse than wicked hands.

Our ears often don't hear what our mouths say.

◄§ Your ears belong to yourself; your tongue is heard by others.

Send [only] your ears into the streets.

If you don't open your mouth, no flies will get in.

When people keep gossiping about something, it may be true.

◄§ Those who think of themselves don't gossip about others.

Run from gossip as you would run from ghosts.

Gossip is the most common of human habits and causes the most trouble.

People eat and drink together, yet pierce each other with the sword of their tongues. TALMUD: *Yomah,* 9b

Gossip comes from peddlers—and vermin from rags.
  TALMUD: *Berakoth,* 51b

Man's fingers are shaped like nails, so that he can put them in his ears when ugly words reach them.
  TALMUD: *Kethuboth,* 5a

Your friend has a friend, and your friend's friend has a friend [so be discreet]. —adapted from TALMUD: *Kethuboth,* 109b

◄§ Gossipers start with praise and end with derogation.
  MIDRASH: *Tanhuma Shelah,* 9

◄§ Even if all of a slander is not believed, half of it is.
  MIDRASH: *Genesis Rabbah,* 56 : 4

The whisperer separates friends. *Book of Proverbs* 16 : 28

What your eyes have seen
Report not hastily to the mob. *Book of Proverbs*

He who overlooks an offense promotes good will;
He who repeats a tale separates friends.
  Book of Proverbs 17 : 9

Where there is no wood, a fire goes out;
And where there is no whisperer, a quarrel dies down.

> *Book of Proverbs* 26 : 20

From a man's mouth you can tell what he is.   *Zohar*

Men's eyes and ears don't always depend on will power; but a
man's tongue always is subject to his will.   *Zohar*

You enclose your vineyard with thorns: put doors and bolts on
your mouth.   BEN SIRACH: *Ecclesiasticus,* 28 : 24

ᵉᶳ Gossip: nature's telephone.   SHOLEM ALEICHEM

See also: CRITICISM, FOOLS, LIES/LIARS, RUMOR, SCANDAL, SECRETS,
SLANDER, TALK

GOVERNMENT

Note. Ancient Israel created a commonwealth (1200–586 before
the Christian Era) that is rather remarkable in the history of
man's political institutions. The political theory imbedded in
Deuteronomy and Leviticus (much neglected by students of
political science) gave the Hebrews the basis for a state with
a "built-in" constitution in which certain rights of the people
enjoyed priority, and in which the *duties* of a ruler to his
people were delineated with as great force as were his powers or privileges.

    Dr. J. H. Hertz compares the stable, undespotic kingdoms
of Israel to the 158 quarreling, jealous, fratricidal states of
ancient Greece: "The Greeks displayed to the full that fatal
vice of factiousness which imbues politics with fanaticism,
and proscribes opponents by massacre or exile."

    Nietzsche called the Greeks "political fools" because every
political experiment they tried failed; and portions of the
Greek population were oppressed whether a city-state was
built on a theory of republic, aristocracy, oligopoly, democracy, or some other. By contrast to Greece, Egypt, or the
despotisms of the East, Israel's theocratic state was stable,
unified, and uniquely democratic.

—L.R.

A fool in office is an ass tied to the sun.

Co-rulers become over-rulers.

Sages are superior to kings.

◄§ Don't live in a city run by scholars.
                                        AKIBA in TALMUD: *Pesahim*, 112a

◄§ Fish die out of water; men die without law and order.
                                        TALMUD: *'Abodah Zarah*, 4a

The real guardians of a state are the teachers.
                                        TALMUD J.: *Hagigah*, 1 : 7

The power of great men can be used for evil no less than good.
                        —adapted from TALMUD: *Sukkah*, 52a

Safety lies in the counsel of multitudes.
                                        Book of Proverbs, 24 : 6

Where there is no vision, the people perish.
                                        Book of Proverbs, 29 : 18

◄§ Pray for political stability, for if not for fear of the government men would swallow each other alive.
                                        Sayings of the Fathers, 3 : 1

Do not place trust in princes.   *Book of Psalms*, 146 : 3

What kind of man is fit to govern? Either a sage given power, or a
king who seeks wisdom.   IBN GABIROL

A government can fall because of one injustice.
                                        "THE CHOFETZ CHAIM"

See also: AUTHORITY, BARBARIANS, COMMUNITY, COMPROMISE, DE-
MOCRACY, EQUALITY, FREEDOM, LAW, POLITICS, POWER

GRAMMAR

Grammar is to speech what salt is to food.
                                        IBN EZRA, *Shirat Yisrael*

God created grammar according to the principles of nature.
                                        —adapted from ABRAVANEL

See also: LANGUAGE, SPEECH, WORDS

GRATITUDE

We never know all we should be grateful to God for.

It was for my good that my cow broke her leg.

Be grateful to the beggar: he gave you the chance to do good.

✒ If a Jew breaks his leg, he thanks God that he did not break both legs; if he breaks both legs, he thanks God he did not break his neck.

Rab declared: "We give thanks unto Thee, oh Lord our God, because we are able to give thanks."   TALMUD: *Sotah,* 48

See also: CHARITY, COMPASSION, ENVY, GOOD DEEDS, GENEROSITY, INGRATITUDE, JEALOUSY, PRAYER

GREAT MEN

✒ The man who is surrounded by dwarfs looks like a giant.

If a great man says something that seems illogical, don't laugh; try to understand it.   TALMUD: *Berakoth,* 19b

The greater the man, the greater his potential for evil (no less than good).   TALMUD: *Sukkah,* 52a

As long as light comes from the great, the light of the lesser is unseen; once the light of the great disappears, the light of the lesser shines.   MIDRASH: *Deuteronomy Rabbah,* 5

Little sins are great when great men commit them.
                                        —adapted from ABRAHAM IBN EZRA
                                        Commentary to Genesis, 32 : 9

The man who can't accept criticism can't become great.

NACHMAN OF BRATSLAV

See also: CRITICISM, GOOD MEN, POWER, SAGES, WISE MEN

GREED

Men are always close—to their pockets.

ఆ§ The eye is small, but devours all.

ఆ§ If eyes did not see, hands would not take.

If you look for cake, you'll lose your bread.

What is grabbed will be lost.

Don't desire what you can't acquire.

ఆ§ When the paupers start dancing, the musicians stop playing.

Show a dog a finger, and he wants your whole hand.

A handful does not satisfy a lion.   TALMUD: *Berakoth,* 3b

When the camel demanded horns, they cut off his ears.

TALMUD: *Sanhedrin,* 106a

Some men begin with a pitcher and end with a barrel.

TALMUD: *Baba Kamma,* 27a

If you grasp too much, you cannot hold it; when you take a little,
   you can.   TALMUD: *Rosh Hashanah,* 4b

Those who increase their flesh only increase food for the worms.

Sayings of the Fathers, 2 : 8

The man who loves silver won't remain satisfied with silver.

SAADIA GAON

More die from overeating than from undereating.

NACHMAN OF BRATSLAV

See also: ANIMALS, COMPLAINT, CIRCUMSTANCES, DESIRE, GIVING AND TAKING, GLUTTONY, GOLD, HEALTH, JEALOUSY, SELFISHNESS, SIN

GRIEF

◄§ All things grow with time—except grief.

Grief may affect one's words the way wine would.

◄§ God is closest to those with broken hearts.

To grieve alone is to suffer most.

Outer garments can hide inner grief.

The deeper the grief, the less words can express it.

No man should be held responsible for the words he utters in his grief.   TALMUD: *Baba Bathra,* 16a

◄§ The man who offers sympathy to someone bereaved a year ago is like a doctor who asks a man who has broken a leg to break it again—so that the doctor can mend it to show his skill.
TALMUD: *Mo'ed Katan,* 21b

Don't try to console a man while the corpse is still in the house.
Sayings of the Fathers, 4 : 25

Bereavement is like a wheel that goes around the world.
RASHI, *Commentaries on the Pentateuch: Genesis*

Everything that grows begins small and becomes big; but grief starts big and becomes small—and disappears.
IBN GABIROL, *Ethics*

◄§ Children, luckily, can't tell good from evil; if they did, they would die of grief.
—adapted from BAHYA IBN PAQUDA, *Duties of the Heart*

◄§ If we could not forget, we would never be free from grief.
—adapted from BAHYA IBN PAQUDA, *Duties of the Heart*

See also: COMPASSION, CONSIDERATION, EMOTION, GOOD DEEDS, GROWTH, HEART, SUFFERING, TEARS

GROOMS

Three kinds need to be protected from others: a patient, a bride, and a groom. TALMUD: *Berakoth,* 54b

See: BACHELORS, MARRIAGE, WEDDING, WIVES

GROWTH

The man who does not grow grows smaller.
—adapted from HILLEL in *Sayings of the Fathers,* 1 : 14

Be not in a hurry, like the almond, first to blossom and last to ripen. Be rather like the mulberry, last to blossom and first to ripen. APOCRYPHA: *Ahikar,* 2 : 7

See also: GRIEF, KNOWLEDGE, LEARNING, POWER

GUESTS

◄§ Guests, like fish, begin to smell on the third day.

A guest for a day can see quite a way.

◄§ We are delighted with a good guest the minute he arrives— and with a bad one, the minute he leaves.

◄§ Who is the most despicable of guests? The one who brings another guest along.

A guest is like rain: too long is a nuisance.

◄§ The first day, a guest is fed roast chicken; the second day, eggs; the third day, beans.

A woman recognizes the character of a guest sooner than her husband does. TALMUD: *Berakoth,* 10

See also: HOSPITALITY

GUILT

If you don't steal, you won't feel guilty.

A guilty man runs when no one is chasing him.

The guilty are uneasy [self-conscious].

⋙ If you do something wrong, at least enjoy it.

On the thief's head, the hat burns. [For years, I was puzzled by this. Why a hat? Why does it burn? Does a thief feel as *if* a hat is burning on his head? . . . The Yiddishists I consulted were as baffled as I; but I found the explanation in a charming story in Ignaz Bernstein's *Jüdische Sprichwörter und Redensarten:* It seems that during a country fair, an old Jew put his broad-brimmed hat down for a moment to wipe his brow; when he reached for his hat, it was gone. He looked around anxiously and, to his dismay, saw a sea of hats similar to his own. What to do? In a stroke of insight that deserves the immortality he unwittingly acquired, the old Jew cried out: "Look! Look! The hat on the thief's head is on fire!" At once, one man swept his hat off his head and betrayed his larceny.]

Silence may be equivalent to confession.
TALMUD: *Yebamoth,* 87b

⋙ The guilty man who denies his guilt doubles it. TALMUD

Guilt has its home among fools. *Book of Proverbs*

A broom sweeps clean, and itself becomes soiled; cleanse yourself of those offenses of which you may be guilty.
BAAL SHEM TOV

See also: BLAME, CONSCIENCE, GOOD DEEDS, HEREAFTER, INNOCENCE, LAW, LIARS/LIES, SHAME, TRUTH, VIRTUE

HABIT

A dog without teeth still gobbles at a bone.

◦§ When a habit begins to cost money, it's called a hobby.

If you always drink vinegar, you don't know there's anything sweeter.

The most common habit is gossip—and it causes the most trouble.

◦§ Sins repeated seem permitted.
                              —adapted from TALMUD: *Yomah,* 86b

Men cling to the opinions of habit.
                    MAIMONIDES, *Guide to the Perplexed,* 1 : 31

Those who live near a waterfall are not disturbed by its roar.
                                    JUDAH ARYEH MOSCATO

It is harder to break evil habits than to split rocks.
                                    THE RIZINER RABBI

See also: CONTENTMENT, CUSTOMS, EVIL, EXPERIENCE, TRADITION

HAPPINESS

A heavy purse makes a light heart.

Not every heart that gives forth laughter is happy.

Those who are happy despite poverty can prevail against anything.

◦§ From happiness to sorrow takes a moment; from sorrow to happiness takes years.

Melancholy creates nervous ailments; cheerfulness cures them.

Happiness vanishes when envy appears.

◦§ While we pursue happiness, we flee from contentment.
> Hasidic saying

Three things make a man happy: a good home, a good wife, and good enough possessions.
> —adapted from TALMUD: *Berakoth,* 57b

Happy is he who knows his place and stands in his own place.
> TALMUD

The miserable man is unhappy every day; but the cheerful man enjoys a constant feast.   *Book of Proverbs* 15 : 15

Bright eyes gladden the heart;
Good news fatten the bones.   *Book of Proverbs* 15 : 30

One day's happiness makes a man forget his misfortune; and one day's misfortune makes him forget his past happiness.
> BEN SIRACH: *Ecclesiasticus,* 11 : 25

When someone tells me he is making a living "but it wouldn't hurt if things were a little better," I ask, "How do you know it wouldn't?"   "THE CHOFETZ CHAIM"

See also: ADVERSITY, AMBITION, CONTENTMENT, FAITH, FORTUNE, HOME, JOY, LIFE, LUCK, TORAH, WIVES

HASTE

◦§ The only thing speed is good for is catching flies.

No good comes from hurrying.

If you measure fast, you'll cut ten times; if you measure slowly, you need cut but once.

Quickly got, quickly lost.

◈§ Sleep faster: we need the pillows.

See also: CAUTION, FORESIGHT, SENSE

HATE

Where you are loved, go rarely; where you are hated, go never.

Hatred usually joins lies.

◈§ Hatred is the fruit of fear.

◈§ The hatred that comes from envy lasts.

◈§ If you are fair, your fairness will destroy your hate.

A man should hate only his own shortcomings.

To hate a man is as if to hate God.

Hate ruins the savor of food and the peace of sleep.

Hate is like a channel made by water: it widens continually.
TALMUD: *Sanhedrin,* 7a

Hate is like the plank of a bridge: once put in place, it stays there.
TALMUD: *Sanhedrin,* 7a

Hatred for insufficient reason is the greatest of sins.
TALMUD: *Yomah,* 9b

The Holy Temple was destroyed because of baseless hatred.
TALMUD: *Yomah,* 9b

The hatred of other men destroys your own world.
Sayings of the Fathers, 2 : 15

Better a dish of herbs, where love is,
Than a fatted ox served with hatred.
Book of Proverbs, 15 : 17

Righteous lips cover up hatred.   *Book of Proverbs,* 10 : 18

If you will remember the end of all things, you will cease hating.
> Ben Sirach: *Ecclesiasticus*, 25 : 6

The man who talks rashly [in railing speech] is hated.
> —adapted from Ben Sirach, *Ecclesiasticus*, 9 : 18

ᴥᕽ People usually hate what they do not understand.
> Moses ibn Ezra, *Shirat Yisrael*

ᴥᕽ Love blinds us to faults, but hatred blinds us to virtues.
> Ibn Ezra, *Shirat Yisrael*

ᴥᕽ A man who hates men is hated by them.
> Ibn Gabirol, *Choice of Pearls*

The man who sows hatred reaps remorse.
> Ibn Gabirol, *Choice of Pearls*

Unfounded hate only multiplies quarrels.
> Nachman of Bratslav

See also: ANGER, ENVY, FRIENDS/FRIENDSHIP, FIGHTING, HOSTILITY, LOVE, REMORSE, VIRTUE

HEALTH

Too much is unhealthy.

ᴥᕽ Your health comes first—you can always hang yourself later.

What a fat belly cost, I wish I had; what it does, I wish on my enemies.

True, God sends us colds—but according to our clothes [were you dressed warmly enough?].

Don't put a healthy head on a sick pillow.

ᴥᕽ When the head is a fool, the body is in trouble.

A great doctor does not work alone; a great angel is always at his side.

Worms eat you when you're dead; worries eat you up when you're
alive.

The man who takes as good care of himself as he does of his livestock won't get sick.

ê§ What soap is for the body, tears are for the soul.

If you chew well with your teeth, you'll feel it in your toes.
TALMUD: Shabbath, 152a

Three things drain a man's health: worry, travel, and sin.
TALMUD: Gittin, 70a

A fox does not die from breathing the dust of his own den.
TALMUD: Kethuboth, 71b

Eat a third and drink a third, but leave the remaining third of your
stomach empty: for then, if anger overtakes you, there will be
room for your rage.   TALMUD: Gittin, 70a

Six things are good omens for the sick: sneezing, perspiring, open
bowels, emission of semen, sleep—and a dream.
TALMUD, Berakoth, 57b

The science of medicine is authorized by God Himself.
TALMUD: Berakoth, 60a

The purpose of maintaining the body in good health is to [make it
possible for you to] acquire wisdom.
MAIMONIDES: Commentaries on the Mishnah, v

See also: ANGER, DISEASE, DOCTORS, ENVY, EXCESS, GREED, JEALOUSY,
MEDICINE, MODERATION, SUFFERING

HEART

ê§ A stab in the heart leaves a hole.

ê§ God is closest to those with broken hearts.

ê§ The heart sees better than the eye.

Trouble tears the heart in two.

⋅⋛ Pearls around the neck may be like stones upon the heart.

⋅⋛ A heavy purse makes a light heart.

The heart is small yet embraces the world.

⋅⋛ The eye reveals what the heart would say.

When the heart is full, it is the eyes that overflow.

A man's heart is a lock, but even a lock can be opened with the
   right key.

⋅⋛ God looks at a man's heart before He looks at a man's brains.

The heart is a half-prophet.

⋅⋛ The culture of the heart is greater than the culture of the mind.

The heart of man and the bottom of the sea are unfathomable.

When you pour your heart out, it feels lighter.

God knows that the best synagogue is the human heart.
                                                    Hasidic saying

Man can see his reflection in water only when he bends down close
   to it; and the heart of man, too, must lean down to the heart of
   his fellow; then it will see itself within his heart.
                                                    Hasidic saying

If you want to endure this world, equip yourself with a heart that
   can withstand suffering.   MIDRASH: *Leviticus Rabbah*, 30

⋅⋛ The heart can ennoble any calling: A kind jailer may exceed
   the saintly in true merit, and a jester may be first in the kingdom of heaven, if they have diminished the sadness of human
   lives.   RABBI BAROKA in TALMUD

⋅⋛ Any wound is better than a wound in the heart.
                                    BEN SIRACH, *Ecclesiasticus*, 25 : 13

The tongue is the pen of the heart.
> BAHYA IBN PAQUDA, *Duties of the Heart*

Words that come from the heart enter the heart.
> MOSES IBN EZRA, *Shirat Yisrael*

⮜ Man is a holy Temple, and his heart is the holy of holies.
> JONATHAN EIBESCHUTZ, *Yaarot Dvash*

See also: COMPASSION, CONSIDERATION, EMOTION, GOOD DEEDS, INTEL-
LIGENCE, REASON

HEATHEN

The heathen is your neighbor, your brother; and to wrong him is a
sin.   MIDRASH: *Tana de Rabbi Eliyahu*, 284

See also: BARBARIANS, GOOD MEN, JEWS, LOVE, NEIGHBORS, SIN, VIRTUE

HEAVEN

Note. Very orthodox Jews are persuaded that there is a literal
heaven. (Cabalists claimed there were two, one on earth and
one "in the highest.") *Gan Eden,* "the garden of Eden," is a
synonym for the Paradise to come. The Talmud lists seven
heavens. (The recurrence of seven as a favored, virtuous,
lucky or magical number is, of course, familiar to students of
history, philosophy, and the mythology of peoples around the
globe: e.g., the Seven Against Thebes, the Seven Deadly Sins,
the Seven Gifts of the Spirit, the Japanese Seven Gods of
Luck, the Seven Years of Tannhäuser, the Seven Virtues, the
Arabs' Seven Viziers, etc. The ancient Hebrew scribes had
Seven Names for God, out of the many by which He was
called, which required especial care in copying—and during
the Middle Ages, the Lord was sometimes referred to as "The
Seven.")

Rab, the great savant, said Paradise would entail no eating, drinking, business, envy, hatred, ambition—or cohabitation: The righteous would simply sit around, crowns on their

heads, basking in the blazing glory of the Divine Presence. Of this concept, Maimonides dryly noted: "To believe so is to be a schoolboy, who expects nuts and sweetmeats as compensation for his studies. Celestial pleasures can neither be measured nor comprehended by a mortal being, any more than a blind man can distinguish colors, or the deaf appreciate music."

—L.R.

⋰⟋ It is worse to be in heaven with a fool than in hell with a sage.

The smallest grass on earth has its guiding star in heaven.

⋰⟋ A special place is reserved in Heaven for those who can weep, but not pray.

⋰⟋ In Heaven, they do not grant half-favors.

TALMUD: *Yomah*, 69b

⋰⟋ There are halls in heaven that open only to the voice of song.

Zohar

Better an hour of happiness in heaven, than a lifetime of pleasure on earth.   *Sayings of the Fathers*, 4 : 22

A clown may be first in the kingdom of heaven, if he has helped lessen the sadness of human life.

RABBI BAROKA in TALMUD

See also: **GOOD DEEDS, HELL, HEREAFTER, PARADISE, VIRTUE**

HELL

Note. Gehenna, the word derived from the Hebrew *gehinom* ("hell"), comes from the name of that accursed "valley of the sons of Hinnon" where child sacrifices were made to the idol Moloch. Talmudic literature is unclear about a literal location for a literal Hell to which the wicked shall be sent after death. Except for the very orthodox, and pious clusters of hasidim, Jews do not, I believe, think very much about a fiery abode of unremitting torments for those who were sinners on earth. I must add that Jews are equally ambiguous, or allegorical, about Paradise: its location, daily routines, and unimaginable bliss. (See headnote for HEAVEN.)   —L.R.

◁§ Hell is not so bad as the road to it.

One path leads to Paradise, but a thousand lead to Hell.

In Hell you can buy an ox for a penny, but what man there has one?

In Hell, the wicked, too, rest on the Sabbath.

Isaiah asked the Lord, "What must a man do to be saved from Hell?" And the Lord said: "Let him give charity, sharing his bread with the poor, giving money to the scribes and the students; let him not behave arrogantly to his fellow men; let him steep himself in the Torah and in its commandments; let him live by humility; let him not speak in puffed-up spirit. Whoever has these qualities will inherit the future life."
   —adapted from MIDRASH: *Pesikta Rabbah*, 198a

The unrepentant go to Hell, the shamed to Eden.
                         Sayings of the Fathers, 5 : 20

A man's enemy cannot harm him as much as he can harm himself; for his enemy cannot cast a man into Gehenna, as he does himself.   SAADIA GAON

There is no hell like an evil woman [wife].   IBN ZABARA

See also: GOD, HEAVEN, HEREAFTER, SATAN, SIN

HELP

◁§ Those who do not help others need doctors to help them.

To help a stranger may be to help an angel.

The man who helps others with no desire for praise deserves the highest of honors.

To help a fellow man may be to tip the scales (of God's reckoning)
for the entire world.
                         —adapted from Talmud: *Kiddushin,* 40 : 2

If you do not help a man with his troubles, it is equivalent to
bringing troubles to him.   Nachman of Bratslav

⋙ Always help those who are being persecuted.
                                  Nachman of Bratslav

See *also:* altruism, compassion, consideration, cooperation,
good deeds, service, virtue

HEREAFTER

The scoffer, the liar, the hypocrite, and the slanderer can have no
share in the future world.

The man who has a son in this world does not feel lonely in the
world to come.

⋙ The world is like an inn, the world to come like home.
                                  Talmud: *Mo'ed Katan,* 9b

Men who are just, whatever their nation, will be rewarded in the
world to come.   Talmud: *Sanhedrin,* 105a

⋙ When a man appears before the Throne of Judgment, the first
question he will be asked is not "Have you believed in God?"
or "Have you prayed and observed the ritual?"—but "Have
you dealt honorably with your fellow man?"
                                  Talmud: *Shabbath,* 31a

In the hereafter, men will be called to account for depriving themselves of the good things the world offered.
                                  Talmud J.: *Kiddushin,* end

A bastard can have a place in the world to come.
                                  Midrash: *Ecclesiastes Rabbah*

A man must not rely on the virtues of his ancestors: if he does
not do good in this world, he cannot fall back on the merit

of his fathers, for in the time to come no man will eat off his fathers' works, but only of his own.

> MIDRASH: *Midrash Psalms*, 146 : 3

This world is no more than the vestibule of the world to come, so prepare in life to enter the hereafter.

> *Sayings of the Fathers*, 4 : 16

When a man departs from this world, neither silver nor gold nor jewels accompany him—only Torah, and his good deeds.

> *Sayings of the Fathers*, 6 : 9

ⴷ Conquerors here are conquered in the hereafter.

> *Sefer Hasidim*

The prosperity that the wicked enjoy here is a measure of the rewards that the righteous will receive in the hereafter.

> MIDRASH: *Midrash Psalms*, 37 : 3

We must expect that even in the millennium, though evil will be weakened—it will not be entirely destroyed.   *Zohar*

In the world to come, there will be neither famine nor war, jealousy nor strife: Prosperity will be everywhere, and the sole task will be to know the Lord. And then men will know things that are now hidden; and they will attain all of that knowledge of the Holy Creator that is within the capacity of mortals.   MAIMONIDES: *Mishneh Torah*, end

ⴷ Plan for this world as if you hope to live forever; but plan for the hereafter as if you expect to die tomorrow.

> IBN GABIROL, *Choice of Pearls*

See also: BASTARDS, DEATH, EVIL, FATE, FUTURE, GOD: COMPLAINTS ABOUT, GOOD DEEDS, GOOD MEN, GUILT, HEAVEN, HELL, RESURRECTION, SIN, VIRTUE

HEREDITY

You need luck to inherit brains.

Don't take credit for what you inherited.

It is not for us to ask why God made some men smart and some
    men stupid.

A fool is not responsible for the brain he was given.

To do good is better than to inherit intelligence.

The worm in horseradish who thinks he's in heaven is only express-
    ing the worms' capacity for imagination.

What environment can do, heredity cannot do.
                                    MIDRASH: *Tanhuma, Vayetze* 13

See also: ANCESTORS, DEEDS, FAMILY, GOD: COMPLAINTS ABOUT

HERETICS

⋙ The heretic has closed his heart, not his mind.

Sailors are not heretics: they live in daily peril.

When he was warned about his associations with a known heretic,
    Rabbi Meir answered, "I enjoy the sweetness of fruit, but
    throw away the rind."   TALMUD: *Hagigah,* 15b

All Israelites have a share in the future world [except] he who
    says there is no resurrection, he who says the Law has not
    been given by God, and an *apikoros* [heretic].   *Mishnah*

⋙ If all the ancient sacred writings had been preserved, some
    would be found to be heretical.   NACHMAN OF BRATSLAV

See also: APOSTATES, FAITH, GOD: COMPLAINTS ABOUT, RELIGION

HEROES

Note. "The castle [at York, in 1190] had sufficient strength for
    [the Jews'] defence . . . but the cruel multitude . . . felt such a
    desire of slaughtering those they intended to despoil, that . . .
    the attacks continued, till at length the Jews perceived they
    could hold out no longer. . . .

"When the Jewish council was assembled, the *Haham* [Rabbi] rose and addressed them . . . 'Men of Israel! . . . Death is before our eyes; and we have only to choose an honourable and easy one. If we fall into the hands of our enemies, which we cannot escape, our death will be ignominious and cruel. It is therefore my advice that we elude their tortures; that we ourselves should be our own executioners; that we voluntarily surrender our lives to our Creator. God seems to call for us; let us not be unworthy of that call.' Having said this, the old man sat down and wept.

"The assembly was divided in its opinions. Again the Rabbin rose . . . 'My children, since we are not unanimous in our opinions, let those who do not approve of my advice depart from this assembly.' Some departed, but the greater number . . . now employed themselves in consuming their valuables by fire; and every man, fearful of trusting to the timid and irresolute hand of the women, first destroyed his wife and children, and then himself . . .

"All this was transacted in the depth of the night. In the morning the walls of [York] castle were seen wrapt in flames, and only a few . . . beings, unworthy of the sword, were viewed on the battlements, pointing to their extinct brethren. When they opened the gates of the castle, these men verified the prediction of their late Rabbin; for the multitude, bursting through the solitary courts, found themselves defrauded of their hopes, and in a moment avenged themselves on the feeble wretches who knew not how to die with honor."
—Isaac d'Israeli, *Curiosities of Literature,* 1793, vol. 2

See INQUISITION, INTOLERANCE, MARTYRS, PERSECUTION, POGROMS

No man is a hero to his *mishpokhe* [relatives].

Who is a hero? He who suppresses a wisecrack.

The soldiers fight—and the kings are called heroes.

The greatest hero is the man who turns his enemy into a friend.
Abot de Rabbi Nathan, 23

See also: COURAGE, ENEMY, GLORY, GREAT MEN, HONOR/HONORS, WAR

HISTORY

Note. "We are so old that in our history everything has happened
and nothing new can occur."   MAX NORDAU

"Jewish history is a history of martyrdom and learning."
HEINRICH GRAETZ

Many pens are broken, and seas of ink consumed, to describe
things that never happened.   MIDRASH: *Tanhuma*

The Jews are God's stake in human history.   A. J. HESCHEL

See ISRAEL, JEWS

HOLIDAY

◄§ After a holiday, only debts and dirty dishes remain.

HOLINESS

If you sanctify yourself a little, you are sanctified much.
TALMUD: *Yomah*, 39a

We may add to the sacred from the profane.
TALMUD: *Yomah*, 81b

In holy matters, we may promote, but not demote.
TALMUD: *Shabbath*, 21b

There are sparks of holiness in everything; they constitute our
spirituality.   THE MEZERITZER RABBI

See also: FAITH, GOD: COMPLAINTS ABOUT, GOOD DEEDS, PIETY, SAINTS,
VIRTUE

HOME

Note. The Jewish home is considered a temple, sanctified by God.
Each Friday the poorest domicile is scrubbed from stem to

stern for the eve and celebration of the holy Sabbath. To call
a Jewish woman "a real *baleboste*" means to honor her as a
true homemaker.

—L.R.

Things can be good anywhere, but they're even better at home.

There is no greater honor than to stay at home.

⋅⋖§ Pity the home where everyone is the head.

A man who never leaves his home is like a man who spends his
life in prison.

Woe to the house that serves to carry the load of a whole family's
quarrels.

Anger in a home is like rottenness in fruit.

TALMUD: *Sotah*, 3b

Immorality in a home is like a worm in fruit.

TALMUD: *Sotah*, 3b

First build a home, then marry.   TALMUD: *Sotah*, 44a

⋅⋖§ Home? The wife.   TALMUD: *Yomah*, 2a

⋅⋖§ In his home, even a weaver is a ruler.

TALMUD: *Megillah*, 12b

Dine on onions, but have a home; reduce your food and add to
your dwelling.   TALMUD: *Pesahim*, 114a

Like a bird that strays from her nest
Is a man who strays from his home.

Book of Proverbs, 27 : 8

Let your house be an assembling place for the wise: Powder yourself in the dust of their feet, and drink in their words with
zest.   *Sayings of the Fathers*, 1 : 4

⋅⋖§ In his own home, every man is king.

Abot de Rabbi Nathan, 28

The man who builds his home with the wealth of others builds
   his own grave.   BEN SIRACH: *Ecclesiasticus*, 21 : 9

The trip is never too hard, if you know you're going home.
                                          "THE CHOFETZ CHAIM"

See also: CHILDREN AND PARENTS, HUSBANDS, MARRIAGE, MEN AND
   WOMEN, WIVES

HOMELAND

There is a divine covenant in everyone's heart: to love his native
   soil—despite its climate.
                           MIDRASH: *Genesis Rabbah*, 34 : 15

Some men long more for their homeland than for their food.
                           MOSES IBN EZRA, *Shirat Yisrael*

See also: ISRAEL

HONESTY

&⁊ A man is not honest just because he has had no chance to
   steal.

&⁊ Locks keep out only the honest.

It is not the rich who pay; it is the honest.

&⁊ An honest slap is better than a false kiss.

If you walk straight, you won't fall.

Treasures unjustly acquired are of no avail;
But honesty saves from death.
                              Book of Proverbs, 10 : 2

See also: CHARACTER, DISHONESTY, FALSEHOOD, LAW, LIARS/LIES, SIN-
   CERITY, THIEVES

HONOR AND HONORS

Note. The more learned or influential a Jew, the greater is his responsibility to serve as an example of rectitude. The concept of common *noblesse oblige* (if you will pardon the oxymoron) is strong in Jewish life, but Judaic aristocracy entails not pedigree (which is prized) but knowledge plus morality plus good deeds.

The most honored figure in the life and culture of traditional Jewry was the *talmid khokhem*: the scholar of scholars, one of the rare, spiritual sages fit to be called "a disciple of the wise," one of those who might contribute to the awesome accumulated thought and ruminations known as "the sea of the Talmud." (See headnote for SCHOLARS.)

—L.R.

Honors are like a shadow: the harder you chase them, the further they run from you.

&§ Honor is measured by the one who gives it, not by the one who receives it.

Your honor is dearer than your money.

&§ It is better to die on your feet than to live on your knees.

Faith pulls us to Heaven, honor pulls us to earth.

To pledge yourself is to sell yourself.

The man who does good and does not pursue *koved* [honors], him will *koved* overtake.

Flee from an insult, but don't hurry after honors.

The man who gives with a smile is more honorable than the man who gives with a wince.

Who is honored? He who honors Mankind.

It is more honorable to help a cripple than a scholar.

No labor, however humble, dishonors a man.
                                    TALMUD: *Nedarim,* 49b

▪§ All men should rise when a sage passes.
                                    TALMUD: *Kiddushin,* 33a

The place does not honor the man; the man honors the place.
                                    TALMUD: *Ta'anith,* 21b

Like snow in summer, or rain in harvest,
Honor is unseasonable for a fool.
                                    Book of Proverbs, 26 : 1

The crown of a good name is greater than the crown of learning.
                                    Sayings of the Fathers, 3 : 13

It is better to be a footstool to a king than a king of fools.
                    BERECHIAH BEN NATRONAI, HA-NAKDAN, *Fox Fables*

▪§ I am below what people say, and above what they think.
                                    MOSES IBN EZRA, *Shirat Yisrael*

See also: ANCESTORS, COURAGE, DECORUM, GLORY, HEROES, MONEY,
    REPUTATION, RICHES, SHAME, VALOR, WEALTH

HOPE

▪§ It is good to hope, but bad to depend on it.

▪§ Hoping and waiting turn wise men into fools.

▪§ Too much hope can drive you crazy.

The longer the wait, the greater the disappointment.

The grave is already open, yet man still hopes.

As long as a man breathes he should not lose hope.
                                    TALMUD J.: *Berakoth,* 9 : 1

Hope deferred makes the heart sick;
But desire fulfilled is a tree of life.
                                    Book of Proverbs, 13 : 12

Number me the days that are not yet come, gather me the rain-
  drops that are scattered, make me the withered flowers to
  bloom again.
                                    APOCRYPHA: *II Esdras,* 5 : 36

Hope is a liar.   SHOLEM ALEICHEM

HOSPITALITY

Note. Great stress was placed on hospitality, a prime good deed,
  among Jews. Every synagogue had a hostel, attached or near
  to it, for wayfarers. The food offered to a guest had to be as
  abundant as possible, even if (as was often true) a family
  had to "go without" for many a day to come. *Hakhnose-
  sorkhim,* a recurrent Hebrew phrase for hospitality, was considered Abraham's salient virtue—and is in the liturgy recited
  each morning. The Passover service emphasizes this, too.
      The head of a Jewish household usually tried to bring a
  stranger home from the synagogue to share the Sabbath dinner. A Jewish stranger in a community on a Friday night was
  fairly certain to receive an invitation to "come home and make
  shabbes with us."

                                                —L.R.

Hospitality is one form of worship.

᭦ He who has fed a stranger may have fed an angel.

Men like guests more than women do.
                                    TALMUD: *Baba Mezi'a,* 97a

Hospitality to strangers shows reverence for the name of the Lord.
                                    TALMUD: *Shabbath,* 127a

To welcome a fellow man is to welcome the *Shekhinah* [Divine
  Presence].   MIDRASH: *Mekilta to Exodus,* 18 : 12

Welcome everyone—with joy.   *Sayings of the Fathers,* 1 : 15

See also: CHARITY, COMPASSION, DUTY, GUESTS, OBLIGATION

HOSTILITY

~§ Hostility is like an itch: the more you scratch, the more it itches.

~§ Hostility is like the plank of a bridge: the longer it endures, the firmer it becomes.

Hostility ruins sleep.

Hostility is like a stream: once it opens a path, it swiftly widens.

~§ Never try to pacify a man at the height of his hostility.

Hostility blinds you to others' virtues.

The hostile man engenders hostility against himself.

~§ Hostility makes an easy alliance with lies.

Hostility comes from fear.

The hostility that is rooted in envy lasts.

In time, hostility becomes hate.

Hostility is curable—unless it rests on envy.
                    —adapted from IBN GABIROL, *Choice of Pearls*

~§ The world goes on because of those who close their lips when they meet hostility from others.   NACHMAN OF BRATSLAV

~§ I conquered my hostility by putting it away until the day I might need it.   THE KORETSER RABBI

See also: ANGER, CRITICISM, HATE, MAN, QUARRELS, PEACE

HUMILITY

~§ Too humble is half proud.

The fruits of humility are love and peace.

Just as water leaves a high place to travel to a low one, so do
the words of Torah find a resting place only in the man of
humble spirit.   Talmud: *Ta'anith,* 7a

The larger cluster of grapes hangs down lower than the smaller;
so is it among Israel: the greater the man, the humbler he is.
                          Midrash: *Leviticus Rabbah,* 36 : 2

It is better to be humble with the lowly
Than to share spoils with the proud.   *Book of Proverbs,* 16 : 19

ᥫᶲ Humble yourself here, and you won't be humbled hereafter.
                          Midrash: *Exodus Rabbah,* 30 : 19

Be not like a large door, which lets in the wind, or like a small
door, which makes the worthy stoop; be rather like the
threshold, which all men are able to cross.
                          Tana de Rabbi Eliyahu, 193.

The bashful go to Paradise; the brazen go to Purgatory.
                          Sayings of the Fathers, 5 : 31

Be very humble, for man's destiny is the worm.
                          Sayings of the Fathers, 4 : 4

ᥫᶲ The summit of intelligence is reached in humility.
                          Ibn Gabirol, *Choice of Pearls*

ᥫᶲ The green shoots of humility are love.
                          Ibn Gabirol, *Choice of Pearls*

I find humility a greater help to me than all my fellow men.
                          Ibn Gabirol, *Choice of Pearls*

Wisdom begets humility.   Abraham ibn Ezra

ᥫᶲ A sage said: "I never met a man in whom I failed to recognize something superior to myself: if he was older, I said he
has done more good than I; if younger, I said I have sinned
more; if richer, I said he has been more charitable; if poorer,
I said he has suffered more; if wiser, I honored his wisdom;
and if not wiser, I judged his faults lighter."
                          The Testament of Judah Asheri

⠶ The man who acts humble in order to win praise is guilty of the lowest form of pride.   NACHMAN OF BRATSLAV

See also: ARROGANCE, CONCEIT, LOVE, MODESTY, PRIDE, RIGHTEOUS-NESS, TORAH, WISDOM

HUNGER

⠶ When you're hungry, sing; when you're hurt, laugh.

⠶ Those who are sated don't believe those who are hungry.

When the stomach is empty, so is the brain.

Lazy? Hungry.

The stomach has no windows.

⠶ When hunger comes through the door, love flees through the window.

Hunger is an insistent landlord.

An empty stomach cannot tolerate anything.

⠶ You die of hunger only during a famine.

⠶ When a Jew is hungry, he sings; when a nobleman is hungry, he whistles; when a peasant is hungry, he beats up his wife.

Love and hunger can't live together.

A hungry man can have sixty toothaches while a well-fed one smacks his lips.   TALMUD: *Baba Kamma,* 92b

He who is sated with food disdains the honeycomb;
But to the hungry man every bitter thing is sweet.
                    Book of Proverbs, 27 : 7

The workman's appetite works for him,
For his hunger urges him on.   *Book of Proverbs,* 16 : 26

Don't approach a hungry man for a favor: before his meal he is
like a voracious animal; after it, like a contented lamb.
SHOLEM ALEICHEM

See also: POOR MEN, POVERTY

HUSBANDS

◦§ When a man is too good for this world, it's too bad for his wife.

◦§ The man who marries for money earns it.

It is better for a woman to have one husband, though he be
useless, than ten wealthy children.

◦§ An old man who marries a young wife grows younger—but she
grows older.

A faithless husband makes a faithless wife.   TALMUD: *Sotah,* 10a

A man should not become the husband of a pregnant woman or
divorcee until her child is born.   TALMUD: *Yebamoth,* 36b

◦§ A henpecked husband can't get relief in a court.
TALMUD: *Baba Mezi'a,* 75b

See also: DIVORCE, MARRIAGE, MEN AND WOMEN, WIVES

HYPOCRISY

An insincere kiss is worse than an honest blow.

If you want to be considered smart, just agree with everyone.

The hypocrite will never see God's face.   TALMUD: *Sotah,* 42a

There are four classes of men who cannot see the Holy Spirit:
mockers, hypocrites, slanderers, and liars.
MIDRASH: *Midrash Psalms,* 101 : 7

An idolater worships one object, but there is no limit to the number of men whom the hypocrite will worship.

BAHYA IBN PAQUDA, *Duties of the Heart*

◆§ Beware the man who has two faces—and two hearts.

MOSES IBN EZRA, *Shirat Yisrael*

See also: GOSSIP, LIARS/LIES, SLANDER

IDEALS

If I do not acquire ideals in my youth, when will I? Not in old age.

MAIMONIDES

Everyone is dedicated to that which he desires and chooses.

SAMUEL HA-NAGID

A generation in which human ideals do not improve must perish.

THE KORETSER RABBI

See also: ALTRUISM, COMPASSION, SELFISHNESS

IDEAS

Those on the other side of a fence have different ideas.

◆§ Corrupt ideas are worse than corrupt money.

Fooling people with words is more contemptible than cheating
them out of money.

See also: CUSTOM, INTELLIGENCE, JUDGMENT, REASON

IDLENESS

◦§ The hardest work of all is to do nothing.

Idlers get busy when other men sleep.

Rip and sew, but don't stay idle.

Through slothfulness the rafters sink in, and through idleness of
hands the house leaks.   *Ecclesiastes*, 10 : 18

The sluggard will not plow in autumn;
So in harvest he seeks a crop in vain.   *Book of Proverbs*, 20 : 4

As vinegar to the teeth, and smoke to the eyes,
So is the sluggard to those who send him on an errand.
                                    Book of Proverbs, 10 : 26

◦§ Whoever does no work will suffer all his life.
                        MAIMONIDES: *Mishneh Torah*, Deot 4

Man dies of idleness—and boredom.   *Abot de Rabbi Nathan*, 11

◦§ The idle man, even a king, ends in weakness, sickness, or madness.

                        —adapted from SAADIA GAON

See also: BOREDOM, BUSINESS, CHARITY, SHIRKERS, THRIFT, WORK

IDOLATRY

Roman pagan to a rabbi: "Your God abominates idolatry; why then
does He not destroy the idols?"
"Would you have God destroy the sun and moon because of the
foolish people who worship them?"
                        TALMUD: *Abodah Zarah*, 54b

See also: FAITH, GOD, HYPOCRISY/HYPOCRITES

IGNORANCE

Note. An *am ha-arets* (from the Hebrew: "people of the soil") is
described in the Talmud as one who does not respect the Law,
and by Maimonides as "a boor in whom is neither learning nor
moral virtue." Rabbi Nathan ben Joseph called an *am ha-arets*
"one who has children and does not educate them . . ."

—L.R.

Only the ignorant are really poor.

The greatest luck of an *am ha-arets* [ignoramus] is this: he
doesn't know that he doesn't know.

Beware of those whose ignorance is joined with piety.

When a scholar seeks a bride, he should take an ignoramus
along to advise him.

Even a blind hen sometimes finds a grain.

Wise men, grown older, grow wiser; ignorant men, grown older,
grow more foolish.

For the ignorant, old age is winter; for the learned, old age is the
harvest.   Hasidic saying

The man who hides his ignorance is better than the *khakhem*
(wise man) who parades his wisdom.

The ignorant think less clearly as they grow older; scholars think
more clearly as they age.   TALMUD: *Kinnin,* 3 : end

The ignorant cannot really be pious.
Sayings of the Fathers, 2 : 5

Do not say, "I will love the learned and hate the ignorant"; love
them both.   —adapted from *Abot de Rabbi Nathan,* 16

He who refuses to learn deserves extinction.
HILLEL in *Sayings of the Fathers*

Don't make fun of the ignorant: you may be maligning your ancestry. BEN SIRACH, *Ecclesiasticus,* 8 : 4

See also: **ADVICE, FOOLS, ILLOGIC, NEBBEKH, SHLEMIELS, STUPIDITY**

ILLOGIC

◆§ A deaf man heard a mute tell him how a blind man saw a cripple run—on water.

Sleep faster, we need the pillows.

Beating your wife with the paddle won't make the sheets white.

Food is cooked in a pot, but the plate gets the praise.

See also: **FOLLY, FOOLS, NONSENSE, SENSE, STUPIDITY**

ILLUSION

◆§ A worm in a jar of horseradish thinks he's in Paradise.

A mirror fools no one except the homely.

◆§ Illusions are comforting; just don't act upon them.

Some things smell sweet and taste bitter.

◆§ He's half a millionaire: he has the air, but not the million.

◆§ We always think that others are enjoying themselves.

Illusions drive men mad.

See also: **ADVICE, FOLLY, IMAGINATION, REALITY, SENSE**

IMAGINATION

◆§ The deaf imagine what they cannot hear.

Things can be imagined more quickly than they can be achieved.

See also: **ILLUSION, REALITY, SENSE**

IMMORALITY

Men hate moralists, without being immoral.

Immorality in a house is like a worm in a plant.
> TALMUD: *Sotah,* 3b

See also: GOOD, GOOD AND EVIL, HONESTY, HONOR/HONORS, SIN, VIRTUE

IMMORTALITY

⋙ The good die but live on, in the example they provided.
> —adapted from TALMUD: *Berakoth,* 18b

Whoever lives by Torah, good deeds, humility and the fear of God
will be saved from eternal doom.
> MIDRASH: *Pesikta Rabbati,* 198a

Live as if you expect to live forever, but plan as if you expect to
enter the hereafter tomorrow.
> IBN GABIROL, *Choice of Pearls*

God, the Source of Life, endowed us with the blessed hope of immortality, so that we can console ourselves over the vanity of
life, and contend with the dread of death.
> JEDAIA BEN BEDERSI

See also: DEATH, ETERNITY, HEREAFTER, PARADISE, SALVATION, SOUL

IMPUDENCE

⋙ Impudence [*chutzpa*] is sovereignty without a crown.
> TALMUD: *Sanhedrin,* 105a

See also: ARROGANCE, CONCEIT, HUMILITY, VANITY

IMPULSE

See: MAN, PASSION, TEMPER

INDEPENDENCE

Better independent than humiliated.

Better a pushcart with your own money than a store with someone else's.

Rather than become dependent, do work even if it is beneath you.
                                                    TALMUD: *Pesahim*, 113a

See also: CHARITY, DEPENDENCE, HONOR, POWER, SELF-ESTEEM, VIRTUE

INDIVIDUALITY

◀§ If I am like someone else, who will be like me?

Not all horses enjoy the same thing.

Rabbi Zusya said, before his death: "In the world-to-come I shall not be asked: 'Why were you not Moses?' but 'Why were you not Zusya?'"   Hasidic saying

◀§ Some prefer vinegar and some prefer wine.
                                                    TALMUD: *Kiddushin*, 48b

Even one ear of corn is not exactly like another.
                                                    TALMUD: *Sanhedrin*, 4 : 9

The Creator made all men different in features, intelligence, and voice, in order to promote honesty and chastity.
                            RABBI MEIR in TOSEPHTA: *Sanhedrin*, 8 : 6

Men's features are not alike; nor are their opinions.
                            MAIMONIDES: *Mishneh Torah*, Deot 1

See also: ADAM, INDEPENDENCE, MAN, and individual character traits

INDUSTRIOUSNESS

He who comes first grinds first.

He who needs the fire must fan it.   *Midrash Samuel*

If a man does not plow in the summer, what will he eat in the
   winter?   *Midrash Proverbs*

He who tills his ground will have plenty of food;
But he who follows empty pursuit lacks sense.
                              Book of Proverbs, 12 : 11

See also: DETERMINATION, EFFORT, WILL, WORK

INEVITABILITY

ఆ§ The stone fell on the pitcher? Woe to the pitcher. The pitcher
   fell on the stone? Woe to the pitcher.
                      MIDRASH: *Esther Rabbah*, 7 : 10

See also: CAUSE AND EFFECT, CONSEQUENCES, REALITY

INFLUENCE

One egg can whiten a whole bowl of borsht.

To be in the company of a wise man is like going into a perfumery:
   you may not buy a thing, but the sweet scent will cling to you
   for a day.   *Abot de Rabbi Nathan*, 11 : 14b

See also: AUTHORITY, CAUSE AND EFFECT, CONSEQUENCES, POWER

INFORMER

An informer should be hanged by his tongue.

See also: LIARS, SLANDER

INGENUITY

ఆ§ Some things are clever only the first time.

An impudent young Pole put both hands behind his back and
   challenged a rabbi in this way: "Your attention! I hold a little
   bird in one of my hands. Guess which one. If you guess right,

I'll let the bird go free; if you guess wrong, I'll strangle it, and its death will be on your head! . . . What does your precious Talmud tell Jews about a dilemma such as this?"

The rabbi studied the young man dolorously, then sighed: "Our Talmud tells us that the awful choice between life and death—is in your hands."   Hasidic story

See also: **LOGIC, REASON, RESOURCEFULNESS**

INGRATITUDE

When he was a puppy I fed him, and when he became a dog he bit me.

∞§ If you give people nuts, you'll get shells thrown at you.
                                        Yemenite proverb

See also: **CHARITY, GRATITUDE, GREED**

INHERITANCE

∞§ If you come for the legacy you may have to pay for the funeral.

The richest inheritance can become a burden.

Dowries and legacies bring no luck.

Dogs fight over a bone, and mourners over a will.

To dissipate your inheritance, wear white linen, use glass, or be an absentee employer.   TALMUD: *Hullin,* 84b

See also: **LUCK**

INIQUITY

All iniquity is like a two-edged sword;
A blow from it cannot be healed.
                         BEN SIRACH, *Ecclesiasticus,* 21 : 3

See also: **EVIL, SIN**

INJUSTICE

The best morsels are given to the worst dogs.

Better suffer an injustice than commit one.

See also: EVIL, HONOR, JUSTICE, LAW, SIN

INNOCENCE

◄§ God looks into our hearts before he looks into our minds.

Innocence goes with peacefulness.

Don't try to identify the Tree of Knowledge: you may cast suspicion on one innocent. MIDRASH: *Genesis Rabbah,* 15 : 7

See also: CHILDREN, GOOD DEEDS, GUILT, MAN, VIRTUE

INQUISITION

Note. "Would you believe that as the flames were consuming these innocent victims, the inquisitors . . . were chanting our prayers? These pitiless monsters invoked the God of mercy and kindness and pardon while committing the most atrocious, barbarous crime, acting in a way which demons in their rage would not use against brother demons."
                                  —VOLTAIRE, *Sermon du Rabin Akib'*

"In 1390 . . . the Catholics of Seville being excited by the eloquence of a great preacher . . . attacked the Jews' quarter, and murdered 4,000 Jews. . . . About a year later, similar scenes took place at Valentia, Cordova, Burgos, Toledo, Barcelona . . . the Inquisition was established [and] numbers of converted Jews were massacred. Others, who had been baptized during past explosions of popular fury, fled to the Moors, to practise their religious rites, and at last, after a desperate resistance, were captured and burnt alive."
          W. E. H. LECKY, *Rationalism in Europe,* 1865, chap. 6

See: ANTI-SEMITISM, INTOLERANCE, PERSECUTION, POGROMS, PREJUDICE

INSANITY

The *entire* world isn't crazy.

> There is no man without his own kind of *meshugas* (craziness).

Even the man who has everything dare not stay idle, for the idle man, be he even a king, will end in weakness, sickness, or insanity.　　　　　—adapted from SAADIA GAON

See also: DISEASE, ILLOGIC, ILLUSION, NONSENSE, REASON

INSIGHT

In sleep, thoughts come to your mind to reveal the thoughts of your heart.　　　—adapted from the *Book of Daniel,* 2 : 29–30

Where there is no knowledge there can be no insight, and where there is no insight there can be no knowledge.
　　　　　　　　　Sayings of the Fathers, 3 : 2

The beginning of wisdom is to desire it.
　　　　　　　　　IBN GABIROL, *Choice of Pearls*

See also: INTELLIGENCE, REASON, SENSE, UNDERSTANDING

INTELLECT

> Man's best companion is his intellect; his worst enemy is his lust.

The man who wishes to attain human perfection should study Logic first, next Mathematics, then Physics, and lastly Metaphysics.　　　MAIMONIDES, *Guide to the Perplexed,* 1

Intellect is the dividing line between man and beast: it masters natural impulses and subdues passions.
　　　　　　　　　IBN GABIROL: *Choice of Pearls*

There is no [genuine] distinction except in the intellect.
HAYYIM VITAL

Intellect is a man's guard; without it he is like an infant.
THE KORETSER RABBI

See also: INTELLIGENCE, PASSION, REASON, UNDERSTANDING

INTELLIGENCE

When brains are needed, muscles won't help.

Any man can count his own teeth.

Of what use are gray hairs, when the brains are still green?

Eggs may be smarter than hens, but they rot faster.

We don't need intelligence to have luck, but we do need luck to
have intelligence.

Borrowed brains are of no use.

Silence is the only good substitute for intelligence.

As face reflects face in water,
So the mind of Man reflects Man.   *Book of Proverbs,* 27 : 19

The senseless man pours contempt on his neighbor;
But the intelligent man keeps silent.
Book of Proverbs, 11 : 12

The spiritual perfection of man consists in his becoming an intelligent being—one who knows all that he is capable of learning.
And such knowledge is obtained not by virtue or piety, but
through inquiry and research.
MAIMONIDES: *Guide to the Perplexed,* 3

Seykhl [good sense] is a gift, but intelligence is an acquisition.
IBN GABIROL

Sweet of voice, but short of brains.
IMMANUEL OF ROME, *Mahberot*

Brains to the lazy are like a torch to the blind—a useless burden.

BEDERSI, *Behinat ha-Olam*

See also: IGNORANCE, INTELLECT, INSIGHT, KNOWLEDGE, REASON, STU-
PIDITY, UNDERSTANDING

INTOLERANCE

Note. "Insulted, plundered, hated, and despised by all Christian
nations, banished from England by Edward I, and from France
by Charles VI, they found in the Spanish Moors . . . a special
sympathy for a race whose pure monotheism formed a marked
contrast to the scarcely disguised polytheism of the Spanish.
. . . Jewish learning and Jewish genius contributed very largely
to that bright but transient civilization which radiated from
Toledo and Cordova, and exercised so salutary an influence
upon the behalf of Europe. But when, in an ill-omened hour,
the Cross supplanted the Crescent on the heights of the Al-
hambra, this solitary refuge was destroyed, the last gleam of
tolerance vanished from Spain, and the expulsion of the Jews
was determined."
—W. E. H. Lecky, *Rationalism in Europe,* 1865, chapter 6.

⊷ No one is as deaf as the man who will not listen.

See also: ANTI-SEMITISM, INQUISITION, JEWS, PERSECUTION, PREJUDICE

IRONY: EXAMPLES

Any man can count his own teeth.

Too bad: The bride is too beautiful.

There are two involved in feasting on a chicken: me and the
chicken.

⊷ The fool who shuts up sounds like a sage.

⊷ The daughters of the rich are always beautiful.

A pretty thanks—to your navel. [Thanks for nothing.]

One father manages to support ten children; but ten children don't seem to be able to support one father.

The can of a tinsmith is full of holes, and the shoemaker goes barefoot.

Even the unlucky need luck.

A Litvak is so clever that he repents *before* he sins.

Men become more brotherly during prosperity.

❧ A broken clock is still better than one that goes wrong: at least it is right twice a day.

It's worth as much as a blown-out egg.

The world would burst with philanthropists—if giving cost nothing.

❧ He is a good man—according to his epitaph.

❧ All corpses look pious.

Many men are generous—with other people's money.

❧ God gave me such a good brain that in one minute I can worry more than others do in a year.

Miracles do happen—but they rarely provide food.

To judge according to beards or girth is to conclude that goats are the wisest creatures on earth.
                                          —adapted from JOSEPH SOLOMON DELMEDIGO

See also: ADAGES, ADVICE, SARCASM

IRRATIONALITY

See: FOLLY, ILLOGIC, ILLUSION, REASON

ISRAEL

Note. Since the exile of the Jews to Babylonia, Zion or Israel has
continued the idea of a reunited Jewish people returned to
their homeland. "By the rivers of Babylon, there we sat down,
yea, we wept when we remembered Zion" (Psalm 137). Wherever they lived, when Jews prayed they turned in the direction of Jerusalem.

    Erets Yisroel ("the land of Israel") is the believing Jews'
"Promised Land," promised by God to Abraham's descendants, the kingdom of David and Solomon, the land in which
Holy Jerusalem was built, the land where the Messiah will
appear.

—L.R.

❧ Whatever will happen to all Israel will happen to Mr. Israel.

Burial in Israel is like burial under the altar of the Temple.
                       TALMUD: *Kethuboth,* 11a

Israel has no *mazel* [lucky star], because it is under God's direct
    protection.   TALMUD: *Shabbath,* 156a

Israel is shielded and lifted by its precepts as a dove by its wings.
                       TALMUD: *Shabbath,* 130a

The community is Israel's rampart.   TALMUD: *Baba Bathra,* 7a

Israel is like a vine: the people are the branches, the unlearned
the leaves, and the learned are the fruit.
                       TALMUD: *Hullin,* 92a

Israel is like a vine: trodden underfoot; but some time later its
wine is placed on the table of a king. So, Israel, at first oppressed, will eventually come to greatness.
                       TALMUD: *Nedarim,* 49b

As everyone treads on dust, so does every nation tread on Israel;
but dust lasts longer than metal, and so shall Israel outlast
the others.   MIDRASH: *Genesis Rabbah,* 41 : 9

 Why is Israel like a dove? Other birds, when tired, rest on a
branch; but when the dove tires, she rests one wing and flies
with the other.   MIDRASH: *Genesis Rabbah,* 39 : 10

God told Moses and Aaron: "Accept my mission, but be prepared
for stones and curses."   MIDRASH: *Exodus Rabbah,* 7

Myrtle is sweet to the one who smells it, but bitter to the one
who bites it; so Israel brings prosperity to those who grant
it kindness, and depression to those who afflict it with evil.
                    MIDRASH: *Esther Rabbah,* 6 : 5

Why is Israel like sand? As in the sand you dig a pit, and in the
evening find it filled up, so is it with Israel.
                    —adapted from MIDRASH: *Pesikta*

Sand mixed in bread injures the teeth: so will those who persecute
Israel suffer for it.   —adapted from MIDRASH: *Pesikta*

 When trouble comes into the world, Israel feels it first: when
good comes, Israel feels it first, too.
                    MIDRASH: *Lamentations Rabbah,* 2 : 3

The death of a sage is worse for Israel than the death of a king;
for a sage cannot be replaced, but all Israel is eligible to
succeed a king.   —adapted from MIDRASH

Why is Israel like a worm? Because the worm's sole strength lies
in its mouth. So is it with Israel [for it has the power of
prayer].   *Zohar*

 A tent cannot stand without pegs and cord, and Israel cannot
stand without scholars.   *Seder Eliyahu Rabbah*

 Living in Israel is itself an atonement for one's sins.
                    RABBI MEIR in *Sifre—Deuteronomy*

Among the nations Israel is like the heart amidst the organs of
the body: both the sickest and the healthiest of all.
                    JUDAH HA-LEVI, *Kuzari,* ch. 2

 The real slavery in Egypt was this: the Israelites learned to
endure it.   SIMCHA BUNIM

As sand is moved from place to place without a sound, so Israel
is exiled from place to place without complaint.
                          SAMUEL BUBER, *Introduction to Tanhuma*, 134

See also: JEWS, SABBATH, SCHOLARS

J

JEALOUSY

❧ Love may be blind, but jealousy sees too much.

❧ We anger God with our sins, and men with our virtues.

The jealousy [competition] of scribes helps increase wisdom.
                                    TALMUD: *Baba Bathra*, 21a

Jealousy in the heart makes the bones rot.
                                    Book of Proverbs, 14 : 30

Wrath is ruthless, and anger a torrent;
But before jealousy who can stand?   *Book of Proverbs*, 27 : 4

Jealousy is as cruel as the grave.   *Song of Solomon*, 8 : 6

❧ The man who loves without jealousy does not truly love.
                                                        Zohar

See also: ENVY, LOVE, SUSPICION

JERUSALEM

Note. Jerusalem was established because of administrative and
    military necessities: the great city, like the monarchy, was

not an aspect of the early life and dreams of ancient Israel. Urban life was a challenge of no small proportions in the religious tradition of Israel, until then a semi-nomadic and agricultural people.

David captured Jebus/Jerusalem in the 11th century before the Christian Era and made the city the center of a united Israel. He moved the holy Ark of the Covenant to his new capital—which became the head of an empire that, at its apogee, stretched from the Red Sea to the Euphrates.

In the Diaspora, Jews all over the world looked towards, and dreamed of, Jerusalem as the spiritual heart of Judaism and the symbolic capital of Jewry.

L.R.

"The Assyrians burnt it and deported its population; the Romans slew a million of its inhabitants, razed it to the ground, passed the ploughshare over it, and strewed its furrows with salt; Hadrian banished its very name from the lips of men, changed it to 'Aelia Capitolina,' and prohibited any Jew from entering its precincts on pain of death. Persians and Arabs, Barbarians and Crusaders and Turks, took it and retook it, ravaged it and burnt it; and yet, marvellous to relate, it ever rises from its ashes to renewed life and glory."

—J. H. Hertz, at the Thanksgiving service for
the capture of Jerusalem by British forces, 1917.

To dwell in the Holy Land tends to prevent sin.

Talmud: *Kethuboth,* 111a

Jerusalem was destroyed because its children did not attend school.　　　　　　　Talmud: *Shabbath,* 119b

See: ISRAEL

JEWS

Note. What is a Jew? Morris N. Kertzer's lucid answer, in a book bearing that question as its title,* takes up 207 pages. One can list a bibliography of staggering length on the topic. A

---

* *What Is A Jew?,* World Publishing Co., New York, 1953.

refreshing lucidity distinguishes the following passage from Dr. Morris Adler:

> Jews do not constitute a church but a people. One of the reasons the modern Jew finds it difficult to define his identity is that the English language offers no term to suggest the complex of ethnic, national, cultural and religious elements that constitute the collective life of the Jew. The irreligious Jew is not read out of the community. Affiliation ... is not a matter of creed. The religion of the Jew embraces areas that modern man would call secular. There is no instance, in the Western world, of an ethnic group whose religion emerged out of its own history ... the word church does not fit the Jewish situation.*

I sometimes remember Mark Twain's words:

> The Jew made a marvelous fight in this world, in all the ages; and has done it with his hands tied behind him. The Egyptian, the Babylonian, and the Persian rose, filled the planet with sound and splendor, then faded to dream stuff and passed away. The Greek and the Roman followed, and made a vast noise, and they are gone. Other peoples have sprung up and held their torch high for a time, but it burned out, and they sit in twilight now, or have vanished. The Jew ... is now what he always was—exhibiting no decadence, no infirmities of age ... no slowing of his energies, no dulling of his alert and aggressive mind.**

Allow me one final, arresting quotation, from Heine:

> I see now that the Greeks were only handsome youths, whilst the Jews were always men—powerful, indomitable men—who have fought and suffered on every battlefield of human thought.***

—L.R.

◢§ When a Jewish farmer eats a chicken, one of them is sick.

◢§ The Jew who can't be a cobbler dreams of becoming a professor.

◢§ Jews are just like everyone else—only more so.

---

* *The World of the Talmud,* B'nai Brith Hillel Foundations, 1958, p. 124.
** "Concerning the Jews," *Harper's Monthly,* September 1899.
*** In *A Book of Jewish Thoughts,* ed. J. H. Hertz, Oxford, London, 1920, p. 66.

Better a Jew without a beard than a beard without a Jew.

&ε If a Jew breaks a leg, he thanks God he did not break both legs; if he breaks both legs, he thanks God he did not break his neck.

The joy of Jews is never free of anxiety.

A Jew is always short one day. ["If I only had one more day."]

&ε When a Jew is hungry, he sings; when a peasant is hungry, he beats his wife.

The nobleman thinks of his horse and dog; the Jew thinks of his wife and child.

&ε "Thou hast chosen us from among all the nations"—but why did You have to pick on the Jews?

&ε When trouble comes, Jews feel it first; when fortune smiles, Jews feel it last.

&ε Every Jew has his own brand of madness.

A Jew on a desert island will build two synagogues—so that he will have one he does not want to go to.

Gentiles aren't used to Jewish troubles.

&ε A nation that persecutes Jews cannot last long.

Tie my four limbs, but throw me among my own.

Jewish wealth is like a March snow.

Misfortune seldom misses a Jew.

A Jew answers a question with a question.

If a Jew be right, he is beaten all the more.

One is not doomed among Jews.

&ε Whoever renounces idol worship may be called a Jew.
                                        TALMUD: *Megillah,* 13a

Poverty is the ornament of the Jews.   TALMUD: *Hagigah*, 9b

A Jew is prohibited from deceiving even a worshipper of idols.
                                         TALMUD: *Baba Kamma*, 113b

"They are my servants" [Lev., 25 : 55]—not servants' servants.
                                         TALMUD: *Baba Mezi'a*, 10a

What is permitted one Jew is permitted another.
                                         TALMUD: *Bezah*, 25a

If a group of Jews on a long journey are overtaken by barbarians
    who say, "Give us one of your number, or we shall kill you
    all," let all be slain: for no Israelite may deliberately be de-
    livered to barbarians.   TALMUD: *Sanhedrin*, 84a

❧ We (Jews) must not appoint a leader in any community
    without first consulting the people.
                                         TALMUD: *Berakoth*, 55a

There are three impudent creatures: among beasts, the dog; among
    birds, the cock; among people, Israel. But Rabbi Ammi added:
    "Do not consider this as blame; it is praise, for to be a Jew
    means to be ready to be martyred."
                                         MIDRASH: *Exodus Rabbah*, 42 : 9

Is a Jew an alien anywhere? Wherever he goes, his God is with
    him.   MIDRASH: *Deuteronomy Rabbah*, 2 : 16

❧ If all the seas were ink, and all the reeds pens, and all the
    people scribes, it would not be enough to record all the mis-
    fortunes of the Jews in a single year.
                                         MIDRASH: *Megillath Ta'anith*

Ye shall be a peculiar treasure unto me among all peoples.
                                         Book of Exodus, 19 : 5

God found the Jews as one finds grapes in the desert.
                                         Book of Hosea, 9 : 10

A true Jew is distinguished by three characteristics: sympathy,
    modesty, benevolence.   *Sayings of the Fathers*, 5 : 22

No Jew, however learned and pious, may consider himself one
whit better than a fellow Jew, however ignorant or irreligious.
Simcha Bunim

The best weapons of a Jew are his prayers.
NACHMAN OF BRATSLAV

The real "Jewish Question" is this: From what can a Jew earn a
living?   SHOLEM ALEICHEM

Though Pesach [Passover] comes but once a year, Jews ask questions all year long. [The Passover feast features "the four
questions," usually asked by the youngest son.]
SHOLEM ALEICHEM

We are God's stake in human history.   A. J. HESCHEL

It is no challenge to die like a Jew; the true challenge is to live
like a Jew.   THE CHOFETZ CHAIM

See also: ISRAEL, PERSECUTION, REFUGEES, SABBATH, SYNAGOGUE

JOY

Joy finds its completion in success.
IMMANUEL OF ROME, *Mahberot*

A man's joy is greatest when his family is with him.
EPHRAIM LUNTSHITZ, *Keli Yakar*

Joy and sadness are as close as day and night.
HAYYIM OF VOLOZHIN

See also: CONTENTMENT, FAMILY, HAPPINESS, PIETY, PLEASURES

JUDAISM

Note. It has been said that whereas the core of Christianity is the
figure of Jesus, the core of Judaism is the Law—as set forth
in the Torah, the Oral Tradition, the Talmud. It was a Chris-

tian scholar who made this interesting distinction: Christianity is a religion built around an ideal person; Judaism is a religion of ideals.

Not even Moses is considered divine by Jews; nor is he worshipped; nor is he sanctified. There is one passage in the Talmud, indeed, in which the learned agree that the patriarch Ezra was entirely virtuous—virtuous enough to receive the holy tablets on Mount Sinai from the Lord, but that Moses happened to precede him. In the Book of Nehemiah (8 : 8) we are told that at a great convocation of the Jews, after their return from slavery in Babylonia (in the middle of the fifth century before the Christian Era), Ezra read the Torah before the Jews and "they read in the book, in the law of God, distinctly; and they gave the sense and caused them to understand the reading." What Ezra had decided to do was translate the laws of God into ordinances (Ezra, 7 : 10), so that the Holy Torah would be *applied*, given the authority of Law—which was continually to be increased by close study and interpretation. The word *"Midrash,"* which means "interpretations," comes from the root of the word Ezra himself employed as "to seek": *lidrosh,* which can also be translated as "to interpret."

So began the long tradition and practice of teachers, scholars, rabbis, sages, interpreting and teaching the Law. (See GUIDENOTES for Talmud, Mishnah, Midrash.)

—L.R.

See: JEWS, RELIGION, TORAH

JUDGES

Note. Every Jewish community in Europe usually had its own civil court (*Beth Din*), presided over by a chief rabbi or a *dayan.* (In rabbinic literature, *dayan* means either "sage" or "rabbinical judge"; every *dayan* was a rabbi, but only a rare rabbi was a *dayan.*) These Jewish courts dealt with religious and local (Jewish community) problems, and with those disputes (marriage, divorce, legacies, debts) in which the disputants sought advice or arbitration. These courts had no legal authority: Jews came to them voluntarily and accepted their judgments. The first question asked of litigants was: "Do you wish law or arbitration?"

When a dispute involved formal litigation, at least three rabbi-judges were required to sit on the bench of the *Beth Din.* In the Middle Ages, special "guild" courts governed different trades and occupations. In Israel today, these courts are official: they operate in the office of the central Rabbinate; they have exclusive jurisdiction over certain areas: legal status, marriage, inheritances, etc.

—L.R.

✑ Don't blame the judge for the law.

When a judge sits in judgment over a fellow man, he should feel as if a sword is pointed at his own heart.
TALMUD: *Sanhedrin,* 8a

✑ Two scholars who dislike each other may not sit together as judges.   TALMUD: *Sanhedrin,* 29a

Judgment delayed is judgment voided.
TALMUD: *Sanhedrin,* 95a

No man can be declared guilty in his absence.
TALMUD: *Kethuboth,* 11a

A habitual borrower is unfit to be a judge.
TALMUD: *Kethuboth,* 105b

As Rabbi Samuel was boarding a ferry, a man rushed up to help him; the rabbi asked why he was so attentive, and the man said, "Because I have a lawsuit that will come up in your court." To which Rabbi Samuel replied, "Then I am forbidden to be your judge."   TALMUD: *Kethuboth,* 105b

✑ I cannot try the case of one of my students, because I love him as myself, and no one can see a fault in himself.
TALMUD: *Shabbath,* 119a

✑ A judge who has drunk a quart of wine may not sit in judgment: He will condemn the innocent and acquit the guilty.
MIDRASH: *Leviticus Rabbah,* 1 : 4, 8

❧ If there be no officer to enforce the law, what power do judges possess?   MIDRASH: *Tanhuma, Shofetim*

He who passes judgment on fools is himself judged a fool.
MIDRASH

The judge who knows other judges have erred, but agrees because he does not want to shame them, will end in *Gehenna*.
Sefer Hasidim

Don't sue a judge, for he will have it his way.
BEN SIRACH, *Ecclesiasticus*, 8 : 14

Just as you listen to the poor man, listen to the rich man, for it is written, "Ye shall not favor persons in judgment."
Abot de Rabbi Nathan, 20 : 22a

❧ The rabbis said about capital cases: "We decide by a majority of one for acquittal, but only by a majority of at least two for conviction."
RASHI, *Commentaries on the Pentateuch, Exodus*

See also: COURTS, EVIDENCE, JUSTICE, LAW, REASON

JUDGMENT

Before you start up a ladder, count the rungs.

❧ A chicken in the hand is better than an eagle in the sky.

❧ When shnaps [liquor] goes in, judgment goes out.

Ask advice wherever you will, but act according to your own judgment.

❧ Don't try to fill a sack that's full of holes.

It is better to measure ten times and cut once, than measure once and cut ten times.

❧ Judge a man not by the words of his mother, but from the comments of his neighbors.   TALMUD

Judge a man only by his own deeds and words; the opinions of others can be false.   TALMUD

It is better to have one bird in a cage than a hundred in the air.
                              MIDRASH: *Ecclesiastes Rabbah*, 4 : 6

If you come too close to fire, you get burnt; if you stray too far, you'll be cold; the art [of judgment] is to find the right distance.   *Mekilta on Jethro*

Judge every man charitably.   *Sayings of the Fathers*, 1 : 6

The man who accepts tradition without applying his own intelligence and judgment is like a blind man following others.
                              BAHYA IBN PAQUDA, *Duties of the Heart*

⋙ If you can't have what you want, want what you can have.
                              IBN GABIROL, *Improvement of Character*

See also: ABILITY, FORESIGHT, PRUDENCE, REALITY, SENSE

JUSTICE

The just way is always the right way.

Justice delayed is worse than injustice.

Give every man the benefit of the doubt.
                              Sayings of the Fathers, 1 : 7

The Roman Emperor Antoninus once said to Rabbi Judah the Prince, "On the Day of Judgment, Soul and Body will stand before the Heavenly Judge, and the Body will say, 'It is the Soul, not I, who sinned; for without the Soul, I am as lifeless as a stone.' And the Soul will say, 'How canst Thou impute sin to me? It is the body that dragged me down.' . . . What say you to that?"

    Answered Rabbi Judah: "A king once had a garden of wonderful fruits and put two men to guard over it—a blind man and a lame man. One day, the lame man said, 'I see some luscious fruit, but cannot reach it.' 'Then get on my back,' said the blind man. 'I can carry you there, then you stand on my shoulder and we shall both enjoy plenteous fruit.' When the king discovered the fruit gone, he haled both men before him. The lame one said, 'I could not have been the thief: I cannot walk!' And the blind man said, 'I could not have been the thief; I cannot see a thing!' But the king was very wise and asked the lame man to climb on the shoulders of the blind man—and sentenced them both. In the same way, your Majesty, will the Divine Judge of the Universe mete out judgment—to body and soul together."

—adapted from TALMUD

Abraham said to God: "If you want the world to exist you cannot insist upon complete justice; if it is complete justice you want, the world cannot endure."

MIDRASH: *Genesis Rabbah*, 49 : 20

Don't try to identify the Tree of Knowledge: Heaven forbid that we cast suspicion on any [innocent] tree!

MIDRASH: *Genesis Rabbah*, 15 : 7

When Rabbi Ammi's hour to die came, he wept bitterly; and his nephew asked, "But why do you weep? Is there any Torah you have not learned and taught? Is there any kindness you have not practiced? And you never accepted public office, or sat in judgment on others." The rabbi replied: "That is why I weep: I was given the ability to extend justice, but never carried it out."

—adapted from MIDRASH: *Tanhuma on Mishpatim*

If you see wicked men perverting justice, do not say: "Since they are many, I must follow after them."

RASHI, *Commentaries on the Pentateuch, Exodus*

To arbitrate is to temper justice with charity.

NACHMAN OF BRATSLAV

See also: GOOD, RIGHTEOUSNESS, VIRTUE

KILLING

Whoever destroys a single life is as guilty as though he had destroyed the entire world; and whoever rescues a single life earns as much merit as though he had rescued the entire world.   TALMUD: *Sanhedrin,* 37 : a

Someone came before Raba and said: "The mayor of my town has told me, 'Go and kill so and so; if you do not, I will have you killed.'
    Raba said to him: "Let him kill you. Do you think your blood is redder than another man's? Perhaps his blood is redder than yours."   TALMUD: *Sanhedrin,* 72b

If a man kills a thief, it is not murder, since a thief is like one who has been dead from the beginning.
    RASHI, *Commentaries on the Pentateuch, Exodus*

See also: ADAM, COMPASSION, GOOD DEEDS, KINDNESS, TORAH, VIRTUE

KINDNESS

Kindness is the beginning and the end of the Law.

A kindness is remembered, a meanness is felt.

Kindness is better than piety.

ఆర్ God is not kind to those who are not kind.

Kindness is even greater than charity.

A kind word is better than a handout.

One should feed his animals before sitting down to table.

TALMUD: *Gittin,* 62a

The highest form of wisdom is kindness.

TALMUD: *Berakoth,* 17a

Where there is no truth, there is no kindness.

NACHMAN OF BRATSLAV

See also: ALTRUISM, CHARITY, COMPASSION, CONSIDERATION, GOOD
DEEDS, PIETY, VIRTUE

KNOWLEDGE

With knowledge, one is nowhere lost.

Knowledge is the best merchandise.

◈ Some men study so much they don't have time to know.

◈ To know a trade is to own a kingdom.

◈ Every new answer raises a new question.

A man is greater than the knowledge he acquired.

The head of a fool is like a broken dish: it will not hold knowledge.

Those who know much age fast.

◈ It is better to know nothing than to learn nothing.

◈ A light for one is a light for a hundred.

TALMUD: *Shabbath,* 122a

◈ If thou hast acquired knowledge, what canst thou lack? If
thou lackest knowledge, what hast thou acquired?

MIDRASH: *Leviticus Rabbah,* 1

◈ Man enters the world with a whimper and exits with a cry: for
he enters the world without knowledge, and leaves it without
knowledge.   MIDRASH: *Ecclesiastes Rabbah,* 5

When wine comes in, knowledge goes out.
                    MIDRASH: *Tanhuma Yashan on Leviticus*, 7

◦§ Knowledge is a hoard from which nothing can be lost.
                                                IBN GABIROL

He who increases knowledge, increases sorrow.
                                        Ecclesiastes, 1 : 18

◦§ When one's deeds are greater than one's knowledge, knowledge is effective; but when one's knowledge is greater than
one's deeds, the knowledge is futile.
                            Sayings of the Fathers, 3 : 14

◦§ Knowledge should have no other purpose than to know what
is true   —adapted from MAIMONIDES

◦§ Through intelligence, man achieves . . . knowledge and comes
to . . . bear a resemblance to the character of the angels.
                                                IBN GABIROL

Knowledge: A little light expels much darkness.
                    BAHYA IBN PAQUDA, *Duties of the Heart*

The man of knowledge who has no fear of sin is like a carpenter
without tools.   *Abot de Rabbi Nathan*

◦§ Knowledge that is paid for will be longer remembered.
                                    NACHMAN OF BRATSLAV

See also: EDUCATION, FOOLS, GOOD DEEDS, INTELLIGENCE, LEARNING,
STUDY, TORAH, WISDOM

KOSHER

See: FOOD AND DRINK

LABOR

See: WORK

LANGUAGE

God created language—and man according to its principles.

ABRAVANEL

A language is a dialect that has an army and a navy.

MAX WEINREICH

See also: EDUCATION, KNOWLEDGE, LEARNING, SCHOLARS, STUDY, TRANS-LATION

LAUGHTER

Not every heart that laughs is cheerful.

Too much laughter can deaden the mind.

Laughter is heard further than weeping.

We laugh alone and we weep alone.

Man should not fill his mouth only with laughter in this world.
—adapted from TALMUD: *Berakoth,* 30b

A fool raises his voice when he laughs, but a wise man smiles quietly. BEN SIRACH, *Ecclesiasticus,* 21 : 20

See also: CONTENTMENT, PLEASURE, SUFFERING, TEARS

LAW

Note. When the rabbis and philosophers of Judaism used "the Law" or "Torah," a complicated concept was involved. For the Law includes the Written Law, in the five books of Moses, and the "traditions of the elders" or "the Oral Law"—that is, the practices and beliefs developed around, or attached to, the Written Law. There is yet a third meaning: that of a spirit or connection between Written and Oral Law that unifies the two into one all-encompassing body of faith, principles, and precepts for living.

"The Law," i.e., the Torah, offered no explicit suggestion as to the way many juridical conflicts could be resolved. It was the rabbis and scholars, in their extraordinary discussions, who found answers to countless problems. They interpreted the Law by reinterpreting the Torah's text. (See guidenotes: TALMUD, MISHNAH, MIDRASH.) It takes no expert to present a hundred passages from the Torah or the Talmud that present uncertainty or inconsistency or imprecision (see, for instance, the headnote on SABBATH).

In countries where Jews were forced to live apart from the general population, the government often granted judicial authority (in cases involving only Jews) to rabbinical judges (*dayanim*).

The Talmud is full of explicit and impressive instructions for the administration of justice: A judge may not listen to the arguments of one litigant in the absence of the other; equality before the law is so underscored that preference must not be shown even to the learned; the first question put to litigants was: "Do you wish law or arbitration?" (See headnote for JUDGES.) The legal sophistication and modernity of many legal passages in the Talmud would impress any historian of jurisprudence.

—L.R.

ঞ্চ Without law, civilization dies.

ঞ্চ A new king makes new laws, but new laws cause new transgressions.

&8 The beginning and the end of the Law [Torah] is kindness.

Don't use the conduct of a fool as a precedent.

TALMUD: *Shabbath,* 104a

Anyone through whom another man has been falsely punished will be barred from Heaven's gates.   TALMUD: *Shabbath,* 149a

The law of the land is the law of the Jew.

TALMUD: *Baba Bathra,* 113a

To break an oral agreement which is not legally binding is morally wrong.   TALMUD: *Baba Mezi'a,* 44a

&8 Only such decrees should be issued which the majority of a community can endure.   MIDRASH: *Midrash Psalms*

&8 If there be no officer to enforce the law, what power do judges have?   MIDRASH: *Tanhuma, Shofetim*

The falling of rain is an event greater than the giving of the Law, since the Law is for Israel, but rain is for the whole world.

MIDRASH: *Midrash Psalms,* 117

The Law forbids revenge.

—adapted from *Abot de Rabbi Nathan*

&8 What is hateful to you, do not to your fellow: that is the whole Law; all the rest is interpretation.

HILLEL in TALMUD: *Shabbath,* 31a

See also: COURTS, EVIDENCE, JUDGES, JUSTICE, TORAH

LAW AND ORDER

&8 Fish die when they are out of water, and people die without law and order.   TALMUD: *'Abodah Zarah,* 4a

See how the people act, and that is the Law.

TALMUD: *Berakoth,* 45a

◂§ Just as it is forbidden to permit that which is prohibited, so it is forbidden to prohibit that which should be permitted.

TALMUD J.: *Terumoth*, 5 : 3

If there be no officer to enforce the Law, of what avail is the judge?

MIDRASH: *Tanhuma*, Shofetim

See also: COURTS, EVIDENCE, JUDGES, JUSTICE

LAZINESS

◂§ The man who looks for easy work always goes to bed tired.

A lazy messenger finds many excuses.

The lazy dance while others slave.

One's the type who chops the wood, the other's the type who does the grunting.

The hardest work in the world is doing nothing.

As vinegar to the teeth, and as smoke to the eyes, so is the sluggard to those who send him on an errand.

Book of Proverbs, 10 : 26

A lazy man is like a stone covered with rot: men flee from the stench.   BEN SIRACH, *Ecclesiasticus* 22 : 1

Rest has value only after toil; rest without toil is not rest, but indolence; so the sluggard never attains the rest for which he craves.   SAADIA GAON

◂§ Brains to the lazy are like a torch to the blind—a useless burden.   BEDERSI, *Behinat ha-Olan*

See also: IDLENESS, SELFISHNESS, SHIRKERS, SIN, WORK

LEADERS/LEADERSHIP

Beware of the chief seat, because it shifts.

He who has a co-ruler has an over-ruler.

Woe to the ship whose captain has been lost.
TALMUD: Baba Bathra, 91b

A man is led the way he wishes to follow.
TALMUD: Makkoth, 10b

The body follows the head.   TALMUD: <i>Erubin,</i> 41a

◆§ Too many captains will sink a ship.   TALMUD

The serpent was dragged into a ditch, into fire, and amidst thorns,
when its head followed its tail!
MIDRASH: Deuteronomy Rabbah, 1 : 10

When the shepherd blunders, his flock blunders after him.
MIDRASH: Pirke de Rabbi Eliezer, 42

◆§ A wise man is a greater asset to a nation than a king.
MAIMONIDES

◆§ A king is like fire, necessary when far, scorching when near.
IBN GABIROL

The man most fit for high station is not the man who demands it.
MOSES IBN EZRA, Shirat Yisrael

A little sin is big when a big man commits it.
—adapted from ABRAHAM IBN EZRA,
Commentary to Genesis, 32 : 9

A leader must not think God chose him because he is great: Does a
peg in the wall, on which the king hangs his crown, boast that
its beauty attracted the king's attention?
MOSES OF KOBRYN

When a man is able to take abuse with a smile, he is worthy to
become a leader.   NACHMAN OF BRATSLAV

A place becomes known far and wide if it is the home of a great
man.   THE ROPSHITZER RABBI

See also: AUTHORITY, GOVERNMENT, GREAT MEN, LAW, POWER

LEARNING

Note. "Learning was for two thousand years the sole claim to distinction recognized by Israel. 'The scholar,' says the Talmud,
'takes precedence over the king.' Israel remained faithful to
this precept throughout all her humiliations. Whenever, in
Christian or Moslem lands, a hostile hand closed her schools,
the rabbis crossed the seas to reopen their academies in a distant country. Like the legendary Wandering Jew, the flickering
torch of Jewish scholarship passed from East to West, from
North to South, changing every two or three hundred years
from one country to another.

"Whenever a royal edict commanded them to leave the
country in which their fathers had been buried and their sons
born, the treasure Jews were most anxious to carry away with
them was their books. Among all the *autos-da-fé* which the
daughter of Zion has had to witness, none has cost her such
bitter tears as those flames which, during the Middle Ages,
greedily consumed the scrolls of the Talmud."
——A. Leroy Beaulieu, *Israel Among the Nations*, Heinemann, New York, 1893

See headnote: BOOKS

⋙ The man who lacks learning lacks everything.

Learning is a lifelong occupation.

⋙ The man who understands least asks the most questions.

⋙ First learn; then teach.

Learning requires a talent for sitting.

Don't act the philosopher before you have learned enough to be
one.

You can get more water from one deep well than from ten shallow
ones.

In time, even a bear can learn to dance.

◄§ He who seeks to know everything grows old quickly.

Whoever tries to profit from learning will be punished.

It is worse to learn nothing than to know nothing.

If you go into many houses, you are sure to carry something out [learn something].

Where there is learning there is wisdom.

Don't look for more honor than your learning merits.
                                        Rabbinical saying

◄§ For the ignorant, old age is winter; for the learned, it is the harvest.   Hasidic saying

Learning is more important than action—when it leads to action.
                                        TALMUD: *Megillah,* 26

◄§ Once an error is learned, it is hard to unlearn.
                                        TALMUD: *Baba Bathra,* 21a

Learning advances from the rivalry of scholars.
                                        TALMUD: *Baba Bathra,* 21a

If you are a man of the sword, you can't claim to be a man of the book; and if you are a man of the book, you will not be a man of the sword.   TALMUD: *'Abodah Zarah,* 17b

◄§ Much have I learned from my teachers, more from my colleagues, but most from my students.
                                        TALMUD: *Ta'anith,* 7b

If you understand the why and wherefore of what you learn, you do not forget it quickly.   TALMUD J.: *Berakoth,* 5 : 1

A man should not say, "I will love the learned and hate the unlearned"; he should say, "I will love them all."
                                        Abot de Rabbi Nathan, 16

◄§ A learned bastard stands higher than an ignorant High Priest.
                                        MIDRASH: *Numbers Rabbah,* 6 : 1

Do not say: I will learn when I will have leisure; you may never
    have it.   *Sayings of the Fathers,* 2 : 5

Learning is not obtained by the bashful.
                      Sayings of the Fathers, 2 : 6

Warm yourself at the fire of the learned, but beware of their glow-
    ing coals, lest you get scorched. [Don't delve too deeply into
    profundities you may not understand; you may draw the wrong
    conclusions.]   *Sayings of the Fathers,* 2 : 14

∾ Learning is one thing that can't be bequeathed.
            —adapted from *Sayings of the Fathers,* 2 : 16

The crown of learning is not so great as the crown of a good name.
                  Sayings of the Fathers, 3 : 13

Do not make learning into a crown to flaunt, nor into a spade with
    which to dig [for money].   *Sayings of the Fathers,* 4 : 5

∾ Move to a place where there is learning; you can't expect
    learning to move to you.   *Sayings of the Fathers,* 4 : 20

What you learn as a child is like ink on fresh paper; what you learn
    when old is like ink on used paper.
            —adapted from *Sayings of the Fathers,* 4 : 27

He who learns from the immature is like the man who eats unripe
    grapes and drinks fresh wine; he who learns from the old is
    like the man who eats ripe grapes and drinks old wine.
                  Sayings of the Fathers, 4 : 28

He who possesses both learning and piety is like an artist with all
    his tools at hand.
          JOHANAN BEN ZAKKAI in *Abot de Rabbi Nathan,* 22

He who does not increase knowledge diminishes it; and he who
    refuses to learn deserves extinction.
HILLEL in *Sayings of the Fathers* (*Note:* It was not uncommon for
    the sages to stress the importance of a duty by exaggerating
    the punishment for its nonperformance.—L.R.)

◄§ A man should have no purpose in learning except this: to learn
wisdom itself.   MAIMONIDES

A man should never stop learning, even on his last day.
                                                            MAIMONIDES

◄§ For learning, the ear is more useful than the eye.
                                                              GERONDI

◄§ The learning for which you pay will be remembered longer.
                                                  NACHMAN OF BRATSLAV

See also: IGNORANCE, ISRAEL, KNOWLEDGE, LOGIC, PIETY, REASON,
TRUTH, VIRTUE

LENDING

Note. Lending money for interest was expressly forbidden in
Deuteronomy (23 : 20 ff.) between "brother and brother"—
whether Jew to Jew (or, as interpreted later by Catholic Church
fathers) between Christian and Christian. But Deuteronomy
goes on to say (28 : 12) that it is a blessing to lend to a needy
nation—and a blessing not to need to borrow.

For the curious and tragic story of the Jews' role as moneylenders and their reputation as "usurers," see the headnote
for USURY. Jews were often forced into moneylending—barred
from all other trades, crafts, occupations, or professions—then
were taxed prohibitively. Jews were often ordered to administer a king's or prince's moneylending—to shield the noble
from the Catholic sin of usury. Jews were drafted to raise
money for the building of cathedrals, palaces, armies, crusades.

The economically invaluable services performed, through
the lending of money, did not spare the Jews from paying a
terrible price for the function they were persuaded, forced, or
seduced into serving: In Strasbourg, in 1349:

> On Saturday—St. Valentine's Day—they burnt the Jews
> on a wooden platform in their cemetery. There were about
> two thousand people of them.... And everything that
> was owed to the Jews was cancelled, and the Jews had to

surrender all pledges and notes that they had taken for
debts.... The money was indeed the thing that killed the
Jews. If ... the feudal lords had not been in debt to them,
they would not have been burnt.

JACOB R. MARCUS. *The Jew in the Medieval World, A
Source Book: 315–1791;* Atheneum, New York, p. 47.

See also headnotes for **BORROWING, MONEY, USURY.**

—L.R.

◦§ If you lend money, you buy enemies.

◦§ If you lend someone money and he avoids you, you've gotten
off cheap.

Lend before witnesses, but give without them.

◦§ Interest grows without rain.

A long loan is still not a gift.

◦§ If you have received a plow or a pillow as collateral for a loan,
return the plow each morning and the pillow each night.
                              TALMUD: *Baba Mezi'a,* 114b

He who gives pledges for a stranger will suffer; but he who hates
giving pledges is secure.   *Book of Proverbs*

◦§ The interest on borrowed money is like the bite of a snake.
            RASHI, *Commentaries on the Pentateuch, Exodus*

◦§ Don't lend to a man stronger than you; and if you do, act as
though you had lost it.   BEN SIRACH, *Ecclesiastes,* 8 : 12

See also: **BORROWING, DEBT, MONEY**

LETTERS

A letter is like a body, its meaning like a soul.

◦§ A letter not opened is like a dream not interpreted.

LIARS/LIES

⋞ He only lies twice a year: in summer and in winter.

⋞ A liar is like a mute: neither tells the truth.

You may go a long way through lies—but not back.

⋞ The clever liar gives no details.

⋞ A half-truth is a whole lie.

⋞ A liar believes no one else.

⋞ What he says he doesn't mean, and what he means he doesn't say.

⋞ Hostility makes easy alliances with lies.

⋞ Liars need good memories.

A lie one must not tell, and some truths you should not tell.

⋞ You mustn't tell a lie, but you're not bound to always tell the truth.

⋞ Truth may walk about naked; but lies should be clothed.

A liar tells his story so often that he begins to believe it himself.

⋞ Sometimes truth is the safest lie.

Better say "I don't know" than lie.

⋞ Truth shows in the eyes; lies stay behind them.

When young, a liar; when older, a thief.

With a story or a lie, only children can be rocked to sleep.

A lie has no feet [no leg to stand on].
> TALMUD: *Shabbath*, 104a

Lordly words are not fitting for a fool; much less are lying words for a lord.
> *Book of Proverbs*, 17 : 7

I said in my haste, "All men are liars."   *Book of Psalms,* 116 : 11

◦§ If you wish to strengthen a lie, mix a little truth in with it.
Zohar

Lies are forbidden—unless uttered to make peace.
Baraita Perek ha-Shalom

Since dishonor is habitual with a liar, his shame attends him continually.   BEN SIRACH, *Ecclesiasticus,* 20 : 26

◦§ Do not think a thing proved because it is in a book; the liar,
who deceives men with his tongue, does not hesitate to deceive them with his pen.
MAIMONIDES, *Epistle to the Yemenites*

The man who intends to lie seeks witnesses from far away.
JUDAH ASHERI

◦§ To some men, lying is a profession.
MOSES HAYYIM LUZZATTO, *The Path of the Upright*

◦§ A man who can't lie can't be a marriage broker.
MENDELE MOCHER SEFORIM

He who has no confidence utters falsehoods, and he who utters
falsehoods has no confidence.   NACHMAN OF BRATSLAV

Lies are usually caused by an undue fear of men.
NACHMAN OF BRATSLAV

◦§ For thirteen years, I taught my tongue not to tell a lie; and
for the next thirteen, I taught it to tell the truth.
THE KORETZER RABBI

See also: HONOR, HYPOCRISY/HYPOCRITES, SIN, TRUTH

LIBERTY

See: AUTHORITY, DEMOCRACY, EQUALITY, FREEDOM, GOVERNMENT,
INDEPENDENCE, LAW, MASSES, POLITICS, POWER

LIFE

᪗ Life is a dream—but please don't wake me.

Life is with people.

᪗ A man should go on living—if only to satisfy his curiosity.

Youth is the one thing that never returns.

᪗ Ever since dying came into fashion, life hasn't been safe.

᪗ Life is the greatest of bargains: we get it for nothing.

Life is not what men want, but what God decrees.

Life is bitter as bile—but without bile, no man can live.

In this life, luck won't help you unless you cooperate.

᪗ It's a short way from happiness to sorrow, but a long way from sorrow to happiness.

What you fall into you can fall out of.

Not all the time is life bad—or good.

᪗ When life isn't the way you like, like it the way it is.

᪗ Pray that you will never have to bear all that you are able to endure.

Worse we never need, and better has no limits.

What's new at sea? They're catching fish.

If things don't get better, they may get worse.

᪗ If you sing before you get out of bed, you'll cry before you go to sleep.

What you don't get you can't lose.

᪗ In life, each of us must sometime play the fool.

We all bring a hearty appetite to other people's parties.

◆§ We do not live on joy, nor die of sorrow.

Neither good nor bad lasts forever.

We long remember the good—and longer the bad.

It is better to live in joy than die in sorrow.

◆§ All life ends in weeping.

If you live long enough, you'll see everything.

One man wants to live but can't, another can but doesn't want to.

Three types of men lead lives that are not worth living: he who is too ready to rage; he who is too soft-hearted; and he who is too fastidious.   TALMUD: *Pesahim*, 113a

Don't worry about tomorrow: who knows what may befall you this day?   TALMUD: *Yebamoth*, 63b

◆§ All beginnings are difficult.   *Mekilta on Jethro*

If there were this life only, nothing could be more bitter.
         APOCRYPHA: *II Baruch*, 21 : 13

Our days are scrolls: write on them what you want to be remembered for.   BAHYA IBN PAQUDA, *Duties of the Heart*

◆§ Mobility is one of God's wonders.
         BAHYA IBN PAQUDA, *Duties of the Heart*

A long life without wisdom is worse than a short life with it.
         —adapted from MOSES IBN EZRA, *Shirat Yisrael*, 119

One can learn much about life from a checker game: surrender one to take two; don't make two moves at one time; move up, not down; and when you reach the top, you may move as you like.
         THE TSUPENSTER RABBI

◆§ Life is a dream for the wise, a game for the fool, a comedy for the rich, a tragedy for the poor.   SHOLEM ALEICHEM

See also: **HAPPINESS, HEAVEN, HELL, SUFFERING, VIRTUE**

LIFE: Cynical Comments on

◌⟩ The only thing you get free in this life is garbage.

When a man has it too easy, he starts sliding on ice.

Wise men walk, while fools ride.

There will be mud in front of my door, too, one day.

◌⟩ When there's a wind, garbage flies high.

It's easy to poke a fire with someone else's hand.

The more flesh, the more worms.
                              HILLEL in *Sayings of the Fathers*

◌⟩ April Fool: A joke repeated 365 times a year.
                              SHOLEM ALEICHEM

◌⟩ Life is a blister on top of a tumor, and a boil on top of that.
                              SHOLEM ALEICHEM

LIFE: Rueful or Resigned Comments on

Even the greatest swimmer can drown.

◌⟩ So many hymns—and so few noodles.

In this world, there are more *shokhtim* [slaughterers] than chickens.

All of life is a war.

The fees for circumcision, confirmation, wedding, burial—all come
    due too soon.

The provision is scant, and the road is long.
                              TALMUD: *Kethuboth*

Not everyone who rejoices today will rejoice tomorrow.
                              MIDRASH: *Tanhuma* (Shmini)

The road through life is like the edge of a blade, with the nether-
world on either side.   THE SASSOVER RABBI

See also: DEATH, IRONY: EXAMPLES, RESIGNATION

LIFE: The Purpose of

∽§ There are three lives that are no lives: he who lives off others,
he who is ruled by his wife, he whose body is racked by pain.
(And some say, he who has only one shirt!)
                                    TALMUD: *Bezah,* 32b

The Golden Mean is to love this world, to do good in life, and to
aspire to the world to come.   SAADIA GAON

Many say a man should try to lengthen his life, asking, "What
profit is there after death?"... Yet men who spend their days
in pleasure do not live long. And those who increase their days
also increase their anxiety, their vexation, their guilt, and their
sins.   SAADIA GAON

See also: GOOD DEEDS, HAPPINESS, HEAVEN, HEREAFTER, SOUL, SUFFER-
ING, VIRTUE

LIFE AND DEATH

We all know when we set forth; but we none of us know when we'll
return.

Ask not that all troubles cease, for when troubles end, so does life.

Hurry and eat, hurry and drink, for this world is like a wedding
feast from which we must soon depart.
                                    TALMUD: *Erubin,* 54a

Birth and death are like ships: why do we rejoice over a ship
setting out on a journey [birth] when we know not what she
may encounter on the seas? We should rejoice when the ship
returns safely to port [death].
                    —adapted from *Midrash Tanhuma:* Vayakel, 1

⋐ "Life is a passing shadow," says Scripture. The shadow of a tower or a tree? No: the shadow of a bird—for when a bird flies away, there is neither shadow nor bird.

MIDRASH: *Genesis Rabbah*, 80

⋐ We rejoice over a birth and mourn over a death. But we should not. For when a man is born, who knows what he will do or how he will end? But when a man dies, we may rejoice—if he left a good name and this world is in peace.

—adapted from MIDRASH: *Tanhuma on Exodus*

⋐ A man who lost his brother was asked, "What was the cause of his death?" and replied, "Life."

IBN ZABARA, *Book of Delight*, 7 : 27

⋐ Life is a terrible disease—cured only by death.

HAI GAON, *Musar Haskel*

Heaven is wonderful, but getting there is most of the fun.

"THE CHOFETZ CHAIM"

Why is a man sad when at the end of his life he leaves for his true home in heaven? "THE CHOFETZ CHAIM"

⋐ It is no challenge to die like a Jew; the real challenge is to live like a Jew. "THE CHOFETZ CHAIM"

See also: DEATH, HEREAFTER, TROUBLES

LIGHT

Light is especially appreciated after the dark.

HASDAI, *Ben ha-Melekh ve-ha-Nazir*

The light of a candle is useful when it precedes you; it is useless when it trails behind. BAHYA BEN ASHER, *Kad ha-Kemah*

See also: CAUSE AND EFFECT, CIRCUMSTANCES, KNOWLEDGE

LILITH

Note. Lilith, "the demon of the night," was the Assyrian siren mentioned by Isaiah (34 : 14) and described in the Talmud as having wings (*Niddah,* 24b). In old rabbinical tradition, Lilith flew about in the night, with her long tresses streaming like a demonic owl, and snatched up babies. She sometimes masqueraded as a serpent. *And* she preceded Eve as Adam's wife! More recondite lore fancied the idea that Lilith had been Satan's paramour before she latched on to Adam in unholy wedlock.

Jewish cabalists spoke of Lilith as the epitome of lust, temptation, illicit sex; and many believed that all demons and evil spirits were the children of Lilith, who had forced Adam into the conjugal performance that produced them.... So forceful and fearful was this legend that, in Eastern Europe, Jewish mothers used amulets to protect their newly born from Lilith, who (everyone knew) was driven by a monstrous obsession to kill each of Adam's descendants—as soon as they entered the world.*

The Lilith legend obliged those who believed it to believe that Eve was created by God only *after* Lilith, tired of Adam, harshly dropped him and refused to come back to his desolate arms. (In Greek mythology, Lamia, a Lybian queen, deflowered by Zeus himself, had her children killed by jealous Hera, then sought the same infanticidal revenge Lilith practiced. Lamia was sometimes serpentine and bisexual.) *See* EVE.

—L.R.

LIQUOR

Liquor may muddle the head—but troubles take it off altogether.

Whiskey makes men brawl.

A little brandy warms you in winter and cools you in summer.

The judge who has drunk too much is not fit to judge.

* *New Standard Jewish Encyclopedia, op. cit.,* p. 1226.

The teacher who has had too much to drink is not fit to teach.

Liquor's tongue reveals what is on the mind.

⋅⋛ When whiskey enters, judgment flees.

The drunkard who has no whiskey talks of whiskey.

Men sotted with liquor cannot help harming somebody.

⋅⋛ Teetotalers are rarely wise.

Liquor can make a man an exile from his own family.

See also: **ABSTINENCE, DRUNKARDS, WINE**

LOGIC

⋅⋛ "For instance" is not proof.

To jump to a conclusion is to by-pass the process of proof.

Every "why" has a "therefore."

⋅⋛ Lust is the enemy of logic.

Logic opens a universe of freedom.

Out of snow you can't make cheesecake.

A bachelor matchmaker, a spinster grandmother—these cannot be.

We cannot learn everything from general principles: there may be exceptions. TALMUD: *Kiddushin,* 34a

See also: **ILLOGIC, PREJUDICE, REASON**

LONELINESS

Loneliness eats into the soul.

It's better to be bored than lonely.

⊷ Even in Paradise, it's not good to be alone.

⊷ If you seek a faultless friend, you will remain friendless.

A son in this world prevents loneliness in the world to come.

A man can eat alone, but not work alone.

The man who thinks he can live without others is mistaken; the
    man who thinks others can't live without him is more mistaken.
                                                    Hasidic saying

If I were to cut myself off from those of my brethren who sin,
    I would be alone.   —adapted from IBN GABIROL

In everyone's heart stirs a great homesickness.
                                    RABBI SEYMOUR SIEGEL

See also: **FAMILY, FRIENDS, HEREAFTER**

LOVE

⊷ Three things can't be hidden: coughing, poverty, and love.

Love, like butter, is better with bread.

⊷ Love may be blind, but jealousy sees too much.

Love is sweet—but better with bread.

⊷ Love me a little less, but longer.

⊷ To love mankind is easy; to love man is hard.

To promise and to love cost no money.

If you don't love me don't kiss me.

⊷ Where love is, no room is too small.

Who loves you scolds you.

You can't love God without first loving Man.

Love which never reproves is not love.

⋖ One drop of love can create a sea of tears.

Those who tease you love you.

Love can't be forced.

Love destroys one's mental equilibrium.

Light love, heavy consequences.

For a little love, you can pay your whole life.

When love is strong, a man and woman can make their bed on
    a sword's blade; when love is weak, a bed of sixty cubits is
    not wide enough.   TALMUD: *Sanhedrin*, 7a

A woman prefers poverty with love to riches without love.
                —adapted from TALMUD

Love and hatred exaggerate.   —adapted from TALMUD

Love is the greatest pleasure open to man.
        Seder de Rabbi Eliahu Rabbah

Love is as strong as death.   *Song of Solomon*, 8 : 6

Hatred stirs up strife; but love draws a veil over all transgressions.
             Book of Proverbs, 10 : 12

"Love your neighbor as yourself" is the great principle of the
    Torah.   MIDRASH: *Torath Kohanim on Leviticus*, 19

To obey out of love is better than to obey out of fear.
    RASHI, *Commentaries on the Pentateuch, Deuteronomy*

A cheerful face makes for love.   *Orhot Tsadikim*

What you love for yourself, love also for your fellow man.
        FALAQUERA, *Sefer ha-Mevakesh*

⋖ A fool's love is but a transient whim.   RABBENU TAM

He who truly loves another can read his thoughts.

THE KORETSER RABBI

Don't believe in the love of the one who cast his burdens upon you but denied you his favor.

IBN GABIROL, *Choice of Pearls*

All love has reality, except the love of the stupid.   IBN GABIROL

Love renders one blind and deaf.   IBN GABIROL

⋙ Of what use is love, if you have no one to love?

IMMANUEL OF ROME, *Mahberot*

⋙ Love turns one person into two; and two into one.

ISAAC ABRAVANEL

See also: COMPASSION, COURTSHIP, HATE, KINDNESS, LUST

LUCK

⋙ When a man has luck, even his ox calves.

When Luck enters, give him a seat!

⋙ If you have luck, you don't have to be smart.

⋙ An ounce of luck is better than a pound of gold.

⋙ You don't need intelligence to have luck, but you do need luck to have intelligence.

Too good is bad for you.

⋙ God is a father, luck a stepfather.

⋙ To have luck without sense is like carrying a sack full of holes.

Those with luck hit the bull's-eye without taking aim.

⋙ Even the unlucky need luck.

Luck can't be bought at the grocer's.

◦§ The man who runs after good luck runs away from good peace.

Sometimes a piece of bad luck can come in handy.

◦§ It takes no brains to be lucky.

Beauty is better with luck.

If you don't depend on good luck you will postpone bad luck.

Coins are round: sometimes they roll to you, sometimes to others.

If you have bread and butter, your luck is good.

◦§ Whenever you can, hang around the lucky.

Luck always finds a welcome.

The bright world is darkened by bad luck.

With luck's help, cleverness can succeed.

◦§ From luck to misfortune is only a step; but from misfortune to luck is a long way.

◦§ Luck doesn't help those who won't cooperate.

◦§ Luck makes men think you smart, because luck makes you rich.

◦§ To have bad luck, one still must have luck.

Without luck nothing happens right.

The first winner is the last loser.

Everything depends on *mazl* [luck].

If you don't depend on luck, you will postpone bad luck.
　　　　　　　—adapted from TALMUD: *Berakoth,* 64a

Weep for the man who does not know his good fortune.
　　　　　　　TALMUD: *Sanhedrin,* 103a

If a man becomes sick, he should not tell anyone on the first day,
    lest he have bad luck; but he may reveal his illness after that.
                    —adapted from TALMUD, *Berakoth*, 55b

⊷ Need makes people better; luck makes them worse.
                                                    Hasidic saying

See also: FORTUNE, INTELLIGENCE, RICHES

LUFTMENSH

A *luftmensh* [someone with his head in the clouds] is always
    searching for yesterday.

The *luftmensh* takes a bath and forgets to wash his face.

When a *luftmensh* goes to the market, all the merchants smile.

God protects the *luftmensh;* who else can?

The *luftmensh* does not seem to age.

See also: FOLLY, ILLOGIC, ILLUSION, MAN: HUMAN TYPES, NEBEKH,
    SHLEMIEL

LUST

Lust is like rot in the bones.

A lecherous old man is intolerable.   TALMUD: *Pesahim*, 113b

⊷ Lust and reason are enemies.   IBN GABIROL

Lust is pursued by foolish men because of the immediacy of its
    delight . . . they ignore the suffering and wretchedness that
    follow in its train.   IBN GABIROL

Poverty cannot disgrace the wise, nor can lust enslave them.
                                    —adapted from IBN GABIROL

⊷ Lust should be stifled, for it cannot lead to truth.
                            MOSES IBN EZRA, *Shirat Yisrael*

See also: **DESIRE, ENVY, GREED, JEALOUSY, PASSION, SEX, SIN, SUFFER-
ING**

LUXURY

The spendings of the rich feed more mouths than their philanthropies do.

◦§ We would all live in luxury, if we didn't have to eat.

When luxuries grow, so do necessities.

See also: **EXCESS, RICHES, VANITY, WEALTH**

M

MAN

◦§ Some people are like new shoes: the cheaper they are, the
louder they squeak.

◦§ Man comes into the world with an _Oy!_ and leaves with a
Gevalt!

Only man was endowed with shame.

◦§ If Man is but another animal species, why has no other species produced even one Darwin?

If God really loved Man, would He have created us?

ᤣ It is easier to know ten countries than one man.

ᤣ Every man has his own *meshugas* [craziness].

Every man is blind—to himself.

A man is what he is, not what he used to be.

ᤣ A man is, alas, only a man—and sometimes not even that.

All virtues in one man are nowhere to be found.

Man has two eyes, two ears, but only one mouth.

ᤣ To love mankind is easy; to love man is hard.

Don't pity him who is a man; pity him who is not a man.

ᤣ He is mediocre—not close to wise, and not far from foolish.

ᤣ A man is weaker than a straw and stronger than iron.

To love God, you must first love Man.

ᤣ Animals have long tongues and can't speak; men have short
tongues and dare not.

Man is not like any other single creature; but he is like all of
them collectively.

ᤣ A man is a man because he is a man.

To displease men is to displease God.
                              —adapted from *Sayings of the Fathers*, 3 : 10

Man is endowed by nature with two eyes: one to see his neighbors' virtues, the other to see his own faults.
                                        Hasidic saying

In everyone there is something precious, found in no one else; so
honor each man for what is hidden within him—for what he
alone has, and none of his fellows.   Hasidic saying

ᤣ Man is closest to himself.   TALMUD: *Yebamoth*, 25

It would have been better if man had not been created; but since
he *has* been created, let him examine his works.

TALMUD: *Erubin,* 13b

⋟ Why was man created on the last day? So that he can be told,
when pride takes hold of him: God created the gnat before
thee.   TALMUD: *Sanhedrin,* 37a

Even one ear of corn is not exactly like another.

TALMUD J.: *Sanhedrin,* 4 : 8

Men fall only in order to rise.   *Zohar*

One is really not a man until he reaches the age of twenty-five.

Yalkut Shimoni

Man is like a trumpet that produces a tone if blown into;
If the blower leaves, it can produce no sound.   *Derekh Tsedek*

At one, man is a king, adored by all; at two, he is like a pig, wal-
lowing in dirt; at ten, he skips like a goat; at twenty, he
neighs like a horse; married, he works like an ass; when a
father, he snarls like a dog; and when old, he dodders like
an ape.   MIDRASH: *Ecclesiastes Rabbah,* 1 : 2

Man was made a little lower than the angels.

—adapted from *Book of Psalms,* 8 : 5

⋟ Where there are no men, try to be a man.

Sayings of the Fathers, 2 : 6

A man is a world in miniature.   *Abot de Rabbi Nathan,* 36

One man is equivalent to all creation.   *Abot de Rabbi Nathan*

The power of reasoning, with which God endowed man, makes
man capable of perfection.

MAIMONIDES, *Guide to the Perplexed,* 1 : 2

There is no such thing as two men exactly alike—nor two thoughts.

MAIMONIDES (*probably adapted from*
TALMUD J.: *Berakoth,* 809)

After God created language, He made man—according to its principles.   ABRAVANEL

This world is like a house: the sky a ceiling, the earth a carpet,
the stars lamps . . . and man is its master.
                          BAHYA IBN PAQUDA, *Duties of the Heart*

There is no one who never stumbled.   SAMUEL HA-NAGID

We must always hold the reins of the animal within us.
                                        "THE CHOFETZ CHAIM"

Man is a miracle.   THE KORETSER RABBI

If a man is covered with a blanket, he feels warmer: not so a
stone.   THE RIZINER RABBI

MAN: IRONIC OBSERVATIONS ON

All brides are beautiful—and all dead men are pious.

⋅⋟ Man has large eyes—but cannot see his own faults.

The peasant will cling to his basket even if a crown is placed on
his head.

⋅⋟ The *badkhn* [wedding jester] makes everyone cheerful; only he
is in misery.

⋅⋟ The man who blows the foam off his glass is not really thirsty.
                                        TALMUD: *Sanhedrin,* 100b

Men are like weasels: they hoard and know not for what purpose.
                                    TALMUD J.: *Sabbath,* 14 : 1

MAN: PSYCHOLOGY OF

⋅⋟ To a drunkard, no liquor is bad; to a merchant, no money is
tainted; to a lecher, no woman is ugly.

⋖§ A man's worst enemy can't wish for him what he can think up himself.

⋖§ Man's nature changes every seven years.

⋖§ One man likes sour cream, the other prayer.

What men want, they do not have; what they have, they do not prize.

The world is full of troubles, but each man feels only his own.

To know a man you must ride in the same cart with him.

Man worries over the loss of his possessions, not over the loss of his years; but his possessions cannot help him, and his years will never return.   Rabbinical saying

⋖§ A man shows his character by three things: his tipping, his tippling, and his temper.   TALMUD: *Erubin,* 65b

⋖§ Like fish, like men: the greater swallow the smaller.
                    TALMUD: *'Abodah Zarah,* 4a

In the morning Man says, "Would that it were evening!" and in the evening Man says, "Would that it were morning!"
                    —adapted from *Deuteronomy,* 28 : 67

⋖§ Pallor is a sign of anger, talk is a sign of folly, and self-praise is a sign of ignorance.   *Zohar*

⋖§ By nature we like the familiar and dislike the strange.
                    MAIMONIDES: *Guide for the Perplexed,* 1 : 31

Men like the opinions to which they have been accustomed from their youth; they defend them, and shun contrary views: and this is one of the things that prevents men from finding truth, for they cling to the opinions of habit.
                    MAIMONIDES: *Guide to the Perplexed,* 1 : 31

⋖§ How can you expect me to be perfect ... when I am full of contradictions?   MOSES IBN EZRA, *Shirat Yisrael*

&⁊ Man regrets the past, is anxious about the present, and is concerned for the future.   Ha-Penini, *Behinat Olam,* 13

MAN AND HIS FELLOW MEN

If men knew what one thought of the other, they would kill each other.

We anger God by our sins and people by our virtues.

&⁊ Artists seldom like each other.

For God, have fear; with men, be on guard.

&⁊ The man who believes he can live without others is mistaken; and the man who thinks others can't live without him is more mistaken.   Hasidic saying

Dear God, bless me so that I don't need people.
                    —adapted from the grace after meals

Three kinds of mortals need to be protected from others: a patient, a groom, and a bride.   TALMUD: *Berakoth,* 54b

Condemn no man and consider nothing impossible, for there is no man who does not have his hour.
                    Sayings of the Fathers, 4 : 6

Don't rely on the broken reed of human support.
                              ASHER BEN JEHIEL

MAN: HUMAN TYPES

&⁊ He is the kind of man who first prepares the bandage, then inflicts the wound.   TALMUD: *Megillah,* 13a

Four kinds of men are intolerable: an arrogant poor man, a deceitful rich man, a lecherous old man, and the head of a synagogue who lords it over his congregation.
                              TALMUD: *Pesahim,* 113b

Four types of men may be thought of as dead: the poor, the blind,
the leprous, and the childless.

> TALMUD: *'Abodah Zarah,* 5a

ᴗᔟ Who is wise? He who can learn from every man.
Who is strong? He who can control his passions.
Who is rich? He who is content with his lot.
Whom do men honor? He who honors his fellow men.

> BEN ZOMA in *Sayings of the Fathers,* 4 : 1

There are four types among men:
> The ordinary one says: "What is mine is mine, and what is
> yours is yours."
> The queer one says: "What is mine is yours, and what is
> yours is mine."
> The saintly one says: "What is mine is yours, and what is
> yours is yours."
> The wicked one says: "What is mine is mine, and what is
> yours is also mine."   *Sayings of the Fathers,* 5 : 16

ᴗᔟ There are four types of temperaments: easy to provoke and
easy to calm—here the fault is canceled by the virtue; hard
to provoke, but hard to calm—here the virtue is canceled by
the fault; hard to provoke, and easy to calm—this is the temperament of a good man; easy to provoke, but hard to calm
—this is the temperament of the wicked.

> *Sayings of the Fathers,* 5 : 17

The bashful man cannot learn, the ill-tempered man cannot teach,
and the one who preoccupies himself with worldly affairs
cannot impart wisdom.

> HILLEL in *Sayings of the Fathers,* 2 : 6

ᴗᔟ There are four types of men in this world:
> The man who knows, and knows that he knows: he is wise, so
> consult him.
> The man who knows, but doesn't know that he knows: help
> him not forget what he knows.
> The man who knows not, and knows that he knows not: teach
> him.

Finally, there is the man who knows not but pretends that he knows: he is a fool, so avoid him.

IBN GABIROL, *Choice of Pearls*

A pretty maiden, a cup of wine, a beautiful garden, the song of a bird, the murmur of a brook—these are for the lover, the lonely, the poor, the sick.

ABRAHAM IBN EZRA, *Yesod Mora*

MAN AND GOD

ৎৡ O, Lord—glance down from heaven and take a real look at Your world.

ৎৡ When God wants to break a man's heart, he gives him a lot of sense.

Man is in bondage to his impulses—and to his Creator.

There are three partners in man: God, his father, and his mother.

TALMUD: *Kiddushin*, 30b

Four types of men will never see God's face: the scoffer, the liar, the slanderer, and the hypocrite.   TALMUD: *Sotah*, 42a

Man was created last for a reason: If he is worthy, he will find all nature at his service; if he is unworthy, he will find all nature arrayed against him.   THE KORETSER RABBI

See also: ADAM, CHARACTER, FAMILY, GOD, LIFE, MEN AND WOMEN, OLD AGE, PRIDE, VANITY, YOUNG AND OLD

MANNERS

ৎৡ Good manners will open any door.

Don't push yourself where you shouldn't be.

You may look, but not stare.

Without study, there are no good manners.

Don't taunt your neighbor for your own blemish.

TALMUD: *Baba Mezi'a,* 59b

In a house where someone was hanged, don't say, "Hang this up
for me." —adapted from TALMUD, *Baba Mezi'a,* 59b

A woman will uncover her neighbor's pots in order to see what's
cooking. TOSEPHTA, *Taharoth,* 8

⋐§ At the table of the great, don't gulp.

BEN SIRACH, *Ecclesiasticus,* 31 : 12

There is no truer index to intelligence than the way one acts at the
table. IBN GABIROL, *Choice of Pearls*

⋐§ The test of good manners is to be patient with bad ones.

IBN GABIROL

Say not to your neighbor, "Dine at my house for I dined at yours";
it sounds like usury.

—adapted from MAIMONIDES, *Mishneh Torah*

See also: ANGER, BOASTING, CONSIDERATION, DECORUM, LAUGHTER,
SENSITIVITY, TEMPER, THOUGHTFULNESS

MARRIAGE

Note. The first positive commandment of the Bible is the one
that enjoins man to "Be fruitful, and multiply" (Genesis,
1 : 28). The Hebrews looked favorably upon early marriage:
the Talmud set eighteen as the proper age; some rabbis encouraged marriage as early as fourteen. A rabbi or formal
religious service may be waived, by Talmudic dictum, under
certain conditions. A Jew on a desert isle, it is fondly related,
once wed himself to a woman—and made Heaven and Earth
witnesses: "I call upon Heaven and Earth to witness that I
consecrate you as my wife, according to the laws of Moses and
of Israel."

The idea of marriage as holy and mystical, and of God
as participating in it, has created charming legends. It is said
that when souls are created in heaven, an angel cries: "This

boy for that girl!" Marriage *reunites* the male and female aspects of one soul, the *Zohar* tells us.

Arranging marriages was considered a sacred matter: The union of two souls, and the agreement to have children and raise them as Jews, was part of Israel's obligation in its compact with God. (Commentaries in the Talmudic tractate *Baba Kamma* deal with the role of the matchmaker in perpetuating the existence of Israel itself.)

God is considered the supreme *shadkhn* (matchmaker): there is an old legend that forty days before a Jewish child is born, its mate is selected in Heaven. The professional *shadkhn* performed an important social function, gathering information about eligible mates in far-removed villages, trying to match family standing and pedigree, weighing individual qualities that might strengthen compatibility, etc.

Our modern aversion to the idea of arranged marriages is, of course, a post–eighteenth-century attitude: it did not occur to earlier generations of Jews or their contemporaries that "love and marriage" go together.

Elaborate premarital "arrangements" were once required. A dowry (*nadn*) was, of course, part of every Orthodox nuptial contract. Presents of value were exchanged in advance between bride and groom: the latter usually gave his betrothed a prayer book (*siddur*), a veil, a fine comb, a sash, a ring. The bride-to-be gave her betrothed a prayer shawl (*talis*), a gold or silver chain, even a watch.

Jewish folk sayings on marriage are like those of almost every other people, a mishmash of delightful contradictions: they exalt it, deride it, praise it, scorn it, revere it, and poke fun at its victims.

—L.R.

ᴥᴥ When a young man marries, he divorces his mother.

ᴥᴥ Even a bad match can beget good children.

ᴥᴥ The man who marries for money earns it.

Early to rise and early to wed does no harm.

ᴥᴥ By day they fight, but bed at night.

⋲§ Jews have no nunneries.

Husband and wife are one flesh, but have different purses.

When there is peace in the house, even morsels of food will be enough.

A third person may not interfere between two who sleep on the same pillow.

He who is without a wife dwells without blessing, life, joy, help, good, and peace—and without defense against temptation.
TALMUD: *Yebamoth*, 62b

Whosoever remains unmarried does not deserve to be called a man.
TALMUD: *Yebamoth*, 63a

⋲§ More than man desires to marry, woman desires to be married.
TALMUD: *Yebamoth*, 113a

When a man marries, his sins decrease.
TALMUD: *Kiddushin*, 29b

If you must sell everything . . . marry your daughter to a scholar.
TALMUD: *Pesahim*, 49b

Forty days before the creation of a child, a voice proclaims in heaven: "So-and-so's daughter for so-and-so's son!"
TALMUD: *Sotah*, 2a

⋲§ The female [child] should be married first, for the shame of a woman is greater than the shame of a man.
TALMUD: *Kethuboth*, 67b

⋲§ It was the custom [in ancient Judea] to plant a cedar tree when a boy was born, and to plant a pine when a girl was born; and when they were married, the canopy was made of branches woven from both trees.   TALMUD: *Gittin*, 57a

Before a young man marries, his love goes to his parents; after he marries, it goes to his wife.   *Pirke de Rabbi Eliezer*

Without a hedge the vineyard is laid waste; without a wife, a man is a homeless wanderer; and who trusts an armed band of vagabonds?   BEN SIRACH, *Ecclesiasticus*

&ξ When a soul is sent down from heaven, it contains both male and female characteristics; the male elements enter the boy baby, the female the girl baby; and if they be worthy, God reunites them, in marriage.   *Zohar*

See also: BACHELORS, COURTSHIP, DAUGHTERS, DIVORCE, DOWRY, FATHERS, LOVE, MEN AND WOMEN, MOTHERS, SONS, WIVES

MARRIAGE AND GOD

&ξ God sits above and makes matches below.

Between husband and wife only God should judge.

&ξ The Holy Spirit can rest only upon a married man, for an unmarried man is but half a man, and the Holy Spirit does not rest on what is imperfect.   Rabbinical saying

God creates new worlds constantly—by causing marriages to take place.   *Zohar*

If husband and wife are worthy, the Holy Presence abides with them; if not, fire consumes them.
RABBI AKIBA in TALMUD: *Sotah,* 17a

See also: BACHELORS, DIVORCE, FAMILY, GOD, HUSBANDS, LIFE, LOVE, MEN AND WOMEN, SEX

MARRIAGE: CYNICAL COMMENTS ON

&ξ A man may ride on a coach, but a woman rides on her apron.

For dying or marrying, there's always time.

After the wedding it's too late to have regrets.

The ceremony lasts an hour, but the troubles last a lifetime.

Marry fast and get stuck for good.

&ξ It is as hard to arrange a good marriage as it was to divide the Red Sea.   TALMUD: *Sotah,* 2a

Many a married man hoards—for the future husband of his wife.
IBN GABIROL, *Choice of Pearls*

Honeymoon for a month, trouble for life.
HASDAI, *Ben ha-Melekh ve-ha-Nazir*

A man enters the *khupe* [marriage canopy] living, and comes out
a corpse.   SHOLEM ALEICHEM

See also: ADVICE, COURTSHIP, DIVORCE, HUSBANDS, MEN AND WOMEN,
WIVES

MARRIAGE: ADMONITIONS, ADVICE, AND LEGALITIES

Marriage is made in Heaven; but second marriages are arranged
by people.

⋅§ Better break the engagement than the marriage.

⋅§ When an old man takes a young wife, the man becomes young
and the woman old.

Those who marry while they have no secure livelihood are fools.

A man should not marry a pregnant widow or divorcee until her
child is born.   TALMUD: *Yebamoth,* 36b

The children of the man who married for money will turn out to
be a curse to him.   TALMUD: *Yebamoth,* 37a

A man should not marry a woman with the mental reservation
that, after all, he may divorce her.
TALMUD: *Yebamoth,* 37b

⋅§ A henpecked husband gets no relief in court.
TALMUD: *Baba Mezi'a,* 75b

The old and the young should not be joined in marriage, lest both
the peace and the purity of marriage be destroyed.
TALMUD: *Sanhedrin,* 76a

No marriage contract is made without a quarrel.
TALMUD: *Shabbath,* 130a

Now that the Roman Government seeks to prevent the circumcision of our sons, should we ordain that no one marry and
beget children? No, for then the descendants of Abraham
would die out.   TALMUD: *Baba Bathra,* 60b

See also: BACHELORS, CHILDREN, DIVORCE, FAMILY, HUSBANDS, LOVE,
MEN AND WOMEN, WIVES

MARTYRS

Note. Being a martyr is the highest form of *Kiddush ha-Shem*
("sanctification of God's Name")—that is, enduring torture
and accepting death because of faith in God, or to prevent
a desecration of God's name. The idea of martyrdom as the
ultimate testimonial to one's faith in God seems to have
arisen, as a mass phenomenon, during the Jewish wars against
Hellenization.

—L.R.

See HEROES, INQUISITION, PERSECUTION, POGROMS

MASSES

The masses aren't asses.

The masses are fools.

The public is a clod.

Public safety comes from consulting the multitude.
                         —adapted from *Book of Proverbs,* 11 : 14

~§ When I see no way of teaching a truth except by pleasing one
intelligent man and offending ten thousand fools, I address
myself to the one, and ignore the censure of the multitude.
          MAIMONIDES, *Guide to the Perplexed,* Introduction

See also: DEMOCRACY, FAME, GLORY, HONOR, PEOPLE, POLITICS,
POWER, REPUTATION, STATUS

MEDICINE

Words are like medicine: measure them with care; an overdose
can hurt.

Doors closed to good deeds open to disease.

Love is the best medicine.

Don't judge a doctor; poll his patients.

ᴇᔰ No medicines heal sick souls.

ᴇᔰ Some medicine does in a week what no medicine does in seven
days.

See also: DISEASE, DOCTORS, HEALTH, MODERATION

MEEKNESS

ᴇᔰ Too meek is half-proud. Better be humble with the meek
than share spoils with the proud.
—adapted from *Book of Proverbs,* 16 : 19

There is a type of meekness that brings a man to Gehenna: For
instance, the judge who knows that other judges made an error, but says, "Shall I put them to shame?" . . . Or the man
who hears a congregation speak falsely and says, "Who am
I to correct them?" . . . There is a kind of humility which
is not righteousness.   *Sefer Hasidim*

See also: HUMILITY, LAW, MODESTY, PRIDE, SELF-ESTEEM

MELANCHOLY

ᴇᔰ It is hard to repent of the sin of melancholy—for, in doing so,
we fall into a deeper melancholy, realizing we have sinned.
THE BERSHIDER RABBI

See also: CONSCIENCE, DISEASE, SADNESS, SORROW, SUFFERING

MEMORY

◦§ Two things get weaker with time: your teeth and your memory.

◦§ What's good, we remember; what's bad, we feel.

Habitual liars need a powerful memory.

◦§ Men can forget anything—except when to eat.

There is a difference between learning one's lesson a hundred times and learning it a hundred and one times.

TALMUD: *Hagigah,* 9b

See also: FORGETTING, LEARNING, LIARS/LIES, LOGIC, REASON

MEN AND WOMEN

◦§ Men should take care not to make women weep, for God counts their tears.

A man may ride on a coach; but a woman rides on her apron.

Man's brains are his jewels; woman's jewels are her brains.

Rather talk to a woman and think of God than talk to God and think of a woman.

Women persuade men to good as well as to evil, but they always persuade.

Should a male and a female orphan need to be supported, let the female take precedence, for a boy can beg, but a girl must not.   TALMUD: *Kethuboth,* 67a

It is easier to appease a male than a female—because the first man was created out of dust, which is soft, but the first woman was created out of bone, which is hard.   TALMUD: *Niddah,* 31b

A man likes visitors; not so a woman.

TALMUD: *Baba Mezi'a,* 97a

Man and woman are one body and soul.
                    —adapted from TALMUD: *Menahoth*, 93a

Women want to be married more than men do.
                    —adapted from TALMUD: *Yebamoth*, 113a

Females should be married before males, for the shame of a
    woman is greater than that of a man.
                              TALMUD: *Kethuboth*, 67b

᳇ The ideal man has the strength of a man and the compassion
    of a woman.   *Zohar*

Parsimony, soft-heartedness, and naïveté are vices in a man—but
    virtues in a woman. HASDAI, *Ben ha-Melekh ve-ha-Nazir*

A man without a wife is a homeless wanderer.
                              BEN SIRACH, *Ecclesiasticus*

Elderly men who are popular with young women usually lack
    wisdom.   NACHMAN OF BRATSLAV

᳇ A man is young if a girl can make him happy or unhappy; he
    enters middle age when a woman can make him happy but
    not unhappy; he becomes old when a woman can make him
    neither happy nor unhappy.   MORITZ ROSENTHAL

See also: COURTSHIP, GOD, LOVE, MARRIAGE

MEN AND WOMEN: CYNICAL COMMENTS ON

᳇ Man searches for a mate and finds his own rib.

Pray to God to preserve you from bad women, and preserve your-
    self from the good ones.

᳇ "If you know everything," said the cynic to the *tsadik* [holy
    man], "tell me: What did Eve do whenever Adam came
    home?"
        "She counted his ribs," said the *tsadik*.

᳇ Adam's last testament read: "Don't believe Eve."

If a male dog barks, enter; if a female dog barks, depart.
                                        TALMUD: *Erubin*, 86a

At the time of the Golden Calf, the women refused to use their
    golden ornaments for idolatry; so today they rule over their
    husbands.   *Yalkut Ruveni*

MERCY

◄§ The mercy of the wicked is cruel.
                                    Book of Proverbs, 12 : 10

See also: COMPASSION, GOOD DEEDS, KINDNESS, PIETY, POWER,
RIGHTEOUSNESS

MESSIAH

Note. The history and different connotations of "Messiah" deserve
    careful explanation. The word comes from Hebrew: *ha-ma-
    shiah:* "the anointed." The Hebrew *mashiah* in Greek became
    messias; in translation, *christos;* hence, *messias* = messiah;
    christos = Christ—and each denotes "the anointed one."
        In the Old Testament, *meshiah* was the title given to
    kings ("God's anointed") and priests, who were initiated by
    being anointed with sacred oil. Later, *meshiah* meant a prophet,
    or anyone with a special mission from God. Then *meshiah*
    came to mean the awaited Deliverer of the Jews from their
    bondage and oppression, who will restore the kingdom of
    Israel. Finally, *meshiah* stood for the Savior who will make
    the world of men acknowledge God's sovereignty, and will
    thus usher in the Day of Judgment.
        English translations of the Bible tend to separate the
    idea of "the anointed" from the "Messiah"—the first being
    used for the living, the second for the expected. But the Jew-
    ish concept should be approached historically. The Old Testa-
    ment uses the term *meshiah* or anointed king for Saul, David,
    Zedekiah, and Cyrus of Persia, who was no Hebrew.
        King David established the dynastic principle among the
    Hebrews. And from this developed the idea that some man,
    blessed by God, would come from the House of David to end

Israel's tribulations, enforce justice, and establish peace. As a spiritual leader, the Messiah would establish a messianic age —on earth, be it noted—which the prophets Isaiah and Micah foretold. And in the new Age of Righteousness, all of mankind would be redeemed.

Jews thus distinguished the earthly Messiah from a heavenly Messiah: the earthly Messiah, Deliverer of the Jews, would be a man born of the line of David; but the heavenly Messiah lives in Heaven "under the wings of the Lord" (Enoch, 39) and existed before even the sun and the stars were created. The idea of a *divine* "Son of Man" was not understood by Jews in the later Christian sense.

The doctrine of the Messiah has been one of the most powerful elements in the history of Judaism. Whenever catastrophes—epidemics, starvation, pogroms, wars, expulsions, or any of the torments visited upon the Jews—seemed unendurable, the faithful looked once more into their holy books for some hopeful, hidden sign, some new revelation, some miraculous harbinger of deliverance. Pious mystics, astrologers, cabalists, and, later, some hasidim even predicted the exact time when the Messiah would usher in the Kingdom of God. (So did Christian Millenarians throughout the Middle East, Europe, and England.)

The Romans feared messianic predictions for political reasons, considering them an incitement to, or a camouflage for, rebellion against Rome's rule; and messianic movements often did lead to political militancy.

Whenever an empire under which Jews suffered crumbled—the Persian, the Byzantine, the Roman—the messianic fervors were intensified. A memorable statement on this tragic-hopeful theme is that of Professor Hugh Trevor-Roper: ". . . when Popes and Kings allied themselves with the blind prejudices of the Church and the mob, such patronage availed the Jews no more than the Moriscos of Spain or the Huguenots of France. Whither then were the persecuted remnant to turn for relief? Whither indeed but to that stock refuge of the oppressed: mysticism, the Messiah, the Millennium. As the defeated humanists of Spain sank into private ecstasies, as the *marabout* on his African dunghill promises a Mahdi to the dejected beduin, as the Anabaptists of the seventeenth century manipulated their Scriptural logarithms to hasten the Apocalypse, so also the Jews of the Dispersion deviated into mystical heresies, counted the days to the Millennium, or discovered the Messiah."*

Messianic ideas opposed the sense of resignation, the passive acceptance of Israel's fate on earth that, some Jews felt, was encouraged by Talmudic law. A group called *Neturei Karta,* who today live in Israel, refuse to recognize Israel as an independent state, because they maintain that such a holy sovereignty could only have been established by the *meshiah* —and the *meshiah* has, clearly, not yet arrived.

—L.R.

When the Messiah comes, all the sick will be healed—but fools will remain fools.

See also: HEREAFTER, MIRACLES, PARADISE, SALVATION

MILLENNIUM

In the Millennium we must expect Evil to be diminished, but not abolished.   *Zohar*

See: GOD, HEAVEN, HEREAFTER, PARADISE, SALVATION

MIND

❧ God looks into our hearts before he looks into our minds.

The mind of each man is as unique as his face.
—adapted from TALMUD: *Berakoth,* 58a

Man's mind is the Holy of Holies, and to admit evil thoughts is like setting up an idol in the Temple.
THE BERDICHEVER RABBI

See also: EMOTIONS, INTELLECT, INTELLIGENCE, LOGIC, REASON, SOUL

---

* *Historical Essays,* Macmillan, London, 1963, pp. 148–49.

MIRACLES

Note. The prophet Elijah is the leading miracle man in Jewish
folklore. He is credited with saving the sick, rescuing the
doomed, and countless miraculous deeds. A special symbolic
place in ceremonials (the Passover Seder, circumcision) is reserved for Elijah and his ever-hoped-for appearance on earth.
For it is Elijah who will return to this world, blowing his
horn, to signal the Messiah's appearance and the day of Redemption.

I should remind you that according to Scripture this
once-fierce but since-beloved prophet never died: he was
transported directly to heaven, within a whirlwind and on a
flaming chariot.

—L.R.

If God willed it, brooms would shoot.

You think it a miracle if God does the will of your rabbi; we
think it a miracle if our rabbi does God's will.

If a thousand pious men gathered around a log, it, too, could work
miracles.

Miracles don't happen every day.   TALMUD: *Pesahim,* 50b

Miracles do occur—but they rarely provide food.
TALMUD: *Shabbath,* 53b

Hope for a miracle—but don't depend on one.
—adapted from TALMUD: *Megillah,* 7b

A miracle cannot prove that which is impossible; it is useful
only as a confirmation of what is possible.
MAIMONIDES, *Guide to the Perplexed,* 3

Believe in God through faith, and not because of miracles.
NACHMAN OF BRATSLAV

See also: FATE, FORTUNE, GOD, ILLUSION, LUCK, REASON, SKEPTICISM

MISERS

⋙ Misers worship an idol.

A miser's moneybags are a bed for mice.

A miser is worse than a pauper.

Even the birds in the air despise a miser.

A miserly man is like a fattened ox: he will give of his fat only when he has been deprived of his life.

Some men are like weasels; they hoard and know not its purpose.
TALMUD J: *Sabbath*, 14 : 1

Seeking charity from a miser is like fishing in the desert.
IBN GABIROL, *Choice of Pearls*

⋙ The greatest miser with money is the biggest spendthrift with desires.   MOSES IBN EZRA, *Shirat Yisrael*

Miserliness is an expensive habit.   "THE CHOFETZ CHAIM"

A miserly man and a fat cow are useful only after death.
SHOLEM ALEICHEM

See also: CHARITY, MONEY, THRIFT, WEALTH

MISERY

Many crowd the gate of abundance, but neither brother nor friend enters the door of misery.

See also: CONSCIENCE, DUTY, GOOD DEEDS, MELANCHOLY, REPENTANCE, REVENGE, SORROW, SUFFERING

MISFORTUNE

⋙ Other men's misfortunes are not hard to bear.

The fear of a misfortune is worse than the misfortune.

A boil isn't so bad—on someone else's neck.

Nothing is so bad but that some good may not come of it.

The bitterest misfortune can be concealed with a smile.

◆§ If the house has fallen, woe to the windows.

Whether the stone falls on the pot, or the pot on the stone, woe
    to the pot!   SIMEON BEN JOSE BEN LAKUNIA in
                            MIDRASH: *Esther Rabbah,* 7 : 10

One day's happiness makes misfortune forgotten, and one day's
    misfortune makes a man forget past happiness.
                            BEN SIRACH, *Ecclesiasticus,* 11 : 25

To imagine that no misfortune will befall you is like wishing not
    to live at all, for misfortunes are a necessary part of this
    transient world.   IBN GABIROL

See also: FACE, FATE, FORTUNE, HAPPINESS, LUCK, POVERTY, SORROW,
    SUFFERING

MISOGYNIST

See: HATE, MAN

MITZVAHS

Note. A *mitzvah* ("commandment") means an act meritorious in
    God's eyes, a truly virtuous, kind, compassionate deed. I think
    that "*mitzvah*" is encountered second only to "Torah" in the
    vocabulary of Judaism. There are 613 (!) separate *mitzvoth:*
    248 are positive, 365 negative. The rabbis often used the
    phrase *simha shel mitsvah* ("the joy of fulfilling a pious act")
    to drive home the notion that good deeds which are performed
    out of a sense of duty are not as meaningful as those per-
    formed out of the pure desire to do good. Judaic ethics rest
    on the idea of performing good deeds—as a mandatory obli-
    gation or (better) as a volunteered expression of the desire

to do good. Israel Zangwill called *mitzvoth* "the sacred sociology" of the Jews.

—L.R.

See: CHARITY, COMPASSION, GOOD DEEDS, MAN, VIRTUE

MOCKERY

See: SARCASM, SELF-MOCKERY

MODERATION

You'll suffer more from overeating than from undereating.

Three things are good in small quantities and bad in large: yeast, salt, and hesitation.   TALMUD: *Berakoth,* 34a

◄§ There are eight things of which a little is good and much is bad: travel, mating, wealth, work, wine, sleep, spiced drinks, and medicine.   TALMUD: *Gittin,* 70a

Too much sitting aggravates hemorrhoids; too much standing hurts the heart; too much walking hurts the eyes; so divide your time between the three.   TALMUD: *Kethuboth,* 111b

The Torah may be likened to two paths, one of fire, the other of snow. Turn in one direction, and you die of heat: turn to the other and you die of the cold. What should you do? Walk in the middle.   TALMUD: *Hagigah,* 2 : 1

See also: ASCETICS/ASCETICISM, ENVY, EXCESS, GLUTTONY, GREED

MODESTY

◄§ Too much modesty is half-conceit.

When pride comes, scorn comes; but with the modest is wisdom.
Book of Proverbs, 11 : 2

Modesty is the noblest of all ornaments.   ELEAZAR ROKEACH

See also: BOASTING, HUMILITY, MEEKNESS, PRIDE, WISDOM

MONEY

Note. "It is in the nature of man to long for wealth," says the *Shulhan Aruk* (the "prepared table," or Code of Jewish Law). This was published (1564–65) long before Adam Smith. Jewish law and attitudes to moneylending, interest, and usury (which, I'll wager, are quite different from what you may think) are sketched in the headnotes for BORROWING, LENDING, and USURY.

—L.R.

Gold has a dirty father [the earth] yet is everywhere esteemed.

◄§ If you have money, men think you wise, handsome, and able to sing like a bird.

◄§ The man who thinks that anything can be accomplished by money is likely to do anything for money.

◄§ Shrouds have no pockets.

To be without money is a great mistake.

Bad neighbors count a man's income, not his expenses.

No dollar is a bastard.

Money really adds no more to the wise than clothes can to the beautiful.

◄§ It isn't that a full purse is so good; it's that an empty one is so bad.

It's not that money makes everything good; it's that no money makes everything rotten.

A purse without money is only a piece of leather.

Money can buy anything—except sense.

⋐ To have money is not always so *Ai-yi-yi,* but *not* to have it is *Oy-oy-oy!*

Money can marry off even a grandmother.

⋐ If you can't help out with a little money, at least give a sympathetic groan.

⋐ A heavy purse is light to carry.

⋐ If you have no money, attend no auctions.

When you bribe, you ride.

When the purse is full the stomach is still.

Money is a soap that removes the worst stains.

⋐ Some people are slaves—to gold and silver.

⋐ Money helps Man like reality.

Money without children is riches without savor.

⋐ If you sow money, you reap fools.

A golden key [money] opens all doors.

⋐ You can silence gossip if coins tinkle in your pocket.

Money in the pocket means peace in the house.

The world rests on three things: Money, money, and money.

The Torah gives light, but warmth comes from money.

A good income cures most ills.

⋐ It's easier to make money than to keep it.

To have money is good; to have control of money is still better.

With money, you can do everything.

& 5; Without money, this world is not fit to live in.

A little money lights up my world—like the sun.

Better a steady dime than a rare dollar.

Money goes to money.

He who has money has authority.

The love of money leads to idolatry and causes those who have
it to fall into madness.

When Death summons a man to appear before his Maker, money,
which man most loves, cannot go with him.   TALMUD

There's no money for provisions, but there is for waste.
                                        TALMUD: *Hagigah,* 5a

All the parts of the body depend on the heart, and the heart depends on the purse.   TALMUD J.: *Terumoth,* 8

See also: BUSINESS, FOOLS, FORTUNE, GREED, MISERS, RICHES, THRIFT,
WEALTH

MONOTHEISM

Note. However the history of man is written in the future, one
thing seems to me certain: the Hebrew concept of monotheism represented a most profound *intellectual,* no less than
religious, revolution:
(1) It freed men from a fearful subordination to the
forces of nature, by positing a loving (or punishing) supra-
natural cosmic power; the idea of one God emancipated men
from their terror of many evil demons, supernatural appari-
tions, fiendish hobgoblins, animistic cacodemons, etc.
(2) Monotheism fused *religion and morality:* ethical conduct became a duty to the deity; morality now partook of
the divine.
(3) The love of God was a novel and immense contribution (the Hebrews' predecessors and contemporaries feared,

placated, or made sacrifices to a gallery of gods who were unloving, willful, vain, jealous, angry, petulant—in short, oddly undivine; the *Iliad* is a marvelous chronicle of the curious intramural feuds that raged on lofty Olympus).

(4) The concept of One God ultimately became a stimulus to *science* (even though the rabbis were opposed to the secular and the scientific), because it suggested a unitary, consistent pattern within which everything in nature functioned. Monotheism offered the idea of order, consistency, and meaning in the universe—all waiting for man to explore and understand.

(5) The idea of One God contained within itself the concept of a central cause, a prime reason for things; and the searches for that reason, whether in the analysis of sacred writings or experimental ventures or the cool observation of physical phenomena, became a systematic enterprise. For once cosmic unity is accepted, universal consistencies, regularities, and interrelations follow; and each new discovery adds weight to the view that behind all of the multifarious, mystifying phenomena of the world, there is one final and consistent set of principles. (I am by no means downgrading the surpassing brilliance of polytheistic Greece.)

Von Humboldt shrewdly observed that the love of nature, to say nothing of the sympathetic study of it, could only begin after superfluous pagan gods had been removed from man's intellectual apparatus. And Einstein, in one of his most famous asides about quantum physics, said that he could not believe that God "threw dice"—i.e., that the laws of the universe are random.

See quotations: GOD.

—L.R.

MORALS

"One lesson, and only one, history may be said to repeat with distinctness, that the world is built somehow on moral foundations; that in the long run it is well with the good; in the long run it is ill with the wicked. But this is no science; it is no more than the old doctrine taught long ago by the Hebrew prophets."

> —J. A. Froude, in *A Book of Jewish Thoughts*,
> ed. J. H. Hertz, Oxford, London, 1920, p. 151.

I take comfort from this noble quotation, and only wish that "the long run" were not so long.

> —L.R.

ᴗᶔ The world hates two types: the informer and the moralist.

See also: EVIL, GOOD, GOSSIP, LIARS/LIES, LUST, SEX, SIN, SLANDER, TRUTH

MOTHERS

ᴗᶔ God could not be everywhere, so he created mothers.

A child without a mother is like a door without a knob.

ᴗᶔ A mother has glass eyes [she cannot see her children's faults].

ᴗᶔ A mother understands what a child does not say.

ᴗᶔ One mother achieves more than a hundred teachers.

A mother is a veil: she hides her children's failings.

ᴗᶔ The warmest bed of all is Mother's.

ᴗᶔ When a young man marries, he divorces his mother.

Mothers have big aprons—to cover the faults of their children.

The best fork is Mother's hand.

There is no such thing as a bad mother.

Many a young foal's skin served as a saddle on its mother's back.

Hearing the approaching step of his mother, Rab Joseph would say: "I must stand up, for the *Shekhinah* [Holy Spirit] enters."   TALMUD: *Kiddushin,* 31 : 2

The life of the mother takes priority over the unborn child.

Mishnah: *Ohalot*, 7 : 6

A foolish son is grief to his mother.   *Book of Proverbs*, 10 : 1

A modest woman has good children.   Nachman of Bratslav

See also: CHILDREN, DAUGHTERS, FAMILY, HUSBANDS, MARRIAGE, PAR-
ENTS, SONS, WIDOWS, WIVES

MOTHERS-IN-LAW

If you're angry with your mother-in-law, you yell at her daughter.

A mother-in-law and a daughter-in-law in one house are like two
cats in a bag.

The mother-in-law and the daughter-in-law should not ride in the
same cart.

◄§ Adam was the luckiest man: he had no mother-in-law.

Sholem Aleichem

See also: DAUGHTERS-IN-LAW, SONS-IN-LAW

MOURNING

Note. The sages of the Talmud instruct Jews not to mourn too
long, too deeply, or self-accusingly. They prescribe the proto-
col of grief: three days of weeping, followed by four days of
eulogy of the departed. The seven-day *shiva* period is followed by a thirty-day period (*shloshim*) of lesser mourning,
and an eleven-month period during which the mourner recites
the Kaddish (prayer for the dead) twice daily. The deceased
is remembered each year on the anniversary of his death.

—L.R.

It is better to go to a house of mourning than to a house of
feasting.   *Ecclesiastes*, 7 : 2

◄§ When a sage dies, all men should mourn, for they are his
kinsmen.   TALMUD: *Shabbath*, 105b

See also: DEATH, GOOD DEEDS, SUFFERING

MURDER

See: KILLING

MYSTICISM

See: ASTROLOGY, FOLLY

N

NATURE

God used the principles of nature to create language, and the
principles of language to create Man.   ABRAVANEL

When the first man saw the first little blade of grass, he felt sorry
for it—and the first rains fell.

Not a handful of rain descends from above without the earth
sending up two handfuls of moisture to meet it.
                        MIDRASH: *Genesis Rabbah*, 13 : 13

Don't ask the Lord to change the laws of nature for you.
                                NACHMAN OF BRATSLAV

If Man is worthy, all nature will be at his service; if Man is not
    worthy, all nature will join against him.
                   —adapted from THE KORETSER RABBI

See also: GOD, WORLD

NEBEKH (NEBBECH)

Note. In the vocabulary of character-types, woven out of pity,
    candor and insight, *nebekh* stands (along with *nudnick, shle-
    miel, shlimazl, shnuk, shmendrick, yold, Chaim Yankel, shlep-
    per*) in that pantheon of special Yiddish words coined to de-
    scribe the ineffectuals of this world. (For definitions, see
    Glossary; for longer descriptions, illustrations, and stories
    about each, see *The Joys of Yiddish, op. cit.*)
        "*Nebekh*" is both a noun and an interjection. As a noun,
    it means an innocuous nonentity, a helpless, hapless soul—
    first cousin to a *shlemiel* (*q.v.*). But whereas one may dislike
    a *shlemiel* it is hard to feel anything but sympathy for a
    nebekh.
        As an interjection, *nebekh* means "alas . . . too bad . . .
    unfortunately . . ." expressing affectionate dismay, regret, or
    commiseration. Hence the irony of the story of the Jew in Ber-
    lin who said he would be the happiest man in the world if
    he could only be sitting on a bench with a friend and ex-
    claim, "Look who's there! It's, *nebekh,* Hitler."
                         —L.R.

A *nebekh* (alas) is only a man—and sometimes not even that.

⋙ When a *nebekh* leaves the room, you feel as if someone came
    in.

Better ten enemies than one *nebekh.*

A *nebekh* talks as if whispering secrets to mice.

A *shlemiel* is always knocking things off a table, and the *nebekh*
    always picks them up.

᪥ When a *shlemiel* trips, he knocks down a *shlimazl;* and a *nebekh* repairs the *shlimazl's* glasses.

See also: FOOLS, SHLEMIEL, SHLIMAZL

NECESSITY

When there is no meat, one must pick the bones.

᪥ If things aren't the way you like, like them the way they are.

Necessity can break iron.

When a wave approaches, bend your head.
        —adapted from AKIBA, in TALMUD: *Yebamoth*, 121 : a

See also: ADVERSITY, DESTINY, FATE, LIFE, RESIGNATION

NEIGHBORS

᪥ Love thy neighbor, even when he plays the trombone.

You can judge a man better by the comments of his neighbor than by the praises of his mother.

Before you buy a house, investigate the neighbors.

If you mix with the neighbors, you'll learn what's going on in your own house.

Better a neighbor near at hand than a brother far away.
        Book of Proverbs, 27 : 10

An envious neighbor counts your income, not your expenses.
        Yalkut Shimoni, Deuteronomy

See also: ENVY, FRIENDS

NITPICKERS

The fault-finder will complain that the bride is too pretty.

He's the type of man who wonders whether a flea has a *pupik* [navel].

NONSENSE: EXAMPLES OF

◅§ Sleep faster, we need the pillows.

Let's go to town tomorrow, if we're alive; if not, let's go on Wednesday.

◅§ The best tailor among all the cobblers is Jacob the baker.

There's nothing so nonsensical that it hasn't been written (or printed).

◅§ A mute told a deaf man how a blind man saw a cripple run on water.

If my aunt had wheels, she would be a carriage.

If a grandmother had a beard, she'd be a grandfather.

See also: **FOLLY, FOOLS, ILLOGIC, IRONY: EXAMPLES OF, PARADOXES: EXAMPLES OF, SHLEMIEL**

OBLIGATION

◆§ If you give food to a small child, you must tell its mother.
TALMUD: *Shabbath,* 10b

He who eats of another's bread is afraid to look at him.
TALMUD J.: *Orlah,* 1 : 3

No man may buy a beast, an animal, or a bird until he has provided food for it.   TALMUD J.: *Yebamoth,* 15 : 3

I did not find the world desolate when I entered it; my fathers
planted for me before I was born: so do I plant for those
who will come after me.   TALMUD J.: *Ta'anith,* 23a

See also: CHARITY, CONSCIENCE, DUTY, GOOD DEEDS, HONOR, RESPONSI-
BILITY, VOWS

OCCUPATION

See: BUSINESS, SKILL, TRADE, WORK

OLD AGE

◆§ Gray hair is worthless if the brain is still green.

Fortunate are those who enjoy old age.

◆§ If you don't want to get old, hang yourself while young.

Though old people dye their hair, the roots remain white.

☙§ When asked how he had lived to so long and happy an old age, a rabbi replied: "I have never been angry with my family; I have never envied men greater than I; and I never gloated over anyone's downfall."

The new may be true, but the old is gold.

For the ignorant, old age is as winter; for the learned, it is a harvest.
Hasidic saying

Men worry over the loss of their possessions, not over the loss of their years—which never return.
Rabbinical saying

An old man in the house is a burden; but an old woman in the house is a treasure.
TALMUD: *'Arakin*, 19a

Respect an old man who has lost his learning: remember that the fragments of the Tablets broken by Moses were preserved alongside the new.
TALMUD: *Berakoth*, 8b

The ignorant think less clearly as they age; the wise more clearly as they grow older.
TALMUD: *Kinnin* 3 : end

☙§ To learn from the young is to eat unripe fruit and drink new wine; to learn from the old is to eat ripe fruit and drink old wine.
—adapted from *Sayings of the Fathers*, 4 : 28

Just because I am old, do not forget me, do not neglect me.
Standard Prayer Book

Do not dishonor the old: we shall all be numbered among them.
BEN SIRACH, *Ecclesiasticus*, 8 : 6

To honor an old man one should not sit in his place or contradict his words.
RASHI, *Commentaries on the Pentateuch, Leviticus*

The longest beards and fattest bellies are found in goats, but that does not make them the wisest creatures on earth.
—adapted from JOSEPH SOLOMON DELMENDIGO

☙§ The prosperity of a country can be seen simply in how it treats its old people.
NACHMAN OF BRATSLAV

Suggested inscription for a Hebrew Home for the Aged:
"They suffer from the three worst ailments of mankind: they
are sick, they are old, and they are Jews."

HEINRICH HEINE

See also: AGE, LEARNING, WISDOM, YOUNG AND OLD, YOUTH

OPINION

⋅≨ If men knew what one thought of another, they would kill
each other.

If everybody says so, believe them.

How long halt ye between two opinions?   I Kings, 18 : 21

Moses made agreement between the members of a community a
part of religion.   JOSEPHUS

⋅≨ Men like the opinions to which they have become accustomed
. . . and this prevents them from finding truth, for they cling
to the opinions of habit.

MAIMONIDES, *Guide to the Perplexed,* 1 : 31

See also: EVIDENCE, REASON, TRUTH

OPTIMISM

⋅≨ Let's go to the circus tomorrow, if—God willing—we're alive;
and if not, let's go Tuesday.

When things are not as you like, like them as they are.

Better is he who shows a smiling countenance then he who offers
milk.   TALMUD: *Kethuboth,* 111b

When the going seems rough, look at the jewels you're carrying.

"THE CHOFETZ CHAIM"

See also: COURAGE, HOPE, LUCK, SHLEMIEL

ORPHAN

When an orphan grieves, no one sees it; when he rejoices, the whole world does.

᪥ A *chutzpanik* is a man who, having killed his mother and father, asks the court for mercy because he is an orphan.

One who adopts an orphan is as if he begot him.
                                          TALMUD: *Megillah*, 13a

Between male and female orphans, provide first for the female: the male may beg, but not the female.
                                          TALMUD: *Kethuboth*, 67b

See also: CHILDREN, FAMILY, PARENTS

P

PAIN

᪥ The greatest pains are those you can't tell others.

᪥ A toothache makes you forget a headache.

᪥ Not to have felt pain is not to have been human.

Any ache but heartache; any pain but in the head.
                                          TALMUD: *Berakoth*, 11a

See also: DISEASE, HEALTH, SUFFERING

PARABLES

Let not a simple parable seem trivial in your eyes, for through it
    you acquire an insight into the complex law.
                        MIDRASH: *Song of Songs Rabbah,* 1 : 8

A parable from a fool is worthless because he tells it at the wrong
    time.   BEN SIRACH, *Ecclesiasticus,* 20 : 20

See also: ADVICE, EDUCATION, PEDAGOGY, TEACHING

PARADISE

⋙ Even in Paradise, it's miserable to be alone.

Better to be in Hell with a wise man than in Paradise with a fool.

One day Alexander the Great came to the gate of Paradise and
knocked, and the guardian angel asked, "Who is there?"
    "Alexander."
    "Which Alexander?" asked the angel.
    "*The* Alexander!" thundered the Conqueror. "Alexander the
Great, Conqueror of the world!"
    "He is not known here," said the angel. "He cannot enter; for
this is the Lord's gate and only the righteous may enter here."
    Alexander demanded proof that this was indeed the heavenly
gate. And a fragment of a human skull was thrown out to him, with
these words: "Weigh it."
    So Alexander took it to his Wise Men, who fetched a pair of
scales and placed the bone in one, while Alexander placed gold and
silver in the other. But the small bone outweighed them all. . . .
More and more silver and gold were piled into the scale, until
Alexander's great crown and all of his jewels were there—but they
all flew upwards, like feathers.
    Then one of the Wise Men placed a few grains of dust on the
skull, and now that side of the scale flew up: for the bone had
surrounded the eye, and nothing will satisfy man's eye until it is
covered by the dust of the grave.
                        —adapted from TALMUD

ঙ৯ Those who feel true shame go to Eden.
Sayings of the Fathers, 5 : 20

My thoughts form an Eden in my heart.
Judah ha-Levi, *Kuzari*

God uses a man's good deeds as seeds to plant trees in Paradise: in
this way every man creates his own Paradise.
The Mezeritzer Rabbi

See also: GOD, HEAVEN, HEREAFTER, WORLD TO COME

PARADOXES: EXAMPLES OF

Black earth gives white bread.

Better do nothing than make nothing.

When a miller fights with a chimneysweeper, the miller gets black
and the sweeper turns white.

ঙ৯ Where there's too much, something is missing.

Too good is bad for one.

ঙ৯ If you go a little slower, you'll arrive a little sooner.

Going backwards [in the wrong direction] is still a form of travel.

ঙ৯ A one-eyed man sees more of you than you, with two eyes, see
of him.

The worst libel can be the truth.

ঙ৯ Gold, like children, must sometimes be beaten.
Alphabet of Ben Sira, 4

The only whole heart is the one that has been broken.
"The Chofetz Chaim"

The longer the blind live, the more they see.
Sholem Aleichem

See also: ILLOGIC, IRONY: EXAMPLES OF, LOGIC, REASON

PARENTS

A child should treat his parents as though they were his king and
queen.

Those who are ashamed of their parents can win neither blessings
nor praises.

❧ Not to teach your son to work is like teaching him to steal.
TALMUD: *Kiddushin,* 29a

The child honors his mother more than his father because his
mother affects him by her words—so God set the honoring of
the father before the honoring of the mother; and the child
fears his father more than his mother, because it is the father
who teaches him Torah—so God set the fearing of the mother
before the fearing of the father.
TALMUD: *Kiddushin,* 31 : a

❧ Let us be grateful to our parents: had they not been tempted,
we would not be here.   TALMUD: *'Abodah Zarah,* 5a

Honor your father and mother, even as you honor God; for all three
were partners in your creation.   *Zohar*

He who does not support needy parents bears evil testimony against
himself.   *Tana de Ben Eliahu*

To "fear" one's parents means not to sit in their place, not to speak
in their stead, and not to contradict them.
RASHI, *Commentaries in the Pentateuch, Leviticus*

❧ The man who disobeys his parents will have disobedient sons.
NACHMAN OF BRATSLAV

The troubles parents take for their children are inspired by a form
of selfishness: to be proud of their achievements.
MENDELE MOCHER SEFORIM

See also: ANCESTORS, CHILDREN, DAUGHTERS, FAMILY, FATHERS, MOTH-
ERS, SONS

PARTNERS

The pot that belongs to partners is neither hot nor cold.

See also: BUSINESS, POWER

PASSION

Passion is a master.

A tranquil mind is health for the body; but passion is like rot in the bones.

Man is in bondage to his passions—and his Creator.

Passion leads to prejudice, not reason.

When passion burns within you, remember that it was given to you for good purposes.   Hasidic saying

The pursuit of passion becomes boring.   Hasidic saying

At first, man's passions are like a cobweb's thread; at last, they become like thickest cord   TALMUD: *Sukkah,* 52a

&s Our passions are like travelers: at first they make a brief stay; then they are like guests, who visit often; and then they turn into tyrants, who hold us in their power.
                    TALMUD: *Sukkah,* 52b

Men make a harness for their beasts; how much more should they fashion a harness for their passions.
                    —adapted from TALMUD J.: *Sanhedrin*

&s Who is strong? The man who can control his passions.
                    BEN ZOMA in *Sayings of the Fathers,* 4 : 1

It is easier for an apathetic man to be stirred to enjoyment than for a man burning with passion to curb his lusts.
                    MAIMONIDES: *Eight Chapters,* IV

All passions contain an element of sadness.
>—adapted from JONATHAN EIBESCHUTZ, *Yaarot Devash*

See also: COMPASSION, DESIRE, DISEASE, EMOTION, GRIEF, HEART, LUST, SEX, SIN, SUFFERING, TEARS, TEMPER

PASSOVER

See GLOSSARY: PESACH

PATIENCE

To be patient can be better than being rich.

You can drain a whole brook, or drill through the hardest granite, if only you have enough patience.

See also: HOPE, OPTIMISM, PERSEVERANCE, RESIGNATION

PATRIOTISM

⋈ If not for patriotism, barren lands would be deserted.

See also: ISRAEL, POLITICS, WARS

PAUPER

⋈ To welcome a pauper come only two: a cold wind and a snapping dog.

The pauper who arrives in a town does no favor to the local poor.

⋈ Rejoice, pauper: dirt is cheap.

Paupers at least have good waistlines.

⋈ One good thing about being a pauper: you save on laundry.

God protects paupers—from committing expensive sins.

Paupers are cold in summer and hot in winter.

◄§ The ignorant are the true paupers.

◄§ Paupers serve God's purpose: they make it possible for the rich to perform good deeds.

◄§ God is pleased when a pauper finds a treasure—and returns it.

God is happy when one pauper scratches another's back.

Paupers need no guards, and fear no thieves.

See also: CHARITY, GOOD DEEDS, PHILANTHROPY, THE POOR/POOR MEN, POVERTY, WEALTH

PEACE

Better a bad peace than a good war.

Peace is to man what yeast is to dough.

Three things can't live together in peace: wives, dogs, and chickens.

◄§ For the sake of peace one may lie, but peace itself should never be a lie.

◄§ When you quarrel, do it in such a way that you can make up.

Peace: the wisp of straw which binds the sheaf of blessings.

Peace is important, for God's name is *Shalom* [peace].
                                   MIDRASH: *Exodus,* 9

The Holy Scripture was given to mankind in order to establish peace.   MIDRASH: *Tanhuma, Jethro*

Talmidei hakhamim [saintly wise men] strengthen peace in the world.   *Standard Prayer Book*

Rabban Simeon ben Gamaliel had said: "The world rests on three things: On justice, on truth, on peace." Said Rabbi Mona: "But these three are one and the same: for if there is justice, there is truth, and if there is truth, there is peace."

Perek ha-Shalom

A peace which comes from fear and not from the heart is the opposite of peace.   GERSONIDES

ᴗᵹ Where there is no peace, prayers are not heard.

NACHMAN OF BRATSLAV

ᴗᵹ Whenever a treaty of peace is signed, God is present.

NACHMAN OF BRATSLAV

Work for peace within your family, then in your street, then within the community.   THE BERSHIDER RABBI

Better an insincere peace than a sincere quarrel.

THE LUBLINER RABBI

See also: CRITICISM, FAMILY, FEAR, MARRIAGE, POLITICS, QUARRELS, WARS

PEDAGOGY

ᴗᵹ Open your discourse with a jest, and let your hearers laugh a little; then become serious.   TALMUD: *Shabbath,* 30b

If there are more than twenty-five children in an elementary class, appoint an assistant.   TALMUD: *Baba Bathra,* 21a

A teacher who has drunk a quart of wine may not teach.

MIDRASH: *Leviticus Rabbah,* 1 : 4

To teach what is error is transgression.

—adapted from *Sayings of the Fathers,* 4 : 13

The ill-tempered cannot teach.

HILLEL, in *Sayings of the Fathers,* 2 : 6

Unmarried teachers have childish minds.

—adapted from MIDRASH

৶৯ Of what use is wisdom that is not taught?
                —adapted from BEN SIRACH, *Ecclesiasticus*, 20 : 30

See also: EDUCATION, LEARNING, STUDY, TEACHERS

PEOPLE

৶৯ When people who have led hard lives are given authority, they
    are harder than tyrants.

Where there is no vision, the people perish.
                                    Book of Proverbs, 29 : 18

৶৯ The voice of the people is as the Voice of God.
                            MIDRASH SAMUEL on *Pirke Abot*

See also: DEMOCRACY, FREEDOM, GOVERNMENT, LAW, MAN, MASSES,
    POLITICS, POWER

PERFECTION

There's no such thing as a perfect thing.

৶৯ Perfection is an obsession.

The perfect man has a man's strength and a woman's compassion.
                                                    Zohar
Man is capable of perfection—because of the power of reasoning,
    which God gave him.
                        MAIMONIDES, *Guide to the Perplexed*, I : 2

To seek perfection, in property or health or character, is not a
    worthy human goal; nor is it a proper cause of pride and glory
    for man; the knowledge of God is [the only] true wisdom, and
    the sole perfection man should seek.
                —adapted from MAIMONIDES, *Guide to the Perplexed*

A faultless man is possible only in a faultless world.
                            HASDAI, *Ben ha-Melekh ve-ha-Nazir*

See also: CHARACTER, GOD, GOOD, WISDOM

PERSECUTION

Note. The story of the persecution of the Jews, one of the more
harrowing aspects of Western history, need not be recapitulated
here. ("Oh Lord," runs one folk saying, "do not inflict upon us
all that we may be able to endure.") One passage, of literally
thousands one may read in history books, lingers in my mind:

> Thus were the Jews burnt at Strasbourg, and in the same year
> in all the cities of the Rhine, whether Free Cities or Imperial
> Cities or cities belonging to the lords. In some towns they burnt
> the Jews after a trial, in others, without a trial. In some cities
> the Jews themselves set fire to their houses and cremated them-
> selves. It was decided in Strasbourg that no Jew should enter
> the city for a hundred years, but ... the Jews [were allowed
> to come] back to Strasbourg, in the year 1368 after the birth of
> our Lord.
> Jacob R. Marcus, *The Jew in the Medieval World, A Source
> Book: 315–1791*, Atheneum, New York, 1969 p. 47.

ᴥ�§ It is better to be persecuted than to persecute others.

Persecutors are blind, and no medicine can cure them.

There are so many Hamans, but only one Purim. [Purim, "the Feast
of Lots," commemorates the rescuing of the Jews of Persia from
Haman's plot to exterminate them.]

God loves the persecuted, and hates the persecutors.
                                            Pesikta Rabbati, 193b

The prayers of the oppressed and the poor are the first to reach the
highest heaven.   IMMANUEL OF ROME

See also: ISRAEL, POWER, PREJUDICE

PERSEVERANCE

ᴥ§ Quiet waters wash down cliffs.

A tree can't be felled with one stroke.

Even the hardest granite yields to the drilling of those who persevere.

The man who persists in knocking will succeed in entering.
                                        MOSES IBN EZRA, *Shirat Yisrael*

◄§ A man can transform faults into virtues if he but perseveres.
                                        THE MAGGID OF DUBNO

See also: DETERMINATION, ENDURANCE, WILL

PESSIMISM

◄§ If things don't get better, wait—they'll get worse.

◄§ All sentences that start with "God forbid" describe what is possible.

Remember: every uphill has its downhill.

Buttered bread always falls on its face.

◄§ You don't want to get old? Hang yourself while young.

Expect nothing and you'll never be disappointed.

Even great swimmers drown.

So many prayers—and so few noodles.

◄§ If you have it easy, you'll slide on life's ice.

The only thing you get free is garbage.

Each of us must sometimes play the fool.

◄§ All life ends in weeping.

What doesn't get better can get worse.

What's new at sea? They're catching fish.

Don't worry about tomorrow; who knows what will befall you
    today?   TALMUD: *Yebamoth,* 63b

◄§ April Fool is a joke—repeated 365 times a year.

SHOLEM ALEICHEM

See also: DESPAIR, HAPPINESS, HOPE, ILLUSION, OPTIMISM

PETULANCE

◄§ Because he hates the cantor he doesn't say "Amen!" to the prayer.

◄§ The proud are petulant, and the petulant are foolish.

See also: CHARACTER, ILLOGIC, MAN: HUMAN TYPES, STUBBORNNESS

PHILANTHROPY

◄§ The poor profit more from the luxuries of the rich than from their philanthropy.

If you don't open your door to the poor, you will open it for the doctor.

◄§ To give little with a smile is better than giving much with a frown.

The promise of the generous is a gift; the gift of the miser is a promise.   IBN GABIROL, *Choice of Pearls*

See also: CHARITY, DUTY, GOOD DEEDS, LUXURY

PHILOLOGY

Note. "It must also be admitted that little attention was paid to philology, so that the great Talmudist often mistook a Greek word for an Aramaic, and, *horribile dictu,* sometimes would not even be able to distinguish Aramaic from Hebrew. But while a little grammar would certainly have been of some use to the mediaeval scholar, a larger portion thereof would as little

have made him a Talmudist as it has succeeded in the case of the modern grammarians and philologians."
—Louis Ginzberg in *Students, Scholars and Saints,* Jewish Publication Society of America, 1928, pp. 72–73.

See LANGUAGE, WORDS

PHILOSOPHERS/PHILOSOPHY

∽§ Philosophy is the road to knowledge, and knowledge is the road to freedom.

Philosophers without experience tend to be silly.

If all men were philosophers, the social order would be destroyed and the human race exterminated: men need many material things to survive.   Maimonides: *Eight Chapters*

See also: REALISM, REASON, SAGES, SCHOLARS, STUDY, TALMUD, TORAH, WISDOM, WISE MEN

PHYLACTERIES

See GLOSSARY: TEFILLIN, p. 691

PHYSICIANS

See: DISEASE, DOCTORS, HEALTH, PREJUDICE, SICKNESS, SOUL

PIETY

∽§ Better be good than pious.

A pious man walks in light and is not afraid to walk alone; the impious man walks in darkness and is anxious for company.

It does not matter whether a man does much or little, if only he directs his heart to Heaven.   Talmud: *Berakoth,* 17a

Those who, in their dreams, see the Book of Psalms may hope to
gain piety.   —adapted from TALMUD, *Berakoth,* 57b

Do not act toward the Lord as other people act toward their gods:
honoring them when times are good, but cursing them when
disaster strikes. Israel should praise the Lord no matter whether
He brings good times or evil.

Mekhilta to Exodus, 20 : 30

◄§ Without wisdom there is no piety, without piety there is no
wisdom.   *Sayings of the Fathers,* 3 : 21

Beware the pious who are fools.
—adapted from IBN GABIROL, *Choice of Pearls*

◄§ What I want to know is not why I suffer, but only whether I
suffer for Thy sake.   THE BERDICHEVER RABBI

◄§ I am in constant fear lest I may become too wise to remain
pious.   THE KORETSER RABBI

The pious man is better than the clever man.
THE KORETSER RABBI

See also: FAITH, GOD, GOOD, ISRAEL, RELIGION, VIRTUE, WISDOM

PITY

"It was part of the spirit of Prophecy to be dumbfounded
at human ferocity. . . . In the presence of the iniquities of the
world, the heart of the Prophets bled . . . and their cry of indignation re-echoed the wrath of the Deity. Greece and Rome
had their rich and poor, just as Israel had in the days of
Jeroboam II; and the various classes continued to slaughter one
another for centuries; but no voice of justice and pity arose
from the fierce tumult. . . . The words of the Prophets have
more vitality at the present time, and answer better to the
needs of modern souls, than all the plastic masterpieces of
antiquity."
—JAMES DARMSTESTER, quoted in *The Pentateuch and Haftorahs,* ed. by Dr. J. H. Hertz, Soncino Edition, second
edition, London: 1970, p. 930.

Better be cursed than pitied.

The greatest pity of all is deserved by a very poor woman in child-
birth. [Where will food come from?]

◦ᓚ Pity was invented by the weak.
MENDELE MOCHER SEFORIM

See also: COMPASSION, CONSIDERATION, EMOTIONS, GOD, MAN: HUMAN
TYPES

PLEASURE

◦ᓚ If you're going to eat ham, at least let it be juicy.

◦ᓚ Perpetual pleasure is no pleasure.   Hasidic saying

When a man faces his Maker, he will have to account for those
[God-given] pleasures of life which he failed to enjoy.
TALMUD J.: Kiddushin, end

The lover of pleasure will come to want; the lover of wine and oil
will not grow rich.   *Book of Proverbs,* 21 : 17

The man who pursues pleasure cannot control his life.
SAMUEL HA-NAGID

◦ᓚ Those who spend their days in pleasure don't live long.
SAADIA GAON

◦ᓚ All pleasures contain an element of sadness.
JONATHAN EIBESCHUTZ, Yaarot Devash

You may reach a compromise between evil and good by enjoying
legitimate bodily pleasures—and serving God at the same time.
THE MEZERITZER RABBI

POGROMS

Note. "When Richard I ["The Lion-Hearted"] ascended the throne,
the Jews, to conciliate the Royal protection, brought their

tributes. Many . . . appearing at Westminster, the Court and the mob imagined that they had leagued to bewitch His Majesty. A rumor spread rapidly through the city that in honor of the festival the Jews were to be massacred. The populace, at once eager of royalty and riot, pillaged and burnt their houses and murdered the devoted Jews. The people of York soon gathered to imitate the people of London."
—ISAAC D'ISRAELI. *Curiosities of Literature*, London, 1793.

"The central feature of this year's report [1906, American Jewish Year Book] is the table of massacres of Jews in Russia, during the period whose entrance and exit are guarded by Kishineff and Bialystok as bloodstained sentinels. The figures frightfully arrayed are so heart-rending that one is impelled to apologize for perpetuating them. It would be a wanton harassment of the feelings, were it not a document to stimulate Israel to self-help, and gentiles to self-introspection."
Quoted in *Of Making Many Books*, edited by Joshua Block, J.P.S.A., 1953, p. 83.

See: ANTI-SEMITISM, ISRAEL, JEWS, PERSECUTION, PREJUDICE

POLITICS

A fool in office is like an ass tied to the sun.

⋅§ One is a lie, two are lies, but three lies becomes politics.

He who has a co-ruler has an over-ruler.

⋅§ Fish die out of water, and people die without law and order.
TALMUD: *'Abodah* ZARAH, 4a

Safety lies in the counsel of the multitudes.
—adapted from *Book of Proverbs*, 11 : 14

⋅§ Sages are more important than kings, for if a sage dies, who can replace him? When a king dies, all Israel is eligible to succeed him. —adapted from MIDRASH

When a person is appointed an official among men, he is considered
a man evil in Heaven.
—adapted from *Mishnah Adoyoth*, 5 : 6

Woe to high position, for it takes the fear of Heaven from him who
occupies it.   *Midrash ha-Gadol*

ക§ Kings may be judges of the earth, but wise men are the judges
of kings.   IBN GABIROL

A king is like fire—necessary when far, but scorching when near.
IBN GABIROL

The man who can take abuse with a smile is fit to become a leader.
NACHMAN OF BRATSLAV

See also: DEMOCRACY, FREEDOM, GOVERNMENT, LAW, MASSES, POWER,
STATUS

THE POOR/POOR MEN

Note. A Jewish community in Eastern Europe had at least one
shnorer (beggar), and often a platoon. The *shnorer* was not a
run-of-the-mill mendicant, but a professional man; for many
shnorers considered they had a tacit license from the Lord and
were in fact, doing His bidding: after all, were they not helping Jews discharge the solemn obligation to help the poor?
Beggars made it possible for a Jew to accumulate *mitzvahs*
(good deeds); and any man who served as an agent for the
performance of *mitzvahs* was part of God's marvelous scheme
for improving the human race. The *shnorer* often read a good
deal, could quote Talmud with confidence, was a synagogue
"regular," and took part in discussions of Torah and Talmud
on an equal footing with his benefactors.

—L.R.

ക§ It's no disgrace to be poor—which is the only good thing you
can say about it.

ക§ It's no disgrace to be poor, but it's no honor, either.

Rejoice, pauper: dirt is cheap.

When you cook with straw, the food is raw.

ᴥ§ When a poor man gets to eat a chicken, one of them is sick.

ᴥ§ If you're poor, remember: at least it's good for the waistline.

Only the ignorant are truly poor.

ᴥ§ Those who have nothing are always ready to share it with others.

You don't need teeth to eat borsht.

If you have no linen, at least you save on laundry.

When you have no butter for your bread, it is not yet real poverty.

ᴥ§ A full bag is heavy to carry, but an empty one is heavier.

ᴥ§ The heaviest weight in the world is an empty pocket.

Love not sleep, lest you come to poverty; keep your eyes open, and you will have plenty of food.   *Book of Proverbs*, 20 : 13

THE POOR: IRONIC COMMENTS ON

ᴥ§ The poor have it hard only twice a year: in the summer and in the winter.

God really does help the poor: He protects them from committing expensive sins.

Poor men don't develop pot bellies.

ᴥ§ The poor are always liberal.

The poor fear no thieves.

The Talmud tells us that a fine dwelling, fine clothes, and a beautiful wife broaden a man's understanding: I need all the understanding I can get—to serve God as He deserves.

A poor man is happy when he loses something—and finds it again.

Poor men need no guards.

A poor man can be tempted by a slice of bread.

No one is so miserable as the poor man who is invited to two weddings for the same day.

◆§ For what does a poor man blow his whistle? For nothing, since he owns nothing but a whistle.

The poor are cold in summer and hot in winter.

◆§ The poor child's shoes grow with his feet.

To the poor, bread is more useful than air.

◆§ When a poor man makes a wedding, his dog gets the shivers!

It is easy to offend a poor man.

The poor man is like a sack full of holes.

The poor man also wants to live.

Poor is to rich as crooked is to straight.

The poor are like hunchbacks: they carry what they have on their backs.

A poor man may eat meat and wine yet feel bitterness in his heart.

◆§ Things are never as good with money as they are bad without it.

◆§ Poor relatives are distant relatives.

To the poor, life is bitter—and death more so.

An ox for a penny! But what if you don't have the penny?

Those without shoes recall the comfort in their father's home.

Bad luck chases after the poor.   TALMUD: *Baba Kamma*, 92a

The poor are likened to the dead.   TALMUD: *Nedarim*, 76

◄§ No one is so poor as he who is ignorant.
                                        TALMUD: *Nedarim*, 41a

You can't compare the man who has bread with the man who
    has not.   TALMUD: *Yomah*, 18b

Just as you listen to a poor man, listen to one rich: for it is writ-
    ten, "Ye shall not favor persons in judging them."
                            Abot de Rabbi Nathan, 20 : 22a

Who despises small things shall become poor.
                        BEN SIRACH, *Ecclesiasticus*, 19 : 1

No one is as poor as the man who worries about poverty.
                        IBN GABIROL, *Choice of Pearls*

I have succeeded in half my prayer for the poor: the poor are
    willing to accept gifts—if the rich offer them.
                                THE ROPSHITZER RABBI

God must hate the poor, else why did He make them poor?
                                SHOLEM ALEICHEM

THE POOR: IN DEFENSE OF

◄§ Whoever steals from a poor man steals from God.

He who laughs at the poor will become a laughingstock.

◄§ Honor the sons of the poor for they give science its splendor.

Take heed of the poor, for they produce learning.
                                TALMUD: *Nedarim*, 81a

He who mocks the poor insults his Maker; he who rejoices at
    their calamity will not go unpunished.
                                Book of Proverbs, 17 : 5

The prayers of the poor are heard by God before the prayers of
all others.　　　　　　　　　　　　　　　　　　*Zohar*

He who lengthens the life of a poor man will have his own life
lengthened when his time comes.　　　　　　　　*Zohar*

Despise no man: pearls [of wisdom] may be found in a poor
man's tunic.　　　　　　　Eliezer ben Isaac, *Orhot Hayim*

God is the poor man's advocate.　　"THE CHOFETZ CHAIM"

Beware of discourtesy to the poor: The Lord stands near them.
　　　　　　　　　　　　　　　　　THE SLONIMER RABBI

POOR MEN AND RICH MEN

⮪ If the rich could hire others to die for them, the poor would
make a very nice living.

⮪ The rich man carries his God in his pocket, the poor man—
in his heart.

God loves the poor but helps the rich.

The poor man thinks, the rich man laughs.

A cheap rich man is worse than a pauper.

Before the fat man grows lean, the lean man wastes away.

The rich eat the meat; the poor eat the bones.

Poverty runs after the poor, and wealth runs after the rich.

⮪ Though a rich man's fortune goes down and a poor man's
up, they still do not end up even.

Poor and rich lie in the earth as equals; only on earth arc the
rich better off.

A rich man's wealth is his fortress; the ruin of the poor is their
poverty.　　　　　　　　　　*Book of Proverbs,* 10 : 15

◄§ The rich swell up with pride, the poor from hunger.
>   SHOLEM ALEICHEM

See also: CHARITY, FATE, FORTUNE, GOOD DEEDS, LUCK, MONEY, PAU-
PERS, POVERTY, SUFFERING, STATUS, WEALTH, WISDOM

POPULARITY

◄§ Woe to the one nobody likes, but beware of the one everyone
likes.

If you want to be popular, ask people questions.

To please others always costs a lot.

Those who try to please everyone will die before their time.

◄§ When I see no way of teaching a truth save one that will
please one intelligent man but will offend ten thousand fools,
I address myself to the one and ignore the censure of the
thousands.
>   MAIMONIDES, *Guide for the Perplexed* (Introduction)

See also: FAME, GLORY, HONOR, REPUTATION, STATUS, TEACHING

POSSESSIONS

If possessions are near at hand, their owner consumes them; if
possessions are at a distance, they consume him.

See also: AMBITION, BUSINESS, HAPPINESS, RICHES, STATUS, WEALTH

POVERTY

Note. I think historians would agree that the Hebrews of old
brought a new conception of poverty and the poor to Western
civilization: They subordinated money/property rights to
moral and compassionate obligations.
    We might remember that the glorious Greeks did not

especially pity or respect the poor, the weak, the humble. (We need but recall the chilling candor of the dialogue, recounted in Thucydides, between the Melians and the Athenians, who had besieged the island of Melos, then slaughtered or enslaved every soul thereon.) The noble Romans, powerfully motivated for the public weal, so deeply respected property that they held poverty to be deserved; concern for the poor was considered proper for slaves, perhaps, but not for Roman freemen. (True enough, those who served the republic, though poor, were honored.) Those who could not pay their debts were imprisoned, or sold into slavery, or simply slain. Seneca "recoiled in horror" from the poor; Vergil praises one of his heroes for feeling no sympathy for the starving; and some Romans wrote that it was *cruel* to feed the hungry, because that would only prolong lives of insupportable misery.

Now: In the Jewish Commonwealth (it preceded the Greek and Roman empires), the poor occupied a peculiarly secure place; the community was legally bound to feed, clothe, educate, and protect them. Orphans, widows, poor brides-to-be; the sick, the old, the handicapped; wayfarers, mendicants, mental defectives—all were automatically aided by communal funds. Jewish ownership of property was not absolute (tithing held a superior claim).

Above all, the idea of a freeing Messiah, the Redemption, total equality for the virtuous in a world-to-come—all this promised the poorest and lowliest Israelite ultimate justice, supreme dignity, and priceless favor in the eyes of God. These ideas, incorporated into Christianity, dramatically transformed the world. (See headnote for CHARITY.)

—L.R.

✑ Poverty shows first on the face.

Poverty is no disgrace, but it's no great honor, either.

✑ Doctors have a cure for everything but poverty.

Poverty and laziness are brothers.

Those who are happy despite poverty can prevail against everything.

◄§ Conceit and poverty make a poor combination.

When the poor move, poverty moves right along with them.

◄§ You can often hide poverty with a needle and a brush.

When bread runs out, strife knocks at the door.

◄§ The wife wails and the dog whines and the child cries and poverty howls.

Poverty's head is very hard.

◄§ Poverty in a home is worse than fifty plagues.
TALMUD: *Baba Bathra,* 116a

Poverty is the ornament of the Jews.   TALMUD: *Hagigah,* 9b

◄§ Poverty makes handsome women ugly.
—adapted from TALMUD: *Nedarim,* 66b

Put all other sufferings in one side of the scale, and poverty in the other, and poverty would be heavier.
MIDRASH: *Exodus Rabbah,* 31 : 12

Nothing is more painful than poverty.
MIDRASH: *Exodus Rabbah,* 31 : 12

In all labor there is profit; but mere talk leads only to penury.
Book of Proverbs, 14 : 23

Wise men who are poor are all too often ignored.
Book of Ecclesiastes, 9 : 16

He who fulfills the Torah amidst poverty will fulfill it amidst wealth; he who neglects Torah amidst wealth will come to neglect it amidst poverty.   *Sayings of the Fathers,* 4 : 9

◄§ Poverty was created to give the rich an opportunity for charity.   ANAV, *Maalot ha-Midot*

See also: CHARITY, GOOD DEEDS, LEARNING, THE POOR/POOR MEN, STATUS, VIRTUE, WORK, WISDOM

POWER

ε§ Two dogs can kill a lion.

The man with an ax delivers the whacks.

Money is power.

A stick in the hand is better than a tongue in the mouth.

ε§ Henchmen are worse than their masters.

He who shares power has an over-ruler.

You can't move a mountain with a splinter.

The master is kind—but in his hand is a whip.

As among fish, so among men: the larger swallow the smaller.
                         TALMUD: *'Abodah Zarah,* 4a

If a fox becomes king, bow.   TALMUD: *Megillah,* 16b

Iron axes can break iron.   TALMUD: *Sanhedrin,* 96b

ε§ The obscure endure.
                    —adapted from TALMUD: *Sanhedrin,* 14a

ε§ Where there are no officers to enforce the law, of what avail
   are judges?   MIDRASH: *Tanhuma, Shofetim*

A farmer puts the yoke on his strong ox, not his weak one.
                         MIDRASH: *Genesis Rabbah,* 32 : 3

ε§ A sage takes precedence over a king.
                              —adapted from *Mishnah*

Can you draw out the Leviathan with a hook?
                              Book of Job, 41 : 1

Put not your trust in princes.   *Book of Psalms,* 146 : 3

Gain authority for the purpose of acting as judge of what is right,
   of supporting the poor, of delivering the oppressed from the

oppressor, of removing the spoiler, and of driving off those
who are perverse, for it is written: "Behold, a king shall reign
in righteousness" (Isaiah, 32 : 1).   SAADIA GAON

Don't rely on the friendship of a king—if his minister is your
enemy; but if you are friends with the minister, fear not
the king.   IBN GABIROL

◄§ A tiny fly can choke a big man.
                        IBN GABIROL, *Choice of Pearls*

Kings are judges, but sages judge kings.
                            —adapted from IBN GABIROL

◄§ A giant feels the sting of a bee.   IMMANUEL OF ROME

To work for another is like taking honey from a bee: accompanied
by a sting.   THE ROPSHITZER RABBI

See also: AUTHORITY, GOVERNMENT, POLITICS, STRENGTH, WEAKNESS

PRAISE

A little praise may be uttered in a man's presence; too much
praise should not be uttered in his presence; but all of his
praises may be sung in his absence.
                        —adapted from TALMUD: *Erubin*, 18b

◄§ To eat too much honey is not good; therefore be sparing of
your compliments.   *Book of Proverbs*, 25 : 27

Just as a smelter is for silver, and a furnace for gold, so a man
is tested by what he praises.   *Book of Proverbs*, 17 : 3

Let another man praise you, not your own mouth—
A stranger, and not your own lips.   *Book of Proverbs*, 27 : 2

Only a part of a man's praise should be recounted in his presence;
but in his absence all of his good qualities may be told.
                RASHI, *Commentaries on the Pentateuch, Genesis*

See also: DECORUM, FLATTERY, PRIDE

PRAYER

Note. For some 3000 years, Jews retained a most vivid sense of being part of one uninterrupted prayer to, and dialogue with, the Lord. Chapters of the five books of the Torah ("the Books of Moses") are read in the synagogues, week by week; and when on the festival of *Simhat Torah* ("the day of rejoicing in the Law"), the final words of Deuteronomy arc read—to be allowed to read it is a signal honor given to a learned member of the congregation—the congregation breaks into an excited *"Khazak, khazak, venit khazak!"* ("Be strong, be strong, and gather new strength!")—and at once the year-long cycle of readings is begun anew, with the first verse of Genesis.

By tradition, pious Jews pray at least thrice a day (but see below): *shaharith,* in the morning; *minhah,* in the afternoon; *maareb,* in the evening. Ten male Jews are required for a religious service. Solitary prayer is certainly laudable, but the pious hold that whenever ten males assemble for worship or study, God's Presence dwells among them.

To strictly religious Jews, the ceremonial demands for prayer are very heavy, however deeply the faithful rejoice in them. *Brokhes* (prayers) are recited upon arising, before retiring, before and after every meal, while washing one's hands (which must be done as soon as one gets out of bed, and before praying, and before eating), upon returning from a journey, recovering from an illness, seeing the new moon, donning a new garment, seeing a great scholar or sage, *et cetera.*

The Silent Devotion, a prayer of nineteen benedictions, is offered three times daily by Orthodox (and many Conservative) Jews, but four times on the Sabbath (and two other days) and five times on Yom Kippur. Recited or chanted while standing, this devotion involves three central thoughts: Wisdom, Learning, Immortality. It offers a hope for the welfare of the supplicant, his family, and the community at large; and it thanks the Lord for His blessings.

A devout Jew will not read from the Torah, or study Talmud, or pronounce the name of God unless his head is covered; the truly Orthodox *never* leave their heads uncovered by hat or *yarmlke* (skull-caplet). No rabbinical edict I can uncover directs Jews to cover their heads while praying, though Exodus did prescribe headcovering for the Temple priests.

Reform Jews think that in the Western world it is more appropriate to bare one's head as a sign of respect. Conservative Jews retort that baring the head imitates non-Jewish custom: Christians bare their heads in church since Paul (Saul of Tarsus) wrote that any who covered his head while "praying or prophesying . . . dishonoureth his head." (I have always believed Saul was overreacting against his early training.)

Orthodox and Conservative Jews wear a prayer shawl (*tallith;* "talis" in Yiddish) and phylacteries (tephillin) when praying—except on the Sabbath. Reform Jews do not wear phylacteries.

The *tallith* is striped at the ends, across its width—usually in black. (This may signify mourning over the destruction of the Temple.) In America, most Jews fold the *tallith,* which is made of silk, and wear it rather like a long scarf. But Orthodox Jews use a voluminous, robelike *tallith,* and during the most solemn portions of prayer place part of the shawl over their heads—to shut out anything that might diminish the intensity of their concentration.

> They say that when God finished the world, He asked one of the angels if anything was lacking on land or sea, in the air or in heaven. The angel answered that although everything was perfect, only one thing was wanting on earth—speech, to praise God's works. The Lord approved the angel's words, and soon there appeared the race of man. This is an ancient story, and in its spirit I say: "It is God's work to benefit men, and His creatures' work to thank Him." —PHILO

For the very close connection between prayer and study, in Jewish life, see my headnote for STUDY. See also SIDDUR.

—L.R.

⋙ When I pray, I pray quickly, because I am talking to God; but when I read the Torah, I read slowly, because God is talking to me.

Prayer without devotion [conviction] is like the body without a soul.

God does not listen to the prayers of the proud.

The prayer goes up and the blessing comes down.

⊸§ Nine saints do not make a *minyan* [quorum for prayer] but one ordinary man can—by joining them.

Oh Lord of the Universe: please take a real look at Your world!

A place is reserved in Heaven for those who weep, but cannot pray.

Prayers are heard best at night.

⊸§ Better pray for yourself than curse another.

⊸§ Prayer is the service of the heart.   TALMUD: *Ta'anith*, 2 : 1

Rab declared, "We give thanks unto Thee oh Lord, our God, because we are able to give thanks."   TALMUD: *Sotah*, 48

Don't stop praying even when the knife is placed against your neck.   TALMUD, *Berakoth*, 9a

Give, oh Lord, each one his bread, each body what it needs.
                          TALMUD: *Berakoth*, 29b

⊸§ Even when the gates of Heaven are closed to prayer, they are open to tears.   TALMUD: *Berakoth*, 32a

⊸§ Pray only in a room with windows [to remember the world outside].   TALMUD: *Berakoth*, 34b

⊸§ He who prays for his neighbor will be heard for himself.
                          TALMUD: *Baba Kamma*, 92b

The pious man waits an hour before praying, and concentrates his thoughts upon the Lord; even if a king greets him, he should not answer; and even if a snake winds around his head, the pious supplicant should not interrupt his prayer.
                          —adapted from TALMUD, *Berakoth*, 30b

The gates of prayer are sometimes closed, but the gates of repentance are forever open.
                              MIDRASH: *Deuteronomy Rabbah*, 2 : 7

⋅≶ The prayers of the poor are heard by God ahead of all others.
                                                        Zohar

⋅≶ It is the prayers of the poor and the oppressed that reach
the highest heavens.   IMMANUEL OF ROME

Do not hurry when you leave a place of worship.
                              JOSEPH CARO, *Shulhan Aruk*

The prayer of a sick person is more effective than anyone else's,
and is answered first.
                    RASHI, *Commentaries on the Pentateuch, Genesis*

⋅≶ You don't have to pray loudly; just direct your heart to
heaven.   RABBI CHIA

He who prays without knowing what he prays does not pray.
                    MAIMON BEN JOSEPH, *Letter of Consolation*

O God, I stand before Thee, knowing all my deficiencies, and
overwhelmed by Thy majesty.... Thou knowest what is for
my good. If I recite my wants, it is not to remind Thee of
them, but that I may better understand how great is my dependence upon Thee.... Oh, Lord, my heart is not haughty,
nor are mine eyes lofty.   BAHYA IBN PAQUDA

Gold and silver are purified through fire; if you feel no sense of
improvement after praying, either you are made of base metal,
or your prayer lacked heat.   THE KORETSER RABBI

I love to pray at sunrise—before the world becomes polluted
with vanity and hatred.   THE KORETSER RABBI

Unless we believe that God renews creation every day, our prayers grow habitual and tedious.   BAAL SHEM TOV

Don't petition God to change natural laws for your sake.
                                          THE SASSOVER RABBI

There is a very high rung only one man in a generation can reach: that of having learned all wisdom, then praying like a child. MENDEL OF RYMANOV

Prayers truly from the heart open all the doors in Heaven. NACHMAN OF BRATSLAV

The shophar [the ram's horn sounded on the High Holy Days] is a prayer without words. SAUL LIEBERMAN

PRAYER: IRONIC COMMENTS ON

❧ If prayer did any good, they'd be hiring men to pray.

No one gets slapped for saying "Amen!"

❧ And now, dear God, farewell: I am going to America.

Praying can do no harm. TALMUD J.: *Berakoth*, 1 : 1

See also: AGNOSTICS, FAITH, GOD, HEAVEN, HEREAFTER, PIETY, PRIDE, REPENTANCE, STUDY, WORSHIP

PREJUDICE

❧ No physician can cure the blind in mind.

Prejudice joins hate to fear.

Prejudice is a sickness in the brain.

Prejudice is reason's enemy.

❧ Passion and prejudice are allies.

See also: HATE, JUDGMENT, OPINION, PASSION, REASON

PRIDE

❧ Pride is a mask for faults.

~§ If you harden your heart with pride, you will soften your brain with it, too.

~§ Pride is a prison.

Pride ends on the dunghill.

You may deal in rags yet dress in silks.

Nothing is more dangerous for a poor man than pride.

The proud man thinks, "Wherever I sit is the front."

~§ The proud are petulant, and the petulant are foolish.

God does not listen to the prayers of the proud.

The proud man is disturbed by the slightest wind.

A proud man is not loved even in his own house.
TALMUD: *Baba Bathra,* 98a

Concerning the man of pride, God has said: "I and he cannot abide together."   TALMUD: *Sotah,* 5

Absalom was proud of his hair, and was therefore hanged by his hair.   TALMUD: *Sotah,* 9b

~§ If you must hang, choose a high tree.
—adapted from TALMUD: *Pesahim,* 112a

~§ If ever man becomes proud, let him remember that a flea preceded him in the divine order of creation!
TOSEFTA: *Sanhedrin,* 8 : 8

A proud man never praises anyone.   *Zohar*

~§ King Solomon put a tiny ant in his palm and asked: "Is there anyone in the world greater than I?"
"Yes," answered the ant, "I am, since God sent you to carry me."   *Midrash Vayosha*

When pride cometh, then cometh shame: but with the lowly is wisdom.   *Book of Proverbs,* 11 : 2

⋧ It ill becomes a lion to weep in the presence of a fox.
Tanna de Be Elijah, 17

⋧ Pride is the reservoir of sin.
Ben Sirach, *Ecclesiasticus,* 10 : 13

⋧ He who believes he has not sinned carries pride within himself, and that is worse than sin.
Bahya ibn Paquda, *Duties of the Heart*

The proud man cannot humble himself to learn wisdom.
Saadia Gaon

⋧ The man who acts humble in order to win praise is guilty of the lowest form of pride.   Nachman of Bratslav

The Torah itself becomes coarse in the mouth of a man of pride.
Nachman of Bratslav

⋧ The conceited man is not a sinner but a fool.
"The Chofetz Chaim"

See also: ARROGANCE, CONCEIT, HUMILITY, MEEKNESS, VANITY

PRISON

Envy is a prison.

The proud live in their own prison.

Ignorance is a prison.

Fools do not know what a prison they live in.

The greedy are imprisoned for life.

⋧ Prisoners are free if content with their state; free men who seek more than their lot are prisoners to desire.

Immobility is a prison.

See also: FREEDOM, LIBERTY

PROGRESS

Progress is slow, setbacks are swift.

Moses ibn Ezra, *Shirat Yisrael*

See also: ADVICE, AMBITION, EFFORT, WEALTH

PROMISES

See DUTY, GOOD MEN, RESPONSIBILITY, VOWS

PROOF

ఆ§ "For instance" is not proof.

ఆ§ To give an example only gives an example.

ఆ§ A truth, established by proof, does not gain in force from the support of scholars; nor does truth lose its certainty because of popular dissent.

Maimonides, *Guide to the Perplexed,* Intro. II

ఆ§ Do not regard a thing as proved because you find it in books; for the liar who deceives men with his tongue will not hesitate to deceive them with his pen.

Maimonides, *Letter to the Yemenite Jews*

Those who believe a thing proved because it is in writing are fools.

Maimonides, *Letter to the Yemenite Jews*

ఆ§ A miracle cannot prove what is impossible; it is only useful to confirm what is possible.

Maimonides, *Guide to the Perplexed,* III

ఆ§ God will forget the man who stubbornly rejects proof that he is wrong.   Nachman of Bratslav

See also: EVIDENCE, ILLOGIC, LAW, LOGIC, REASON, TRUTH

PROPERTY

⊷ It is better to be a rich tenant than a poor landlord.

See also: BUSINESS, POSSESSIONS, RICH MEN, WEALTH

PROPHETS

Leave it to the people; if they are not prophets, they are the sons
of prophets.   TALMUD: *Pesahim,* 66a

Sages rank higher than prophets, for the prophecy of power does
not abide with a man every moment, but the power of wisdom does.   *Zohar*

See also: ISRAEL, RABBIS, SAGES, WISE MEN

PROPRIETY

Never accept a present from a thief.

⊷ In a house of the hanged, ask no one to hang up your coat.

Too much courtesy is offensive.

Among those who laugh, do not weep; among those who weep,
do not laugh.
                    HILLEL in *Tosephta Berakoth*

See also: CONDUCT, CONSIDERATION, DECORUM, MANNERS, TACT

PROSELYTES

Note. Jews distinguished forced apostates from Judaism (*anusim*)
from those who join another faith of their own volition (*me-
shumadim*). The most famous and important of Jewish *anusim,* of course, were the *marranos* of Spain.
                                        —L.R.

A convert is neither a Jew nor a gentile.

If anyone desires to become a proselyte, the rabbis ask him: "Why?
Do you not know that the Israelites are harried, hounded,
persecuted?" If he says, "I know, if only I would be worthy,"
they receive him without further argument.

TALMUD: *Yebamoth,* 47a

During a great famine, King Monobaz, a convert to Judaism, un-
locked his ancestral treasures and distributed them among the
poor. His ministers rebuked him: "Your fathers amassed these
treasures, and you squander them."

"No," said the king. "They collected earthly treasures, but
I preserve heavenly treasures. Their treasures could be stolen;
mine are beyond mortal reach. Their treasures were barren;
mine will bear fruit for time without end. They preserved
money; I have preserved lives. Their treasures are of this
world; mine are for eternity."   —adapted from TALMUD

The true proselyte is dearer to God than the Israelites were at
Mount Sinai: for had not the Israelites seen the thunder and
lightning, the quaking mountain and the sounding trumpets,
they would not have accepted the Torah; but the true proselyte, who saw none of these things, has surrendered to the
Holy One. Can anyone be dearer to God?

MIDRASH: *Tanhuma*

See also: CONVERTS, FAITH, ISRAEL, RELIGION

PROVERBS

Acquaint yourself with the proverbs of the wise, for by them shalt
thou be instructed.

Had I not lifted the shard, would you have found the pearl?
[Used to praise a maxim.]   TALMUD: *Yebamoth,* 92 : 2

If you want to know the Creator, study proverbs [Haggadah].

MIDRASH: *Sifre—Ekev,* 45

A proverb has three characteristics: few words, good sense, and
a fine image.   Moses ibn Ezra, *Shirat Yisrael*

A proverb without wisdom is like a body without a foot.
Moses ibn Ezra, *Shirat Yisrael*

See also: ADVICE, WISDOM

PRUDENCE

⇜ Don't sell the hide of a bear that's still in the woods.

The man who rents one garden will eat birds, but the man who
rents many gardens—the birds will eat him. [To attempt too
much is to lose all.]

Whoever moves into a run-down house is preparing a grave for
himself.

Better a chicken in the hand than an eagle in the sky.

If you fight a wave, it overpowers you; let it roll over you.

Better a little pumpkin in your hand than a big one in the field.
Talmud: *Sukkah*, 56b

A man should not hide all his money in one corner.
Midrash: *Genesis Rabbah*, 76 : 3

⇜ Don't run too far; you will have to return the same distance.
Midrash: *Ecclesiastes Rabbah*, 11 : 9

The simple man trusts everything; the sensible man pays heed to
his steps.   *Book of Proverbs*, 14 : 15

⇜ As long as I do not utter a word, I am its master; once I utter
it, I am its slave.   —adapted from Ibn Gabirol

Fortune often attends flight.
—adapted from Ibn Gabirol, *Choice of Pearls*

See also: FORESIGHT, JUDGMENT, SENSE

PUBLIC

It's bitter and bad when the public is wrong.

The voice of the people is as the Voice of God.
Midrash Samuel on Abot

See also: DEMOCRACY, GOVERNMENT, LAW, MASSES, OPINION, POLITICS

PUBLIC WELFARE

If a man is not by temperament a scholar, he should devote his
time to public affairs and the public welfare.
MIDRASH: *Leviticus Rabbah*, 25

See also: AUTHORITY, DUTY, POLITICS

PUNISHMENT

> We forget blows, but not words.

When a calf kicks, it's time to punish the cow.

> The worst punishment is a sleepless night.

If my brother steals, it is the thief—not my brother—who is
hanged.

Scolding doesn't help; a stick does.

> To punish a pupil, use nothing harder than a shoelace.
TALMUD: *Baba Bathra*, 21a

Anyone through whom a man has been incorrectly punished will
be barred from Heaven.   TALMUD: *Shabbath*, 149a

If, in a dream, you see a Book of Job, fear punishment.
TALMUD: *Berakoth*, 57b

A soothing tongue is a tree of life; but wild words break the
spirit.   *Book of Proverbs*, 15 : 4

He who associates with sinners, even if he does not imitate them, shares in their punishment.   *Abot de Rabbi Nathan,* 30

⁔§ A court which executes a man once every seventy years may be called destructive.   Eliezer ben Azariah

Does the Law really intend that the man who tore out another's eye should have his own eye torn out? Some men are weaker than others; and perhaps the guilty one, being weaker, would die as a result of the punishment.

What the Torah says is "An eye for an eye," *not* "A life for an eye." ... It is impossible to inflict on a second man exactly the same wound as was suffered by the first, for the first wound was not measured as to length, depth, and width. If we observe the ruling: "As he did, so shall it be done to him," the injury would have to be exactly the same, neither more nor less.   RABBI HANANEL

See also: JUDGES, JUSTICE, REVENGE

PURPOSE

Even a tree needs a function and search for a task.

Everything is good—in its time.
                    —adapted from *Ecclesiastes,* 3 : 1–8

There is no man who has not his hour, and no thing that has not its place.   *Sayings of the Fathers,* 4 : 3

See also: CAUSE AND EFFECT, CIRCUMSTANCES, GOD AND MAN

QUARRELS

ঌ Quarrels are the weapons of the weak.

ঌ Be sure you have the support of your equals before you challenge your superiors.

When two quarrel, a third grabs the hat.

ঌ A quarrel is like an itch: the more you scratch, the more it itches.

When the maids quarrel, the master learns about the pilferage.

ঌ A quarrel begins with a pitcher and ends with a barrel.

Spread the table and the quarrel will end.

The first quarrel is the best quarrel.

Gossip can estrange the closest friends.

Quarrel (if you must) with someone above you.

Don't interfere in an argument between lovers—or kin.

ঌ When you quarrel, quarrel in such a way that you can make up.

Strife is like the plank in a bridge: the longer it endures, the firmer it becomes.

Strife is like water going through a crevice: the wider the crevice, the stronger the flow.

Discord is like a leak in a cistern: drop by drop, the water escapes.

❧ When two men quarrel, the one who yields first displays the nobler nature.   TALMUD: *Kethuboth*, 71b

A quarrel is like a stream of water: once it opens a way, it becomes a wide path.   TALMUD: *Sanhedrin*, 7a

❧ When men quarrel, even God's anger does not frighten them.
                                                        Zohar

Do not quarrel with a powerful man, or you may fall into his hands.   BEN SIRACH, *Ecclesiasticus*, 8 : 1

❧ Don't quarrel with a loud man.
                        BEN SIRACH, *Ecclesiasticus*, 8 : 3

❧ The world stands firm because of those who close their lips during a quarrel.   NACHMAN OF BRATSLAV

A quarrelsome man deserves no honors. NACHMAN OF BRATSLAV

The greater a man's wisdom the more will he avoid quarrels.
                                        NACHMAN OF BRATSLAV

❧ Better an insincere peace than a sincere quarrel.
                                        THE LUBLINER RABBI

See also: CONTENTMENT, HATRED, PEACE, WAR

R

RABBIS

Note. "Rabbi" means "my teacher." The rabbi (in Yiddish, *rebbe*) is not a priest or minister, in the Christian sense. He is not an intermediary between God and man; nor is he a spiritual arbiter; nor does he exercise any formal religious authority over others; nor does he enjoy hierarchical status. I know that all this is difficult to believe. But the fact is that a rabbi's influence rests on his learning, his character, his personal qualities. Formal ordination, although it has ancient roots (Numbers, 27 : 18, 19) did not even become institutionalized until modern times; a rabbi may be ordained by another rabbi.

The rabbi *rarely leads religious services:* the *hazzan* (cantor) usually does; but any respected, learned layman may be asked to take the pulpit. Only in modern times, incidentally, did rabbis become Sabbath preachers.

The first rabbis were not professional priests at all, but men respected by the community for their superior character and learning. They exercised moral leadership, and acted as judges or counselors, simply because they were recognized to be worthy of teaching and leading. Jewish scholars established the precept that no man should use the Torah as a "spade" with which to dig for wealth. The great names of the Talmud are the names of workmen-scholars: Hillel was a woodchopper; Shammai, a surveyor; Ishmael, a tanner; Abba Hoshaiah, a launderer.

The very title of "rabbi," given to those who taught in the academies, was not used until the beginning of the Christian Era. Ordination (*smikhah:* "the laying on of hands") could, by rabbinical law, be performed only in Israel and by a member of the Sanhedrin. The Romans forbade the ordination of rabbis, under punishment of death. Ordination thus ended in the fourth century of the Christian Era, along with the political and economic decline of Jewry in Palestine. Formal ordination seems to have disappeared, for in the twelfth century Maimonides raised the possibility of renewing ordination—through an assembly of all the rabbis in Palestine, who would give one of their number the power to ordain others.

Such attempts at restoring ordination failed until the institution of modern ordination, which is made official by a certificate (not a license) called *hatarat horaah,* which means "permission to teach" (!), and usually includes the phrase "*Yoreh, yoreh, yadin, yadin,*" which is translatable as "He may indeed judge and give a decision." Ordination confers no sacerdotal powers: the teaching, as authority, extended only to rituals and dietary laws, and the judging only to civil cases.

Modern ordination can be said to have begun in Germany during the fourteenth century, with Rabbi Meir ha-Levi of Vienna. In the fifteenth century, the practice spread to Italy and Poland.

Traditionally, a rabbi is a teacher of Torah (in the broad sense: the Bible, Talmud, and later rabbinic works) and seeks to apply it to daily life. Jewish scholars were expected to share their knowledge with the less learned, and their insights with the less astute. They were expected to instruct, to spread enlightenment, to elevate the moral and religious life of the Jewish community.

What does a rabbi *do?* He performs the ceremonials that attend birth, confirmation, marriage, death; he interprets the tenets of Judaism; he oversees instruction in synagogue or temple; he offers comfort and consolation; he visits hospitals; he counsels families; he tries to "guide the perplexed."

All this may explain the curious mixtures of reverence, amusement, impertinence, and even scorn contained in the sayings Jews love to exchange about the rabbinical community.

—L.R.

◦§ A rabbi whose congregation does not want to drive him out of town isn't a rabbi; and a rabbi they do drive out isn't a man.

Influence with the *rebetsn* [rabbi's wife] is better than with the rabbi.

The moment you ask a rabbi a simple question, he starts to give you a complicated answer.

Every rabbi's wife is a magician: how else can she raise a family on his salary?

◦§ Our rabbi is so poor that if he didn't fast every Monday and Thursday, he'd starve to death.

◦§ If you quarrel with the rabbi, make peace with the bartender.

◦§ A goat has a beard—but that doesn't make him a rabbi.

The crown of a good name is greater than the crown of priesthood.
Sayings of the Fathers, 3 : 13

RABBIS: IRONIC COMMENTS ON

It's good to be important, for then the rabbi delivers your funeral eulogy in person.

You think it a miracle if God does the will of your rabbi; we deem it a miracle if our rabbi does God's will.

It is wiser to deal with a local thief than a strange rabbi.

Since flattery is unavoidable, and a universal necessity, I may as well become a rabbi. THE ROPSHITZER RABBI

◦§ It was hard for Satan alone to mislead the whole world, so he appointed rabbis in different localities.
NACHMAN OF BRATSLAV

Unless you can play baseball, you'll never get to be a rabbi in America. SOLOMON SCHECHTER

See also: PIETY, SCHOLARS, STUDY, TORAH, WISDOM

RANSOM

Note. The number of sayings and legal rulings that deal with ransom seem surprising only if we forget Jewish experience throughout history. An Egyptian satrap, a Roman sheriff, an Arabian brigand, a Bulgarian adventurer or drunken Cossack would kidnap a Jewish worthy, or a group of pilgrims, then blackmail the Jewish community for ransom. The alternatives pictured were not pleasant to contemplate.

And so Jewish community funds—for the needy, the old, the sick; for orphans, widows, the halt and the blind; for free burials, free clothes, dowries for poor maidens—contained a high-priority fund, until quite late into the Middle Ages, called *Pidyon Shebuyim,* a fund set aside for the ransoming of Jews. All other obligations were made secondary to that of freeing Jewish captives. (See Cecil Roth's "A Community of Slaves," in his *Personalities and Events in Jewish History,* pp. 112–35.)

—L.R.

Captives should not be ransomed at exorbitant costs—for the safety of society: otherwise, our enemies will exert every effort to capture victims. But a man may ransom himself at any price.   TALMUD: *Gittin,* 45b

Ransom a captive before you feed the poor. No act of charity is greater: and money collected for any purpose whatsoever may be used as ransom—even if collected to build a synagogue.
                                      JOSEPH CARO, *Shulhan Aruk*

Every moment delayed in ransoming a captive is like shedding his blood.   JOSEPH CARO, *Shulhan Aruk*

See also: CHARITY, FREEDOM, SLAVERY

REALISM

ᴥᎦ Out of snow, you can't make cheesecake.

If you chop wood, chips will fall.

ᴥᴥ You can't put "Thank you" in your pocket.

ᴥᴥ If you can't endure the bad, you won't live long enough to enjoy the good.

ᴥᴥ The man who does not make a choice makes a choice.

When two play, one must win and one must lose.

ᴥᴥ When the wind blows, garbage flies.

You can't pull two hides off one ox.

ᴥᴥ A chicken can't be slaughtered without blood being shed.

There are bones without meat, but no meat without bones.

One log won't even warm the fireplace.

Another man's cloak won't keep you warm.

ᴥᴥ There is no cloth so fine that moths are unable to eat it.

A carpenter without tools is no carpenter.

MIDRASH: *Exodus Rabbah*, 40 : 1

See also: CAUSE AND EFFECT, CIRCUMSTANCES

REASON

Note. Judaism rests on the assumption that piety can be buttressed by reason but not without faith; that God gave men reason—to use; that God gave men the freedom to choose, and the capacity to live good lives or bad lives.

The rabbis held that reason is not enough for man: that the problems of life cannot be solved without faith. In this, they differed from many philosophers of Greece. The Jews, according to one Greek commentator, were "a people of creative skepticism." —L.R.

A principle illustrated by an example only produces an example.

ᴥᴥ "For instance" is not proof.

When Man reasons, God laughs.

To make an assumption is to fool yourself.

◆§ Reason lives in the universe of freedom.

Passion is the friend of prejudice, not reason.

◆§ The man who does not make a choice makes a choice.

Lust and reason are enemies.

God conceals himself from our reason, but reveals Himself to our
hearts.   —adapted from *Zohar*

Reason is the mediating angel between God and man.
ABRAHAM IBN EZRA, *Commentary to Pentateuch*

◆§ Man is not an angel, whose reason always works perfectly,
nor is he a mule whose reason works not at all.
JOSEPH BEN ABBA MARI CASPI, *Yoreh Deah*

It is the power of reasoning [*seykhl*] with which God endowed man
that renders man capable of perfection.
MAIMONIDES: *Guide to the Perplexed*, 1 : 2

See also: BRAINS, FAITH, INTELLECT, INTELLIGENCE, LOGIC

RECONCILIATION

A reconciliation that does not explain that error lay on both sides is
not a true reconciliation.   MIDRASH: *Genesis Rabbah*, 54 : 3

See also: COMPROMISE, PEACE, QUARRELS

REDEMPTION

Redemption, like a livelihood, must be earned each day.
MIDRASH: *Genesis Rabbah*, 20 : 9

See also: HEREAFTER, SABBATH, SALVATION, VIRTUE

REFUGEES

If you change houses, you need only change your shirt; if you change lands, you change your whole life.

The refugee is like a plant without soil or water.

Moses ibn Ezra, Shirat Yisrael

See also: ISRAEL, JEWS, PATRIOTISM, PERSECUTION

REGRET

◆§ You may regret telling the truth.

No one has a monopoly on regret.

◆§ We regret more what we say than what we don't say.

See also: HOPE, REMORSE

RELATIVITY

◆§ The big you have seems small, the small you have not seems big.   Talmud: *Berakoth,* 33b

If there are no small ones, there will be no big ones.

Talmud J.: Sanhedrin, 10

When the home is in flames, one does not worry over the broken windows.   Hillel Zeitlin

See also: CIRCUMSTANCES, ENVY, GREED

RELIGION

Moses did not make religion a part of virtue: but he declared other virtues to be a part of religion—I mean justice, and fortitude, and temperance, and a universal agreement of the members of the community with one another.   Josephus

See also: FAITH, GOD, ISRAEL, PIETY, SABBATH, TORAH, VIRTUE, WISDOM

REMORSE

ᴥᲤ Never mind the remorse; just don't do what causes it.

Revenge begets remorse.

See: CONSCIENCE, DUTY, GOOD DEEDS, REPENTANCE, REVENGE, SUFFER-
ING

REPENTANCE

ᴥᲤ Rob not and repent not.

ᴥᲤ A Litvak is so clever that he repents *before* he sins.

ᴥᲤ When the sin is sweet, repentance is not so bitter.

The ways of repentance are no less hidden than the ways of sin.

The tears of repentance are not shed in vain.

Repentance is a key that opens any lock.

ᴥᲤ When we are young, God forgives our stumblings; when we
    mature, He weighs our words; and when we grow old, He
    waits—for our repentance.

If only one man repents for his sins, the whole world is pardoned.

Repentance prolongs a man's life.   TALMUD: *Yomah,* 86b

One must not say to a man who has repented [and changed his way
    of life], "Remember your former transgressions."
                                    TALMUD: *Baba Mezi'a,* 58b

Consider every day your last and you will always be ready—with
    good deeds and repentance.   TALMUD: *Shabbath,* 153a

Don't criticize a wicked man who abandons his wickedness—and
    repents.   MIDRASH: *Proverbs,* 6 : 30

⋖ The gates of prayer are sometimes open, sometimes closed; but the gates of repentance are open forever.
MIDRASH: *Deuteronomy Rabbah*, 2 : 7

The Lord will accept repentance for everything except giving another man a bad name. —adapted from *Zohar*

Just as the ocean is always open, even so are the gates of repentance.
Yalkut Tehilim, 789

Repent the day *before* you die [which means every day, for who knows the day of his death].
RABBI ELIEZER in *Sayings of the Fathers*, 2 : 10

It is not easy to repent of the sin of melancholy: for when a man begins to repent of it, he falls into a deeper melancholy, realizing he has sinned. THE BERSHIDER RABBI

See also: CONSCIENCE, GUILT, HEREAFTER, PRAYER, SIN

REPRISALS

The dog who is struck by a stone bites—another dog. [The oppressed turn upon the more oppressed.] *Zohar*

See also: RETRIBUTION, REVENGE

REPUTATION

You can rub him with honey and he'll still smell of tar.

In your town, it is your name that counts; in another, your clothes.
TALMUD: *Shabbath*, 145

⋖ No tombstones need be erected on the graves of the righteous; their deeds are their monuments. TALMUD, *Pesahim*, 119a

Happy is the man who leaves a good name.
TALMUD: *Berakoth*, 17a

What is a profanation of the Name? For example, if a scholar does
   not pay the butcher at once. [It sets a bad example.]
TALMUD: Yomah, 86a

∾ Even if all of a slander is not believed, half of it is.
MIDRASH: Genesis Rabbah, 56 : 4

Every man has three names: one his father and mother gave him,
   one others call him, and one he earns himself.
MIDRASH: Ecclesiastes Rabbah, 7 : 1

Beauty wanes, but a name endures.   APOCRYPHA: Ahikar, 2 : 49

The Lord will accept repentance for all sins, except one: giving a
   man a bad name.   —adapted from Zohar

A good name is more desirable than great riches, a good reputation
   than silver and gold.   Book of Proverbs, 22 : 1

He who earns a good name acquired it for his own good.
Sayings of the Fathers, 2 : 7

There are three crowns: the crown of learning, the crown of priesthood, the crown of royalty; but greater than any of these is the
   crown of a good name.   Sayings of the Fathers, 4 : 13

He who advertises his name, loses it.
HILLEL in Sayings of the Fathers, 1 : 13

∾ What you think of others tell us what they think of you.
MOSES IBN EZRA, Shirat Yisrael

A place becomes known far and wide because it is the home of a
   great man.   THE ROPSHITZER RABBI

See also: **FAME, GOOD DEEDS, HONOR, SELF-ESTEEM, SLANDER**

RESIGNATION

Note. The story is told of a rabbi who lost every one of his thirteen
   sons, and in his terrible grief said to their mother, who could
   not be consoled: "But our sons have not died in vain. Think of

it: when great misfortune strikes other men, they will remember ours, and recall that *we* lost thirteen sons; and perhaps they will not be angry with—blessed be His name!—the Lord."

—L.R.

◦§ All utterances prefaced with "God forbid" are possible.

So it goes: one man has a purse, but another has the money.

Fowl become inured to the killings.

◦§ If things aren't the way you like, then like them the way they are.

◦§ It will do about as much good as bleeding [cupping] a corpse.

Let him whose cloak a court of law has taken sing his song and go his way. [He was saved from theft.]

TALMUD: *Sanhedrin,* 7a

When a fox has his hour, bow to him.   TALMUD: *Megillah,* 16

To cry over the past is to offer a vain prayer.

MISHNAH: *Berakoth,* 9 : 3

He who tries to resist the wave is swept away, but he who bends before it abides.   MIDRASH: *Genesis Rabbah,* 44 : 15

◦§ To each wave that approached me, I bent my head.

RABBI AKIBA in TALMUD: *Yebamoth,* 121a

See also: ADVERSITY, CIRCUMSTANCES, HOPE, LIFE, OPTIMISM, PESSIMISM, REALISM

RESPONSIBILITY

If each one sweeps in front of his own door the whole street is clean.

When the shepherd is lame and the goats are fleet, there will be an accounting at the gate of the fold.

◦§ Hold no man responsible for what he says in his grief.

TALMUD, *Baba Bathra,* 16a

A man should not fast excessively (it weakens a man for good
    deeds).   TALMUD: *Ta'anith*, 11a

To deal with a deaf-mute, an idiot, or a minor is bad, for you are
    liable (responsible) and they are not.
                                    MISHNAH: *Baba Kamma*, 8 : 4

The man who warns the wicked, even if his warning goes unheeded,
    has saved himself from blame.   *Zohar*

See also: CAUSE AND EFFECT, CONSCIENCE, CHARITY, DUTY, OBLIGATION

RESOURCEFULNESS

◄§ When things are scarcer than you wish, a herring will have to
    serve as a fish.

When you can't go over, go under.

What you don't have in your head, you have in your feet.

See also: EFFORT, ENDURANCE, INGENUITY

REST

No rest is worth having unless it follows work.   SAADIA GAON

A man's body grows sluggish through too much rest; his stomach
    gets inflated, and disease is created in the lower parts: sciatica,
    gout, even elephantiasis. Even if a man has all he needs, he
    dare not stay idle, for the idle man will end in weakness, in-
    sanity, and sickness; and this truth applies even to a king or
    ruler.   SAADIA GAON

The only truly desirable rest is the rest to be enjoyed in the world-
    to-come.   SAADIA GAON

Only if a man knows himself, and has no illusion about himself, and
    understands every existing thing in relation to itself, will he
    find real rest [of mind].   MAIMONIDES, *Eight Chapters*, 5

Just as the body becomes exhausted by hard labor and is rein-
vigorated by rest, so the mind needs its weariness relieved by
rest.   MAIMONIDES, *Eight Chapters*, 5

See also: CONTENTMENT, HEALTH, WORK

RESURRECTION

Note. The earliest portions of the Bible are vague about the concept of resurrection; the Book of Daniel mentions it (12 : 2);
but Isaiah gave the idea potent, poetical form—as a prophecy
to all of hard-pressed Israel: "The dead shall live, the bodies
shall arise. . . . Awake and sing, ye who dwell in the dust."
Later, the prophet Ezekiel, in Babylon, proclaimed: "Behold, I
will open your graves, and cause you to come out of them, O
my people."

The Pharisees, after the Exile (during the time of the
Second Temple), adopted a belief in the resurrection: i.e., that
the dead would literally rise from their graves at "the end of
days." The Sadducees did not accept this concept. In *Ecclesiasticus* (second century B.C.E.), Jesus ben Sirach, an aristocrat
and a Sadducee, tartly wrote:

> "When the dead is at rest
> Let his memory rest!"

But the Sadducee view did not prevail, for it was from the
ranks of the plainer folk that the Pharisees and, later, most
rabbinical scholars came.

Christianity and Islam, of course, adopted resurrection as
an integral aspect of their creeds. The Talmud accepts resurrection as a basic, sacred tenet of Judaic faith. The rabbinical
tradition agreed that the redemption of man is not possible,
nor divine reward and punishment, nor immortality of the soul,
without that physical resurrection, followed by a reunion of
bodies with their souls, which the Messiah's coming will effect.
The power of these ideas to Jewry for thousands of years was
of incalculable importance in holding their world-dispersed
community together, and in convincing them that divine justice
would be meted out.

For centuries, all of the prayers in the liturgy of Judaism specifically mentioned the resurrection (the second paragraph of the *Amidah,* the part of the prayer recited when standing) and the *Shmona Esra* (the Eighteen—now Nineteen—Benedictions). The daily prayers of observing Jews still contain this passage in the second of these benedictions ". . . You revive the dead with great mercy [and] keep faith with them who lie in the dust. . . . Blessed art Thou, O Lord, who revivest the dead."

But one must always remember that religious ideas were never embalmed beyond changeability in Judaism; Jewish faith underwent constant analysis, exegesis, criticism; every aspect of belief and the Law was debated throughout centuries of disputation—both scholarly and lay. Maimonides, who sometimes departed from traditional rabbinical judgments (and was roundly denounced for it), placed resurrection among his majestic *Thirteen Articles of Faith.* But the dogma of bodily resurrection continued to bother many sages and scholars, who conceived of the world-to-come, of eschatology and perfection, in terms of supernal, eternal bliss of the *soul.*

Orthodox Jews continued to interpret resurrection literally —differing only as to whether it would include all of mankind, only the deserving righteous, or only Jews. Any disbelief in, or skepticism about, the physical actuality of resurrection was condemned by the Orthodox as heresy; and in the end resurrection was held to be the reward of "all the righteous of all nations."

Reform Judaism does not accept bodily revival and refusion with the soul; the Reform liturgy has expunged earlier, Orthodox phrasings. Many Reform scholars point out that the concept of physical resurrection is a carry-over from primitive experience, agrarian societies, pagan fertility cults, Egyptian and Babylonian myths, the mystic religions of the East—and that such a conception should have no place in modern Judaic faith and worship. Among Conservative Jews (who stand midway between the Orthodox and the Reformed), the doctrine of the resurrection has been blended into the larger, comforting precept of the soul's immortality—without bodily attendance or reinforcement. "Eternal Life" has become the phrase adopted in the prayer books of Conservative and Reform Jews instead of "resurrection."

Most modern Jews, I suspect, do not ponder much over whether the coming of the Messiah or salvation, immortality or the world-to-come, are to be taken literally, but are inclined to regard them with ancient, symbolic affection, with a sense of historical respect and continuity, as affirmations of a larger, more important concept—the faith in One omnipotent, compassionate, and forgiving God.

—L.R.

Those who sleep in the dust shall awake.   *Daniel,* 12 : 2

The dead shall live, the bodies shall arise.   *Isaiah,* 26 : 19

⋑ Awake and sing, ye who dwell in the dust. *Isaiah,* 26 : 19

I will open your graves, my people, and cause you to come out of
     them.   *Ezekiel,* 37 : 12

The righteous man has hope in his death.
                              Book of Proverbs, 14 : 32

Death is when two worlds meet with a kiss: this world going out,
     the future coming in.   Talmud J.: *Yebamoth,* 57a

Man is born to die; the dead will live again.
                              Sayings of the Fathers, 4 : 22

⋑ Death is merely moving—from one home to another: and if we
     are wise, we will make the latter the more beautiful.
                              The Kotzker Rabbi

I am going out one door, and shall go through another.
                              Baal Shem Tov

See also: DEATH, HEREAFTER, IMMORTALITY, PARADISE

RETRIBUTION

⋑ God waits long, but he pays with interest.

As you brew, so shall you drink.

Those who sow the wind shall reap the whirlwind.
                                                          Book of Hosea, 8 : 7

He who digs a pit will fall into it, and he who rolls a stone, it will
    come back upon him.   *Book of Proverbs*, 26 : 27

He who can hire a poor worker but does not, shortens the worker's
    life, and his own life will be shortened, too.   *Zohar*

Because you drowned others, you were drowned, and those who
    drowned you shall be drowned, too.
                                          HILLEL in *Sayings of the Fathers*, 2 : 6

See also: ADVICE, CAUSE AND EFFECT, FORGIVENESS, GOD, REVENGE

REVELATION

Only through what is disclosed can man learn what is undisclosed.
                                                          LEOPOLD ZUNZ

See also: HEAVEN, HEREAFTER, REASON, RESURRECTION

REVENGE

Note. All the ancient religions of the Middle East contained *lex
    talionis*, "the law of retaliation." "Thou shalt give life for life,
    eye for eye, tooth for tooth, hand for hand, foot for foot" (Ex-
    odus 21 : 23–24). But many who venerated the Torah's teach-
    ings on lovingkindness, and the loving and forgiving of neigh-
    bors, wondered whether this passage could mean what it
    seems to mean; in the quotations that follow, you will find
    rabbinical interpretation of the "eye for eye" injunction. Note
    especially the remarkable passage by Rabbi Hananel.
                                                          —L.R.

God punishes, men take revenge.

⋙ Revenge begets remorse and remorse begets misery.

The smallest revenge will poison the soul.

Revenge is half consolation.

&§ Blood that has been shed does not rest.

If you take revenge, you will regret it; if you forgive, you will rejoice.

Who takes vengeance destroys his own house.

Thou shalt not avenge.   *Leviticus,* 19 : 18

Say not, "I will pay back evil." Wait for the Lord to help you.
                    Book of Proverbs, 20 : 22

If a man says "I will not lend you my shovel because you refused to lend me your scythe," that is revenge—which the Law forbids.   *Abot de Rabbi Nathan*

Does the Law really intend that the man who tore out another's eye should have his own eye torn out? Some men are weaker than others; and perhaps the guilty one, being weaker, would die as a result of the punishment.

What the Torah says is "An eye for an eye," *not* "A life for an eye.". . . It is impossible to inflict on a second man exactly the same wound as was suffered by the first, for the first wound was not measured as to length, depth, and width. If we observe the ruling: "As he did, so shall it be done to him," the injury would have to be exactly the same, neither more nor less.
                    RABBI HANANEL

See also: CONSCIENCE, FORGIVENESS, RETALIATION, RETRIBUTION

REVOLUTION

&§ One unjust act can cause a revolution.

Revolution is the right of slaves.
                    H. LEIVICK (LEIVICK HALPERN), in *The Golem*

See also: GOVERNMENT, POLITICS, POWER, SLAVERY

RICHES/RICH MEN

The wise know the value of riches, but the rich do not know the
    pleasures of wisdom.

The rich eat when they want to, the poor when they can.

He heapeth up riches, and knoweth not who shall gather them.
                                        Book of Psalms, 39 : 6

A good name is worth more than great riches.
                                        Book of Proverbs, 22 : 1

‮ Listen to the rich no less than the poor, for it is written: "Ye
    shall not favor persons in judging them."
                                        Abot de Rabbi Nathan, 20 : 22a

See also: POOR MEN AND RICH MEN, WEALTH

RIGHTEOUSNESS

‮ The righteous man who says he is righteous—is not righteous.

‮ What is just is always right.

The righteous man gives a little more than a scale indicates.
                                        TALMUD: *Baba Bathra,* 7b

The righteous promise little and perform much; the wicked promise
    much and perform not even a little.
                                        TALMUD: *Baba Mezi'a,* 87a

Gray hairs are a glorious crown which is won by a righteous life.
                                        Book of Proverbs, 16 : 31

Better a little with righteousness than great revenues with injustice.
                                        Book of Proverbs, 16 : 8

As the whirlwind passes, so the wicked man vanishes;
But the righteous one is rooted forever.
                                        Book of Proverbs, 10 : 25

The wicked man earns illusive wages;
But he who sows righteousness has a true reward.
Book of Proverbs, 11 : 18

A righteous man cares for his beast;
But the mercy of the wicked is cruel. *Book of Proverbs,* 12 : 10

Righteousness delivereth from death.
Book of Proverbs, 10 : 2

If a man has two cows, one strong and one weak, he lays the yoke
upon the strong: God does the same with the righteous.
Midrash: *Genesis Rabbah,* 32 : 3

It is beyond our power to explain the prosperity of the wicked or
the troubles of the righteous.
Sayings of the Fathers, 3 : 16

See also: EVIL, GOOD, GOD, HEAVEN, HEREAFTER, PIETY, PRAYER

RIVALRY

Superior work is what results from a man's rivalry with his neighbor.
Midrash: *Ecclesiastes Rabbah,* 3 : 11

ROBBERS/ROBBERY

◄§ A scholar is not a robber, and a robber is not a scholar.
Talmud: *'Abodah Zarah,* 176

See also: THIEVES

RUMOR

◄§ Tongues are more dangerous than swords, for tongues can
hurt from afar.

◄§ When in doubt, shut up.

To repeat what you have not seen is to increase what you only
heard.

If there were no listeners there would be no rumors.

◦ If you hear your neighbor died, believe it; but if you hear he became rich, don't believe it.

◦ What you see and hear, you cannot help; but what you say depends on you alone.   —adapted from *Zohar*

The man who rails is feared, and he who talks rashly is hated.
                    —adapted from BEN SIRACH, *Ecclesiasticus,* 9 : 18

See also: GOSSIP, SCANDAL, SECRETS, SLANDER, TALK

SABBATH

Note. The Torah's laws governing the Sabbath presented considerable difficulties to Jews in the conduct of daily life. Should a physician go to attend a dying man on the Sabbath? Should the injunction against handling money on the Sabbath be waived so that ransom might be paid to save the life of a captive? The male child is supposed to be circumcised on the eighth day after birth, but if the eighth day falls on the Sabbath, during which no work of any kind is permitted ("whosoever doeth any work therein shall be put to death"—*Exodus,* 35 : 2), and if "no man [should] go out of his place on the seventh day" (*Exodus,* 16 : 29)—then what was to be done about circumcision? Or how could Jews defend themselves against, say, the Romans—who, knowing of the Sabbatical injunction, attacked Jews on the holy day?

In these, and a thousand comparable problems, the oral interpretation and amplification of rabbi-scholars made it possible for the Jews to hold to the letter of the Law—by reinterpreting what the letters might mean. (See Guide Notes for TORAH, TALMUD, MISHNAH, MIDRASH, and GEMARA.)

Shabbes (the Sabbath) is called "the Queen of the week," "the Bride." In however bitter a time and place, the Sabbath, to Jews, was the miraculous time when even the lowliest or poorest felt himself in kingly communion with the Almighty, favored by God's special concern: "It is a sign between me and the children of Israel!" (Exodus, 31 : 17).

Each Sabbath, down the generations, in every land in which they have lived, Jews have scrubbed every nook of their dwelling, bathed themselves with care, donned fresh garments, laid out their best linens, glasses, utensils: for *shabbes* brought —each week, throughout a lifetime—a sense of personal splendor, cleanliness, devotion, exaltation. The old rabbis believed that the *neshoma yesera* ("extra soul") descends each Friday when the sun sets. *Shabbes* was redolent with intimations of divinity, the hint of angels, visions of heaven, all the blessed on golden thrones under the sparkling stars. ("Our house was filled with the odor of burning wax, blessed spices," writes Isaac Bashevis Singer, "and with an atmosphere of wonder and miracles.")

What did the Jews do on *shabbes?* They prayed—and studied; they read; they enjoyed sleep—the special Sabbath sleep of bliss; they discussed the Torah and the Talmud. Moses had enjoined them, said Philo, "[to] assemble . . . on these seventh days . . . in a respectful and orderly manner . . . [to] hear the laws read [and explained] so that none should be ignorant of them."

Considered historically, the idea of a workless seventh day was revolutionary. (The Fourth Commandment ordains Sabbath for beasts of burden no less than men.) The Greeks and Romans scorned it. Seneca called the Hebrews "this most outrageous people [who] lose almost a seventh part of their life in inactivity." Juvenal jeered at those Roman Christians "to whom every seventh day is idle." Horace and Martial thought the idea foolish, conducive to laziness.

Every Sabbath morning a portion of the Five Books of

Moses is read in the synagogue, together with a reading from the Prophets, so that the Torah is completed in one year—and the cycle is promptly begun again. In their homes, all summer, fathers and grandfathers traditionally engaged the children in discussions—of the *Sayings of the Fathers* or portions of the Mishnah that discuss ethical problems. How can one appraise the consequences of a people, young and old, spending one day a week, year after year, generation after generation, in such seminars on religion, morals, ethics, responsibility?

Once, when some Falasha Jews were being tortured, and were goaded to name their savior, they cried: "The savior of the Jews is the Sabbath!" Of which England's Rabbi Hertz wrote: "They spoke wiser then they knew."

—L.R.

෴ On the Sabbath, the wicked in Hell, too, rest.

The savior of the Jews is the Sabbath.
                                  Saying of the Falasha Jews

Remember the Sabbath day, to keep it holy. Six days shalt thou labor, and do all thy work: But the seventh day is the Sabbath of the Lord, thy God.
                  the Fourth Commandment, *Exodus*, 20 : 8–10

The Sabbath was delivered unto you, and not you unto the Sabbath.
                                  TALMUD: *Yomah*, 25b

The Sabbath was given for the study of the Torah.
                                  TALMUD: *Pesikta Rabbati*, 22

෴ The Sabbath was given for pleasure [of the scholars].
                                  Pesikta Rabbati, 22

Shabbes (the Sabbath) is the Queen of the week.
                                  TALMUD, *Shabbath*, 119a

[The Sabbath] is a sign between me and the children of Israel.
                                  Exodus 31 : 17

Some rules governing the Sabbath are as scantily supported [in Scripture] as mountains hanging by a hair.
                                  MISHNAH: *Hagigah*, 1 : 8

The Jews, in bondage in Egypt, possessed scrolls, in which they
reveled every Sabbath. These promised them that God would
redeem them because they rested on the Sabbath.

MIDRASH: *Exodus Rabbah,* 5

Blessed art Thou, O lord ... who has commanded us to kindle the
Sabbath light.   *Standard Prayer Book*

More than the Jews kept the Sabbath did the Sabbath [observance]
keep the Jews [alive].   AHAD HA-AM

See also: REDEMPTION, RESURRECTION

SADNESS

A pretty garment can conceal a sad heart.

◦§ The deeper the sadness, the less tongue it possesses.

◦§ "And it came to pass" usually introduces a tale of sadness.

TALMUD: *Megillah,* 10b

Laughter may come from an aching heart. All pleasure contains an
element of sadness.

JONATHAN EIBESCHUTZ, *Yaarot Devash*

See also: HAPPINESS, MELANCHOLY, MISFORTUNE, PLEASURES, SUFFER-
ING

SAFETY

◦§ The wolf does not fear the dog, but his bark.

He who can cringe creeps forward.

◦§ It is worse to live on your knees than die on your feet.

If two are traveling in a desert, and only one has a canteen of
water, if both drink, both will die, but if only one drinks he
will survive; the son of Patura thought: "It is better that both
should drink and die, rather than that one should witness his

companion's death." Rabbi Akiba thought, " 'That your brother may live with you' implies that your life takes precedence over his life." [At least one life is saved.]

TALMUD: *Baba Mazi'a*, 62a

If all men were philosophers, the social order would be destroyed and the human race exterminated: men need many material things to survive.   MAIMONIDES: *Eight Chapters*

The fox feels safe only as long as the leopard has others to prey on.

IBN ZABARA, *Book of Delight*

See also: AUTHORITY, LAW AND ORDER, POLITICS, POWER, STRENGTH

SAGES

Note. Anyone who has read the first five books of the Old Testament (the Torah) may sympathize with the problems that confronted the ancient "book men"—the sages, rabbis, philosophers —who set out to clarify and enforce God's edicts among the Hebrew people. After all, the Torah is held to come directly from God; it is God's word; it can be neither denied, corrected, nor evaded. (See headnote: TORAH.)

The Torah contains injunctions and commandments from On High. But much that is in the Five Books of Moses is obscure in meaning; much is metaphorical; much is in the form of parables the exact meaning of which was not easily agreed upon. Much of the Torah is worded in so generalized a form that the absence of details represents an absence of the procedures to be followed in observing the Law. And the Torah is not free of contradictions: some laws are given more than once, in different form—for reasons never explained in the Torah itself.

Changing problems and crises of the most dreadful nature simply demanded that certain injunctions be reinterpreted so that Israel might live. (See, for instance, the headnotes for REVENGE, SABBATH.) This presented no easy problem. See the Guide Notes: TALMUD, MISHNAH, GEMARA, MIDRASH, and headnote for SCHOLARS.

—L.R.

᪗ They are our sages because we are their fools.

A complete fool is better than a half-sage.

᪗ After the death of Rabbi Moshe, Rabbi Mendel of Kotzk asked one of his disciples: "What was most important to your sage?" The disciple thought, and replied: "Whatever he happened to be doing at the moment." Hasidic story

Some men are stupid: they stand up to honor a Holy Scroll, but do not rise to honor a sage. TALMUD: *Makkoth*, 22b

᪗ When a sage dies, all men should mourn, for they are his kinsmen. TALMUD: *Shabbath*, 105b

Just as a small log may set fire to a large one, so do smaller scholars sharpen the wits of sages. TALMUD: *Ta'anith*, 7a

The curses of a sage even when not deserved will come to pass. TALMUD, *Berakoth*, 56a

To see a sage die is like seeing a holy scroll burn: "On such a day, I fast," said Rabbi Abbabu. TALMUD J.: *Mo'ed Katan*, 3

᪗ A sage takes precedence over a king, for if a sage dies, we have no one like him, but if a king dies all Israel is eligible to succeed him. —adapted from the MIDRASH

Sages rank higher than prophets, for the power of prophecy does not abide with a man every moment, but the power of wisdom does. *Zohar*

See also: KNOWLEDGE, POLITICS, SCHOLARS, WISDOM, WISE MEN

SAINTS

Note. A venerable legend of the Jews concerns the *Lamed-Vov Tsadikim* ("the Thirty-Six Saints"), living men who do not know they are saints but perform such surpassing deeds of kindness and compassion that God allows the world to go on because of them. Not only does each of the Thirty-Six not know how saintly and sainted he is, no one else can ever identify him, either. A member of the Thirty-Six Saints may be a pauper, a cobbler, a hem-stitcher, a seer. A *Lamed-Vov* discloses his identity only in very dire emergencies: When Jews are in mortal peril, one of the *Tsadikim* may swoop in to do God's bidding—suddenly, magically—then will vanish as inexplicably as he appeared.

This idea of doing good for the sake of goodness alone, without intention of reward or recognition or simple gratitude from the one benefited, played a central role in the ethical pantheon erected by generations of rabbinical philosophers. The less self-serving a good deed, the less known or publicized, the less one receives praise or credit or reward, the nobler it is: After all, *God* knows, and must most cherish the pure of heart.

—L.R.

◈ Bad men do well in this world, saints in the next.

◈ If charity cost no money, and favors represented no inconvenience, the world would be bursting with saints.

A vulgar man cannot be a saint.

HILLEL in *Sayings of the Fathers*, 2 : 5

See also: ANGELS, IRONIES, RIGHTEOUSNESS, VIRTUE

SALVATION

Note. There is no satisfactory way of translating the word/concept of "salvation" into Hebrew or Yiddish, for in Jewish thought salvation has simply meant the deserved reward of those who "live Torah," fulfill the commandments, perform the *mitzvahs* of good deeds, kindness, compassion, help to one's fellow men —those mortals, in short, who exemplify true piety and virtue by the way they live on earth.

Jews do not believe that a man inherits the guilt of Adam's Fall, nor that man is born in, with, or out of sin. They hold that personal salvation is achieved by personal conduct. Every man, Jew or not, is believed to be responsible for, and capable of, attaining his own salvation: each can approach God in his own fashion, without a mediating rabbi, priest or minister.

The writings of the rabbis reflect an abiding realism, I

think, about the nature of man's nature: his passions, irrationalities, vanity, willfulness, propensity to evil; but rabbinical writings stress man's power to choose, to act, to overcome his baser impulses. Moreover, man is held to have been created incomplete by God's intention, precisely so that men may themselves cooperate in virtue—thus completing God's work. (See headnote for SIN.)

—L.R.

Whoever lives by Torah, good deeds, humility, and the fear of Heaven, will be saved from doom.
MIDRASH: *Pesikta Rabbati*, 198a

See also: **HEAVEN, HEREAFTER, ISRAEL, JEWS, REPENTANCE, RESURRECTION, SIN, TORAH, VIRTUE**

SARCASM: EXAMPLES OF

⋙ Eggs want to be smarter than hens.

The world is beautiful, shining, bright, and easy—but for whom?

⋙ When a *nebbekh* leaves a room, it feels as if someone came in.

⋙ To avoid all sorrows, just cut off your head.

A hearty thanks—to your navel.

⋙ A crow flies high—and perches on a pig.

Let God worry about tomorrow—who will give me a loan today?

It's about as much help as throwing a bean at a wall.

⋙ Things are going beautifully for me—as they do for a saint in this world.

The rabbi finishes the wine only to make his disciples happy.

⋙ He acts rich: he owns a whole head of cabbage.

To be a millionaire, he'll sell you the shirt off his back.

See also: **ANIMALS, IRONY, PARADOXES, SCHOLARS: AMUSED COMMENTS ON**

SATAN

✺ Satan seduces us in this world, and accuses us in the next.
                              TALMUD: *Sukkah*, 52b

Satan's torment was worse than Job's. He was like a servant told to
    break a cask without spilling the wine.
                              TALMUD: *Baba Bathra*, 16b

When a man is in danger, Satan presses charges against him.
                              MIDRASH: *Genesis Rabbah*, 91

✺ If Satan says, "Sin—for the Lord will forgive you," don't do it.
              —adapted from TALMUD: *Hagigah*, 16a

Satan brought curses on the world through his cleverness.
                                          Zohar

Like iron, out of which man can fashion whatever tools he needs
    when he heats it in the forge, so Satan can be subdued to the
    service of God, if tempered by the Torah, which is like fire.
                              Abot de Rabbi Nathan, 16

It was hard for Satan alone to mislead the world, so he appointed
    rabbis in different places.   NACHMAN OF BRATSLAV

You can't trust Satan: he tries to persuade you not to go to the
    synagogue on a cold morning; and when you do go, he follows
    you there.   THE KORETSER RABBI

See also: DEMON, DEVIL, EVIL, HELL, SIN, TORAH, VIRTUE; **and head-
    notes for** DEVIL, EVIL

SCANDAL

Why were our fingers made flexible? So that we may stop our ears
    with them when evil [scandal] is being spoken.
                              TALMUD: *Kethuboth*, 5

See also: GOSSIP, RUMOR, SLANDER, TALK

SCHOLARS

Note. To study, for Jews, was "to come under the wings of the Divine Presence." Atop the Jewish pyramid of respect, unchallenged, stands the scholar—not the ruler, the prince, the millionaire, the rabbi. (A rabbi can, of course, be a great scholar; but scholars were more respected than rabbis.)

A Jewish mother customarily sang a lullaby of hope that her little son might become not rich or successful, but learned and wise—a *talmid khokhem* ("disciple of the wise," "expert on Talmud"). A student was considered a great matrimonial catch—and families offered dowries or outright support to them during their years at a *yeshiva* (college). High honor was accorded the family in which a daughter married a scholar. "If you must, sell everything [to] marry your daughter to a scholar," comes from the Talmud (*Pesahim,* 49b).

Penurious students were supported by the community. Some students walked "from the banks of the Danube to the banks of the Seine, (defying) hunger and cold, to drink in the words of some far-famed master" (Louis Ginzberg, in *Students, Scholars and Saints,* J.P.S.A., 1928). Those who came from far distances were lodged with local families. It was considered an act of piety to feed a *yeshiva bocher,* many of whom went from home to home, eating and sleeping in a different place each night.

In the old country, before a boy entered a *cheder* (school) he was carried into the synagogue by his father or *melamed* (teacher), and sometimes placed in front of the *bimah* (pulpit) to face the entire congregation; and sometimes the Scroll of the Torah was unrolled and the Ten Commandments were read aloud, addressed to the boy directly, reenacting the scene on Mount Sinai.

On his first day in *cheder,* the boy's mother and father would stand over him as the teacher pointed to the letters of the alphabet. As the lad repeated the names of the letters, his mother might give him a cookie, shaped in the form of that letter. Sometimes, honey would be put on the slate, so that the child should lick it—to learn that "learning is sweet." At the end of this first lesson, the mother would enfold the boy and pray that her son "fulfill his life with years of Torah study, marriage, and good deeds."

The scholar was expected to be immaculate in clothes and person; indifferent to physical comforts or material rewards; gentle in manner; sensitive to others. He had to combine scholarship with rectitude. Indeed, these virtues were assumed to go hand in hand: those who study are virtuous, and those who *know* will not do evil. See headnotes for SCHOLARSHIP, STUDENTS, STATUS.

—L.R.

The table that has fed no scholars is not blessed.

A scholar can't conduct a business.

The fate of Israel depends on its scholars.

The scholar who has abandoned the study of Torah is like a bird that has abandoned its nest.   TALMUD: *Hagigah,* 9b

Just as the kernel of a nut is not despised, even though the shell be marred, so it is with [the appearance of] a scholar.
TALMUD: *Hagigah,* 15b

He who has learning but does not fear God cannot enter Heaven.
TALMUD: *Shabbath,* 31a

A scholar with a spot on his garments deserves the worst.
TALMUD: *Shabbath,* 114a

If you must, sell everything and marry your daughter to a scholar.   TALMUD: *Pesahim,* 49b

A scholar who is the son of a scholar is modest; but a scholar who is the son of an ignoramus trumpets his knowledge abroad.   TALMUD: *Baba Mezi'a,* 85b

A scholar is not a robber, and a robber is not a scholar.
TALMUD: *'Aboda Zarah,* 17b

The ignorant think less clearly as they grow older, but scholars think more clearly with the years.
TALMUD: *Kinnin,* 3 : end

To treat a scholar to wine is like offering a libation to God.
TALMUD: *Yomah,* 71a

A scholar should be like a bottle which lets in no wind; like a
deep garden bed which retains its moisture; like a pitch-coated
jug which preserves its wine; and like a sponge which absorbs
everything. TALMUD: *Derekh Erets,* 1 : 2

To partake of a meal at which a great scholar is present is to
feast upon the refulgence of the Divine Presence.
TALMUD: *Berakoth,* 64a

◆ A scholar who is not as unyielding as iron is no scholar.
TALMUD: *Taanith,* 4a

The man who is not a scholar by temperament should devote his
time to public affairs. MIDRASH: *Leviticus Rabbah,* 25

A scholar who is a bastard [*mamzer*] is preferable to a high
priest who is ignorant. MIDRASH, *Numbers Rabbah,* 6

◆ Just as a tent cannot stand without pegs and cords, so Israel
cannot stand without scholars. *Seder Eliyahu Rabbah*

The "bite" of the learned is like the bite of a fox, their sting is
like a scorpion's, their hiss like a serpent's: all their words
are like coals of fire. [A scholar's words are not to be taken
lightly.] *Sayings of the Fathers,* 2 : 10

◆ There are four types [of students]: the sponge, the funnel,
the strainer, and the sifter: The sponge soaks up everything;
the funnel takes in at one ear but lets out at the other; the
strainer lets pass the wine and retains the lees; and the sifter
holds back the coarse flour and collects the fine.
Sayings of the Fathers, 5 : 15

It is imperative that most men work in [physically] productive
occupations, so that the few who devote themselves entirely
to learning may have their wants provided; in this way, the
human race goes on, and knowledge is enriched.
MAIMONIDES, *Commentary on Mishnah, Introduction*

When you help scholars, you gain a share in their learning.
NACHMAN OF BRATSLAV

SCHOLARS: AMUSED COMMENTS

The most important thing a scholar needs is a small appetite.

◦§ Some scholars study so much that they don't leave themselves time to think.

◦§ When a scholar sets out to look for a bride, he should take an ignoramus along to advise him.

Every scholar has his own peculiarities [eccentricities].

◦§ When a scholar makes a mistake it is a big one.

◦§ The scholar [lost in his thoughts] does not see that borsht is red.

I have been rewarded for what I interpreted—and for what I left uninterpreted.   TALMUD: *Pesahim,* 22b

How does an uneducated man regard a scholar? At first, like a golden ladle; if he talks with him, like a silver ladle; and if the scholar is his beneficiary, like an earthen spoon.
                    TALMUD: *Sanhedrin,* 52b

◦§ Some scholars are both wise and handsome—and would be still wiser were they less handsome.   TALMUD

A carcass is better than a scholar without common sense.
                    MIDRASH: *Leviticus Rabbah,* 1 : 15

A scholar without sensibility is less than an ant.
                    MIDRASH: *Leviticus Rabbah,* 1 : 15

◦§ Some scholars are like camels loaded with silk: neither the silk nor the camel is of any use to the other.
                    ABRAHAM IBN EZRA, *Yesod Mora*

◦§ Some scholars are like donkeys: they only carry a lot of books.
                    BACHYA IBN PAQUDA, *Duties of the Heart*

See also: EDUCATION, ISRAEL, KNOWLEDGE, LEARNING, SABBATH, STATUS, STUDY, TORAH, WISDOM

SCHOLARSHIP

Note. It is most revealing that relatively few of the students at a *yeshiva* (college) in Eastern Europe received (or wanted) a rabbinical degree. The primary purpose of the *yeshiva* was not to produce rabbis, but Jews well-versed in the Talmud: learned men, disciplined in their thinking, who would dedicate themselves to live according to the Torah and spend their lives studying the ever-discussable Talmud.

May I repeat a quotation from W. E. H. Lecky, the Irish historian, who summarized the Jewish ethos in the following passage?

> While those around them were grovelling in the darkness of besotted ignorance ... enthralled by countless superstitions in which all love of enquiry and all search for truth were abandoned, the Jews were still pursuing the path of knowledge, amassing learning, and stimulating progress with the same unflinching constancy that they manifested in their faith. *The Rise and Influence of Rationalism in Europe*, Vol. II, 3d edition; Appleton, New York, 1906, p. 271.

—L. R.

See: ISRAEL, KNOWLEDGE, LEARNING, SCHOLARS, STUDY, TRUTH, WISDOM

SCIENCE

Note. Until the tenth century, there is almost nothing in the literature of the Jews that approximates science or scientific analysis. The marvels of nature excited awe and a veneration of the wonders God had created on earth. Within the Talmud's system of discourse, its exegetical debates and sophistical distinctions, there was no place for science as we know it. The rabbis set their faces against secular knowledge (as did Catholic authorities). Professor Charles Singer points out that although many Greek names are found in the Talmud, not one Greek scientist is included; even Aristotle is not mentioned. Maimonides incurred great hostility, for his writings and range approached scientific method. (See BIOGRAPHIES.)

Yet the Jewish passion for literacy, for learning, for scholarship, the support given any student of promise, the emphasis on study, analysis, reasoning, argument, the profound veneration of knowledge—all these were bound to break through the insulating walls of traditional Talmudic authority.

It was through Arabic thought and Islam, via the Sephardic Spanish intellectuals, that science came to the Jews. Many medieval rabbis became accomplished in mathematics, for instance, or astronomy, medicine, Hellenic philosophy. (See BIOGRAPHIES.)

For the past four centuries, the contribution of Jewish scientists (physicists, mathematicians, biologists, chemists, physiologists, philosophers, economists, etc.) has surely been remarkable; as of 1971, sixty Jews have won Nobel Prizes (first awarded in 1901).

I think that the old tradition of Judaism is neatly symbolized in this anecdote: An agnostic Jew smiled, "But Darwin has proved that man is only another animal"; to which a rabbi responded, "Then why has not a single breed of animal ever produced a Darwin?"

—L.R.

◈§ The sons of the poor give science its splendor.

Science, though it seems to waste Torah, actually confirms and clarifies it.   THE KORETSER RABBI

See also: **INTELLECT, INTELLIGENCE, KNOWLEDGE, SCHOLARS, STUDY, TRUTH, WISDOM**

SCRIPTURE

Where there is Scripture, there is wisdom.

A passage from Scripture can yield many meanings, just as a hammer splits one rock into many fragments.
                                TALMUD: *Sanhedrin,* 34a

See also: **GOD, TORAH, TRUTH, WISDOM**

SECRETS

ᴥ What three know is no longer a secret.

If you tell your secret to three, ten will know it.

Secrets are easier heard than kept.

ᴥ Your friend has a friend: don't tell him.

To be in on a secret is no blessing.

ᴥ The tongue has no bones, so it's very loose.

ᴥ Don't tell a secret in a field of mounds.

Don't tell a secret even to an ape.

ᴥ When wine goes in, secrets come out.

It is easy to get a fool to reveal a secret.

Fools and children cannot keep secrets.

The secrets of men are as different as their faces.
                    —adapted from TALMUD, *Berakoth,* 58a

If you never repeat what you are told, you will fare none the
          worse.   BEN SIRACH, *Ecclesiasticus,* 19 : 9

ᴥ What you hide from an enemy don't tell a friend.
                              IBN GABIROL, *Choice of Pearls*

A sage when asked, "How do you hide a secret?" answered, "I
     make my heart its grave."   IBN GABIROL

ᴥ Your secret is your prisoner; once you reveal it, you become
     its slave.   IBN GABIROL

See also: ADAGES, GOSSIP, SILENCE, SLANDER, TALK

SECURITY

A man who does not own a piece of land is not a complete [secure]
    man.   TALMUD: *Yebamoth,* 63a

See also: MONEY, POWER, SAFETY, STRENGTH, SURVIVAL

SELF

If I shall be like him, who will be like me?

The hen hears the rooster's sermon—and searches for its own
    kernel of corn.

To flee from God is to flee into the self.
                     —adapted from PHILO

℞ If I am not for myself, who will be for me? And if I am
    only for myself, what am I? And if not now—when?
              HILLEL in *Sayings of the Fathers,* 1 : 14

If I am here, all is here; and if I am not here, who is here?
              HILLEL in TALMUD: *Sukkah,* 53a

The I is the soul, which endures.   NACHMAN OF BRATSLAV

See also: CHARACTER, HONOR, INDIVIDUALITY, MAN, SELF-ESTEEM,
    SELFISHNESS

SELF-CENTEREDNESS

℞ When you sit in a hot bath, the whole city feels warm.

In a mirror, everyone sees his best friend.

See: EGOTISM

SELF-DECEPTION

⋅ဢ To assume is to fool oneself.

⋅ဢ At a distance, you fool others; close, you fool yourself.

The girl who can't dance tells herself the orchestra can't keep
time.

Our ears often do not hear what our tongues utter.

He acts like a man of means because he owns a head of cabbage.

The wisest of men can fool himself.

⋅ဢ Those who chase happiness run away from contentment.

Hasidic saying

See also: CHARACTER, CONCEIT, EGOTISM, FOLLY, REASON, VANITY

SELF-ESTEEM

⋅ဢ The sun will set without your help.

⋅ဢ The girl who can't dance says the orchestra can't keep time.

If you lose your self-respect, you also lose the respect of others.

It is better to be alone than demeaned.

Three things enlarge a man's spirit [self-esteem]: a beautiful home,
a beautiful wife, and beautiful garb.

TALMUD, *Berakoth,* 57b

Don't crave to sit at the table of kings: your own table is better
than theirs; and so is your crown.

Sayings of the Fathers, 6 : 5

Don't let your wife, your son, or your friend dominate you.

BEN SIRACH, *Ecclesiasticus,* 33 : 20

Eat less and dress better.   —adapted from IBN TIBBON

See also: CONCEIT, CHARACTER, EGOTISM, HONOR, VANITY

SELF-IMPROVEMENT

"Do better," a peasant said to Rabbi Bunim, when he purchased
some item. This became Rabbi Bunim's motto: "Do better."

If a man makes a harness for his beast, how much more should he
fashion a harness for his impulses—which prompt him to lead
a good or evil life.   TALMUD J.: *Sanhedrin*

It is not enough to appeal to a man to improve his ways; help
him do so.   THE KORETSER RABBI

See also: AMBITION, GROWTH, INTELLIGENCE, SELF-ESTEEM, STUDY,
WISDOM

SELF-KNOWLEDGE

⋰ "Barking dogs don't bite," but they don't know it.
                    SHOLEM ALEICHEM

See also: ANIMALS, MAN

SELF-MOCKERY

⋰ One of life's greatest mysteries is how the boy who wasn't
good enough to marry your daughter can be the father of
the smartest grandchild in the world.

⋰ If a suit doesn't fit, it may be because you have grown smaller.
                    "THE CHOFETZ CHAIM"

SELF-PITY

I felt sorry for myself, because I had no shoes—until I met a man
who had no feet.

See also: EGOTISM, MAN: HUMAN TYPES

SELFISHNESS

◦§ When the streets are muddy, shoemakers rejoice.

He loves everyone—from a distance.

◦§ Better a grape for me than two figs for thee.

To hoard is worse than to steal.

◦§ A man who offers sympathy to someone bereaved a year ago is like a doctor who asks a man who has broken a leg to break it again—so that the doctor can show his skill.

TALMUD: *Mo'ed Katan,* 21b

See also: ALTRUISM, CHARITY, EGOTISM, GOOD DEEDS, KINDNESS, SYMPATHY

SENSE (SEYKHL)

◦§ When the Lord wants to break a man's heart, he gives him *seykhl* [good sense].

You can't live with someone else's *seykhl* [brain].

Seykhl has free will.

◦§ Some things are clever only the first time.

To have luck but no sense is like carrying a sock full of holes.

The angel who mediates between man and God is *seykhl.*

ABRAHAM IBN EZRA

With *seykhl,* you have everything; without *seykhl,* life is a desert.

SAMUEL HA-NAGID

Seykhl is the very root of wisdom.   SAMUEL HA-NAGID

Man's best gift is his *seykhl.*   MOSES IBN EZRA

◦§ When *seykhl* is crooked, who can repair it?   GERONDI

A man of good sense guards his tongue and attends to his own
    affairs.   IBN GABIROL

Lost *seykhl* can't be recovered.   IBN GABIROL

See also: FOLLY, FORESIGHT, INTELLIGENCE, JUDGMENT, REALISM, WIS-
DOM, PRUDENCE

SENSITIVITY

When a student knows that his teacher is able to answer him, he
    may ask a question; otherwise, he should not.
                                              TALMUD: *Hullin,* 6a

Address another man in the language he understands; do not use
    literary speech with the uneducated, nor vulgarity with the
    learned.   *Zohar*

See also: COMPASSION, CONSIDERATION, DECORUM, MANNERS, SPEECH

SENTIMENT

Note. The attitude of Jews to the expression of sentiment is as
    un–Anglo-Saxon as is that of Italians or Hindus. (See Author's
    Preface: "A Word to Non-Jews.") Jews do not regard "a stiff
    upper lip" as a sign of superior character: they expect emo-
    tions to be expressed, shared with (and therefore enjoyed by)
    others. To an Englishman, Jews no doubt seem maudlin, for
    they do love heightened effect, hyperbole, *shmaltz;* and they
    do rush to identify with the suffering or troubles of others;
    and they do not think it "unmanly" to weep or carry on at
    funerals.
        Second generation Jews (in England and the United
    States) learned to restrain their readiness to laugh, cry, moan,
    or gloat. The Waspicization of behavior has led to a marked
    toning-down of visible and audible emotional levels. Such
    deprivation may find special rewards in the Jewish sayings in
    these pages.
                                                            —L.R.

The gift is not as nice as the sentiment.

⋖§ Sweet words can't warm you; sweet thoughts can.

See also: COMPASSION, CONSIDERATION, DECORUM, GIVING, KINDNESS, MANNERS, SENSITIVITY

SEPHARDIM

See GLOSSARY

SERPENT

Note. Many and wondrous are the tales men have spun about serpents, perhaps because the snake sloughs off its skin, apparently rejuvenating itself—thus achieving immortality. The Mesopotamian goddess of life, for instance, was "the divine serpent, lady of life."*

Among the Jews, the reptile symbolized wisdom and even smacked of sanctity: the divine sign of Moses' mission was his staff's turning into a snake (Exodus, 4 : 2–4). The serpent was also believed to possess singular medicinal powers; Moses, you remember, fashioned a snake out of brass to cure the Israelites in the wilderness.

In the Bible, the serpent was not condemned to crawl on its belly until after it had persuaded Eve to eat the apple on the Tree of Knowledge (in Greek mythology, a serpent guarded the golden apples in the Garden of the Hesperides) and Jews were thereafter forbidden to eat reptilian fare (Leviticus, 19 : 26). One of the miraculous aspects of the Great Temple in Jerusalem, said the rabbis, was the fact that the snakes within its capacious precincts never bit a human being (*Pirke Abot,* 5 : 8).

An ancient Brahmin fable recounts that the Lord of the Universe sent an immense snake down to earth, which gave birth to ten thousand others—which became "sins in the hearts of men."

—L.R.

See EVE

---

* See Theodor H. Gaster, *op. cit.,* pp. 338–39.

SERVANTS

The servant is often nobler than the master.

The new [servant] may be true, but the old is gold.

See also: AUTHORITY, CONSIDERATION, SENSITIVITY, STATUS

SERVICE

◂§ A candle lights others, and consumes itself.

See also: CHARITY, COOPERATION, HELP

SEX

Note. The most important single comment one can make about
the attitude of Jews to sex, I think, is that Jews consider sexual
appetites normal, God-given, not sinful, morally satisfiable
within marriage. Judaism raises no serious problems about the
"evil," "impurity," or carnality of the body: Man's body is
holy, being God's creation, God's gift, God's design. How,
then, can man's divinely endowed needs and functions—if
moderately, properly expressed, in marriage—be tinged with
sin? Sex is treated with surprising ease and "modernity" in
rabbinical thinking: Body and soul form a unity; neither is
purer or wickeder than the other; when a mortal commits a
sin the soul is as responsible as the body.

Rabbinical decisions on cohabitation, marriage, divorce,
often anticipate modern psychology and sex hygiene. Chastity
was enjoined as a premarital duty: early marriages were therefore encouraged; girls were not scorned for not marrying, if
they so decided; cohabitation was considered laudable (especially on the eve of the Sabbath), since it would produce
children. Modesty is prized, as in all other aspects of human
conduct. Moderation in sex is considered sensible. The avoidance of temptation is stressed. Illicit sex was held sinful, as
was promiscuity; prostitution was totally rejected. Under Bibli-

cal law, sodomy was a crime; but female homosexuality, though held to be abhorrent and scandalous, was not punishable.

Under rabbinical law, a husband and wife are not permitted to come into close physical contact, much less cohabit, throughout the time of her menstruation, or for seven days afterward. On the seventh day, the wife is required to take a bath in running water, or in a bath expressly built for that purpose: a *mikve*.

A community of Jews was strictly obligated to maintain a community bathhouse. The rules and regulations governing the *mikve* are quite detailed; in fact, a whole section of the Mishnah explores this subject. Today, only very religious Jewish women observe the *mikve* custom—or attend a bathhouse for *mikves* such as were found in profusion in Europe and on the Lower East Side.

—L.R.

◆§ If you're going to do something wrong, at least enjoy it.

Man has a small organ; the more he feeds it the more it needs—
and vice versa.   TALMUD: *Sukkah*, 52

Man's shame is between his legs, a fool's between his cheeks.
MOSES IBN EZRA, *Shirat Yisrael*

See also: LOVE, LUST, MARRIAGE, MEN AND WOMEN, PASSION, WOMEN

SHADKHN

Note. Because of the great importance Jews attached to marriage, as a sacred obligation to God and a necessity for the survival of Israel, the institution of the *shadkhn,* the professional matchmaker and marriage broker, grew up—and thrived. Unmarried girls were a pain in the heart of the Jewish community, no less than her parents; bachelors were considered selfish shirkers of their responsibility to "go forth and multiply."

A *shadkhn* would enter in his record of marriageable males or females a careful list of the scholars, teachers, rabbis, in the family background. The more the learning, the higher the *yikhes* (honor) and the greater the DOWRY (*q.v.*). Successful Jews sought to marry their daughters to promising scholars, not potential rich men. The *shadkhonim* performed a most valuable function in matching marital possibilities, effecting meetings between young men and women who would not otherwise know each other, for they often lived in different villages, and at remote distances. (See headnotes for BACHELORS, MARRIAGE, SCHOLARS.)   —L.R.

See MARRIAGE

SHAME

❧ Only man was endowed with shame.

Better pain in your heart than shame on your face.

❧ Better be ridiculed than shamed.

He who has no shame before the world has no fear before God.

There is always hope for the man who is capable of being ashamed.
                                        TALMUD: *Nedarim,* 20a

❧ To shame a man in public is like shedding his blood.
                                        TALMUD: *Baba Mezi'a,* 68b

Shame not others and you will not be shamed by them.
                                        TALMUD: *Mo'ed Katan,* 9b

It is better for a man to cast himself into an oven than to shame
    a comrade in public.   TALMUD: *Berakoth,* 43b

The man who commits a transgression, and is filled with shame,
    has his sins forgiven.   TALMUD: *Berakoth,* 12b

There is a great difference between the man who feels shame in
    his soul and the man who is ashamed only before his fellow
    man.   TALMUD: *Ta'anith,* 15a

Shame is an iron fence against sin.   *Orhot Tsadikim*

Many precepts of the Torah are fulfilled not because of piety but
only out of shame.   —adapted from Bahya ibn Paquda

Be ashamed before God as you are before His creatures.
Hasdai, *Ben ha-Melekh ve-ha-Nazir*

Since dishonor is habitual with a liar, he is continually attended
by shame.   Ben Sirach, *Ecclesiasticus,* 20 : 26

An undeserved title brings more shame than honor.
"The Chofetz Chaim"

See also: ADVICE, CHARITY, PIETY, REPENTANCE, SIN/SINNERS, SOUL

SHIRKERS

He who is slack at his work is brother to him who destroys.
Book of Proverbs, 18 : 9

The sleeping cat doesn't catch a rat.
Abraham ibn Ezra, *Shirim*

See also: ADVICE, AMBITION, COOPERATION, HELP, LAZINESS, SUCCESS,
WORK

SHLEMIEL

Note. Who knows where this delectable word originated? Perhaps
from Adelbert von Chamisso's 1814 classic, *Peter Schlemihls
Wunderbare Geschichte* (a fable in which Peter sold his soul
to Satan—and lost his shadow); or from the name of the leader
of the tribe of Simeon, one Shlumiel, who (according to Numbers, 2) always lost his battles while other Hebrew generals
were winning theirs; or (possibly) as a variant of *shlimazl.* In
any case, a *shlemiel,* though closely related to a *shlimazl*
(*q.v.*), is more precisely a simpleton, a gull, a pipsqueak;
clumsy, submissive, uncomplaining, naive; a Caspar Milque-
toast writ large—and in Yiddish.

—L.R.

◆§ The *shlemiel* falls on his back and breaks his nose.

◈ When a *shlemiel* takes a bath, he forgets to wash his face.

When a *shlemiel* kills a rooster, it hops; when he winds up a clock, it stops.

◈ A *shlemiel* wonders if a flea has a navel.

When a *shlemiel* scalds his tongue on hot (soup), he then blows on the cold.

When he falls on straw, the *shlemiel* hits a stone.

SHOLEM ALEICHEM

See also: ADVICE, FOOLS, LUCK, MISFORTUNE, NEBBEKH, SHLIMAZL

SHLIMAZL

Note. The word comes from the German *schlimm* ("bad") and the Hebrew *mazl* ("luck"), but a *shlimazl* is thought of as more than simply unlucky. He is the chronic loser, patsy, fall-guy, pigeon. I use these slang words because *shlimazl* is only one of many vivid words, coined in Yiddish, to find a wryly affectionate description for psychological types. A *shlimazl* may also be characterized in psychiatric nomenclature as one predisposed to be victimized, one "accident prone." So *shlimazl* conveys the idea of one doomed (innocently) to fail *and* (perhaps) masochistically inclined to cooperate with the inequitable fates.

—L.R.

◈ If a *shlimazl* [luckless one] sold umbrellas, it would stop raining; if he sold candles, the sun would never set; and if he made coffins, people would stop dying.

◈ A *shlimazl* buys a suit with two pair of pants and promptly burns a hole in the jacket.

When a *shlimazl* sells an umbrella, the sun comes out.

◈ A *shlemiel* is always spilling hot soup—down the neck of a *shlimazl*.

Only *shlimazls* believe in *mazl* (luck).

When a *shlimazl* winds a clock, it stops.

When it rains gold, it is the fate of the *shlimazl* to be under a roof.

See also: FATE, FORTUNE, LUCK, MISFORTUNE, NEBBECH, SHLEMIEL

SHOFAR (SHOPHAR)

The Shofar (ram's horn blown in the Synagogue during Rosh Ha-shanah and Yom Kippur) has a profound meaning. It says: "Awake, ye sleepers, and ponder your deeds. Remember your Creator, and return to Him in penitence. Be not among those who miss reality in their pursuit of shadows, and waste their years in a quest for vain things. Look to your souls. Examine your acts. Forsake evil, all of its ways and thoughts, so that God may have mercy on you."   MAIMONIDES

The shofar is a prayer without words.   SAUL LIEBERMAN

See GLOSSARY: PESACH

SICKNESS

The prayers of the sick are more effective than the prayers of others, and are answered first.
                    RASHI, *Commentaries on the Pentateuch, Genesis*

See also: DISEASE, DOCTORS, HEALTH, MEDICINE

SIDDUR

Note. The *Siddur,* which is the collected "order" of prayers, is the most widely used single book in Judaism. It is curious that although prayers are found in the Torah, in the Prophets (Abraham, Hannah, Jonah) and in the Book of Psalms, Jewish prayers were not formally collected until the year 500 of the Christian Era. Why? Because the rabbinical tradition forbade writing down the Oral Law—which included prayers. The Talmud contains the *meditations* of individual sages and saints, and is crowded with discussions of prayer which fashioned rules and ordinances anent praying. Psalms (55 : 18) alludes to "evening, morning and noon" prayers; Daniel faced Jerusalem and "kneeled ... thrice a day and prayed" (Daniel 6 : 11).

The exact time when formal prayers were instituted among Jews remains obscure. Communal praying may have grown up simply as a substitute for Temple sacrifices. In Babylon, prayer surely served to preserve and intensify religious fidelity. The early *siddurim* included comments on customs, law, religious services, etc. The most famous *siddurim* are the early ones of Rabbi Amram Gaon of Sura (875), Saadia Gaon, Maimonides (for the Sephardic rite), Rashi, Rabbi Simcha (which established Ashkenazic rites).

Today's *Siddur* is an anthology of 4000 years of prayers, poems, liturgical hymns—kept up to date: a prayer for the state of Israel was introduced in 1948. See PRAYER.

—L.R.

SIGH

◄§ If you can't give money, at least give a sympathetic sigh.

A sigh can break a man in two.   TALMUD: *Berakoth,* 58b

See also: EMOTION, FEELINGS, SUFFERING

SILENCE

◄§ Eloquent silence often is better than eloquent speech.

Silence is the fence that encloses wisdom; but mere silence is not wisdom.

◄§ The man who is silent tells us something.

◄§ Speech is difficult, but who can keep quiet?

If a word be worth one shekel, silence is worth two.
                                TALMUD: *Megillah,* 18a

For many afflictions, silence is the best remedy.

TALMUD: *Megillah*, 18a

Silence (may be) equivalent to admission.

TALMUD: *Yebamoth*, 87b

If silence is good for the wise, how much better it is for fools.

TALMUD: *Pesahim*, 98b

◦§ Press your lips together: don't be in a hurry to answer.

TALMHD: *'Abodah Zarah*, 35a

◦§ Silence is restful: it rests the heart, the lungs, the larynx, the tongue, the lips—and the mouth. *Zohar*

◦§ I grew up among wise men and learned that nothing is better than silence. *Sayings of the Fathers*, 1 : 17

Silence protects wisdom.

AKIBA in *Sayings of the Fathers*, 3 : 19

Where words abound, sin will not be wanting; but he who holds his tongue acts wisely. *Book of Proverbs*, 10 : 19

◦§ One [kind of] man remains silent because he has nothing to say; another keeps silent because he knows it is the time for it.

BEN SIRACH, *Ecclesiasticus*, 20 : 6

Both a boaster and a fool miss the fitting time for silence.

BEN SIRACH, *Ecclesiasticus*, 20 : 6

◦§ I am better able to retract what I did not say than what I did.

IBN GABIROL

You may regret your silence once, but you will regret your speech twice. IBN GABIROL

Guard your tongue as you treasure your wealth. IBN GABIROL

◦§ Man was given two ears and one tongue, so that he may listen more than speak. HASDAI, *Ben ha-Melekh ve-ha-Nazir*

Unless you speak wisely, keep silent. IMMANUEL OF ROME

See also: BOASTING, FOOLS, GOSSIP, LIARS, SLANDER, TALK, TRUTH, WISDOM, WISE MEN

SIN/SINNERS

Note. Judaism defines two types of sin: against God, and against other men. A sin against the Deity is expiated by direct confession (a rabbi cannot serve as intermediary), true remorse, and "a return to God." But a sin against man must be "absolved" by a direct plea for forgiveness from the one sinned against: God will not forgive such sins, although he punishes them.

Judaism contains no concept of Original Sin, or inherited guilt, or the innate shame or impurity of man's flesh.
See headnote for YOM KIPPUR   —L.R.

◦ No man suffers for another's sins: he has enough of his own.

◦ If not for fear, sinning would be sweet.

Never mind the remorse; just don't commit the sin.

Sin takes money, too.

The knowledge of Scripture is no obstacle to sin.

◦ A Litvak is so clever that he repents *before* he sins.

As long as a man does not sin, he is feared; as soon as he sins, he is afraid.

◦ When the sin is sweet, repentance is not so bitter.

◦ A sin repeated seems permitted.   TALMUD: *Yomah,* 86b

It is better to sin out of good intentions than to conform with evil [greedy] intent.   TALMUD: *Nazir,* 23b

Whoever can pray on behalf of his neighbor and fails to do so is [called] a sinner.   TALMUD: *Berakoth,* 12b

Three things sap a man's strength: worry, travel, and sin.

TALMUD: *Gittin*, 70a

Man does not commit a sin unless he is possessed by folly.

TALMUD: *Sotah*, 3a

Wives save us from sin. TALMUD: *Yebamoth*, 63b

Tremble before committing a minor sin, for it may lead you to a major one. TALMUD: *Derekh Erets*, 1 : 26

Whoever destroys any useful thing is guilty of a sin.

TALMUD: *Sabbath*, 105

Leave them alone: let men sin unwittingly rather than willfully.

TALMUD: *Shabbath*, 148b

⌗ If the Evil Impulse says: "Sin—God will forgive you," don't heed it. TALMUD: *Hagigah*, 16a

Sinners should not be excluded as unworthy of joining their fellow Jews in prayer; frankincense of an offensive odor was included in the incense used in the holy Temple.

TALMUD: *Kerithoth*, 6b

⌗ The eye and the heart are sin's agents.

TALMUD J.: *Berakoth*, 1

A sinner is like a man who sees open manacles—and puts his hands in them. TALMUD J.: *Nedarim*, 9 : 1

⌗ Sin is sweet in the beginning, but bitter in the end.

TALMUD J.: *Shabbath*, 14 : 3

It is better to be called a fool all of one's days than to sin for one hour. MISHNAH: *Edoyoth*, 5 : 10

To make another man sin is worse than to kill him; for it is to doom him not only in this world but in the next.

MIDRASH: *Numbers Rabbah*, 21

From the moment a man thinks about committing a sin, he is faithless to God. MIDRASH: *Leviticus Rabbah*, 8 : 5

The biggest sinner is the one who regrets his previous goodness.

Zohar

↳ A little sin is big when a big man commits it.

ABRAHAM IBN EZRA, *Commentary to Genesis*, 32 : 9

It is wise to work as well as study Torah, for between the two, you
will forget to sin.   *Sayings of the Fathers*, 2 : 2

Consider three things, and you will avoid sin: Above you is an
all-seeing eye, an all-hearing ear, and a record of all your acts.

Sayings of the Fathers, 3 : 1

Righteousness exalts a nation—but sin is a people's ruin.

Book of Proverbs, 14 : 34

↳ The man who has knowledge but no fear of sin is like a
carpenter without tools.   *Abot de Rabbi Nathan*

Don't kindle the coals of a sinner: you may be scorched by the
flame of his fire.   BEN SIRACH, *Ecclesiasticus*, 8 : 10

Do not envy a sinner: you don't know what disaster awaits him.

BEN SIRACH, *Ecclesiasticus*, 9 : 11

↳ Pride is the reservoir of sin.

BEN SIRACH, *Ecclesiasticus*, 10 : 13

Sin destroys the soul of man.   BEN SIRACH, *Ecclesiasticus*, 21 : 2

Run from sin as from a snake; if you approach, it will bite you.

BEN SIRACH, *Ecclesiasticus*, 21 : 2

The path of sinners is paved smooth, but at its end lies the pit of
Hell.   BEN SIRACH, *Ecclesiasticus*, 21 : 10

Whoever thinks he has not sinned carries great pride within himself
and that is worse than sin.

BAHYA IBN PAQUDA, *Duties of the Heart*

At first, sin is like a spider's web; but in the end, it is like the cable
of a ship.   RABBI AKIBA in MIDRASH: *Genesis Rabbah*, 22 : 6

Let man love man and mercy win, From Thy grace, not his sin!
                    IBN GABIROL, *Choice of Pearls*

ᴇᴈ Beware of the pious fool, and the wise sinner.
                    IBN GABIROL, *Choice of Pearls*

ᴇᴈ Were I to cut myself off from my brethren because of their sins,
    I would be alone.   IBN GABIROL

We are like mice: one man eats the cheese and all men are blamed.
                    IBN VERGA, *Shebet Yehuda*

We should not tempt even an honest man to sin, much less a thief,
    for that is like putting fire next to tow.
                    MARTIN BUBER, MIDRASH: *Tanhuma*, 26b

There is a type of sinner who does evil with a policy, guided by an
    "ism." "I am no ordinary thief or murderer," he says, "I am a
    communist and I believe in communism." But sinning with a
    policy, says the Torah, is unforgivable.
                    "THE CHOFETZ CHAIM"

See also: EVIL, FEAR, GOD, GOOD, HEREAFTER, PUNISHMENT, PIETY,
    RETRIBUTION, SHAME, SUFFERING, VIRTUE

SINCERITY

ᴇᴈ Better an insincere "Good morning" than a sincere "Go to hell."

It is the eye that says what the heart means.

ᴇᴈ An honest slap is better than a dishonest kiss.

Words that come from the heart enter the heart.
                    MOSES IBN EZRA, *Shirat Yisrael*

See also: ALTRUISM, GOOD, HONESTY, HONOR, TREACHERY, TRUTH,
    VIRTUE

SKEPTICISM

The reddest apple can contain a worm.

If God will provide, why doesn't He?

An example is not proof; it is only an example.

What was written and is believed is not thereby proved true.

&ipsum; Once a miracle happens, it shows it's not a miracle.

Why is it that miracles don't provide food?

&ipsum; An act of reason is a miracle.

&ipsum; Rather a skeptic than a fool.

&ipsum; People who say "For instance" do not prove anything—except "for instance."

&ipsum; The Torah does not tell us to believe what is absurd.
                                      JOSEPH AEBO, *Sefer ha-Ikarim*

See also: ADVICE, EVIDENCE, IRONIES, LOGIC, PROOF, REALISM, REASON, SUSPICION

SKILL

To have a skill is to be free from anxiety.

To know a trade is to own a kingdom.

A trade is a shield against poverty.

&ipsum; Nothing is difficult—if you only know how.

That house is blessed where the man has a trade.

&ipsum; It is not good to have too many trades: many trades, few blessings.

◄§ A man at work is the equal of the most learned.

Good tools are half an artisan.

A handicraft honors those who engage in it.
TALMUD: *Nedarim,* 49b

Master a trade, and God will provide.
MIDRASH: *Ecclesiastes Rabbah,* 6

◄§ Together with the study of Torah, learn a trade.
MIDRASH: *Ecclesiastes Rabbah,* 9

The man who has a trade is like a woman who has a husband, or a
vineyard which has a fence.
MIDRASH: *Ecclesiastes Rabbah,* 10 : 6

◄§ A carpenter without tools is not a carpenter.
MIDRASH: *Exodus Rabbah,* 40 : 1

To have a trade is to have a fence: it protects you against tres-
passers. *Tosephta: Kiddushin,* 1 : 11

A famine may last seven years, yet passes the artisan's gate.
RABBI RABA, TALMUD: *Sanhedrin,* 29a

The master craftsman does everything himself; the fool hires a
passer-by. *Book of Proverbs*

See also: BUSINESS, WORK

SLANDER

◄§ The tongue is a dangerous enemy.

◄§ What is candor to your face is slander behind your back.

An angry tongue is worse than a wicked hand.

◄§ If there were no listeners, there would be no backbiters.

◄§ It is better to speak good of yourself than bad about others.

Whoever slanders a fellow man denies God.

⋙ Some men are prone to steal, but all men seem prone to slander.

If you think of yourself, you will not speak badly of others.

⋙ The slanderer, like the liar and the hypocrite, will find no place in the world to come.

⋙ The man who slanders hurts three people: the man slandered, the man to whom the slander is uttered—and himself.
TALMUD: 'Arakin, 15b

⋙ It is a duty to say what should be heard, and a duty not to say what should not be heard.   TALMUD: <i>Yebamoth</i>, 65b

A good man who speaks evil is like a palace next to a tannery: one defect destroys all the grandeur.   TALMUD: <i>Shabbath</i>, 56b

⋙ Slander is in the same category with murder.
TALMUD J.: Pe'ah, 1

⋙ Slander is worse than weapons; for weapons hurt from near, slander from afar.   TALMUD J.: <i>Pe'ah</i>, 1 : 1

Hot coals, cooled on the outside, cool within; but slander, cooled outwardly, does not cool inside.   TALMUD J.: <i>Pe'ah</i>, 1 : 1

⋙ Even if all of a slander is not believed, half of it is.
MIDRASH: Genesis Rabbah, 56 : 4

When Rabban Gamaliel told his servant to buy the best meat in the market, the slave brought home a tongue. The next day Rabban Gamaliel asked him to buy the worst thing in the market and again the servant brought home a tongue, wisely saying, "There is nothing better than a good tongue, and nothing worse than an evil one." MIDRASH: <i>Leviticus Rabbah</i>, 33

Scripture says, "Cursed art thou [serpent] above all creatures," because the serpent uttered slander. MIDRASH: <i>Tanhuma</i>, 24a

If others speak ill of you, let the worst they say seem a trifle; if you speak ill of others, let the trivial seem enormous.
Sifre, 89b

◄§ God will accept repentance for all sins except one: giving another man a bad name.   *Zohar*

A fickle man sows discord, and a whisperer separates friends.
Book of Proverbs, 16 : 28

Righteous lips cover up hatred; but he who lets out slander is a fool.
Book of Proverbs, 10 : 18

◄§ For thirteen years I taught my tongue not to tell a lie; for the next thirteen, I taught it to tell the truth.
THE KORETSER RABBI

See also: FOOLS, GOSSIP, HYPOCRITES, LIES/LIARS, TRUTH, VIRTUE

SLAVERY

Note.

> The Jews, hunted out of Spain in 1492, were in turn cruelly expelled from Portugal. Some took refuge on the African coast. Eighty years later the descendants of the men who had committed or allowed these enormities were defeated in Africa, whither they had been led by their king, Dom Sebastian. Those who were not slain were offered as slaves at Fez to the descendants of the Jewish exiles from Portugal. "The humbled Portuguese nobles," the historian narrates, "were comforted when their purchasers proved to be Jews, for they knew that they had humane hearts." —Morris Joseph, *Judaism as Creed and Life*, 1891.

Wars, captivity, slavery, ransom, selling human bodies— are as old as mankind. The most enlightened Greeks held slaves to be but "animated tools" (the phrase is Aristotle's) who had no rights whatsoever. (In Athens, the ratio of slaves to freemen was about 5 to 1.) To the Romans, defeat clearly justified enslavement, as it did to the Assyrians, Aztecs, Chaldeans, Egyptians, Persians, Chinese, *et alia*.

The attitude of the ancient Hebrews takes on particular significance in an historical context: they purchased Canaanite (non-Hebrew) "servants" from neighboring tribes or peoples— and these slaves became proselytes: the males being circumcised, the females made subject to Jewish laws regarding women, diet, hygiene, marriage, etc. The Hebrew master was admonished by Torah not to be brutal to his "servants" (the word in Scripture often used for slaves)—not to be either unkind or unjust.

In Israel itself, there were no slave markets. The forcible capture, enslavement, or sale of a human was a criminal offense. The Hebrews were obligated to give any fugitive slave asylum, and not to surrender him or her to his owners; and a fugitive who reached Palestine was accorded full legal freedom.

A Hebrew could sell his or her own services to another Hebrew, for six years. Many did so—in order to live, in order to pay their debts, out of a desire to be assured of a home, protection, etc. After the six-year period, the male servant-slave was released. A female servant-slave (if she had not become wed to her owner or his son) could not be sold; she had to be redeemed by her own family. All Hebrew slaves, including those who chose to remain with their masters after their six-year servitude, were legally freed in "the year of Jubilee" (*Leviticus* 25 : 40). Jewish masters and slaves were often on "family" terms; many slaves inherited property, or were accepted as the husbands or wives of their master's children. (All these conditions of servitude became impossible or irrelevant after the Babylonian Exile.)

Centuries later, the Talmud instructs masters to treat their slaves as equals (*Kiddushin* 20): "You should not eat white bread, and he black; you should not drink old wine, and he new; you should not sleep on a feather bed, and he on straw." The master's feet could be washed by a disciple, a student, or his son—but not by his slave (*Mekilta,* a midrashic tract, on Exodus 21 : 2).

Small wonder that it was said that "he who gets a Hebrew as a slave gets a master."

—L.R.

⋙ A man can have nothing worse over him than another man.

⋙ A slave should never be addressed as "slave," for the very name is contemptible.

To be immobile is to be in chains.

MOSES IBN EZRA: *Shirat Yisrael*

❧ Ransom a captive before you feed the poor: no act of charity
   is greater.   JOSEPH CARO, *Shulhan Aruk*

Every moment of delay in ransoming a captive is like shedding his
   blood.   JOSEPH CARO, *Shulhan Aruk*

Revolution is the right of slaves.
                    H. LEIVICK (LEIVICK HALPERN) in *The Golem*

See also: FREEDOM, INDEPENDENCE, POWER

SLEEP

❧ Sleep is the best doctor.

❧ The one-eyed need sleep, too.

Less sleep, more living.

No punishment is worse than a night without sleep.

❧ Sleep is a thief.

Sleep faster, we need the pillows.

When you go to sleep on an empty stomach, you count the beams
   on the ceiling.

Sleeping is one-sixtieth part of death.   TALMUD, *Berakoth,* 57b

He who reaps in the summer acts wisely; he who sleeps during
   harvest acts shamefully.   *Book of Proverbs,* 10 : 5

If a man can't learn without napping at noon, let him nap—but not
   too long.   JOSEPH CARO

Even in a brief sleep, do not be intent on your pleasure, but on
   restoring your body to serve God.
                    —adapted from JOSEPH CARO, *Shulhan Aruk*

See also: DREAMS, HEALTH, MEDICINE

SNAKES

See SERPENT

SOCIETY

See: COMMUNITY, GOVERNMENT, ISRAEL, LAW, MAN, POLITICS, SAFETY

SOLDIERS

Soldiers are braver after eating.

Soldiers do the fighting and generals are called heroes.

If one soldier knew what the other [enemy] thinks, there would be
   no wars.

Better be a dog in peace than a soldier at war.

Those who hate the smell of powder should not go to war.

Men of the sword can't claim to be men of the Book.
                                          TALMUD: *Abodah Zara,* 17b

See also: COURAGE, VIOLENCE, WAR

SONS

Note. Apart from the preference for sons found in any primitive,
   agricultural, or nomadic society (as workers, warriors, defenders, and perpetuators of the tribe), Jewry considered a son
   their *"Kaddish"*—*i.e.,* the reciter of that prayer for a dead
   parent which helps the departed soul find peace. Jewish
   couples who had no sons would adopt an orphan to serve as
   their *Kaddish.*
       The *bar mitzvah* ("son of the commandment" or "man of
   duty") is a ceremony, *not* a confirmation. It is held in a synagogue or temple when a thirteen-year-old Jewish boy reaches

the status, and assumes the duties, of a "man." The *bar mitzvah* signifies that a young male is now a "man of duty," committed to lifelong religious and ethical obligations. He can now be counted as an adult in the *minyan* of ten males required before religious services can begin, and he can be called to the pulpit to recite a passage from the Torah.

The *bar mitzvah* ceremony is not an ancient one; it did not exist until the fourteenth century; and it is not a sacrament, nor a sacramental rite, for Orthodox Jews consider Jewishness something that does not require confirmation.

Ancient rabbinical sources hold that after his thirteenth birthday, a Jewish boy is responsible for observing the 613 (!) holy commandments. With all due respect to the elders, I feel obliged to record my wonder whether a careful accounting of this is kept, even in heaven.

—L.R.

To strike a grown son is to drive him to sin.

May you live to introduce your son to Torah, to marriage, and to good deeds. (Traditional blessing which is part of the circumcision ceremony.)

∽§ Even if a man is a rabbi, when his father enters, the son must rise [in the presence of his pupils].   TALMUD: *Horayot,* 13b

∽§ The only time a son should disobey his father is when [if] the father orders him to commit a sin. TALMUD: *Yebamoth,* 5b

A son is his father's foot.   TALMUD: *Erubin,* 70b

Should a father order his son to throw gold into the sea, the son should obey.   TALMUD: *Kiddushin,* 32a

∽§ One father can support ten sons, but ten sons seem unable to support one father.

There are four types of sons: the wise, the simple, the wicked—and the one who does not yet know how to ask questions.
   Mekilta to *Exodus,* 13 : 14 (in the Haggada for Passover)

He who spares the rod hates his son.   *Book of Proverbs,* 13 : 24

A wise son makes a glad father;
But a foolish son is a grief to his mother.

Book of Proverbs, 10 : 1

A father is to be treated as a king.   *Pirke de Rabbi Eliezer*, 39

A bad son is like a sixth finger; to cut it off hurts, and to leave it is
to be beset with a blemish.   IMMANUEL OF ROME

At five your son is your master, at ten your slave, at fifteeen your
double; after that, he is your friend or your enemy, depending
on how he was raised.

HASDAI, *Ben ha-Melekh ve-ha-Nazir*

See also: CHILDREN, EDUCATION, FAMILY, FATHERS, ISRAEL, LEARNING,
MOTHERS, PARENTS, SCHOLARS, SONS-IN-LAW

SONS-IN-LAW

One of life's greatest mysteries is how the boy who wasn't
good enough to marry your daughter can be the father of the
smartest grandchild in the world.

Lighter than bran [worthless] is a son-in-law who lives in the house
of his father-in-law.   TALMUD: *Baba Bathra*, 98b

He who lives in his mother-in-law's house for thirty days deserves a
flogging.   TALMUD: *Kiddushin*, 12b

See also: DAUGHTERS-IN-LAW, MARRIAGE, MOTHERS-IN-LAW, PARENTS

SORROWS

No one knows the sorrow of another.

Sorrows thin our bones.

The deeper the sorrow, the less voice it has.

Cut off the head and you'll end the sorrow.

Sorrows create ailments; happiness cures them.

One man can carry more sorrows than ten horses could bear.

The man who increases knowledge increases sorrow.

Ecclesiastes, 1 : 18

See also: **MISFORTUNE, SUFFERING, TEARS**

SOUL

Note. In the Talmud it is said that God created individual souls—
when He created the world. When a child is born, his or her
preassigned *neshomeh* (spirit) joins the body. But the Talmud
nowhere mentions transmigration of the soul—i.e., its leaving
the body after death. Many rabbis considered such stuff superstition—and a denial of monotheism. Yet mystics and ordinary
folk clung to the idea. (The "mystery religions" of the East—
in Persia, India, Egypt, among Greek cults—are full of trans-
migratory souls, who inhabit the bodies of mortals or animals.)

No precise distinction existed between body and soul until
rabbinical (i.e., post-Biblical) days, when the Hebrew *neshomeh*
came to mean that aspect of man that is spiritual, noncorporeal
—and immortal. (The Jews were influenced in these metaphysical niceties by Greek thought.)

In the Middle Ages, Jewish cabalists were attracted to the
idea of souls wandering around, as punishment, to atone for
their sins; the concept (*galuth*) even filtered into an explanation for the dispersion of Jews from the Holy Land; and
prayers referred to this as God's punishment "for our sins." In
Orthodox Judaism, the idea of resurrection is important; the
conception of bodily resurrection is linked to the immortality
of the soul.

—L.R.

◦§ Those who find a difference between soul and body have
neither.

The body is a sponge; the soul is an abyss.

What soap is to the body, tears are to the soul.

◦§ The smallest revenge poisons the soul.

A blind man lifted up a lame man to rob the King's orchard, and
  could not escape either complicity or punishment: in the same
  way, the soul and the body will be reunited for judgment.
                              MIDRASH, *Leviticus Rabbah,* 4 : 5

Is not the soul a guest in the body?
                              MIDRASH: *Leviticus Rabbah,* 32

My soul was also on Mount Sinai.
                              MIDRASH: *Exodus Rabbah,* 28 : 4

ᴥ When a soul is sent down from Heaven, it contains both male
  and female elements: the male part enters the male child, the
  female enters the female; and if they are worthy, God reunites
  them in marriage.   *Zohar*

ᴥ The soul is the Lord's candle.   *Book of Proverbs,* 20 : 27

(When dust returns to the earth), the spirit shall return to God,
  who gave it.   *Ecclesiastes,* 12 : 7

The man who injures the soul of another injures his own.
                              APOCRYPHA: *II Enoch*

Wisdom is to the soul as food is to the body. ABRAHAM IBN EZRA

I have stilled and quieted my soul, and like a babe with his mother,
  my soul is now with me like a weaned child.
                              BAHYA IBN PAQUDA

Upon death, the soul goes out of one door and enters another.
                              —adapted from BAAL SHEM TOV

See also: GOD AND MAN, HEALTH, HEAVEN, HELL, HEREAFTER, RESUR-
  RECTION

SPEECH

ᴥ If a horse had anything to say, he would speak up.

The heart of fools is in their mouth; the mouth of the wise is in their
  heart.

All the world is on the tip of the tongue.

Had I been on Sinai, I would have asked God for two mouths: one
for ordinary speech, and one for Torah; but now I think that
since the world is ruined by man's one mouth, how much
worse would it be if he had two!
TALMUD J.: *Berakoth*, 1 : 2

Let thine ears [too] hear what thy mouth speaketh.
TALMUD J.: *Berakoth*. 2 : 4

From a man's mouth you can tell who he is.   *Zohar*

A soothing tongue is a tree of life.   *Book of Proverbs*, 15 : 4

The mouth of the righteous is a fountain of life;
But the mouth of the wicked is filled with violence.
Book of Proverbs, 10 : 11

✒ What is lofty can be said in any language, and what is mean
should be said in none.   MAIMONIDES

✒ The tongue is the heart's pen and the mind's messenger.
BAHYA IBN PAQUDA, *Duties of the Heart*

Consider the speech, not the speaker.
CASPI, *Commentary on Yoreh Deah*

The worst of men is he whose tongue is mightier than his mind.
MOSES IBN EZRA, *Shirat Yisrael*

✒ Man's chief superiority over animals is his power of speech; if
he abuses it, he is no higher than they.
THE SASSOVER RABBI

✒ If a horse with four legs can sometimes stumble, how much
more can a man with only one tongue.   SHOLEM ALEICHEM

See also: GOSSIP, GRAMMAR, LIARS, SENSITIVITY, SLANDER, TALK, WORDS

SPIRIT

A broken spirit is hard to heal.

✒ Loneliness breaks the spirit.

When you have no choice, mobilize the spirit of courage.

See also: **MAN, SOUL, SUFFERING**

STATUS

Note. The most respected members of a Jewish community were pious scholars (see headnote: SCHOLARS) and laymen called *balbatim.* These leaders possessed outstanding character and reliability: the vulgar, however rich; the ill-mannered, however successful; the nonrespecters of learning, however flourishing —these were not *balbatish,* and were not accorded the deference and esteem enjoyed by *balbatim.*

—L.R.

⋗ Not everyone on the dais is distinguished.

⋗ He is a *shammes* [guard] in a pickle factory. [Low man on anyone's totem pole.]

Be a servant to noblemen rather than chief of the vulgar.

⋗ Food is cooked in a pot, but people praise the plate.

Better a footstool for a king than a king of fools.

The servant of a king is something of a king.

⋗ A sage takes precedence over a king.
                                —adapted from MISHNAH

⋗ When a sage enters, all men should rise (unless they are at work).   TALMUD: *Kiddushin,* 33a

Before I was elected to the court, I would have thrown to the lions anyone who said, "Become a candidate"; afterwards, I would throw boiling water on anyone who suggested I resign.
                                TALMUD: *Menahoth,* 109

⋗ If you must hang, choose a high tree.
                    —adapted from TALMUD: *Pesahim,* 112a

~§ God loves those who do not insist upon their privileges.
—adapted from TALMUD: Pesahim, 113a

Better a man of low rank who works for his living than one who
puts on airs but has nothing to eat.   Book of Proverbs

Burning thorns make much noise, as if to say: "We, too, are wood."
MIDRASH: Ecclesiastes Rabbah, 7

Rather be the tail among lions than the head among foxes.
Sayings of the Fathers, 4 : 15

Don't crave to sit at the table of a king; your own table is better—
and so is your crown.   Sayings of the Fathers, 6 : 5

The sons of sages are not always sages—so that no one can think
Torah is inherited, and so that the sages' sons do not hold
themselves superior to others.
—adapted from Sayings of the Fathers, 2 : 12

See also: ANCESTORS, CHARACTER, FAME, GOD, HONOR, HUMILITY,
MONEY, POLITICS, POVERTY, POWER, RICHES, SAGES, TORAH

STRANGERS

Note.
"Love the stranger and the sojourner," Moses commands, "because you have been strangers in the land of Egypt." And this
was said in those remote, savage times when the chief ambition of races and nations consisted in crushing and enslaving
one another.   —Leo Tolstoy

~§ A big blow from a stranger hurts less than a small blow from
a friend.

He who has fed strangers may have fed angels [as did Abraham].

~§ The troubles of a stranger aren't worth an onion.

~§ A stranger's folly creates laughter; your own folly produces
shame.

Respect a stranger, but suspect the stranger.

It is hard to eat bread at a stranger's table.   TALMUD: *Bezah*, 32

How shall we sing the Lord's song in a strange land?
Book of Psalms, 137 : 4

See also: CHARITY, DUTY, GOOD DEEDS, FRIENDS, KINDNESS, NEIGHBORS

STRENGTH

Separate reeds are weak and easily broken; but bound together they
are strong and hard to tear apart [like Israel's unity].
MIDRASH: *Tanhuma, Nizavim:* 1

See also: ENDURANCE, ENERGY, POWER, WEAKNESS

STUBBORNNESS

⊷ There is no cure for stubbornness.

⊷ Some men go from Heaven to Hell out of sheer stubbornness.

⊷ Stubbornness is a disease.

He who stiffens his neck against many reproofs will suddenly be
broken beyond repair.   *Book of Proverbs*, 29 : 2

God forgets the man who stubbornly rejects proof that he is wrong.
NACHMAN OF BRATSLAV

See also: ARGUMENT, BOASTING, CONCEIT, ERROR, SELFISHNESS

STUDENTS

What sacrifices was he not ready to bring, the Jewish youth
who trudged afoot from the banks of the Danube to the banks
of the Seine, bidding defiance to hunger and cold, only to
drink in the words of some far-famed master! How he would
wander about, a restless wayfarer, for half a year, across
ditches and mountains and among brigands on his journey

from Cologne to Venice for the sake of the Talmud explanations to be had from an Italian scholar?
—Louis Ginzberg, in *Students, Scholars and Saints*. The Jewish Publication Society of America, 1928, pp. 68–69.

See EDUCATION, KNOWLEDGE, LEARNING, SCHOLARS, STUDY, TEACHERS

STUDY

Note.

Centuries before the modern idea of adult education was evolved, Jews regarded it as a religious duty to band themselves together for study every morning before the labors of the day began, and every evening when the ghetto gates closed them off from association with the outside world.
—Cecil Roth. In *Essays on Jewish Booklore*, KTAV, New York, 1971, p. 179.

The tradition of study, the reverence for ideas, the inculcated passion to analyze and *know* has led many Jews, since the Middle Ages, to distinguish themselves in secular literature, secular philosophy, medicine, law, science. But the intellectual tradition began in faith—and was long hostile to the secular.

The Jews structured an entire culture around the core of prayer and study—and the latter flowed out of the former, as a co-equal part of man's sacred obligations. In studying or discussing Torah or Talmud, the pious Jew believed he was actually earning "a portion of bliss." So male Jews were always reading—even in markets, at country fairs, while "minding the store." Itinerant Jews—peddlers, salesmen—usually carried some part of the Talmud, Mishnah, or some collection of Midrashim, to read while away from home, to fulfill the "appointment" they had pledged.

The synagogue, from its inception (around 586 before the Christian Era, when Nebuchadnezzar drove the Jews into exile), was a place for both prayer and study (some experts say) and became the mortar of Jewish society, the carrier of cultural continuity, the motor that constantly regenerated the Jews' sense of identity. Prayer-and-study lent hope and meaning to poverty, persecution, perpetual insecurity, and repeated banishments. Study-prayer illuminated the hardest life, compensated for the harshest adversities, gave life a sense of purpose, admitted the humblest Jew to the company of prophets, sages, and saints. There was a certain ecstasy in the singsong verbalization of Talmud which a passer-by would hear issuing from a synagogue, a *Bet Midrash*, a Talmud Torah (school)—or a Jew's home.

The *shul*, the Yiddish word for "school," which the synagogue was called, was the capital, the center, the forum of Jewish communal life. Day and night men sat, read, prayed, studied, discoursed, debated there. Many synagogues never closed their doors. A pious Jew began and ended each day there. Men would drift from group to group in the *shul*, between prayers, listening with one ear to catch a word from those reciting or arguing.

The Talmud holds that God Himself goes from one *Bet Midrash* to another, and made it mandatory for Jews to build a *shul* as soon as a community contained ten males (a *minyan*)—and to support ten *batlanim* if need be: i.e., men who do no work but devote all their time to prayer-and-study, for the good of all Israel.

It was considered best to study in groups, because true learning could only be achieved, the Talmud said (*Berakoth*, 63), in group study. So virtually all of Jewry participated in a perpetual seminar on Torah and Talmud—which means a perpetual seminar on the most complex aspects of faith, metaphysics, truth, morals, duties, epistemology, etc. Every boy past the age of six (except for mental deficients) could read and write. They all became exegetes, dialecticians, amateur theologians. And *their* descendants enriched the knowledge, the technology, and the science of the West in proportions far greater than their number. (See headnote for SCHOLARS.)

—L.R.

◆§ When I pray, I pray swiftly, because I am talking to God; when I study, I read slowly, because God is talking to me.

◆§ Some men study so much, they don't have time to know.

Prayer without study is like a soul without a body.

&§ A scholar can't conduct a business; and a merchant has not enough time to study.

&§ Jerusalem was destroyed because the children did not attend school.   TALMUD: *Shabbath,* 119b

He who studies but does not repeat his lessons is as one who plants but does not enjoy the fruit.
                                        TALMUD: *Sanhedrin,* 90

Blessed were our ancestors, for their discipline was such that they were punished for falling asleep during their studies.
                                        TALMUD: *Tamid,* 28a

Study is worth as much as ritual sacrifice.
                        —adapted from TALMUD: *Menahoth,* 110a

&§ The chief thing is not to study but to do.
                                Sayings of the Fathers, 1 : 17

Don't say, "I shall study when I find the time," because you may never find time.   HILLEL in *Sayings of the Fathers,* 2 : 4

If there is no bread there is no study [so support the students].
                                Sayings of the Fathers, 3 : 17

Do not neglect study because of your pleasures, or even for your occupation.   —attributed to MAIMONIDES

If a man can't learn without sleeping at noon, let him sleep—but not too long.   JOSEPH CARO

I weep because I can study God's law no more.
                                        A blind rabbi

Happy is the man who devotes his time to study, and he who resists temptation.   THE SLONIMER RABBI

See also: **CHILDREN, EDUCATION, LEARNING, PEDAGOGY, TEACHERS**

STUPIDITY

⋙ Approach a goat from the back, a horse from the front, and a stupid man from no direction whatsoever.

⋙ Some are so stupid they must search for a notch in a saw.

Don't ask the stupid a question, and don't give them an explanation.

Drunkards can sober up, but the stupid remain stupid.

⋙ Why don't the stupid turn gray?

⋙ No cure exists for stupidity.

⋙ The stupid do not even understand stupidity.

To praise the stupid is to nourish their stupidity.

⋙ Educating the stupid does not teach them how to be smart.

To the stupid, this world is very pleasant.

When the smart talk to the stupid, both act like fools.

You confront lions and ask of foxes?!   TALMUD J.: *Shebi'it*, 9 : 4

On the lips of a sensible man wisdom is found;
But a man without sense needs a rod for his back.
                                        Book of Proverbs, 10 : 13

⋙ Some scholars are like donkeys: they only carry a lot of books.
          BAHYA IBN PAQUDA, *Duties of the Heart*

Sweet of voice but short of brains.   IMMANUEL OF ROME

See also: COMMON SENSE, FOOLS, INTELLIGENCE, SCHOLARS, SENSE, WISDOM

SUCCESS

◄§ The door to success has two signs: PUSH—and PULL.

Failures are the pillars of success.

◄§ Success is intoxicating—even without wine.

Even to fall from a fine horse is worthwhile.

You won't get ahead by keeping quiet.

See also: BUSINESS, EFFORT, ENDURANCE, LUCK, PERSISTENCE, RICHES,
WEALTH

SUFFERING

Note. Suffering is man's lot in a world where God's purposes are
never wholly revealed; and the rabbinical philosophers were
driven to conclude that suffering serves divine purposes: it
purifies, it teaches, it is itself an agency of God's plan. Virtue, besides, is divine—and its own reward to mortals who
practice it and are transmogrified by its grace. The noblest
comment on this is, oddly, "secular": Maimonides' statement
that to do right and avoid evil, whatever the suffering, is to
be a man, for each man owes it to his humanness to seek to
purify his desires and perfect his conduct.

—L.R.

No man knows another's sorrows.

◄§ A stab in the heart leaves a hole.

God is closest to those with broken hearts.

The one who suffers alone suffers most.

One man can bear more than ten oxen can carry.

◄§ From happiness to suffering is a step; from suffering to happiness seems an eternity.

Suffering creates nervous ailments; happiness cures them.

Things are going very well for me—as they do for a saint in this world.

Suffering can also make one laugh.

Suffering [sorrow] makes bones thin.

From happiness to misery is a short step; from misery to happiness is quite a way.

If you cut off the head, you'll abolish the pain.

ᴥ§ The deeper the sorrow, the less tongue it has.

Garments conceal the suffering underneath.

The paths to a cemetery are paved with suffering.

ᴥ§ The stars in heaven weep with him who weeps at night.
TALMUD: *Sanhedrin*, 104

ᴥ§ "And it came to pass" usually introduces a tale of woe.
TALMUD: *Megillah*, 10b

Not to know suffering means not to be a man.
MIDRASH: *Genesis Rabbah*, 92

ᴥ§ If you want to live in this world, equip yourself with a heart that can endure suffering. MIDRASH: *Leviticus Rabbah*, 30

ᴥ§ We can understand neither the suffering of the good nor the prosperity of the wicked.
—adapted from *Sayings of the Fathers*, 4 : 21

Even in laughter the heart may be aching, and the end of joy may be sorrow.   *Book of Proverbs*, 14 : 13

Like one who drops vinegar upon a wound is he who sings songs to a sorrowing heart.   *Book of Proverbs*, 25 : 20

Suffering is precious, for it is a divine covenant. *Mekilta*, 20 : 20

❧ One day's happiness makes us forget suffering, and one day's suffering makes us forget all our past happiness.
—adapted from BEN SIRACH, *Ecclesiasticus,* 11 : 25

❧ Any wound is better than a wound in the heart.
BEN SIRACH, *Ecclesiasticus,* 25 : 13

What I want to know is not why I suffer, but whether I suffer for Thy sake. THE BERDICHEVER RABBI

❧ The only whole heart is a broken one.
"THE CHOFETZ CHAIM"

A lack of accomplishment is the greatest suffering.
"THE CHOFETZ CHAIM"

See also: **EMOTIONS, ENDURANCE, HAPPINESS, HEALTH, LAUGHTER, PAIN, SORROW, TEARS**

SUICIDE

Note. Suicide is a crime, like murder, in traditional Judaism; and suicides were denied proper mournng and burial rites. Yet the rabbis realized that many (if not most) of those who took their lives were mentally sick—and not responsible for their deeds, hence could not rightly be condemned. Unless a suicide was clearly unbalanced of mind, the body was buried in a special place at one side of a cemetery.

Samson and Saul committed suicide, as did the whole garrison at Masada, in 73, to escape capture by the Romans—all 960 Zealots, under Eleazar ben Jair, men, women, and children perished in one mass destruction. In England, in 1190, the Jews besieged in York castle exterminated themselves, except for a few. (See Isaac d'Israeli's moving account, in the headnote to HEROES, above.) The sacred prohibition of suicide was waived, in these and many other historic disasters, and in the eyes of Jews those driven to suicide, under such hopeless circumstances, became heroes, legends of courage and resolute faith.

The number of Jews who have committed suicide to

escape torture, incineration, forcible conversion, slavery or slaughter is simply uncountable. The toll of self-destruction in Austria, Czechoslovakia, Germany, Poland, France and all the places on which the horrors of Nazi rule fell—no one dare estimate the number.

—L.R.

He who commits suicide bit by bit, day by day, has lost both this world and the next one.

Suicide is more reprehensible than homicide [the latter may have justification].   *The Testament of Judah Asheri*

The man who puts his talents to selfish uses commits spiritual suicide.
—adapted from HILLEL in *Sayings of the Fathers*, 1 : 13

See also: KILLING, SIN, VIOLENCE

SUPERSTITION

Note.
Say what you will of the Judaism of the Middle Ages; call it narrow; deride it as superstitious ... [but] for sweetness and spirituality of life, the Jew of the Ghetto, the Jew of the Middle Ages, the Jew under the yoke of the Talmud, challenges the world.
—E. G. Hirsch, in *A Book of Jewish Thoughts*. Ed. J. H. Hertz, Oxford, London, 1920, p. 10.

Where there are many women there is much superstition.

An unbeliever went into a synagogue, stared at the Ark, the Scrolls, the Eternal Light, and declaimed: "These are just superstitions! If I'm wrong, let God correct me."
And a great voice came down from Heaven, saying "You're right."

See also: ASTROLOGY, BELIEF, FOLLY, ILLUSION, LUCK, MIRACLES, MYS-TICISM, REASON

SURVIVAL

◄§ To endure, be obscure.

See also: SAFETY

SUSPENSE

The suspense is often worse than the ordeal.

SUSPICION

◄§ Respect the stranger—and remain suspicious.

Man is not suspected of a deed unless he did it—at least partially;
   or thought of doing it; or saw others doing it and enjoyed it.
                              TALMUD: *Mo'ed Katan,* 18

If you bring suspicion on yourself, don't condemn anyone who
   thinks ill of you.   IBN GABIROL

See also: EVIDENCE, GUILT, JEALOUSY, JUDGES, LAW

SYMPATHY

◄§ If you can't help, at least make a sound of sympathy.

A man devoid of sympathy is not a man but a monster.

◄§ Sympathy doesn't provide food, but it makes hunger more
   endurable.

The capacity to sympathize raises man above the animals.

Sympathy is a little medicine to soothe the ache in another's heart.

See also: COMPASSION, CONSIDERATION, GOOD DEEDS, GRIEF

SYNAGOGUE

Note. See headnote for STUDY.

—L.R.

✦ If there were only two Jews left in the world, one would summon the other to the synagogue—and he would go.

A Jew on a desert island will build two synagogues—so that there is always one he does not want to go to.

✦ Two Jews on an island will build three synagogues—one for each, and the third neither wants to attend.

The best synagogue is the heart.

See headnote for STUDY, and entries under FAITH, PIETY, PRAYER, WORSHIP

T

TACT

✦ Better one word in time than two ill-timed.

If someone in a man's family was hanged, don't say, "Hang this up for me."   TALMUD: *Baba Mezi'a,* 59b

When a student knows that his teacher is able to answer him, he may ask a question; otherwise, he should not.

TALMUD: *Hullin,* 6a

◄§ Where wisdom enters, subtlety accompanies it.

TALMUD: *Sotah,* 21b

Don't rebuke your fellow in such a way as to shame him in public.

RASHI, *Commentaries on the Pentateuch, Leviticus*

A word without thought is like a foot without muscles.

MOSES IBN EZRA, *Selected Poems,* 92

See also: CONSIDERATION, DECORUM, MANNERS, SENSITIVITY

TALK

The heart does not mean everything the tongue utters.

◄§ Those who talk a lot usually talk about themselves.

◄§ If you have nothing to say, say nothing.

◄§ Speech is hard, but who can keep quiet?

An embittered heart talks much.

The tongue is more dangerous than a dagger.

◄§ All mutes have a great deal to say.

What's said should not be barked: talking is not barking.

On the tips of tongues the fate of the world rests.

Women are nine times more talkative than men.

One word too many serves no purpose.

Your friend has a friend: don't tell.

◄§ Shoemakers talk about their lasts, sailors about their sails.

To have no tongue is like having no [warning] bell.

◄§ A tongue can be a dangerous enemy; so can yours—to your-self no less than to others.

❧ In good times it's good to talk: in bad times, not to.

The less you talk, the healthier.

Talk is a shekel; silence is two.   TALMUD: *Megillah,* 18a

Before you take leave of a friend, offer some serious comment [in philosophy or law] so that he will remember you thereby.
                          —adapted from TALMUD, *Berakoth,* 31a

My tongue is the pen of a ready writer.   *Book of Psalms,* 45 : 1

A man of learning spares his words. *Book of Proverbs,* 17 : 27

❧ If you talk too much, you'll say what you didn't intend to.
                          —adapted from *Book of Proverbs*

In all labor there is profit; but mere talk leads only to poverty.
                                        Book of Proverbs, 14 : 23

Where words abound, sin will not be wanting.
                                        Book of Proverbs, 10 : 19

Our eyes and ears do not always depend upon our will power, but a man's tongue does.   *Zohar*

What is the sign of a foolish man? He talks too much.   *Zohar*

❧ If you talk too much, you talk nonsense.
                                        MAAMAR MORDECAI

It is better to abstain from talking than from eating.
                                        Rosh Hagivah

❧ As long as words are in your mouth, you are their lord; once you utter them, you are their slave.
                          IBN GABIROL, *Choice of Pearls,* 33

A man's ear belongs to himself; his tongue belongs to others.
                                        IBN GABIROL

❧ You may regret your silence once, but you will regret your talk twice.   IBN GABIROL

❧ The mouth is a door, and should be kept closed.
                          BAHYA BEN ASHER, *Kad ha-Kemah*

Men detest the man who talks too much.

> BEN SIRACH, *Ecclesiasticus,* 20 : 8

The tongue is the mind's messenger.

> BAHYA IBN PAQUDA, *Duties of the Heart*

❧ Why did God give man two ears and one mouth? So that he will hear more and talk less.   —adapted from HASDAI

The chief superiority of man over animals lies in his power of speech; but if we speak folly, we are no better than animals.

> THE SASSOVER RABBI

But how can you say, "It was *only* talk, so no harm was done"? Were this true, then your prayers, and your words of kindness, would be a waste of breath.   NACHMAN OF BRATSLAV

❧ Gossip is nature's telephone.   SHOLEM ALEICHEM

See also: **ARGUMENT, FOOLS, GOSSIP, SILENCE, SLANDER, SPEECH, WORDS**

TALMUD

Note.

> Even the Bible itself did not come so close to the daily life of the Ghetto as the Talmud and the Mishna. The Bible was a thing eternal, apart, unchanging. The Talmud was a daily companion, living, breathing, contemporary, with a hundred remedies for a hundred needs. A nation persecuted, lives through time of stress rather by its commentaries than by its Scriptures. In the Ghetto the Talmud was a door into the ideal, always open.   —A. Mary F. Robinson, "Social Life in France in the Fourteenth Century," *Fortnightly Review,* vol. 57, 1892.

For a description and history of the Talmud, see GUIDE NOTE B (pp. 68).

R. Travers Herford, distinguished student of the Talmud, has observed that the rabbi-teachers took the Judaism of the prophets, and "brought it to bear upon the lives of the people in a way and to an extent which the prophets had never been able to accomplish." It is not far from the truth to say that if it had not been for the rabbis, the prophets might have been forgotten.

The reason that the Talmud grew as it did is that it was the work of rabbis, generation after generation, to try to adapt the Law, the Torah, to new problems and the transformed realities which Jews faced—in captivity or in freedom, as rulers or ruled, as men and women and parents, or as subjects of the Romans or Catholic sovereigns, Muslim Spain or the brutal hegemony of the tsars. (See headnote for RABBIS.)

—L.R.

To know one virtue is greater than to know all of the Talmud.

See also: JEWS, LAW, RABBIS, STUDY, TORAH

TAXES

Taxes grow without rain.

See also: GOVERNMENT, POLITICS

TEACHERS: I

◄§ First learn; then teach.

He who teaches a child is as if he had created it.
TALMUD: *Sanhedrin,* 19b

Whoever teaches his son also teaches his son's son—and so on to the end of man's generations.   TALMUD: *Kiddushin,* 30a

The calf wants to suckle, but even more does the cow want to give suck. [The teacher may need to teach more than his pupils need to learn.]   TALMUD: *Pesahim,* 112a

◄§ God said: You must teach, as I taught, without a fee.
TALMUD: *Nedarim,* 37a

In teaching, do not favor the children of the rich—and teach the children of the poor without compensation.
TALMUD: Ta'anith, 24a

The bad teacher's words fall on his pupils like harsh rain; the good teacher's, as gently as the dew.
TALMUD: Ta'anith, 7a

Blessed is the son who studies with his father, and blessed is the father who teaches his son.
TALMUD

The man from whom people learn must be especially strict with himself.
—adapted from TALMUD: Bezah, 2 : 6

A teacher who has drunk a quart of wine may not teach.
MIDRASH: Leviticus Rabbah, 1 : 4

A pupil receives but a fifth of the reward that accrues to the teacher.
MIDRASH: Song of Songs Rabbah

Be very careful in teaching, for an error in teaching is tantamount to a willful transgression.   Sayings of the Fathers, 4 : 13

—§ The ill-tempered cannot teach.
HILLEL in Sayings of the Fathers, 2 : 6

When I see no way of teaching a truth but one that will please one intelligent man but will offend ten thousand fools, I address myself to the one, and ignore the censure of the thousands.
MAIMONIDES: Guide to the Perplexed, Introduction

—§ In seeking knowledge, the first step is silence, the second listening, the third remembering, the fourth practicing, and the fifth—teaching others.
IBN GABIROL

TEACHERS: II, CRITICAL COMMENTS ON

One mother can achieve more than a hundred teachers.

—§ When a teacher fights with his wife, it's tough on his students.

The man who can't even tie a cat's tail can become a *melamed* [teacher of elementary subjects].

The man who learns but does not teach is like a myrtle in the desert: no one profits from it.
TALMUD: *Rosh Hashanah*, 23a

Unmarried teachers are as arrogant as kings, but their minds are like those of children.   —adapted from MIDRASH

Hidden wisdom and concealed treasure—of what use is either?
BEN SIRACH, *Ecclesiasticus*, 20 : 30

He who has not studied enough and teaches imperfect knowledge is to be treated as if he has sinned intentionally.
MAIMONIDES: *Guide to the Perplexed, Introduction III*

See also: LEARNING, PEDAGOGY, RABBIS, SCHOLARS, STUDY, WISE MEN

TEARS

ᥱᔌ When we laugh, everyone sees it; when we weep, no one does.

ᥱᔌ What soap is for the body, tears are for the soul.

ᥱᔌ Caution at first is better than tears at last.

ᥱᔌ There is a special place in Heaven set aside for those who can weep, but cannot pray.

ᥱᔌ Laughter is heard further than weeping.

All of life ends in tears.

ᥱᔌ Ink dries fast; tears do not.

When you pour your heart out [in tears] it feels lighter.

ᥱᔌ What good is the golden urn that is full of tears?

The gates to our tears are never locked.   *Zohar*

See also: LAUGHTER, LIFE, SORROW, SUFFERING

TEPHILLIN

See GLOSSARY: TEPHILLIN, p. 691

TEMPER

❧ A man who can't control his temper is like a city without defenses.

You can tell a man by his tipping—and his temper.

A forbearing man is better than a warrior; and he who rules his temper is better than one who takes a city.
Book of Proverbs, 16 : 32

He who spares his words has true wisdom; and he who holds his temper is a man of sense. *Book of Proverbs,* 17 : 27

If a man cannot control his temper, how much less can he control others? —adapted from IBN GABIROL

See also: ANGER, IMPULSE, PASSIONS

TEMPERANCE

It's healthier to undereat than overeat.

To the extremist, there is no midway between extremes.

Man, who can make a harness for his beast, should make one for his appetites. TALMUD J.: *Sanhedrin,* 10 : 1

Temperance enlarges understanding.
—adapted from MAIMONIDES, *Responsa* II : 39a

See also: EXCESS, FOOD: EATING AND DRINKING, GLUTTONY, MODERATION, PRUDENCE, TORAH, WINE

TEMPTATION

✑ If girls were not pretty, men would completely ignore temptation.

✑ In a maiden, temptation sleeps; in a wife, it's wide awake.

A man without a wife has no defense against temptation.
                    —adapted from TALMUD: *Yebamoth,* 63a

Never put yourself in temptation's path; for even King David could
    not resist it.   TALMUD: *Sanhedrin,* 107a

✑ Be grateful to your parents; had they not been tempted, you
wouldn't be here.
                    —adapted from TALMUD: *'Abodah Zorah,* 5a

✑ The most effective defense against temptation is this: Shut
your eyes.   IBN GABIROL, *Choice of Pearls*

✑ Temptation laughs at the fool who takes it seriously.
                    "THE CHOFETZ CHAIM"

See also: LUST, MEN AND WOMEN, PASSION, VIRTUE

THEFT

See: THIEVES

THIEF/THIEVES

✑ A man is not honest simply because he had no chance to steal.

✑ Not only did he break the commandment not to steal, he
stole the Bible.

A thief has long hands and short pockets.

When thieves fight, the peasant keeps his cow.

A thief has an easy job but bad dreams.

⋙ When a crook kisses you, count your teeth.

A thief has to be clever.

Minor thieves are hanged; major thieves are thanked.

A thief takes one path, but his pursuers confront ten.

⋙ It's hard to rob a thief.

⋙ Never accept a present from a thief.

⋙ If my brother steals, what they hang is not my brother but the thief [in him].

If you need a thief badly enough, cut him from the gallows.

Don't steal and you won't have to repent.

When servants quarrel, masters learn about the pilferage.

⋙ If you steal from a thief, you taste of thieving.

Don't mention the gallows in the presence of a thief.

To hoard is worse than to steal.

Stolen waters are sweet, and bread eaten in secret is pleasant.
Book of Proverbs, 9 : 17

For a Jew to cheat a Gentile is worse than cheating a Jew; for in addition to violating the moral law, it brings Jews into contempt.   TALMUD: *Baba Kamma*, 113b

You can't protect yourself against a thief in your own home.

⋙ It is not the mouse but the hole that's the thief.
TALMUD: *Gittin*, 45a

To rob one's fellow of a penny may be as bad as robbing him of his life.   TALMUD: *Baba Kamma*, 119a

Not to teach your son a trade is like teaching him to steal.
TALMUD: *Kiddushin,* 29a

Do not steal your property back from a thief, lest you seem a
thief yourself.   TALMUD J.: *Sanhedrin,* 8 : 3

The thief who finds no chance to steal considers himself law-abid-
ing.   —adapted from TALMUD: *Sanhedrin,* 22a

◄§ "What most encourages theft?" asked a teacher.
"Hunger," replied one pupil.
"Envy," said another.
"Extravagance," said a third.
But a fourth student answered best: "Those who buy stolen
goods."
—adapted from MIDRASH: *Leviticus Rabbah,* 6 : 2

The man who steals men's confidence is the worst of thieves.
MIDRASH: *Mekilta Mishpatim*

All thievery depends upon a receiver.
MIDRASH: *Leviticus Rabbah,* 6

To kill a thief is not murder, for a thief is like one who has been
dead from the beginning.
RASHI, *Commentaries on the Pentateuch, Exodus*

A thief invokes God's aid while breaking into a house.
IMMANUEL OF ROME

A thief is better than a liar, but they are both doomed.
BEN SIRACH, *Ecclesiasticus,* 20 : 25

See also: DECEIT, HONESTY

THOUGHT

◄§ Thought is a universe of freedom.

◄§ My thoughts form an Eden in my heart.
JUDAH HA-LEVI, *Kuzari*

Dive into the sea of thought, and find there pearls beyond price.
MOSES IBN EZRA, *Shirat Yisrael*

Thought serves as a mirror: it shows us the ugliness and the beauty within.
MOSES IBN EZRA, *Shirat Yisrael*

Words are but the shell; meditation is the kernel.
BAHYA IBN PAQUDA, *Choice of Pearls*

৶ Thinking is more precious than all five senses.
NACHMAN OF BRATSLAV

Those who are pure of heart find new thoughts whenever they meditate.
NACHMAN OF BRATSLAV

Thought is nobler than words, because it guides them.
THE MEZERITZER RABBI

See also: INTELLECT, KNOWLEDGE, LOGIC, REASON, STUDY

THRIFT

৶ If you eat your bagel, you'll have nothing left but the hole.

It is easier to earn than to save.

Those who don't save pennies don't have dollars.

Don't throw away a shirt because of one worn place in a corner.

৶ The thriftiest with money are the most spendthrift with desires.
MOSES IBN EZRA, *Shirat Yisrael*

See also: BORROWING, EXTRAVAGANCE, FORESIGHT, LENDING, MONEY

TIME

৶ In time even a bear can learn to dance.

Time can transform everything.

◦§ Time brings wounds and time heals wounds.

Yesterday is your past; today is your future—for your tomorrow has yet to be known.

The greatest of doctors is time.

With time, fowl get used to the killing.

◦§ "And if not now, when?" asked Hillel. When will the "now" be? The now that is now, this moment, never existed before—from the time the world was created; and this moment will never exist again. Formerly there was another "now," and later there will be another "now," and every "now" has its own special import and function.   Hasidic saying

Snow begins pure white but turns into slush, and all beauty will in time change into corrupted matter.   *Sefer Hasidim*

There is a time to love, and a time to hate.   *Ecclesiastes*, 3 : 8

Though a plague last seven years, no one dies before his time.
                    Ashi in Talmud: *Sanhedrin*, 29a

Time is of short duration and flies away swifter than the shades of evening. We are like the child who grasps a sunbeam in his hand, and when he opens it finds it empty, to his amazement, and all the brightness gone.   Jedaiah ben Bedersi

People say "Time is money" but I say "Money is time," for every luxury costs so many precious hours of your life.
                            "The Chofetz Chaim"

See also: DESTINY, FATE, FORTUNE

TOLERANCE

◦§ When three men cry "You're crazy!" the fourth should say "Bim bom." [This can mean either "Confirm the verdict," or "Give them the answer they want—what harm will it do?"]

See also: COMPASSION, CONSENSUS, KINDNESS, OPINION, PREJUDICE

TORAH

Note. The word "Torah" (Hebrew: "doctrine" or "teaching") has several significant meanings in the usage of that sacred word by Jews.

(1) Technically, Torah refers to the Pentateuch, or "the Five Books of Moses" (Genesis, Exodus, Leviticus, Numbers, and Deuteronomy).

(2) In another sense, "the Torah" designates the actual scroll, containing the Five Books of Moses, handwritten on parchment, from which readings are publicly annunciated in the synagogue on the Sabbath festivals, Mondays and Thursdays.

(3) In a general sense, Torah is all of Jewish law and religious studies. (Torah *she-bealpeh* refers to the oral teachings of the rabbis, as contrasted to Torah *sheh-biksav*, the written teachings.)

(4) In the largest usage, Torah means Judaism—as a religion, a philosophy, a commitment, a set of values: hence the phrases to "live," "live by," or "practice" Torah.

For the rabbinical interpretations that were needed to enforce the Torah's laws and moral edicts, see the Guide Notes for TALMUD, MISHNAH, MIDRASH, GEMARA (pp. 67–68), and see the entries under COURTS, JUDGES, LAW.

When scholars approached the Torah, ordinary rules of textual analysis were excluded: obviously, no rabbi, however wise, could dismiss an unclear or contradictory passage by saying that the Author of the Holy Book was unclear, uncertain, or wrong.

The rabbis held that ambiguities or contradictions in the sacred text were the result of insufficient knowledge, insufficient study, insufficient understanding. How could these be overcome? By continuing, rigorous reexamination and reanalysis of the text—for meanings beneath the surface, for significance disguised by language, for precepts concealed within old words and old phrases.

The laws which grew to govern the ways in which the Torah could be interpreted forbade the reading *into* any passage of something that was not actually (or inferentially) apparent. Rules of interpretation (hermeneutics) were refined to protect the sanctity of the holy Torah and to give authority to particular explications of that text. As Morris Adler puts it, the work of rabbinical scholars "was a work of discovery, not of innovation. They saw themselves ... as interpreters, not legislators." (*The World of The Talmud, op. cit.,* p 25.)

—L.R.

Torah is the best of wares [possessions, merchandise].

ᥩ The Torah lives—even in a hovel, up to its neck in dirt.

The Torah begins with acts of loving and ends with kindness; it begins with God clothing Adam and Eve, and ends with God burying Moses.   TALMUD: *Sotah,* 14a

ᥩ The beginning and end of Torah is performing acts of loving-kindness.   TALMUD: *Sotah,* 14a

The words of the Torah abide with him who regards himself as nothing.   TALMUD: *Sotah,* 21b

The Torah may be likened to two paths, one of fire, the other of snow. Turn in one direction, and you die of heat; turn to the other and you die of the cold. What should you do? Walk in the middle.   TALMUD: *Hagigah,* 2 : 1

ᥩ God weeps over anyone who could have occupied himself with Torah and did not.   TALMUD: *Hagigah,* 5 : 2

Even an idolator who studies Torah is like the high priest.
                     TALMUD: *Baba Kamma,* 38a

The study of Torah outweighs all sacrifices.
                     TALMUD: *Menahoth,* 110a

The words of the Torah are compared to water, wine, and milk (Isaiah 55 : 1), because just as these are kept only in the simplest of vessels, so the Holy Words are preserved in the humblest of men.   TALMUD: *Ta'anith,* 7a

The Torah can be interpreted in forty-nine different ways, and God instructed Moses, "Decide according to the majority."
                     TALMUD J.: *Sanhedrin,* 4 : 2

The Torah says: "If thou forsakest me for one day I shall forsake thee for two days." TALMUD J.: *Berakoth,* end

There is no end [no bottom] to Torah.
—adapted from *Book of Job,* 11 : 9

Wine cannot stay sweet in gold and silver vessels, but only in cheap earthenware; in the same way, the words of the Torah will keep only with the man who makes himself lowly.
Sifre—Deuteronomy, Ekeb, 48

◄§ Like wine, the Torah pleases the heart and improves with age.
MIDRASH: *Sifre—Deuteronomy,* 48

◄§ He who loves Torah is never satiated.
MIDRASH, *Deuteronomy Rabbah,* 7

When two men sit together and fail to discuss Torah—lo! there is the seat of the scornful. But when two men do discuss Torah, the Holy Spirit rests on them.
Sayings of the Fathers, 3 : 2

One should not make an ax of the Torah.
Sayings of the Fathers, 4 : 5

Where there is no Torah there is no good conduct, and where there is no good conduct there can be no Torah.
Sayings of the Fathers, 3 : 17

◄§ Where there is no food there can be no Torah; but where there is no Torah, there will be no food.
Sayings of the Fathers, 3 : 17

He who honors the Torah is honored by mankind.
Sayings of the Fathers, 4 : 6

He who fulfills the Torah amidst his poverty will in the end fulfill it amidst wealth; he who neglects the Torah amidst wealth will in the end neglect it amidst poverty.
Sayings of the Fathers, 4 : 9

◄§ The only free man is he who engages in the study of Torah.
Sayings of the Fathers, 6 : 2

You want me to teach you the whole Torah? This is its basic principle: What is hateful to yourself do not do to your fellow man. If you want no one to harm you, do not harm him; if you want no one to take what is yours, do not take from him what is his.   *Abot de Rabbi Nathan,* 27a

⋖§ The man who studies the Torah in his old age is like an old man who has married a young woman.
Abot de Rabbi Nathan, ch. 23

What is hateful to thee, never do to thy fellow man: that is the entire Torah; all the rest is commentary.
HILLEL in TALMUD: *Shabbath,* 31a

The more Torah, the more life.
HILLEL in *Sayings of the Fathers,* 2 : 7

⋖§ The Torah does not tell us to believe absurdities.
JOSEPH ALBO, *Sefer ha-Ikarim*

The Torah is our life and the length of our days. While loving and studying the Torah, we may be in great danger from our enemies; but if we gave up our studying, we should disappear and be no more.   AKIBA in TALMUD

Torah should lead to good deeds, not only to faith, not only good intentions.   ELIJAH DELMEDIGO, *Behinat ha-Dat*

How long are we required to study Torah? Until the day of our death ... Some of Israel's wisest men were woodchoppers, other drawers of water, some even blind men—and all of them studied Torah day and night.
MAIMONIDES, *Mishneh Torah*

The words of Torah heal the soul, not the body.
MAIMONIDES: *Mishneh Torah*

⋖§ The Torah is truth, and the purpose of knowing it is to live by it.   MAIMONIDES

⋖§ Men who see Torah collapsing should have their eyes examined.   "THE CHAIM CHOFETZ"

◦§ Every living soul is a letter of the Torah.

NATHAN OF NEMIROV

◦§ There are seventy ways of studying Torah; one is in silence.

THE TCHARKOVER RABBI

See also: FAITH, GOD, PIETY, SABBATH, SCHOLARSHIP, STUDY, RELIGION,
TRUTH, VIRTUE, WISDOM

TRADE

A trade is a kingdom.

To know a trade is to own a mine.

See also: BUSINESS, WORK; for OCCUPATIONS, see SKILL

TRADITION

Tradition protects the Torah [the Law].

Sayings of the Fathers, 3 : 13

The man who accepts tradition without examining it, with his own
intelligence and judgment, is like a blind man led by others.

BAHYA IBN PAQUDA, Duties of the Heart

See also: CONFORMITY, CONSENSUS, INTELLECT, SKEPTICISM

TRANSGRESSION

◦§ New laws cause new transgressions.

If a man thrice guards himself against transgression, God guards
him against it thereafter.   TALMUD J.: Kiddushin, 1

◦§ Transgression is forgiven by shame.

—adapted from TALMUD: Berakoth, 12b

If the man who walks in the ways of the Lord accidentally trans-
gresses, then every creature—below and above him—helps to
conceal it.   Zohar

◢§ The heart and the eyes are like spies for the body: the eye
   sees, the heart covets, and the body commits the transgression.
   RASHI, *Commentaries on the Pentateuch,* Numbers

◢§ A silk thread begins as the weakest of things, the mucus of a
   worm; yet how strong it becomes when entwined many times!
   . . . So it is with transgressions: they grow strong with repetition.   BAHYA IBN PAQUDA, *Duties of the Heart*

See also: EVIL, FAITH, LAW, PIETY, SIN, TEMPTATION

TRANSLATION

Reading poetry in translation is like kissing a woman through a veil.
                                   —adapted from CHAIM BIALIK

TRAVEL

The fool who traveled is better off than the wise man who stayed
   home.

◢§ No matter what happens, travel gives you a story to tell.

Travel leads to three things: it diminishes the marital relationship,
   it decreases wealth, and it lessens one's fame.
                        RASHI, *Commentary on Genesis* (Abraham)

See also: CIRCUMSTANCES, EXPERIENCE, LIFE

TREACHERY

◢§ Those who betray their cause support the other's.

The side that breaks a truce during a war will lose.
                                   NACHMAN OF BRATSLAV

Trees are cut down by their own kind. [Ax handles are made of
   wood.]

See also: DECEIT, HYPOCRISY, LIARS

TROUBLE

◆§ Troubles are drawn to wetness—to tears and to brandy.

◆§ Troubles that don't show on the face lie on the heart.

It's easier to endure trouble with soup than without soup.

◆§ Chopped liver is better than chopped troubles.
[*Gehokte tsores*—"chopped troubles"—is a popular way of saying troubles compounded.]

Nothing causes more trouble than the tongue.

◆§ Bygone troubles are a pleasure to discuss.

Man should remember: Not all trouble comes from Heaven.

We do not live on joys, or die of troubles.

◆§ Though the world is full of trouble, each man feels only his own.

Troubles are to man what rust is to iron.

◆§ Ask not that all troubles end, for when troubles end, life ends, too.

The longer the life, the more the troubles.

Man grows accustomed to troubles.

◆§ Trouble tears the heart apart.

Troubles are as common as wood, but they can't heat up the oven.

Every day brings its own troubles.

The world is big, its troubles still bigger.

Trouble is a thorn in the heart.

Troubles bind people together.

Troubles don't come alone.

Man is born unto trouble, as the sparks fly upward.
                                        Book of Job, 5 : 7

The man who knows that deterioration is the rule of life won't take
    his troubles too seriously.   FALAQUERA

◄§ Little troubles are really not so bad—for someone else.
                                        SHOLEM ALEICHEM

See also: CONTENTMENT, HAPPINESS, HOPE, JOY, LIFE, PAIN, SUFFERING,
    WORRY

TRUST

◄§ He who lives on trust is lost.

Trust not in yourself until the day of your death [because you may
    undo your good deeds].
                    HILLEL in *Sayings of the Fathers,* 2 : 4

See also: FAITH, GOD, LIFE, PIETY, SKEPTICISM

TRUTH

◄§ The truth never dies—but it lives a wretched life.

◄§ Truth rests with God alone—and a little with me.

◄§ When you tell the truth you don't have to remember what you
    said.

If you add to truth, you enter the domain of lies.

◄§ Truth is heavy, so few men carry it.

◄§ Truth is neither alive nor dead: it just aggravates itself all the
    time.

Man finds God through truth.

Truth shows in the eyes; lies stay behind the eyes.

Nothing is more harmful to a new truth than an old error.

Ultimately, truth rises, like oil on water.

 Many love truth, but not many speak it.

Half a truth is a whole lie.

A lie one must not say; and some truths you should not tell.

 The worst libel can be the truth.

 Truth creeps; lies race.

Lust cannot lead to truth.

Truth may walk around naked; but lies should be clothed.

Children and fools tell the truth.

A joke is a half-truth.

Heaven and earth have sworn that nothing shall remain lost [i.e., the truth].

 The truth lights, but money warms.

You may regret having told the truth.

Truth can be the greatest deceiver.

If you are proved right, you achieve little; but if you are proved wrong, you gain much—for you learn the right.

Truth is its own witness.

Passion and truth are enemies.

Better the ugly truth than a beautiful lie.

God loves the truth.

Everyone boasts of the truth, but few [none] have it.

Ⱄ The truth has every charm—but is very shy.

A hint can hurt more than the truth.

Truth wears many faces.

Death reveals the truth.

Ⱄ When you add to the truth, you subtract from it.
TALMUD: Sanhedrin, 29a

Truth is God's seal.   TALMUD, Shabbath, 54

Truth, justice and peace are one.
—adapted from Perek ha-Shalom

At times even liars speak the truth.
MOSES IBN EZRA, Shirat Yisrael

A truth, established by proof, does not gain in force from the support of scholars; nor does it lose its certainty because of popular dissent.
MAIMONIDES, Guide to the Perplexed, Intro. II

Ⱄ No other purpose should be attached to truth than that you should know what is true.   MAIMONIDES

Ⱄ A truth does not become greater by repetition. MAIMONIDES

Men cling to the opinions to which they are accustomed from youth; this prevents them from finding the truth, for they cleave to the opinions of habit.
MAIMONIDES: Guide to the Perplexed, 1 : 31

The Torah is truth, and the purpose of knowing it is to live by it.
MAIMONIDES

Truth should be neither cowardly nor bashful.
JOSEPH BEN CASPI, Sefer ha-Mussar

Ⱄ Truth is not nullified because unbelievers deny it.
SAADIA GAON

◄§ Hope and fear are not proper tests of truth.

MOSES MENDELSSOHN

◄§ Truth has a halo.   SAMUEL HA-NAGID, *Ben Mishle*

The truth hurts like a thorn, at first; but in the end it blossoms like
a rose.   SAMUEL HA-NAGID, *Ben Mishle*

◄§ Perfection demands of us not so much the capacity to tell good
from evil, as truth from falsehood.

FALAQUERA, *Commentary on [Maimonides']*
Guide to the Perplexed.

Truth is the very seal of life.

JONATHAN EIBESCHUTZ, *Yaaroth Dvash*

Victory cannot tolerate truth.   NACHMAN OF BRATSLAV

Where there is no truth there is no grace.

NACHMAN OF BRATSLAV

◄§ For thirteen years, I taught my tongue not to tell a lie; for the
next thirteen years I taught it to tell the truth.

THE KORETSER RABBI

Everything can be imitated, except truth; for imitated truth is no
longer truth.   THE KOTZKER RABBI

See also: DECEIT, GOSSIP, LIES, PROOF, SLANDER, TALK, VIRTUE

UGLINESS

There is no one so ugly as the man who is satisfied with himself.

Hasidic saying

See also: **ARROGANCE, BEAUTY, CONCEIT, SELF-ESTEEM, VANITY**

UNDERSTANDING

The heart sees better than the eye.

The man who has understanding has everything.

The wise man hears one word—but understands two.

The less a man understands, the happier he is.

You can look into someone else's eyes, but not into someone else's heart.

Many see, but few understand.

Carry your own lantern and you need not fear the dark.

The Talmud tells us that a fine home, fine clothes, and a good wife will broaden a man's understanding: I need all the understanding I can, to serve God as He deserves.   Hasidic saying

Wisdom is with aged men, and understanding in length of days.

Book of Job, 12 : 12

How much better is wisdom than gold, and understanding than silver.   —adapted from *Book of Proverbs*, 22 : 1

The discourse of a fool is like a burden on a journey; but pleasure
    comes from the lips of a man of understanding.
                              BEN SIRACH, *Ecclesiasticus,* 21 : 16

Whoring and wine remove understanding.   SAADIA GAON

The more a man understands, the more is expected of him.
                                        "THE CHOFETZ CHAIM"

⋖§ The longer a blind man lives, the more he sees.
                                        SHOLEM ALEICHEM

See also: COMPASSION, HEART, INSIGHT, INTELLIGENCE, KINDNESS,
    KNOWLEDGE, PROOF, REASON

UNHAPPINESS

See: EMOTIONS, FATE, FORTUNE, HEALTH, LUCK, MISFORTUNE, SORROW,
    SUFFERING

UNIVERSE

The universe is always unfinished ... It calls for our continuous
    labor and unceasing renewal—for we are partners of the
    Creator.   SIMCHA BUNIM

See also: ETERNITY, GOD, HEAVEN, HEREAFTER, NATURE, WORLD

USURY

Note. Deuteronomy (23 : 20) forbids lending money at interest,
    "between brother and brother," but rabbinical modifications in
    the Talmud, which laid down some remarkably sophisticated
    guides to economic activity, forbade Jews from taking "exces-
    sive" interest; rabbis were responsible for advising what was
    fair to both lender and borrower. Maimonides said that lending
    money at interest was necessary and beneficial: an economy
    grows for the benefit of all.

To economists, the medieval Christian Church gravely erred in considering banking "usurious," no matter how proper or acceptable the interest rate charged. How, except through borrowing money, could men buy tools, seed, livestock? Pay taxes? Recover from drought, accident, disease?

Kings and barons and the clergy often built palaces and churches by raising money from Jews, who were then reviled for "usury." The Church considered it a sin to accept interest; but since Jews were doomed to perdition anyway, it let them take on one more sin. Barred from the land, and often from trade and crafts as well, the Jews in medieval Europe were often forbidden to earn a living *except* through moneylending.

Most of the interest earned on money was then taken from the Jews—via exorbitant taxes. In time, the lending of money became a state monopoly—which Jews were compelled to administer for the royal purse. And whenever Jews were forced out of banking/investment/moneylending, interest rates ("usury") everywhere *rose*. Several popes denounced Christian moneylenders for their "heartless" rates; seventeenth-century monarchs asked Jews to lend them money so as to break the monopoly interest rates being charged by Christian bankers; Pitt enlisted the aid of English Jews against English financiers, whose high interest rates were "strangling" the Treasury.

In the nineteenth and twentieth centuries, the anti-Semitism that had once forced Jews into banking operated to bar them from the inner circles of the financial-social elite.

See also headnotes for BORROWING, LENDING, MONEY.

—L.R.

⋖§ Usury is one form of murder.

The man who does not lend money on interest, either to Jew or Gentile, walks with honor.   TALMUD: *Makkoth,* 24a

The testimony of a usurer is not valid in a court of justice.
                                        TALMUD: *Sanhedrin,* 24b

⋖§ A man who is careful to greet his creditors warmly is guilty of usury in words.   TALMUD: *Baba Mezi'a,* 75b

Consider the folly of the usurer: were a man to call him a scoundrel, he would fight him; yet he takes pen and ink and in the presence of witnesses gravely writes himself down as a scoundrel and a denier of God's word.

TALMUD: Baba Mezi'a, 71a

Usury, like the bite of a poisonous snake, looks small, but its effects are deadly.   MIDRASH: Exodus Rabbah, 31

The usurer has no fear of God . . . for God says, "He who lives on usury in this world shall not inhabit the world to come."

MIDRASH: Exodus Rabbah, 31 : 6

See also: BORROWING, BUSINESS, MONEY, LENDING

UTILITY

◄§ An ugly patch is nicer than a beautiful hole.

◄§ As long as a cow can be milked, it is not slaughtered.

A tree serves no use until it is chopped into wood.

New brooms sweep cleaner.

The animals whose meat we eat, and from whose hide we get shoes . . . are more useful than most of our fellow men.

MOSES IBN EZRA: Shirat Yisrael

See also: CAUSE AND EFFECT, FUNCTION, VALUE

V

VALOR

Valor means persevering in the right, and mastering your desires, until you feel that to die in the best way is better than to live in the worst.   IBN GABIROL

See also: COURAGE, ENDURANCE, FORTITUDE, HONOR

VALUE

It is worth as much as a blown-out egg.

Pearls are not sold along with vegetables.

A pearl remains a pearl anywhere: and if lost, it is lost only to its owner.   TALMUD: *Megillah,* 15a

If you achieve wisdom, what do you lack; and if you lack wisdom, what do you have?   MIDRASH: *Leviticus Rabbah,* 1

⋙ Verbal disparagement does not diminish the value of silks.
                                    SAADIA GAON

See also: CIRCUMSTANCE, GOOD DEEDS, KINDNESS, KNOWLEDGE, LEARNING, MONEY, WISDOM

VANDALISM

Note. As far back as the time of Syrian King Antiochus IV (175–163 B.C.E.), the Scrolls of the Torah were ripped to pieces and burned. The destruction of the Second Temple of course con-

sumed priceless manuscripts. In 1242, the religious authorities
of Paris burned no less than twenty-four cartloads of Talmuds
and Talmudic manuscripts. In 1288, the city of Troyes burned
ten Jewish martyrs—and their libraries. Pope Clement IV proclaimed in a bull that Talmuds be confiscated by the Church
and destroyed by pious monks. England burned Jewish books in
1299. Pope Benedict XIII in 1415, Emperor Maximilian in
1510; a Bishop Dembowski in the eighteenth century—each
ordered the destruction of Hebrew books and manuscripts. As
for the holocaust of the Nazis, in Germany, Austria, Czechoslovakia, Poland, Denmark, Holland, Norway, the Ukraine: it
is safe to say that every Jewish home contained books . . .

—L.R.

See headnotes: BOOKS, INQUISITION, JEWS, LEARNING, POGROMS.

VANITY

True, "All is vanity"—but who can get along without it?

❳ Many complain of their looks, but no one complains of his
brains.

❳ If you want to see your best friend, look in the mirror.

A mirror can be the greatest deceiver.

❳ Even the man with big eyes does not see his own failings.

No man is as ugly as the man who is self-satisfied.

Hasidic saying

Absalom was vain about his hair, therefore was he hanged by his
hair.   TALMUD: *Sotah*, 9b

A giant in your eyes may be a dwarf in ours.

MIDRASH: *Genesis Rabbah*, 65

There is no room for God in the man who is filled with himself.

BAAL SHEM TOV

See also: APPEARANCE, ARROGANCE, CONCEIT, FLATTERY, MAN, PRAISE

VENGEANCE

See: RETALIATION, RETRIBUTION, REVENGE

VICE

◄§ God created only one man so that no one could call virtue
  or vice hereditary.   TALMUD: *Sanhedrin,* 38a

The wise man turns vices into virtues, but the fool turns virtues
  into vices.   *Orhot Tsadikim*

Each virtue in its extreme becomes a vice.
                    JOSEPH BEN HANAN EZOBI, *Karaiat Kesef*

◄§ If you hide your vices, hide your virtues, too.
              —adapted from IBN ZABARA, *Book of Delight*

See also: EVIL, GOOD, LUST, PASSION, SIN, VIRTUE

VIOLENCE

Violence in a house is like a worm in fruit.

If the Book, then no sword; if the sword, then no Book.
                        TALMUD: *'Abodah Zarah,* 17b

See also: ANGER, ARROGANCE, LIFE, MAN, QUARRELS, REASON, WAR

VIRTUE

◄§ God first looks at a man's heart, then at his mind.

A saloon won't harm a good man, a synagogue won't help a bad
  one.

No man possesses all virtues.

◄§ We anger God with our sins, and men with our virtues.

To know all of the Talmud is a great thing; to learn one virtue is greater.

⋙ Not in your ancestry, nor in your inheritance, but in your self seek holiness.

⋙ Why did God create only one man? So that virtue and vice would not be called hereditary. TALMUD: *Sanhedrin,* 38a

⋙ The heart of virtue is good intentions.
                                        TALMUD: *Megillah,* 20a

The man who thinks wisdom is more important than virtue will lose his wisdom.   *Sayings of the Fathers,* 3 : 5

If you conceal your vices, conceal your virtues.
                        IBN ZABARA, *Book of Delight*

The little that is pure is much; the much that is impure is little.
                    BAHYA IBN PAQUDA, *Choice of Pearls*

⋙ Man's finest virtue is that of which he is unaware.
                    MOSES IBN EZRA, *Shirat Yisrael*

An ugly face is the only effective guardian of a woman's virtue.
                    IMMANUEL OF ROME, *Mahberot*

⋙ The man who is pure of heart will find new thoughts whenever be meditates.   NACHMAN OF BRATSLAV

A man can transform a fault into a virtue, if he only perseveres.
                        THE MAGGID OF DUBNO

Be not entirely offended by one who seeks to harm you: he may have virtues you do not possess.   THE SASSOVER RABBI

I don't like those who are "pure as snow"—for snow is not long white and pure, but soon turns muddy and soiled.
                        —adapted from THE RIZINER RABBI

See also: COMPASSION, EVIL, GOOD, HUMILITY, INNOCENCE, KINDNESS, MAN, SIN

VISION

Your old men shall dream dreams, your young men shall see vis-
    ions.   *Book of Joel*, 2 : 28

Where there is no vision, the people shall perish.
                                      Book of Proverbs, 29 : 18

See also: DREAMS, FORESIGHT, IMAGINATION, LEADERS, POWER, WISDOM

VISITING

⋙ Guests, like fish, begin to smell on the third day.

The woman sees the guests' faults before the man does.

Visiting is like rain: prayed for when absent, but tiresome when
    overdone.   IBN GABIROL, *Choice of Pearls*

See also: GUESTS, HOSPITALITY

VOWS

Note. Judaism attaches the most solemn, weighty importance to
    the fulfillment of personal promises. Jews are required by the
    law to fulfill every vow, even if that entails extreme sacrifices.
        Consider the text of Kol Nidre, the prayer that ushers
    in the holiest day of the year, Yom Kippur, "the Day of Atone-
    ment." The invocation is not a paean to God—it is a legal
    document (in Aramaic, not Hebrew), which is recited three
    times, with awesome solemnity, as the Torah Scroll is held
    aloft before the congregation:
        "Kol Nidre [all vows], obligations, oaths, anathemas, be
    they called *konam* or *konas* or by any other name, which we
    may vow or swear or pledge . . . from this Day of Atonement
    until the next . . . we do repent. May they be deemed to be for-
    given, absolved, annulled, or void—and made of no effect. They
    shall not bind us nor have power over us [and] the vows shall

not be considered vows nor the obligations obligatory, nor the oaths oaths."

If the latter part seems confusing, remember that Jews were often not allowed to swear by their God, while in a court; and in Kol Nidre they were referring to oaths they were often brutally forced to take, under the most humiliating circumstances (wearing thorns, kneeling, standing on a pig-skin, teetering on a three-legged stool from which one peg had been removed, etc.). Kol Nidre also absolved Jews (they hoped) from the conversions to Catholicism they had been tortured into undergoing.

The rabbis made it clear that Kol Nidre's appeal for dispensation applied only to vows involving the vower, and did not affect his duty toward others. Vows of conscience, directed to God, were differentiated from promises made to men: the former could be remitted, but not the latter.

—L.R.

Vows are a fence for abstinence.
                    RABBI AKIBA in *Sayings of the Fathers,* 3 : 13

See also: DUTY, FAITH, OBLIGATION, PIETY

VULGARITY

To parade one's learning or one's virtues is vulgar.

Better be a servant to a nobleman than a captain of the vulgar.

Don't use vulgarity with men of learning.   *Zohar*

See also: CONSIDERATION, DECORUM, MANNERS, SAINTS, TACT, VIRTUE, WISDOM

WAR

❧ A small war may cause a large chaos.

If one soldier knew what the other [enemy] soldier thinks, there would be no war.

One word can start a war.

It is better to be a dog in peacetime than a soldier in war.

Don't consult a merchant about a bargain, or a coward about war.

❧ If you can't stand the smell of gunpowder, don't go to war.

❧ Even on the threshold of war, we [Jews] are bidden to begin in no other way than with peace, for it is written: "When you draw near a city to fight, first offer it peace."

MIDRASH: Leviticus Rabbah, 9

When men war, even God's anger does not frighten them.

Zohar

See also: **ANGER, FIGHTING, PEACE, QUARRELING, VIOLENCE**

WEAKNESS

❧ Quarrels are the weapons of the weak.

❧ When a cow falls, everyone sharpens his knife.

Separate reeds are weak and easily broken; when bound together, they are hard to tear apart.

MIDRASH: Tanhuma Nizavim, 1

See also: **COMPASSION, POWER, STRENGTH, WEAKNESS**

WEALTH: I

◦§ We would all be rich—if we didn't have to eat.

◦§ The rich have heirs, not children.

◦§ A poor man's roast and a rich man's death are smelled far away.

What good is a silver urn if it is full of tears?

◦§ Sad is the man who has nothing but money.

◦§ Pearls around the neck [may represent] stones upon the heart.

Better be a rich tenant than a poor landlord.

While a rich man sleeps, his profits increase.

A heavy purse makes a light heart.

◦§ Wherever there is too much, something is lacking.

◦§ When a wallet grows, so do necessities.

A lazy hand brings poverty; but the hand of the diligent brings wealth.   *Book of Proverbs,* 12 : 24

Some people are chained—to gold and silver.
                    TALMUD: *Shabbath,* 54a

Not everyone is privileged to enjoy two tables [wealth and wisdom].   TALMUD: *Berakoth,* 5b

Gold and silver, precious jewels and pearls are left behind when God calls you.   *Sayings of the Fathers,* 6 : 9

Who is really rich? The man who is satisfied with his share.
                    Sayings of the Fathers, 4 : 1

◦§ When told of a man who had acquired great wealth, a sage replied, "Has he also acquired the days in which to spend it?"   IBN GABIROL, *Choice of Pearls*

⋙ When a man's wealth diminishes, even his children don't accept his opinion. IBN GABIROL

⋙ The more money you have, the harder it is to part with it.
"THE CHOFETZ CHAIM"

WEALTH: II—IRONIC COMMENTS ON

⋙ If you rub elbows with a rich man, you'll rub a hole in your sleeve.

⋙ What a fat belly cost, I wish I had; what it's worth, I wish on my enemies.

⋙ To be a millionaire, he'd be glad to sell you the shirt off his back.

If you steal enough eggs, you, too, can become rich.

⋙ Rich people are wise, handsome—and sing like angels.

⋙ The rich may go down and the poor up—but they still don't end up even.

⋙ The rich are often thin and the poor are often fat.

A rich man, though foolish, is treated like a lord.

You can live like a lord and die like a fool.

See also: CONTENTMENT, HAPPINESS, LAZINESS, MONEY, POVERTY, RICH MEN, TORAH

WEAPONS

Words are weapons.

⋙ When you are weaponless at least act brave.

The tongue is the most dangerous of weapons.

Slander is worse than weapons, for weapons hurt from near, but slander hurts from afar.   TALMUD J.: *Pe'ah*, 1 : 1

See also: GOSSIP, RUMORS, SLANDER, WAR

WEDDINGS

Note. Wedding customs among Jews varied greatly throughout the world. In ancient Greece, a Jewish bride and groom wore garlands and wreaths; in Roman times, Jews used lighted torches. Jews in Germany once married only under a full moon, Jews in Spain only under a new moon.

    The custom of the groom's breaking a glass (after the rabbi has pronounced his benediction) has many interpretations: some say it commemorates the destruction of the Temple. The Talmud counsels Jews to remember that all happiness is transient; that Jews must never forget the sufferings of their ancestors; that a thoughtful father once was so disturbed by the frivolity of the guests at his son's wedding that "he broke a fine glass . . . and they became sad."

    Orthodox Jews "celebrate" the couple for seven days (following the Bible's account of the festivities after the marriage of Jacob and Leah). Teachers used to adjourn classes to join a wedding party, with their students: it was a *mitzvah* to participate in the happiness of a bride and groom.

                    —L.R.

If you dance at every wedding, you'll weep at every funeral.

❧ To a wedding, walk; to a divorce, run.   SHOLEM ALEICHEM

See also: DIVORCE, MARRIAGE

WICKED/WICKEDNESS

❧ The wicked do well in this world, the saints in the next.

The good pay, the bad demand.

When the wicked are in power, crime increases.

◦§ A good man needs no recommendation; a bad one, it won't help.

A word helps a good man; but even a stick can't help the wicked.

◦§ The mercy of the wicked is cruel.
Book of Proverbs, 12 : 10

The tongue of the righteous is choice silver;
The mind of the wicked is of little worth.
Book of Proverbs, 10 : 20

He who walks honestly walks safely;
He who walks crookedly will be found out.
Book of Proverbs, 10 : 9

He who seeks good will win forever;
But he who aims at the harmful will bring it upon himself.
Book of Proverbs, 11 : 27

The righteous promise little and perform much; the wicked promise much and perform not even a little.
TALMUD: *Baba Mezi'a,* 87a

Seven pits lie open before the good man—and he escapes: only one lies before the wicked man—and he falls into it.
TALMUD: *Sanhedrin,* 7a

When they are in trouble, the wicked repent; once the trouble is over, they return to their evil ways.
MIDRASH: *Tanhuma,* Exodus

◦§ It is forbidden to pray that a wicked man die: Had Terah died while he worshiped idols, Abraham [his son] would not have come into the world.　　*Midrash ha-Neelam*

It is beyond man's power to explain the prosperity of the wicked, or the troubles of the good.
Sayings of the Fathers, 3 : 16

The wicked are easy to provoke and hard to calm.
—adapted from *Sayings of the Fathers,* 5 : 17

The good die young, so that they may not degenerate; but the wicked live on so that they may repent, or produce virtuous progeny.   *Zohar*

◄§ The quintessence of wickedness is foolishness.
                                        "The Chofetz Chaim"

◄§ I love more the wicked man who is aware of his wickedness, than the good man who preens himself on his goodness.
                                        The Lubliner Rabbi

See also: EVIL, GOOD, SIN, TRANSGRESSION, VIRTUE

WIDOWS

Note. In the Torah, a widow is given legal protection (Exodus 22 : 21 and Deuteronomy 27 : 19). Her property cannot be taken from her by creditors; she cannot be denied any sum stipulated in her marriage contract; she must be supported by her husband's heirs, if destitute. Later rabbinical decrees further ruled that a bride could not in her marriage contract surrender the lien which her claim (on her dead husband's estate) represented.
    See also headnote for WOMEN.
                                        —L.R.

◄§ Better a young widow than an old maid.

◄§ A widow with a golden roof is still a widow.

The man who comforts a beautiful young widow does not only intend to perform a good deed.

Do not take in pawn a widow's possessions—even if she be rich.

See also: DEATH, MARRIAGE, WIVES

WIFE

See WIVES

WILL

Man is in bondage to his impulses—and his creator.

☙ Our eyes and ears are not subject to our will—but our tongues
are.   —adapted from *Zohar*

Skill is nil without will.   IBN TIBBON, *A Father's Admonition*

See also: **EFFORT, ENDURANCE, SKILL**

WINE

Wine helps open the heart to reason.

☙ When wine goes in, secrets come out.

Better old wine than old strength.

Wine is the greatest medicine.

Rabbi Meir said: "The tree of which Adam ate was a vine; wine
brings sorrows to man."   TALMUD: *Sanhedrin,* 70a

☙ Where there is no wine, drugs are necessary.
                              TALMUD: *Baba Bathra,* 58b

The judge who has drunk a quart of wine may not sit in judgment,
for he will condemn the innocent and acquit the guilty.
                        MIDRASH: *Leviticus Rabbah,* 1 : 4, 8

Wine is an unreliable messenger! I sent it down to my stomach,
and it went up to my head!   AL-HARIZI, *Tahkemoni*

Wine, though bitter, sweetens all bitterness.
                              MOSES IBN EZRA, *Selected Poems*

☙ The Talmud declares that wine, in moderation, unfolds a man's
brain: A teetotaler rarely possesses great wisdom.
                              THE KORETSER RABBI

See also: **DRUNKARDS, HEALTH, REASON**

WISDOM

Note. In Jewish thought, wisdom is not simply the fruit of intelligence, scholarship, or knowledge; wisdom is held to involve basic attributes of character and conduct toward one's fellow men. The highest *khakhmah* (wisdom) lies in being learned *and* righteous *and* spreading lovingkindness.

—L.R.

If a man does not try to reach wisdom, wisdom will not come to him.

ᨄ Wisdom is better than piety.

With wisdom alone, don't go to market.

ᨄ Of what use is wisdom when folly reigns?

Wisdom not acted upon is like a tree without fruit.

Wisdom is gentle.

ᨄ Wisdom is a tree whose fruit is virtue.   Rabbinical saying

Teach us [to] apply our hearts unto wisdom.
                                        Book of Psalms, 90 : 12

The wisdom of the poor is despised. *Book of Ecclesiastes,* 9 : 16

If, in a dream, you see the Book of Proverbs, you may hope to gain wisdom.   TALMUD, *Berakoth,* 57b

Wisdom is more precious than pearls. *Book of Proverbs,* 3 : 15

Where wisdom enters, subtlety comes along.
                                        TALMUD: *Sotah,* 21b

ᨄ The jealousy [competition] of scribes helps increase wisdom.
                                        TALMUD: *Baba Bathra,* 21a

Wisdom, like wine, keeps best in a plain vessel.
                                        —adapted from TALMUD

৵৳ Without experience there is little wisdom.

> BEN SIRACH, *Ecclesiasticus*

Wisdom is the consciousness of self.

> MAIMONIDES, *Guide for the Perplexed*, 1

To seek perfection in property or health or character is not a
worthy goal, nor a proper cause of pride and glory; the
knowledge of God is true wisdom, and is the only perfection
man should seek.

> MAIMONIDES, *Guide for the Perplexed*, 3 : 53

Wisdom must not be pursued with any ulterior motive: to obtain
honors, or to gain money, or to improve one's material state
by the study of Torah.   MAIMONIDES, *Mishneh Torah*

Wisdom, like gold ore, is mixed with stones and dust.

> MOSES IBN EZRA, *Shirat Yisrael*

Wisdom is like fire: a little enlightens, much of it can burn.

> MOSES IBN EZRA, *Shirat Yisrael*

In seeking wisdom, the first step is silence, the second listening,
the third remembering, the fourth practicing, the fifth—teaching others.   IBN GABIROL

Wealth brings anxiety, but wisdom leads to peace of mind.

> IBN GABIROL

৵৳ Wisdom is a hoard from which nothing is lost.

> IBN GABIROL

৵৳ The beginning of wisdom is to desire it.

> IBN GABIROL, *Choice of Pearls*

To seek wisdom when old is like making a mark in the sand; to
seek wisdom when young is like hammering an inscription
on stone.   —adapted from IBN GABIROL

Wisdom is to the soul as food is to the body. ABRAHAM IBN EZRA

Wisdom is God's power in action; for without it, everything is but
theory.   THE MEZERITZER RABBI

᪥ Wisdom is God's raiment.   THE MEZERITZER RABBI

Old men who are popular with young women usually lack wisdom.
                                     NACHMAN OF BRATSLAV

WISDOM: WISE MEN/THE WISE

Note. A *khokhem* is one who possesses or displays *khakhma* (wisdom); he need not be an intellectual; many a butcher or
barber was known as a *khokhem,* and the early sages almost
invariably toiled in humble occupations.

    The wisest of the wise was the *talmid khokhem,* "the dis-
ciple of the wise," the lifelong student of Torah and Talmud.
No formal agency could make one a *talmid khokhem.* The
title came via recognition from peers. As a young scholar demonstrated greater and greater sagacity, deeper insight, nobler
humility—he began to be called a *khokhem.* The *talmid khokhem* remained a student throughout his life, be it noted. The
Jews exempted many a *talmid khokhem* from paying communal taxes, not only because *khakomim* were notoriously
poor, but because Jews wanted them to spend every moment
in Talmud study. A *khokhem* studied for the community, as
it were, and for its welfare: for learning, and the study of
Torah, were noted by the Lord Himself. So the Talmud
scholar was supported by the community and by his wife,
whom the community accorded great respect because her labors enabled her husband to study without being distracted
by concern for mundane wherewithal. (See headnotes for
SCHOLARS, LEARNING.)

                                                    —L.R.

᪥ The wise man hears one word—and understands two.

Wisdom increases with the years, but so does folly.

The wise know the value of riches, but the rich do not know the
pleasures of wisdom.

᪥ Some wise men are handsome; and they would be more wise
had they been less handsome.

~§ If you want to be considered smart, agree with everyone.

The wisest man can fool himself.

To recognize your folly is the first step towards wisdom.

~§ That fools love sweets was a discovery of the wise.

~§ A wise man lowers a ladder before he jumps into a pit.

The wise man who parades his wisdom is worse than the fool who, ashamed, conceals his ignorance.

When a wise man makes a mistake, it's a whopper.

~§ Wise men report what they have seen, fools what they have heard.

It is good to look at the fair but live with the wise.

A fool sees a man's clothes; a wise man sees a man's spirit.

The man who understands his foolishnesses is wise.

Old men who marry young women usually lack wisdom.

~§ The wise measure ten times before cutting once; fools cut ten times before measuring once.

God grants wisdom only to those who can be wise.

Silence is a fence enclosing wisdom; but silence alone is not wisdom.

Money adds no more to the wise than clothes do to the beautiful.

Say unto wisdom, "Thou art my sister."   *Book of Proverbs*, 7 : 4

~§ When a wise man is angry, he is no longer wise.
TALMUD, Pesahim, 66a

The wise do not rest either in this world or in the world to come [for they always strive for greater wisdom].
—adapted from TALMUD: Berakoth, 64a

Wisdom is with aged men, and understanding in length of days.
Book of Job, 12 : 12

The man who thinks wisdom is greater than virtue will lose his
wisdom.   *Sayings of the Fathers,* 3 : 5

The wise man is he who can learn from every man.
Sayings of the Fathers, 4 : 1

Make your home an assembling place for the wise, and drink their
words with zeal.   *Sayings of the Fathers,* 1 : 4

If you acquire wisdom, what do you lack; if you lack wisdom,
what do you have?   MIDRASH: *Leviticus Rabbah,* 1

To be in the company of a wise man is like going into a perfumery; you may buy nothing, but the scent will cling to you
for a day.   *Abot de Rabbi Nathan,* 11 : 14b

Man is wise only while searching for wisdom; when he thinks he
has found it, he is a fool.   IBN GABIROL, *Choice of Pearls*

The wise man blames neither himself nor others, for he is pious.
IBN GABIROL, *Choice of Pearls*

❧ A wise man's question contains half the answer.
IBN GABIROL, *Choice of Pearls*

Poverty cannot disgrace the wise man, nor can lust enslave him.
IBN GABIROL

❧ The wise are pleased when they discover truths; fools are
pleased when they discover falsehoods.
—adapted from IBN GABIROL

Kings may be judges of the earth, but wise men are the judges
of kings.   IBN GABIROL

No man is wise unless he possesses three qualities: never to scorn
one less learned who seeks wisdom; never to envy someone who
is richer; and never to accept a fee for his learning.
IBN GABIROL

The sage is wise because he spent more on oil [on lamps to read by] than others spent on wine.

—adapted from IBN GABIROL

~§ A wise man is a greater asset to a nation than a king.

MAIMONIDES

A short life with wisdom is better than a long life without it.

MOSES IBN EZRA, *Shirat Yisrael,* 119

The truly wise man is as liberal with his wisdom as clouds are with their rains.   MOSES IBN EZRA, *Shirat Israel*

Wisdom is the light in man.   MOSES CORDOVERO

Wine and women: they put wise men on guard.

BEN SIRACH, *Ecclesiasticus*

If you judge men by their beards and their girth, then goats are the wisest creations on earth. JOSEPH SOLOMON DELMEDIGO

Everyone is wise—in his own eyes.   BARUCH SPINOZA

If you cling to wisdom, you cannot cling to [impure] desires.

THE MEZERITZER RABBI

I am in constant fear lest I become too wise to remain pious.

THE KORETSER RABBI

See also: AGE, FOOLS, GOD, KNOWLEDGE, LEARNING, PIETY, SAGES, TORAH, TRUTH

WITNESSES

Four eyes see more than two.

~§ Lend before witnesses, but give without them.

The man who intends to lie will look for witnesses from afar.

JUDAH ASHERI

See also: ADAGES, EVIDENCE, LAW, LIARS/LIES

WIVES: I

Note. Despite many "antifeminist" aspects of Judaism, wives enjoyed rights rarely accorded their non-Jewish sisterhood. Where wife's "conjugal rights" and to satisfy her if he saw her centuries, Jewish Law forbade it, and Jewish courts could punish and even anathematize a wife-beater.

The code of law (Shulhan Aruk) forbade a husband from being "unduly familiar" with his wife, or injuring her dignity, or (Heaven forfend!) beating or selling her. Further, a husband was enjoined not to cohabit with his wife "unless she desires it" (!) and was "certainly forbidden to force her," or to have intercourse if she hated him, or said she did not want his attention, or was intoxicated, or was asleep. A husband was forbidden to cohabit with his wife if she had decided he wanted to divorce her. He was commanded not to deny his wife's "conjugal rights" and to satisfy her if he saw her "primping and coquetting, even if it is not the appointed time."

One of the most interesting Rabbinical decrees declared that a new husband must not leave his town, even to serve in the army, for the first year of marriage—"in order that he may rejoice with her."

For the singularly advanced conceptions of Divorce among the Hebrews, see that category. And for the high status of women in Judaism, see the long headnote for WOMEN.

—L.R.

◆§ Give your ear to all, your hand to your friends, but your lips only to your wife.

Old maids make devoted wives.

◆§ The man who is too good for the world is no good to his wife.

A gentle girl makes a dove of a wife.

A maiden should pretty herself for the boys she may meet; a wife should be pretty for her husband.

◆§ When the wife is fat, the loaves she bakes are round.

Why is it that fools have pretty wives?

Between a husband and wife only God can judge.

It does no harm to listen to one's own wife.

A shrewish wife can, alas, be right.

A little table, a little bench—oh, to be a *balebuste* [housewife].

⋙ It is better to have an ugly wife for one's self than a beautiful wife for others.

An old maid who gets married becomes a young wife.

If you love your wife, you love her family, too.

⋙ When a young girl marries an old man, he gets younger but she gets older.

If you're faithful to your wife, you have a healthy body.

House and wealth are inherited from our fathers;
But a sensible wife is a gift from the Lord.
Book of Proverbs, 19 : 14

⋙ Love your wife as you love yourself—and honor her more.
Talmud: *Yebamoth,* 62 : b

A beautiful wife makes for happiness and her husband's days are doubled.   Talmud: *Yebamoth,* 63b

⋙ Wives save men from sin.   Talmud: *Yebamoth,* 63b

⋙ When a young man's wife dies, the altar of God is draped in mourning.   Talmud: *Sanhedrin,* 22a

There is a substitute for everything except the wife of your youth.   Talmud: *Sanhedrin,* 22a

⋙ Home is the wife.   Talmud: *Yomah,* 2a

⋙ A man without a wife is not perfect [complete].
Talmud: *Yomah,* 12a

⋐§Tears fall on God's altar for whoever divorces his first wife.
TALMUD: Gittin, 90a

Husband and wife are like one flesh.   TALMUD: Menahoth, 93b

Three things broaden a man's mind: an attractive house, attractive
furniture, and an attractive wife. TALMUD: Berakoth, 57b

A beautiful wife enlarges a man's spirit.
—adapted from TALMUD: Berakoth, 57b

Be careful to honor your wife, for blessing enters the house only
because of the wife.   TALMUD: Baba Mezi'a, 59a

⋐§ Thy wife is short, so bend down and consult her.
TALMUD: Baba Mezi'a, 59a

⋐§ I never call my wife "wife": I call her "home"—for it is she
who makes my home.
—adapted from TALMUD: Shabbath, 118b

Man is not even called man until he is united with woman.
Zohar

⋐§ Before you take a wife, study her brothers.
RABBI RABA, TALMUD: Baba Bathra, 110a

A man without a wife is a homeless wanderer.
BEN SIRACH, Ecclesiasticus

⋐§ Better your wife's kisses than those of your neighbor's wife.
SHOLEM ALEICHEM

WIVES: CRITICAL COMMENTS

⋐§ If you give the bear a wife, he will stop dancing.

⋐§ A wife is a bit of a dove and a bit of a devil.

Pretty faces don't produce good wives.

The first wife pulls the wagon; the second wife rides on the seat.

A wife can make a man a master—or a slave.

&ε§ When the wife wears the pants, the husband washes the floor.

When the wife wears the pants, the husband rocks the child.

&ε§ Where the wife is a slob, the cat is a glutton.

A man's wife has scarcely stopped living before another woman is ready to take her place.

&ε§ Some men get along with their wives like stonemasons with their stone.

A young wife is like a bird: she should be kept in a cage.

&ε§ A short wife can have a big mouth.

If a wife wants her husband to stay home, she should talk less and clean more.

A second wife is like a wooden leg.

A shrewish wife is a scourge.

&ε§ A heavy rain chases you into the house; a mean wife chases you out.

The wife of a righteous man is herself righteous; and the wife of a murderer is as he is.

"Rebbe, since you know all things, tell us what did Eve do whenever Adam returned home late?"
"She counted his ribs."   Hasidic story

It is better to live in a corner of the roof, than share a large house with a quarrelsome wife.   *Book of Proverbs*, 21 : 9

A foolish son is his father's ruin; and a quarrelsome wife is like a constant drip.   *Book of Proverbs*, 10 : 9

A good wife is a crown to her husband; but one who acts shamefully is like rot in his bones.   *Book of Proverbs*, 12 : 4

Hell awaits the man who always follows the advice of his wife.

TALMUD: *Baba Mezi'a*, 59a

◦§ A bad wife is like a dreary, rainy day.

TALMUD: *Yebamoth*, 63

The woman who does not adorn herself for her husband deserves the worst. HAI GAON

How can an intelligent man test himself? By enduring the company of a bad wife. IBN GABIROL

A bad wife is like a wolf: she may change her hair but not her nature. IBN GABIROL

See also: DIVORCE, GIRLS, HUSBANDS, LOVE, MARRIAGE, MEN AND WOMEN, WOMEN

WOMEN

Note. There are so many misconceptions about the status of women in Judaism that I trust you will forgive a lengthy headnote for this category. Start with the Bible: the mother is placed on equal footing with the father in the Ten Commandments; Miriam is acclaimed one of the emancipators of the Israelites from the Egyptians (Micah, 6 : 4); Deborah was a leader in the war of independence; the praises of women and mothers are sung and resung in Proverbs.

The loftiest word in Hebrew is held to be *rahamanut:* "mercy, compassion;" literally, the word means "mother love." An old Jewish saying goes "God could not be everywhere, so he created mothers."

The rabbis often said that women are superior to men— in chastity, compassion, and piety. "Man is not even called man until he is united with woman," says the *Zohar.* "The ideal man has the strength of a man and the compassion of a woman."

The infrequency of infidelity or divorce among Jews is well-known. It is no small thing that the Talmud tells Jewish men: "Love your wife as yourself, and honor her more than yourself. . . . Cause no woman to weep, for God counts her tears. . . . Israel was redeemed because of the virtue of its women." "God's blessing does not descend upon the unmarried man—for he is imperfect" is an old rabbinical saying; the Talmud (*Yebamoth,* 63a) says: "The man who remains unmarried does not deserve to be called a man."

Each week of each year, on the eve of the Sabbath, Jewish women for centuries have been "Queens of the Sabbath," and their husbands sang a tribute, *Eshes Hayil* ("A Woman of Valor"):

> Strength and honor are her clothing . . .
> She openeth her mouth with wisdom . . .
> Her children arise up, and call her
>   blessed; her husband also, and he
>   praiseth her.

The mother lights the candles and offers a benediction: and in this she becomes a priestess of the Lord.

Or consider this: "Between a male and female orphan, provide first for the female: the male may beg, but not the female" (Talmud, *Kethuboth* 67b).

Perhaps the simplest illustration of the advantages enjoyed by Jewish women is the rarity of wife-beating—a custom much practiced and admired in the ethos of peoples among whom the Jews lived. Wife-beating—in Europe no less than the Middle East—was very common; many tribes, town statutes, even Catholic canon law, expressly made it legal. In England, wives were legally beaten into the late fifteenth century—and *sold* throughout the nineteenth (read Hardy's *The Mayor of Casterbridge*) and into the twentieth. In the Middle East, Africa, and Eastern Europe, a man's right to beat his wife was as natural as rain.

But very early, Jewish Law ordered the *Beth Din* to punish any wife-beater; and, if need be, to anathematize him; if necessary, to force him to give his wife a divorce—maintaining her full legal, monetary compensation. An old folk saying goes: "When a Jew is hungry, he sings; when a nobleman is hungry, he whistles; when a peasant is hungry, he beats his wife."

Other legal protections the Jews give to women are notable: by rabbinical law, a man was required to marry a girl he had seduced, and was never permitted to divorce her. Jewish husbands were forbidden to use their wives as unwilling sexual receptacles. Maimonides said that a woman is not a slave "compelled to consort with a man against her will," and declared that, if a husband did not satisfy his wife's conjugal rights, she could divorce him. Jewish women were legally protected against desertion or capricious divorce; and they could obtain a divorce where a marriage had become intolerable: Jewish women were not forced to endure husbands who were drunkards, gamblers, libertines.

Alimony was given to Jewish women long, long before that institution was widespread in the west. Widows were specially protected and supported. Women's property rights under Jewish law were considerably superior to those of other nations; "in respect to possessing an independent estate, the Jewish wife was in a position far superior to that of English wives before the enactment of recent legislation" (Israel Abrahams).

Jewish women ran their households with a degree of independence unknown to their contemporaries; they managed the household budget, carried on financial transactions outside the home, and were frequently given community funds to dispense or invest according to their discretion.

It is in the *educating* of females that the Jews displayed all-too-familiar masculine bias. Jewish girls' education was, for centuries, far inferior to that given Jewish boys. But it is not true that Jewish females were *barred* from education. As early as 1475, a Talmud Torah (school) for girls existed in the Jewish settlement in Rome; and periodically, through history, travelers and commentators remarked on the fact that, compared to non-Jewish females, very few Jewish women were illiterate. (See Cecil Roth's essay in *The Jewish Library: Woman*, edited by Leo Jung, Soncino Press, London, 1970.)

Jewish women were expected to make it possible for Jewish males to study Torah—by raising, feeding, sheltering, healing, even supporting them. The women of Israel were held responsible for the basic moral supervision and training of children; they were indoctrinated to indoctrinate the young with a love of study, learning, and obligation to others. Women were not required to study Torah, as men were—although the Mishnah (*Nedarim*, 4) advises instruction in Scripture for both boys and girls, and Judah the Pious declared: "Everyone should know the Divine Law and commandments; youths . . . in Hebrew; women and girls . . . in their mother tongue."

The most widely read work in Yiddish literature is the *Tseno-Ureno* ("Go Out and See") by Jacob ben Isaac Ashkenazi (1550–1628). It was directed to Jewish women, and became a sort of woman's Bible. Ostensibly a translation of the Pentateuch, the *haphtarahs,* and the Five Scrolls, the *Tseno-Ureno* is a charming mosaic of legend, allegory and ethical observations. It became the chief source of Jewish knowledge for generations of mothers who, Sabbath after Sabbath, absorbed its cabala-flavored philosophy of life. In an important sense, this book reflected the triumph of individual interpretation over literal translation, the prominence of the woman's role in everyday Jewish life, and the emphasis of Polish ritual over that of the more worldly Germanic Jews. It overshadowed all previous works in Yiddish, and it affected the life of Ashkenazic Jews more deeply and more lastingly than any other.

Isaac Yanover wrote an unpretentious "home book" for women, in the sixteenth century, that became immensely popular in Eastern and Central Europe: the *Teitsh-Chumash,* an engaging array of material from the Bible and Talmud, and from folklore, humor, allegories, superstitions and legends. In its pages, Jewish women found their devotional guide, their ethical counselor, their household almanac on every conceivable problem from dress and dancing to prayer and behavior.

The status of Jewish women has changed dramatically, needless to say, in the last century. They have taken on greater and greater prominence in trade unions, politics, community organizations. The transformation of the female's status is obvious if one but thinks of Israel, where the Prime Minister is a woman and where women receive equal educational opportunities, the right to vote, etc. (See also headnotes on DIVORCE, FAMILY, WIDOWS, WIVES.)

—L.R.

WOMAN/WOMEN: I

◦§ God did not create woman from man's head, that he should
command her; nor from his feet, that she should be his slave;
but from his side, that she should be nearest his heart.
                                    as the source adapted from TALMUD

A woman may wear pearls around her neck, though she have stones
on her heart.

Culture in a woman is worth more than gold.

◦§ Women persuade men to do good as well as to do evil—but they
always persuade them.

Don't deny a pregnant woman's wish.

Women don't blame the tailor when he sews their shrouds.

◦§ A woman of sixty, like a girl of six, will run at the sound of
wedding music.

◦§ Blessed art Thou, oh Lord, who hast made me according to
Thy will.   Morning prayer

A woman is a better appraiser of guests than a man is.
                                    TALMUD, *Berakoth,* 10b

◦§ The death of a woman is felt by no one so much as her husband.   TALMUD: *Sanhedrin,* 22

◦§ A woman prefers poverty with love to riches without love.
                                    —adapted from MISHNAH: *Sotah,* 3 : 4

Everything derives from woman. MIDRASH: *Genesis Rabbah,* 17

Alexander the Great came to a city inhabited by women, to make
war on them, but they said: "If you kill us, people will say:
'He conquered women;' and if we kill you, they will say:
'What a king: Women killed him!'"
         Then Alexander said: "Bring me bread; I am hungry."
         But they brought him a loaf of gold.
         "Can I eat gold?" asked Alexander angrily.

The women answered: "If you wanted bread, was none in your kingdom? Did you have to march to so far a place?"

So Alexander departed, having inscribed on the gates of their city: "I, Alexander, was a madman, to come to Africa to be taught by women."

　　　　　　　—adapted from MIDRASH: *Tanhuma Buber*

◆§ After they were divorced, the man married a bad woman, and she made him bad; the woman married a bad man, and she made him good; this proves that all depends upon the woman.

　　　　　　　MIDRASH: *Genesis Rabbah*, 17 : 7

The ideal man has a man's strength and the compassion of a woman.

　　　　　　　Zohar

If a man and a woman ask for food or clothing, always give the woman preference.　　　　　JOSEPH CARO, *Shulhan Aruk*

A woman is like a garden.　　　　　*Pirke de Rabbi Eliezer*, 1

◆§ Be careful not to make women weep, for God counts their tears.

　　　　　　　TALMUD: *Baba Mezi'a*, 59a

◆§ A woman can be evaluated by her cooking, her dressing—and her husband.　　　　　SHOLEM ALEICHEM

WOMEN: NEGATIVE COMMENTS ON

◆§ When a woman dies, people find out how many children she had.

◆§ Where there are many women there is much superstition.

Women are nine times more talkative than men.

◆§ A woman can argue even with the Angel of Death.

◆§ May God protect you from bad women: protect yourself against good ones.

A woman, it is said, has long hair and short sense.

⇜ Test gold with fire, and a woman with gold.

Where there are many women there is much superstition.

The best horse needs a whip; the wisest man, advice; the most chaste woman—a man.

A woman who turns into a witch is worse than a woman who was born one.

⇜ There is a key for every door, and one for every woman.
TALMUD: *Berakoth*, 45b

God cursed woman, but all men pursue her.
TALMUD: *Yomah*, 75a

A woman will uncover her neighbor's pots to know what's cooking.
TOSEPH, *Taharoth*, 8

⇜ Hell can lie between the lashes of a beautiful woman's eyes.
Sefer ha-Hinukh

Like a golden ring in the snout of a sow is a beautiful woman lacking in taste. *Book of Proverbs*, 11 : 22

A contentious woman is like a continual dripping on a rainy day.
—adapted from *Book of Proverbs*, 27 : 15

⇜ There is no hell like an evil woman [wife]. IBN ZABARA

Don't associate with a woman singer; you may be captured by her wiles. BEN SIRACH, *Ecclesiasticus*, 9 : 4

I would rather dwell with a lion or serpent than with an evil woman. BEN SIRACH, *Ecclesiasticus*, 25 : 16

⇜ Wine and women put wise men on guard.
BEN SIRACH, *Ecclesiasticus*

⇜ An ugly face is the only effective guardian of a woman's virtue.
IMMANUEL OF ROME, *Mahberot*

⇜ A woman's tears are a form of bribery.
THE SHATZOVER RABBI

⋙ Women? You suffer before you get them, while you have them, and after you lose them.   SHOLEM ALEICHEM

See also: DOMESTICITY, EVE, GIRLS, GOD, HAPPINESS, HOME, MARRIAGE, MEN AND WOMEN, WIVES

WORDS

⋙ Words should be weighed, not counted.

⋙ You can forget a blow, but not a word.

A slap disappears; a word does not.

One word can start a war.

A word is like an arrow: in a hurry.

⋙ Words are like medicine: they should be measured with care, for an overdose may hurt.

⋙ Like a bee, a word may have honey in its sting.

Learned men spare words.

Fools love to use words.

Pleasant words are as a honeycomb, sweet to the soul, and health to the bones.   *Book of Proverbs,* 1 : 24

Who . . . darkens counsel by words without knowledge?
          Book of Job, 38 : 2

Like apples of gold in a setting of carved silver is a word that is aptly spoken.   *Book of Proverbs,* 25 : 11

⋙ A soothing tongue is a tree of life; but wild words break the spirit.   *Book of Proverbs,* 15 : 4

An apt utterance is a joy to a man, and a word in season—how good is it!   *Book of Proverbs,* 15 : 23

The instruments of both life and death are contained within the power of the tongue.   *Book of Proverbs,* 18 : 21

One word can be canceled by another.   TALMUD: *Gittin,* 32b

≈§ The righteous need no tombstones; their words are their monuments.   TALMUD: *Pesahim,* 119a

Words are the guide to acts: the mouth makes the first move.
                    LEONE DA MODENA, *Tsemah Tsadik*

≈§ Looks explain words.
                    —adapted from MOSES IBN EZRA, *Shirat Yisrael*

≈§ Words are like bodies; meanings are like souls.
            MOSES IBN EZRA, *Commentary on Exodus,* 20 : 1

As the length of a tree's branches depend on its roots, so right words depend on a man's good sense.   IBN GABIROL, *Poems*

≈§ If I do not utter a word, I am its master; once I utter it, I am its slave.   —adapted from IBN GABIROL

≈§ You may regret your silence once, but you will regret your words often   —adapted from IBN GABIROL

Words are the shell; meditation is the kernel.
                BAHYA IBN PAQUDA, *Choice of Pearls*

A word without thought is like a foot without muscles.
                MOSES IBN EZRA, *Selected Poems,* 92

≈§ Thought is better than words, because it guides them.
                    THE MEZERITZER RABBI

A kind word is no substitute for a piece of herring or a bag of oats.
                    SHOLEM ALEICHEM

See also: ARGUMENT, CRITICISM, FOOLS, GOSSIP, SLANDER, TALK, WISDOM, WISDOM: WISE MEN/THE WISE

WORK

≈§ The hardest work is being idle.

Bread does not come from flour alone.

◄§ Work is easy—for those who like to work.

◄§ When a furrier is out of work, he too is cold.

The cobbler who sticks to his job keeps his pot full.

◄§ Men at work are not obliged to stand up when a sage passes
by. [Other men are.]   TALMUD: *Kiddushin,* 33a

◄§ Not to teach your son to work is like teaching him to steal.
TALMUD: *Kiddushin,* 29a

If you are told, "I toiled [in study] and I didn't get," believe it not;
if told, "I didn't toil and I got," believe it not; but if told, "I
toiled and I got," believe it.   TALMUD: *Megillah,* 6b

No labor, however humble, dishonors man.
TALMUD: *Nedarim,* 49b

◄§ To earn a living can be as hard as to part the Red Sea.
TALMUD: *Pesahim,* 118a

The workman's rights always take precedence over those of his
employer.   TALMUD: *Baba Mezi'a,* 77a

Weeds spring up and thrive; but to get wheat, how much toil we
must endure!   MIDRASH: *Genesis Rabbah,* 45 : 4

Superior work results from a man's rivalry with his neighbor.
MIDRASH: *Ecclesiastes Rabbah,* 3 : 11

The man who works is blessed.   MIDRASH: *Psalms,* 23

It is wise to work as well as study Torah: between the two, you
will forget to sin.   *Sayings of the Fathers,* 2 : 2

◄§ A man can die if he has nothing to do.
Abot de Rabbi Nathan, 11 : 23a

It is imperative that most men engage in productive occupations,
so that the few men who devote themselves entirely to learning
may have their wants provided; for in this way, the human race
goes on—while knowledge is enriched.
MAIMONIDES, *Commentary on Mishnah,* Introduction

ও§ To work for another man is often like taking honey from a bee: accompanied by a sting.   THE ROPSHITZER RABBI

See also: LAZINESS, POVERTY, SKILLS, THRIFT, TRADE

WORLD

ও§ The world is beautiful, shining bright, and easy—but for whom?

ও§ This world is a dream—but please don't wake me up.

ও§ O, Lord of the Universe—please take a real look at Your world!

ও§ God has said: "Do not corrupt My world; for if you do, who will set it right after you?"

ও§ We can have both heaven and hell in this world.

The world is God's looking-glass.

This world can be changed neither by cursing nor by laughing.

ও§ If all men pulled in one direction, the world would keel over.

The world is a collection of cogs: each depends on the other.

ও§ The entire world is not crazy.

Without money, this world is not fit to live in.

God created a world that is full of many little worlds.

ও§ So it goes in this world: one man has the purse, the other the money.

ও§ The world itself rests upon the breath of the children in our schools.   TALMUD: *Shabbath,* 119b

ও§ The world is in the hands of fools. TALMUD: *Sanhedrin,* 46b

Hurry and eat, hurry and drink, for this world is like a wedding feast from which we must soon depart.
                TALMUD: *Erubin,* 54a

The world is like a ladder: one man goes up while another goes
    down.   MIDRASH: *Tanhuma, Numbers,* 49

God created many worlds and destroyed many worlds before he
    created this one of heaven and earth.
                                        MIDRASH: *Genesis Rabbah*

⋙ Rabban Simeon ben Gamaliel had said: "The world rests on
    three things: On justice, on truth, on peace." Said Rabbi
    Mona: "But these three are one and the same: for if there is
    justice, there is truth, and if there is truth, there is peace."
                                        Perek ha-Shalom

⋙ This world was created for those who are ashamed to do evil.
                                        Introduction to *Tikune Zohar*

This world is like a house: the sky is a ceiling, the earth a carpet,
    the stars lamps . . . and man is its master.
                        BAHYA IBN PAQUDA, *Duties of the Heart*

This world is like a fair: people gather for a while, then part.
                        BAHYA IBN PAQUDA, *Duties of the Heart*

⋙ A faultless man is possible only in a faultless world.
                        HASDAI, *Ben ha-Melekh ve-ha-Nazir*

The world is a tree, and man is its fruit.   IBN GABIROL

⋙ Just as a house testifies to a builder, a dress to a weaver, a door
    to a carpenter, so the world proclaims its creator, God.
                        RABBI AKIBA, *Midrash Temura,* chapter 3

The man who despises this world is a hero: only a weakling honors
    it.   MOSES IBN EZRA, *Shirat Yisrael*

⋙ Just as your hand, held before the eye, can hide the tallest
    mountain, so this small earthly life keeps us from seeing the
    vast radiance that fills the core of the universe.
                                        NACHMAN OF BRATSLAV

The world is a tempestuous sea, immense in its depth and its
    breadth, and time is a frail bridge built over it—its beginning

fastened with those cords of chaos that preceded existence, but the end is eternal bliss, lighted by God's countenance.

JEDAIA BEN BEDERSI

◄§ The world is new to us every morning—that is God's gift, and a man should believe he is reborn each day.

BAAL SHEM TOV

See also: GOD, HEAVEN, HEREAFTER, NATURE

WORLD-TO-COME

Note. The idea of the immortality of the soul served to reconcile man to the sufferings and injustices of this world, which Job, Jeremiah, Ecclesiastes, so eloquently protested. And the Hebrew masses, from the time of the Maccabees, nourished their hopes and salved their sorrows by the retention of faith in a world to come—in which the good will at last be rewarded.

The pious Jew spent an enormous amount of his time in prayer and study (of Torah and Talmud) in order to earn "a portion of bliss" in the eternal hereafter.

—L.R.

This world was created for the wicked; the world-to-come for the righteous.   —adapted from RAB in TALMUD, *Berakoth,* 61b

See: HEREAFTER, IMMORTALITY, RESURRECTION

WORRY

◄§ It is better to have ten worries than one.

The greatest of worries can't pay the smallest of debts.

A horse has a huge head, so let him worry.

◄§ Worms eat you when you're dead; worries eat you up alive.

◄§ The good Lord gave me a brain that works so fast that in one moment I can worry as much as it would take others a whole year to achieve.

Noblemen worry about their horse and dogs; Jews worry about their wife and children.

ઌ Only one kind of worry is proper: to worry because you worry so much.

Worry saps a man's strength.   TALMUD: *Gittin*, 70a

ઌ Don't worry about tomorrow; who knows what will befall you today?   TALMUD: *Yebamoth*, 63b

ઌ It is a serious disease to worry over what has not occurred.
                                                    IBN GABIROL

Why should you be anxious about a world that is not yours?
                                          THE SASSOVER RABBI

See also: ANXIETY, CONSCIENCE, MAN, MELANCHOLY, MISFORTUNE, TROUBLES

WORSHIP

Note. There is an old, delightful story that "the three pillars" of Judaism, *Torah* (learning), *Avodah* (worship), and *Gemilus hasadim* (kind deeds) came before God; and they cried that with the dispersion of the Jewish people they would be forgotten. "Not so," answered the Lord. "I shall tell the Jews to build synagogues. The rabbi will teach them Torah; the cantor will lead them in Avodah."

"But how will *I* be remembered?" asked Kind Deeds.

"Ah," said the Lord, "during the service, each Jew will turn toward his neighbor and offer him a pinch from his snuffbox."
                                                    —L.R.

Could we fill the seas with ink
And use each blade of grass as quill,
And were all the world of parchment
And was every man a scribe:
To write the love of God
Would drain the seas dry,
And the scroll would reach from sky to sky.
                                    MEIR BEN ISAAC NEHORAI

The best worship is silence and hope.   IBN GABIROL

See also: PIETY, PRAYER, SYNAGOGUES

Y

YOM KIPPUR

Note. It long was the custom for Jews on the eve of Yom Kippur,
the last of the annual ten days of penitence, to hurry to all
whom they had offended or been unfriendly—to beg their
pardon. Families would solemnly assemble to ask forgiveness
of one another for any slights or selfish acts they might have
committed in the preceding year. All this was done so that
one might enter upon Yom Kippur with a clean conscience.

On Yom Kippur, observing Jews confess their sins collectively—for on that awesome day, say the pious, all men stand
before the Lord for His judgment. The confession, which is
repeated several times during the day, involves a cataloguing of
no fewer than fifty-six (!) categories of sin: "For the sin we
have committed before Thee by [stating one of fifty-six
varieties], oh God of Forgiveness, forgive us, pardon us, grant
us remission." Note that the confession of guilt is recited as a
collective "we," not as an individual "I." On Yom Kippur, Jews
"share" one another's transgressions—plus a feeling of general
responsibility for the misdeeds of mankind.

—L.R.

The Yom Kippur liturgy has many occasions for confession. There
are the great confessionals, *Ashamnu* and *Al Chet*. The confessional has two interesting characteristics: First, it is in alphabeti-

cal order, and, second, it is in the plural. For if we were to
recount all our sins, we would never complete the list; therefore, we use the alphabetical form, for the alphabet has a beginning and an end. The confessional is in the plural because
all Jews are responsible for all other Jews.

SEYMOUR SIEGEL

❧ The *Shofar* [the ram's horn sounded on the High Holy Days]
is a prayer without words.   SAUL LIEBERMAN

See also: CONFESSION, ISRAEL, JEWS, SINS

YOUNG AND OLD

❧ Old boys become young men.

❧ If you don't want to get old, hang yourself while young.

What you become accustomed to do in your youth, you do in your
old age.

❧ When an old man takes a young wife, he gets young and she
gets old.

Young trees bend; old trees break.

Youth is a crown of roses, but old age is a crown of willows.

What the old chew, the young spit out.

The old often survive the young.

When one is young, God forgives his stumblings; when one is a
man, God weighs his works; when one grows old, God waits
for his repentance.

❧ Wise men, when older, grow wiser; ignorant men, when older,
become more foolish.

❧ The old maid who marries becomes a young wife.

At seven, a boy skips like a goat; at seventy, a man dodders like an
ape.

The glory of the young is their strength: the beauty of the old is
their gray hair.   *Book of Proverbs,* 20 : 29

If old men tell you "throw down" and young men tell you "build
up," throw down and do not build up, because destruction, by
the old, is construction, and construction, by the young, is
[often] destruction.   TALMUD: *Megillah,* 31a

&~§ Old camels often carry young hides [as cargo].
                                      TALMUD: *Sanhedrin,* 52a

When you learn as a child, it is like ink on fresh paper; when you
learn as an old man, it is like ink on used paper.
                              Sayings of the Fathers, 4 : 27

&~§ To seek wisdom in old age is like a mark in the sand; to seek
wisdom in youth is like an inscription on stone.
                                              IBN GABIROL

Old men who are popular with young women usually lack wisdom.
                                      NACHMAN OF BRATSLAV

See also: ADVICE, AGE, LIFE, MAN, YOUTH, WISDOM

YOUTH

&~§ Trees bend only when young.

Youth is a wreath of roses.

When cucumbers are young, you can tell whether they will grow
into good food.

&~§ Youth is one thing that never returns.

If I do not acquire ideals when young, when will I? Not when I am
old.   MAIMONIDES

See also: AGE, LIFE, YOUNG AND OLD

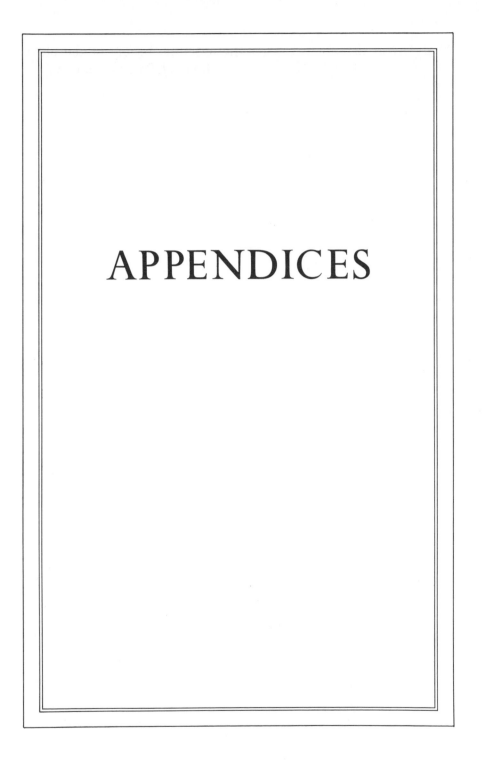

APPENDICES

I · On the English Spelling of Hebrew and Yiddish Words*

E VERY translator must decide what English letters to use in spelling certain Hebrew/Yiddish words. For the reader's convenience I offer the alternative spellings of words, names, and books, as they may be found in other English works. Problems arise with:

(1) English "t" or "s" to end a word (*Bet* or *Bes*); if indicating the Hebrew spelling and pronunciation of a Hcbrew word, I use the "t," but in rendering the Yiddish pronunciation of a Hebrew loan-word, one is obliged to use the "s."

(2) English "b" or "v" (e.g., *Baba* or *Bava*); I prefer the "b."**

(3) English "a" or "ah" to end a word (*Zara* or *Zarah*); I follow the usage of the author I am quoting.

(4) English "t" or "th" to end a word (*Berakot* or *Berakoth*); I prefer the "t," but in quoting I follow the form used by the author of the quotation.

(5) "Ch" or "ḥ" or "kh" or "ḥ" for the back-of-the-throat fricatives (approximated by the *ch* of the German *ach* or the Scottish *loch*); although the use of "ḥ" or "ḥ" in English is increasing, I retain the "ch" at the beginning of a word *if* it is one that many readers of English have already become familiar with

---

* For a fuller explanation and historical background, see my *The Joys of Yiddish, op. cit.,* pp. xxiv–xxviii, and pp. 514–15.

** Hermann L. Strack's authoritative *Introduction to the Talmud and Midrash* uses "b"; so does the Soncino Press edition of the *Babylonian Talmud* and the *Minor Tractates of the Talmud;* so does Herbert Danby's monumental *The Mishnah. The New Standard Jewish Encyclopedia,* edited by Cecil Roth, uses the "v," as do many contemporary writers (*e.g.,* E. J. Lipman, *The Mishnah*).

(*chutzpa, cheder, Chaim*). I use "kh" rather than "ḥ" in the middle or at the end of a word, to insure it will be pronounced, e.g. *mishpokhe, nebekh*. But note:

(6) I spell "ḥasid," "ḥasidic," "ḥasidim" with an "ḥ" (not a "ch") because that is becoming standard practice in Jewish source materials; I suppose the reader who cannot manage the guttural *kh* sound, or who would pronounce "chasid" with the "ch" of "Chinese," comes closer to the comprehensible (orally) in uttering "ḥasid" with the "ḥ" of "house" than with the "ch" of "choose."

(7) "Z" or "tz" or "ts" to begin a word (e.g., *zaddik*) which is pronounced "ts"; I prefer the "ts," to discourage the readers' use of the "z" sound, as in "zebra."

(8) Hebrew, Arabic, or Aramaic names are often rendered in English with an apostrophe, inverted apostrophe, hyphen, space, or successive capital letters; I prefer to use the space or hyphen, but follow the form used by the author or editor being quoted.

In all of the above, the lack of consistency, which I regret, is both necessary and expedient.

Some of these "rules" represent a reversal from those I followed in *The Joys of Yiddish;* in making the changes, I was simply bowing to the growing consensus among linguists about how Hebrew/Yiddish orthography should be standardized.

II · On Translating Hebrew

C OMPARED with Yiddish, Hebrew* is wholly alien to, and remote from, the languages of the Indo-European family—
which were the tongues of nearly all immigrants from the
Old World to the New. Those languages are often cousins, sometimes siblings, so millions of new Americans could swiftly learn
that, say, "book" or "house" were the English versions of the Ger-
man/Yiddish *buch* or *Haus* or *hoiz*. This was impossible with Hebrew, where "book" is *sepher* and "house" is *bet*. Hebrew found no
cognates in English.

Nor is vocabulary the decisive point; Hebrew changes words
according to their function; and the order in which Hebrew sets
words, to frame a sentence, so differs from English that even expert translators often moan over their difficulties.

The Hebrew which has been translated for this anthology is
almost entirely ancient or medieval. This means that the very
tone and stance of the content differ from today's ways of thinking and writing. The wisdom imbedded in Hebrew aphorisms is
rooted in, and tied to, the Law; the philosophical sayings mediate,
as it were, between the Law and the people. Every word (or even
syllable) of a Hebrew sentence may possess an internal association

---

* The word "Hebrew" possibly stemmed from *ibri*, or *ivri*, which denoted
"one from the other side" (of the Jordan). What language was spoken by the
people whose history is recorded in the Old Testament? The Old Testament tells
us only "the lip of Canaan" and "Judaic." The word "Hebrew," to describe the
original language of the Old Testament, does not occur until around 130 of the
Christian era—in a Greek translation of the work of Jesus ben Sirach.

with some principle of the Law. Translation simply cannot preserve all these linkages and echoes.

In contrast, *Yiddish* folk sayings, though often rooted in a Talmudic insight, branch out exuberantly and take their shape and meaning from the earthy experience of the masses.

More specifically: Hebrew texts originally contained no vowels: rabbis added diacritical marks (in the margins) above or below a consonant to signal its pronunciation. (These vowel signs followed different patterns, so different scholars resolved the resulting ambiguities in different ways until a uniform system was adopted, in Tiberias, in the fifth–sixth century of the Christian era.) *

In Hebrew, as in certain other languages, like Hopi, tenses as we know them in English do not exist; instead, there are "aspects of tense" (one for processes, one for endings). Masculine and feminine gender change blithely. The singular is freely used to represent the collective. Letters such as *tof* and *shin* were often used interchangeably. Because there are no relative pronouns in Hebrew, possessive adjectives change their endings—say, where dependent clauses appear without benefit of an introductory conjunction.

Nor is this all: A Hebrew sentence often runs verb-subject-object ("Plucked he daisies"), or entirely omits a verb: "To her a child" means "She bore a child."

Hebrew employs many connectives, but especially uses the letter *vov*—added as a conjunction; the combination is often translated as "and." But it can also mean "however ... but ... when ... because ... despite ... accordingly ... yet ... thereupon ..." etc.

The editors of the new translation of the Torah for the Jewish Publication Society of America (1962) say that to render the particle *waw* as "and," which was customary in old translations, "is

---

* Hindu priests faced the same problem when the popular pronunciation of their oldest hymns (in Vedic Sanskrit) began to diverge from the esoteric norm; this was a special problem because the faith required that rites employ exact chanting pronunciation, to be effective. Worse, whereas altered vocalizations represented a "corruption" of faith in the mystery religions, as in Greece, changes in the sound of Hindu texts were tantamount to sacrilege. So the Hindu priests, like the ancient Hebrew priests, were obliged to write down standard phonetic signs, to avoid the capriciousness of orally transmitted, memorized but unwritten pronunciations. (See David Crystal, *Linguistics, Language and Religion*, Burns and Oates, London, 1965, p.20.)

to misrepresent the Hebrew rather than to be faithful to it" (p. iii).

Hebrew sentences which contain *vov* were often given a *causal* content in English which is not justified by the Hebrew. To illustrate:

"He went into the garden and wept"

can also mean

"He went into the garden because he was weeping"

or

"He went into the garden after he wept"

or

"He went into the garden and, because of that, wept"

or

"Even though he went into the garden, he wept."

So I have changed "and" to whichever connective best conveys the meaning of the original text. For instance:

"Sin is sweet in the beginning and bitter in the end"

takes on greater force, I think, as

"Sin is sweet in the beginning *but* bitter in the end."

Before indignant experts rush in to remind me that "the original" of one or another Hebrew text is far better than the one from which I quote a passage, let me confess that for the sake of clarity or impact: (a) I have adapted or paraphrased as often as I have quoted; (b) I often use translations from Hebrew that were made specifically for me; (c) "original texts" may sound impressive, but they often turn out to be woefully deficient in accuracy or completeness.

Professor Benzion Halper, who edited the excellent anthology *Post-Biblical Hebrew Literature,* cautions us to remember that the old scribes themselves often used abbreviations, dropped occasional letters at the end of occasional words, and that individual words are not clearly divided, one from another, in old Hebrew manuscripts.

"Even the most careful manuscript or edition contains erroneous readings, and the most slovenly work sometimes preserves
correct passages. . . . In a vast number of cases . . . the texts
are hopelessly corrupt . . . the manuscripts and editions offer
no aid [and] I was obliged to resort to emendations."*

Puns were popular among the Hebrews, and prophecy via puns
will be found in Micah, Isaiah, Jeremiah, just as they were in the
Greek oracles, among the vestal virgins of Rome, and in Arabic
fables.** But puns are rarely preserved in translation, and where
tried are pitifully tortured.

---

* Benzion Halper, *Post-Biblical Hebrew Literature*, Jewish Publication Society
of America, Philadelphia, 1921, pp. xi–xii.
** *Jewish Encyclopedia, op. cit.*, vol. 10, p. 227. Professor Theodor H. Gaster
holds that Micah's lovely "Tell it not in Gath" rose from the phonetic similarity
of "Gath" and the Hebrew word for "tell" (*ta-gidhu-ū*); Isaiah deliberately called
the city of Dibon "*Dimon*," which would be filled with blood, for which the
Hebrew is "*dam*"; when Ezekiel says Gilgal "will be driven into exile" he is playing on *Gilgal* and *galah*, the Hebrew word for "exile." See Gaster, *Myth, Legend
and Custom in the Old Testament*, Harper and Row, New York, 1969, pp. 657–58.

III · Biographical Vignettes of the Authors Quoted

I HAVE tried in these vignettes to give the reader a succinct account of the life and teachings of the leading rabbis/ philosophers/scholars/poets who are named, in the preceding pages, as authors of individual quotations.

The profusion of Jewish scholars and philosophers called "rabbi" should be understood in its historical context. "Rabbi" means "my teacher," not "priest" or any version of a mediator between God and man. The title "rabbi" was not used until the beginning of the Christian Era.

Formal ordination, incidentally, ended in the fourth century and was not resumed until the fourteenth (see Headnote for RABBIS). And since formal ordination, by tradition, could only be performed in Palestine, and by a member of the Sanhedrin (which disappeared before the end of the fourth century), Jewish medieval scholars, Talmudists, philosophers, were called "rabbi," by their disciples or correspondents or laymen, as a tribute to their learning—not because of any ecclesiastical status or office. Jewish communities often conferred the title of "rabbi" on scholars or saintly wise men who had no diplomas of formal ordination—nor were they expected to have.

—L.R.

NOTE. Readers may wish to remember that, *"ben," "bar"* and *"ibn"* mean "son of" (respectively, in Hebrew, Aramaic, Arabic); that *"abba"* is Hebrew for "father of"; that when "i" ends a Hebrew name it means "son of."

Where "ibn" appears within a name, I do not capitalize it; when it appears as the initial word (e.g., "Ibn Tibbon"), I do.

ABRAVANEL (ABARBANEL, ABRABANEL), ISAAC A. (*1437–1508*)

Descended from an illustrious family of Spanish Jews, Abravanel, born in Lisbon, was a philosopher, scholar, and statesman who served Alfonso V of Portugal as treasurer and adviser. He was forced to flee to Spain, on charges of conspiracy, in 1483. He entered the court service of Ferdinand and Isabella. The 1492 decree expelling Jews from Spain (unless they converted to Catholicism) drove him to Italy, where he entered the service of King Ferdinand of Naples as diplomatic adviser. When the French took Naples, Abravanel went to Sicily, then Corfu, finally to Venice, where he served as a diplomatic negotiator for the government. He died in Venice in 1508.

Abravanel's copious, lucid writings include a commentary on the Bible (which influenced seventeenth- and eighteenth-century Christian exegesis), and religious writings that stressed belief in divine revelation and the Messiah. Sometimes called "the last Jewish Aristotelian," Abravanel was anti-Maimonidean; but what is confusing about him is his alternating defense of and attack upon rationalism and secular philosophy. His writings were important during the Messianic movements that swept Jewry (and Christian millenarian sects) in the sixteenth and seventeenth centuries.

AHAD (ACHAD) HA-AM (*"One of the People"*): *pen-name of ASHER GINZBERG. (1856–1927)*

A brilliant essayist, editor, and polemicist, of great influence in the late nineteenth and early twentieth centuries, Ginzberg was born in the Ukraine, settled in Odessa, and began to write essays critical of Theodor Herzl's "political" Zionism; for these he used the pseudonym "One of the People." He criticized the colonization of Palestine, which he visited several times; he advocated a revival of Judaism via "spiritual Zionism" for which a Jewish state in Palestine would be but a beginning.

He was active in the negotiations that led to the Balfour Declaration (1917) that committed England to the establishment of a Jewish "national home" in Palestine. In 1922, he moved to Tel Aviv. There he published his memoirs and correspondence (six volumes), which are invaluable as documentation in the history of modern Jewish politics and literature.

AKIBA (AKIVA): *AKIBA BEN JOSEPH.* (*40–135*)

The greatest Biblical scholar of his day, a true giant in the history of Judaism, Akiba was one of the *Tannaim* (a teacher during the period between Hillel's death and the generation after Judah ha-Nasi). He is often called "the father of Rabbinical Judaism." He single-handedly collected, collated, and arranged the entire body of "Oral Law" according to subject matter. This collection of the individual *halakot* served as the basis for the Mishnah. He also definitively fixed the canon of the Old Testament. (He opposed including *Ecclesiasticus*, which he admired.)

Akiba's was a work of incalculable importance, considering the disorganized and confused state of *halakot* (logical support for, and amplifications of, *halaka*). Akiba was driven by a desire to correct misinterpretations of Torah which resulted from the inaccuracies of Greek translations and were affecting the Jewish community. He developed a system of analysis that assigned every word, letter, or symbol of the Torah some specific significance, usable in rabbinical decisions. He insisted that the wording of the Torah was entirely different from all other books.

The brilliance of Akiba's work effected many changes in Jewish law, customs, and social life (e.g. he changed prevailing attitudes to women, slavery, intermarriage—all in a liberal direction). There is not an aspect of the Judaic conception of God, heaven, the origin of man, freedom of will, eschatology, ethics, justice that was not profoundly affected by Akiba.

All this is the more astonishing if we consider that Akiba was virtually uneducated until he was forty, and for years was an *am ha-arets* (ignorant man) who detested the "pedantry" of the rabbis. Born in Lydda, Palestine, Akiba was a shepherd who, with a large family dependent upon him, enrolled at forty in the academy headed by Eliezer ben Hyrcanos). After thirteen years of study, he became a teacher, then established his own school in Bene Berak, near Jaffa. Akiba's academy, said to have had 24,000 students, produced some of the greatest *Tannaim* of the second century (Eleazer ben Shammai, Rabbi Meir, Simeon ben Yohai) and an immense number of followers and disciples.

Rabbi Akiba was a man of spotless character, vast kindness, great humility; his teachings stressed modesty and scorned anyone "who esteems himself for his knowledge." He traveled widely among the Jewish communities in and outside Palestine. He considered the greatest precept of Judaism to be: "Thou shalt love thy neighbor as thyself" (Leviticus, 19), yet turned nationalist in politics. He hailed Bar Kochba (*q.v.*) as the Messiah, and supported the Jewish revolt against Roman rule. When the Roman authorities forbade the teaching of Torah, Akiba publicly ignored it. He was imprisoned, then condemned to death, in Caesarea, by one of Hadrian's officials.

Akiba was flayed alive. As the skin was raked from his living body, he recited his *Shema* (the Hebrew prayer that begins "Hear, O Israel, The Lord our God, the Lord is One"); he was asked how he could endure such pain, and whether he was some sort of magician. Akiba replied: "No, but I rejoice at this chance to love my God 'with all my life,' having until now only been able to serve him 'with all my means.'" That scene has become part of Jewish tradition: The association of the *Shema* with Akiba's death has made the prayer a common death-bed affirmation of faith.

ALBO, JOSEPH. (*c. 1380–c. 1435*)

Spanish religious philosopher, a disciple of Hasdai Crescas, the Crown Rabbi of Aragon. Albo participated in the famous "Disputation of Tortosa" (1414) between Christians and Jews. His *Sefer ha-Ikkarim* ("Book of Principles") is an outstanding statement of medieval Jewish philosophy and faith, concerned with those questions of the Messiah and salvation with which Christian theologians were challenging Judaism. Albo distinguished between secular, natural, and Divine law—and assigned sacred primacy to the third. Like many medieval philosophers, he tried to use reason and experience as guides to finding God's will, and ended by stressing faith, revelation, and miracles.

ALFASI, ISAAC BEN JACOB; *also known as ISAAC BEN JACOB HA-KOHEN. Acronym: "Rif."* (*1013–1103*)

This illustrious scholar-judge was called "Alfasi" ("man of Fez") because he came from Fez and taught there until he was driven to Cordoba, Spain, at the age of seventy-five. He attracted many disciples (among them, Maimonides' future teacher) and composed distinguished *responsa* from North Africa and Spain. He concentrated on the study of the Talmud and collected its legal data and judgments in the *Sefer ha-Halakhot* ("Book of Legal Decisions"), colloquially called *Alfas.* This massive work, the most authoritative text on Talmud until Maimonides superseded it, was so important (during the period when the reading, study, or discussion of the Talmud was prohibited by secular authorities) that it was called "the little Talmud." Alfasi omitted all Haggadic material. In cases of conflict between the Babylonian and Jerusalem Talmuds, he chose to follow the former. The *Sefer ha-Halakhot* inspired a great many commentaries and critical analyses. Alfasi was greatly admired by Maimonides, who, in his *Commentary on the Mishnah,* called Alfasi's juridical decisions "unassailable" (except for a handful). Alfasi died at ninety; on his gravestone is inscribed:

> ". . . the angels of God approached thee
> And wrote the Torah on the tablets of thy heart . . ."

"AL-HARIZI": JUDAH BEN SOLOMON BEN HOPHNI; *also known as "ALHARIZI."* (*c. 1170–c. 1235*)

"Al-Harizi," born in Spain, is one of the leading lights and poets of medieval Hebrew literature. He used an informal humorous style, typical of medieval Arabic and Hebrew literature, traveled widely, and wrote about a great variety of subjects. He was the author of *Takhemoni* ("Apothecary"), which consists of fifty *makamot,* or narratives in rhymed prose—an Arabic literary form which he introduced into Hebrew literature. He translated many books from Arabic into Hebrew, including Maimonides' *Guide for the Perplexed.*

ANAV (ANAU, ANAW), JEHIEL BEN JEKUTHIEL: *Hebrew name: Min Ha-Anavim. (Thirteenth century)*

This family, presumably settled in Rome by the emperor Titus, and known in Italian as Piatelli or Mansi, produced many scholars, physicians and poets. Jehiel Ben Jekuthiel was an author, poet, and copyist of sacred texts. He wrote a liturgical poem to commemorate the burning of the synagogue in Rome in 1268. His most popular work is *Maalot ha-Midot* ("The Merit of the Rules").

ARAMA, ISAAC: ISAAC BEN MOSES ARAMA. (*c. 1420–1494*)

Born in Spain (probably in Zamora, where he was head of a rabbinical academy), he served as rabbi in Tarragona, in Fraga, in Calatayud. He sought to counteract the effects of the Christian sermons which the Jews in Spain were compelled to attend. The 1492 decree, expelling all Jews from Spain, drove him to Naples, where he worked and where he finally died.

His major efforts were devoted to refuting philosophers who emphasized Judaism's philosophical, rather than theological, content, or who denied the special nature of God's revelation to the Jews. His best-known book is *Akedat Yitshak* ("The Offering [or "Binding"] of Isaac"): a tract on the relationship between theology and philosophy.

ASHER BEN JEHIEL (JECHIEL); *also known as HA-ASHER and ASHERI (both meaning "the Asherite"), or by the acronym "the RoSH" (from "Rabbenu Asher"). (1250–1327). Do not confuse him with Judah ben Asher (q.v.), his son, or Jacob, his brother.*

Asher ben Jehiel was born in Germany, lived in southern France, then went to Toledo, where he became a rabbi. A leading student of Rabbi Meir of Rothenburg, he followed his teacher's absolute opposition to "liberal" interpretations of Talmud. Asher violently opposed all but Talmudic thought, held religion and philosophy to be incompatible, and hewed to the theological conservatism dominating German Jewry. He fought the influence of Maimonides and even tried to persuade the Toledo synod to forbid Jews to read Greek, Latin, or Islamic books. His influence weakened the contemporary movement in which Jewish students and scholars were acquainting themselves with the classics, secular literature, and works in science.

Asher's abstracts of *halakot* (Talmudic laws), which deliberately excluded the Haggadic (non-legalistic) aspects and debate, are attributed in most editions of the Talmud to "Rabbenu Asher"—from which comes the acronym "Rosh." The rabbinical *decisions* which he himself handed down were separately collected and published (by his son Jacob) as *Piske ha-Rosh.* Asher's *responsa* (answers to questions on Judaic law) provide rich, first-hand information about Jews in Spain in the first decades of the fourteenth century.

ASHI: *RAB ASHI.* (*c. 352–c. 427*)

The *Rab* ("master") tells us Ashi was a very great rabbi; in fact, he was the leader of the academy at Sura for over fifty years —and chief editor of the Babylonian Talmud, which he arranged, collated, and edited (with the assistance, in so monumental a task, of many scholars and students). He collected all the interpretations of the Mishnah which had been handed down in Babylonian rabbinical academies—to compose the Gemara (*see Glossary*). The Gemara incorporated into the Babylonian Talmud the pertinent discussions of the *Amoraim* (Jewish lecturer–scholar–law-givers in Palestine and Babylon).

Ashi's phenomenal erudition and rigorous judgment make him one of the cardinal figures in all Talmudic thought. He revived Sura as a center of rabbinical thought, and reconstructed both the academy and the synagogue so that their physical splendor became legendary.

"BAAL SHEM TOV (TOB)" *or* "BA'AL SHEM-TOV" (*"Master of the Good Name"*) *or* " *the BeSHT*" (*the acronym*): IS-RAEL BEN ELIEZER. (*1700–1760*)

The founder of the remarkable Hasidic movement; a revered, immensely influential, legendary figure, credited with many miraculous cures. *"Baal Shem"* was the name given to men of saintly deportment whom Eastern European Jews believed to possess magical powers (presumably attained through recondite manipulations of the letters that form God's Name), men chosen by the Lord Himself for divine purposes.

Israel ben Eliezer was the most important of these "holy men," a Polish Jew, a *melamed* (teacher of children), a lime-burner turned evangelist. He was a visionary who preached simple sermons in an ecstatic, "God-possessed" style. He traveled about spreading a simple gospel: "Love God, love Torah, love Man." He urged his faithful to celebrate the Lord by enjoying life—in song, laughter, spontaneous dancing, ecstatic states, unrestrained evidence of adoration of the Holy One. All of this infuriated orthodox rabbis and scandalized traditionalists.

Eliezer was a gifted aphorist who scoffed at the learned, whom he called sterile pedants: "They spend so much time studying Talmud they have no time to think about God." The Lord, said Eliezer, is served by deeds and joy, by living out the precepts of the Torah—*not* by obsessive reading and academic preoccupations with texts.

The Baal Shem's adoring disciples grew until they numbered some 10,000 semi-frenzied souls; their sanctified leader, branded a mountebank or a heretic by the rabbis of Poland and Galicia, was formally excommunicated by the illustrious Gaon of Vilna, who banned all of Eliezer's teachings. But Eliezer's influence continued to grow, for

> the Besht said to the poor and the ignorant: God is in everything, including man. Every man, therefore, is good, and even a sinner can approach God with devotion. It does not matter that a simple Jew is unlearned—honest prayer is as important as erudition. . . . Man must enjoy human passions, not repress them or run from them. . . . An entire culture within the culture of the *shtetl* grew up around the liberating visions of the *Baal Shem Tov*—and ended, as movements begun by simple men often do, in a cult."*

The Baal Shem "rejuvenated" Jewry, says Professor A. J. Heschel; for through Rabbi Israel ben Eliezer Jews "fell in love with the Lord and felt such yearning for God that it was

---

* *Joys of Yiddish*, p. 24.

unbearable. . . . In the days of Moses, Israel had a revelation of God; in the days of the Baal Shem, God had a revelation of Israel."*

Eliezer never wrote down his sermons, parables and sayings. They were included in the various works of his disciples, especially in the publications (about twenty years after the Besht's death) of Jacob Joseph of Polonya. They constitute a remarkable body of homely acumen, exalted aspiration, and touching phrasing.

The Baal Shem carried on the cabalistic teachings of Isaac ben Solomon Luria (*q.v.*), sometimes known as "Ari," whose teachings were posthumously presented in the writings of a disciple, Hayyim Vital (*q.v.*).

BACHYA (BAHYA) BEN ASHER: *full name BACHYA BEN ASHER IBN HALAWA. (d. 1340)*

He was born in Saragossa and was a student of Solomon ben Adret, but was more influenced by the works of Ben Adret's teacher, Nachmanides (*q.v.*), whose example Bahya followed in using the cabala as a basis for interpreting scripture. His best known work is a commentary on the Pentateuch. He also wrote *Kad ha-Kemah* ("The Jug of Flour"), an ethical work based on cabalistic concepts.

BAHUR. *See LEVITA, ELIJAH.*

BAR KOCHBA or BAR COCHBA or BAR KOKHBA (*Hebrew: "Son of the Star"*); *the popular name for SIMEON BAR (or BEN) KOSIBA or COZIBA. (d. 135 of the Christian Era)*

For centuries, the heroic figure of Bar Kochba has been a part of Jewish folklore, but "more myth than man." Scholars and historians possessed scanty data about "the Second Revolt" of the Jews against the Roman oppressors of Jerusalem. But the Dead Sea caves yielded a priceless cache of letters, 1800 years old, which have authenticated Bar Kochba, his warriors, his successes against the Roman legions, his brief restoration of a Jewish state.

---

* A. J. Heschel, *The Earth Is the Lord's,* Abelard-Schuman, New York, 1964, pp. 76–98.

A great revolutionary leader, Bar Kochba claimed to be the Messiah, descended from David, and led the revolt against Hadrian in 132. The revered Rabbi Akiba became his shield-bearer, and acclaimed him the Messiah, but others disputed this overly optimistic view. The ultra-orthodox called Bar Kosiba "Bar Coziba" ("son of deceit") because he once cried, before going into battle: "O Lord, don't help us—and don't spoil it for us!"

Bar Kochba captured Jerusalem, proclaimed a new Jewish state, and held off large, superior Roman armies for over three years. In 135, a Roman counterattack, commanded by Julius Severus, defeated Bar Kochba's forces in their last stronghold, Betar, where Bar Kochba was slain. Records of the time say that 985 villages were destroyed and that 580,000 Jews died in the long fighting (apart from the thousands who perished of hunger and disease).

Rather little is known of Bar Kochba's personal life and characteristics; the anecdotes about him in the Talmud picture him as daring, impetuous, and autocratic—attributes confirmed by the testimony of the letters recently found near the Dead Sea. (See Yigael Yadin, *Bar-Kokhba,* Random House, New York, 1971.)

"THE BELZER RABBI": *SHALOM BEN ELEAZAR.* (*19th cent.*)

Little has been published in English, so far as I can discover, about this hasid who lived in the Galician town of Belz for fifty years, from about 1816 to 1856, and there "founded a hasidic dynasty"; his office passed down to his son, grandson, and great-grandson. Like most hasidic rabbis, his sayings were transmitted orally and recorded by later disciples. Sayings and anecdotes concerning the Belzer Rabbi have appeared in a number of hasidic works: *Dober Sholom* is a collection devoted mainly to him; a recent biography, *Ha-Rab mi-Belz* ("The Rabbi from Belz"), was published in Israel.

BENJAMIN BEN JONAN, OF TUDELA (*BENJAMIN OF TU-DELA*). (*Twelfth century*)

This celebrated rabbi, merchant, traveler-memoirist was the first European to describe the Far East—as far, that is, as the bor-

ders of China. He lived in Tudela, northern Spain, and between
1160 and 1165 set forth from Saragossa on journeys from which
he did not return for seven or eight (some say thirteen)
years. He kept clear, carefully detailed notes, from which his
travelogue was compiled (by another hand) in 1543. It was
translated into Latin, German, French, Dutch, English (in
1625). Benjamin visited almost 300 different places—from
France and Italy to Corfu, Greece, Palestine, Turkey, Syria,
Egypt, Iraq, and Sicily. He was at one time believed to have
entered China, before Marco Polo, but present experts doubt
that he went beyond India and Ceylon.

His travel book, *Masaot shel Rabi Binyamin,* contains invaluable data and astute observations on the politics, commerce, geography, and customs of the places he visited—plus
the information he collected, in his travels, about places to
which he never went. Like all travelers in those days, he
made many errors and accepted some tall stories. But his descriptions of Constantinople or Genoa or Alexandria, his observations on Greeks, Turks, Druzes, his comments on officials of
the Byzantine court, the Baghdad caliphate—all have proved
to be accurate and are invaluable to historians.

Benjamin was especially interested in the communities of
Jews, wherever he went, and his accounts of medieval Jewish
life are among the best and richest available; they testify to
a far-ranging curiosity about everything from schools and synagogues to civil status and occupations. He collected statistical
data on the number of Jews in various places—among the
first numerical facts gathered on Jewish populations. He catalogued Jewish trades and tradesmen (silk, dyeing, glass-mak-
ing, ship-building, etc.). He described special Jewish sects in
Cyprus, Damascus, Caesarea, etc. His story of David Alroy
(Menachim ben Solomon), a famous false messiah of Mesopo-
tamia, is the principal source of our information on that colorful, learned, dubious character who led a messianic movement that began among the "Mountain Jews" of Persia.

The appendix to Benjamin of Tudela's book contains unusual information he had gathered about places and people
he did not visit: Slavic lands, the Jews in Germany, northern
France. A sample of Benjamin's travelogue is included in *Jewish Travellers,* edited by Elkan N. Adler (Hermon Press, 1966,

pp. 38–63); the full text was translated and critically examined by Marcus Nathan Adler, London, H. Froude, 1907 (out
of print, alas).

BEN NATRONAI. *See BERECHIAH BEN NATRONAI, HA-
NAKDAN.*

**BEN SIRACH, JESUS, or JESHUA BEN ELEAZAR BEN SIRA,
or SIMEON BEN SIRACH;** *his Hebrew name, SIMEON, was
given in Greek as JESUS or JESHUA. (fl. around 180 before
the Christian Era)*

He is the author of the immortal *Ecclesiasticus* (also known as
the *Book of Proverbs* or *Sayings of Jesus ben Sirach*) which
was composed around 180 B.C., was translated into Greek in
132 B.C. by his grandson, and was subsequently included as
as major part of the Apocrypha.

A remarkable lyrical poet and a brilliant aphorist, Ben
Sirach belonged to an elite group of scholars and scribes in
Jerusalem. He was a renowned teacher in his own school. His
work belongs to the "Wisdom Literature" of the Hebrews, in
which the recounting of proverbs, parable and fables played
an important role. Ben Sirach modestly said he was a "grape-
gatherer," but he embroiders earlier proverbs with much
beauty and originality. He was a worldly man, widely traveled,
forever inspired and enthralled by the services in the Temple.
His poetic apothegms contain striking, shrewd, pragmatic observations on man's nature, good and evil, wisdom, free will,
parents, children, even commerce.

It is fascinating to note that even though the Talmud
(Sanhedrin: 100b) lists Ben Sirach as one of the forbidden
books, "outside" the canon, the rabbis often quoted him, and
his book was translated from Hebrew into Aramaic—which
was the vernacular of Hebrews in Palestine in that time. So
well known was Ben Sirach that many of his proverbs, when
quoted, simply began "It has been written" or "It is said"—
the formal phrase used to introduce sayings from the Old
Testament.

He tried to demonstrate the superiority of Judaism over
Hellenistic thought, but shows the influence of the latter. (For
instance, he considers earthly wisdom part of the Law, the

wise virtuous, the foolish wicked—whereas preceding philosophers of Judaism sharply separated divine from human wisdom.)

Ben Sirach's original Hebrew text, which took the Book of Proverbs as its model, was lost in the late tenth century. In 1896, many manuscripts were discovered in the *genizah* ("hiding place") of the Fostat (Cairo) Synagogue; it was from these and later discoveries (over 100,000 leaves) that Ben Sirach's great work was reconstructed, by Professor Solomon Schechter. In the Masada excavations (1964) under Yigael Yagin, five more chapters were unearthed. But no single manuscript to this day contains the complete Hebrew text of that masterpiece, *Ecclesiasticus*.

BEN ZOMA, SIMEON. (*fl. early 2nd cent. of the Christian Era*)

A famous *Tanna* (teacher) and mystic, famed and acclaimed for his erudition. It was said: "Whoever sees Ben Zoma in his dream is assured of scholarship." Only a few of his written paragraphs have come down to us (most of what we know comes from the disciples who quoted him), but they are enough to indicate his skill and fecundity as an aphorist. It is believed that his theosophical ventures into "the garden of esoteric knowledge" caused Ben Zoma finally to display signs of mental aberration.

"THE BERDICHEVER RABBI": *LEVI ISAAC OF BERDICHEV, or LEVI ISAAC BEN MEIR. (1740–1809)*

This chasidic luminary led congregations in Pinsk and Berdichev (or Berdychev) in the Ukraine, and wrote a compilation of ethical sayings. His prayers, Yiddish poems, and songs were widely loved; his Hebrew work *Kedushat Levi* ("The Holiness of Levi;" "The Holy Prayer of Rabbi Levi"), a commentary on the Pentateuch, is considered a classic of hasidic literature. Many legends surround his name and life.

BERECHIAH BEN NATRONAI, HA-NAKDAN (*"the Translator" or "Punctuator"*); *also known as Berechya ben Natronai, and Benedict le Pointeur ("Punctuator"). (Twelfth–thirteenth century)*

Berechiah, a scribe-punctuator of Bible texts, was a leading writer of fables. He lived in France and England, knew Latin, French and (perhaps) English as well as Hebrew, and is best known for his very popular *Mishle Shualim* (*"Fox Tales"*). This charming collection of 119 folk stories leaned heavily on Aesop, though it includes fables from Hebrew, the Talmud, Midrash—plus many tales Berechiah probably invented. The stories are neatly satirical, offering moral homilies about animals and insects and even the Leviathan which depict quite human foibles and failings. Berechiah achieved delightful comic effects through his allusions to Hebraic sayings and Talmudic passages, having a dog or wolf, say, calmly quote a well-known passage from one of the Prophets. In the original, the prose is rhymed—which suffers greatly, I am told, in translation. (Incidentally, the Fox does not appear in every story, as one would expect from the book's title: Berechiah was simply using the Talmud's generic name, "fox tales," for fables of any sort.)

"THE BERSHIDER RABBI": *RAPHAEL (RAFAEL) OF BERSHID or BERSHAD.* (*d. 1816*)

All I can find out about "The Bershider" is that he was a disciple of "The Koretser Rabbi" (*q.v.*). Like many hasidic rabbis, he wrote little or nothing, but is remembered through the sagacities, uttered to his flock, that were widely repeated and carried down the oral stream of attributions.

THE "BESHT." See *BAAL SHEM TOV.*

BET HILLEL (*"School of Hillel"*).

"BET HILLEL" and "BET SHAMMAI" were the contending schools of *Tannaim* (teachers) during the first century of the Christian era. They differed sharply in their approach to, and decisions on, several hundred cases. We are told that the clash of philosophical premises almost led to a small civil war among the Jews; but it should be remembered that philosophical differences often were enmeshed with political disagreements —especially about rebellion against Roman rule. The school of Shammai represented an ultra-nationalistic political position.

In general, the school of Shammai held the more conservative position, and the Hillelites what may be called the liberal, humanistic view. But in some cases, the positions were reversed; sometimes one faction would adopt the analytic method and conclusions of the other. The doctrines of the School of Hillel eventually prevailed in most cases involving Jewish law. One legend holds that a proclamation supporting the Hillel school was issued by a BAT KOL, "divine voice," from heaven itself. Such advocacy was difficult to contest.

BIALIK, CHAIM NACHMAN, *or HAYYIM NAHMAN BIALIK.* (*1873–1934*)

A great Hebrew poet, a commanding figure in modern Jewish literature, and a central force in twentieth-century Judaic culture. Born in Russia, Bialik moved to Berlin and founded several publishing houses. He became Chairman of the *Vaad ha-Lashon* ("Hebrew Language Council") in Tel Aviv, where he went to live in 1924. Bialik was a spearhead in reviving and modernizing Hebrew—as writer, publisher, editor, translator, anthologist. He translated Shakespeare, Cervantes, *The Dybbuk,* and *William Tell* into Hebrew.

He wrote many exquisite poems and stories, a classic anthology of Midrashic literature (with Y. H. Rabnitsky), and edited the poems of Moses ibn Ezra and Solomon ibn Gabirol. He was a discerning anthologist of Jewish folk tales and played an important role on the board of editors of The Hebrew Technical Dictionary (1929).

"THE BRATSLAVER RABBI". *See NACHMAN OF BRATSLAV.*

BUBER, MARTIN (*1878–1965*)

One of the great philosopher-theologians of the modern era, Martin Buber was born in Vienna, raised in Lvov, Poland, studied at German universities, was profoundly influenced by hasidic thought, and envisioned religion as a continuing dialogue between God and man: In this, he exercised a profound and enduring influence on Christian theology.

Buber edited the Zionist journal *Die Welt* ("The World") and founded the so-called "democratic faction" of the Zionist movement. With Franz Rosenzweig, he made a German translation of the Bible. Buber served as Professor of the Philosophy of Jewish Religion and Ethics at the University of Frankfurt. He settled in Jerusalem in 1938, and became Professor of the Sociology of Religion at the Hebrew University. He was a strong advocate of *rapprochement* between Jews and Arabs.

His best known works, in English, are *Tales of the Chasidim* (or *Hasidim*), *I and Thou, Between Man and Man, The Prophetic Faith.*

BUBER, SOLOMON (1827–1906)

Grandfather of Martin Buber, Solomon Buber was a scholar of Talmud who earned his livelihood as a businessman in Lvov, Poland. He discovered important ancient *midrashim* in obscure manuscripts and published them with comprehensive notes. Buber wrote many essays on the history of the Polish Jews, and edited medieval masterworks by Rashi (*q.v.*), Saadia Gaon (*q.v.*), and others.

BUNIM (BUNAM), SIMCHA: *SIMCHA BUNAN (BUNAM) BUNEHART; also known as "the Cosmopolitan Rebbe."* (1765–1827)

This exceptional rationalist, the son of a *maggid* (itinerant teacher-preacher), disciple of such seers as Rabbi Moses Leib of Sassov (*q.v.*), followed the advice of Rabbi Israel of Kozienice, and went to work as the representative of an industrialist. He led a rich, secular life, abandoning his hasidic clothes and enjoying the Polish and German theater. Then he became a factor in lumber, then a chemist. But his interest in Talmud and hasidism did not die; each night, he closed his apothecary shop and consulted "the Jew of Bunim Pzysha," Rabbi Jacob Isaac; and when that worthy soul died, Bunim succeeded him as rabbi.

Bunim emphasized Maimonides and Judah ben Low ben Bezalel of Prague—against those who were following the Baal Shem (*q.v.*). Bunim placed little faith in cabalism—and none in popularly touted "miracles." Indeed, his scorn for "the cult of the *tsadik* [saint]" was expressed in a dry epigram: "A fur hat and an illustrious father do not make a *tsadik*."

Bunim went blind, accepting this fate philosophically:

"What is good for me to see, I see—with 'the inner light.' That which would not be good for me to see, I do not wish to see at all." Rabbi Bunim was a prolific producer of parables which are quoted to this day; they explain the admiration he has continued to enjoy.

CARO (KARO), JOSEPH: *or JOSEPH BEN EPHRAIM CARO. Not to be confused with at least eight other rabbis or historians, in Poland, German, Russia, Turkey, who bear the distinguished family name of Caro. (1488–1575)*

Joseph Caro was the last of the great codifiers of the rabbinical laws and interpretations of the Law. His *Shulhan Arukh* ("The Prepared Table"), published in 1564, is still accepted in orthodox circles as the final code of authority on Judaic law, ethics, and ritual.

Caro was born in either Portugal or Spain and went to Turkey with his parents. He became strongly interested in mysticism, though not (oddly enough) in the cabala; and he even yearned for a martyr's fate "to sanctify God's sacred Name." (In this, he was influenced by Solomon Molcho, a Portuguese-Spanish convert to Judaism.) Caro had many dreams, which he called revelations from a divine mentor who was the Mishnah personified.

He emigrated to Palestine, after several years in Salonica and Constantinople. In Safed, under Jacob Berab, who ordained him, Caro founded his own *yeshiva*. His *Bet Yosef* ("House of Joseph"), an extraordinary commentary and analysis of Talmudic and post-Talmudic literature from which the *Shulhan Aruk* was digested, brought him tremendous prestige —and an authority such as had not honored any Jewish intellectual since Maimonides. Rabbis wrote to him from Italy and France for his judgment on complex cases—despite recurring discontent with his messianic strain.

He alleged that he was being made privy to great secrets confided to him by an angel. But his codifications of Judaic Law show no signs of his mystical predilections. And the sheer range and detail of his "Table" can only elicit admiration; he instructs the reader in such matters as Thoughts While Shampooing Hair; Tatooing and Depilation; Can Interest Be Taken on Loans?; The Taboo on Excessive Displays of Excessive Grief; Promises and Vows and Oaths, etc.

The historic *Shulhan Aruk* survived violent attacks from the rabbis of Poland and the influential Solomon Luria; the Ashkenazic rabbis thought that the Sephardim, of whom Caro was of course one, were prone to introduce "dangerous" innovations in ritual and liturgy. The hostility to the *Shulhan Aruk* raged for a century after its appearance, but in the middle of the seventeenth century the classic began to be accepted by even Polish Talmudists.

Some authorities consider Caro too rigid and his Judaism, therefore, "a strait-jacket." But no one questions his massive scholarship or his achievement in reconciling Sephardic and Ashkenazic religious practices.

CASPI, JOSEPH BEN ABBA MARI *Not to be confused with his namesake, Joseph Caspi ben Shalom of the sixteenth century.* (*c. 1280–c. 1340*)

Born and raised in the south of France, Caspi (which stands for "made of silver," a surname derived from his birthplace, Largentière) traveled widely in France, Spain, and Egypt. His Provençal name was Don Bonafous de Largentera.

A philosopher and grammarian, he was greatly influenced by Aristotle and Averroes, whose teachings he found entirely consonant with Judaism: This did not endear him to medieval rabbis. Many of Caspi's works (he was a prolific author) were lost; his most important two books are commentaries on Maimonides' *Guide for the Perplexed*. Strict Talmudists reprove Caspi for his belief that the universe is eternal—*i.e.*, was not made by God.

CHAIM OF VOLOZHIN. *See HAYYIM BEN ISAAC.*

CHIA, RABBI. *See HIYYA.*

"CHOFETZ CHAIM" or HAPHETZ HAYYIM ("He who desires life"); *also called RABBI HACOHEN. ISRAEL MEIR KAHAN.* (*1838–1933*)

A formidable rabbi, one of the most respected leaders of Ashkenazic Jewry, "The Chofetz Chaim" told and invented hundreds of homely folk stories, each with a moral designed to underline a total preoccupation with Torah and service to the Almighty.

His pen-name comes from a story in the Talmud ('Abodah Zarah, 19b): Rabbi Alexandrai stretches out his hands to the people and asks: "Who wants life?" As they flocked to him, Rabbi Alexandrai told them to re-read King David's words [34th Psalm]: "Who is the man who desires life, and wants to enjoy happiness for many days? Keep your tongue from evil and your lips from deceit. Avoid evil and do good; seek peace and pursue it."

A bearded, formidable figure, Rabbi Hacohen wrote a considerable number of books—mostly meant for laymen: as guides to living; to reinforce piety, prayer, purity of devotion, the sanctity of the family, one's primary duty to God; or to discourage gossip, encourage charity; or to lift the hearts of Jewish soldiers drafted into foreign armies, or to comfort Jews lonely in far-off lands.

All of his tales and writings were permeated by absolute fundamentalism, unswerving orthodoxy, insistence on every jot and tittle of gospel truth.

One story illustrates this patriarch's acting-out of one of the 613 *mitzvahs:* A thief stole a parcel from the rabbi's person and shot away—and "Chofetz Chaim" ran after him, frantically yelling, "I forgive you! I forgive you!"

He died at the age of ninety-five.

CORDOVERO, MOSES BEN JACOB; *also known as RAMAK or REMAK.* (1522–1570)

Moses Cordovero, rabbi of Safed, came from a Spanish Jewish family, no doubt from Cordoba's illustrious colony of Jews. He studied under the great Caro (*q.v.*) and proceeded to explore the cabala and its mysteries. Extremely competent in Arabic philosophy as well as Judaic thought, Cordovero became a leader of the mystical school in Safed. His expositions of the fundamentals of cabalistic theology (divine emanations, the Names of God, hidden significances attributed to letters of the Hebrew alphabet, etc.) won him great renown. Cordovero echoed Aristotle's ideas that the thinking of the Lord must be different, in kind, from human modalities of reason—that in divine thinking, the thought and the material objects thought

of, are inseparable, one, absolute. Spinoza probably read
Cordovero with profit: their conceptions of God are strikingly
similar. *Pardes Rimonim* ("Orchard of Pomengrates") is the
work by which Cordovero is best remembered.

DELMEDIGO, ELIJAH: *ELIJAH CRETENSIS BEN MOSES ABBA DELMEDIGO. Do not confuse with Joseph Solomon ben Elijah Delmedigo (q.v.). (1460–1497)*

Delmedigo (from the Italian "del Medico") is the name of a famous
Jewish family of scholars and physicians who emigrated from
Germany to Crete, in the late fourteenth century, and were
rabbis on that island for generations.

Elijah ben Moses was born in Candia, as a child showed
unusual intellect, and in his early twenties was invited to head
a Talmudic school in Padua. His Latin was elegant. He held
chairs in philosophy at the universities of Padua, Venice, Peru-
gia and Florence. (Pico della Mirandola, the great Renaissance
humanist, was one of his students—and was to translate the
Zohar into Latin.)

Elijah Delmedigo became one of the stars in the brilliant
galaxy of talent in Florence. He expounded the theories of
Maimonides and Averroes, whose work he translated, and wrote
learned commentaries on Plato and Aristotle. In Judaic matters,
he attacked cabala ("an intellectual swamp"), upheld the
halakic portions of Talmud as divine, but said the Haggadic
portions could claim no sanction higher than that of mortal
judgments. Jealousies, intrigues, and a quarrel with the rabbi
of Padua, who distrusted Delmedigo's secular writings and disliked his staunch independence in religion, drove Delmedigo
to return to Crete. He taught philosophy there. His reputation
grew so great that upon his death "crowds of learned Christians, clad in mourning" attended his funeral.

His best-known book, an effort to separate philosophy and
religion, is *Behinat ha-Dat* ("Examination of Religion"), from
which the quotations in the present anthology were taken.

DELMEDIGO, JOSEPH SOLOMON BEN ELIJAH; *also known by the acronym YaSHaR (from JOSEPH SOLOMON ROFE). Do not confuse with Elijah ben Moses Delmedigo (q.v.). (1591–1655)*

Born in Candia, Crete, of the distinguished Jewish Italian family of physicians and scholars, Joseph Solomon Delmedigo, son of the rabbi of Candia, entered the University of Padua when fifteen, and specialized in mathematics and astronomy. He was a physician, philosopher, mathematician, Talmudic scholar, and astronomer (he studied under Galileo). He often visited Leone da Modena (*q.v.*) in Venice, and was influenced by that ingenious, erratic figure.

Delmedigo's somewhat secular views made life in Crete difficult for him; he went to Cairo, to find books to add to his library; and there met Karaite Jews—and wrote a book on mechanics. In Turkey, he studied the cabala. Then he visited or worked in Germany, Holland, Bohemia, Poland (he was personal physician to Prince Radziwill, in Vilna); was for a time a teacher of Sephardic Jews and a rabbi in Hamburg and Amsterdam; served as town physician of Frankfurt; and settled in Prague, in 1648, where he lived until his death.

Joseph Delmedigo's reputation was marred by the fact that he defended the Cabala publicly but scoffed at it in private. For all his piety and erudition, he won a reputation for insincerity; I think he feared being accused of heresy.

But he was a far-ranging intelligence, of notable versatility and outstanding scholarship. He wrote on logic, chemistry, geometry, harmony, ancient science, astronomy, metaphysics, optics. He translated Hippocrates' Latin aphorisms into Hebrew, and some of Philo's and Abravanel's writings. His *Sefer Elim* ("Book of Elim," an allusion to Exodus, 15 : 27) answers twelve questions in science, gives seventy paradoxes in mathematics, and is a collection of various writings.

EIBESCHUTZ, JONATHAN (*EYBESHITZ, EYBESCHITZ, EYBENSCHUTZ*). (*c. 1690–1764*)

Born in Cracow, Eibeschutz became one of the leading scholars and Talmudists of his time. He presided over a *yeshiva* in Prague and became the chief rabbi of Metz, Germany. He was an authority on the cabala. Some thought him a follower of the legendary, notorious Sabbatai (or Shabbetai) Zvi (or Zvei or Zevi), "the Messiah of Izmir," one of the more amazing mystics and mountebanks of the seventeenth century. (See my *Joys of Yiddish*, pp. 503–7).

ELEAZAR (ELIEZER) HA-KAPPAR; *not to be confused with his son, Bar Kappara. (Second century)*

This fourth-generation *Tanna* is quoted several times in the Mishnah (*Aboth*, 4, 21–22). His lucid exhortations on peace, virtue, envy, ambition, evil, and the judgment of God are cited in the *Pirke d'Rabbi Nathan* (xxiv, 4), in *Derekh Erets Zuta* (9, 1), and in *Sifre Be-Midbar* ("Sifre on the Book of Numbers").

Authorities caution us that Eleazar's son, Bar Kappara, may have coined some of the precepts attributed to his father. Bar Kappara collected *The Mishnah of Bar Kappara*. He was a brilliant maker of fables and conversationalist, and headed an academy near Lydda (Lod).

ELEAZAR BEN JUDAH of WORMS: *also known as ELEAZAR ROKEACH (ROKEAH). (c. 1160 or 1176–1238)*

This Talmudic scholar, a native of Mayence, and a rabbi in Worms, was descended from the famous Kalonymus family. In 1196, two Crusaders broke into his home and murdered his wife and two daughters (and possibly his son, too) before his eyes.

Eleazar ben Judah was immensely erudite, studied astronomy and, as a liturgist, wrote over fifty psalms and dirges. Absorbed in cabala, he stressed the confession of sin and its heartfelt repentance. He popularized an haggadic mysticism that was to be profoundly influential among the Ashkenazim. In 1233, he participated in the historic Synod of Mayence, which produced a body of important Judaic enactments.

Eleazar published many treatises: on the unity of God, gematria, confession, mystical ruminations about different passages of Torah and the psalms, commentaries on the prayers of other Talmudists (*e.g.*, Delmedigo), on the different names of God, on angels, on seventy-three "Gates [chapters] to the Torah." But it is his exquisite ethical sayings, which echo the style of the prophets, that are most remembered. His best-known work (1505) is *Sefer ha-Rokeakh* ("The Book of the Dealer in Spices"), from which he came to be known as Eleazar Rokeach.

ELIEZER BEN ISAAC, HA-GADOL: *also called ELIEZER GAON, "ELIEZER THE GREAT." (Eleventh century)*

A famous German rabbi, often quoted by no less than Rashi (*q.v.*), Eliezer ha-Gadol was believed by some to be the author of *Orhot Hayim* ("Paths of Life"); but this work is now credited to Eliezer ben Hyrcanos (or Hyrcanus), *q.v.*, in the *Jewish Encyclopedia* (vol. v, p. 115). Eliezer ha-Gadol may be the author of a penitential prayer, *"Elohai Baser Ameka"* ("My God, fortify your people"), which very orthodox Jews recite in the *Yom Kippur Katan* ("Minor Days of Atonement") prayers/ fasts before the new moon.

ELIEZER, ISRAEL BEN. *See "BAAL SHEM TOV."*

EZOBI, JOSEPH BEN HANAN *(Thirteenth century)*

A poet who lived in Perpignan, Ezobi wrote liturgical passages about the Feast of Pentecost and Jewish martyrs under Hadrian. His most important poem was *Kararat Kesef* ("Bowl of Silver"), which advised his son on how to live and study— warning him against Greek thought and urging him to read Talmud and study Maimonides. *Kararat Kesef* has been translated into English by I. Freedman (*Jewish Quarterly Review*, vol. viii, p. 535).

FALAQUERA (PALQUERA), SHEM-TOV BEN JOSEPH; *also known as SHEM TOB PALQUERA, or IBN FALAQUERA. (1225–c. 1290)*

This Spanish philosopher-poet-translator came from a distinguished family of Jews in Toledo. His life and personal characteristics remain virtually unknown. From his treatises on religion, philosophy, psychology, metaphysics, it is clear the Falaquera was extremely knowledgeable about Plato, Aristotle, Greek and Arabic philosophy. He made Hebrew translations and scholarly abridgments of Averroes and Avicenna. His works embrace a very wide range, from dreams and the nature of body and soul to the compatibility of Torah with secular science. He defended Maimonides and urged Jewish scholars to study the great Greek thinkers. He even attempted prose-poetic summation of all human knowledge. It is no wonder he was called "*Shem Tob*" (Good Name).

GABIROL. *See IBN GABIROL.*

"THE GERER RABBI": *ISAAC MEIR BEN ISRAEL ALTER (of Rothenburg); also known as "The Old Gerer Rabbi" and "Hiddushe ha-Rim". (1799–1866)*

This rabbi, one of the leading Talmudists of Poland, was so esteemed that forty years after his death his followers were said to number over 100,000. At the age of seventeen, he had written extensive notes for several tractates of the Talmud; they are known as *Hiddushe ha-Rim* ("New Interpretation of Rabbi Isaac Meir").

GERONDI, JONAH BEN ABRAHAM: *or GERONDI "THE PIOUS." Not to be confused with Gersonides (q.v.). (d. 1263)*

Jonah ben Abraham Gerondi, called "the Pious," headed the important Toledo *yeshiva* (rabbinical college). He was a cousin of Nachmanides (*q.v.*), wrote ethical treatises, and produced commentaries on the Talmud that influenced later scholars. Gerondi, incidentally, was the surname given to families from Gerona (or Gerunda) in Catalonia, an important Jewish community from the eleventh century until the expulsion of the Jews in 1492.

GERSONIDES: LEVI BEN GERSON (GERSHON); *also known by the acronym "RaLBaG;" as Leon de Bagnols; and (in Latin) Magister Leo Hebraeus. (1288–1344)*

Very little is known about the life of this remarkable French Jewish philosopher, physician, Talmudist, scholar, mathematician and astronomer. He was a master of the works of Aristotle and Averroes, wrote important books on geometry (he is said to have laid the foundations of modern trigonometry), invented a nautical device called "Jacob's Staff," and improved the *camera oscura*. His writing on astronomy criticized Ptolemaic assumptions. He is said to have been the last Jewish Aristotelian. His views were severely criticized by Hasdai Crescas, the Spanish Jewish philosopher who was Crown Rabbi of Aragon (and whose disciple was Joseph Albo, *q.v.*). Gersonides' chief work, insofar as this anthology is concerned, was *Milhamot Adonai* ("Wars of the Lord").

GINZBERG ASHER. *See "AHAD HA-AM."*

HA-ASHERI. *See ASHER BEN JEHIEL.*

HA-GADOL. *See ELIEZER BEN ISAAC, HA-GADOL.*

HAI GAON: *or HAI (Gaon means "Eminence").* (939–1038)

The *geonim* (plural of *gaon*) were the intellectual leaders of the Jewish community in Babylon from the sixth to the eleventh century. They led the studies of the academies in Sura, Nehardea, and Pumbedita, and exercised great judicial-legal-temporal power among Jews everywhere.

Hai, son of an influential *gaon*, was the last *gaon* of Pumbedita. He was appointed head of the ecclesiastical court, the *Bet Din,* in 998. Hai made his academy the leading center of Jewish scholarship; students from all of Europe and Asia flocked to Pumbedita. Theologians and rabbis often wrote to Hai, whose responses interpreting the Law were accepted as definitive. He wrote learned commentaries (in Arabic) on Torah and Talmud until his death, past the age of ninety-nine.

HA-KAPPAR, ELEAZAR. *See ELEAZAR HA-KAPPAR.*

HA-LEVI, AARON OF BARCELONA. (*c. 1300*)

The author, probably, of *Sefer ha-Hinukh* (*Hinnukh*), "the Book of Education," a classic which enumerates and analyzes the 613 divine precepts. The text was early translated into Latin and into French.

HA-LEVI, JUDAH: *JUDAH BEN SAMUEL HA-LEVI, or JE-HUDA HALEVI or HA-LEVI. Do not confuse ha-Levi with the French writers, Elie or Joseph Halevy. (c. 1075–1141)*

By profession a physician ("We heal Babylon, but it cannot be healed," he said), ha-Levi, a Spanish Jew born in Toledo, won a reputation as a poet-philosopher. A master of Arabic, he introduced Arabic forms and meter into Hebrew verse. His *Zionides* ("Songs of Zion") are lovely, lyrical expressions of the Jews' longings to return to the holy land. He used much symbolism in his poetry and included many quotations from the Bible and rabbinical literature. His "sacred" poems were so beautiful that they became part of many Jewish liturgies.

Ha-Levi's most important work was *The Kuzari* (or *Ha-Kuzari*)—written (1130–1140) in Arabic, just before ha-Levi left Spain. The title alludes to a discussion between a rabbi and a king of the Khazars, a Turkish or Finnish sect settled along the lower Volga. (The king was converted to Judaism, according to legend—400 years before ha-Levi began his masterwork.) *The Kuzari* is a long defense of, and sustained argument for, the faith of the Jews. The subtitle, "An Argument for the Faith of Israel," tells us this was a defense of a severely harassed religious group, caught within the struggle of Catholics and Muslims for the domination of Spain—and Holy Palestine (where the Crusaders appeared to have doomed Israel to extinction). Ha-Levi often used the dialogue form, reminiscent of Plato, in his account of the debate between the Khazars and "the Rabbi." Translated into Hebrew by Judah ibn Tibbon (*q.v.*), *The Kuzari* exercised a world-wide influence on Jews: it is considered a classic in the literature of Judaism. It has been translated into English (Schocken Books, 1964), and the introduction by Henry Slonimsky is well worth reading.

HA-LEVI, JUDAH HASID. *See JUDAH the PIOUS.*

"HA-NAKDAN." *See BERECHIAH BEN NATRONAI, HA-NAK-DAN. (Third century)*

It was said of this great Babylonian halakist (expert on the Law) that he could recite the entire body of rabbinical Law from memory. He was a scribe, a disciple of Rab (Abba Arika), and his name is found often in the Talmud (in both the Babylonian and Jerusalem texts) because he taught many scholars the tradition and responsibilities of the scribe.

"HA-PENINI." *See BEDERSI, JEDAIAH BEN.*

HAPHETZ HAYYIM. *See "CHOFETZ CHAIM."*

HASDAI, ABRAHAM BEN SAMUEL HA-LEVI, or IBN HAS-DAI. (*fl. first part of thirteenth century*)

This Barcelona Jew, supporter of Maimonides and a vigorous polemicist in his behalf, translated many works into Hebrew from
Arabic; some classic Arabic works became known only through
Hasdai's translations. He translated Maimonides' famous *Letter
to Yemen* from Arabic into Hebrew. He wrote in an elegant
style.

His story of the Buddha (*Ben ha-Melekh ve-ha-Nazir*),
taken from Arabic sources (themselves translated from Indian
or Persian, and probably embellished by Hasdai), played an
important part in acquainting Western Europe with Buddhism.

HAYYIM BEN ISAAC, OF VOLOCHIN; *also known as CHAYIM OF VOLOZHIN.* (*1749–1821*)

A leading Lithuanian Talmudic scholar, a student of the great Vilna
Gaon, Chayim ben Isaac founded a *yeshiva* (rabbinical academy) in Volozhin, in 1802. He was extremely influential,
amongst the Jews of Lithuania, in opposing both the hasidic
and Haskalah (enlightenment) movements.

HILLEL. (*flourished first century of the Christian Era*)

Called "the Elder," (*ha-Zakan*) and the leader of the Pharisees,
Hillel was a peerless scholar, teacher, judge, legalist, unsurpassed in intellect and influence, renowned for the saintliness
of his character and conduct. He stressed humility, charity,
love, fear of God, and—above all—love of one's fellowmen and
a passion for peace. He is credited with the Golden Rule,
albeit in reverse form, saying to a non-believer: "What is hateful to thee, do not unto thy fellow man. That is the whole
Law: all the rest is commentary." (Jesus was certainly influenced by many anecdotes told about Hillel; and Paul, the
evangelist, was a pupil of Hillel's grandson, Gamaliel.)

Details of Hillel's early life are scant. Born in Babylonia,
he is nowhere called, as was common practice, "Hillel, son of
[his father's name]." Some held him to be descended from
David. In the days of King Herod, Hillel, suffering great hardships, received a Doctor of Laws degree in Jerusalem. There

he worked for about forty years. Many Jews drew parallels between the life of Moses and the life of Hillel; both presumably died at the age of 120. Hillel's descendants led Judaism in Palestine for five centuries.

Legend holds that Hillel became the head of the Sanhedrin (the highest ecclesiastical court of the Jews). He did create the basic seven rules of hermeneutics used to determine the full meaning of passages, prescriptions and laws in the Old Testament, and the prestige of his name was so potent that it often endowed his interpretations of the Law with the status of decrees. Hillel's "school" (called *Bet Hillel*, "the School of Hillel") came to prevail over the contrary interpretations of Shammai, his colleague and opponent, and "the Shammai school." It is a curious tribute to Hillel's wisdom and character that the profound respect and affection he enjoyed among Jews was never embroidered (as other sages' names were) with legends about putative wizardry, miraculous cures, or necromantic capacities.

Hillel's many marvelous sayings are preserved in the Babylonian Talmud, partly in Hebrew and partly in Aramaic (at that time the language of the masses). His style is lucid and epigrammatic; his thought is permeated by singular compassion and an almost mystical consciousness of God; his emphasis on brotherly love and peace were basic formative elements in the gospel of Christianity. His conceptions of duty, honor, righteousness, learning are unsurpassed for simplicity of phrasing and nobility of substance: "If I am not for myself, who is for me? And if I am only for myself, what am I? And if not now—when?" He must surely be ranked among the wisest and noblest men in human history.

HIYYA (CHIA) BAR ABBA: *called HIYYA RABBAH, the Great, or HIYYA THE ELDER, to distinguish him from Rabbi Hiyya bar Abba (bar-Wa, bar-Ba)—whose biography follows this one. (second century of the Christian Era)*

Often quoted in the literature of the Haggadah, Hiyya was the author of many important, conservative legal decisions (*halakot*), and was highly regarded in Babylon as a physician. He edited several historic *halakot* that had not been included in the Mishnah (*Baraitot de Rabi Hiya, Mishnayot Gedolot,*

Mishnah de Rabi Hiya), and exerted great influence in founding rabbinical schools and furthering the practices of learning.

HIYYA (CHIA), RABBI: *HIYYA BAR ABBA; also known as HIYYA BAR WA or HIYYA BAR BA. Not to be confused with the elder, Rabbah Hiyya—above. (End of third century of the Christian Era)*

He is referred to, in the Palestinian/Babylonian Talmuds, as Rabbi Hiyya, Hiyya bar-Ba, Hiyya bar-Wa. A native of Babylon, descended from priestly Amoraim (scholar-teachers), he went at an early age to Palestine, where he became a disciple of Rabbi Johanan. He became a master, so acknowledged, of *halaka* (Law). He recited the words of the masters with such fidelity that his renditions were preferred to all others for accuracy and reliability. He was so fanatical about the sanctity of Oral law that he castigated those who sought to write down his own profound commentaries—but it was, nonetheless, sensibly done.

IBN EZRA, ABRAHAM BEN MEIR; *also known as ABEN EZRA. (1092–1167)*

A scholar and poet, Ibn Ezra lived in Spain until he was fifty-one, then traveled widely in France, Italy, England and (possibly) Palestine. He wrote many poems, both secular and sacred, and produced a great many Hebrew aphorisms and paradoxes. His interpretations of the Law were exceptionally sophisticated in textual and linguistic analysis. He wrote several works in astrology, a commentary on Exodus, and translated many Arabic works into Hebrew.

IBN EZRA, MOSES BEN JACOB *(known in Arabic as ABU HARUN MUSA). Do not confuse with Solomon ben Moses ibn Ezra. (1055–after 1135)*

Born in Granada, of a great Spanish Jewish family, he fled after the Amoravides, a Muslim sect, captured that town. He was a distinguished linguist, a melancholy poet, a philosopher of acumen, close to Judah ha-Levi (*q.v.*) who said "Moses ibn Ezra draws pearls from the wells of thoughts." After his flight from Granada, he endured much suffering. He wrote in Arabic and in Hebrew: many religious and secular poems, a book on rhetoric, another on poetry which includes valuable material on Hebrew poets and the history of poetry in Spain, and a philosophical treatise on Neo-Platonism. He included many aphorisms in his writings.

Moses ibn Ezra is an acknowledged master of Hebrew and Arabic; his *Tarshish* (1210 lines) and *"Anak"* are vivid secular excursions into beauty, wine, love, the countryside, friends, love-sickness, misfortune and death. Yet a current of gravity ran through all of his work, even where the subject is gay, even frivolous.

IBN FALAQUERA. *See FALAQUERA.*

IBN GABIROL: *SOLOMON BEN JUDAH IBN GABIROL (GE-BIROL); also known as ABU AYYUB SULAIMAN IBN YAH-YA IBN JABIRUL. (c. 1021–about 1058)*

Born in Saragossa, orphaned, sickly—for the rest, little is known of the early years of this immortal medieval poet and essayist. He began to write poetry at sixteen, greatly influenced by mystical literature, earlier Spanish Hebrew poetry, and Sufism, a Muslim sect.

Ibn Gabirol wrote many cheerful verses, celebrating love and drinking; many intensely introspective, gloomy poems; and many noble, lyrical works that exalt humility, submission to God, and a spiritual yearning for the redemption of man: many of the latter became part of Jewish liturgy. His great *Keter Malkhut* ("Crown of Kinship with the Divine") was a lofty tribute to the Lord—and a revelation of Ibn Gabirol's sense of insignificance in the cosmos. Several of his neo-Platonic treatises, written in Arabic and translated into Latin, influenced the Catholic scholastics and—later—Spinoza. His most important philosophical treatise is *Tikun Midot ha-Nefesh* ("The Improvement of the Moral Qualities").

His work was not collected until the nineteenth century, and was not published *in toto* until 1924–32 (by Chaim Bialik and Y. Ravnitsky). He is one of the poets most loved by readers of Hebrew, and is one of the aphorists most often quoted in this anthology.

IBN HASDAI. *See HASDAI.*

IBN PAQUDA (PAKUDA), BAHYA BEN JOSEPH; *or BACHYA IBN PAQUDA; sometimes called "the Saint". (c. 1050–c. 1120)*

A *dayan* (ecclesiastical judge) in Saragossa, Ibn Paquda was a philosopher-theologian about whose life very little is known. But his influence on Jewish moralists and mystics has been enormous, chiefly because of his masterpiece *Hovot ha-Leva-vot* (*"The Duties of the Heart"*), perhaps the first Jewish systematic treatise on ethics.

Bahya divided the duties of man into those which are physical (and visible) and those which are spiritual—including faith, compassion for others, the avoidance of jealousy, hostility, vengefulness. He tried, as he said in his preface, to synthesize for the first time "the duties of the mind and the duties of the heart." The work is simple in style, natural in phrasing and feeling, employs charming parables, and directs personal appeals (for which he gently apologizes) to the reader.

Duties of the Heart was written in Arabic, translated into Hebrew and Ladino and Yiddish, bridging the Sephardic and Ashkenazic worlds with equal popularity. Bahya ibn Paquda became so beloved by the Jewish masses that he was dubbed "the Saint." The book was gracefully translated into English by Moses Hyamson.

Ibn Paquda said that self-examination, asceticism, humility and love of God are as important as observing the commandments. He was greatly influenced by Saadia Gaon (*q.v.*), and quotes Aristotle and Muhammed (after all, the sages had said that many a wise man is to be found among the gentiles). Bahya is quoted on many topics in the present anthology.

IBN TIBBON, JUDAH BEN SAUL; *or JUDAH IBN TIBBON. (c. 1120–d. sometime after 1190)*

Not to be confused with others, contemporary and later, whose patronym is "Ibn Tibbon": namely Abraham, Jacob ben Machir, Judah ben Moses, Moses, Moses ben Isaac, Samuel,

Samuel ben Judah. The family of Spanish Jewish scholars were translators and commentators of great importance in the history of Hebrew literature.

Judah ben Saul ibn Tibbon was a physician, born in Granada, from which he was driven in 1150 to settle in Lunel, in southern France. He translated Arabic works by Spanish Jews into Hebrew—most notably Saadia Gaon, Bahya ibn Paquda, and Judah ha-Levi. Ibn Tibbon has been criticized for taking excessive poetic license in these translations, but praised for his ingenuity in concocting Hebrew terms for technical concepts in philosophy. Perhaps his own best-known work (not translation) was his "ethical will" to his son, Samuel: a paternal, moralistic guide to duty and faith—with careful advice about the preservation of manuscripts.

IBN VERGA, JUDAH (JOSEPH). (*Fifteenth to sixteenth century*)

The *Jewish Encyclopedia* and the *New Standard Jewish Encyclopedia* differ on identifying Ibn Verga. Sources also differ about whether one Solomon ibn Verga was the son of Judah (or Joseph); Judah is presumed by some students to have been Solomon's grandfather; and some scholars cite a second Joseph ibn Verga—of Avlona, Spain. (I'm sorry if all this confuses you; it does me.)

Judah ibn Verga was an historian, astronomer and rabbi who left Seville in 1492, at the time of the catastrophic (to Spain no less than to Jewry) expulsion. He went to Lisbon, where he suffered martyrdom. He wrote *Shevet Yehudah* ("The Rod of Judah")—a title also used in Italy by Solomon ibn Verga, who had also fled Spain.

IBN ZABARA, JOSEPH BEN MEIR. (*c. 1140–c. 2100*)

A physician in Barcelona and a Spanish Hebrew poet, Ibn Zabara's *Sefer Shaashuim* ("Book of Delight") contains many delightful parables and anecdotes, in rhymed verses, and is a treasury of folk lore—which he said he had collected during his extensive travels. He has been translated into English, beautifully, by the late Professor Moses Hadas of Columbia University.

"IMMANUEL of Rome": *IMMANUEL BEN SOLOMON; also known as IMMANUEL BEN SOLOMON BEN JEKUTHIEL, or as the Italian poet MANOELLO GIUDEO. (1260–c. 1328)*

A poet and teacher, Immanuel traveled widely through his native Italy. He wrote many philosophical commentaries on the Old Testament, but only a portion were ever published. His vast body of poetry contains majestic hymns—and surprisingly candid erotica.

He is believed to have been the first poet to introduce the form of the sonnet into Hebrew literature. He also wrote an "imitation" of Dante. His *Mahberot Immanuel* ("Compositions of Immanuel"), which is the work quoted in the present anthology, was a collection of miscellaneous writings and verse on the model of Al-Harizi's *Tahkemoni,* proscribed by some Italian rabbis because of its occasionally earthy content. He worked in the rhymed prose (interspersed with poetic excursions) structure known as *makamot.*

ISRAEL BEN ELIEZER. *See "BAAL SHEM TOV."*

JABIRUL. See *IBN GABIROL.*

JEDAIA BEN BEDERSI; *also known as JEDAIAH of BEZIERS; pen-name "HA-PENINI" ("Dispenser of Pearls"). (c. 1270– c. 1340)*

Physician, philosopher, poet, from a well-known family in Beziers (south France), Bedersi was an advocate of philosophical inquiry. He wrote many books, the best known, reprinted in over eighty editions, being *Behinat Olam* ("Examination of the World"). His poetry includes a 1,000-word prayer in which each word begins with the letter *aleph*(A).

JOSEPHUS: *FLAVIUS JOSEPHUS; his Hebrew name was Yoseph ben Mattityahu ha-Cohen. (c. 38–c. 100)*

Josephus came from a distinguished priestly family in Palestine, was a political scientist of distinction, and became the Jewish military commander in Galilee, which the Romans attacked in the year 67. He was captured and became a turncoat, in the eyes of Jewish patriots, when he urged the Jews to end their rebellion. He even accompanied Vespasian and Titus to the siege of Jerusalem, and there tried to persuade the Jews to make peace.

Josephus is, of course, a leading authority on the events in the rebellion of the Jews against Roman rule, but historians question his objectivity: His historical writings defend his own role in the hostilities and try to justify his integrity—both as a Jewish patriot and an advocate of the Roman position. His *Autobiography* denied the charges of Justus of Tiberius, who attacked Josephus as the prime "cause" of the Jewish wars. Josephus' *The Jewish War* and *The Antiquities of the Jews* cover the history of the Jews from the first century before the Christian Era through the wars against Roman government from 66–79 of the Christian Era. His *Contra Apion* is an eloquent, if apologetic, answer to Apion's nasty anti-Semitic charges. (Apion, an Alexandrian historian, was part of a delegation to the emperor Caligula that opposed the delegation of Jews led by Philo.)

In sum: Josephus is a gifted historian, writer and polemicist. His politics may be criticized for an expediency that testified to poor character—or may be defended as the sagacity of a political realist who had the courage to offend popular opinion and bring calumny upon his name.

JUDAH BEN ASHER; *also known as JUDAH ASHERI. Do not confuse with his brother Jacob, author of* Arbah Turim, *a famous codification of Talmudic decisions.* (*1270–1349*)

Son of the great Talmudist Asher ben Jehiel (*q.v.*), "the Rosh," Judah ben Asher was born in Germany, went to Spain at the age of thirteen, returned to Germany and again to Spain—to arrange for his father's settlement in Toledo as rabbi. Upon his father's death, he became rabbi of Toledo's Jewish community. He was greatly esteemed for his firmness in Talmudic discussions. His eloquent "ethical will," translated as the *Testament of Judah Asheri,* is quoted in the present anthology.

"JUDAH the PIOUS," JUDAH HASID HA-LEVI. *Do not confuse with Judah ha-Levi.* (*1638–1700*)

A cabalist, born in Podolia, the Ukraine, Judah headed a sect which practiced hasidic rites, praying in visible and audible ecstasies, emphasizing man's sinfulness, the necessity for true penitence, and the imminence of the Messiah and the re- demption of the world.

Judah's reputation as a *tsadik* and oracle spread so wide that he made a pilgrimage to Palestine with no less than 1,500 ardent disciples. It was an ill-fated journey, many dying or being killed long before they reached the Holy Land (1700). And Judah himself perished only a few days after reaching his goal. His followers, treated as believers in "the false Messiah," Sabbetai (or Shabbatai) Zvi (or Zevi), were so vigorously persecuted, by those who feared and hated the Sabbetaian movement, that they straggled back to Russia and Poland.

Judah the Pious is known for his charming parables and sayings, which have been orally transmitted for several hun- dred years.

KAHAN, ISRAEL MEIR. *See "CHOFETZ CHAIM."*

KARO. *See CARO.*

"THE KORETSER RABBI": *PHINEAS BEN ABRAHAM OF KO- RETS.* (*1726–1791*)

A Lithuanian Chasidic rabbi, he departed from his traditional Ju- daic education after coming under the influence of the Baal Shem Tov (*q.v.*). He opposed *pilpul* (casuistic) methods of exegesis. He preached a simple gospel of humility and venera- tion of the Lord.

"The KOTZKER RABBI": *MENAHEM MENDEL OF KOTZK; full name Menahem Mendel Heilprin—later Morgenstern.* (*1787–1859*)

A brother-in-law of "the Gerer Rabbi" (*q.v.*), Menahem Mendel Heilprin supported the 1830 revolution of the Poles against the Czars and, to evade capture and punishment, changed his name to Morgenstern. He was a formidable, if not ferocious, character whose acolytes often hid under their tables to escape the wrath of his censure. He spent the last two decades of his life in total isolation—in the study of his home. None of his writings survive: he destroyed them all—whether out of misguided piety, excessive humility, or anxiety about their possible misinterpretation, I do not know. His shrewd, tart sayings were orally transmitted, and printed in 19th and 20th century books.

KRANZ, JACOB BEN WOLF. *See "The Maggid of Dubno."*

LEONE DA MODENA, "LEON of MODENA," LEONE MODENA: *LEON JUDAH ARYEH.* (*1571–1648*)

This brilliant, erratic figure, was a rabbi, a superb preacher, an inexhaustible writer, a poet, a compulsive gambler, a theater director, a sophisticate who headed a gambling syndicate in the ghetto of Venice and moved in the loftiest circles of Venetian society. Leone's sermons were so eloquent that Catholics and members of the nobility attended them; his fame as a teacher attracted many aristocratic students from France, including an archbishop. His personal life and multifarious activities are the stuff of picaresque fiction.

He was born in Venice, the scion of a distinguished family of Jews (his grandfather had been knighted by Charles V). A child prodigy, he knew the classics, mathematics, much natural history. He wrote a tract *against* gambling (before he was fourteen) that was good enough to go into Latin, German, French translations, and into that Judaeo-German vernacular that would become Yiddish. He became a hopelessly addicted gambler, which he blamed, with great poise, on astrological influences. At one time or another, he practiced no less than twenty-six professions; he squandered his income at the gaming tables and suffered many tragedies in his private life. (One of his sons was killed in a brawl; another went to Brazil and disappeared; Leone's wife was insane for years.)

The Venetian rabbinate tried to excommunicate Leone for his gambling, but his brilliant moralistic essay of defense persuaded them that they were acting arbitrarily—and contrary to Talmudic Law.

This gifted fantast published an enormous number of tracts, treatises, poems and books—in Hebrew and Italian, including a collection of 400 of his sermons, a system of mnemonics, commentaries on the Pentateuch, translations of Ecclesiastes, a collection of Hebrew poems, "enigmas and remedies," moral maxims, prayers, abridgements of the Passover Haggadah, a primer on the technical terminology of logic, etc. His work is not distinguished by profundity. But his autobiography (one of the very early autobiographies to be written in Hebrew) and his vivid, voluminous letters provide an extraordinary and truly invaluable picture of Venice in its golden seventeenth century, and the life of the Jews during that period.

LEVITA, ELIAS, or ELIJAH BAHUR, ELIJAH MEDAKDEK, ELIJAH TISHIBI: *ELIJAH BEN ASHER HA-LEVI ASHKENAZA.* (*1468–1549*)

He was born in Neustadt, Germany and died in Venice. In Rome he was supported, with his family, by a Cardinal, to whom he gave lessons in Hebrew in exchange for lessons in Greek. He spent thirteen years in the palace, writing the works which won him a wide reputation. When Rome was sacked in 1537, Elijah was driven out, back to Venice. One of his students now was the French ambassador, later a Bishop, who subsidized Levita's great concordance of the Masoretic texts, *Sefer ha-Zikhronot* ("Book of Remembrance"). It took him twenty years to complete.

Elijah was important as lexicographer and grammarian; his writings on the Hebrew language are considered models of methodology. He propounded the unpopular theory that the "vocalizations" in Bible texts were post-Talmudic. He wrote a lexicon to the Talmud, *Tishbi* ("The Tishbeite"), and the first known dictionary of Yiddish-Hebrew, plus two novels in Italian verse, and Hebrew poems. He translated into Yiddish many works—especially the extraordinary *Bovo Bukh*, an Italian romance (based on an English cycle by one Bevis of

Hampton) that played an enormous role in the education of Jewish women. (See my *Joys of Yiddish,* pp. 46–7.)

"THE LUBLINER RABBI": *JACOB ISAAC HOROWITZ, "The Lubliner."* (1745–1815)

Known as "the seer of Lublin," acclaimed for his purity and clairvoyance, "The Lubliner" (also called "Our holy rabbi") was a hasid possessed by a conviction that he was personally struggling against the agents of the Evil Impulse. For seven years, he literally shielded his eyes against the possibility of seeing anything unworthy or tempting. He was obsessed by a fear of falling into sin and even feared his own powers as a preacher and *tsadik* ("holy man").

His gospel emphasized joyousness in worship and humility in conduct. He attacked affluent Jews for their vainglory, and won a large following among the poor of Lublin, Poland— especially after he proclaimed that the sufferings of the Napoleonic wars were a sign of the immanent coming of the Messiah. He wrote three books, of which *Divre Emet* ("Words of Truth") was of particular interest to the present anthology.

LURIA, ISAAC BEN SOLOMON: *known as "ARI" (Hebrew: "the holy lion," also an abbreviation for "Ashkenazi"). Do not confuse him with such notables as Berman Ashkenazi, Bezalel Ashkenazi, Jacob Ashkenazi, Solomon Ashkenazi (all sixteenth-century Talmudists or authors) and Tzevi (Zevi) Ashkenazi.* (1534–1572)

"Ari" came from Jerusalem, was educated in Egypt, and achieved fame in Safed, where he taught and won fame by identifying certain ancient graves. He greatly impressed the community by his saintliness, asceticism, and explorations of mysticism. Countless legends of miracles, during his life and afterwards, have been woven around "Ari"—not least because of his self-proclaimed familiarity with supernatural familiars. His teachings were extremely influential, reviving and invigorating earlier cabalistic trends in Judaism.

The pupils of the Ari ("the holy lion"), of blessed memory, once asked him why he had never written a book on the Kabbalah. He replied that it was impossible, because the moment he plunged into a subject a veritable torrent of thoughts overwhelmed him, one subject leading him irresistably to another and another and another. Even when he speaks to his disciples, said the Ari, he must exert strenuous effort to keep his thoughts to one subject.*

Luria's lectures and ideas were written down after his death, by Hayyim Vital (*q.v.*): *Ets Hayim* ("Tree of Life"), *Sefer ha-Gilgulim* ("Book of Wheels") and *Peri Ets Hayim* ("Fruit of the Tree of Life").

LUZZATTO, MOSES HAYYIM: (*often abbreviated into the acronym "RaMHal"*). (*1707–1747*)

Poet, mystic, probably paranoid (he thought Biblical figures were dictating secrets to him, and sometimes was persuaded he was the Messiah), Luzzatto was born in Padua of a wealthy family. He was educated in Latin and several other languages, was an indefatigable reader of Talmud, and grew especially attracted to its cabalistic, metaphysical portions. He wrote at least 150 poetic psalms, hymns, poems, and a drama about Samson. His Hebrew was so pure, his style so Biblical, that some thought his psalms were rediscovered Biblical text; this caused considerable annoyance among the elders, who held Luzzatto to be presumptuous in modeling his poems on the Bible.

To his disciples, Luzzatto often confided mysteries and revelations which, he believed, Biblical heroes were communicating to him. His reputation as a cabalist spread through and beyond Italy, but he was severely denounced by Venetian and German rabbis, who (remembering the harm done by Shabbatai Zvi), persuaded him to renounce his teachings of the cabala. His works were thereupon locked in a stout casket. Luzzatto was given the official title of rabbi, but later was pressed into leaving for Amsterdam. He died in Palestine.

His most enduring work is *Mesillat Yesharim* ("The Way of the Righteous"), a work on ethics of great beauty, undoubtedly a classic, read and studied to this day, and admirably translated into English by Mordecai M. Kaplan.

---

* Adapted from a collection by S. Y. Agnon, in *Essays on Jewish Booklore*, KTAV, New York, p. 171.

"THE MAGGID OF DUBNO": *JACOB BEN WOLF KRANZ.*
(*1740–1804*)

One of the most impressive preachers of his time, the Maggid
("preacher-teacher") of Dubno traveled throughout Poland
and Galicia. The many parables and aphorisms with which he
brightened his sermons were collected and published after his
death.

"THE MAGGID OF MEZERITZ": *DOB BAER OF MEZHIRICH
or DOB BAER OF MEZERITZ; known also as "the Preacher
[Maggid] of Mezeritz" or "the Mezeritzer".* (*1710–1772*)

Originally a simple folk preacher or *maggid,* never ordained as a
rabbi, Dob Baer was greatly influenced by the mystical teachings of Solomon Luria. He lived an ascetic life, fasted much,
"prayed with copious tears and self-abasement," and succumbed
to the charismatic influence of the Baal Shem (*q.v.*), whom
he went to meet in person; after that worthy's death, "the
Mezeritzer" became the leader of the hasidic movement. He
was believed to be a worker of miracles. He appeared in public
only on the Sabbath, clothed in white. He was singularly effective in attracting not only simple folk to "vulgar" hasidic
practices of ecstatic veneration, but influenced younger rabbis,
scholars, and cabalists as well. Indeed, virtually all of the
hasidic rabbis or preachers of the next generation were his
acolytes and became his emissaries. Hasidism spread throughout Poland, Lithuania, Galicia, the Ukraine.

"The Mezeritzer" established the idea that the *tsadik*
("holy" or "righteous man") is more than a pious, virtuous
figure—he is a holy intermediary between the Lord and the
Jews. His teachings were entirely oral; he wrote neither
sermons, essays, nor books. His sayings were published by one
of his disciples, Rabbi Solomon ben Abraham of Lutsk, who
freely admitted that he did not himself understand many of
the great hasid's more mystical sayings.

MAIMON (MAIMUM) BEN JOSEPH. *Not to be confused with
MAIMONIDES, (q.v.), who was his son, Moses; nor with
Solomon Maimon, Lithuanian Jewish philosopher of the eight-
eenth century. (c. 1110–1165)*

Maimon ben Joseph was a scholar of Cordoba (or Cordova), Spain, where he was a *dayan* ("rabbinical judge"). He fled Cordoba in 1148 with his family, wandered about Spain for twelve years, emigrated to Fez, North Africa, and eventually moved to Egypt (his son Moses having written an article that incurred official suspicion; see Maimonides). He wrote a commentary, in Arabic, on the Pentateuch, and on many aspects of Judaic religious rites. The most important surviving work of Maimon ben Joseph's is a letter of consolation (long attributed to his son): *Igeret ha-Shemad* ("The Epistle of Conversion"—from Judaism to other religions). This eloquent affirmation was addressed to those Jews who had been subjected to so much persecution, suffering and exile that their faith was shaken, faltering, or renounced.

MAIMONIDES: *MOSES BEN MAIMON; also known by the acronym "RaMBaM," for Rabbi Moses ben Maimon.* (1135–1204)

One of the commanding minds in Jewish history, Maimonides (known in Arabic literature as "Abu Imran Musa ben Maimum ibn Abd Allah") has been called "the second Moses." He was born in Cordoba (Cordova); was first educated by his father, Maimon ben Joseph (*q.v.*) in rabbinical fashion; and was then placed to study with Arabic masters. At an early age, Maimonides was introduced to almost every branch of learning then known.

The Maimon family fled Cordoba (which fell into the hands of a fanatical Muslim sect, the Almohades), wandered through Spain for twelve years, and then moved to Fez, where they passed for a time as Muslims. But young Maimonides' writings (on reason and faith) attracted the attention of the authorities when an informer accused him of having defected from Islam (!). Only the help of a friendly Arabic poet-theologian saved Maimonides from execution. The family swiftly left Fez for Accra, then Jerusalem, and then (since Jerusalem was still possessed by passions pro and con the Crusaders) settled in Fostat (Cairo).

Now Maimonides studied to become a physician (he thought it unseemly to earn his living by writing about religion). He became personal physician to the vizier of Saladin, through whom he attended the royal family, and administered the affairs of the Jews of Cairo, who acknowledged him as their leader.

Scholarly writings—in philosophy, jurisprudence, Talmudic law, astronomy, medicine—poured from his pen. He always thought the medical knowledge of his day superficial and empirically dubious, but he wrote on many medical subjects, including a treatise on sexual intercourse; and he made a notable collection of medical axioms. His medical writings and opinions were used extensively (in Latin translation) in the universities of Europe for four centuries.

By 1158, Maimonides had produced several works on technical logic, his classic catalogue of the 613 Talmudic precepts, a commentary on the Mishnah, and his *Thirteen Articles of Faith*—all in Arabic. His insightful *Epistle to Yemen* (1172), responding to questions written to him from that south Arabian community of Jews (where many were being forced to convert, and others were beginning to follow one or another false Messiah), made so profound an impression that many Yemenite congregations included the name "our teacher Moses" in their *Kaddish* ("prayer for the dead").

From 1170 to 1180 he worked on *Mishneh Torah* ("Repetition of the Law"), a massive fourteen-volume Hebrew codification and compendium of the entire *halaka* (the legal part of the Talmud and later literature). Contemporary critics railed that Maimonides was trying to make his own laws, was not citing his rabbinical authorities, and was, in effect, trying to supplant the Talmud—a view made easier because in the introduction Maimonides said readers could now consult his book on any aspect of the Law, without laborious reading in other texts. (He also promised to publish a revised edition, with references, but never found the time to do so.) The *Mishneh Torah* remains unsurpassed for range, detail, depth, and systematic coordination of the Babylonian and the Jerusalem Talmuds, the Midrash, and the decisions of the *gaoim*. It was a staggering feat of erudition and energy.

In 1190, Maimonides wrote his most famous book, in Arabic, *Dalalat al-Ha'irin* ("*Guide of the Perplexed*"*), which set

---

* This classic is also called "Guide to the Perplexed" and "Guide for the Perplexed."

forth the faith of Judaism in a lucid, powerfully reasoned structure and tried to synthesize philosophy and religion. Maimonides, though thoroughly steeped in neo-Platonic and Aristotelian ideas, opposed many of Aristotle's arguments about the creation of the universe, the nature of God, prophecy, etc. He considered "the perfect man," one who contemplates the divine as a philosopher but remains animated, as a man, by passionate love of the Lord. The *Guide for the Perplexed* made a very strong impression on Muslim and Christian thinkers, especially on Aquinas and Leibnitz. Maimonides insisted that Judaism rested on reason; he even asserted that Judaism could be thoroughly comprehended only on Aristotelian principles: to worship or to have faith on other grounds, Maimonides held, was a form of idolatry. This created a furore, understandably, among the learned and anti-secular Jews of Europe. In 1305, the reading of philosophical works of Maimonides' sort was forbidden to Jews until they were twenty-five years old; excommunication was threatened to any under twenty-five who did so.

During the Haskalah (Jewish Enlightenment) movement of 1750–1880, Maimonides again became the spearhead of anti-traditionalist positions and the authority for Jewish rationalist emphases; his great *Guide* was called "The Bible of the *Maskilim*" ("enlightened ones"), and has remained so to this day.

MEIR, RABBI: *also known as MEIR BA'AL HA-NES ("Meir the Miracle Worker"); his original name may have been "ME'-ASHA," according to the Babylonian Talmud; he is also known, in Aramaic, as "Nehorai." Not to be confused with twenty-four other "Meirs" listed in the* Jewish Encyclopedia. *(fl. second century of the Christian Era)*

The commanding importance of the great Rabbi Meir is demonstrated by the fact that his Mishnah became the basis for the larger Mishnah of Judah ha-Nasi, the ultimate authority in Judaic law. Rabbi Meir was one of the most brilliant of the Tannaim (teachers of the first two centuries, named in the Mishnah, beginning after the death of Hillel and concluding with the generation that followed Judah ha-Nasi). "Meir" means "one who enlightens"; and the Talmud states that the name was *given* him because he taught the Law so profoundly to the wisest men of his day, "opening their eyes" to the deepest meanings and subtleties of *halaka* ("law").

Meir's origins are uncertain. He was born somewhere in Asia Minor. (He is believed, in legend, to have been descended from the emperor Nero and converted to Judaism after Nero's fall.) He became a student of Akiba and Ishmael, and was a member of the Sanhedrin after the savage persecution launched by Hadrian.

Meir was thoroughly at home in Greek and Latin, traveled widely, and enlivened his lectures with memorable fables, aphorisms, and parables. (These, and many stories of his sufferings, generosity and ingenuity, are often mentioned in midrashic literature.) He was a man of great modesty and a champion of peace (he stayed clear of Bar-Kochba's rebellion). It may be said that he hated only ignorance. He coined a great many aphorisms, repeated to this day ("When in Rome, do as the Romans do"). His wife was a noted scholar, too.

Rabbi Meir was an exegete and dialectician of phenomenal power: The Talmud says he could present 150 reasons for declaring something ritually clean, under the Law—and 150 proving the reverse. Indeed, some of his rulings did not become laws because the rabbis could not tell, so thorough and dazzling were his explications, which of two opposing views he himself preferred.

So revered was Rabbi Meir's name among religious Jews that in Poland and Russia, special little boxes for alms bore the name: *"Meir Baal ha-Nes Pushke."* (For the meaning of *pushke* or *pishke* see my *Joys of Yiddish,* pp. 301–2.)

MENAHEM MENDEL, OF VITEBSK: *"MENDEL OF VITEBSK."* (*1730–1788*)

A hasidic rabbi who, in 1777, left Russia for Palestine with over 300 devout and devoted followers. They settled first in Safed, then in Tiberias. Mendel of Vitebsk was admired for the metaphysical aspects of his teachings.

"**MENDEL OF RYMANOV**"; *MENAHEM MENDEL "OF RY-MANOV." Not to be confused with other rabbis named Mendel, who are identified with other place-names.* (*b. ?–d. 1815*)

Rabbi "Mendel of Rymanov" was a hasid whose sermons and orthodoxy attracted thousands of Jews to his little town in Galicia. He was a strict traditionalist who insisted on the preservation of the smallest rites observed by Jews throughout the centuries. He declared that the Messiah would appear during (or soon after) the Napoleonic wars of his time. His prophecy has not been fulfilled.

"**MENDELE MOCHER SEFORIM**" (*"Mendele the Book-Seller"*): *SOLOMON (SHALOM) JACOB ABRAMOWITSCH.* (*c. 1836–1917*)

If any one man can be called the founder of Yiddish literature, it is "Mendele Mocher Seforim." Sholem Aleichem aptly dubbed him the "Grandfather" of Yiddish letters.

Born in Russia in 1836, Abramowitch studied in a *yeshiva*, but soon began to write poetry and articles for Hebrew journals. He wrote the first short story, in the modern sense, published in Hebrew. Then he applied his talents to the uses of Yiddish as a literary vehicle. His satirical stories and adaptations, his astute and ironic delineations of the conflicts between the orthodox elders and the rising generation of Jews, brought him criticism so severe that he moved to Zhitomir on the Ukrainian border. He translated the Psalms into Yiddish and wrote extensively on the life of the Jews in Russia, on the savagery of pogroms, on the nature of anti-Semitism. With Bialik and Ravnitzsky, he translated the Pentateuch into Yiddish.

Abramowitch perfected a modern, literary Hebrew which opened new vistas to Jewish authors; and it was he who made Yiddish an authentic, energetic literary tongue. His best-known work is the *Travels of Benjamin III*, which is immensely popular with the Jewish masses and a classic of humor and characterization. Among his other writings are *In the Days of the Storm, The Little Man,* and *Fishke the Lame.*

MENDELSSOHN, MOSES: *or "MOSES DESSAU," as he signed his name; or by the acronym "RaMBeMaN." (1729–1786)*

He is sometimes called "the third Moses" (Maimonides being the second) and is the central figure around whom and because of whom a new era in Judaism began. The most important representative of the Jews in Germany, the leading figure of the Enlightenment, a distinguished philosopher, Moses Mendelssohn's erudition and character achieved such standing in Germany that the city of Berlin exempted him from paying taxes. He was a passionate exponent of civil rights and an eloquent expositor of Judaism as a religion and a philosophy. His intervention stopped or prevented the legal discrimination and oppression that threatened Jews in Dresden and in Switzerland.

Mendelssohn, born in Dessau, was a poor young man; after many hardships, he became a tutor, a book-keeper, and, at last, a successful businessman. He first came to prominence with a letter that defended the Jews against the savage critics of Gotthold Lessing's play, *Die Jüden,* a plea for tolerance written by a non-Jew. Mendelssohn became the model for Lessing's famous drama, *Nathan the Wise.*

At home in German, Hebrew, Latin, French, and English, Mendelssohn won the Academy of Science (Berlin) prize for an essay on metaphysics—no small feat if we know that one of his rival entrants was Immanuel Kant. Mendelssohn annotated Ecclesiastes, translated the Pentateuch and the Psalms into German, and wrote a brilliant analysis of Maimonides' book on logic. His *Phädon,* a discourse on immortality, won him the extraordinary sobriquet: "the German Socrates."

MOSCATO, JUDAH ARYEH (LEONE). *(Sixteenth century; d. before 1594)*

Rabbi, poet, philosopher, student of ancient civilizations, Moscato was born near Ancona, Italy, and fled to Mantua (after Pope Paul IV expelled the Jews from the pontifical states), where he became chief rabbi. He was a typical scholar of the Renaissance, well-versed in Latin and Greek literature. He was a great admirer of Maimonides, and a student and exponent of the cabala. He wrote the first important book (published posthum-

ously) about Judah ha-Levi's (*q.v.*) *The Kuzari*. He held that
the civilizations of Egypt, Greece and Rome were predomi-
nantly the products of Judaic thought.

MOSES, JACOB BEN. *See "RABBENU TAM."*

MOSES OF KOBRYN. (*d. 1858*)

The town of Kobryn, in Grodno province, Russia, contained a Jewish colony as far back as the sixteenth century, and a *yeshiva*,
of over 400 students, that produced many rabbis of repute.
Moses of Kobryn was a hasidic rabbi—which is all I can find
out about him.

"NACHMANIDES" (NAHMANIDES); *MOSES BEN NAHMAN; acronym RaMBaN; in Spanish he was known as Bonastruc de Portas.* (*1194–c. 1270*)

In 1263, when Rabbi Nachman of Gerona was sixty-nine, King
James I of Aragon summoned him to the court in Barcelona
—to defend Judaism in a disputation with the Dominican Fra
Pablo (Paul) Christiani, a fulminating apostate from Judaism.
The confrontation took place before an illustrious audience of
ecclesiastical officials, court dignitaries, and prominent Jews.

Rabbi Nachman asked for freedom of speech (and im-
munity from its consequences), which the King graciously
granted. Nachman's later account of this dramatic meeting
attests to his knowledge, his equanimity (he had already debated the fanatical, rather ignorant Fra Pablo in Gerona), his
good humor—and his courage, for he did not hesitate to preach
a sermon, on the following Sabbath, against the King's con-
versionist efforts. Nachman even dared question the King on a
cardinal article of Christian faith: the miraculous conception
of Jesus.

So effective was Nachman's reasoning, scholarship and
character that King James rebuked Fra Pablo, congratulated
the rabbi, and even gave him a parting gift. But the publication of the text of the debate was too much: Catalonians
accused Nachmanides of blaspheming their faith, burned his
pamphlet in public, and—despite King James' promise—
brought the old rabbi to trial. He was exiled from Spain. After
three years of wandering about (he was a physician as well as

a rabbi), he settled in Palestine, in 1267. One of his letters states there were only two Jewish families in post-Crusade Jerusalem!

Nachmanides established a synagogue and a *yeshiva* in Jerusalem, corresponded widely, delivered sermons, and wrote a popular commentary on the books of the Torah. He also wrote poetry and books about the Law, in which he tried to reconcile rational and cabalistic interpretations of the Pentateuch. It is worth noting how many medieval intellectuals, theologians, mystics, and preachers wrestled with the same problem.

"NACHMAN OF BRATSLAV": *NACHMAN BEN SIMCHA OF BRATSLAV; known as "The Bratslaver."* (*1770–1811*)

A leading hasidic rabbi, founder of the sect called "the Bratslaver hasidim," Nachman was born in Poland—a grandson of the famous Baal Shem Tov (*q.v.*). He was an ardent cabalist and ascetic who won acclaim in Palestine, where he traveled for study, then returned to Poland. His teachings emphasized self-abnegation, penitence and fasting. He held the Evil Impulse (*yezer ha-ra*) to be necessary, because it makes possible man's perfection.

Nachman won a huge following: because of the power of his personality, his fervent sermons, his ingenious parables and his countless aphorisms. His followers were criticized and, in some cases, excommunicated—on the ground that Nachman was a follower of Shabbetai Zvi, "the Baal Shem," and the notorious charlatan, Jacob Frank, a sybarite who held that redemption could be achieved via impurity of conduct. Nachman's sermons and sayings were published after his death by a disciple, Nathan ben Naphtali Herz of Nemirov. His profound and epigrammatic observations on man, life, God, the hereafter insure his immortality.

NATHAN, OF NEMIROV (NEMROV): *NATHAN BEN NAPH-TALI HERZ (HIRZ).* (*d. 1830*)

Rabbi Nathan of Nemirov appears in this anthology chiefly because he acted as Boswell to his Dr. Johnson: Rabbi Nachman of Bratslav (*q.v.*)—whose sermons, parables, and sayings he recorded. Nathan wrote these, and many of Nachman's stories, in Yiddish. He describes the particular sermon or occasion that caused Rabbi Nachman to make up a given story. Rabbi Nathan opened his own printing press in 1821, to print Hebrew works he had transcribed or edited: collections of prayers, legal rulings, treatises on morals, the *Shulhan Aruk* ("Set Table"), etc.

NEHORAI. *See MEIR, RABBI.*

PALQUERA, SHEM TOB. *See FALAQUERA.*

PAQDA or PAQUDA. *See IBN PAQUDA.*

PHILO: *PHILO JUDAEUS. (c. 20 before the Christian Era–died after 40 of the Christian Era)*

We know little about the particular events of his life, except that he was born in Alexandria and was a member of the delegation of Jews sent to Rome, in 40 of the Christian Era, to seek Caligula's protection against the anti-Semitic activities of Alexandrian Greeks.

Philo was a philosopher and a philosopher of science, who produced many works in metaphysics, theology, ethics, epistemology, natural science. As an observer-historian, he has left us vivid descriptions of the persecutions of Flaccus, governor of Egypt; and he recorded the story of the Jewish deputation to Caligula in Rome and the controversy there.

Philo was more familiar with Greek philosophy than with Judaism (he seems to have had little formal education in Judaic theology or law). It was long believed that he knew no Hebrew (he read the Greek translation of the Old Testament); yet he wrote interesting etymological expositions of Hebrew names. Interestingly enough, he held the Old Testament to be the basic source and sole measure of truth—whether in religion or in science.

Despite his emphasis on human brotherhood, wisdom, and the purest devotion to God, Philo was never influential in Judaic thought, during his time or later; but his role in the origins of Christianity was immense. He wrote extensively on the nature of God and man, reason and the soul, his thinking heavily permeated with the ideas of Plato and the Stoics. He

held that perfection can be achieved only through a renuncia-
tion of the sensuous and "the soul's irrational" propensities, and
that true wisdom is possible only in the mastery of philosophy,
which in its highest stages makes it possible to see the divine
—even God Himself.

Philo was the deepest thinker produced within that branch
of Judaism that was Hellenistic. The Palestinian Jews soon shed
Greek philosophical influences in theology; but the new religion that sprang up around Jesus of Nazareth, propelled by
the titanic evangelism of Paul of Tarsus, was enormously affected by Philo's doctrines.

RABA: RABA JOSEPH BEN HAMA (280–352)

This famous Babylonian Amora ("interpreter," "explainer") headed
the Rabbinical academy at Mahoza—at that time the only one
in Babylon. He became renowned as an authority on *halaka*
(Law) and Haggadah (interpretative ethics, legends, etc.)
He was admired by the mother of the Persian king (Sapoo II),
became very wealthy, and was praised for many philanthropies
to the non-Jewish poor.

RAB ASHI. *See ASHI.*

RABBAH: RABBAH BAR BEN HANAH. *Do not confuse with Midrash Rabbah. See Glossary. (dates unknown)*

A third-generation Amora ("scholar" of the third–sixth century), he
was the grand-nephew of Hiyya (or Chia) the First, who had
also been called "Rabbah"—a title reserved for academy heads.
Rabbah Bar Ben Hanah was famous for his florid accounts of
his many travels. He has been fondly dubbed "the Jewish
Sinbad."

RABBAN. *See ZAKKAI, JOHANAN BEN.*

"RABBENU TAM" (*"Our perfect Master"*): *JACOB BEN MEIR TAM. (c. 1100–1171)*

Acclaimed "Our perfect Master," Jacob ben Meir Tam was the
greatest authority on Talmud among the Jews of France and

Germany, the most eminent Tosaphist. (*Tosophot*, Hebrew for "addenda," refers to exegetical notes on Talmud made, from the twelfth to the fourteenth centuries, by rabbinical scholars in Germany and France, which criticized Rashi's monumental commentary and used supplementary discussions for the explication of law.) The Talmud contains both the Tosaphists' revisions of Rashi and Rashi's exegesis itself. This bears particular meaning for "Rabbenu Tam"—whose mother was Rashi's daughter—and whose older brother was the illustrious Samuel ben Meir, known as "RaSHBaM."

Jacob ben Meir Tam headed a rabbinical academy in Ramerupt, where his home was wrecked by French crusaders; he was almost killed by their blows. He became the leading rabbinical figure of his time and won the official protection of the King of France. He attended the assembly of French rabbis in Troyes who decreed that thereafter all disputes between Jews be settled in Jewish courts.

His major work is *Sefer ha-Yasher* ("Book of the Straight Path"), which contains thirty treatises on the Talmud plus his written responses to questions of rabbinical law and ritual. (Present editions are said to contain only a portion of Tam's original, plus material not certain to be his.) Rabbenu Tam sought, as he wrote, "to reconcile the [differing] traditions of the text [of Talmud] with the original..." He inveighed against expository innovations: "My grandfather [Rashi] made one correction, and [my brother] Samuel made twenty more..." He particularly opposed the use of texts where erasures or new entries occurred.

As French and German Jews developed more harmonious relations with their neighbors, it was necessary to find religious support for newer ways of living in a Christian world. Rabbenu Tam tried to be realistic about changes, and often defended contemporary departures from old ritual—*if* he could but find a Talmudic justification for them. He particularly permitted changes in dietary practices, marriage ceremonies, and the formation of a *minyan* (quorum). His influence among later rabbis was greater than that of even Maimonides. He and Rashi are sometimes called "the two highest mountains" in European Judaism.

"RASHI": *acronym for RABBI SHLOMO BEN ISAAC; SOLO-MON YITSHAKI ("son of Isaac" is indicated by the "i" at the end of Yitshak); or SOLOMON BAR ISAAC. (1040–1105)*

This illustrious scholar, whose lucid commentaries on the Bible and the Babylonian Talmud made the latter "an open book," is the giant on whose work Nachmanides and Abraham ben Ezra based their historic interpretations of the Torah. The first book ever printed in Hebrew (in Reggio, Italy, in 1475) was Rashi's *Commentary on the Pentateuch.*

Many legends once surrounded his name, his fame, his life, and his work. He was born in Troyes, France, studied in the Rhineland with various teachers, and returned to establish a school in Troyes. But Rashi earned his living not by using his immense knowledge as a "spade" for a livelihood (an activity frowned upon in rabbinic tradition) but by working in his vineyard. His academy produced many notable scholars and disciples. Despite popularly believed stories, he did not travel throughout Europe and Asia—nor did he meet Maimonides. But he met many foreign luminaries in Troyes, a thriving commercial center.

Rashi's scholarship was unsurpassed, his style lucid, his approach to any problem brisk and direct. His reasoning was a model for all who followed him. He was thoroughly familiar with existing methodologies of textual analysis—Palestinian, Babylonian, Italian, and Ashkenazic. His commentary on the whole of Talmud, liberally lightened by many *midrashim,* is a monument in Judaic thinking, and a *tour de force* of analytic skill. He established revised, parallel texts, based on early manuscripts, the oral tradition, and the research of contemporaries. He was exceptionally gifted in defining theological and philosophical terms, in clarifying difficult or unusual phrasings, and in providing linkages between different, differing passages in the Torah or Talmud. He cut through complexities and quibblings with the confidence—and the bluntness—of a true master. His judgment was as balanced as his reasoning was clear.

He was a master of style, combining grace with precision. His mixing of Hebrew, Aramaic, and French (he used 3,000 words in the vernacular) still provide philologists with an invaluable source for medieval usages. Despite legend, Rashi seems to have known no Latin or Greek—which makes his achievement all the greater: his exegetical brilliance is his own, not beholden to scholarly works in those languages.

Rashi had three daughters, who married pupils of his—and his family and descendants became important disseminators of Rabbinical learning. When the Jews were expelled from France (Hebrew books were burned in Paris in 1240) and later from Spain, "the Bible and the Talmud, with the commentaries of Rashi, were their inseparable companions . . . often their supreme as well as their only solace, and the chief bond of their religious unity" (Morris Liber, in *Jewish Encyclopedia,* KTAV, New York [no date], vol. 10, p. 328).

The importance of Rashi's contributions to an understanding of the Pentateuch is seen in the fact that Christian scholars translated his work into Latin, German and other languages, and often cited him as an authority. Rashi's insistence on clarity and common sense led him to make drawings of many objects he described; he incorporated these drawings into his explications of Torah and Talmud—but they were omitted by hidebound copyists, so that Rashi's phrases "like this" were followed by blank spaces in the texts.

Through the writings of Nicolas de Lyre (or Lyra), a French monk, Martin Luther was greatly influenced by Rashi's work. The King James translators of the Bible made constant use of Rashi's commentaries.

Is is no exaggeration to say that Rashi is the most widely quoted authority in Judaic scholarship. He was dubbed "Parshandata," which means "the interpreter of the Torah." His pellucid observations on Hebrew were said by experts to revive and reveal the truest nature of that ancient tongue. In fact, many scholars refined their Hebrew grammar and syntax by studying Rashi.

Countless editions of his commentaries have been published; laymen (such as I) who have not studied him in the original will find a valuable, simplified introduction to Rashi's work in the translation and selections by Chaim Pearl (Norton & Co., New York, 1970). Modern texts of this great rabbi's work sometimes combine Old French (for which his eleventh-century manuscripts are an invaluable source), Hebrew and Yiddish. No body of commentary on Torah or Talmud remains more popular with the laity, and more widely used by theologians.

REGGIO, ISAAC SAMUEL: *also known by the acronym "YaSHaR." Not to be confused with his father, Abraham or Vita ben Azriel Reggio; or Issachar Ezekiel Reggio; or Leone Reggio.* (*1784–1855*)

Born in Austria, of Italian-Jewish ancestry, Isaac Samuel Reggio was a mathematician who became interested in the study of Talmud after his professorship (in geography and history) was revoked by Austrian anti-Semitic legislation. He translated the Pentateuch into clear, simple Italian, studied the cabala (to which, unlike his father, he developed a strong aversion), became a follower of Moses Mendelssohn, and was a leading figure in the Haskalah (Enlightenment) in Northern Italy. His critical commentaries on Torah drew strong negative reactions from German scholars.

In Venice, he published an appeal for a Jewish seminary, which was established in Padua and for which Reggio devised the curriculum—which included the study, by rabbinical students, of Western and classical philosophy. Reggio opposed hair-splitting parades of dexterity in exegesis. He wrote many books, hoping to join modern thought and science to Judaic scholarship. He held that most of the ordinances in the Talmud were the product of the Pharisees, and should not be considered observances of perpetual, unchanging validity.

"THE RIZINER" or "THE RIZINER RABBI" (REBBE): *ISRAEL OF RUZHIN.* (*1797–1851*)

A famous hasidic rabbi and *tsadik* ("holy or righteous man"), "the Riziner" succeeded his father in the prestigious post. He regarded himself, as did many of the leading hasidim, as a sort of sovereign, a messenger of the Messiah, who deserved to live in considerable luxury. His piety, wisdom, and aphoristic skills made his reputation; his sayings, cherished and lovingly repeated by his flock, have come down to us.

"THE ROPSHITZER RABBI": *NAFTALI (NAPHTALI) OF ROPSHITZ (ROPCZYCE). (1760–1827)*

Books about the hasidim give us almost no facts about the life and works of "the Ropshitzer." He won a reputation as a wit, no less than a hasid and a learned student of Talmud. He voiced strong views against Napoleon and his conquests in Eastern Europe.

"THE ROSH." *See ASHER BEN JEHIEL.*

SAADIA GAON: *SAADYAH BEN JOSEPH; also known as SAADYAN ("Saadiah" may be the Hebrew equivalent of the Arabic name "Sa'id"). (882–942)*

A *gaon* was a leading scholar, in Babylon, during the "post-Talmudic" era (sixth to eleventh centuries). The *geonim* were the eminences who led the three great Rabbinical academies (at Sura, Nehardea, and Pumbedita); their secular authority over Jews everywhere was very great.

He was born in Dilaz, in upper Egypt; almost nothing is known of his youth. (His detractors said he was not born a Jew, but Saadia stressed his lineage as being noble, of the family of Shelah, the son of Judah.) By the time he was twenty, Saadia had completed a great Hebrew dictionary, *Agron*. He wrote polemical attacks against the Karaites and other heretical sects, strongly defending traditional Judaism. He left Egypt for Palestine, then Babylon. Appointed to a post in Sura, the first "foreigner" to be a *gaon*, he pursued his duties with stupendous energy and found himself involved in bitter intramural disputes that ended with reciprocal excommunications.

Saadia ben Joseph was the Gaon of Sura, so admired that after his death the academy was closed—for over forty years. His intellectual and philosophical range astounded his colleagues. He is the father of the scientific study of the Hebrew language and Biblical texts. He brought Arabic and Muslim thinking into Judaic thought, and wrote many scientific papers: most have disappeared, but are known through references to them by contemporaries, disciples and other scholars.

He wrote widely on philology, law, philosophy, lexicography, and liturgy. He translated most of the Bible into Arabic, appending his commentary in Arabic. (He seems to have planned this translation for Muslims as well as Jews). His best-known philosophical work is *Amanat wa-i 'Tiqadat* ("Beliefs and Opinions") which was translated from Arabic into Hebrew by Judah ibn Tibbon (*q.v.*), and into English, in 1948, by S. Rosenblatt.

SAMUEL HA-NAGID (*"The Chief" or "Prince"*): *SAMUEL HA-LEVI BEN JOSEPH IBN NAGRELA or NAGDELA.* (*993–1056*)

He was born in Cordoba (or Cordova), was educated in rabbinical literature, and learned Latin, Arabic and Berber. Driven out of Cordoba by the Berber conqueror, Suleiman, Samuel emigrated to Malaga, where his penury forced him into selling spices. His skill in Arabic, and the beauty of his calligraphy, won the attention of the Vizier in Granada, who found "the Levite" so astute a diplomatist that he made him his chief counsellor.

Samuel became the beloved chief or *Nagid* of the Jewish community in Granada, serving as both chief rabbi and liaison to the Muslim court. The Vizier's successor, Habus (or Habbus), placed Samuel in charge of all diplomatic and military matters. After Habus' brother became king, Samuel acted, in effect, as head of state, and was privately called "king of Granada."

He was a gentle, modest man, interested in furthering knowledge, and most bountiful in his benefactions. (He purchased enormous numbers of books for scholars who could not afford them.) He was the patron of many Spanish Jewish writers and poets, notably Solomon ibn Gabirol (*q.v.*). Moses ibn Ezra (*q.v.*) wrote that Samuel ha-Nagid "raised the kingdom of science from its lowliness, and the star of knowledge [in Spain] once more shone forth." Samuel had so many admirers among Muslim scholars and state officials that he remained Vizier, despite conspiracies against his authority, and was succeeded in that high office by his son.

Few of his writings have survived. He wrote an introduction to the Talmud printed in all standard editions, poetical works in the manner of Psalms and Ecclesiastes, and a large number of undistinguished poems. (There was a saying: ". . . as cold as the songs of Samuel the Levite.") What has been preserved, fortunately, is a portion of his collection of maxims, *Ben Mishle;* from this book come those aphorisms credited to him in this anthology.

"THE SASSOVER RABBI": *MOSES LEIB OF SASSOV (SA-SOB); also known as Rabbi Moshe Yehuda Leib of Sassov.* (*1745–1807*)

The rabbi of Sassov or Sasov, in Tsarist Russia, Rabbi Moses Leib was affectionately dubbed "the father of widows and orphans." He was tireless in his efforts to raise money for the poor and the bereaved, and to ransom Jews held as hostages.

SCHECHTER, SOLOMON. (*1850–1915*)

A major leader of Conservative (as distinguished from Orthodox and Reform) Judaism, president of the Jewish Theological Seminary in New York, Solomon Schechter was born in Rumania, studied in Vienna and Berlin, and lectured on Talmud in Cambridge, England. His identification of a long-lost Hebrew manuscript of *Ecclesiasticus,* discovered in Cairo in 1896, and his subsequent analyses of the contents of that *genizah* ("hiding place") won him a world-wide reputation among Biblical scholars. His three-volume *Studies in Judaism* is outstanding. He also edited texts of historical importance (*Abot de Rabbi Nathan*) and contributed major interpretations of Judaism.

"THE SHATZOVER RABBI": *ABRAHAM SACHATZOUER or ABRAHAM OF SOCHASZEW; known as "The* Tzaddik *of Sochochov" (or Sochaszew).* (*1839–1910*)

He came from very poor beginnings and as a rabbi was helped each week by the fifteen rubles Rabbi Isaac Meir Alter sent him. He became the son-in-law of "the Kotzker Rabbi" (*q.v.*), is known as "the holy man of Sochochov," and was the head of the hasidic court in his town. His *yeshiva* attracted (and produced) many gifted scholars; his personal following, doing homage to their illustrious *tsadik,* was very large. His two works on *halaka* were used in some Lithuanian seminaries as "companion texts" in the study of Talmud and post-Talmudic rabbinical literature.

"SHMELKE (SCHMELKE) OF NICKELSBURG": *SAMUEL (or SHMELKE) OF NICHELSBURG. (1726–1778)*

A disciple of Dob Baer, "the Meritzer Rebbe" (*q.v.*), Shmelke was an ordained rabbi whose scholarship was so great that he won the special favor of the great Elijah Gaon (*q.v.*) of Vilna. He was the teacher of "the Lubliner . . . the seer of Lublin" (*q.v.*), served as rabbi in several communities, and was the brother of Rabbi Phineas of Frankfurt.

SHOLEM (SHOLOM) ALEICHEM: *pen-name of SHALOM (or SOLOMON) RABINOVITZ. (1859–1916)*

There is but one Sholem Aleichem, although the phrase, which means "Peace Unto You," is the conventional salutation among Jews, heard whenever Jews meet—or part (when they say *Aleykhem sholem:* "and unto you, peace"). In Hebrew, *sholem* is pronounced *sha-lóm*, in Yiddish *shó-lem*.

Sholem Aleichem, often called "the Mark Twain of Yiddish literature," is the best-known, most beloved and most influential Yiddish writer of the twentieth century. He is a master of humor, characterization and sheer narrative enchantment. His style is limpid, his characters matchless; his mixture of compassion, irony and ruefulness is a delight. He never tried for "big" effects or pretentious works. His work has the quality of conversation—and has achieved the status of folklore. He is, *par excellence,* the master of the re-creation of life in the *shtetl.*

The sensationally successful *Fiddler on the Roof* is based on one of Sholem Aleichem's characters: Tevye, the milkman (and his wife and five daughters); but those who think well of this amiable play would be astonished by the greater range, humor, and universality of the character types Sholem Aleichem created. Translations of this great artist are, alas, never quite satisfactory. (Isaac Bashevis Singer attributes this, in part, to the difficulties of translating Sholem Aleichem's mischievous mingling of accurate and deliberately bowdlerized Biblical or Hebrew sayings, whose humor depends on a knowl-

edge of what is being satirized; and, in part, to the fact that
it takes a humorist to translate humor.) For a superb re-creation of Sholem Aleichem's unique people and locales, one can
do no better than read Maurice Samuel's classic, *The World
of Sholom Aleichem* (Schocken paperback, 1965). Translations
of interest: *Inside Kasrilevke,* translated by Isidore Goldstick
and others (Schocken paperback, 1968); *The Adventures of
Menahem-Mendel,* translated by Tamara Kahana (Putnam,
1969); *Old Country Tales,* translated by Curt Leviant (Putnam,
1966); and *Stories and Satires,* translated by Curt Leviant
(Thomas Yoseloff, 1963).

Shalom (or Solomon) Rabinovitz was born in Russia in
1859. In Kiev, he wrote stories, novels and essays, in Hebrew
and Russian; but he came into his own when shaping and
adorning Yiddish as a vehicle for narration. He subsidized an
annual, *Di Yiddishe Folksbibliotek,* in which he published and
encouraged a whole generation of writers in Yiddish. His
greatest works were written in New York, where he lived for
a decade until his death in 1916. His writings about the life
of Jewish immigrants in the *goldene medine* of America are
unmatched for reportage, understanding and impish humor.

SIMEON BEN JOSE BEN LAKUNIA (or LEKONYA). (*Fourth century*)

A *Tanna* "of the fourth generation," brother-in-law of Eleazar ben
Simeon (*q.v.*), most of Ben Lakunia's commentaries on *halaka* have not survived. The two sayings attributed to him in
this anthology may be sentences he quoted from then-current
folk sayings.

"THE SLONIMER RABBI": *AVRUM (ABRAHAM) OF SLO-NIN.* (*1804–1883*)

A disciple of "the Kobriner," Rabbi Moshe of Kobryn, Rabbi Avrum founded "the Slonim dynasty" of *tsadikim* ("holy men").
He wrote many letters to his disciples in Palestine. His *Yesod
ha-Avodah* ("The Principle of Service"), published in 1892, is
of great importance in the history of the hasidic movement:
It virtually canonized the role of the *tsadik* as the core of religious activity in a Jewish community. Avrum drew heavily

on parables and illustrative anecdotes from history and every-day living; quoted lavishly from the Babylonian and Jerusalem Talmuds, from the mystical Zohar, from Maimonides, etc. He wrote midrashic homilies on Exodus: notably *Beer Avraham* ("The Well of Abraham"); and of special interest is his collection of letters, *Hesed le-Avraham* ("The Grace of Abraham"), which, because of its cabalistic views on creation and Judaism, was not published until after his death. He feared it would be misinterpreted or would serve to mislead the naïve or the immature.

SPINOZA (DE SPINOZA or ESPINOSA), BARUCH (or BENE-DICT). (*1632–1677*)

"Spinoza" comes from the name of a town, Espinosa, near Burgos. Spinoza's grandfather and father had escaped to Holland and were leaders of the Jewish Sephardic community there. Spinoza received his training in a *yeshiva* in Amsterdam, and went on to learn Latin, mathematics, physics, astronomy, chemistry, and medicine. Thoroughly acquainted with Aquinas and scholasticism, he was influenced by Jewish medieval and renaissance philosophers, especially Maimonides (*q.v.*), and Hasdai Crescas.

What was decisive in Spinoza's thinking was his discovery of Descartes; the idea that reason, not tradition or texts, should govern philosophy made so great an impression on him that he was suspected of heresy in the Jewish community, and was "called up to the Law." In 1656 he was formally excommunicated (he was twenty-three)—after an interrogation, to parts of which he answered that according to Holy Scripture angels were phantoms, that the soul is mortal, that God has "extension" or body. . . . (The excommunication—rescinded centuries after his death—was based not only on Spinoza's heresies, but on the fears of the Jews that Dutch freedom might not be elastic enough to countenance Spinoza's views, and that the Jewish community would be made to suffer for them.)

Spinoza moved outside of Amsterdam and became part of a Mennonite circle whose doctrines were similar to those of Quakers. He became a lens-grinder, an optician, a tutor of philosophy, Latin and Hebrew. In Leyden, he began his

Ethics (written in Dutch and published posthumously), a great exposition of pantheism. His *Tractatus Theologico-Politicus,* published anonymously, exposed contradictions in the Bible and made incisive distinctions between piety and reason, faith and truth. It created a furore and was proscribed in many parts of Holland; but it is the foundation of all modern Bible criticism. Spinoza was consulted, by letters, by the leading intellectuals and scientists of his time. His influence on Leibniz, who visited him, was tremendous.

He was a gentle man, exceptionally calm, kindly, philosophical. In spirit, he remained isolated from both Judaism and Christianity. His use of Euclidean methods; his opposition to the authority of rabbis or priests, synagogue or church; his insistence that the state guarantee freedom of thought in religion, no less than politics; his belief that nothing is "supernatural" or outside of nature; his view that God is an infinite substance "causing" itself—or Himself—all made a profound impression on thinkers of the seventeenth and eighteenth centuries.

He held that true freedom lies in the power and purity of the intellect, and that happiness is achieved through the *intellectual* (not mystical or traditional or non-reasoning) love of God. He remains one of the truly seminal names in philosophy, theology, ethics, and political theory.

"THE TCHARKOVER RABBI": *ZEVI HIRSCH HA-LEVI HURWITZ. (d. 1758)*

A great Talmudist, "the Tcharkover" was the rabbi most respected by the Baal Shem (*q.v.*). He was the father of Shmelke of Nickelsburg.

TIBBON. *See IBN TIBBON.*

"THE TSUPENSTER RABBI": *NAHUM TSUPENSTER. (d. 1868)*

I can find little about this hasidic rabbi who was (probably) the same as the one known as "Nahum of Stepinesht." He was a faithful follower and disciple of "the Riziner Rabbi" (*q.v.*); his sayings were repeated by his admirers and descendants.

VERGA. *See IBN VERGA.*

VITAL, HAYYIM. *Not to be confused with JOSEPH, MOSES, SAMUEL BEN HAYYIM, or DAVID BEN SOLOMON VITAL.* (1543–1620)

Hayyim Vital, descended from a famous family of southern Italian Jewish scholars, was born in Safed. His life is surrounded by legends of his powers as a worker of miracles. He was a mystic and cabalist who sometimes claimed his soul was the soul of the Messiah.

Vital was a disciple of Isaac Luria. In Damascus, where he worked from 1590 on, he mastered Lurianic *cabala* and preached the immanent appearance of the Messiah. His *Ets Hayim* ("Tree of Life") was published without his permission (his notes, locked in a strongbox, were taken therefrom by his brother and another disciple). This work was important in spreading Luria's esoteric mysticism throughout Jewish communities in the Middle East and Europe. He wrote essays on repentance, holiness, the future world, the transmigration of the soul, and cabalistic interpretations of various passages from the Bible.

WEINREICH, MAX. (1894–1969)

A scholar-editor pioneer in the world of Yiddish, its history, linguistics, literature, and folklore; he was one of the founders of *YIVO* (Yiddish Scientific Institute) in Vilna, and became Professor in City College of New York.

YOM-TOB LIPPMANN. *See Zunz, Leopold.*

ZABARA. *See IBN ZABARA.*

ZAKKAI, JOHANAN BEN: titled *"Rabban"* (*"our master"*). (*first century of the Christian Era*)

Leader of the Pharisees, disciple of and successor to Hillel, founder of the great *yeshiva* at Jabneh (or Yabneb), Johanan ben Zakkai was called "Rabban" to emphasize his eminence over other rabbi-scholars. His rulings on questions of law were usually accepted against their Sadducee alternatives. His sayings, in Haggadah, are still famous. He included many proverbs and fables in his writings. It is said that Hillel, just before his death, named Johanan, his youngest pupil, to succeed him, calling him "the father of coming generations."

Ben Zakkai's reestablishment of the academy of Jabneh was of immense importance, for it continued the Judaic tradition despite the end of services in the Temple, where religious activity had centered. Jabneh replaced Jerusalem as the seat of the Sanhedrin. Johanan was an important secular leader of the Palestinian Jews, a tower of strength, despite his age, in keeping Judaism alive and in purifying it, as it were, from "the Temple cult." Among his students was Akiba, who became the intellectual giant of Jewry in the next generation.

ZEITLIN, HILLEL (1872–1943)

This writer-philosopher is considered the leading exponent of hasidic thought in recent Yiddish literature. He was born in Russia, was an ardent Zionist, and initially wrote his works in Hebrew. In Vilna, he began to publish in Yiddish. He strongly opposed assimilationist and secular trends in Jewish life. He perished in the holocaust of the Warsaw ghetto.

ZOMA. *See BEN ZOMA, SIMEON.*

ZUNZ, LEOPOLD: *also known by his Hebrew name YOM-TOB LIPPMANN. (1794–1886)*

Philologist, historian and scholar, Zunz (from "Zons," the name of a town on the Rhine) is called "the founder of the science of Judaism" ("*Jüdische Wissenschaft*")—i.e., the systematic study of Judaica. He revealed the widespread inaccuracies of books, written by non-Jews, about Judaism. Zunz pioneered modern Judaica research in historic works on rabbinical literature, homiletics, Jewish names, the history of the liturgy, medieval hymns and poems, Jewish contributions to science, studies of the Torah, etc.

His *Gottesdienstliche Vorträge der Juden* (Lectures for Jewish Religious Services) is often called the most influential single book about Judaism of the nineteenth century. The preface attacked the authorities of Germany for their failure to give Jews full citizenship, for excluding research about Judaism from government patronage, etc. So powerful was the preface, a plea for the return of the sermon into German synagogues, that the authorities suppressed it. Zunz exercised a tremendous influence on the growth of Reform Judaism.

IV · Glossary

'ABADIM. A Minor Tractate added to the Talmud.

ABBA. Aramaic word for "father," "my father." In Babylonia, *Abba* became fused to the "r" of "*Rab*," to become "Rabba" or "Raba"; in Palestine, this was shortened to "Ba"/"Va."

'ABODAH ZARAH. Hebrew: "idolatry." The eighth tractate in NEZIKIN, fourth order of the Talmud.

ABOT DE RABBI NATHAN. A Minor Tractate added to the Talmud. There are two versions of *Abot de Rabbi Nathan;* one has forty-one chapters, the other forty-eight; they stem from the times of the *Tannaim.*

ABOTH (ABOT, AVOTH, AVOT). Hebrew: "the fathers." The ninth tractate in NEZIKIN, *ibid. Aboth,* the only tractate without argument or debate, is also known as *Pirke Abot,* "Sayings of the Fathers." See *Av* and *Pirke Abot.* (Scholars consider "*Abot de Rabbi Nathan,*" below, to be a commentary to *Pirke Abot.*)

ADAM. Hebrew: "man." The Biblical name for the first man. Genesis, II : 7 says God created a man of *adamah* ("earth" or "dust of the ground").

ADDITIONS TO DANIEL. A book in the Apocrypha.

ADDITIONS TO ESTHER. A book in the Apocrypha.

ADONAI. Hebrew: "My Lord." The sacred title of God; usually translated as "Lord" in English. *Adonai* is plural in form (*Adoni* is the singular), but Hebrew, like many Western languages, uses the plural for the singular in formal or reverential situations.

ADOSHEM. From Hebrew *ha-shem:* "the name." The name of God used in ordinary discourse, not in formal religious services, instead of *Adonai.*

AGGADAH. See HAGGADAH.

AKEDAT YITSHAK (pronounced yits-*hok*). Hebrew: "The binding of Isaac." Also the title of a book by Isaac Arama (*q.v.*). The title refers to Abraham's attempt to sacrifice Isaac on Mount Moriah.

ALAV HA-SHALOM (*aleha ha-shalom:* feminine). Hebrew: literally, "On him (or her) peace." The phrase used automatically when referring to someone who is dead—as, in English, one says "of blessed memory," or "May he rest in peace."

ALIYAH (plural ALIOT). Hebrew: "going up . . . ascent." (1) A spiritual pilgrimage, usually to Jerusalem. (2) The honor of being called to the pulpit during a synagogue service, or to recite the blessings before and after the reading of a section of the Torah. (3) Migration to the State of Israel.

AM HA-ARETS. Hebrew: literally, "people of the soil." An ignoramus, an unlettered, uneducated boor. (In Biblical times, these Israelites were drifting away from Judaism, and marrying outside the faith.) The Talmud describes an *am ha-arets* as one who does not respect the Law and the rabbis. Maimonides defined him as "a boor in whom is neither learning nor moral virtue." Rabbi Nathan ben Joseph called an *am ha-arets* "one who has children and does not educate them. . . ."

AMIDAH. Hebrew: "standing." The principal prayer of Jews, usually: *Shemona Esra,* or the Eighteen Benedictions, recited while standing.

AMORA (plural AMORAIM). From Aramaic and Hebrew: *amar;* "speak." Scholar-teacher-lecturers who lived chiefly between 200 and 500, and whose opinions are cited in the GEMARA (*q.v.*). An *amora* often explained to an audience in popular language (usually Aramaic) what an erudite scholar lectured about.

APOCRYPHA. Greek: "hidden," "obscure." Works not in the canon of Jewish sacred writings, though clearly kin. The books of Ecclesiasticus, Judith, Tobit, Esdras, Maccabees I and II, Daniel, Wisdom of Solomon. (Greek translations of the Apocrypha included other books, such as the story of Susanna). These works were written during the period of the Second Temple and following its destruction and the rebellion led by Bar Kochba (*q.v.*). Some of these "post-Biblical" books were incorporated into the Septuagint, canonized by the Roman Catholic Church. Other books outside the canon are in the PSEUDEPIGRAPHA (*q.v.*), which also includes works by unknown and probably invented authors.

  The books of the Apocrypha, although written by and for Jews, were preserved by the Christian Church; in the Middle Ages they were virtually unknown to rabbis and Jewish scholars. (An authoritative work on this subject is R. Travers Herford's *Talmud and Apocrypha*, KTAV Publishing House, New York, 1970.)

'ARAKIN. Hebrew: "Vows . . . evaluating." The fifth tractate in KODASHIM, the fifth order of the Talmud.

ARAMAIC. The language used by most Jews during the Babylonian Exile (536 B.C.E.). The Gemara and first translations of the Bible were written in Aramaic, the *lingua franca* of the Middle Eastern world.

ARI. Popular name for Isaac Luria, "the Ashkenazi" or "the Lion." (See BIOGRAPHIES.)

ASHKENAZI. From *Ashkenaz:* Hebrew for "Germany." A Jew or Jewish tradition in, or from, Central and Eastern Europe; contrasted with Sephardi or Sefardi (*q.v.*)—Spanish or South

European Jewry; the name once used for a kingdom in ancient Armenia. The name Ashkenazim has been applied, since the sixteenth century, to the Jews of central and Eastern Europe—ancestors of the vast majority of Jews in the United States (the first Jewish immigrants to America were Sephardim).

Ashkenazim and Sephardim are the two main branches of Jewry. The Sephardic Jews lived in, or come from, Africa, Portugal, Spain, and southern France, and some in the Orient. The Ashkenazim moved from northern France to Germanic cities along the Rhine, then to Central and Eastern Europe, where they found settlements of Jews who had emigrated, long before, from Babylon and Palestine.

Medieval rabbis dubbed Germany *"Ashkenaz"* after a passage in Jeremiah (51 : 27), and decided that, after the Flood, one of Noah's great-grandsons, named Ashkenaz, had settled in Germany.

The Ashkenazim followed the religious practices and traditions of the rabbi-scholars of Palestine; the Sephardim continued and elaborated the practices and traditions of Jews in Babylonia.

Ashkenazic Jews are distinguished from Sephardic Jews in their style of thought, their pronunciation of Hebrew, aspects of their liturgy, many customs, food habits, ceremonials. YIDDISH is the Ashkenazic language—and universe: the vernacular of Sephardic Jews is Ladino, a dialect of Spanish.

The Ashkenazim created a distinctive civilization—in a Yiddish literature that Sephardic Jews could not understand—about a kind of person the Sephardim had never seen, celebrating passions and visions Sephardim could comprehend only by an effort. It was in the Ashkenazic world that *Yiddishkeit* ("Jewishness") reached its golden age. The culture of Ashkenazim is markedly different from that of Sephardim (see SHTETL). At the core of Sephardic thought, wrote Abraham Menes, lay the question: "What must a Jew know?" At the heart of Ashkenazic life, stirred the challenge: "What must a Jew do?" (For more details see my *Joys of Yiddish,* pp. 19–20, 460–461.)

You may hear it said that the Sephardim were the aristocrats of Judaism, the deepest philosophers, the first Jewish mathematicians and astronomers, the vanguard of rationalism, enlightenment, and critical inquiry. In this context, the words of the late Professor Louis Ginzberg (in *Students, Scholars and Saints,* J.P.S.A., 1928, p. 64.) are particularly pointed:

> Modern historians [praise] the well-ordered studies of the Sefardim, and [censure] the topsy-turvy methods in vogue among the Ashkenazim, which embarked a ten-year-old lad on the "sea of the Talmud" and kept him there until he became a master navigator. [But] is it not startling to find that since the time of Rabbi Joseph Caro (d. 1575) the Sefardim cannot show a single name in the realm of the Talmud comparable with the distinguished scholars of Poland? . . . There must have been method in the methodlessness of the Polish Jew.

AV (plural: AVOT). Hebrew: "father." (1) A teacher of Mishnah who helped establish the methods of legal interpretation. These important scholar-legalists were called *Tannaim* (*q.v.*). They lived during the last 200–250 years before, and the first two centuries of, the Christian Era. (2) The ethical precepts and aphorisms of these teachers, as recorded in *Pirke Abot* (*q.v.*). (3) In the Bible, the *avot* are Abraham, Isaac, and Jacob.

BAAL SHEM. Hebrew: "Master of (God's) Name." The name given a holy man, healer, saintly magic-worker, especially in Eastern Europe. See Baal Shem Tov (Israel ben Eliezer), in BIOGRAPHIES.

BABA (BAVA). Hebrew: "gate" (see below).

BABA BATHRA. Hebrew: "the last gate." The third tractate in NEZIKIN, the fourth order of the Talmud dealing with civil law.

BABA KAMMA. Hebrew: "the first gate." The first tractate in NEZIKIN, *ibid.*

BABA METZI'A. Hebrew: "the middle gate." The second tractate in NEZIKIN, *ibid.*

BABYLONIAN TALMUD. See Guide Note B, pp. 68–71.

BAMIDBAR. The oldest name for *Numbers,* the fourth book of the Pentateuch (the five books of Moses), which describes the numbering of the Israelites; later *Bamidbar* was replaced by the fourth word in the opening sentence, *Be-Midbar,* "In the Wilderness."

BAR. Aramaic for Hebrew word "ben," denoting membership in a class, usually meaning "son" or "son of."

BARAITHA. Hebrew: "that which is external." A Tannaitic teaching, not included in the official *Mishnah.*

BARUCH. A book of the Apocrypha of the Old Testament.

BAVA. See BABA.

BEKOROTH. Hebrew: "first born . . . firstlings." The fourth tractate in KODASHIM, the fifth order of the Talmud.

BEL AND THE DRAGON. A book in the Apocrypha.

BE-MIDBAR. See **BAMIDBAR.**

BEN. Hebrew: "son" or "son of."

BERAKOTH. Hebrew: "blessings . . . benedictions." The first tractate in ZERAIM, the first order of the Talmud.

BERESHITH (BE-RESHIT). Hebrew: "In the beginning." (1) The Hebrew name for the First Book of Moses, originally, "Book of Creation," rendered into Greek by *Genesis,* "origin," because it gives an account of the creation of the world and the beginnings of life. *Bereshith* is the first Hebrew word in its opening sentence. (2) *Bereshith* is also the name of the first of the fifty-four weekly Torah readings (*Sedrahs*) on Sabbath mornings. (3) *Shabbath Bereshith* can also refer to any ordinary Sabbath.

"BESHT." The acronym for Baal Shem Tov. (See BIOGRAPHIES.)

BETH DIN. Hebrew: "house of law." A Jewish court. Three main levels of Jewish courts existed during the Mishnaic period: one with three judges, one with twenty-three judges, and the great Sanhedrin—of seventy-one. After 425 C.E., only courts of three, five, or seven judges continued to function.

BEZAH. Hebrew: "[an] egg." The seventh tractate in MO'ED, second order of the Talmud; the tractate is also known as *YOM TOV.*

BIBLE. From Greek: *biblia,* "little books." The Hebrew Bible, "the sacred canonical books," originally structured as twenty-four books, divided into three sections: *Torah, Neviim, Ketuvim* (i.e., "Torah, Prophets, Hagiographa"). See Guide Notes, TORAH, TALMUD, MISHNAH, MIDRASH, GEMARA, pp. 67–76.

BIKKURIM. Hebrew: "first fruits." The eleventh and last tractate in ZERAIM, the first order of the Talmud.

CABALA (CABBALAH, KABBALAH). Hebrew: "tradition." A mystical system based upon the permutations of numerical values assigned to letters of the Hebrew alphabet, and believed in this way to reveal "hidden" meanings to words and phrases. Feats of divination, numerology, and esoteric thought became influential among Jews during the Middle Ages. The *Zohar* (*q.v.*), probably written in the thirteen century (translated into Latin 200 years later by Pico della Mirandola), made cabalism a movement of considerable consequence.

Originally, cabalism meant the Oral Tradition; in the twelfth century, Jewish mystics asserted that there was an unbroken link between their ideas and those of ancient days. God was known to the cabalists as *En Sof* (Infinite One); His existence was made known through ten *sefirot,* or "divine emanations."

The cabalists held that reason alone could never penetrate the exalted, mystical experience involved in their perception of God's mysteries. Occult formulae and numerological acrobatics went into the cabalists' efforts to comprehend God's will, and many a prediction excitedly hailed the imminent appearance of the Messiah and the Day of Judgment. Some cabalists mortified the flesh; others set themselves prodigious tasks of fasting, penitence, prayer—to atone for evil, purge the soul of sin, redeem the spirit. The center of cabalistic teaching in the sixteenth century was Safed, Palestine, which was the seat of a sizable community of mystics. Isaac Luria (see BIOG-RAPHIES) was the outstanding cabalist (known as the "Ari" —the "Lion"), a visionary who claimed to speak with the Prophet Elijah, presided over fervent disciples to whom he expounded arcane invocations containing many secret, "hidden Names" of God, upon which the faithful were exhorted to meditate. Esoteric and minatory rituals were ordained over every conceivable interpretation of passages from the Torah or the names of prophets.

(NOTE: It is not so hard to understand why mystical doctrines attracted Jews, in the later Middle Ages, given the poverty and abiding terror under which they lived. Many devout souls became convinced they would be delivered from their terrible tribulations only by the Messiah. What, except the miraculous, was there to place hope in? See Hugh Trevor-Roper's brilliant analytic description, in *Historical Essays,* Harper and Row, New York, 1957, 1966, pp. 146 ff.)

CHACHEM. See HAKHAM.

CHANNUKAH. See HANUKKAH.

CHASID (CHASSID). See HASID.

CHEDER (HEDER). Hebrew: "room." The room or school where boys learned/learn elementary Hebrew. The *cheder* was often the free school for boys who could not afford to attend a YESHIVA (*q.v.*).

CHUTSPA. Hebrew: "insolence." Gall, brazen effrontery, indescribable presumption-plus-arrogance. The classic definition of *chutspa* is this: *Chutspa* is that quality enshrined in a man who, having killed his mother and father, throws himself on the mercy of the court because he is an orphan.

COHEN. See KOHEN.

DARKE TSEDEK. Hebrew: "Paths of Justice." A book of homilies by Zechariah Mendel of Yeroslav.

DEMAI. Hebrew: "doubtful crops . . . produce not certainly tithed." The third tractate in ZERAIM, the first order of the Talmud.

DEREKH ERETS. Hebrew: "the way of the land . . . local customs and courtesies." The title of two minor tractates appended to the Talmud. See below.

DEREKH ERETS RABAH (RABBAH) (*rabah:* Hebrew: "large.") A collection published in translation in the Soncino edition of the *Minor Tractates of the Talmud;* it emphasizes rules of decorum, modesty, manners—through stories of the lives of the Sages.
Technically, the minor tractates are not "of the Talmud" but are appended to it.

DEREKH ERETS TSUTA (*tsuta:* "small") Published in the minor tractates "of" the Talmud; a collection of ethical teachings, plus the praising of peace, with advice to the learned about their religious and teaching duties. Although printed after DEREKH ERETS RABBAH, there is no substantive progression from the one to the other.

DEUTERONOMY. The Greek name for the fifth book of the Torah. See Guide Note: TORAH (pp. 67–68) and DVARIM, below.

DEUTERONOMY RABBAH. See Guide Notes A and C (pp. 67–68, 72–73.

DEVARIM. See DVARIM, below.

DIASPORA. Greek: "dispersion"; in Hebrew, *galuth:* "exile." Literally, the dispersion of Jews from the holy land, and their settlement in other lands; but the word carries profound overtones of recurrent persecutions, misery, and tragic expulsion from one land after another, sometimes after centuries of residence. Since the sixth century B.C.E., when the ancient kingdom of Judah was conquered and the Babylonians effected forcible deportations (to what is now Iraq), Jews have lived "in exile."

(I use quotation marks because of the great number of Jews who elected not to return to live in Palestine, or to the State of Israel.) Jewish colonies thrived all through the Middle East and along the northern coast of Africa. The conquests of Alexander the Great and the Romans tended to unify the culture of Mediterranean and Middle Eastern people; but political/religious repression drove Jewish groups into the Balkans, into Italy, Spain, France, the Rhineland, the Netherlands, England.

During the Middle Ages, fanatical harassments drove Jews more and more into Eastern Europe—Poland, the Ukraine, Turkey. In the nineteenth and twentieth centuries, drastic discrimination, poverty, and pogroms made the Jews leave "the Pale" of Russia and Poland, and many settlements in Austria, Rumania, Hungary—for England, the United States, South America, South Africa, Australia, and Palestine.

DVARIM. Hebrew: "words." The name of the fifth book of the Torah, from the opening phrase in the Hebrew text; but the oldest name, contained within the book itself, was "*Mishneh Torah*": "The Repetition of the Torah." Greek-speaking Jews translated this as *deuteros nomos* or *Deuteronomion*, i.e., "Second Law." This title was given in the Latin Bible as *Deuteronomium* and then, in English versions, as Deuteronomy.

'EDUYYOTH (EDUYOTH, EDUYYOT, EDYOT). Hebrew: "testimonies," (collection of *mishneot*). The seventh tractate in NEZIKIN, the fourth order of the Mishnah, known as *Behirta* ("chosen") in the Talmud. The tractate covers proceedings of the high court in Javneh; but the same materials appear in other tractates.

ELOHIM. A generic name for God, used among many ancient peoples in the Near East. In the Hebrew Bible, *Elohim* is one of the names of God most frequently used—along, and sometimes combined, with YHVH (*q.v.*). Medieval Jewish philosophers maintained that *Elohim* refers to that aspect of God found in nature.

EPISTLE OF JEREMY. A book in the Apocrypha (*q.v.*).

'ERUBIN (ERUVIN). Hebrew: "Sabbath travel regulations . . . the fusion of Sabbath limits." The second tractate in MO'ED, the second order of the Talmud; it embraces many regulations concerning the Sabbath. (Some authorities consider *Erubin* to be a continuation of *Shabbat,* the first tractate in MO'ED.)

ESDRAS. Two books in the Apocrypha (*q.v.*), usually attributed to the prophet Ezra. The books are called Esdras III and IV because Ezra I and II are ascribed to Ezra and Nehemiah.

ESTHER. A book (*Megillat[h] Esther*) in the Bible (*q.v.*), probably written around 330 B.C.E.; it describes the role of Esther, wife of Ahasuerus, in saving the Jews of Persia from extermination. See PURIM, below. The name "Esther" ("star") is the Persian or Babylonian form of *Hadassah.* See MEGILLAH.

ETS HAYIM. Hebrew: "tree of life." (1) The wooden sticks around which a Torah scroll is rolled; the words come from a verse in the Book of Proverbs; "It [Torah] is a tree of life to them who hold it." (2) The name of a book presenting the ideas of Isaac Luria. (See BIOGRAPHIES.)

EXODUS. Greek: "road out." The second book of the Torah, called in Hebrew *shmot* ("Names") after its opening word. See Guide Note A, (pp. 67–68).

EXODUS RABBAH. A midrashic commentary on Exodus in the Midrash. See Guide Note D, (pp. 74–75).

GALUTH. Hebrew: "exile." In Yiddish, pronounced *goles.* See DIASPORA.

GAN EDEN. Hebrew: "paradise . . . Garden of Eden." "God planted a garden eastward, in Eden," says Genesis. Popular tradition placed Eden between the Tigris and Euphrates rivers. The Talmudists and cabalists were persuaded that there were two gardens of Eden: the luxuriant garden on earth; and the one in the heavens, the eternal abode of the righteous after death. When a mortal dies, his or her good deeds are weighed against bad deeds. See GEHENNA.

GAON. Hebrew: "genius," "pride," or "excellency" (plural: *geonim*). (1) The head of a Talmudic academy. (2) A rabbi whose learning was so great that he was given the honorary title of *gaon*. (3) A scholar-genius. The title *gaon* was held by the heads of the Talmudic academies of Babylonia from 589 to 1040, then fell into disuse; it was revived and applied to a rabbi of exceptional learning or an authority unquestioned by world Jewry. The *geonim* ruled on religious questions; questions were sent them from all parts of the Diaspora; they provided *responsa* (*q.v.*).

GEHENNA. Greek for the Hebrew: "Gehinnon . . . the valley of Hinnom." (1) The name of a valley, southwest of Jerusalem, where human sacrifice was practiced. (2) The name of the place where the wicked will abide, after death, to expiate their misdeeds. One description in the Talmud pictures Gehenna as a dark place, filled with everlasting fire and sulfurous fumes. ("Purgatory" is nowhere named in the Bible; this name entered official Roman Catholic Church usage in the thirteenth century; back in the third century, Origen had said that souls wait in a fearful place to be "purged of evil" so they may enter the Kingdom of Heaven undefiled. The Church of England has scorned Purgatory as "grounded upon no warranty of Scripture, but rather repugnant to the Word of God." See Gustav Davidson's learned and unique *A Dictionary of Angels*, Free Press, 1967.)

GEMARA. Hebrew: "completion" or "learning." The discussion—lengthy, discursive, difficult, and still often charming—of the *Mishnah*, which together with it constitutes the Talmud. See Guide Notes D and F: GEMARA (pp. 74–75, 76–78).

GEMATRIA. From Greek: *gamma*, the third letter in the alphabet, and *tria*, "three." In Hebrew, the letters of the alphabet also served the ancients as numbers: *aleph* = 1, *bet* = 2, etc. Each letter, hence each word or phrase, possessed a numerical "value." Mystics converted numerical values into supposed keys to the meanings of passages in the holy texts, to reveal a new meaning or resolve an old ambiguity. Example: The Hebrew word for "pregnancy," *herayon,* has a numerical value of 271, which is "the total number of days a woman carries a child." The manipulation of numbers became a popular mode of Biblical and Talmudic interpretation during the Middle Ages. Many scholars employed *gematria* in the hope of discovering the exact date on which the Messiah would arrive. So far, the Messiah has not confirmed the researches and expectations of the gematriasts.

GENESIS. The Greek name for the first book of the Torah; in Hebrew: "Bereshith" or *"Be-Reshit."* See Guide Note A: TORAH (p. 67–68).

GENESIS RABBAH. A book in the Midrash (see Guide Note E: p. 76), containing 100 passages from Genesis which are extensively interpreted.

GITTIN (GITIN). Aramaic: "divorces . . . bills of divorce." The fifth tractate in NASHIM, the third order of the Talmud; its nine chapters discuss Judaic laws of divorce.

GOLEM. Hebrew: "yet-unformed thing." A robot, a simpleton, a clod. (For legends and dramas, see my *Joys of Yiddish,* pp. 137–38.)

HAGGADAH. Hebrew: "tale" or "narration." (1) The narrative, read aloud at the Passover *seder,* which recounts the story of Israel's bondage in, and flight from, Egypt; the material comes from many sources, and contains prayers, psalms, hymns, and songs for the children. (2) The vast, colorful repository of allegories, historical episodes, folklore, prayers, parables, witticisms, anecdotes about martyrs, saints, sages, etc., found in the Talmud, very popular with Jewish people. Also called Aggadah. See Guide Note D (pp. 74–75). (*The Passover Anthology,* by Philip Goodman, J.P.S.A., 1961, is an invaluable and comprehensive collection of material about every aspect of Passover.)

HAGIGAH. Hebrew: "festival sacrifice . . . the festal offerings." The twelfth tractate in MO'ED, the second order of the Talmud.

HAGIOGRAPHA. Greek: "holy writings;" in Hebrew, *ketuvim:* "writings." The third/final part of the Old Testament, which follows the Prophets and consists of twelve books: the five "Scrolls" (*megilloth*) read in the synagogue on special days (Ruth, the Song of Songs, Lamentations, Ecclesiastes, Esther) and Psalms, Proverbs, Job, Daniel, Ezra-Nehemiah, Chronicles I and II.

HAKHAM. Hebrew: "wise man"; "one who exemplifies or practices *hakhmah*." (See below.)

HAKHMAH. Hebrew: "wisdom." (1) The divine spirit of Wisdom which, according to the Midrash, preceded the creation of the world. (2) Wisdom, profundity, astuteness. (3) The total reservoir of rabbinical knowledge. (4) Wisdom handed down by tradition and impossible to learn by experiment. (5) Cabalistic knowledge.

HALAKA (HALAKHA, HALACHA). Hebrew: "guidance" or "step." (1) The legalistic parts of the Talmud as distinguished from the ethical, poetic, allegorical, anecdotal materials known as the *Haggadah*). (2) The decisions of the rabbis on disputes about ritual, obligations, duties. (3) The Law that governs devout Jewry's conduct in religious-ethical-social matters. (4) The accumulated jurisprudence of Judaism—without Biblical citations. *Halaka* encompasses all the laws to which observing Jews are bound. But the rabbis did not "create" *Halaka;* they interpreted, clarified, and codified legal teachings, constantly adapting them to changed historical and social circumstances. Many rabbis believed the source of all Law was the Revelation at Sinai.

HALITSAH (Hebrew: "taking off"). The ceremony, described in Deuteronomy 25 : 5–10, in which a childless widow releases her brother-in-law from the ancient requirement to marry her.

HALLAH. Hebrew: "dough offering." (1) The ninth tractate in ZERAIM, the first order of the Talmud. (2) The braided white bread, glazed with egg white, which is a Sabbath delicacy. Orthodox Jews place two *challahs* (*challa, challeh,*—many spellings) on the table on the eve of Sabbath, uncut until after the blessing. (This perpetuates the memory of the Temple in Jerusalem, where two rows of bread were set before the altar.)

HAMAN: See PURIM.

HA-NAGID. See *NAGID.*

HANUKKAH (CHANNUKA, HANNUKAH). Hebrew: "The Feast of Dedication," more colloquially known as "The Feast of Lights." One of the less solemn Jewish festivals, this eight-day holiday falls on the 25th of the Hebrew month of Kislev and continues into the month of Tevet (in December, according to our calendar). Hanukkah commemorates the historic victory of the Jewish Maccabees over Syrian despots (167 before the Christian Era), a fight for religious freedom that rescued Judaism from annihilation. The Apocrypha tells the story (Maccabees I and II). The rebellion, led by a priest, Mattathias, and his son, Judah the Maccabee ("the Hammer"), continued for three years against the armies of Antiochus IV, who wanted to turn the Hebrews to Greek polytheism. Antiochus desecrated the great Temple, ordered the Jews to build shrines for idols and to stop circumcising male babies.

Guerrilla groups of Jews, equipped with primitive weapons, fought the Seleucid soldiers—and won a surprising victory at Emmaus. They returned to Jerusalem and set about restoring the burned Temple. On the twenty-fifth day of the Hebrew month of Kislev, in 165 B.C.E., Judah the Maccabee rededicated Zion's Temple—lighting the eternal light.

Each Hanukkah, Jews around the world light candles for eight days—one the first evening, adding one light each night on a nine-branched menorah. The ninth candle, called the *shames* (servant), stands apart from the rest and is used to light the others; this is interpreted to show that one can give love and light to others without losing any part of one's own radiance. (*Hannukah,* edited by Emily Solis Cohen, Jr., J.P.S.A., 1965, is a comprehensive and invaluable collection covering every aspect of "the Feast of Lights.")

HAPHTARAH (HAPHTORAH, HAFTORAH). Hebrew: "end
. . . conclusion." A chapter from the Prophets, read in the
synagogue on Sabbaths and festivals after the reading from the
Torah. When the Romans prohibited the Torah reading, a
common evasion was to read a *haphtarah* containing a reference to the appropriate part of the Torah.

HASID (CHASID, HASSID). Hebrew: "pious," "pious one." (1)
A most pious man. (2) A follower of the Hasidic philosophy
and way of life (a disciple of a great rabbi). In the days of
Roman rule, the Hasidim were militant Pharisees. But the term
usually refers to the extraordinary Hasidic movement of the
seventeenth–eighteenth centuries which raced through Jewish
communities of eastern and central Europe. This movement
was founded by Israel ben Eliezer (called "the Baal Shem
Tov"—see BIOGRAPHIES), who preached a folk gospel that
had enormous appeal to small-town Jews, because it opposed
the rabbinical emphasis on formal learning and scholastic cas-
uistry. Israel ben Eliezer extolled simple faith, joyous worship,
everyday pleasures; God requires no synagogues, except "in the
heart." Prayers should be spontaneous, personal, happy. The
Hasidim danced and clapped hands while singing the Lord's
praises. Hasidic rabbis, often not ordained, preached with delightful parables, anecdotes and folk sayings. They angered
many of Jewry's rabbinical establishment. The Gaon of Vilna,
head of the rabbinical academy, formally anathematized the
Hasidim.
     A Hasidic leader was treated by his followers with greater
awe than Jews customarily gave a rabbi. Disciples repeated a
Hasid's every phrase, imitated his every gesture. Hasidism's
leaders became known as *tsadikim* (*q.v.*)—seers, near-saints,
prophets believed to possess supernatural powers. The title
tsadik even became hereditary. Hasidism still has passionate
adherents, in small, lively enclaves in Israel, South America
and the United States.

HASMONEAN: See MACCABEE.

HEBREW. From the Hebrew root *ivri*, which may originally have
meant "one from the other side of the river [Jordan]." To be

exact, "Hebrew" should be applied only to Israelites and Judeans before the Babylonian Exile (586 B.C.E.); after that date, the name "Jew" (from "Judah") became accepted.

HERMENEUTICS. From Greek: "interpretation;" the Hebrew is *midot* ("rules" or "measurements"). Hermeneutics is the system of rules that govern the linguistic/exegetical ways by which a word, phrase, or passage of sacred writings may be interpreted. These rules were first set down by Hillel (see BIOGRAPHIES) in seven principles, dealing with permissible and nonpermissible inference, deduction, limitations on textual particulars/generalizations. Rabbi Ishmael enumerated thirteen rules; Rabbi Eliezer ben Rabbi Yose ha-Galili enumerated three (but the latter appear only in post-Talmudic literature). Other curious methodologies for hermeneutics were emphasized later: e.g., *gematria* (*q.v.*) and *notarikon,* which treated some words as abbreviations for larger phrasings. (See Akiba in BIOGRAPHIES.)

HORAYOTH. Hebrew: "decisions . . . instructions." The tenth tractate in NEZIKIN, the fourth order of the Talmud. The tractate discusses legal errors committed by the Sanhedrin (*q.v.*) or by a high priest.

HULLIN. Hebrew: "unconsecrated animals . . . animals killed for food." The third tractate in KODASHIM, the fifth order of the Talmud, which sets forth the ritual and techniques to be followed in slaughtering animals.

IBN. Arabic for "son [of];" *ibn* became *"ben"* or *"bin"* when used between the proper names of father-and-son.

ISRAEL. Hebrew: "Champion of God." (1) Precisionists used "Israel" only to name the people of the Northern Kingdom, where the so-called "Ten Tribes of Israel" dwelt. (2) The name of the state created on May 14, 1948. (3) Jewry as a whole. (4) Popular Jewish first name.

JERUSALEM TALMUD. Hebrew: *"Talmud Yerushalmi."* See Guide Note B: TALMUD (pp. 68–71).

JESUS. See Guide Note D: MIDRASH (p. 74–75).

JESUS BEN SIRACH. See BIOGRAPHIES: *BEN SIRACH.*

JUDITH. A book in the Apocrypha; it describes a siege in Samaria and the beheading of Holofernes, the Assyrian general, by the pulchritudinous Judith. The book was written in Hebrew, but has survived only in a Greek translation. Many experts regard the text as unreliable.

KABALA (KABBALA). See CABALA.

KADDISH. Aramaic: *Kadosh,* "holy." In Hebrew: "consecration." (1) A prayer glorifying God's name, recited at the close of synagogue prayers. (2) The mourner's prayer. (3) A son, called affectionately *"my Kaddish."*

The *Kaddish* was originally a doxology, recited after completing a reading from the Bible or a religious lesson from the Mishnah, that glorifies God's name, affirms faith in the establishment of His Kingdom, and expresses hope for peace. The language of the prayer is Aramaic, which was spoken by the Jews in their Babylonian exile and during the days of the Second Temple or Commonwealth. In time, a belief grew that the praises of God in the *Kaddish* would help the souls of the dead find lasting peace; and the prayer became known as the Mourner's Prayer (even though it contains no reference to death). The *Kaddish* is recited at the grave, and, for varying months after a death, by the children, parents, siblings of the deceased, then each year on the anniversary of death (*Yortsayt*). There are five separate *kaddish* forms: the short, the whole, the mourners', the rabbinical, and the "kaddish of renewal," which is given at the grave. The *kaddish* is recited only when a *minyan* (*q.v.*) attends. Females may recite the *kaddish* in Conservative and Reform services.

KALLAH. Hebrew: "bride." (1) A bride. (2) One of the Minor Tractates, containing material on marital relations. *KALLAH* is now included in virtually all editions of the Talmud.

KALLAH RABBATHI. A larger tractate of *KALLAH* (see above), in the Minor Tractates.

KARET (KARETH). Hebrew: "excision." A punishment for sin—not ordered by a *Beth Din* (ecclesiastical court) but divinely imposed, presumably, through an "accident," disease, sudden death, etc. Such punishment presumably cut the offender from a place in the world-to-come.

KEDUSHAH (plural: *kedushot*). Hebrew: "sanctification." (1) This is a form of doxology contained in the repetition of the *Amidah* (*q.v.*). (2) The name of the third of the Eighteen/Nineteen Benedictions. (3) Noun, meaning "holiness."

KELIM. Hebrew: "utensils" or "vessels." The first tractate in TOHOROTH (TOHOROT), the sixth order of the Talmud, which deals with ritual laws on the purification of glass, earthenware, and metal utensils.

KERITHOTH. Hebrew: "divine punishment . . . extirpation." The seventh tractate in KODASHIM, the fifth order of the Talmud; it deals with *karet* (see above).

KETUBAH (KETTUBAH). Hebrew: "written document." The traditional, marriage contract, specifying the wife's legal rights in the estate, if her husband dies or divorces her.

KETHUBOTH (KETUBBOT). Hebrew: "marriage contracts . . ." The second tractate in NASHIM, the third order of the Talmud; it deals with monetary aspects of divorce or widowhood, and the reciprocal duties of husbands and wives.

KIDDUSH. Hebrew: "sanctification." (Do not confuse with *Kaddish*, above.) The prayer and benediction that celebrates the Sabbath and Jewish holy days. The father of the family recites Genesis 2:1–3, which tells how God rested on the seventh day and made it holy. Two *brokhes* (blessings) follow: praising God for having created wine; thanking Him for having created the Sabbath "as a memorial of the Creation" and "in remembrance of the departure from Egypt." Some Jews recite the *Kiddush* without wine (and without the blessing for wine), using the *challe* loaf instead (thousands of Jews were too poor to afford wine every Friday). The *Kiddush* ceremony predates the Christian Communion and Eucharist; the first

Christians adapted the ritual of a communion (or "love feast") that was used among the sect of Jews called Essenes.

KIDDUSH HA-SHEM. Hebrew: "sanctification of God's Name." (1) Hebrew term for martyrdom. (2) Righteous acts performed in public. (3) Doing more than is required in order to praise God before Gentiles.

KIDDUSHIN. Hebrew: "sanctifications" or "betrothals," "marriage rites." (1) The Jewish rite of marriage. (2) The seventh tractate in NASHIM, the third order of the Talmud; it deals with prohibited and permitted engagements, specifying legal regulations.

KIL'AYIM. Hebrew: "diverse kinds." The fourth tractate in ZERAIM, the first order of the Talmud; it discusses prohibited "minglings" of animals, seeds, fabrics.

KINNIN. Hebrew: "bird nests ... bird offerings." The eleventh (last) tractate in KODASHIM, the fifth order of the Talmud; it deals with regulations concerning Leviticus 5 and 12:8, on offerings after the birth of a child; the tractate discusses the pairs of birds, "two turtles or two young pigeons," which were made obligatory as offerings to expiate certain offenses—and certain unclean conditions.

KLEE YAKAR. Hebrew: "beloved vessel." A commentary on the Torah by Rabbi Ephraim Lunchitz (Luntshitz), in the seventeenth century. Lunchitz was head of the *yeshiva* in Lvov, and chief rabbi of Prague.

KODASHIM. Hebrew: "sacred" or "hallowed things." The fifth order of the Talmud. It contains eleven tractates on ritual, sacrifices, slaughtering.

KOHELETH. Hebrew: meaning uncertain, but probably a name; the Greek, chosen by Jerome, is best rendered as "collector of wise sayings for teaching." A part of the HAGIOGRAPHA which expounds gloomy ideas about life, faith, reason, oppression. The authorship ("Koheleth, son of David," whom the rabbis took to be Solomon) prevented the rabbis from banning this great lyrical, pessimistic masterpiece, which is today read in synagogues during the Feast of Tabernacles. Contemporary experts on the Bible consider Koheleth a pseudonym and date the book somewhere around the third century before the Christian Era.

KOHELETH RABBAH. The Midrash on the Book of Ecclesiastes, included in the Midrash Rabbah and dated by scholars as a post-Talmudic work.

KOHEN (COHEN). Hebrew: "priest." Before the Exodus, the head of every Israelite family was a consecrated, priestly mediator between God and man; and the first-born male possessed authority as legatee of his father's estate. After the Exodus, the tribe of Levi was selected as the priesthood, in place of sons in general—partly because of the traumatic experience of the Golden Calf episodes; and the descendants of Aaron (Moses' brother), were made responsible for supervising laws of hygiene, instruction in the laws, maintaining the Tabernacle, etc. To estop a priesthood from achieving *political* hegemony, the tribe of Levi was not allotted land in Israel; they lived on tithes, portions of sacrifices, and land apportioned from other tribes. (One must admire the political foresight and sophistication this entailed.)

There were seven grades of priesthood (see Exodus, 30:22–33 and Deuteronomy 20:2–12) from the High Priest (*kohen gadol*) to deputies, war-priests, Temple treasures, ordinary *kohens*.

The Kohens hold a special status in Orthodox Jewry to this day; they arc the first called up to read from the Torah; they may not marry divorcees; they must not go to cemeteries (except for nearest blood relations), etc.

KOL NIDRE. Aramaic: "all vows." This plaintive prayer (in Aramaic) ushers in the holiest of days, Yom Kippur (*q.v.*); it is uttered, just before sunset, by the cantor—three times, first softly, then louder, the congregation reciting it softly along with him. Throughout, the Torah scroll is held aloft by three men. The melody is exceptionally moving, and seems to recapitulate the history of Jewish suffering and persecutions.

(Beethoven placed part of *Kol Nidre* in his *Quartet in C♯ Minor;* Tolstoy characterized the prayer as an "echo of the martyrdom of a grief-stricken nation.") But the words of *Kol Nidre* are severely legalistic:

Kol Nidre [all vows], obligations, oaths, anathemas, be they called *konam* or *konas* or by any other name, which we may vow or swear or pledge . . . from this Day of Atonement until the next . . . we do repent. May they be deemed to be forgiven, absolved, annulled or void—and made of no effect. They shall not bind us nor have power over us [and] the vows shall not be considered vows, nor the obligations obligatory, nor the oaths oaths.

Kol Nidre was originally regarded with contempt by rabbi/ scholars. It was Rabbi Yehudai the Gaon, an eighth-century sage of Babylonia, who introduced *Kol Nidre* into the synagogues. For the special importance which Jews attach to promises, see Headnote: VOWS in the collected quotations of this volume, which then explains why certain vows "shall not be considered vows" and why certain oaths (forced out of Jews by threat and torture) were not to be treated as legitimate or binding.

KOSHER. Hebrew: *kasher:* "fit." The rabbinical regulations which govern the dietary laws of observing Jews, based on the tractate *Hullin* (*q.v.*) and the second part of the *Shulhan Aruk* (*q.v.*). See FOOD AND DRINK in the collected quotations.

KUNI LEMMEL. German: *Lümmel,* "bumpkin." A yokel, a Simple Simon. (For the subtle and ironic differences between a *Kuni Lemmel* and a *shlemiel,* a *nebekh,* a *Chaim Yankel, et alia,* see *The Joys of Yiddish.*)

KUTHIM (KUTIM). One of the Minor Tractates added to the Talmud, it discusses the relations between Jews, Samaritans (*Kuthim* was the Talmudic name for Samaritans and any who did not accept the Oral Law) and non-Jews. In censored editions of the Talmud, *Kuthim* was used to replace various appellations for non-Jews, and vice versa.

KUZARI. A classic, written in Arabic, variously called *Kitab al-Khazari, The Kuzari, Ha-Kuzari,* by Judah ha-Levi, recounting the discussions 400 years earlier between a rabbi and the king of the Khazars, a Tatar people on the lower Volga, which ended with the king's conversion to Judaism. See BIOGRAPHIES: *HA-LEVI.*

LEVITICUS. Greek: *Leuitikos;* late Latin: *Leviticus*: "book of the Levites"; in Hebrew: *Va-Yikra,* after the opening word of this third book of the Pentateuch. Leviticus is also known as *Torat(h) Kohanim* ("the priestly code" or "laws of the priests") for it contains much of the Mosaic law concerning priests, sacrifices, and ritual purity. Scholars differ on the dating of parts of Leviticus: some hold it to be a collection of isolated works and commandments, some think it preceded the Exile; parts clearly seem traceable to the Sinai period. See Guide Note A: The Torah, (pp. 67–68).

LEVITICUS RABBAH. (Complete title: Midrash Leviticus Rabbah.) The third book in the Midrash Rabbah (see below): one of the earliest *midrashim* (fifth–sixth century). It consists of thirty-seven chapters concerning the weekly readings from Leviticus, the third book of the Torah—at a time when these readings covered a triennial cycle.

LOSHN-KADOSH. Yiddish from Hebrew: "sacred language." The language of the Torah. Yiddish is called *mama-loshn* ("mother tongue"; see below.)

MAALOT HA-MIDOT. Hebrew: "The merit of the rules." See *ANAV*, in BIOGRAPHIES.

MAAMAR MORDECAI. Hebrew: "Mordecai's essay (or sermons)."

MA'ASER SHENI. Hebrew: "second tithe." The eighth tractate in ZERAIM, the first order of the Talmud; it consists of five chapters on tithes in Jerusalem.

MACCABEES. Derivation unknown. (1) The Maccabees (or Hasmoneans), a dynasty of priests, founded by Mattathias, called *Hasmonai*—possibly after an ancestor, or after the place mentioned in the Book of Joshua (15:27). Mattathias's five sons, of whom Judah the Maccabee was the oldest, led the revolt of the Jews in Palestine against the Syrian autocrat Antiochus Epiphanes (75–164 B.C.E.). (2) Four individual books in the Apocrypha; that is:

Maccabees I; describes the Hasmonean family's history— from Antiochus, who made martyrs of seven children (called Maccabees by later Christians) who refused to perform idolatrous rites; their mother, Hannah (Salome), is honored in many shrines throughout the Christian world. The original Hebrew text of the book has been lost; the Greek translation survived in the Septuagint.

Maccabees II; written probably in the second century B.C.E., describes the Hasmonean uprising, and revolves around the extraordinary story of Judah the Maccabee; this account apparently is a shortened version of a Greek work, written by one Jason of Cyrene.

Maccabees III; written in Greek, describes the persecutions of Ptolemy IV (Philopator) and the miraculous deliverance of the Temple. (Some authorities believe the data referred to Caligula's persecutions in Egypt.)

Maccabees IV; an eloquent philosophical work extolling reason, as against passions. Clearly influenced by the philosophy of the Stoics, the book was written in Greek by a Jew, sometime in the last century before, or the first century of, the Christian Era; its only connection with "Maccabees" is that the author quotes II Maccabees from time to time.

MAGEN (MOGEN) DAVID. Hebrew: "Shield of David." The 6-pointed Star of David, symbol of Israel; no one is sure why, how, or when it became a symbol of Jewry. The Zionist Congress adopted it in 1897. No reference to the *Magen David* is found in rabbinical writings until the thirteenth century; and the first explicitly Jewish association did not occur until the seventeenth.

MAGID. Hebrew: "teacher" or "preacher" (plural: *magidim*). A teacher/preacher, usually itinerant. The *magid* played a significant role in Jewish communities in Eastern Europe in the eighteenth and nineteenth centuries. A shabbily clothed "country preacher," he wandered about, on foot or by cart, from *shtetl* to *shtetl.* Note that the *rabbis* were not expected to preach sermons; they were occupied with study, teaching, interpreting the law, stimulating discussion of the Torah. In earlier times, a *darshan* ("expounder") was paid to deliver sermons in the synagogue on Sabbath afternoons; the *darshan* was also a learned man, a rabbi, whose preachings were in Hebrew, erudite, often pedantic.

The *magidim* came to play a cherished role among the poor laity; the *magid* generally used Yiddish, was informal in his sermons, and lived off contributions. Some *magidim* were orators of the fire-and-brimstone school, but the most beloved were homey types, mixing jokes and parables into their sermons. The lore of Ashkenazic Jews was vastly enriched by the delightful fables and moralistic tales circulated by the *magidim.*

MAKKOTH. Hebrew: "punishment by flogging." The fifth tractate in NEZIKIN, the fourth order of the Talmud; it deals with lashings, perjury, and places of refuge for persons guilty of involuntary manslaughter (*shogegim*).

MAMA-LOSHN. Yiddish: "mother language" or "mother tongue." (1) The colloquial name for Yiddish. Since the holy books were in Hebrew, and generally only Jewish males were taught to read Hebrew, Yiddish became "the mother's tongue" in Eastern European Jewish homes. Yiddish derives from the German brought by medieval German Jews into Poland, mixed with words from Hebrew and Eastern European tongues. Yiddish is incomprehensible to Sephardic Jews, whose vernacular, Ladino, is derived from Spanish. (2) Candid, truthful talk: "Let's talk *mama-loshn*" means "Get down to brass tacks."

MARRANO. Spanish: "pig." (Derivations other than Spanish are sometimes suggested.) The contemptuous name used by Spanish and Portuguese Catholics, five hundred years ago, for Jews converted by force—who remained "secret Jews." Popes Clement VI, Boniface IX, Nicholas V opposed such persecutions and expressly forbade forcible or threat-induced conversions; but the Church in Spain, Portugal, France, Mexico carried on an effective Inquisition. In Spain, many Marranos rose to positions of great influence: ". . . the majority of distinguished Spanish families married into newly converted Christian families."* One family came to include a minister of finance in Navarre, a vice-chancellor of Aragon, a speaker of the *Cortes* (Parliament), a bishop, a judge of the high court. In the fifteenth century, Spain burned "new Christians," and pious fanatics devised hideous tortures. Torquemada, the Chief Inquisitor, persuaded Isabella and Ferdinand to expel all Jews. Between 150,000 and 500,000, including many at the very heart and mind-center of Spanish culture, were driven out; about 100,000 found their first sanctuary in Portugal (whence they were later expelled); a few thousand went to Italy, to North African cities, and some roamed as far as Poland and Turkey. Spain never recovered from the disastrous excision. Marranos founded important Jewish communities in Amsterdam and London.**

MASORAH. Hebrew: "tradition" (but this translation is uncertain). (1) The traditional readings of the text of the Hebrew Bible. (2) The traditions governing the writing, reading, spelling of words and phrases in the Bible.

MASSEROT (MA'ASEROT, MASSEROTH). Hebrew: "tithes." A tractate in ZERAIM, the first order of the Talmud.

MAVIN (MAYVIN). Hebrew: "understanding." Yiddish for a true expert, a seasoned judge of quality, a connoisseur.

MEGILLAH. Hebrew: "scroll, roll volume . . ." (plural: *megilloth*). (1) The Scroll of Esther, which is read in synagogues during Purim (*q.v.*). (2) The tenth tractate in MO'ED, the second order of the Mishnah, which describes the time and manner of the public reading of the Scroll of Esther during the feast of Purim, and also discusses the public reading of other portions of Scripture. There are five *megilloth* in the Bible: The Song of Songs, the Book of Ruth, Lamentations,

---

* Paul Borchsenius, *History of the Jews,* Vol. III, Simon & Schuster, 1966, pp. 212–13.
 ** See Professor Cecil Roth's *History of the Marranos,* third edition, Oxford, 1959; also B. Netanyahu, "The Marranos of Spain," in *Proceedings of the American Academy for Jewish Research,* XXXI, 1963.

Ecclesiastes, and Esther. (3) In popular usage, anything very long, verbose, a rigmarole. (The Book of Esther wanders in interminable details.)

MEKILTA (MEKHILTA). Aramaic: "measure" or "rule"; Hebrew, *midah*: "rules by which to interpret." The *Mekilta* is an ancient collection of both halakic and haggadic *midrashim* (first and second centuries B.C.E.) on some thirteen chapters of Exodus, from the School of Rabbi Ishmael; it is often called *Rabbi Ishmael's Mekilta* (*Mekilta d' Rabbi Yishmael*), or *Mekilta,* or simply "M." Another *Mekilta* has been discovered: that of Rabbi Shimon (Simeon) ben Yohai.

MELAMED (plural: *melamdim*). Hebrew: "teacher." A teacher —of elementary Hebrew. *Melamdim* were an impecunious lot, teaching by rote and repetition; a Jew who had no other way of making a living, or who had failed, would often become a *melamed.*

MENAHOTH (MENAHOT). Hebrew: "flour offerings . . . meal offerings." The second tractate in KODASHIM, the fifth order of the Talmud. It discusses the preparation of meals and bread.

MENTSH (MENCH). Yiddish, from German: "person." An upright, honorable person; someone of consequence; someone to admire and emulate. Jewish children often hear the admonition: "Behave like a *mentsh!*" or "Be a *mentsh!*" The key to being "a real *mentsh*" is—character: rectitude, dignity, a sense of what is right, the fulfillment of ethical obligations.

MESHUGE. Hebrew: "crazy." Insane, eccentric, obsessed, absurd; such a man is a *meshugener;* such a woman is a *meshugene.*

MESILLAT YESHARIM. "The Way of the Righteous." (See Moses Hayyim Luzzatto in BIOGRAPHIES.)

MESSIAH. See Headnote: MESSIAH (p. 363).

MEZUZA. Hebrew: "doorpost." (1) One of the seven Minor Tractates added to the Talmud; it contains only two chapters

on how *mezuzot* should be copied, written, or applied. (2)
The little oblong container affixed to the right doorjamb of an
observing Jew's home. The *mezuza* consecrates the home as
a temple. An Orthodox Jew touches his fingers to his lips,
then to the *mezuza*, each time he enters or leaves his home.
Inside the *mezuza* is a tiny rolled-up parchment on which
are verses from Deuteronomy 6:4–9, 11:13–21, beginning with,
"Hear, O Israel, the Lord our God is one." Inscribed passages
contain the command to "love the Lord your God . . . with
all your heart and soul," and includes the reminder that God's
laws are to be observed away from, as well as at, home.

MIDRASH. Hebrew: "exposition . . . homily." See Guide Note D,
(pp. 74–75).

MIDRASH CANTICLES RABBAH: Canticles: from Latin:
"chant." The Song of Songs (in Hebrew, *Shir ha-Shirim*). The
first of the five scrolls included in the Hagiographa (*q.v.*).
The Midrash on Canticles is part of the Midrash Rabbah (see
below).

MIDRASH DEUTERONOMY RABBAH. In Hebrew: *Dvarim
Rabbah.* A homilectic, nonlegalistic Midrash on Deuteronomy.
(See Midrash Rabbah, below).

MIDRASH EXODUS RABBAH. In Hebrew: *Shemoth Rabbah.*
The part of the Midrash Rabbah that deals with the book
of Exodus.

MIDRASH GENESIS RABBAH. In Hebrew: *Bereshith Rabbah.*
The portion of the Midrash Rabbah that interprets, or homi-
lectically expounds, the Book of Genesis.

MIDRASH HAGGADAH (AGADAH). (1) The homiletic (folklore, fables, parables, theological speculations) portions of the
Midrash, as contrasted to the legalistic. (See HAGGADAH
and HALAKA.) (2) A compendium of rabbinical interpretations of the first five books of the Old Testament (the Torah)
edited from manuscripts by Solomon Buber, who dates these
midrashim as having been composed in the sixteenth century.
Midrashic materials form a literature stretching over a thousand years.

MIDRASH HALAKA. The legalistic portions of the Midrash, as contrasted with the Midrash Haggada (*q.v.*), which contains folklore, parables, ethical allegories—from which rabbinical rulings and laws were often derived. (See Guide Note D, pp. 74–75).

MIDRASH LAMENTATIONS RABBAH. In Hebrew: *Ekhah Rabbat* (h). The Midrash on the third of the five *megilloth* or scrolls; part of the Midrash Rabbah (see below).

MIDRASH LEVITICUS RABBAH. In Hebrew: *Va-yikra Rabbah.* See Midrash Rabbah (below) and Guide Notes B, D and E (pp. 68–71, 74–75, 76).

MIDRASH NUMBERS RABBAH. In Hebrew: *Be-Midbar* ("in the wilderness") *Rabbah.* The Midrash on the Book of Numbers, included in the Midrash Rabbah (see below) and Guide Notes B and E (pp. 68–71, 76).

MIDRASH RABBAH. This title is actually a misnomer for:

(1) The collection of *midrashim* ("commentaries" or "investigations") on the Torah and the five *megilloth* (Song of Songs, Ruth, Lamentations, Ecclesiastes, Esther). The unapt title *Midrash Rabbah* grew out of a set of complicated facts: Genesis begins with *Be-Reshit* or *Bereshith* ("In the beginning"); the Midrash for Genesis became identified as *Bereshith Rabbah*—("Bereshith: the Great Work"); and "*Rabbah*" began to be tacked on to all the other collections of midrashic materials, such as those on the *megilloth* mentioned above.

(2) The Midrash named after a rabbi who collected *midrashim;* "rabbi" in Aramaic is "*rabbah.*"

The entire *Midrash Rabbah* was translated into English by H. Freedman and Maurice Simon, published in London in 1939.

MIKVE (MIKVAH). Yiddish from Hebrew: "ritual bath . . . immersion pool." The bath, prescribed by ritual, which religious Jewish women take (a) at the end of their menstrual period, (b) before being married, (c) after bearing a child. The woman recites a benediction while in the water. A community of Jews was obligated by rabbinical law to maintain a community *mikve*. The regulations governing the *mikve* are quite detailed and are set forth in the sixth tractate of TOHOROTH.

MILHAMOT HA-SHEM. Hebrew: "Wars of the Lord." A book by Gersonides (see BIOGRAPHIES).

MINOR TRACTATES OF THE TALMUD. (See Guide Note B 6, p. 71). The use of "of" is inexact; the Minor Tractates are appendages to, and not all accepted parts of, the Talmud.

MINYAN (MINYON). Hebrew: "number" or "counting." The ten male Jews required for religious services. No congregational rites can begin "until we have a *minyan*"; to have ten men is to have a "synagogue." (In certain special circumstances, exceptions to a *minyan* are permitted for a wedding, circumcision, etc.)

Solitary prayer is laudable, but a *minyan* possesses special merit to the observant, who have held from antiquity that when ten male Jews assemble for study or worship, God's Presence (*Shekhinah*) dwells among them. The Lord said He would spare Sodom if ten truly righteous men could be discovered there. And since God exempted Joshua and Caleb from His castigation of the spies who returned from Canaan, a congregation is twelve minus two—or ten (Numbers, 14:22–38), according to Mishnah.

MISHLE. Hebrew: "proverbs." This is the name in Hebrew for the Book of Proverbs.

MISHLE SHUALIM. Hebrew: "Fox Tales." (See Ha-Nakdan in BIOGRAPHIES.)

MISHNAH (MISHNA): See Guide Note C (pp. 72–73).

MISHNEH TORAH. Hebrew: "repetition of the Law". (1) The book of Deuteronomy. (2) The great codification of Jewish laws by Maimonides (see BIOGRAPHIES).

MISHPOKHE (MESHPOCHE). Hebrew: "relatives . . . extended family." The closest synonym in English is "clan." See *Joys of Yiddish*.

MITZVAH (plural *mitzvot*). Hebrew: "commandment." (1) Commandment; divine commandment. (2) A meritorious act, a "good work," a truly virtuous, kind, ethical deed.

    Mitzvah is second only to *Torah* in the vocabulary of Judaism. *Mitzvot* are of various kinds: those of positive performance (e.g., caring for the widow and orphan), and those of negative resolve (e.g., not accepting a bribe); those between man and God (fasting on *Yom Kippur*) and those between man and man (paying a servant promptly).

    Mitzvoth are regarded as profound obligations, but must be performed not from a sense of duty but with "a joyous heart." There are 613 separate *mitzvot* listed in the *Sefer Mitzvot Gadol*, of which 248 are positive and 365 negative. Maimonides listed all the *mitzvot* in his *Book of the Mitzvot;* he remarked that the man who performed only one of the 613 deserved salvation—*if* he did so not to win credit, but entirely for its own sake. The potential number of *mitzvot* is endless. Israel Zangwill called *mitzvot* the Jews' "sacred sociology."

MO'ED. Hebrew: "set feast." The second order of the Talmud, dealing with festivals, fasts and the Sabbath.

MO'ED KATAN. Hebrew: "minor festival days." The eleventh tractate in MO'ED, the second order of the Talmud.

MOGEN DAVID. See MAGEN DAVID.

MOISHE KAPOYR. Yiddish for one who must do things backwards, who persists in being contrary and contradictory. For a longer description see *Joys of Yiddish.*

MOREH NEVUHIM. Hebrew: "Guide for the Perplexed." The philosophical classic by Maimonides (see BIOGRAPHIES). In English, the title is often given as "guide of . . ." or "guide to . . ."

NAGID (HA-NAGID). Hebrew: "leader, prince." This word appeared in Muslim and some Christian countries in the Middle Ages as the title, recognized by the state, for a head of a Jewish community. (Compare "Nasi.")

NASHIM. Hebrew: "women." The third order of the Talmud; seven tractates on betrothals, weddings, marital vows, husbands and wives, Levirate marriages, divorces.

NASI. Hebrew: "prince." (1) The president of the Sanhedrin. (2) Today, the title of the president of the State of Israel.

NAZIR. Hebrew: "a Nazirite," from *nazar*, "to dedicate (oneself)." The fourth tractate in NASHIM, the third order of the Talmud; nine chapters on Nazirite vows as prescribed in the Bible (Numbers 6:1–21). These vows have virtually disappeared. The Nazirites were ascetics who eschewed wine or intoxicants, did not cut their hair, and avoided contact with even a relative's corpse. Samson and Samuel were Nazirites.

NEDARIM. Hebrew: "vows." The third tractate in NASHIM, the third order of the Mishnah.

NEVIIM. Hebrew: "Prophets," which became the name for "the Prophetic Books." The *neviim rishonim* ("the former [first] prophets") are the books of Joshua, Judges, Samuel, Kings—which relate the history of the Israelites from their time in Canaan to the destruction of the First Temple (586 B.C.E.), covering both Hebrew kingdoms: Israel and Judah. The *neviim aharonim* ("later prophets") are Isaiah, Jeremiah and Ezekiel. The other twelve or "Minor Later Prophets" are sometimes grouped together as one book, *The Minor Prophets*, in English; or as *T're Asar* ("The Twelve") in Hebrew.

NEZIKIN. Hebrew: "damages . . . civil and criminal law." The fourth order of the Talmud; ten tractates which govern oaths, court damages, criminal law. NEZIKIN contains the great and beloved collection of ethical sayings, *Pirke Abot* (*q.v.*), "The Sayings of the Fathers."

NUMBERS. See Guide Note B (pp. 68–71).

NUMBERS RABBAH. The Midrash on the Book of Numbers (see above); the Midrash Numbers Rabbah.

OLEVASHOLEM. Yiddish form of ALAV HA-SHOLOM, above.

ORHOT HAYIM. Hebrew: "Paths of Life." The name of an important book by Eliezer ben Isaac ha-Gadol (See BIOGRAPHIES).

ORHOT TSADIKIM. Hebrew: "The Ways of the Righteous."

OTSAR. Hebrew: "treasure . . . treasure trove."

OTSAR MIDRASHIM. A collection of 200 midrashim, annotated by David Eisenstein.

PASSOVER. See PESACH.

PE'AH. Hebrew: "gleanings . . . corner . . . edge of the field." The second tractate in ZERAIM, the first order of the Talmud. The produce of the corners of a field had to be left for the poor; no maximum area or amount was specified. *Peot* (Yiddish: *peyes*) refers to the "corner" curled earlocks worn by Hasidic and other very orthodox Jews, in conformity with Leviticus 19 : 27.

PERAKIM: See Guide Note B (pp. 68–71).

PEREK. Hebrew: "chapter." This is also a common name for *Sayings of the Fathers.*

PEREK HA-SHALOM. Hebrew: "Chapter of Homilies on Peace." One of the Minor Tractates attached to the Talmud.

PESACH. Hebrew: *Pessah:* "passover," "sparing." The Passover holiday and celebration, one of the most cherished of Jewish holidays, the Festival of Freedom. It lasts eight days (seven in Israel) and commemorates Israel's deliverance from enslavement in Egypt over 3200 years ago, as recounted in Exodus. (To be exact, the "passing over" of the houses of Hebrews, during the plague Exodus describes [12:13] as afflicting the first-born, refers to the sacrifice, on the eve of the Exodus, of a lamb.) Hence, *pesach* means the first day of the "Feast of the Unleavened Bread."

On the first and second nights of Passover (Israeli Jews

and Reform Jews celebrate only the first), a family *seder* is held. This combination of banquet and religious service is the highlight of the holiday—and, to many, of the year. Nothing containing leavening, or which has come in contact with a leavening agent, may be used during the festival; special china and utensils are used during the Passover week. On the table are matzos (unleavened bread), a reminder of the haste in which the Israelites left Egypt, without waiting for their bread to rise; bitter herbs, marking the bitterness of slavery; an egg and bone, symbolic of the offerings brought to the Temple; *haroset,* a mixture of chopped nuts, apples, cinnamon, and wine, representing the clay from which the Israelites made bricks while in slavery. Each setting has a wineglass, including the one placed for Elijah. The father half-reclines at the head of the table, propped up on pillows or on a sofa; this dramatizes freedom and ease. Guests are customarily invited.

Following the *Kiddush,* the grandfather, father, or oldest son opens the *seder* with a prayer in Aramaic:

This is the bread of affliction that our fathers ate in the land of Egypt. All who are hungry, let them come and eat; all who are needy, let them come and celebrate Passover with us. Now we are here: next year may we be in Israel. Now we are slaves: in the year ahead may we be free men."

This prayer was probably composed shortly after the Romans crushed Judea, in the year 70, and the Jews went into *galut* —exile. The Haggadah, the narrative read at the *seder,* includes rabbinical comments, hymns, prayers, four stylized questions and answers—the whole constituting a ceremony of celebration and praise to the Lord.

PESAHIM. Hebrew: "Paschal lambs; feast of Passover." The third tractate in MO'ED, the second order of the Talmud; ten chapters describe the Passover rites.

PESHAT. Hebrew: "the literal meaning." The simplest interpretation of any passage in Holy Scriptures; distinguished from *derash,* which is an exhortation or moral read into a passage; *remez,* a tenuous allusion; and *sod,* an arcane or mystical meaning.

PESIKTA. Hebrew: "section."

PESIKTA d'RAB KAHANA. A collection of thirty-one homilies about holidays, festivals, and Sabbaths—dating back to the seventh century. The work was ingeniously reconstructed by Leopold Zunz (see BIOGRAPHIES) and has been newly edited by Professor Bernard Mandelbaum.

PESIKTA RABBAH. Homilies included in the MIDRASH RABBAH. (See above.)

PESIKTA RABBATI. A collection of forty-seven homilies about festivals and special occasions, compiled (apparently) in Palestine around the seventh century; translated into English in 1968 (by W. G. Braude.) Often catalogued as *Midrash Pesikta Rabbati.*

PIRKE. Hebrew: "chapters of . . ."

PIRKE ABOT (AVOT). Hebrew: "Sayings of the Fathers." An ethical tractate included in the Mishnah, in the order NEZIKIN, and immensely popular among Jews. It contains profound sayings of rabbis across six centuries—from the third century before, to the third century after, the Christian Era. *Pirke Abot* is part of the liturgy: Sephardic Jews recite it at home each Sabbath between *Pesach* (*q.v.*) and Pentecost; Askenazic Jews every summer Sabbath day from Passover to Rosh Hashana. Countless commentaries on, and translations of, this beautiful, aphoristic work have been published.

PIRKE ABOT (AVOTH) DE RABBI NATHAN. A later, larger edition of *Pirke Abot;* translated into English by Judah Goldin (Yale University, 1955).

PIRKE HA-ROSH: See ASHER BEN YEHIEL in BIOGRAPHIES.

PRAYER OF AZARIAH AND SONG OF THE THREE CHILDREN. In the Apocrypha (*q.v.*).

PRAYER OF MANASSES. In the Apocrypha (*q.v.*).

PSEUDEPIGRAPHA. Greek: "falsely ascribed title." Apocalyptic and eschatological writings, not accepted in the Biblical canon; the best known are the Psalms of Solomon, the Testament of the Twelve Patriarchs, the Apocalypse of Baruch, the Ascension of Isaiah, the Book of Enoch. Scholars firmly differ on which writings belong in the Pseudepigrapha and which in the Apocrypha. Pseudepigrapha were known only in translations until the discovery of the Dead Sea Scrolls, where originals were found. See APOCRYPHA.

PURIM. Hebrew: *pur:* "lot." The Feast of Lots, which commemorates the rescue of the Jews of Persia from Haman's plot to exterminate them (5th century B.C.E.). Lots had been drawn by Haman, first Minister to King Ahasuerus (possibly Artaxerxes II), to set the date on which the Jews would be slaughtered. A miraculous deliverance was effected by beautiful Queen Esther and Mordecai, her uncle and guardian. Haman ended on the gallows he had erected to dispatch Mordecai. The story is told in the Book of Esther. Since the Middle Ages, an enemy of the Jewish people has been known as a "Haman."

In synagogues and temples, the *Megillah* (Scroll of Esther) is read on the eve and morning of Purim. Whenever the name of Haman is uttered, the children set up a racket of jeers, and spin ratchety noisemakers. In some communities, Haman's name is written upon the soles of one's shoes, so that the name may literally be wiped out. Among the customs associated with Purim are the sending of gifts (food and money) to the poor, and the exchanging of gifts with friends. The symbolic food of Purim is the *hamntash,* a three-cornered sweet pastry filled with prunes or poppy seeds.

Purim is not a truly religious holiday and, like Channukah, is not universally treated as such: e.g., work, business, secular life is not greatly altered in most, but not all, Jewish communities.

RAB: With Samuel, the first of the Babylonian *Amoraim* (*q.v.*), active between 220 and 250.

RABA: A great Babylonian *Amora;* he lived in the first half of the fourth century.

RABBA (RABBAH). (1) The title usually indicating Rabbah bar Nahmani (third–fourth century), the great Babylonian *Amora,* head of the academy at Pumbedita. (2) The title also given Rabbah Bar Bar Hannah (third–fourth century), the Palestinian rabbi-traveler known as "the Jewish Sinbad."

RABBAN. Hebrew: "our master." (1) A form of "rabbi," a title higher than "rabbi," accorded to four outstanding scholars of early Mishnaic times: Gamaliel I and II, Simeon ben Gamaliel, and Johanan ben Zakkai. (2) The president of the Sanhedrin.

RABBENU. Hebrew: "our master," "our teacher." Moses is called "Moishe Rabbenu."

RABBENU TAM. Hebrew: "our perfect master." The title given Jacob ben Moses, twelfth-century *Tosephist.* (See BIOGRAPHIES.)

RABBI. Hebrew: "my teacher." A title of respect adopted by the Hebrews in Palestine during the first century of the Christian Era; it became the form by which ordained members of the Sanhedrin (*q.v.*) were addressed. In Babylon, scholar-authorities were called *Rav:* "master." In time, "rabbi" came to signify the religious leader in a synagogue or temple.

RALBAG. The acronym for Rabbi Levi ben Gershon (see BIOGRAPHIES).

RAMBAM. The acronym for Maimonides (Moses ben Maimon; see BIOGRAPHIES).

RAMBAN. The acronym for Moses ben Nahman; see BIOGRAPHIES.

RAMHAL. The acronym for Moses Hayyim Luzzato; see BIOGRAPHIES.

RASH. See ROSH.

RASHBAM. The acronym for Samuel ben Meir; see BIOGRA-
PHIES.

RASHI. The acronym for the great Rabbi Solomon Yitzhaki; see
"Rashi," in BIOGRAPHIES.

RAV. "Master." The Babylonian form of "rabbi."

RESPONSA. In Hebrew: *sheelot u-teshuvot,* "questions and answers." The replies written by authoritative scholars in answer
to letters inquiring about a thousand-and-one aspects of Jewish Law, Torah, and Talmud. More than 500,000 *responsa,*
appearing in over 1,000 compilations, have been published.
(Disciples of the rabbis made copies of their masters' correspondence.) Many manuscripts (in Hebrew and Arabic)
were discovered in 1896–1897 in the *Genizah* ("hiding place,"
where religious literature—which is never thrown away—is
deposited) of a synagogue in Cairo.

The *responsa* form of communication is mentioned in the
Talmud (*Sanhedrin,* 11b and 29a) and the Jerusalem Talmud
(Talmud J.: *Kedoshin,* 82 : 12). *Responsa* began in Babylonia,
with the *geonim's* juridical replies to questions; they encouraged correspondence as a way of preserving bonds with distant
communities. From the twelfth to the fifteenth century, the
problems Jews faced in adjusting to new political, social, and
economic vicissitudes required that rabbinical authorities re-
interpret the Law; innumerable problems were encountered
which had not been covered in the Talmud and are not to be
found in the Torah. The influence of *responsa* is seen in the
correspondence of such luminaries as Alfasi, Rashi, Maimonides, the Tosephists, Rabbi Meir of Rothenberg, and Joseph
Caro, who assembled the comprehensive *Shulhan Aruk* (*q.v.*).
The *responsa* of various great scholars proved invaluable during times when the reading of the Talmud was proscribed by
hostile political authorities.

In addition to describing the life and religious problems of
Jews in the widespread communities of the Diaspora, the *responsa* contain invaluable data on historical events, social conditions, intellectual life, and philosophical/theological schools

of thought. *Responsa* are still being written: for some striking examples, see Guide Note F (pp. 76–78).

RIF. The acronym for Rabbi Isaac Ben Jacob Alfasi (1013–1103) of Fez; see BIOGRAPHIES.

RIM. The acronym for Rabbi Isaac Meir; see BIOGRAPHIES.

ROSH. The acronym for Rabbenu Asher; see BIOGRAPHIES.

ROSH HASHANAH (ROSH HA-SHANAH). Hebrew: "The head of the year . . . New Year Observance . . . Feast of the New Year." (1) The eighth tractate in MO'ED, the second order of the Talmud, on the new Moon's celebration, the prayers for the holy day, etc. (2) The commemoration of the birthday of— the world, according to the rabbis, in the Talmud and Midrash.

Rosh Hashana, like all Jewish holy days, is determined by the lunar calendar: it falls in late September or early October and opens the Ten Days of Penitence (the Days of Awe), which end with Yom Kippur (*q.v.*) During these ten days of prayer, all mankind presumably passes before God, who looks into their deeds and hearts.

On Rosh Hashana, the *shophar* (ram's horn) is blown several times: first to celebrate God's kingship; secondly, to stress the role of the individual; third, to remind the congregation of all the events associated with the blowing of the ram's horn. (In ancient Judea, the ram's horn was used to send signals from one mountain to another.) In the Talmud, one rabbi ventures the reassuring comment that the blowing of the *shophar* helps to confuse Satan and his hosts.

Rosh Hashana is a happy time; families gather from everywhere for the holiday and feast; bread or apple is dipped in honey to symbolize a hoped-for "sweetness" in the year ahead. The traditional Rosh Hashanah greeting is *"Le-shana tova tikasevu,"* "May you be inscribed for a good year." Orthodox and Conservative Jews observe two days of Rosh Hashanah; Reform Jews celebrate only one.

ROV. See RABBI.

SABORAIM. (SEBORAIM). See TANNA, and Guide Note D (pp. 74–75).

SACHEL. See SEYKHL.

SANHEDRIN. From Greek: *synedrion:* "assembly." (1) "The High Court . . . the Sanhedrin." (2) Fourth tractate in NEZIKIN, the fourth order of the Mishnah; it deals with legal aspects of the courts, judicial procedure, criminal law—and lists the sins for which one will be excluded from the world-to-come. (3) The seventy elders, plus a Patriarch or President (Nasi), who sat in the Temple in Jerusalem as a combination of Supreme Court and College of Cardinals, ruling on theological, ethical, civil, and political matters. After the year 70, when the Temple was destroyed, the Sanhedrin met in Yavneh; tradition assigns further meeting places, the last being Tiberias, where the Sanhedrin was outlawed, in 425, by the Roman authorities.

Modern scholars think there must have been two Sanhedrins: one of aristocrats and priests, the other a court of Pharisees who attended to matters of ritual, the calendar, etc. After the year 425, the Sanhedrin's functions were replaced by those of the *Beth Din* (*q.v.*). After the State of Israel was founded, in 1948, a movement tried to revive the Sanhedrin, but this was not achieved because of constitutional problems.

SEDER. Hebrew: "order." (1) An order of the Talmud. (2) The Passover feast. See PESACH.

SEFARDI. See SEPHARDI.

SEFER (SEPHER). Hebrew: "book."

SEFER ELIM: "Book of Elim." See Delmedigo, Joseph Solomon, in BIOGRAPHIES.

SEFER HA-GILGULIM. "Book of Transmigrations") or "Metamorphoses"). See Isaac Luria, in BIOGRAPHIES.

SEFER HA-HINUKH. Hebrew: "Book of education." A classic of the thirteenth century, by Rabbi Aaron ha-Levi of Barcelona (see BIOGRAPHIES).

SEFER HASIDIM. Hebrew: "Book of the Pious" or "Saintly." Written by Rabbi Yehuda he-Hasid of Regensburg in the thirteenth century, this famous work on ethics has appeared in an early, long, unorganized text, and as a later, briefer, more orderly presentation. The *Sefer Hasidim* may be the work of more than one author; some authorities attribute it to the great Judah he-Hasid ("the Pious"), a major force in medieval Jewry. The work is a mirror of medieval Judaic thought, containing folklore, anecdotes, legends, a great deal of demonology and superstition—and aphorisms, quoted in the present anthology, about everything from praying to paying taxes; the respect due to parents and the seductive perils of secular writings; the sin of slander and the proper attitude to non-Jews; the raising of children and the virtues of modesty.

SEFER HA-YASHAR. Hebrew: "Book of Yashar" or "Book of the Straight Way." See Rabbenu Tam in BIOGRAPHIES.

SEFER IKARIM (HA-IKKARIM). Hebrew: "Book of Principles." See Joseph Albo in BIOGRAPHIES.

SEFER SHAASHUIM. Hebrew: "Book of Delights." See Ibn Zabara in BIOGRAPHIES.

SEFER TORAH. Hebrew: "Book of the Torah." (1) A book in the Minor Tractates added to the Talmud. (2) The Scroll containing the Five Books of Moses, kept in the Ark at the front of a synagogue or temple. Readings from the *Sefer Torah* are made in synagogues or temples each Sabbath and festival, on Mondays, Thursdays and fast days. The Scroll is of parchment, hand-lettered, in Hebrew; in Ashkenezic communities it is covered with a mantle of silk or velvet, often adorned with a breastplate and crown of silver.

SEFIRAH (SEFIRAT[H] HA-OMER). Hebrew: "counting." The forty-nine-day period that begins with the second day of Passover (when the *omer,* a sheaf of new barley, was traditionally brought to the Temple in Jerusalem as an offering) and ends on Shevuoth, the feast of the first-fruit harvest. The "omer is counted" during daily prayers, followed by the recitation of

Psalm 67. The forty-nine days of *Sefirah* have become a period of mourning because of the misfortunes which, tradition holds, the Jews suffered during this period: the persecutions under Roman rule, the martyrdom of Rabbi Akiba, the slaughter of Jews by the Crusaders. The famous revolt of the Warsaw Ghetto against Nazi troops occurred during *Sefirah*.

SEMAHOT. Hebrew: "joyous occasions"—but this is a euphemism for *Evel Rabati (Rabbati)*: "Great [tractate on] mourning." A book in the Minor Tractates added to the Talmud.

SEPHARDI (plural, SEPHARDIM). Hebrew: *"Sepharad,"* the name found in Obadiah (9:20), which early medieval rabbis identified as Spain. Spanish and Portuguese Jews, and the descendants of the Jews of Spain, Portugal, and the Middle East. The Sephardic tradition, culture, liturgy, etc., differ in many important ways from those of the Ashkenazim (*q.v.*) of Eastern Europe. The Sephardim were beholden to the Babylonian tradition (as were the Jews in all places on the Mediterranean); the Ashkenazim followed the rabbi-scholars of Palestine.

Sephardic Judaism was elitist, intellectual, and dominated Jewish culture from around 600 until the expulsion of the Jews from Spain at the end of the fifteenth century. It was a sophisticated blend of Talmudic thought, Greek philosophy, Aristotelianism, science (as it then existed), and the ideas of Averroës, the great Islamic scholar whom medieval Christians were forbidden, by formal Church prohibition, to read. Sephardic scholars and rabbis were acquainted with Latin, Spanish, French, and they broadened Judaic thought with knowledge from geometry, algebra, astronomy, medicine, metaphysics, music, mechanics.

Sephardic Jews rose to positions of considerable eminence in Spain, Portugal, North Africa—as physicians, philosophers, poets, financiers, diplomats, advisers to kings and courts. The Sephardic Jews wrote mostly in Arabic, even when writing about Torah and Talmud.

When the Sephardic Jews were expelled from the Iberian countries, they moved on to settle along the coastline of the Mediterranean (they soon dominated the culture and religious practices of Jewish communities in North Africa and the Middle East), and to Holland and England—and their colonies.

The Sephardim were sophisticates, enlightened, cosmopolitan; the Ashkenazim (who lived under very harsh Russian, Polish, Austrian rulers, confined to the Pale, excluded from owning land or entering a profession, subjected to repeated pillaging and ghastly pogroms) were peasants, peddlers, proletarians, fundamentalist in faith, steeped in poverty, bound to orthodox tradition, filled with fervent Messianic dreams, and hostile to secular knowledge (partly because education in Christian countries was clerical, therefore not available to and for Jews). Professor Louis Ginzberg remarks: "For the Sefardim, learning was a matter of sentiment; for the Polish Jew, it was an intellectual occupation."*

Today, Sephardic designates any Jews following Sephardic rites, whether from Spanish ancestry or not. Middle Eastern, North African and Oriental Jews are Sephardic.

Communities of Sephardic Jews are today found throughout Asia Minor, in Israel, Turkey, Greece, and in England, Holland, Latin America and the United States (Sephardim were the first Jewish immigrants). Sephardic Jews claim that their liturgy stems from the academies of Babylonia; Ashkenazim follow the Palestinian ritual. The vernacular used by Old World Sephardic Jews, as opposed to the Yiddish (Judeo-German) of Ashkenazic Jews, is Ladino, a form of Spanish.

SEYKHL. Yiddish from Hebrew: "understanding." Native good sense, common sense, judgment.

SHABBATH (SHABBAT). Hebrew: "rest . . . cessation from labor . . . Sabbath." (1) The first tractate in MO'ED, the second order of the Talmud; twenty-four chapters on the rules governing the Sabbath. (2) The Sabbath, which became more than a weekly respite from servitude, labor, anxiety. *Shabbes* (Yiddish for "*Shabbat*") is called "the Queen of the Week," "the Bride." In however bitter a time and place, the Sabbath was the miraculous day when even the lowliest, poorest Jew could feel himself in kingly communion with the Almighty,

---

* *Students, Scholars and Saints,* J.P.S.A., 1928, p. 64.

favored by God's special concern: "It is a sign between me and the children of Israel" (Exodus, 31:17). To "make Shabbes" means to be festive.

The Mishnah sets forth a sizable number of Sabbath prohibitions: baking, plowing, writing, carrying, even tying a knot. On the Sabbath, Jews prayed—and studied; they read; they discussed Torah and Talmud. A rabbi or elder read the laws, to "expound them point by point, until the late afternoon, when [all] depart, having gained knowledge . . . and an advance in piety" (Philo). Every Sabbath morning, a portion of the Torah is read in the synagogue, together with a reading from the Prophets; the entire Torah cycle is completed each year.

On the six Sabbaths between Passover and Shevuoth (Pentecost) and Rosh Hashanah (among the Ashkenazim), fathers and grandfathers would traditionally engage their children, at home, in discussions of the *Sayings of the Fathers* (*Pirke Abot*) or portions of the Mishnah. Cultural historians may appraise the magnitude of the consequences of an entire people, young and old, spending one day a week, year after year, century after century, in a seminar on morals, ethics, responsibility, reason, faith.

Jews try to invite a stranger, traveler, student, or poor man to share the *shabbes* meal. This served to make Jews everywhere feel part of one universal fellowship.

Shabbes ends after sundown Saturday, with a home religious service called *Habdalah,* the "separation" of the Sabbath from week days.

SHALOM (SHOLEM, SHOLOM). From the Hebrew root meaning "whole . . . entire . . . peace." (1) Peace. (2) The greeting and leave-taking word or phrase used by Jews—*Shalom aleykhem* ("peace unto you") being responded to by *Aleykhem shalom* ("and to you, peace"). In Yiddish, "*shalóm*" is pronounced *"shólem."*

SHAS. Hebrew initials for *Shishah Sedarim:* "the six orders" of the Mishnah, which form the foundation of the Talmud. When Catholic censorship in the sixteenth century outlawed the use of the word "Talmud," Jews used *Shas* instead.

SHEKEL (plural: **SHKOLIM**). Hebrew: "coin," "weight." (1) A coin. (2) Money. The *shekel* was the most important silver coin in Biblical times.

SHEMA. Hebrew: "hear." The opening word of Deuteronomy: 6, 4: "Hear, O Israel, the Lord our God, the Lord is one . . ." This has become the name of three selections from the Bible (beginning with Deuteronomy: 6:4–9, and containing 11:13–21, Numbers: 15:37–41) which are recited morning and evening, every day, as dictated in Deuteronomy: 6:7 . . . "You shall speak of them . . . when you lie down and when you rise up."

SHEVET YEHUDAH. Hebrew: "The Rod of Judah"; see Ibn Verga, Judah, in BIOGRAPHIES.

SHEBI'IT. Hebrew: "the Seventh Year." The fifth tractate in ZERAIM, the first order of the Talmud; ten chapters deal with sabbatical years, debts, and legal documents.

SHIDUKH (**SHIDDACH**). Hebrew, from Aramaic: *shidukha*: "marital match." (1) An arranged marriage; a "match" or betrothal. (2) Talmudic term for premarital discussions between the parents of those to be betrothed.

SHIRAT YISRAEL. Hebrew: "The Poetry of Israel."

SHIR HA-SHIRIM. Hebrew: "The Song of Songs."

SHMOT. Hebrew: originally *Sefer Y'Ziat Mizraim:* "the Book of the Going out of Egypt." At an early date, this book of the Torah was known by its opening phrase, *Ve-Eleh Shmot* ("And these are the names"). Its English designation is Exodus, the name used in the Septuagint. See Guide Note A (pp. 67–68).

SHOPHAR. Hebrew: "trumpet," "horn"; specifically "ram's horn." The ram's horn (usually 10 to 12 inches long), blown in the synagogue during Rosh Hashanah and Yom Kippur, which reminds the pious how Abraham, offering Isaac in sacrifice, was reprieved when God said Abraham could sacrifice a ram instead. The man who blows the *shophar* must be of blameless character; in some traditions, the elaborate ritual adds up to about one hundred *tekiot* (arrangements of *shophar* sounds) for *Yom Kippur.* The *shophar* was used in ancient Palestine to signal danger, call for defense, announce a holiday, call together convocations. In Israel today the *shophar* is used on high official occasions. See YOM KIPPUR.

SHULHAN ARUK (SHULCHAN ARUKH). Hebrew: "set table." The title of a most influential and popular compilation of rabbinic laws that regulate the practice of Judaism; written by Joseph Caro (Karo) in 1555; see BIOGRAPHIES.

SIBYLLINE ORACLES. A series of prophecies, in Greek hexameter verse, combining pagan, Hebrew, and Christian legends from the second century before, to the fourth century after, the Christian Era. The text attacks Israel's oppressors, especially Rome, projects the history of the peoples around the Mediterranean, and predicts wars and catastrophes that will precede the Messiah's coming and the redemption of mankind.

SIDDUR. Hebrew: "arrangement," "order." The daily and Sabbath prayer book. It contains the three daily services, the Sabbath prayers, *Sayings of the Fathers,* and special readings. The *Siddur* is based on a compilation made during the ninth century in an academy in Babylonia. Additions and emendations have since been inserted and communities have developed different liturgies. The first printed *Siddur* appeared in 1486—thirty years after the Gutenberg Bible; its colophon reads: "Here is completed the sacred work for the special *minhag* (ritual) of the Holy Congregation of Rome, according to the order arranged by an expert."

Sephardic Jews refer to the *"tephillah,"* and not the *"siddur."*

SIDRA. Aramaic: "order." That part of the Pentateuch which is read in the synagogue each Sabbath. The reading of the entire Torah consumes one year, and is promptly begun again, on the same day the final passage is read.

SIFRA (SIPHRA). Aramaic: "the book." (Do not confuse with *Sifre,* below.) A legal commentary or *midrash* on the book of Leviticus; also called *Torat Kohanim* ("the law of the priests") or *Sifra de-Ve-Rav* ("the book of the School of Rav"). It is the work of Rabbi Akiba's academy and expounds the position of Rabbi Judah, one of Akiba's students.

SIFRE. Aramaic: "the book." A Tannaitic commentary on the books of Numbers and Deuteronomy—the former *halakic,* the latter *haggadic.* This book is the work of Rabbi Ishmael's school—opposed to Rabbi Akiba's on many points.

SIMHAT (SIMCHAT) TORAH. Hebrew: "the day of rejoicing in the law." A festival, observed on the ninth and final day of SUCCOTH (in Israel, on the eighth night), which honors the Torah; a gay occasion, with feasting and dancing. The last chapters of Deuteronomy are read—and immediately the congregation cries, *"Chazak, chazak, venit chazak!"* ("Be strong, be strong, and let us summon new strength!" And then the first chapter of Genesis is begun, to show that the Torah has neither beginning nor end. The holy scrolls are removed from the synagogue's Ark on the eve of Simhat Torah and each male in the congregation takes his turn carrying them; the congregation sings; the men carrying the Torah scrolls "dance."

SIRACH (SIRAH, SIRA), JESUS BEN; see BIOGRAPHIES.

SOPHER (SOFER); plural: SOPHERIM or SOFERIM. Hebrew: "scribe." In the kingdom of Judea, the scribe held the highest office. Scribes transcribed the Scrolls of the Law and wrote all legal documents. The scribe was the community's leading scholar; rabbis were not called scribes; but in time, scribes were replaced as teachers and scholars by rabbis. (See RABBI). The *Sopherim* developed many regulations from Scripture: on prayer, feasts, liturgy. They also changed Hebrew texts (in 18 places), to minimize references to God which they considered anthropomorphic. Their efforts to make the Torah *the* authority served to reduce the powers of the priests, who inherited their position. Torah no longer remained the esoteric monopoly of a caste. This revolutionized Judaism, opening the study of the Law to philosophers and teachers, "democratizing" the mysteries which, in ancient religions, were jealously guarded by hereditary priesthoods. The *Sopherim* were Sadducees; the *Tannaim* were Pharisees.

Note: The word "scribes," for *Sopherim*, developed unfortunate associations; in the New Testament, "scribes" is often used as a synonym for hypocrites. To be both accurate and just, *Sopherim* should be translated as "men of the book."

SOPHERIM (SOFERIM). Hebrew: "men of the book"; plural of *sopher* (*sofer*). (1) The scribes. (2) A book in the Minor Tractates added to the Talmud.

SOTAH. Hebrew: "Wife who has erred . . . suspected adultress." (1) The fifth tractate in NASHIM, the third order of the Talmud. (2) A wife suspected of adultery, who undergoes the ordeal of "the bitter waters" (Numbers 5:12–31).

SUCCOTH (SUKKOTH). Hebrew: "booths." The Feast of Tabernacles (or Booths), the holiday that starts on the fifth day after Yom Kippur (*q.v.*) and is celebrated for nine days by the Orthodox, and for eight days in Israel and among Reform Jews. Throughout the week, a pious family eats its meals in a *sukkah* (booth) set up out of doors, roofed with branches and decorated with flowers and fruit. The booth, intended to look temporary, represents the hastily erected dwellings Jews used during the forty years of wandering in the wilderness. ". . . your generations may know that I made the children of Israel to dwell in booths, when I brought them out of the land of Egypt." (Leviticus 23:43). Philo considered the *sukkah* a democratic institution because there all Jews, rich or poor, dwell in a primitive shelter.

Hoshanah Rabbah, "the great Hosanna," is observed on the seventh day by a procession around the synagogue; the men carry palm and willow branches, and the entire congregation chants verses praising God and requesting His saving powers.

SUKKAH. Hebrew: "booth." The sixth tractate in MO'ED, the second order of the Talmud, whose five chapters present laws about the Feast of Tabernacles (see above).

SUSANNA. A book in the APOCRYPHA.

TA'ANITH (TAANIT): Hebrew: "fast . . . first day of fasting." The ninth tractate in MO'ED, the second order of the Mishnah; it deals with fasting, droughts, petitions to God for rain.

TABERNACLES, FEAST OF. See SUCCOTH.

TAHKEMONI. Fifty narratives, in rhymed prose, written by Judah al-Harizi; see BIOGRAPHIES. The *Tahkemoni* describes the experiences in many places to which the author had traveled, or the tales he heard there. *Tahkemoni* is sometimes translated as "Apothecary" (e.g., *New Standard Jewish Encyclopedia, op. cit.,* p. 73.)

TALLITH (TALIT, TALIS). Hebrew: "covering." The prayer shawl used by Jewish males, according to some practices at their Bar Mitzvah, to others, upon marriage and at morning prayers. The *tallith katan,* a smaller garment, is worn by very orthodox Jews under their shirts, at all times. The Torah tells Jewish males to wear a garment fringed at the four corners. The fringes are called *zizith* (*q.v.*).

   The *tallith* reminds a Jew of his bond and duty to God. At one time, the *tallith* was a gown or cloak worn in public; but because of repeated humiliations, the rabbis decreed that it be used in the synagogue or at home, during prayer services. Black or blue bands cross the prayer shawl, to memorialize the destruction of the Temple and mourn it forever. An observing Jew gives his son a *tallith* on the latter's Bar Mitzvah; his bride or parents-in-law may give him one for his wedding; and he is buried in a shroud with his *tallith.*

TALMID HAKHAM (CHACHEM). Hebrew: "wise in study"; more exactly, "a disciple of the wise." One who is greatly learned in Talmud. The *talmid hakham* represented the ideal man, highest in the Jewish hierarchy of respect.

TALMUD. See Guide Note B (pp. 68–71).

TALMUD TORAH. Hebrew: "Study of Torah." (1) One of the cardinal concepts and values of Judaism: religious study and lifelong dedication to it. (2) A Hebrew school which, in the United States, offered a daily two-hour Hebrew session, after the public schools closed, and classes on Sunday morning; Talmud Torahs have greatly declined in number, many of their activities having been absorbed into the synagogue and temple.

TAMID. Hebrew: "daily sacrifice . . . the daily or perpetual offering." (1) The ninth tractate in KODASHIM, the fifth order of the Talmud. (2) The burnt-offering, each morning and afternoon in the Temple, as described in Numbers 28:1–8.

TANAKH. Hebrew: "the Bible." The name constructed from the first letters of the Hebrew names for the three major sections of the Bible: *Torah, Neviim* (Prophets), and *Ketuvim* (Writings or Hagiographa).

TANHUMA or TANHUMA RABBAH: The Midrash of Rabbi Tanhuma bar Abba, a fourth-century Palestinian scholar, who wrote many *midrashim* and advanced the forms of homiletics.

TANNA (plural: TANNAIM). Aramaic: "one who teaches by repetition." The name for the Talmudic scholars whose work was recorded in the Mishnah. The *Tannaim* are distinguished from the *Sopherim* (*q.v.*) in that the *Tannaim* were Pharisees, the *Sopherim,* Sadducees. After the destruction of the Second Temple (70), the Tannaim became the leaders "of such Jewish life as survived." When written forms of the Law were prohibited by political authorities, the Tannaim became "living libraries." Judaism may be said to be the product of the Tannaim; their Mishnah is the central Judaic authority. Rabbis identified with the Gemara are called *Amoraim* (*q.v.*); later commentators are called *Saboraim,* or "opinion expressers."

TARGUM. Aramaic, from Assyrian: "interpretation or translation in another language." The Aramaic translation of the Bible. The practice of public oral Aramaic translation of the passages read from the Torah probably began around the time of Ezra. (See Talmud: *Megillah,* 3a.)

TARSHISH. See Moses Ibn Ezra, in BIOGRAPHIES.

TEBUL YOM (TEVUL YOM). Hebrew: "he who has bathed that day." The tenth tractate in TOHOROTH, the sixth order of the Talmud.

TEFILLAH. Hebrew: "a prayer." (1) The Amidah (*q.v.*). (2) One of the *Tefillin.* (3) The Sephardic name for a prayer book.

TEFILLIN (TEPHILLIN). Aramaic: "attachments." (1) A "pseudo-Talmudic" small treatise in the Minor Tractates. (2) Phylacteries (from the Greek *phylakterion:* "protection" or "fortress"; see Matthew 23:5): two tiny boxes, containing portions of the Torah inscribed on parchment, that are affixed to the head and left arm while praying during morning services, except on Sabbath and festivals.

    The custom of donning *tefillin* is derived from the injunction in Exodus 13:16 and in Deuteronomy 6:8, etc. The process of putting on *tefillin* is elaborate, and carefully prescribed: the *Shulhan Aruk* (*q.v.*) lists 160 (!) details.

TEMURAH. Hebrew: "exchanges"; "the substituted offering." The sixth tractate in KODASHIM, the fifth order of the Talmud.

TERUMOTH. Hebrew: "heave-offerings." The sixth tractate in ZERAIM, the first order of the Talmud.

TISHA BOV (TISHA B'AV, TISHA B'AB). Hebrew: "the ninth day of the month *Ab* (or *Av*)." The day of fasting and mourning that commemorates the destruction of both the First and the Second Temples in Jerusalem. (The Babylonians razed the first Temple in 586 B.C.E.; the Romans destroyed the second in the year 70.) Reform Jews do not observe this day of communal lamentation, known as "the blackest day in the Jewish calendar"—which has added post-Temple disasters, catastrophes, and horrors: the slaughter of Bar Kochba's followers in 138; Hadrian's leveling of Jerusalem; the death of Rabbi Akiba and nine other martyrs; the Crusades and their unholy massacres, rapes and depredations; England's expulsion of the Jews in 1290; Spain's expulsion of the Jews in 1492, etc.

Tisha Bov usually falls in August, and climaxes nine days of mourning, during which meat is not eaten, marriages not performed, smiles or laughter forbidden to the orthodox. Those who enter the synagogue do not greet one another; they sit on the floor or on low benches; a black curtain is draped over the Ark; one flickering light barely illuminates the synagogue. The Book of Lamentations is recited by the cantor in a low, depressing chant. (In Sephardic communities, the Book of Job is also read.) Poems of immense sadness (some date from the Middle Ages) are intoned; but the service ends on a note of hope, with the reading of Judah ha-Levi's *Zionide*.

TISHBI. "The Tishbeite." Lexicon to the Talmud by Elijah Levita (see BIOGRAPHIES.)

TOBIT. A book in the Apocrypha. It includes a version of the Golden Rule. It is found in Greek, Latin, Syrian, and Aramaic; no early Hebrew manuscript exists. It tells the story of Tobias, sent to Persia, who marries Sarah (whose previous seven husbands had been killed on their wedding nights by the infatuated demon Ashmedai); the marriage was effected only with the help of the Archangel Raphael. Tobias was a most pious man, exiled with the Ten Tribes, who was blind— until Raphael, the angel, restored his sight. The Book of Tobit was put together around the second to first centuries B.C.E.

TOHOROTH. Hebrew "cleanliness." (1) The ritualistic regulations of cleanliness of body and foods. (2) The sixth order of the Mishnah, consisting of 12 tractates. (3) The name of the fifth tractate of the order of the Talmud (Mishnah) of the same name, with ten chapters dealing with presunset prohibitions on uncleanliness.

TORAH. See Guide Note B (pp. 68–71).

TOSEFOTH (TOSEPHOT): See Guide Note E (p. 76).

TOSEPHTA (TOSEFTA). A supplement-commentary on the Mishnah, from compendia written by Rabbi Hiyya (Chia)

bar Abba (see BIOGRAPHIES) and Hashaiah (third and fourth century), or by one of Akiba's disciples, Rabbi Nehemiah. It contains six orders; some paragraphs, called *Baraitot,* are versions of paragraphs from Mishnah, others follow passages from Talmud, and others seem independent of major sources.

TOV. Hebrew: "good."

TSADIK (plural: TSADIKIM). Hebrew: "righteous man." A term of respect for particularly pious, learned, saintly elders. The Talmud tells us that it is the virtues of thirty-six *tsadikim,* in each generation, that keep the world going. (See Headnote: SAINTS.) The idealization of the *tsadikim* was a central aspect of Hasidism (*q.v.*) and led to attributions of miracles, mystical powers, and divine revelation.

The hasidic *tsadik* was considered a blessed intermediary between God and man; his advice was treasured and followed; his words were virtually sanctified by disciples. In time, the title became hereditary, and Eastern European "dynasties" have been carried over into the United States, Israel, etc.

TSORES (TSOURIS). Yiddish from Hebrew *tsarah:* "trouble." Troubles, woes, worries. The singular is *tsore* or *tsure.* Especially aggravating adversities are called *gekokhte* (chopped-up) *tsores.*

VAV. The sixth letter of the Hebrew alphabet, pronounced "v".

VA-YIKRA (VAYIKRA). Hebrew word: "And He called." This opens Leviticus (once known as *Torat Kohanim,* "the code of priests"). "Leviticus" is a Latin word, derived from the Greek *leutikos* in the Septuagint.

VITSEN. Yiddish: "witticisms, wisecracks."

WISDOM LITERATURE. The books of Proverbs, Job, Ecclesiastes, Psalms—plus "apocryphal" writings: The Wisdom of Solomon, Ecclesiasticus by Jesus ben Sirach (see BIOGRAPHIES), and Maccabees. See APOCRYPHA.

WISDOM OF SOLOMON. The book, attributed to King Solomon, eulogizing wisdom and virtue. Originally written in Greek, probably by a Hebrew from Alexandria, its date is uncertain. It is in the Apocrypha.

YADAYIM (YADAIM). Hebrew: "hands." The eleventh tractate in TOHOROTH: it roams from the cleanliness of hands to problems of wisdom literature (see above), Hebrew and Aramaic, the Sadducees and Pharisees.

YAROT DEVASH: a collection of sermons of Rabbi Jonathan Eibeshutz (see BIOGRAPHIES).

YAHVEH. See YHVH.

YALKUT SHIMONI. The most comprehensive of Midrashic collections; attributed to Rabbi Simeon ha-Darshan of Frankfurt (thirteenth century).

YEBAMOTH (YEVAMOT). Hebrew: "brother's wife, sister-in-law." The first tractate in NASHIM, the third order of the Talmud; it deals with childless widows whom their brothers-in-law must marry, according to Deuteronomy 25:5, or "release" through a ceremony (*halitsah*) described in Deuteronomy 25:7–10. The Sephardim upheld obligatory marriage; the Ashkenazim preferred and adopted *halitsah*.

YESHIVA. Hebrew: "seat." (1) A rabbinical college or seminary. (2) In the United States, a Hebrew day school in which both religious and secular subjects are studied. The *yeshiva* was an outgrowth of the *Beth Midrash*, the "house of study" in every Jewish community.

One of the earliest *yeshivot* was established in Palestine, at Javneh, by Rabbi Johanan ben Zakkai (see BIOGRAPHIES). After the destruction of Jerusalem, the Sanhedrin moved to Javneh; the academy attracted scholars and became the seat of Jewish scholarship. During the Talmudic period, *yeshivot*, established elsewhere in Palestine and Babylonia, were the creative source of Jewish theology, law and moral guidance.

From the tenth century on, *yeshivot* were formed wherever Jews migrated: North Africa, Italy, Spain, France, Germany, England, Holland—but especially in Ashkenazic centers in Eastern Europe. The *yeshiva* was for centuries not simply a religious school, but the college for general education.

YESHIVA BOCHER. Hebrew: *bahur:* "young man"; hence, a young man who is a student at a *yeshiva* (see above); hence a scholarly, unworldly type, whether attending a *yeshiva* or not.

YETSER (YEZER) HA-RA. Hebrew: "the Evil Impulse (or Inclination)." Often used in Talmudic literature to signify sexual desires, as well as other "sinful" propensities.

YETSER (YEZER) HA-TOV. Hebrew: "the Good Impulse (or Inclination)."

YHVH. The "Tetragrammaton," the four letters representing the most sacred name of the God of Israel, pronounced only by the High Priest of antiquity, on Yom Kippur, when he entered "the sanctuary of the Holy of Holies" to seek forgiveness for himself and his people. But no one really knows how YHVH was pronounced; probably as "Yahveh." ("Jehovah" is the erroneous tranliteration of a German papal scribe in 1516). In prayer, the name of God is pronounced *Adonai*. In other circumstances, a variety of names have evolved, according to the aspect of the Lord intended: His power, His compassion, His wrath, etc. Maimonides lists these names-by-attribute as seven: YHVH, *El, Eloha, Elohim, Elohai, Shaddai,* YHVH *Tsevaot*. But other names are used by Jews: *Boreh Olam* (Creator of the World), *El Elion* (Most High One), En Sof (Infinite One), etc.

YIDDISH. From the German: *"jüdisch:"* "Jewish." The vernacular of East European Jews; sixteenth-century Middle High Germas at its base, with 15–20% Hebrew words and names, and an equal or greater amount of loan-words from Slavic tongues. Today, Yiddish contains many adapted English words and phrases. (For the distinctive characteristics of this delight-laden tongue, see my *"Joys of Yiddish,"* McGraw-Hill, 1968; Pocket Book edition, 1970.)

YIKHES. Yiddish, from the Hebrew *yihus:* "pedigree . . . ancestry." Family prestige, which must be retained and deserved through virtue, learning, good deeds, charity.

YISROEL (YISRAEL). Hebrew: "Israel." (1) The land of Israel (*Erets Yisroel*). (2) The people of Israel. (3) The name assumed by Jacob after he fought the Angel of the Lord (Genesis 32:29). (4) The collective name for the twelve tribes who left Egypt and settled in Canaan. (5) The name of the Northern Kingdom of Israel (933–722 prior to the Christian Era), formed when ten tribes seceded, after the death of King Solomon. (6) The name of the State of Israel (*Medinat Yisroel*). In Jewish literature, *Yisroel* is used interchangeably with "Jew" and "Hebrew."

YIZKOR. Hebrew: "May [God] remember." Memorial service for the dead, held in a synagogue or temple. *Yizkor* is the shortened name for the memorial service, *Ha-Zkarat Neshamot,* "Remembrance of Souls," recited on the eighth day of Pesach, the second day of *Shevuoth,* the eighth day of Succoth, and on Yom Kippur. Deceased ancestors and parents, "the crown of our head and glory," are extolled. Private prayers are then made in memory of close relatives; those reciting *Yizkor* pledge themselves to perform "acts of charity and goodness." The service continues with a congregational prayer, *El Maleh Rahamim,* which petitions God to grant peace and eternal life to the departed souls. Part of the *Yizkor* service is a memorial to martyrs of all generations.

YOMA. Aramaic: "the day"; Hebrew: *"Yom ha-Kippurim:"* "the Day of Atonement." The fifth tractate of Mo'ed, the second order of the Mishnah, which describes the Yom Kippur services, fast, atonement and repentance.

YOM KIPPUR. Hebrew: "Day of Atonement." (Some scholars trace *kippur* to the Babylonian word for "purge," "wipe off.") The last of the annual Ten Days of Penitence; one of the two high Holy Days of the Jewish calendar; the day which has the strongest hold on the Jewish conscience. Rosh Hashanah marks the first of the Days of Penitence (*Yamim Noraim*), when, say the Orthodox, all men stand before God for judgment; but His decision is made on the last of the Ten Days: Yom Kippur. The synagogue service begins just before nightfall the evening before Yom Kippur. The cantor stands before the Ark; on each side stands an honored member of the congregation, carrying a large Scroll of the Torah. The three men act as spokesmen for the congregation and recite:

> With the . . . permission of the Lord, blessed be He, and this sacred congregation, we declare it lawful to pray with those who have transgressed.

This is thrice repeated; then the cantor intones Kol Nidre (*q.v.*). Prayers continue from the next morning until after sunset. Since purity of conscience is the theme of the day, the curtain of the Ark is white; the rabbi and cantor wear white robes; many men in the congregation wear white skullcaps (*yarmlkes*) and white robes.

Confession, repeated several times during the day, involves a cataloguing of fifty-six categories of sin. Tradition-observing Jews repeat: "For the sin we have committed before Thee by (stating one of the fifty-six varieties), O God of forgiveness, forgive us, pardon us, grant us remission," and beat their breasts. The confession is recited as a collective "we," not an individual "I." Jews "share" each other's transgressions —plus general responsibility for the misdeeds of mankind. Yom Kippur ends with the blowing of the *shophar*.

YOREH DEAH. See Joseph Caro, in BIOGRAPHIES.

YORTSAYT (JOHRTZEIT). Yiddish (from German): "anniversary." The observances to commemorate the death of someone in the family: with an annual prayer, the lighting of a ceremonial candle, etc. Orthodox Jews fast all day.

Yortsayt is the one Jewish religious ceremony for which no Hebrew name is exactly equivalent.

ZABIM (ZAVIM). Hebrew: "those who suffer from bodily discharges [flux]." The ninth tractate of TOHOROTH, the sixth order of the Mishnah.

ZADDIK. See TSADIK.

ZEBAHIM. Hebrew: "animal sacrifices . . . animal offerings." The first tractate in KODASHIM, the fifth order of the Talmud; in the Tosephta (see above) it is called *Korbanoth* ("sacrifices").

ZERAIM. Hebrew: "seeds." The first order of the Talmud, pertaining to laws of prayer and minute details of laws governing agriculture.

ZIONIDES: "Songs of Zion." See Judah ha-Levi, in BIOGRAPHIES.

ZIZITH (Yiddish: Tsitsis). Hebrew: "fringes." The fringes at the corners of the prayer shawl (*tallith*)—or the *tallit katan*—the short garment worn by Orthodox males under their shirt or vest. See TALLITH, above.

ZOHAR. From the Hebrew: *Sefer ha-Zohar:* "Book of Splendor." The most important book of the cabalistic movement; probably written in the thirteenth century; believed to have been written/assembled by the Spanish rabbi Moses (Moshe) de Leon—who deliberately attributed the work to a second-century rabbi, Simeon ben Yohai.

The *Zohar*, nominally a commentary on the Torah, is a fantastic compendium of superstitions, mysticism, folklore, and numerology to reveal hidden meanings in the Bible: abstruse codes, dreams, symbols; cryptic excursions into demonology (and angelology); ways of exorcising devils; the transmigration of souls. (It should be noted that such preoccupations were common to the Christian world of that time, as well.) The *Zohar* is especially beholden to a "science of numbers" (see GEMATRIA, above): a numerical value is assigned each Hebrew letter and a text from the Bible is arranged vertically, backwards, diagonally, upside down, in a triangle, a palindrome, an acrostic, etc.

The *Zohar* also contains wonderful folk stories, ethical dicta, and moving prayers. The book exerted an enormous influence on large sectors of Jewry, particularly the hasidim (q.v.). Rabbis often warned Jews not to court mental dangers by too-deep immersion in the *Zohar*. Among Yemenite Jews, the Zohar is what the Talmud is to Ashkenazic Jews.

V · Selected Bibliography

My son, make your books your companions. Let your shelves be your treasure grounds and gardens. When you are weary, change from garden to garden. Your desire will renew itself, and your soul will be filled with delight.　　　JUDAH IBN TIBBON (c. 1120–1190)

1. Books and Articles Published in English

In this Bibliography, the following abbreviations are used:

H.E.W.　　*Hebrew Ethical Wills*, 2 vols., Jewish Publication Society, 1948

J.P.S.A.　　Jewish Publication Society of America.

P.B.H.L.　　*Post-Biblical Hebrew Literature*, B. Halper, ed., 2 vols., Jewish Publication Society of America, Philadelphia, 1921

ABRAVANEL, ISAAC. "The Advantages of a Republic Over a Monarchy," in *P.B.H.L.*

ADLER, MORRIS. *The World of the Talmud*, Schocken Books, New York, 1963

HA-AM, AHAD (Asher Ginzburg). *Essays, Letters, Memoirs*, tr. L. Simon, Oxford, East and West Library, London, 1946
——. *Selected Essays*, tr. and ed. Leon Simon, J.P.S.A., 1962

ALBO, JOSEPH. *Sefer ha-Ikkarim* (1428), tr. I. Husik, J.P.S.A., 1929
——. *"The Various Ranks of Prophecy,"* in P.B.H.L.

AL-HARIZI, JUDAH BEN SOLOMON, "Seven Young Men Discuss the Merits of the Various Virtues," in *P.B.H.L.*

The Apocrypha and Pseudepigrapha of the Old Testament in English, ed. R. H. Charles, Oxford University Press, London, 1968

JUDAH BEN ASHER. "Ethical and Moral Admonitions," in *P.B.H.L.*

———. "The Testament of Judah Asheri," in *H.E.W.*

BAAL SHEM, ISRAEL. "In Defiance of Despondence," in *H.E.W.*

BAR HIYYA, ABRAHAM, HA-NASI. *The Meditation of the Sad Soul,* tr. Geoffrey Wigoder, Schocken Books, New York, 1969

BARON, SALO. *A Social and Religious History of the Jews,* vol. II, Columbia University Press, New York, 1937, pp. 215–321

JEDAIA BEN-BEDERSI. "The Nothingness of Man and His Pursuits," *P.B.H.L.*

BENJAMIN OF TUDELA. "Description of Jerusalem and Its Surroundings," in *P.B.H.L.*

BEN SIRACH, JESUS. "In Praise of the High Priest Simeon, the Son of Johanan," in *P.B.H.L.*

———. "Wisdom Is a Source of Happiness," in *P.B.H.L.*

BICKERMAN, ELIAS. *From Ezra to the Last of the Maccabees: Foundations of Post-Biblical Judaism,* paperback, Schocken Books, New York, 1968

BIRNBAUM, PHILIP. *Jewish Concepts,* Hebrew Publishing Co., New York, 1964

———, editor. *A Treasury of Judaism,* Hebrew Publishing Co., New York, 1962

BLAU, JOSEPH L. *The Story of Jewish Philosophy,* Random House, New York, 1962

Book of Delight, tr. Israel Abrahams, J.P.S.A., 1912.

A Book of Jewish Thoughts, arr. by Joseph Herman Hertz, Bloch Publishing, New York, 1954

BORCHSENIUS, PAUL. *The History of the Jews* (5 vols.), Simon and Schuster, New York, 1965

BUBER, MARTIN. *The Legend of the Baal-Shem,* tr. by Maurice Friedman, paperback, Schocken Books, New York, 1969

———. *Tales of the Hasidim: Early Masters,* paperback, Schocken Books, New York, 1961

Cambridge History of the Bible (vol. I): *From the Beginning to Jerome,* eds. P. R. Ackroyd and C. F. Evans, Cambridge University Press, London and New York, 1970

CHAJES, Z. H. *The Student's Guide Through the Talmud,* tr. and ed. Jacob Shachter, Phillip Feldheim, Inc., New York, 1960

COHEN, REVEREND A. *Ancient Jewish Proverbs,* John Murray, London, 1911

———. *Everyman's Talmud,* Dutton, New York, 1949

COHEN, I. *Parallel Proverbs*, Dvir, Tel Aviv, 1954

"Deuteronomy Rabbah (MIDRASH)." *Midrash Rabbah* (vol. VII), tr. J. Rabbinowitz, Soncino Press, London, 1961

Dictionary of the Bible, ed. James Hastings, Scribner's, New York, 1963

Ecclesiastes. The Holy Scriptures, according to the Masoretic text, J.P.S.A., 1917, 1945, 1955

"Ecclesiastes Rabbah (MIDRASH)." *Midrash Rabbah* (vol. VIII), tr. by A. Cohen, Soncino Press, London, 1961

ELEAZAR OF MAYENCE. "The Ideals of an Average Jew," in *H.E.W.*

ELIJAH GAON (of Vilna). "Letter of Elijah (Gaon) of Wilna," in *H.E.W.*

The Encyclopedia of the Jewish Religion, eds. R. J. Zwi Werblosky and Geoffrey Wigoder, Holt, Rinehart, Winston, New York, 1966

Ethics of the Fathers, ed. and tr. Joseph Herman Hertz, in *The Daily Prayer Book*, Bloch Publishing Company, 1957

The Ethics of the Talmud: Sayings of the Fathers: Pirke Aboth, ed. and tr. R. Travers Herford, paperback, Schocken Books, New York, 1962

"Exodus Rabbah (MIDRASH)." *Midrash Rabbah* (vol. III), tr. S. M. Lehrman, Soncino Press, London, 1961

The Fathers According to Rabbi Nathan, tr. Judah Goldin, Yale University Press, New Haven, Connecticut, 1955

FINKELSTEIN, LOUIS. *New Light from the Prophets*, Vallentine, Mitchell, London, 1969

FLEG, EDMOND. *The Jewish Anthology*, tr. Maurice Samuel, Harcourt, Brace, New York, 1925

FRENKEL, RABBI ISSER. *Men of Distinction* (vol. I), Sinai Publishing, Tel Aviv, Israel, 1967

GANZFRIED, RABBI SOLOMON. *Code of Jewish Law*, tr. Hyman E. Goldin, Hebrew Publishing Company, New York, 1961

GASTER, THEODOR H. *Myth, Legend and Custom in the Old Testament*, Harper and Row, New York, 1969

"Genesis Rabbah (MIDRASH)." *Midrash Rabbah*, 2 vols., tr. H. Freedman, Soncino Press, London, 1961

GERONDI, JONAH. *The Gates of Redemption*, tr. Shraga Silverstein, Phillip Feldheim, New York, 1967

GINZBERG, LOUIS. *Legends of the Bible*, J.P.S.A., 1909, 1968

———. *On Jewish Law and Lore*, paperback, Atheneum, New York, 1970

———. *Students, Scholars and Saints*, J.P.S.A., 1945

Give Us Life: Mesholim and Masterwords of the Chofetz Chaim, coll. and ed. Mendel Weinbach, Feldheim Publishers, Jerusalem, New York, 1969

GLATZER, NAHUM N. *Hillel the Elder: the Emergence of Classical Judaism,* Schocken paperback, New York, 1970

GLUSTROM, SIMON. *The Language of Judaism,* Jonathan David, New York, 1966

GOODMAN, PHILIP, editor. *Essays on Jewish Booklore,* KTAV, New York, 1971

GRAETZ, HEINRICH. *History of the Jews* (vol. VI), J.P.S.A., 1949

GRAYZEL, SOLOMON. *A History of the Jews,* J.P.S.A., 1968.

Great Ages and Ideas of the Jewish People, ed. Leo Schwarz, Random House, New York, 1956

The Great Jewish Books and Their Influence on History (3 vols.), eds. Samuel Caplan and Harold U. Ribalow, Horizon Press, New York, 1952

HA-LEVI, JUDAH. *The Kuzari,* tr. Hartwig Hirschfeld, paperback, Schocken Books, New York, 1964; also *Book of Kuzari,* tr. Hartwig Hirschfeld, Pardes Publishing House, Inc., New York, 1946

——. *Selected Poems,* tr. Nina Salaman, J.P.S.A., 1924

Hammer on the Rock: A Midrash Reader, ed. Nahum N. Glatzer, tr. Jacob Sloan, Schocken Books, New York, 1948

The Hasidic Anthology: Tales and Teachings of the Hasidim, tr. and compiler, Louis I. Newman, paperback, Schocken Books, New York, 1963

Hebrew Ethical Wills (vols. I and II), ed. Israel Abrahams, J.P.S.A., 1926, third impression, 1948

Hebrew Poems from Spain, tr. David Goldstein, Schocken Books, New York, 1966

Hebrew Proverbs and Their Origin, compiled by Lazar Blankstein, ed. Samuel Ashkenazi, Riryath-Sepher Ltd., Jerusalem, 1964 (several languages)

HERFORD, R. TRAVERS. *Talmud and Apocrypha,* KTAV, New York, 1970

HESCHEL, ABRAHAM J. *The Earth Is the Lord's,* Abelard-Schuman, New York, 1964

HIRSCH, SAMSON RAPHAEL. *The Nineteen Letters of Ben Uziel,* tr. B. Drachman, Funk & Wagnalls, New York, 1899

HORODEZKY, S. A. *Leaders of Hasidism,* Hasefer Agency for Literature, London, 1928

HURWITZ, SIMON. *The Responsa of Solomon Luria* (*Maharshal*), Bloch Publishers, New York, 1938

HUSIK, ISAAC. *A History of Mediaeval Jewish Philosophy,* Macmillan, New York, 1916

IBN AL-FAYYUMI, NATHANAEL. *The Bustan Al-Ukul,* ed. and tr. David Levine, Columbia University Press (reprint, AMS Press, Inc., New York, 1966)

IBN EZRA, ABRAHAM BEN MEIR. "Plaintive Song," in *P.B.H.L.*

IBN EZRA, MOSES BEN JACOB. "Dirge on the Death of His Brother," in *P.B.H.L.;* "Poem Addressed to One of His Noblest Friends," p. 101.

IBN GABIROL, SOLOMON. *Choice of Pearls (Mibhar ha-Peninim)*, tr. B. H. Ascher, London, 1895

———. *Improvement of the Moral Qualities*, tr. S. S. Wise, Columbia University Press, New York 1902; reprinted, AMS Press, New York, 1966.

———. *The Kingly Crown*, tr. Bernard Lewis, Vallentine, Mitchell, London, 1961

———. *Selected Religious Poems of Solomon Ibn Gabirol*, tr. Israel Zangwill, ed. Israel Davidson, J.P.S.A., 1923

IBN PAQUDA, BAHYA. *Duties of the Heart* (2 vols.), tr. Moses Hyamson, Phillip Feldheim, Inc., Jerusalem and New York, 1970

———. "Pious Reflections and Admonitions to the Soul," in *P.B.H.L.*

IBN TIBBON, JUDAH. "A Father's Admonition," in *H.E.W.*

———. "Why the Jewish Religion Does Not Especially Encourage Asceticism," in *P.B.H.L.*

IBN TIBBON, SAMUEL BEN JUDAH. "On the Limitations of Man's Intellect," in *P.B.H.L.*

IBN ZABARA, JOSEPH BEN MEIR. *The Book of Delight*, tr. Moses Hadas, Columbia University Press, New York, 1932, paperback, 1962

———. "Jacob the Broker and the Necklace," in *P.B.H.L.*

IMMANUEL OF ROME. "The Poet Visits Paradise," in *P.B.H.L.*

———. *Tophet and Eden*, tr. H. Gollancz, University of London Press, Ltd., London, 1921

The Jewish Encyclopedia: A Descriptive Record of the History, Religion, Literature, and Customs of the Jewish People from the Earliest Times (12 vols.), ed. Isidore Singer, Funk & Wagnalls, 1901–1951, KTAV Publishing House reprint (no date)

The Jewish Library (vol. III), "Woman," ed. Leo Jung, Soncino Press, London and New York, 1970

A Jewish Reader: In Time and Eternity, ed. Nahum N. Glatzer, paperback, Schocken Books, New York, 1961

The Jews: Their History, Culture and Religion (2 vols.), ed. Louis Finkelstein, Harper, New York, 1960

Josephus: The Jewish War, tr. G. A. Williamson, Penguin Books, London, revised edition, 1970

KLAPHOLTZ, YISROEL. *Tales of the Baal Shem Tov*, Feldheim, Jerusalem-New York, 1970

KOGOS, FRED. *1001 Yiddish Proverbs*

Language of Faith: A Selection from the Most Expressive Jewish Prayers (original text and new English verse), Schocken Books, New York, 1947, 1967

LIBER, MAURICE. *Rashi,* tr. Adele Szold, Hermon Press, New York, 1970, (first edition: J.P.S.A., 1906)

LIPSCHITZ, MAX A. *The Faith of a Hassid,* Jonathan David, New York, 1967

LUZZATTO, MOSES HAYYIM. *Mesillat Yesharim:* "The Path of the Upright," tr. Mordecai M. Kaplan, J.P.S.A., 1966

MAIMON, SOLOMON. *Solomon Maimon: An Autobiography,* tr. J. C. Murray, London, 1888 (Schocken Books, New York, 1947, ed. M. Hadas)

Maimonides: His Wisdom for Our Time, ed. and tr. Gilbert Rosenthal, Funk & Wagnalls, 1969

MAIMONIDES, MOSES. *The Eight Chapters of Maimonides on Ethics,* tr. J. I. Gorfinkle, Columbia University Press, New York, 1912

────── *Guide for the Perplexed,* tr. M. Friedlander, George Routledge & Sons, London, 1904 (2nd Edition)

────── *Iggeret Teman* ("Epistle to Yemen") ed. A. S. Halkin, tr. B. Cohen, New York, 1952

MARCUS, JACOB R. *The Jew in the Medieval World: A Source Book: 315–1791,* Temple Book, Atheneum, New York, 1969

McKANE, WILLIAM. *Proverbs: A New Approach,* SCM Press, London, 1970

Memoirs of My People: Jewish Self-Portraits from the 11th to the 20th Centuries, ed. Leo W. Schwarz, paperback, Schocken Books, New York, 1963

Midrash Rabbah (vol. X), tr. and ed., Harry Freedman and Maurice Simon, Soncino Press, London, 1961

The Minor Tractates of the Talmud (2 vols.), tr. A. Cohen, Soncino Press, London, 1965

MINTZ, JEROME. *Legends of the Hasidim,* University of Chicago, 1968

The Mishnah, tr. Herbert Danby, Oxford University Press, London, 1933

The Mishnah, tr. and selected by Eugene J. Lipman, Norton, New York, 1970

MOORE, GEORGE FOOTE. *Judaism in the First Centuries of the Christian Era: The Age of the Tannaim* (vol. III), Cambridge, Mass., 1927–1930

NASH, WALTER. *Our Experience of Language,* B. T. Batsford, London, 1971

NEWMAN, LOUIS I. *Maggidim and Hasidim: Their Wisdom,* Bloch Publishers, New York, 1962

Orchot Zadikkim ("The Ways of the Righteous"), ed. and tr. Seymour Cohen, Phillip Feldheim, Inc., Jerusalem and New York, 1969

Peake's Commentary on the Bible, ed. Matthew Black and H. H. Rowley, Nelson, London, 1962, reprinted 1967

The Pentateuch and Haftorahs (with Hebrew Text, English Translation and Commentary), ed. J. H. Hertz, Soncino Press, London, second edition, 1960

The Pharisees, ed. R. Travers Herford, Macmillan, New York, 1924

Pirke d' Rabbi Eliezer, tr. Gerald Friedlander, Hermon Press, New York, 1916

Post-Biblical Hebrew Literature: An Anthology, tr. and selected by B. Halper, J.P.S.A., 1921

PRINZ, JOACHIM. *Popes from the Ghetto: A View of Medieval Christendom,* first paperback edition, Schocken Books, 1968

PRITCHARD, JAMES B., editor. *The Ancient Near East,* Princeton University Press, 1969

A Rabbinic Anthology, eds. C. G. Montefiore and H. Loewe, J.P.S.A., 1960

RABINOWICZ, HARRY M. *The World of Hasidism,* Vallentine, Mitchell, London, 1970

RABINOWITSCH, DR. WOLF ZEEV. *Lithuanian Chasidism,* Vallentine, Mitchell, London, 1970

RAPAPORT, SAMUEL. *Tales and Maxims from the Midrash,* KTAV, New York, 1968

——. *A Treasury of the Midrash,* KTAV, New York, 1968

RASHI. *Commentaries on the Pentateuch,* tr. and selected by Chaim Pearl, Norton, New York, 1970

The Rest Is Commentary, ed. Nahum N. Glatzer, Beacon Press, Boston, 1961

ROSTEN, LEO. *The Joys of Yiddish,* McGraw-Hill, New York, 1968, paperback Pocket Books, 1970

ROTH, CECIL. *A History of the Jews: From Earliest Times through the Six Day War,* Schocken Books, New York, revised edition, 1970

—— *The Jewish Contribution to Civilization,* Macmillan, London, 1938

—— *Personalities and Events in Jewish History,* J.P.S.A., 1953

Saadia Gaon: The Book of Beliefs and Opinions, tr. Samuel Rosenblatt, Yale University Press, New Haven, 1948

SAMUEL, MAURICE. *In Praise of Yiddish,* Cowles, New York, 1971

Sayings of the Jewish Fathers, Comprising Pirque Aboth in Hebrew and English, ed. Charles Taylor, KTAV, New York, 1969

SCHECHTER, SOLOMON. *Studies in Judaism,* Meridian Books, Cleveland and New York, 1958

"Shulhan Aruk of Rabbi Karo," in *Anthology of Medieval Hebrew Literature,* ed. Louis Feinberg, The Burning Bush Press, New York, 1961

The Standard Hebrew Prayer Book (The Siddur), the Rabbinical Assembly of America, and the United Synagogue of America, New York, 1960

The Standard Jewish Encyclopedia, ed. Cecil Roth, Doubleday, Garden City, New York, 1966, new revised edition, Cecil Roth and Geoffrey Wigoder, Doubleday, 1970

STRACK, HERMANN L. *Introduction to the Talmud and Midrash,* J.P.S.A., Philadelphia, 1931 (paperback, Temple Book, Atheneum, New York, 1969)

The Sybilline Oracles, tr. in blank verse by Milton Tovey, Hunt and Eaton, New York, 1890

Talmud: The Babylonian Talmud (12 vols.), ed. I. Epstein, Soncino Press, London, 1936

Talmud: Seven Minor Treatises (Sefer Torah, Mezuza, Tefillin, Zizith, Abadim, Kutim, Gerim, and Soferim II), ed. M. Higger, Bloch, New York, 1930

TAUBENHAUS, G. *Echoes of Wisdom,* Haedrich & Sons, Brooklyn, 1900

Three Jewish Philosophers: Philo, ed. Hans Lewy; Saadia Gaon, "Book of Doctrines and Beliefs," ed. Alexander Altman; Judah ha-Levi, "Kuzari," ed. Isaak Heineman, J.P.S.A. (reprint, Atheneum, New York, 1969)

The Torah: A New Translation of the Holy Scriptures According to the Masoretic Text, J. P. S. A., 1962

Tosefta, ed. M. S. Zuckermandel, Bamberger & Wahrmann, Jerusalem, 1937

Tractate Avoth: Ethics of the Fathers, tr. Philip Blackman, Judaica Press, New York, 1964

TRATTNER, ERNEST R. *Understanding the Talmud,* Nelson, New York, 1955

A Treasury of Jewish Quotations, ed. Joseph L. Baron

Universal Jewish Encyclopedia, ed. Isaac Landman, The Universal Jewish Encyclopedia, Inc., New York, 1943

VERMES, G. *The Dead Sea Scrolls in English,* Penguin Books, Harmondsworth, England, 1968

The Wisdom of Israel, ed. Lewis Browne, Random House, New York, 1945

Wit and Wisdom of the Talmud, ed. Madison C. Peters, Baker and Taylor, New York, 1900

The World of Translation: Papers Delivered at the Conference on Literary Translation under the Auspices of P.E.N., American Center (no publisher cited), 1971

Yiddish Proverbs, ed. Hanan J. Ayalti

ZBOROWSKI, M., and E. HERZOG. *Life Is With People: The Culture of the Shtetl,* paperback, Schocken, New York, 1962

The Zohar, tr. Harry Sperling and Maurice Simon, Soncino Press, London, 1949

Zohar: The Book of Splendor, ed. Gershon G. Scholem, paperback, Schocken, New York, 1963

2. Books Published in Yiddish Only

BERNSTEIN, IGNAZ. *Jüdische Sprichwörter und Redensarten* ("Jewish Proverbs and Sayings"), printed by Josef Fischer, Warsaw, 1908, reprinted by Georg Olms, Hildesheim, Germany, 1969

JEUSZOHN, B. *Fun Untser Alten Oytser* ("From our old treasure"), Moshe Justman, (8 vols.) Warsaw, 1932–1938

LAZEROV, JUDAH LOEB. *Encyclopedia of Jewish Wit,* Pardes, New York, 1928

MEKLER, DAVID LOUIS. *Fun Rebins Hawf* ("From the Rabbi's Store of Knowledge"), Jewish Book Publishing Co., New York, 1931

Or Olam ("Light of the World"), A. Kahana, Warsaw, 1928

Peyer Yisroel ("Glory of Israel"), S. Freund, Prezemysl, 1925

RAWNITZKI, JOSHUA CHAIM. *Yidishe Vitsn* ("Jewish Wit"), 2 vols., Sklarsky, New York, 1950

Sipurey Besht ("Collection of the Besht"; author unknown), A. J. Kleiman, Piotrkov, 1911

STUTCHKOFF, NAHUM. *Der Oytser fun der Yidisher Shprakh* ("The Treasury-Thesaurus of the Yiddish Language"), Yiddish Scientific Institute-YIVO, New York, 1950

WISSEON, M. A. *Khokhma un Harifut* ("Wisdom and Witticisms"), published by the author, Vienna, 1927

3. Books Published in Hebrew Only

For books in Hebrew only: Wherever possible, I cite the place and date of publication, and the name of the publisher or "printer"; the *edition* named is the one used by Dr. Solomon D. Goldfarb in his research assistance; since many of the books listed are quite old (collections of essays, sermons, tales, interpretations of the law, legends), they have often been reprinted. A short description of the more important Hebrew books referred to in the preceding pages will be found in the GLOSSARY.

NOTE: The publishing centers for Hebrew and Yiddish books (until the twentieth century) were located in Eastern Europe. Books about the life or teachings of a famous hasid or *tsadik* appeared in the locality in which they were active: Vilna, Koretz, Warsaw, Prezemysl, etc. Experts on hasidic literature (Buber, Kahana, Horodetzky) edited and compiled much of the hasidic material.

AHAD HA-AM. *Al-Parashat Derakhim* ("At the Crossroads"), Jüdischer Verlag, Berlin, 1920

AL-HARIZI, JUDAH. *Tahkemoni* (possibly "The Apothecary" or "The Wise One"), ed. Max Emmanuel Stern, printed by Edlen von Schmidt und Holzwarth, Vienna, 1854

ARAMA, ISAAC (ISAAC BEN MOSES). *Akedat Yitshak* ("The Binding of Isaac"): Sermons on the weekly sections of the Torah and of the five Megilloth; V. Kittseer, Pressburg, 1849

————. *Mishalim* ("Proverbs"), printed by L. Schnauss, Leipzig, 1859

ATAR, HAYIM IBN. *Or Ha-Hayim* ("The Light of Life"), printed by Gershon Madpis, Zolkiew, 1858

BAAL SHEM, ISRAEL. *Midrash Ribash Tov* ("Midrash of the Good Rabbi Israel Ben Eliezer"), printed by Marton Abraham, Kecskemet, 1927

BAHYA BEN ASHER (BACHYA). *Kad Hakemah* ("Jug of Flour"), in *Kitvei Rabenu Bahya* ("Collected Writings of Rabbenu Bahya"), ed. Charles B. Chavel, Mosad Harab Kook, Jerusalem, 1969

BERECHIAH BEN NATRONAL, HA-NAKDAN. *Fuchsfabeln* (*Mishle Shualim:* "Fox Fables"), Erich Reiss Verlag, Berlin, 1921

BIALIK, CHAIM, and J. RAVNITZKY. *Sefer Ha-Agadah* ("Book of the Narrations"), Dvir Co. Ltd., Tel Aviv, 1936

COHEN, AARON (AARON BEN ZEBI HIRSCH HA-KOHEN OF OPATOW). *Keter Shem Tov Ha-Shalem* ("The Complete Crown of the Good Name"), Lvov, 1864

CORDOVERO, (MOSES BEN YAKOV) MOSES. *Pardes Rimonim* ("Orchard of Pomegranates"), Amsterdam, 1708; Munkacz, 1905–1906, Harav Mordecai Ati, Jerusalem, 1961–1962

DARKHE TSEDEK ("Paths of Justice"), Zechariah Mendel of Yeroslav; Honigson's, London, 1958

DAVIDSON, ISRAEL. *Otsar ha-Mishalim ve-ha Pitgamim* ("Thesaurus of Proverbs and Parables" from medieval Jewish Literature), Mosad Harav Kook, Jerusalem, 1956–1957

DELMEDIGO, ELIJAH. *Behinat ha-Dat* ("Examination of Religion"), printed by Anton Edlen von Schmid, Vienna, 1833

EIBESCHUTZ, JONATHAN. *Yaarot Dvash* ("Honeycombs with Honey"): A Collection of Hebrew Sermons, Lemberg 1858 edition, printed by M. F. Poremba

ELIEZER BEN HYRCANOS. *Pirke de Rabbi Eliezer* ("Ethics of Rabbi Eliezer"), Vilna, 1838 (photocopy of Warsaw 1852 edition, O.M. Pblg., New York, 1946)

EPHRAIM SOLOMON BEN AARON OF LENCZYCZA (LUNTSHITZ). *Klee Yakar* ("Beloved Vessel"): Commentaries on the Pentateuch, Amsterdam, 1709, 1767, Zolkiew, 1799

FALAQUERA, SHEM-TOB BEN JOSEPH. *Reshit Hakhmah* ("The Beginning of Wisdom"), Fafelever, Berlin, 1902

———. *Sefer Ha-Mevakesh* ("Book of the Seeker"), Traklin, Warsaw, 1924

———. *Sefer Ha-Nefesh* ("Book of the Soul"), printed by Alexander Gins, Warsaw, 1864

HA-LAHMI, DAVID. *Hochmei Yisrael* ("The Wise Men of Israel"), A. Zioni, Tel Aviv, 1957

HALEVI, AARON (authorship disputed). *Sefer ha-Hinukh* ("Book of Education"), Eshkol, Jerusalem, 1958

HASDAI, ABRAHAM BEN SAMUEL, HA-LEVI. *Ben ha-Melekh ve-ha-Nazir* ("The Son of the King and the Hermit"), Mosad Harav Kook, Zhitomir, 1850, Tel Aviv, 1950

HAYYIM BEN ISAAC, OF VOLOZHIN. *Sheelot u-Teshuvot Hut ha-Meshulah* ("Questions and Answers"): "The Triple Braided Reply", J. C. Metz, Vilna, 1882

HORODETZKY, SAMUEL A. *Ha-Hasidut ve-ha-Hasidim* ("Hasidism and the Hasids"), 4 vols., Dvir, Berlin, 1922–1928

IBN EZRA, MOSES. *Shirat Israel* ("The Poetry of Israel"), in Arabic and Hebrew, tr. Al Muhadonah wal Mudhakarah, Styble, Leipzig, 1924

IBN GABIROL, SOLOMON BEN JUDAH. *Keter Malkhut* ("Crown of Kingship"), Mosad Harav Kook, Jerusalem, 1950

JUDAH BEN SAMUEL HE-HASID. *Sefer Hasidim* ("Book of the Pious"), ed. J. Wistinetzki, 2nd edition, Frankfurt a/M, M.A. Wahrmann, 1924

MAIMONIDES, MOSES. *Teshuvot ha-Rambam* ("*Responsa* of Rambam"), ed. Alfred Freimann, Mekirze Niramim, Jerusalem, 1934

Mekhilta de Rabbi Simeon ben Yohai, ed. David Hoffman, Jüdisch-Literarische Gesellschaft, Frankfurt a/M, 1905

Midrash Agadah, ed. Solomon Buber, Vienna, 1894, Madah, New York, 1959–1960

Midrash: Agadat Bereshit, ed. Solomon Buber, Vilna, 1902 (2nd edition, 1925, Menorah, New York, 1959)

Midrash Rabah, ed. Romm, Vilna, 1878

Midrash Tanaim (in Hebrew and German), ed. David Hoffman, Nord-Ost, Berlin, 1913

Midrash Tehilim ("*Shoher Tov*": "Seeker of the Good"), ed. Solomon Buber, photo-offset edition, Vilna, 1891

Midrash Yalkut Shimoni ("Collection of Simeon"—homilies on the Midrash), collected by Simon ha-Darshan (also known as Simeon Kara, Berrl Lorje, and Leib Matfe), Zolkiew, 1858

Midrash Zuta ("Small Midrash"), ed. Solomon Buber, printed by H. Itzkowski, Berlin, 1894, photo-offset: Vilna, 1925, Tel Aviv, 1963–1964

Mishle Yisrael ("Proverbs of Israel"), ed. Meyer Waxman, printed in Jerusalem, 1933

NACHMAN OF BRATSLAV. *Torat Rabi Nahman* ("The teachings of Rabbi Nachman"), ed. S. Horodetzki, Deviv, Berlin, 1923

Otsar Midrashim (a "treasury" of two hundred *midrashim*, annotated), ed. J. D. Eisenstein, The Editor, New York, 1915

Otsar Midrashim ("Treasury of *Midrashim*"), ed. Adolf Jellinek, Vienna, 1883

Pesikta Rabati (Midrashic collection of discourses for the festivals and the special Sabbaths), edited in 1880 by Meir Freidman (no publisher cited; probably the press of Y. Kaiser)

Pesikta Zutarta: Lekah Tov ("Good Teaching"), Midrashic commentary on the Torah and the *Hamesh Megillot*, by Rabbi Tobias ben Eliezer, ha-Gadol, Prague, 1725

REGGIO, ISAAC SAMUEL. *Torah ve-ha-Filosofia* ("Torah and Philosophy"), printed by Anton Edlen von Schmid, Vienna, 1828

SCHARFSTEIN, ZVI. *Otsar Ha-Rayonot ve-ha-Piteamim* ("Lexicon of Ideas and Epigrams"): quotations from classical and modern Hebrew literature, 3 vols., Jabneh, Tel Aviv, 1966

VITAL, HAYYIM. *Ets Hayim* ("Tree of Life"), Korets, 1819

4. Books Published in German Only

FURMAN, ISRAEL. *Jüdische Sprichwörter und Redensarten* ("Jewish Proverbs and Sayings"), Menorah, Tel Aviv, 1968

LIPPERHEIDE, WILHELM. *Sprichwörterbuch* ("Book of Proverbs"), 3rd edition, Dorner, Berlin, 1934

Midrash Tanaim (in Hebrew and German), ed. David Hoffman, Nord-Ost, Berlin, 1913

Index

Abraham, Testament of, 92
Abravanel, Isaac A., 265, 322, 343, 349
Abaye, 63
Abot de Rabbi Nathan, 134, 148, 202,
    234, 282, 284, 294, 295, 299, 316,
    321, 324, 328, 329, 348, 402, 421,
    440, 441, 451, 475, 517, 546, 561
Adler, Morris, Dr., 310
Aebo, Joseph, 477
Agnon, S. Y., 127
Ahad ha-Am, 446
Akiba, ben Joseph, 72, 73, 154, 250, 264,
    357, 434, 517, 534, 563
Albo, Joseph, 255, 517
Alfasi, Isaac Ben Jacob, 77
Al-Harizi, Judah ben Solomon ben
    Hophni, 541
Anau, Jehiol ben Jukrithiel, 406
Apocrypha
    Ahikar, 112, 134, 156, 215, 249, 268,
        433
    II Baruch, 174, 335
    II Enoch, 487
    II Esdras, 288
    II Maccabees, 217
    Psalms of Solomon, 209, 259
Arama, Isaac ben Moses, 107, 131
Asher ben Jehiel, 202, 351
Asher, Bahya ben. *See* Bachya ben Asher
Asheri, Judah, *Testament of,* 211, 225,
    290, 333, 499, 547
Ashi, Rab, 76, 200, 513

Baraita Perek ha-Shalom, 333
Baal Shem Tov, 113, 131, 220, 239, 249,
    269, 412, 438, 487, 530, 564
Bachya, Ben Asher (Bahya), 204, 218,
    250, 338, 503
Bahur. *See* Levita, Elijah
Bar Kochba, 79
Baroka, Rabbi, 275, 277
Beaulieu, A. Leroy, 327
Bedersi, Jedaia Ben, 325, 351, 564

Belzer Rabbi, The, 159, 259
Ben Azariah, Eliezer, 421
Ben Sira, Alphabet of, 385
Ben Sirach, Jesus (or Simeon), 112, 115,
    126, 130, 131, 134, 145, 152, 154,
    171, 176, 178, 193, 199, 202, 204,
    213, 214, 221, 230, 232, 238, 239,
    244, 245, 263, 271, 273, 275, 285,
    296, 300, 316, 322, 325, 331, 333,
    354, 356, 362, 368, 381, 384, 391,
    402, 415, 423, 443, 458, 460, 468,
    472, 475, 498, 503, 507, 511, 526,
    543, 547, 550, 558
Ben Zoma, Simeon, 352, 387
Berdichever Rabbi, The, 249, 260, 360,
    365, 396
Berechiah ben Natronai ha-Nakdan, 97,
    144
Bershides Rabbi, The, 390, 432, 494
Besht, The. *See* Baal Shem Tov
Bet Hillel. *See* Hillel
Bialik, Chaim Nachman, 519
Book of Saints, 118, 119, 139
Bratslaver Rabbi, The. *See* Nachman of
    Bratslav
Buber, Martin, 476
Buber, Solomon, 308
Bunim, Simcha, 307, 313, 526

Campanton, Judah, 118
Caro, Joseph, 77, 139, 226, 412, 427, 482,
    494, 557
Caspi, Joseph ben Abba Mari, 98, 429,
    488, 523
Chaim of Volozhin. *See* Hayyim ben Isaac
Chefetz, Moses, 231
Chia, Rabbi. *See* Hiyya
Choice of Pearls. See Ibn Gabirol
Chofetz, Chaim, 55, 155, 181, 196, 215,
    250, 265, 271, 285, 313, 338, 349,
    367, 383, 385, 403, 415, 461, 468,
    476, 498, 509, 513, 517, 526, 537,
    540

Cordovero, Moses ben Jacob, 547
Croce, Benedetto, 34

Delight, Book of. See Ibn Zabara
Daniel, Book of, 191, 302, 438
Derekh Tselek, 348
Deuteronomy, Book of, 350
Duties of the Heart. See Ibn Paquda
Danby, Dr. Herbert, 73
Darmsteter, James, 396
Delmedigo, Elijah, 517
Delmedigo, Joseph Solomon ben Elijah,
    104, 117, 211, 305, 381, 517, 547
Denham, John, 34
d'Israeli, Isaac, 282, 398
Dresner, Samuel H., 223
Duran, Profiat, 119

Ecclesiastes, 117, 174, 175, 210, 258, 294,
    321, 375, 406, 421, 486, 487, 513,
    542
Ecclesiasticus. *See* Ben Sirach
Eibeschutz, Jonathan, 276, 328, 397, 446,
    524
Eleazer ben Azariah. *See* Ben Azuhum
Eleazar ben Judah (of Worms). *See*
    Rokeach
Eliezer Ben Isaac, Ha-Gadol, 403
Eliezer, Israel ben. *See* Baal Shem Tov
Eleazar ha-Kappar, 63
Exodus, Book of, 312, 445
Ezekiel, Book of, 438
Ezobi, Joseph ben Hanan, 531
Ezra, 74

Falaquera, Shem Tov ben Joseph, 157,
    211, 225, 342, 521, 524
Froude, J. A., 374

Gabirol, *See* Ibn Gabirol
Gerer Rabbi, The, 249
Gerondi, Jonah ben Abraham, 197, 214,
    330, 402
Gerson, Levi ben, 131, 158, 178, 390
Gersonides. *See* Levi ben Gerson
Ginzberg, Asher. *See* Ahad ha-Am
Ginzberg, Louis, 394, 395, 492
Graetz, Heinrich, 283

Ha-Asheri. *See* Asher ben Jehiel
Ha-Hinukh, Sefer, 558
Ha-Gadol. See Eliezer Ben Isaac
Hai Gaon, 119, 171, 221, 338, 552
Ha-Kappar, Eleazar. *See* Eleazar ha-
    Kappar
Ha-Levi, Aaron (of Barcelona), 558. *See*
    Ha-Hinukh, Sefer
Ha-Levi, Judah, 117, 307, 385, 511

Halevi, Judah Hasid. *See* Judah the
    Pious
Ha-Mevakesh, Book of. *See* Falaquera
"Ha-Nakdan." *See* Berechiah ben
    Natronai
Hananiel, Rabbi, 421, 440
Ha Nagid, Samuel, 233, 293, 349, 462,
    524
"Ha-Penini." *See* Bedersi, Jedaiah Ben
Haphetz Hayyim. *See* Chofetz Chaim
Hasdai, Abraham ben Samuel ha-Levi,
    99, 154, 232, 338, 358, 362, 391,
    468, 472, 485, 563
Hayyim, Ben Isaac (of Volochin), 313
Heine, Heinrich, 113, 250, 310, 382
Hertz, J. H., 309
Heschel, A. J., 283, 313
Hillel, 47, 73, 93, 115, 119, 156, 158, 178,
    179, 238, 268, 295, 324, 329, 330,
    352, 390, 417, 433, 439, 449, 459,
    499, 506, 517, 521
Hirsch, E. G., 499
Hiyya, Bar Abba, Rabbi, 412
Hosea, Book of, 130, 312, 439

Ibn Ezra, Abraham ben Meir, 225, 249,
    265, 290, 326, 353, 429, 455, 462,
    468, 475, 487, 543
Ibn Ezra, Moses ben Jacob, 132, 152,
    176, 179, 181, 197, 214, 218, 236,
    241, 264, 273, 276, 285, 287, 293,
    326, 335, 345, 350, 367, 393, 416,
    419, 430, 433, 462, 466, 476, 481,
    488, 502, 512, 523, 528, 532, 541,
    543, 547, 560, 563
Ibn Falaquera. *See* Falaquera
Ibn Gabirol, 63, 97, 98, 103, 112, 113,
    148, 152, 153, 159, 165, 184, 185,
    186, 197, 202, 203, 230, 232, 233,
    235, 238, 264, 267, 273, 280, 289,
    290, 297, 302, 303, 317, 321, 326,
    341, 343, 345, 353, 354, 358, 367,
    368, 394, 396, 399, 402, 408, 419,
    458, 463, 472, 476, 500, 503, 506,
    508, 509, 529, 533, 536, 537, 543,
    546, 547, 552, 560, 563, 565, 566,
    568
Ibn Hasdai, *See* Hasdai
Ibn Paquda, Bahya ben Joseph, 90, 130,
    132, 134, 151, 157, 179, 202, 234,
    267, 276, 293, 317, 321, 335, 349,
    412, 415, 455, 468, 475, 487, 488,
    495, 504, 512, 518, 519, 560, 563
Ibn Tibbon, Judan ben Saul, 118, 119,
    130, 150, 460, 541
Ibn Verga, Solomon, 183
Ibn Verga, Judah, 476

Ibn Zabara, Joseph Ben Meir, 128, 162,
    176, 177, 239, 278, 338, 447, 531,
    532, 558
"Immanuel" (of Rome), 214, 303, 313,
    343, 392, 408, 412, 472, 485, 495,
    511, 532, 558
Isaiah, Book of, 438
Israel, Ben Eliezer. *See* Baal Shem Tou

Jabirul. *See* Ibn Gabirol
Jedaia ben Bedersi, 176, 297, 513
Job, Book of, 93, 170, 202, 407, 516, 521,
    525, 546, 559
Joel, Book of, 533
José, Rabbi, 76
Joseph, Morris, 480
Josephus, 139, 382, 430
Joshua, Book of, 250
Judah ben Asher. *See* Asheri, Judah,
    Testament of, 3, 245
Judah ha-Nasi (the Prince), 72, 73, 317
Judah of Regensburg, 118, 119
"Judah the Pious," 119

Karo. *See* Caro
Kahan, Israel Meir. *See* Chofetz, Chaim
Kings, Book of, I, 382
Korbriner, Rabbi, The, 250
Koretzer Rabbi, The, 195, 222, 225, 252,
    261, 289, 293, 303, 333, 343, 349,
    353, 377, 396, 412, 451, 457, 461,
    480, 524, 541, 547
Kotzker Rabbi, The, 174, 261, 436, 524
Kranz, Jacob ben Wolf. *See* Maggid of
    Dubno

Lecky, W. E. H., 88, 183, 301, 304
Leivick, H., 440, 482
Leone da Modena, 140, 181, 238, 239,
    560
Levita, Elias, 132
Leviticus, Book of, 440, 481
Lieberman, Saul, 413, 470, 567
Lubliner Rabbi, The, 99, 239, 261, 390,
    423, 540
Luntshitz, Ephraim, 313
Luzzatto, Moses Hayyim, 333

Maamar Mordecai, 503
Macaulay, Thomas Babington, 148
Maggid of Mezeritz, The, *See* Mezeritzer
    Rabbi, the
Maggid of Dubno, The, 393, 532
Maimon ben Joseph, 412
Maimonides
    Commentary on Mishneh, 117, 136,
        157, 274, 454, 501
    Eighteen Chapters, 276, 293, 321, 326,

    330, 387, 395, 435, 436, 447, 470,
        488, 494, 517, 523, 547, 568
    Guide to the Perplexed, 74, 97, 120,
        121, 134, 145, 151, 249, 270, 302,
        303, 348, 350, 359, 366, 382, 391,
        404, 416, 429, 506, 523, 543
    Laws of Repentance, 106, 258
    Mishnah Torah, 105, 139, 150, 156,
        179, 185, 220, 280, 294, 298, 354,
        517, 543
    Responses, 136, 208, 211, 226, 336,
        416, 508
Marcus, Jacob R., 330–1
Meir, Rabbi Ben Isaac, 72, 298, 307, 565
Mekilta (Exodus), 252, 288, 317, 335,
    396, 481, 484, 497, 511
"Mendel of Rymanov," 413
"Mendele Mocher Seforim," 63, 143, 166,
    333, 386, 397
Mendel of Vitebsk, 204
Mendelssohn, Moses, 524
Mezeritzer Rabbi, The, 259, 283, 385,
    397, 512, 543, 544, 547, 560
Midrash, 74, 104, 307, 316, 398, 448
    Canticles, 20
    Deuteronomy Rabbah, 213, 242, 265,
        312, 320, 412, 432, 516
    Ecclesiastes Rabbah, 98, 115, 138, 155,
        175, 209, 230, 256, 279, 317, 320,
        348, 419, 433, 442, 478, 490, 561
    Eliahu Rabbah, 179, 258, 307, 342, 454
    Esther Rabbah, 299, 368
    Exodus Rabbah, 102, 138, 150, 157,
        170, 188, 209, 220, 290, 307, 312,
        389, 406, 428, 446, 478, 487, 528
    Genesis Rabbah, 90, 97, 114, 129, 138,
        142, 143, 145, 175, 179, 184, 203,
        207, 210, 239, 259, 260, 262, 285,
        301, 306, 307, 318, 338, 376, 407,
        419, 429, 432, 433, 434, 451, 475,
        479, 530, 556, 557, 561, 563
    Ha-Gadol, 339
    Haneelam, Genesis, 111, 539
    Lamentations Rabbah, 307
    Leviticus Rabbah, 114, 196, 258, 275,
        290, 315, 320, 390, 420, 454, 455,
        474, 479, 487, 497, 506, 511, 529,
        535, 541, 546.
    Numbers Rabbah, 111, 328, 454, 474
    Otsar, 222
    Pesikta Rabbah, 278, 307
    Proverbs, 144, 232, 233, 299, 431
    Psalms, 151, 199, 225, 249, 258, 280,
        292, 324, 433, 561
    Ruth Rabbah, 134
    Samuel, 101, 420
    Samuel Rabbah, 201, 298
    Sekel Tov, 220

Midrash (*cont.*)
  Sifre Deuteronomy, 123, 138, 260, 306,
    418, 479, 516
  Sifre Kedoshim, 196
  Shekalim, 196, 245, 261
  Song of Songs Rabbah, 258, 384, 506
  Megillath Ta'anith, 102, 312
  Tana de Rabbi Eliyahu, 276, 290, 386,
    415
  Tanhuma, 91, 92, 95, 161, 196, 215,
    233, 262, 281, 308, 316, 318, 321,
    325, 336, 337, 338, 389, 407, 418,
    476, 479, 491, 535, 539, 557, 563
  Temura, 250, 563
  Torath Kohanim on Leviticus, 342
  Vayosha, 414
Mishnah, 72, 281, 407, 489
  Edoyoth, 397, 474
  Berakoth, 434
  Hagigah, 445
  Ohalot, 375
  Sotah, 556
Moscato, Judah Arizeh, 213, 270
Moses ben Abraham Dari, 119
Moses, Jacob ben. *See* "Rabbenu Tam"
Moses of Kobryn, 326

"Nachman of Bratslav," 99, 104, 117, 126,
    134, 139, 140, 143, 144, 145, 154,
    165, 195, 204, 205, 210, 215, 216,
    220, 222, 225, 245, 255, 258, 261,
    266, 273, 279, 281, 289, 291, 313,
    318, 320, 321, 326, 330, 333, 362,
    366, 375, 376, 381, 386, 390, 399,
    413, 415, 416, 423, 426, 451, 459,
    491, 504, 512, 519, 524, 532, 544,
    563, 568
Nathan (of Nemirov), 518
Nehorai. *See* Meir, Rabbi
Nordau, Max, 101, 283
Numbers, Book of, 191

Orhot Tsadikim, 342, 467, 531

Paquda. *See* Ibn Paquda
Paquera, Shem Tob. *See* Falaquera
Philo, 249, 459
Plato, 190, 410
Perek ha-Shalom, 390, 523, 563
Pesikta Rabbati, 138, 297, 392, 445, 450
Pesikta de Rabbi Kahana, 249
Pious, Book of the, 115, 154, 241, 280,
    360, 513
Pirke de Rabbi Eliezer, 220, 239, 252,
    326, 356, 485, 557
Poor Richard's Almanac, 255
Psalms, Book of, 98, 106, 195, 248, 249,

    252, 333, 348, 407, 441, 491, 503,
    542
Proverbs, Book of, 99, 112, 113, 115, 121,
    123, 125, 138, 143, 144, 145, 158,
    161, 165, 169, 178, 179, 184, 192,
    195, 198, 200, 202, 204, 209, 214,
    217, 219, 221, 229, 230, 232, 236,
    241, 252, 260, 262, 263, 264, 269,
    271, 303, 308, 325, 331, 332, 342,
    359, 360, 363, 369, 375, 378, 381,
    397, 398, 400, 402, 403, 406, 408,
    414, 419, 420, 433, 439, 440, 441,
    468, 475, 478, 480, 482, 484, 485,
    487, 488, 490, 491, 495, 497, 503,
    508, 510, 525, 533, 536, 539, 542,
    545, 549, 551, 558, 559, 568

Rab, 63, 564
Rab Ashi. *See* Ashi
Raba (Raba Joseph ben Hama), 319, 478
Rabbon. *See* Zakka, Johanan ben
"Rabbenu Tam," 230
"Rashi," 76, 77, 98, 106, 121, 122, 126,
    146, 158, 166, 182, 184, 193, 213,
    221, 234, 267, 316, 318, 319, 331,
    342, 381, 386, 408, 412, 470, 502,
    511, 519
Reggio, Isaac Samuel, 104
Riziner Rabbi, The, 261, 270, 349, 532
Robinson, A. Mary F., 504
Rokeach, Eleazar, 259, 370
Ropshitzer Rabbi, The, 326, 402, 408,
    426, 433, 562
Rosenthal, Moritz, 362
Rosh, The. *See* Asher ben Jehiel
Rosh Hagivah, 503
Roth, Cecil, 115, 197, 492

Saadia Gaon, 107, 185, 226, 234, 245, 255,
    266, 278, 294, 302, 325, 337, 397,
    408, 415, 435, 523, 529
Samuel ha-Nagid, 176
Samuels, Maurice, 29, 167
Sartre, Jean-Paul, 101
Sassover Rabbi, The, 259, 337, 412, 428,
    504, 532, 565
Sayings of the Fathers, 95, 103, 105, 115,
    134, 138, 156, 184, 203, 210, 236,
    238, 245, 249, 257, 258, 260, 261,
    264, 266, 267, 268, 272, 277, 278,
    280, 284, 287, 288, 290, 295, 302,
    312, 317, 321, 329, 336, 347, 351,
    352, 391, 385, 387, 390, 396, 406,
    421, 426, 433, 438, 439, 442, 449,
    454, 459, 460, 464, 472, 475, 490,
    494, 497, 499, 506, 516, 517, 518,
    521, 532, 534, 536, 539, 546, 561,
    568

Schechter, Solomon, 426
Schreiner, Olive, 101
Shatzover Rabbi, The, 558
Shirat Yisrael. *See* Moses ibn Ezra
"Shmelke" (of Nickelsburg), 140
Sholem Aleichem, 63, 122, 140, 171, 200,
    205, 213, 225, 231, 244, 263, 288,
    292, 313, 335, 336, 358, 367, 375,
    385, 394, 402, 404, 461, 469, 488,
    504, 521, 526, 538, 550, 557, 559,
    560
Shulhan Aruk. *See* Joseph Caro
Sibylline Oracles, 91
Siegel, Seymour, 156, 224, 341, 566–67
Slonimer Rabbi, The, 403, 494
Song of Solomon, 174, 308, 342
Spinoza, Baruch, 547
Steinbach, Alan, 149

Talmud, 68, 102, 145, 149, 154, 175,
    201, 271, 316, 326, 342, 372, 384,
    418, 455, 506, 542
  Abudah Zarah, 144, 165, 251, 264, 294,
    324, 328, 350, 352, 386, 398, 407,
    442, 453, 472, 483, 509, 531
  Arakin, 381, 479
  Baba Bathra, 90, 137, 138, 145, 185,
    188, 205, 267, 306, 308, 324, 326,
    328, 359, 390, 406, 414, 420, 434,
    441, 451, 485, 541, 542, 550
  Baba Kamma, 153, 156, 188, 242, 260,
    266, 291, 312, 402, 411, 435, 510,
    515
  Baba Mezi'a, 114, 121, 158, 165, 178,
    184, 186, 202, 288, 292, 312, 324,
    331, 354, 358, 361, 431, 441, 447,
    453, 467, 501, 527, 528, 539, 550,
    552, 557, 561
  Berakoth, 25, 91, 93, 98, 123, 124,
    143, 150, 157, 159, 165, 169, 170,
    174, 178, 180, 185, 191, 192, 193,
    199, 211, 214, 218, 225, 235, 251,
    260, 262, 265, 266, 268, 269, 271,
    274, 297, 312, 320, 322, 324, 328,
    344, 345, 351, 365, 369, 381, 383,
    395, 396, 411, 420, 430, 432, 448,
    454, 458, 460, 467, 471, 473, 482,
    502, 518, 536, 542, 545, 550, 556,
    558, 564
  Bezah, 153, 312, 337, 506
  Derekh Frets Zuta, 154, 234, 454, 474
  Erubin, 97, 126, 163, 164, 211, 225,
    326, 337, 348, 350, 363, 408, 484,
    562
  Gittin, 130, 137, 187, 225, 274, 320,
    356, 369, 427, 474, 510, 550, 560,
    565
  Hagigah, 137, 182, 229, 281, 312, 361,

    369, 372, 406, 451, 453, 474, 515
  Hirayat, 219, 484
  Hullin, 96, 300, 306, 463, 501
  Kerithoth, 474
  Kethuboth, 121, 123, 132, 137, 158,
    163, 184, 185, 244, 262, 274, 306,
    309, 315, 336, 356, 361, 362, 369,
    382, 383, 423, 451, 553
  Kiddushin, 108, 111, 209, 219, 257,
    279, 287, 298, 340, 353, 356, 374,
    386, 481, 484, 485, 489, 505, 511,
    561
  Kinnim, 295, 381, 453
  Makkoth, 151, 326, 448, 527
  Megillah, 126, 133, 166, 284, 311, 328,
    351, 366, 383, 407, 434, 446, 471,
    472, 497, 502, 529, 532, 561, 566
  Menahoth, 362, 429, 494, 515, 550
  Mo'el Katan, 124, 267, 279, 448, 462,
    467, 500
  Nazir, 89, 473
  Nedarim, 89, 99, 142, 154, 260, 287,
    306, 402, 406, 467, 478, 505, 561
  Niddah, 93, 133, 164, 254, 361
  Pesahim, 99, 126, 148, 165, 187, 248,
    264, 284, 298, 335, 345, 351, 356,
    366, 414, 417, 432, 453, 455, 472,
    457, 490, 505, 545, 560, 561
  Rosh Hashana, 180, 266, 507
  Sanhedrin, 90, 91, 92, 95, 104, 105,
    130, 148, 151, 163, 174, 180, 181,
    202, 207, 209, 229, 238, 242, 248,
    257, 266, 272, 279, 297, 298, 312,
    315, 319, 342, 344, 348, 349, 358,
    407, 423, 434, 455, 457, 494, 497,
    505, 509, 511, 513, 523, 527, 531,
    539, 541, 549, 556, 562, 568
  Shabbat, 98, 130, 137, 149, 150, 174,
    179, 198, 199, 200, 224, 233, 250,
    252, 274, 279, 283, 288, 306, 309,
    315, 320, 324, 332, 358, 366, 376,
    380, 390, 420, 431, 432, 445, 448,
    453, 474, 478, 479, 494, 517, 523,
    536, 550, 562
  Shebu'oth, 163, 256
  Sotah, 122, 126, 146, 222, 257, 265,
    284, 292, 297, 353, 356, 357, 411,
    414, 474, 502, 515, 530, 542
  Sukkah, 142, 144, 182, 209, 257, 264,
    265, 387, 419, 451, 459, 466
  Ta'anith, 95, 98, 146, 152, 218, 287,
    290, 328, 411, 435, 448, 454, 467,
    506, 515
  Tamil, 494
  Yebamoth, 95, 142, 146, 161, 163, 169,
    187, 219, 269, 292, 335, 347, 356,
    358, 362, 378, 393, 418, 434, 459,

Talmud (*cont.*)
    472, 474, 479, 484, 509, 549, 552,
    553, 565
  Yoma, 129, 144, 195, 224, 262, 270,
    272, 277, 283, 284, 402, 431, 433,
    445, 454, 473, 549, 558

Talmud J., 68
  Baba Mezi'a, 246
  Berakoth, 112, 138, 242, 248, 287, 348,
    413, 474, 488, 516
  Gittin, 242
  Hagigah, 264
  Kiddushin, 229, 279, 397, 518
  Nedarim, 89, 112, 474
  'Orlah, 380
  Pe'ah, 126, 258, 479, 538
  Sanhedrin, 134, 348, 387, 430, 461,
    508, 511, 515
  Shabbath, 209, 349, 367, 474
  Shebi'it, 495
  Sotah, 229
  Ta'anith, 249, 252, 380
  Yebamoth, 174, 372, 380
Tcharkover Rabbi, The, 512
Thackeray, William Makepeace, 22
Tibbon, *See* Ibn Tibbon
Tolstoy, Leo, 129, 490
Tosephta
  Berakoth, 158, 178, 417
  Kiddushin, 478
  Sanhedrin, 104, 298, 414
  Tohoroth, 354, 538

Tsupenster Rabbi, The, 335
Twain, Mark, 310

Ussher, Arland, 101

Verga. *See* Ibn Verga
Vital, Hayyim, 303
Voltaire, 101, 301

Way of the Saints, 134
Weinrich, Max, 322
Whitman, Walt, 113

Yom-Tob, Lippman. *See* Zunz, Leopold
Yalkut Ruveni, 138, 175, 363
Yalkut Shimoni, 175, 348, 378
Yalkut Psalms, 211

Zabara. *See* Ibn Zabara
Zakkai, Johanan ben, 329
Zangwill, Israel, 194
Zeitlin, Hillel, 430
Zohar, 90, 99, 101, 108, 134, 138, 147,
    155, 175, 191, 196, 210, 215, 220,
    225, 250, 263, 277, 280, 307, 308,
    333, 348, 350, 355, 357, 362, 365,
    386, 391, 403, 412, 414, 417, 423,
    429, 432, 433, 435, 439, 443, 448,
    451, 463, 472, 475, 480, 487, 488,
    503, 507, 518, 534, 535, 540,
    541, 550, 557
Zohar Tikkune, 210, 563
Zoma, *See* Ben Zoma, Simeon
Zunz, Leopold, 439

LEO ROSTEN, a writer of remarkable versatility and intellectual range, is the creator of the immortal H*Y*M*A*N K*A*P*L*A*N, *Captain Newman, The Joys of Yiddish* and fifteen other books. His name has often appeared on the movie screen. His pioneering studies of Hollywood and the Washington correspondents are considered social-science classics. *A Most Private Intrigue, The Story behind the Painting,* and *People I Have Loved, Known or Admired* have delighted legions of readers, in a dozen languages.

A Ph.D. from the University of Chicago, Mr. Rosten studied at the London School of Economics, has taught at Yale, was Ford Visiting Professor of Political Science at the University of California, and is a Faculty Associate of Columbia University.

His writings have won many honors: the Freedoms Foundation Medal, the George Polk Memorial Award, the Alumni Professional Achievement Award of the University of Chicago, the Commonwealth Club Medal, and a special citation from the National Conference of Christians and Jews.

Mr. Rosten has served the government as Deputy Director of the Office of War Information, consultant to the Executive Office of the President and the Commission on National Goals.

IIe is a member of the Savile Club (London), the Chaos Club (New York), and the Authors Club (London).